ANALYSIS OF CONIFEROUS FOREST ECOSYSTEMS IN THE WESTERN UNITED STATES

US/IBP SYNTHESIS SERIES

This volume is a contribution to the International Biological Program. The United States effort was sponsored by the National Academy of Sciences through the National Committee for the IBP. The lead federal agency in providing support for IBP has been the National Science Foundation.

Views expressed in this volume do not necessarily represent those of the National Academy of Sciences or the National Science Foundation.

Volume

1 MAN IN THE ANDES: A Multidisciplinary Study of High-Altitude Quechua/*Paul T. Baker and Michael A. Little*

2 CHILE-CALIFORNIA MEDITERRANEAN SCRUB ATLAS: A Comparative Analysis/*Norman J. W. Thrower and David E. Bradbury*

3 CONVERGENT EVOLUTION IN WARM DESERTS: An Examination of Strategies and Patterns in Deserts of Argentina and the United States/*Gordon H. Orians and Otto T. Solbrig*

4 MESQUITE: Its Biology in Two Desert Scrub Ecosystems/*B. B. Simpson*

5 CONVERGENT EVOLUTION IN CHILE AND CALIFORNIA: Mediterranean Climate Ecosystems/*Harold A. Mooney*

6 CREOSOTE BUSH: Biology and Chemistry of *Larrea* in New World Deserts/*T. J. Mabry, J. H. Hunziker, and D. R. DiFeo, Jr.*

7 BIG BIOLOGY: The US/IBP/*W. Frank Blair*

8 ESKIMOS OF NORTHWESTERN ALASKA: A Biological Perspective/*Paul L. Jamison, Stephen L. Zegura, and Frederick A. Milan*

9 NITROGEN IN DESERT ECOSYSTEMS/*N. E. West and John Skujins*

10 AEROBIOLOGY: The Ecological Systems Approach/*Robert L. Edmonds*

11 WATER IN DESERT ECOSYSTEMS/*Daniel D. Evans and John L. Thames*

12 AN ARCTIC ECOSYSTEM: The Coastal Tundra at Barrow, Alaska/*Jerry Brown, Philip C. Miller, Larry L. Tieszen, and Fred L. Bunnell*

13 LIMNOLOGY OF TUNDRA PONDS: Barrow Alaska/*John E. Hobbie*

14 ANALYSIS OF CONIFEROUS FOREST ECOSYSTEMS IN THE WESTERN UNITED STATES/*Robert L. Edmonds*

15 ISLAND ECOSYSTEMS: Biological Organization in Selected Hawaiian Communities/*Dieter Mueller-Dombois, Kent W. Bridges, and Hampton L. Carson*

US/IBP SYNTHESIS SERIES | 14

ANALYSIS OF CONIFEROUS FOREST ECOSYSTEMS IN THE WESTERN UNITED STATES

Edited by

Robert L. Edmonds
University of Washington

Hutchinson Ross Publishing Company

Stroudsburg, Pennsylvania

Copyright © 1982 by **The Institute of Ecology**
Library of Congress Catalog Card Number: 80-26699
ISBN: 0-87933-382-0

84 83 82   1 2 3 4 5
Manufactured in the United States of America.

Library of Congress Cataloging in Publication Data
Main entry under title:
Analysis of coniferous forest ecosystems in the Western
   United States.
   (US/IBP synthesis series; v. 14)
   Includes index.
   1. Forest ecology—The West. 2. Conifers—The West—
Ecology. 3. Stream ecology—The West. 4. Lake ecology—
The West. I. Edmonds, Robert L. II. Series.
QK133.A5   581.5′2642′0978   80-26699
ISBN 0-87933-382-0   AACR1

Distributed world wide by Academic Press,
a subsidiary of Harcourt Brace Jovanovich,
Publishers.

CONTENTS

Foreword ix
Preface xi
List of Contributors xv

1: **Introduction** 1
R. L. Edmonds

General Features of the Western Coniferous Forest
Biome, 2   Research Sites, 9   Highlights of the
Coniferous Forest Biome Research Program, 20
Management Implications of the Coniferous
Forest Biome Program, 26

2: **Relations Between Vegetation**
and Environment 28
G. M. Hawk, J. N. Long, and J. F. Franklin

Introduction, 28   Vegetation Classification and
Ordination, 30   Distribution of Species and
Communities Along Environmental Gradients,
32   Summary and Conclusions, 41

3: **Ecological Indexes as a Means of Evaluating**
Climate, Species Distribution,
and Primary Production 45
W. H. Emmingham

Introduction, 45   Background, 46   Study Areas,
47   Comparison of Ecological and Productivity
Indexes Across the Coniferous Biome, 54
Conclusions, 64

4: The Niche and Forest Growth   **68**
K. L. Reed and S. G. Clark

Introduction, 68   Development of Niche Theory,
69   The Niche and Succession, 72   The Forest
Growth Model (SUCSIM), 74

**5: Productivity of Western
Coniferous Forests**   **89**
J. N. Long

Introduction, 89   Development of Individual Crowns
and Stand Canopies, 90   Stem Development, 99
Understory Development, 99   Changes in the
Return of Organic Matter to the Forest Floor, 102
Root Biomass, 105   Stand Productivity, 105
Comparisons with Other Environments and
Vegetation Types, 110   Summary, 118

6: Physiological Activity in Douglas-Fir   **126**
J. P. Lassoie

Introduction, 126   Physiological Activity and Its
Control, 127   Temporal and Spatial Variations in
Physiological Activity, 148   Summary, 170

**7: Nutrient Cycling in Forests of the
Pacific Northwest**   **186**
*D. W. Johnson, D. W. Cole, C. S. Bledsoe,
K. Cromack, R. L. Edmonds, S. P. Gessel,
C. C. Grier, B. N. Richards, and K. A. Vogt*

Introduction, 186   Key Processes in Forest Nutrient
Cycles, 187   Nutrient Cycles in Different Forest
Ecosystems in the Biome in Contrasting Environments,
199   Nutrient Accumulation and Cycling During Stand
Development, 209   Effects of Site Disturbance on
Nutrient Cycling and Its Management Implications,
214   Conclusions, 225

**8: Material Transfer in a Western Oregon
Forested Watershed**   **233**
*F. J. Swanson, R. L. Fredriksen, and
F. M. McCorison*

Introduction, 233   Definition of Processes, 234
Material Transfer in an Old-growth Forest, 240
Erosion Under Forested Conditions, 252   Effects
of Ecosystem Disturbance, 257   Summary, 260

**9: Land—Water Interactions:
The Riparian Zone**   **267**
*F. J. Swanson, S. V. Gregory, J. R. Sedell,
and A. G. Campbell*

Introduction, 267   Structure and Composition of
Riparian Vegetation, 268   Functions of the Riparian
Zone, 274   Spatial Variation of Terrestrial/Aquatic
Interfaces, 282   Temporal Variation in the Riparian
Zone, 283   Summary, 288

10: Coniferous Forest Streams   **292**
F. J. Triska, J. R. Sedell, and S. V. Gregory

Introduction, 292   Stream Structure and Function,
293   Particulate Organic Matter Budgets, 304
Temporal Aspects, 311   A Spatial Perspective, 314
Forest Land-use Implications, 323

**11: Lake Ecosystems of the Lake Washington
Drainage Basin**   **333**
*R. C. Wissmar, J. E. Richey, A. H. Devol,
and D. M. Eggers*

Introduction, 333   Elemental Cycles in Lakes of the
Lake Washington Drainage Basin, 335   Elemental
Transfers Within Lakes, 341   Phytoplankton
Physiological Responses to Changing Nutrient Regimes,
352   Determinants of Consumer Community Structure

and Production in Lake Washington, 362   Comparison
of Aquatic Ecosystems in Different Biomes, 369
Summary, 374

Appendix: Coniferous Forest Biome
                    Program Publications   387
Index   413

FOREWORD

This book is one of a series of volumes reporting results of research by U.S. scientists participating in the International Biological Program (IBP). As one of the fifty-eight nations taking part in the IBP during the period of July 1967 to June 1974, the United States organized a number of large, multidisciplinary studies pertinent to the central IBP theme of the biological basis of productivity and human welfare.

These multidisciplinary studies (Integrated Research Programs), directed toward an understanding of the structure and function of major ecological or human systems, have been a distinctive feature of the U.S. participation in the IBP. Many of the detailed investigations that represent individual contributions to the overall objectives of each Integrated Research Program have been published in the journal literature. The main purpose of this series of books is to accomplish a synthesis of the many contributions for each principal program and thus answer the larger questions pertinent to the structure and function of the major systems that have been studied.

Publications Committee: US/IBP
Gabriel Lasker
Robert B. Platt
Frederick E. Smith
W. Frank Blair, Chairman

PREFACE

Coniferous forests occupy about one-third of the land area of the western United States including Alaska, and the products from this area, such as wood, water, fish, and wildlife, are extremely important to the economic well-being of the nation. In addition, large areas are used for diverse recreational purposes by increasing numbers of people.

Arguments about the management of these lands have gone on for years. Debates have focused on single versus multiple use, the balance between the various uses, and the management procedures best suited to maintaining and increasing forest productivity. More recently, fundamental questions have been raised about the impact of widely accepted practices such as clearcutting on environmental quality and long-term forest productivity.

In the late 1950s, many biologists recognized that individual scientists pursuing their own interests and supported by small grants were not making much progress in solving the major problems of mankind, particularly those involving management of forest lands. They felt that a large coordinated international research program on a worldwide scale would lead to a better understanding of ecosystems. Because of the complexity of ecosystems and because of the skills and knowledge required, no one person or even a small group of persons could encompass all of the required specialties to undertake ecosystem studies.

In response to this need the International Biological Program (IBP) was initiated in 1964 under the auspices of the International Council of Scientific Unions (ICSU). The U.S. Ecosystem Analysis program was begun officially in 1965, and was organized into five biomes: grassland, eastern deciduous forest, western coniferous forest, desert, and tundra. The first program to begin research was the Grasslands Biome in 1969. The operating philosophy in each biome was to study ecosystems as functional units, with the assumption that small segments of information could be synthesized into a describable whole, the ecosystem, and that this integrative approach would be of much greater value and utility than merely summing up the component segments.

The Coniferous Forest Biome program, under the directorship of Dr. Stanley P. Gessel of the University of Washington, was the last of the US/IBP biome programs to be initiated and major research efforts did not commence until 1971. It terminated in December 1978. The major goal of the program

was to understand the composition, structure, and functioning of western coniferous forest ecosystems and associated aquatic ecosystems. In addition,
relations between terrestrial and aquatic ecosystems were studied. Finally, the
impact of man's manipulation of natural ecosystems was assessed.

The material in this volume does not represent an integration of all Biome
data, but rather represents an attempt to convey our understanding of productivity; nutrient cycling; and producer, consumer, and decomposer dynamics in
natural and manipulated terrestrial and aquatic ecosystems. Emphasis was
placed on ecosystems in the Douglas-fir region of Oregon and Washington. A
total list of all Coniferous Biome literature is presented in the Appendix.
Although a considerable modeling effort was mounted in the Biome we have
not made modeling the focus of this book. Rather it is focused on synthesis of
experimental and monitoring data.

ACKNOWLEDGMENTS

I wish to thank all the people who contributed to the volume either directly
or indirectly and the reviewers who made my job considerably easier.

Although the research was carried out mostly by scientists at the University
of Washington and Oregon State University, scientists from many other uni-
versities and research establishments in nine western states collaborated in the
research and many of their results are integrated into this volume.

Financial support for the research conducted by the Coniferous Forest Biome program was provided by the National Science Foundation (grants no.
GB-12075, GB-20963, GB-36810X2, BMS74-20744, DEB74-20744 A02,
DEB74-20744 A03, DEB74-20744 A04, DEB74-20744 A05, DEB74-20744
A06). Contributions from the U.S. Department of Agriculture Forest Service
in providing the H. J. Andrews Experimental Forest in Oregon and other
research sites, and the City of Seattle Water Department for providing the
research sites in the Cedar River watershed in Washington, are greatly appre-
ciated.

The many supporting personnel, particularly those in the central laborato-
ries, are thanked, especially Frances Olzewski (University of Washington)
and Robert Rydell, Lorraine Noonan, Elly Holcombe, Joanne Kristaponis,
and William Hess (Oregon State University).

William Emmingham wishes to thank Drs. H. W. Steinoff, E. W. Mogren,
and C. P. P. Reid, Colorado State University; Drs. F. D. Johnson and G.
Deitschman, University of Idaho; Dr. K. Van Cleve, University of Alaska;
Drs. E. A. Kurmes, C. Avery, and D. E. Wommack, Northern Arizona Uni-
versity; Dr. L. K. Forcier and R. F. Wambach, University of Montana; and
Dr. T. W. Daniels, Utah State University.

James P. Lassoie wishes to acknowledge certain individuals for their special
involvement during preparation of Chapter 6. Program conceptualization and

guidance was facilitated through the efforts of many persons including Drs. L. J. Fritschen, D. R. M. Scott, and R. B. Walker, University of Washington; and Dr. R. H. Waring, Oregon State University. Their active participation is acknowledged. The author also acknowledges and thanks the following individuals for readily supplying the unpublished data contained in this chapter: Dr. R. Amundson, Boyce Thompson Institute, Yonkers, N.Y.; Dr. P. C. Doraiswamy, Texas A & M University; Dr. J. A. Helms, University of California, Berkeley; Dr. J. W. Leverenz, University of Edinburgh, Scotland; Dr. S. W. Running, Colorado State University; Dr. D. J. Salo, Mitre Corporation; Dr. R. B. Walker, University of Washington; and Dr. R. H. Waring, Oregon State University. In addition to the official editors, the author thanks Drs. Leverenz, Walker, and Waring for their editorial comments and suggestions during the writing of this chapter. Finally, the typing skills and dedication of Ms. L. G. Nash are acknowledged.

Dale W. Johnson wishes to thank the following for providing information for the nutrient cycling chapter: Dr. John Turner, New South Forestry Commission, Beecroft, N.S.W., Australia; Dr. C. Gilmour, University of Idaho; Dr. Mark Behan, University of Montana; Drs. L. H. Pike, W. C. Denison, and G. C. Carroll, University of Oregon; Dr. R. Fogel, University of Michigan; Dr. P. Sollins, Forestry Sciences Laboratory, Corvallis, Oregon; Dr. H. Riekerk, University of Florida, Gainesville; Dr. F. Ugolini and P. J. Riggan, University of Washington; and Drs. D. W. Rains and M. J. Singer, University of California, Davis.

F. J. Swanson, R. L. Fredriksen, and F. M. McCorison thank R. J. Janda, D. N. Swanston, R. L. Beschta, R. D. Harr, J. R. Sedell, F. J. Triska, L. F. Glenn, and many others for their valuable contributions of ideas, data, and editorial help in producing Chapter 8. The U.S. Department of Agriculture Forest Service Pacific Northwest Forest and Range Experiment Station Research Work Unit PNW 1653 generously supplied equipment and facilities.

The synthesis of research projects described in the stream chapter (Chapter 10) represent the contribution of numerous people engaged in team research, and without whom a holistic view of the coniferous forest stream would not have been possible. Frank Triska, James Sedell, and Stanley Gregory would first like to extend thanks and gratitude to colleagues in the field who generously contributed both time and ideas that made the project possible. They include: James Hall for his leadership in the project and for his expertise in fisheries; Norman Anderson for his major contribution in entomological research; Fred Swanson for widening our perspective to the total landscape; Jack Lyford for his initial contributions in primary production; David McIntire for his effort in modeling major biotic functions; Richard Fredriksen for streamflow records and water chemistry data; Ken Cummins for advice and ideas that helped establish the program; Robin Vannote, author of the river continuum theory; Rick Larson for data on Sephadex extraction and DOM characterization; and Robert Naiman for contributing data on the spatial aspects of benthic detritus. We would also like to thank our research assistants who have served for as long as five years, providing support in both the laboratory and the field in processing samples and preparing data for publications. These persons include: Barbara Buckley, Linda Roberts, Dale McCullough, Karen Luchessa, and Charles Hawkins. Finally, we would like to thank the graduate students who have contributed so much in both time and ideas to the stream research program. These persons include Mike Murphy, Edward Grafius, Richard Aho, and Clifford Dahm.

Jeff Richey and Bob Wissmar would like to thank the following for their contribution to the lakes chapter: E. Wold, F. Curren, D. Lowman, B. Doble, T. Packard, M. Perkins, A. Litt, and L. Male. Frieda Taub is particularly thanked for her initial efforts in preparation of the chapter.

Finally, Eleanor Connolly, Roberta Dayton, and Beverly Lynner are thanked for their typing, Martha Ellis for her editorial services, and Nancy Morris for illustrations.

Robert L. Edmonds

LIST OF CONTRIBUTORS

Caroline S. Bledsoe
  College of Forest Resources, University of Washington, Seattle,
  Washington 98195

Alsie G. Campbell
  School of Forestry, Oregon State University, Corvallis, Oregon 97331

Stanley G. Clark
  Center for Quantitative Studies, University of Washington, Seattle,
  Washington 98195

Dale W. Cole
  College of Forest Resources, University of Washington, Seattle,
  Washington 98195

Kermit Cromack, Jr.
  Forestry Sciences Laboratory, USDA Forest Service, Corvallis, Oregon
  97331

Alan H. Devol
  Fisheries Research Institute, University of Washington, Seattle,
  Washington 98195

Robert L. Edmonds
  College of Forest Resources, University of Washington, Seattle,
  Washington 98195

Douglas M. Eggers
  Fisheries Research Institute, University of Washington, Seattle,
  Washington 98195

William H. Emmingham
  Forest Research Laboratory, Oregon State University, Corvallis, Oregon
  97331

Jerry F. Franklin
Forestry Sciences Laboratory, USDA Forest Service, Corvallis, Oregon 97331

Richard L. Fredriksen
Forestry Sciences Laboratory, USDA Forest Service, Corvallis, Oregon 97331

Stanley P. Gessel
College of Forest Resources, University of Washington, Seattle, Washington 98195

Stanley V. Gregory
U.S. Fish and Wildlife Service, Department of Fisheries and Wildlife, Oregon State University, Corvallis, Oregon 97331

Charles C. Grier
College of Forest Resources, University of Washington, Seattle, Washington 98195

Glenn M. Hawk
Forestry Sciences Laboratory, USDA Forest Service, Corvallis, Oregon 97331

Dale W. Johnson
Environmental Sciences Division, Oak Ridge National Laboratory, Oak Ridge, Tennessee 37820

James P. Lassoie
Department of Natural Resources, Cornell University, Ithaca, New York 14853

James N. Long
College of Natural Resources, Utah State University, Logan, Utah 84322

F. Michael McCorison
Forestry Sciences Laboratory, USDA Forest Service, Corvallis, Oregon 97331

Kenneth L. Reed
H.D.R. Sciences, 804 Anacapa Street, Santa Barbara, California 93101

Bryant N. Richards
School of Natural Resources, University of New England, Armidale,
N.S.W., Australia

Jeffrey E. Richey
Fisheries Research Institute, University of Washington, Seattle,
Washington 98195

James R. Sedell
Forestry Sciences Laboratory, USDA Forest Service, Corvallis, Oregon
97331

Frederick J. Swanson
Forestry Sciences Laboratory, USDA Forest Service, Corvallis, Oregon
97331

Frank J. Triska
U.S. Geological Survey, Menlo Park, California 94025

Kristiina Vogt
College of Forest Resources, University of Washington, Seattle,
Washington 98195

Robert C. Wissmar
Fisheries Research Institute, University of Washington, Seattle,
Washington 98195

ANALYSIS OF CONIFEROUS FOREST ECOSYSTEMS IN THE WESTERN UNITED STATES

1

Introduction

R. L. Edmonds

The coniferous forests of western North America, particularly those in coastal areas, are unique—individual trees are unrivaled in size, longevity, and biomass accumulation. They are among the most productive forests in the world and have great economic value. In addition, they also lie in a region of great aesthetic value. Although these forests represent a renewable resource, they must be managed on a sound biological basis if economic and recreational values are to be preserved. That is, a sound knowledge of the biology of these forests and their associated aquatic ecosystems is essential for correct management.

Although many aspects of western coniferous forests have been studied by scientists, an integrated study at the ecosystem level had not been conducted before the inception of the Coniferous Forest Biome program. This program was the most intense interdisciplinary scientific study yet mounted of coniferous forests in the western United States, particularly those dominated by Douglas-fir *(Pseudotsuga menziesii)*. The primary program goal was understanding the composition, structure, and functioning of natural coniferous forest ecosystems and associated aquatic ecosystems, with a secondary goal of assessing man's impact on these ecosystems.

This volume is a synthesis of many data collected during the program. It brings together our current understanding of vegetation distribution in the biome (Chapters 2, 3, and 4), forest productivity and its physiological controls (Chapters 5 and 6), nutrient cycling in terrestrial ecosystems (Chapter 7), the physical stability of coniferous ecosystems, particularly with respect to erosion processes (Chapter 8), relations between terrestrial and aquatic ecosystems and the importance of the riparian zone (Chapter 9), and productivity and nutrient cycling in stream (Chapter 10) and lake (Chapter 11) ecosystems. The effects of forest management practices, particularly clearcutting and fertilization, on structure and behavior of natural ecosystems are also discussed.

Included in this introductory chapter are: (1) brief descriptions of the general features of the western coniferous forest biome (2) descriptions of the study sites; (3) some of the highlights of our research findings; and (4) discussion of the use of our research findings for forest management. The total complement of biome publications is listed in the Appendix.

GENERAL FEATURES OF THE WESTERN CONIFEROUS FOREST BIOME

Physical Features

Forests in the western coniferous biome occur mostly in mountainous country (Figure 1.1) where the geology, physiography, and soils are locally and regionally complex. Relief ranges from sea level to over 4300 m; conifer forests range from sea level to about 1700 m in the Cascade Mountains and to about 3300 m in the Sierra Nevada and Rocky Mountains. Vulcanism and glaciation have shaped much of the landscape formed from volcanic, intrusive igneous, sedimentary, and metamorphic rocks.

The oldest rock strata are Precambrian and are found in the northern Rocky Mountains (Figure 1.1). They consist of sandstone, shale, and limestone and are slightly metamorphosed. Some Paleozoic and Mesozoic rock formations occur throughout the central section of the biome and in the northern Cascades, but it is the Cenozoic record that is of the most interest. During that period considerable volcanic activity occurred. The great Cascade Mountain volcanoes were formed at that time, and much of the sedimentary Cenozoic materials are composed of volcanic materials derived by erosion. Many formations include volcanic ash.

Glaciation also occurred during the Cenozoic. Today, however, glaciers exist only in higher mountains and are only remnants of the once vast ice sheets that covered a great deal of the western coniferous biome. Glaciation and volcanic activity have had considerable influence on the current soils and vegetation in the biome.

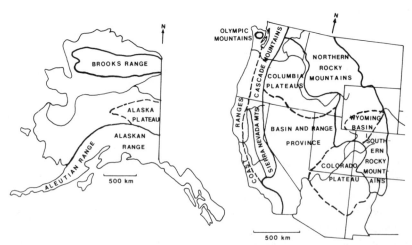

FIGURE 1.1 *Physiographic features of the western coniferous forest biome.*

Climate, Soils, and Vegetation

The western coniferous biome (Figure 1.2) covers wide geographic and climatic ranges. Annual precipitation varies from 20 cm to over 300 cm and annual average temperatures range from close to 0°C to over 20°C. In most of the area precipitation occurs mainly in winter, particularly in the form of snow at higher elevations. There is little precipitation in summer.

Soil types in the biome are extremely varied and include Inceptisols (brown forest and sol brun acids), Spodosols (podzols), and Ultisols (red-yellow podzols and reddish brown laterites). Glaciation has had an influence on soil formation, especially in the northern part of the biome, and the soils derived from the most recent glacial deposits tend to be immature. The great relief in the extensive mountainous regions of Oregon and Washington results in soil creep, landslides, or both.

In terms of vegetation the coniferous forests of western North America consist of a mosaic of ecosystems dominated by different tree species, not all of which are conifers. Some are deciduous, such as red alder *(Alnus rubra)*. Others are evergreen hardwoods such as tanoak *(Lithocarpus densiflora)* and madrone *(Arbutus menziesii)*. Five main vegetation divisions can be distinguished (Figure 1.2): coastal, subalpine, Sierra, Rocky Mountain, and boreal. Most of the research in the Coniferous Forest Biome program was concentrated in the coastal and subalpine division forests, more specifically those west of the Cascade crest in Washington and Oregon. The vegetation, climate, and soils in this area are described below. Subalpine forests also occur at high elevations in the Sierra and Rocky mountains.

Vegetation, Climate, and Soils in the Area West of the Cascade Crest in Oregon and Washington

The vegetation in the area is conventionally described in terms of zones named for a single tree species thought to be the major climax dominant, for example, western hemlock *(Tsuga heterophylla)*. Within each of the zones several associations can exist, each of which represents a climatic climax. Vegetation zones in the area west of the Cascade crest are shown in Figure 1.3. The important forested zones are the Sitka spruce *(Picea sitchensis)*, western hemlock, Pacific silver fir *(Abies amabilis)*, and mountain hemlock *(Tsuga mertensiana)* zones.

Despite its name, large areas of the western hemlock zone are forested with the pioneer species Douglas-fir, since it is the dominant species in seral stands developed after logging and burning. Even old-growth stands quite commonly maintain a major component of Douglas-fir. The climate, soils, and vegetation of these zones are summarized in Table 1.1. Further details can be found in Franklin and Dyrness (1973).

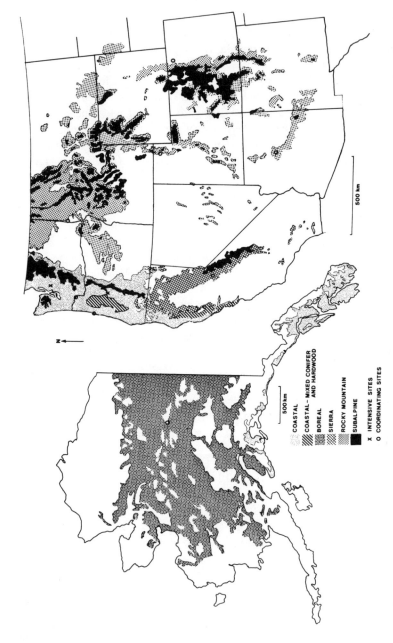

FIGURE 1.2 *Main vegetation divisions in the western coniferous forest biome and the location of intensive and coordinating sites.*

4

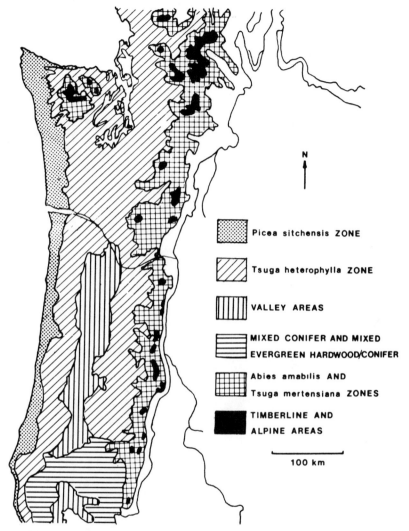

FIGURE 1.3 *Generalized vegetation map of the area west of the Cascade Mountain crest in Oregon and Washington.*

Vegetation in Other Areas of the Biome

On the dry eastern side of the Cascade Mountains, pines are most important, particularly ponderosa *(Pinus ponderosa)* and lodgepole *(Pinus contorta)*. Douglas-fir and western larch *(Larix occidentalis)* are also widespread. In coastal northern California, Douglas-fir and coastal redwood *(Sequoia sempervirens)* dominate. In the Sierras, conifers are mixed, with white fir *(Abies*

TABLE 1.1 Features of the four important forests zones in the coastal vegetation division west of the Cascade crest in Oregon and Washington.

	Zone[a]			
Feature	Picea sitchensis (Sitka spruce)	Tsuga heterophylla (Western hemlock)	Abies amabilis (Pacific silver fir)	Tsuga mertensiana (Mountain hemlock)
Climate	Mild, maritime, 2000–3000 mm/yr; rainfall mostly in winter; fog drip occurs	Mild, maritime, 1500–3000 mm/yr; mostly in winter; 6–9% in summer	Cold, montane, 1500–3000 mm/yr; winter snowpacks 1–3 m	Cold, montane, 1600–3000 mm/yr; winter snowpacks >3 m
Elevation	Sea level–160 m	Sea level–1000 m	600–1500 m	1300–2000 m
Soils	Haplohumults[b] (brown laterites, and reddish brown laterites). Surface soils high in organic matter and total nitrogen, low in base saturation	Dystrochrepts (sols bruns acides), Haplohumults (reddish brown laterites), Haplumbrempts (brown forest soils), Haplorthods (brown podzols) and Xerumbrepts and Vitrandepts (regosols)	Cryorthods (podzols) and Haplorthods (brown podzolics). Organic accumulations from 5 to 30 cm	Cryorthods (podzols) and Haplorthods (brown podzolics)
Major tree species				
Conifers	Sitka spruce, western red cedar (Thuja plicata), western hemlock, and Douglas-fir (Pseudotsgua menziesii)	Douglas-fir, western hemlock, western red cedar, grand fir (Abies grandis), Sitka spruce, western white pine (Pinus monticola), and Pacific silver fir	Pacific silver fir, western hemlock, noble fir (Abies procera), Douglas-fir, western red cedar and western white pine	Varies with locale, few species are found as dominants, mountain hemlock dominates old-growth forests and subalpine fir (Abies lasiocarpa) dominates seral or older stands; white fir (Abies concolor) and Pacific silver fir are also important.

6

Deciduous	Red alder (*Alnus rubra*) and evergreen hardwoods	Red alder, big leaf maple (*Acer macrophyllum*), chinkapin (*Castanopsis chrysophylla*), Oregon white oak (*Quercus garryana*), Oregon ash (*Fraxinus latifolia*), and black cottonwood (*Populus trichocarpa*)	
Other features			
	Mature forests have lush under stories of shrubs, herb cryptograms; sand dunes, tidal marshes, prairies, and forested swamps are included	Understories are dominated by ericaceous shrubs	Understory species belong mainly to the Ericaceae, Rosaceae, and Compositae

[a]From Franklin and Dyrness (1973).
[b]U.S. Department of Agriculture (1972) Soil Classification.

7

concolor), California red fir *(Abies magnifica)*, incense cedar *Libocedrus de-currens)*, ponderosa pine, Jeffrey pine *(Pinus jeffreyi)*, sugar pine *(Pinus lam-bertiana)*, Douglas-fir and giant redwood *(Sequoia gigantea)* occurring. In the Rocky Mountains, grand fir, subalpine fir, lodgepole pine, ponderosa pine, Engelmann spruce *(Picea engelmannii)*, western white pine *(Pinus monticola)*, and Douglas-fir dominate. The driest coniferous ecosystems, pinyon-juniper woodlands, extend from the central Rockies to the arid uplands of central Mexico and down the eastern slope of the Cascade-Sierra ranges from Oregon to Mexico.

In boreal forests white spruce *(Picea glauca)*, and black spruce *(Picea mariana)* are the dominant conifers. Tamarack *(Larix laricina)* is common in wet muskeg areas. Paper birch *(Betula papyifera)*, balsam poplar *(Populus balsamifera)* and quaking aspen *(Populus tremuloides)* are common deciduous species. In interior Alaska, taiga forests cover broad expanses of lowland, which grade into the Arctic tundra.

Lakes and Streams

The lakes and streams of most interest in the program occur in the coastal division. Most of the lakes in the coastal division are found in the state of Washington, where more than 7800 lakes, ponds, and reservoirs occur. In the Puget Sound lowland of western Washington, most lakes occupy depressions in the surface of glacial drift—the sand, gravel, silt, clay, and till laid down by the Puget lobe of continental glaciers during the last ice age. These depressions are either elongate troughs cut by the passing ice sheet or are more circular kettles formed by the melting of stagnant ice blocks. In the adjacent foothills of the Cascade Range and Olympic Mountains, most lakes occur in depressions eroded into the bedrock by the passing continental glacier, while lakes in the higher mountains are in basins cut by local alpine glaciers (Washington State Department of Ecology 1975).

A majority of the lakes are shallow, with mean depths of 3.6 to 7.6 m, although some of the larger lakes, such as Lake Washington in Seattle and Crater Lake in Oregon, are considerably deeper. Mean summer temperatures of the photic zone range from 15°C to 16°C. Most lakes are clear and mesoeu-trophic or mesotrophic.

The coastal division is also rich in streams and rivers. Many of the streams are characterized by high gradients, especially toward their headwaters, and experience strong spring freshets and low summer flows.

Common fish species resident in lakes and streams are: Dolly Varden *(Salvelinus malma)*, rainbow trout *(Salmo gairdneri)*, peamouth *(Mylocheilus caurinus)*, threespine stickleback *(Gasterosteus aculeatus)*, yellow perch *(Perca flavescens)*, longfin smelt *(Spirinchus thaleichthys)*, prickly sculpin *(Cottus asper)*, and northern squawfish *(Ptychocelilus oregonensis)*. Anadro-mous fish also utilize northwestern lakes and streams for part of their life cycle.

Common species include sockeye salmon *(Oncorhynchus nerka)* and steelhead trout *(Salmo gairdneri)*.

RESEARCH SITES

It became obvious in the organizational phase of the program that not all the diverse ecosystems in the biome could be studied. Thus attention was focused on a few selected terrestrial ecosystems and their associated aquatic ecosystems. Most of the research was carried out in the productive western hemlock zone forests, which are dominated by Douglas-fir. Research efforts were concentrated at two intensive sites, the H. J. Andrews Experimental Forest in Oregon and the Lake Washington drainage in Washington (Figure 1.2). Both are in the Cascade Mountains. Limited research was conducted at the other sites indicated in Figure 1.2. Research activities at all the research sites are summarized in Table 1.2.

The H. J. Andrews Experimental Forest

The H. J. Andrews Forest (Figure 1.4) is administered by the U.S. Department of Agriculture Forest Service, Pacific Northwest Forest and Range Experiment Station, and is a 6080-ha drainage ranging in elevation from 460 to 1615 m. A general site description is given in Table 1.3. Work on the Andrews Forest has centered on hydrologic and nutrient cycles in watersheds dominated by mature old-growth (450-year-old) Douglas-fir/western hemlock stands (Figure 1.5) and on stream ecosystems. Stream side vegetation is dominated by red alder. The gauged watersheds of the forest range in size from 10 to 100 ha and provide excellent areas in which to study ecosystem responses. Considerable effort was focused on watershed 10 (Figure 1.4), which is located adjacent to the H. J. Andrews Forest. Extensive data on climate, soils, geology, flora, plant communities, mammals, birds, hydrology and stream biology, and the impact of forest management practices, such as clearcutting, were obtained for this site during the biome program. Soils in the H. J. Andrews Forest are generally derived from basic volcanic parent material. They are generally Dystrochrepts (deep, well-drained, brown to dark brown loams developed from andesitic (basic) tuffs and breccias) and are high in potassium and calcium. Nineteen reference stands were established in the Andrews forest and the soils in each were characterized. A typical soil profile at an elevation of 490 m in reference stand 2 is shown in Table 1.4 (see page 13).

Forest community composition, especially that of understory vegetation, is strongly influenced by moisture. For example, sites characterized by understories of ocean spray *(Holodiscus discolor)* or salal *(Gaultheria shallon)* are dry. More mesic sites are typified by Oregon grape *(Berberis nervosa)*, vine maple *(Acer circinatum)*, and sword fern *(Polystichum munitum)*. Wet sites

TABLE 1.2   *Summary of research activities at the two intensive sites (H.*
J. Andrews Experimental Forest, Oregon, and Lake
Washington drainage basin, Washington) and the
coordinating and environmental grid sites.

Terrestrial studies	Aquatic and aquatic/terrestrial studies

H. J. Andrews Experimental Forest

Forest type: old-growth (450 years old) Douglas-fir/ western hemlock, some young growth

Research: Unit watershed studies concerning hydrologic and nutrient cycles, assessment of impact of clearcutting; assessment of water relations and stand productivity; plant and animal community analysis; decomposition; erosion

Stream biology (litter processing, primary and secondary production, impact of clearcutting); relations between stream and forest ecosystems

Lake Washington Drainage Basin

A.E. Thompson site

Forest type: young-growth (10 to 100 years old) Douglas-fir/red alder/western hemlock

Research (conducted at the stand and process levels): primary production and water relations; stand productivity; nutrient cycling; plant and animal community analysis; decomposition

Lake biology (Litter processing, primary and secondary production, succession); relations between lake and forest ecosystems at Findley Lake

Findley Lake

Forest type: old-growth (170 years old) Pacific silver fir

Research: stand productivity; nutrient cycling; plant community analysis; decomposition

Coordinating Sites

Blodgett Forest, Calif.: tree photosynthesis

Fairbanks, Alaska: stand productivity and nutrient cycling

Flagstaff, Ariz.: stand productivity extant data synthesis

Fort Collins, Colo.: extant data synthesis

Logan, Utah: extant data synthesis

Missoula, Mont.: fire, nutrient cycling

Moscow, Idaho: litter decomposition

Cascade Head, Oreg.: productivity, nutrient cycling, log decomposition

Wildcat Mt., Oreg.: productivity, litter decomposition

Longview, Wash.: experimental stream studies

Note: An additional twenty-one sites in eight states were involved in the biome environmental grid (see Chapter 3 for site descriptions).

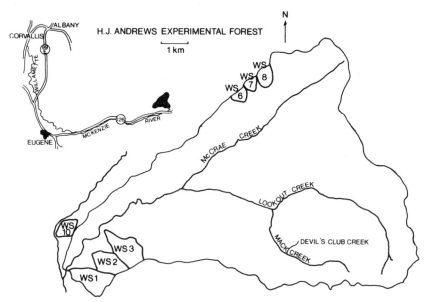

FIGURE 1.4 *Map of the H. J. Andrews Experimental Forest, Oregon, showing the location of gauged watershed and main study creeks.*

FIGURE 1.5 *A 450-year-old Douglas-fir stand in the H. J. Andrews Experimental Forest, Oregon.*

TABLE 1.3 *General site descriptions for the A. E. Thompson Research Center and Findley Lake, Washington, and the H. J. Andrews Experimental Forest, Oregon.*

Site	Latitude	Longitude	Elevation (m)	Mean annual radiation (cal/m^2)	Mean annual temperature (°C)	Mean annual precipitation (mm)	Precipitation during growing season (mm)	Forest type	Soil type & geology	Soil pH
A. E. Thompson Research Center	47°23' N	121°57' W	210	99 280	9.4	1140	670	Young-growth Douglas-fir	Typic Haplorthod derived from glacial till; good drainage	5.4–5.9
Findley Lake	47°19' N	121°35' W	1128	71 540	5.4	2730	270	Old-growth Pacific silver fir	Cryandepts (Podzols), Andesite	4.6–5.6
H. J. Andrews Experimental Forest	44°15' N	122°20' W	430–900	141 970	8.5	2300	<300	Old-growth Douglas-fir	Regasol, reddish brown lateritic intergrade; good drainage, Miocene tuffs & breccias	5.5–6.2

TABLE 1.4   *Description of a typical soil profile in the H. J. Andrews Forest (reference stand no. 2—Typic Dystrochrept).*

Horizon	Depth (cm)	Description
011	4–3	Twigs, needles, cones and so forth (L)
012	3–0	Partially decomposed twigs, cones, and so forth (F)
A1	0–15	Dark-brown, gravelly silt loam, very fine granular structure, very friable, gradual smooth boundary, few pumice grains, pH 5.5
A3	15–33	Dark-brown gravelly silt loam, very fine granular structure, very friable, gradual smooth boundary, few pumice grains, pH 5.5
IIB1	33–53	Brown, dark-brown, silty clay, very fine subangular blocky structure, friable gradual wavy boundary, common pumice grains, pH 5.8
IIB2	53–74	Brown, dark-brown, silty clay, fine subangular blocky structure, friable, gradual wavy boundary, common pumice grain, pH 5.8
IIB3	74-94	Brown, dark-brown, gravelly silty clay, fine subangular blocky structure, friable, abundant pumice grains, pH 5.8
IIC	94–119+	Brown, dark-brown, gravelly silty clay, massive structure, friable, pumice grains common, pH 5.8

Source: R. B. Brown and R. B . Parsons, 1973, *Soils of the Reference Stands, Oregon,* IBP Coniferous Forest Biome Internal Report 128, 76 p.

TABLE 1.5   *Physical characterization of streams in and near the H. J. Andrews Forest.*

Stream	Mean width (m)	Mean depth (m)	Stream gradient (%)	Water shed area (km²)	Stream length (km)	Freshets/yr 5 × base flow	Freshets/yr 10 × base flow	Stream order	Elev. (m)
Watershed 10 stream	1.0	0.05	45.0	0.1	0.5			1	430
Devil's Club Creek	0.6	0.05	40.0	0.2	0.5	32	13	1	810
Mack Creek	3.0	0.22	13.0	6.0	12.0	5	5	3	800
Lookout Creek	12.0	0.90	3.0	60.5	14.4	6	2	5	420
McKenzie River	40.0	1.60	0.6	1024.0	57.6	0	2	6	420

often have western red cedar *(Thuja plicata)* as the dominant tree species with devil's club *(Oplopanax horridum)* as the major understory species. A more comprehensive description of the vegetation of the Andrews Forest is given in Hawk et al. (1978).

Three of the five stream study sites are within the Andrews Forest (Devil's Club Creek, Mack Creek, and Lookout Creek) and the others are adjacent to the forest (watershed 10 and McKenzie River). The characteristics of these streams are shown in Table 1.5 and a representative section of Mack Creek is shown in Figure 1.6

FIGURE 1.6   *A section of Mack Creek, in the H. J. Andrews Forest, Oregon.*

In addition to studies of terrestrial and stream biology, erosion studies were also carried out throughout the H. J. Andrews Forest. The impact of road construction on erosion and the effect of erosion on streams was assessed.

Lake Washington Drainage

The Lake Washington drainage basin (Figure 1.7) is composed of two distinct subdrainages, the Sammamish valley, which includes Lake Sammamish, and the Cedar River valley. Findley Lake at 1128 m elevation and Chester Morse Lake at 470 m (a larger reservoir system) are in the Cedar River valley. Both valleys drain into Lake Washington. The landforms of the lower Cedar River watershed are primarily the result of continental glaciation. The upper Cedar River watershed reflects alpine glaciation during the Pleistocene.

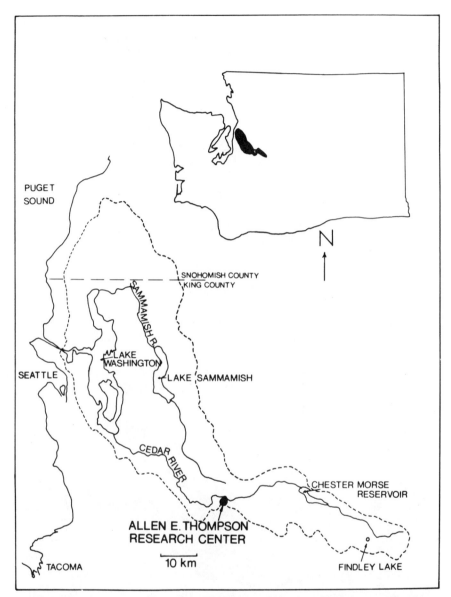

FIGURE 1.7 *Map of the Lake Washington drainage, Washington, showing the location of the Allen E. Thompson Research Center and the four study lakes.*

Terrestrial research was carried out at the Allen E. Thompson Research Center in the lower Cedar River watershed and at Findley Lake (Figure 1.7). General site descriptions are given in Table 1.3. Research at the Thompson site, elevation 210 m, focused on process studies of primary productivity (including gas-exchange studies); consumers; decomposers; and mineral, carbon, and water cycling in young-growth (10- to 100-year-old) Douglas-fir stands. Vegetation and vertebrate and invertebrate consumer surveys were made in the whole watershed. Findley Lake, in the upper watershed (Figures 1.7 and 1.8), was the primary site for research concerning the transfer of nutrients, energy, and water from land to lake. These studies were complemented by sedimentation and decomposition measurements in the lake.

Three forest community types can be delineated at the Thompson site. These seral communities are, in order of increasing soil moisture: Douglas-fir/salal, Douglas-fir/sword fern, and red alder/sword fern. A forty-three-year-old Douglas-fir/salal community is shown in Figure 1.9.

Soils at the Thompson site are typically derived from glacial outwash deposits and are gravelly, sandy loams. The Douglas fir/salal community generally occurs on the Everett series (Typic Haplorthod). A profile is given in Table 1.6. The Alderwood soil series occurs in moister areas at the Thompson site.

The Findley Lake study area is an approximately 150-ha cirque basin containing a small (10-ha) cirque lake. Elevations in the study area range from 1128 m at lake level to about 1450 m along the ridges bordering the cirque.

Vegetation of the basin is diverse, ranging from dense, 170-year-old Pacific silver fir/western hemlock stands through *Alnus sinuata* (Sitka alder) brushland to wet meadows, avalanche tracks, and talus slopes (del Moral 1973). Primary understory species are beargrass *(Xerophyllum tenax)* and several species of huckleberry *(Vaccinium membranecium* and *V. ovalifolium).*

FIGURE 1.8 *Findley Lake, Washington.*

FIGURE 1.9 *A 43-year-old Douglas-fir stand at the Allen E. Thompson Research Center, Washington.*

TABLE 1.6 *Description of the Everett soil profile (Typic Haplorthod) occurring at the Allen E. Thompson research site.*[a]

Horizon	Depth (cm)	Description
Forest		
floor	2.5–0	Undecomposed moses, twigs, needles
A1	0–8	Decomposed organic matter
		Dark brown gravelly, sandy loam; weak granular structure; friable; clear wavy boundary; many roots; pH 5.4
B21	8–24	Dark brown gravelly, sandy loam; massive to very weak structure; very friable; clear wavy boundary; many roots; pH 5.6
B22	24–45	Brown gravelly, loamy sand; massive structure; very friable; an abrupt wavy boundary; many roots; pH 5.85
C1	45–72	Yellow brownish gray very gravelly sand; single grain structure; friable; clear wavy boundary; few roots; pH 5.85
C2	>72	Variegated colored very gravelly sand; single grain structure; friable; no roots

[a]From Edmonds 1974.

Bedrock geology consists primarily of fractured andesitic lava flow overlain near the lake outlet by terminal and lateral moraines, which are also composed primarily of andesite. A number of volcanic ash layers have been deposited on both the bedrock and glacial moraines. Soils of the watershed, primarily podzols, have developed in these deposits. A typical soil profile is shown in Table 1.7.

Characteristics of the four study lakes (Findley, Chester Morse, Sammamish, and Washington) are shown in Table 1.8. Within these lakes, primary and secondary production, nutrient cycling, and the life histories, energetics, and population dynamics of resident and migratory fishes were studied. All but Findley Lake contain fish.

The four lakes drain substantially different basins. Findley Lake and its forested watershed have not been subjected to any significant human disturbance. Chester Morse Lake, which is a reservoir, is surrounded by second-growth Douglas-fir forests. Lake Sammamish is characterized by second-growth Douglas-fir forests, small farms, and residential areas. Lake Washington is located within the boundaries of metropolitan Seattle and receives intensive recreational use. The lake has a well-documented history of change, including lowering of the lake level during construction of a ship canal as a new outlet in 1916. This was followed by a period of human-caused eutrophication through about 1963 with subsequent recovery in recent years (Edmondson 1972).

TABLE 1.7 *Description of a typical soil profile at Findley Lake.*[a]

Horizon	Depth (cm)	Description
01	5–3	Partially decomposed conifer needles and broken twigs
02	3–0	Well-decomposed and humified organic matter
A2	0–11	Gray sandy clay loam; weakly structured, very friable, clear irregular boundary, plentiful roots, Mt. St. Helens volcanic ash; pH 4.3
IIB2hir	11–31	Dark yellowish-brown coarse sandy loam, weakly structured, very friable, abrupt broken boundary, plentiful roots, Mazama volcanic ash; pH 4.7
IIIB31	31–53	Dark yellowish-brown very gravelly clay loam, moderate structure, clear wavy boundary, few roots, Mazama volcanic ash; pH 4.8
IVB32	53–100	>90 percent coarse (>5 cm in diameter) fragments mostly of broken andesite rocks, rock fragments coated with both organic and clayey material; pH 4.6
IVC	>100	Fragmented andesite; gravelly in the upper 5 cm, becoming bouldery below

[a]Adapted from Ugolini et al. 1977.

TABLE 1.8 *Physical characteristics of lakes Findley, Chester Morse, Sammamish, and Washington.*

Lake	Maximum depth (m)	Mean depth (m)	Euphotic zone depth (m)	Lake area (ha)	Volume (m³)	Turnover (per yr)	Ice cover duration (mo)	Annual precipitation (cm)	Drainage basin area (ha)	Elevation (m)	Stratification	Annual temperature range Surface (°C)	Bottom (°C)
Findley	27	7.8	27.0	12	$8.6 \cdot 20^5$	7.0	7–9	273	10^2	1128.0	Summer & winter	2.5–20	4–6
Chester Morse	35	19.0	14.0	681	$1.35 \cdot 10^8$	0.4	0–1	266		470.0	June to October	4–20	7–9
Sammamish	32	17.7	7.3	1980	$3.5 \cdot 10^8$	1.8	0	90	$2.5 \cdot 10^7$	12.0	Summer	5–20	7–9
Washington	65	33.0	10.0	8760	$4.9 \cdot 10^9$	0.3	0	90	$1.2 \cdot 10^5$	6.5	June to October	4–22	7–9

Other Sites

Although limited data were obtained from other regions in the biome, these data have been used to compare the structure and function of coniferous forest ecosystems across the biome with those of the intensive sites. To provide the geographic dimension, research projects were carried out as part of the coordinating sites (Figure 1.2) and environmental grid programs. These activities are indicated in Table 1.2.

HIGHLIGHTS OF THE CONIFEROUS FOREST BIOME RESEARCH PROGRAM

Broad-scale ecological questions can be answered adequately only by a multidisciplinary ecosystem approach such as that undertaken by the Coniferous Forest Biome research program. Because of this approach we now have a better understanding of how coniferous forests in the western United States behave in natural and managed situations. Extensive use was made of conceptual and mathematical models to structure and direct the research toward specific goals.

Most of our efforts were concentrated on investigating three questions: Why do coniferous species dominate in the western United States? How is forest productivity related to the physical environment, particularly climate and soil nutrients? What impact do forest management practices such as clearcutting have on these coniferous forests, especially with respect to nutrient losses and effects on aquatic ecosystems? These questions are discussed below.

Dominance of Coniferous Species in the Western United States

The forests in the western United States, particularly along the Pacific coast, are unique among the temperate forests of the world. These evergreen coniferous forests contrast sharply with the deciduous hardwood forests that dominate elsewhere in the North Temperate Zone (Waring and Franklin 1979). The few hardwoods in these forests typically are pioneer species slowly replaced by conifers or occupy environmentally marginal habitats such as lakeshore or streambanks.

We believe that the dominance of coniferous species is due to past climatic events, including glaciation, periods of dryness, and changes in the annual distribution of heat. Certain structural features of western conifers have enabled them to compete well against hardwoods.

Structural Features of Western Conifers

Structural features of conifers, such as evergreen habit, needleshaped leaves, large leaf areas, conical crowns, massiveness, and the ability to grow to great ages are all advantageous in the western United States. Western conifers seem well suited to the present climate where summer drought and winter rainfall dominate. They seem to do well in stressful environments, particularly where fire is important. Fire frequencies, however, are low in coastal forests. Adaptations to temperature, light, moisture, wind, and nutrients are apparent.

The evergreen habit is well adapted to conditions in the biome. Conifers can assimilate over a broad temperature range. Since winter temperatures are mild (above freezing daytime temperatures are not uncommon even in montane environments) photosynthesis can proceed year-round. In fact, as much as half the annual net carbon assimilation by lowland Douglas-fir may occur between October and May. This period is entirely lost to deciduous hardwoods. Long conical crowns further assist by intercepting a great amount of radiation during low winter sun angles.

Favorable winter moisture in the biome allows conifer photosynthesis to proceed, but dry summer conditions constrain it. Stomata are forced to close to reduce water loss by transpiration and at the same time CO_2 uptake is reduced. Stomatal closure is induced both by low soil moisture and high evaporative demand. Dry summer conditons, however, are even more unfavorable for deciduous hardwoods since this is their growing season.

The water storage capacity of the large volume of sapwood possessed by many western conifers tends to lessen the effect of dry summers. It is a significant buffer against transpiration extremes and may partially recharge after summer rain. Large leaf areas also help the summer water balance since they serve as condensing surfaces for fog or dew.

It is likely that the general lack of hurricane-strength winds, except close to the coast or on ridgetops, allows conifers to grow to large sizes and ages. Many of the twenty-five coniferous species in the Pacific Northwest are extremely long-lived. For example, Douglas-fir can live to 1000 years and giant redwood may live for over 3800 years. The oldest living plant, a bristlecone pine *(Pinus aristata),* is 4600 years old. In addition, in coastal areas insect epidemics are rare, heart rots act slowly, and fire frequency is low.

Conifers generally have lower nutrient requirements and use nutrients, particularly nitrogen, more efficiently than hardwoods. The reduction of annual nutrient requirements through foliage retention is an obvious advantage for conifers, particularly on low-nitrogen soils. Also decomposition and nutrient release are low during the summer in the biome and it is at this time that hardwood nutrient demand is high. Therefore, it is not surprising that one of the most widespread deciduous species in the biome, red alder, is a nitrogen fixer.

The dominance of evergreen conifers in western United States forests appears to be an evolutionary response to a climate with warm, dry summers and cool, wet winters. These forests are well adapted to such an environment. The adaptation is extremely successful; they are among the most productive forests in the world.

Determination of plant productivity and of the factors influencing it was one of the major objectives of the International Biological Program. Biome scientists now have considerably better estimates of the productivity of western coniferous forests. Certainly a large amount of information now exists for Douglas-fir forests as discussed below.

Forest Productivity in the Biome and the Factors Influencing It

Biomass Accumulation and Productivity of Conifers in the Biome

Biomass accumulations in old-growth coastal forests of the biome are huge. For example, estimates of total standing biomass excluding roots may be as high as 1700 t/ha for Douglas-fir and noble fir. Maximum values for coastal redwood are about twice that for Douglas-fir (3500 t/ha). These values greatly exceed accepted norms for temperate forests. Maximum reported values for temperate deciduous, temperate evergreen hardwood, and tropical forests in contrast are 422, 575, and 415 t/ha, respectively (Art and Marks 1971).

Annual above-ground net primary production ranges from 5.7 to 13.1 t/ha for Douglas-fir, with maximum rates in young stands. Higher annual above-ground rates have been recorded for western hemlock (32.2 t/ha) and red alder (26 t/ha). The major factors influencing this productivity are leaf surface area, rates of canopy closure, and moisture and nutrient regimes.

Factors Influencing Productivity

Leaf surface area. Accumulations of biomass result from carbon fixation in the photosynthetic process in the tree canopy. The amount of photosynthesis occurring in an ecosystem is related to the amount of leaf surface area exposed to sunlight. Other things being equal, the more leaf area an ecosystem can maintain, the more photosynthesis it can carry on. Clearly, then, the leaf area of a stand is an important factor determining its productivity (Grier et al. 1979). Sites capable of supporting large leaf areas are in general more productive than those supporting smaller leaf areas.

The maximum leaf area of a stand is related to a number of factors. Among these are climate, soil nutrition, and species. Typically, as trees in a developing stand get larger, the leaf area increases until it reaches a plateau at canopy closure. Peak production of a stand occurs at canopy closure.

The major factor influencing maximum leaf area appears to be the site water balance. A summer dry period in the Pacific Northwest is common and this period coincides with the growing season. This means that water required by forests for growth and survival through the summer is provided mainly by water stored in the soil at the beginning of the growing season. Normal growth of a stand in the early growing season causes leaf area to overshoot levels the climate can support. As soil water levels become low later in the growing season, trees react by closing their stomata; this halts photosynthesis but does not stop other necessary life processes of individual trees. The life processes are sustained by photosynthate reserves stored in the trees. If the reserves of a tree are exhausted the tree dies, lowering the total stand's leaf area. *Weaker* trees have smaller reserves; thus they are more likely to die than the *dominant* trees in a stand. This is one of the reasons for a continuing decline in stand density with increasing tree size. Growing trees are continuously putting pressure on an essentially fixed resource. Other factors also having a potential influence on maximum leaf area are winter water balance, gross nutrient deficits or imbalance, and mechanical damage by wind or snow.

Rate of canopy closure. The rate at which the canopy closes also influences forest productivity. Our studies have shown that the rate at which a forest canopy closes on a given site is related to three primary factors: (1) initial stocking density; (2) soil nutrient status; and (3) competition from brushy and herbaceous species. The influence of brush competition on tree growth is obvious—seedling growth is suppressed by heavy competition for light, water, and nutrients.

In some parts of the Pacific Northwest, reliable stand regeneration is virtually impossible without pre- or postplanting herbicide treatment. The influence of initial stocking density on canopy closure rate is relatively straightforward. In a stand with low initial stocking each individual tree contributes a relatively large proportion of a total crown. The time required for each tree to develop its proportion of the total canopy is greater than in a dense stand where much less growth is required before between-tree competition begins.

Nutrition. Nutrition is another important factor influencing the rate of canopy closure and, at least over the short term, leaf area. The foliage of a tree contains large amounts of nutrients. For a stand to reach maximum productivity it must take up enough of the various nutrients required to develop a full canopy. Time is required for a canopy to develop. Some of the nutrients required to grow new foliage and increase the canopy each year are supplied by the soil; the remainder are translocated to the new foliage from older parts of the tree. If nutrients are only sparingly available from the soil, then the amount translocated from older tissues is large; if nutrients are readily available then translocation is small. Thus translocation serves to conserve within the tree nutrients that are in short supply.

In spite of translocation, if nutrients such as nitrogen are in short supply, the amount of new foliage that can be produced each year is less than could be produced if nutrients were more available. Hence the rate at which a full canopy can develop is in many cases limited by the rate at which nutrients are made available to the trees.

Probably the most important single factor in the mineral nutrition of forests is the availability of nutrients. This subject was one of the major areas of biome research. Many forests have large amounts of the various plant nutrients present but, because they are not in the proper chemical form—that is, generally ionic—they are not available to the trees.

Nutrients must be mineralized before they can be taken up and mineralization can be influenced by a number of factors. Some of the more important results of our research concerned the influence of litter quality on decomposition and nutrient mineralization. Forests produce a variety of different kinds of litter ranging from tree needles to whole logs. Biome researchers have shown substantial uptake and immobilization of nitrogen by decomposers inhabiting woody material such as branches and fallen logs. These observations imply that addition of woody residues to a forest ecosystem by precommercial thinning or a harvest operation could serve to reduce the availability of nutrients while the material is decomposing. This could serve both to reduce nutrient losses by leaching and reduce nutrient availability for residual trees or seedlings. In fact, undisturbed coniferous forests are strongly conservative of nutrients that are present in limited amounts, such as nitrogen.

Biome scientists have demonstrated that the native forests in the biome are well adapted to a climate where summer drought dominates and nutrients, particularly nitrogen, are in poor supply. Despite these apparent handicaps they are still among the most productive forests in the world. Many of the original old-growth forests, however, have been removed as a result of forest management and converted to young-growth plantations with rotation ages of sixty to eighty years. Forests in the biome have changed drastically in the last fifty years and the nature of this change was investigated by biome researchers. Particular attention was paid to clearcutting and its impacts as discussed below.

Impact of Forest Management Practices on Western Coniferous Forests

Man was quick to realize the economic value of forests in the western coniferous biome, particularly the coastal forests, and cutting large areas of old-growth forests for lumber and pulp has been widely practiced since before the turn of the century. Clearcutting is now viewed as a routine forest management tool, especially in coastal Douglas-fir, western hemlock, and redwood forests. It is not the only forest management tool used, but the others, such as fertilization, thinning, and the exclusion of fire, have not created the public outcries that clearcutting has invoked. Hence only clearcutting is discussed here.

Although clearcutting and the conversion of old-growth stands to rapidly growing young-growth stands has been practiced for over seventy years throughout the biome, we have only recently begun to assess its impact. An opportunity to examine the impact of clearcutting an old-growth Douglas-fir ecosystem arose in the Coniferous Forest Biome program with the cutting of trees in watershed 10 adjacent to the H. J. Andrews Experimental Forest in the summer of 1975. Changes in forest structure, nutrient losses, productivity, and aquatic ecosystems were examined.

Changes in Forest Structure

One of the major impacts of clearcutting is the change in the structure of forests. Resulting young-growth stands are distinctly different from old-growth stands. There is less diversity in both animal and plant species in young-growth stands, although annual productivity is higher. Establishment of artificial plantations tends to reduce diversity further since they generally contain one tree species such as Douglas-fir.

Old-growth forests have greater variations in tree sizes. Canopies are usually multilayered and patchiness occurs in the understory. Three structural components of old-growth forests are of major ecological importance: living old-growth trees, standing dead trees (snags), and large logs on the forest floor. Standing dead trees form important ecological compartments, particularly for birds, and logs on the forest floor represent large pools of nutrients and organic matter. They also provide sites for seedling regeneration, bacterial nitrogen fixation, and wildlife. Furthermore they assist in preventing erosion. For example, large woody debris in streams stabilizes streambeds and banks, and influences sediment routing and the distribution of aquatic habitats.

Changes in Forest Function and Productivity

Clearcutting has changed the structure of forests in the coniferous forest biome, but how has it affected their functioning? It has been proposed that clearcutting increases nutrient losses from forests because of increased decomposition, nitrification, runoff, and erosion. Erosion in particular is greatly aggravated by road construction associated with log removal.

Increased nutrient losses potentially reduce forest productivity and many people have proposed that clearcutting be ceased for this reason. Others believe wildlife habitats are destroyed, although certain animals such as deer and elk may thrive in clearcuts as long as they can gain shelter in adjacent forested areas. Although it is still too early to make a final assessment of the effect of clearcutting of watershed 10 on nutrient losses, nitrate losses to the stream were not dramatically increased after clearcutting. The maintenance of a zone of streamside vegetation was extremely important in preventing nitrate losses.

Assessments of the effects on forest productivity are not yet available and will take many more years. If nutrient losses are not great, however, it may be anticipated that clearcutting by itself will have little impact on productivity. The impact of whole tree harvesting and short rotations may have additional effects.

Impact on Streams

Clearcutting also has an impact on streams. Fish productivity may be affected positively or negatively. For example, trout production may increase because of higher stream temperatures and nutrient levels, resulting in an increase in algae and insects, which act as food sources for fish. On the other hand, torrents may remove debris dams and destroy spawning sites, and the increased turbidity will adversely affect fish production. Careless clearcutting can result in erosion, nutrient losses, stream degradation, and potential loss of forest productivity; however, many of the negative aspects can be minimized if clearcutting is carried out carefully.

MANAGEMENT IMPLICATIONS OF THE CONIFEROUS FOREST BIOME PROGRAM

It is difficult to deal completely with the full range of potential management implications of a program as large and complex as the Coniferous Forest Biome. Some of the contributions are indirect. Problem-solving methods and analytical tools such as modeling developed by biome scientists are now being incorporated into the training of foresters and many have been exposed to the concept of ecosystem analysis.

Direct contributions of biome research to understanding the functioning of forests have been far ranging. For example, we now know how strongly forests influence streams and lakes and the stability of the physical landscape. Other studies have clarified the processes involved in regulating nutrient availability, and we have a clearer understanding of the processes responsible for forest growth and development and how forest management influences growth.

Studies of forest productivity point the way for the development of a more accurate classification of the production potential of forest sites and the ability to predict growth response to various thinning regimes. Management practices that hasten canopy closure also may hasten the point during the rotation at which maximum productivity is achieved.

Research in forest nutrition has yielded a clearer understanding of the relation between growth and nutrition. Further research in this area could easily result in: (1) the ability to predict growth response to fertilizer applications; or (2) development of management techniques that can increase nutrient availability without the need for fertilization.

As research results are directly applied to the solving of silvicultural problems, new methods of assessing site potential and forest growth will probably emerge. The forester of the future will likely be as familiar with the meaning of plant and soil analysis as agronomists are today.

Results from the Coniferous Forest Biome program have provided further insight into the changing nature of western coniferous forests and the impact of man. The program established the use of ecosystem analysis as a means of studying coniferous forests. The approach is now firmly established and it should help in the development of sensible land-use management schemes.

LITERATURE CITED

Art, H. W., and P. L. Marks, 1971, A summary table of biomass and net annual primary production on forest ecosystems of the world, in *Forest Biomass Studies,* H. E. Young, ed., Life Sci. and Agric. Exp. Stn. Misc. Publ. 132, University of Maine, Orono, pp. 3–32.

del Moral, R., 1973, The vegetation of the Findley Lake basin, *Am. Midl. Nat.* **89:**26–40.

Edmonds, R. L. (ed.), 1974, An initial synthesis of results in the Coniferous Forest Biome, 1970–1973, *Coniferous Forest Biome Bulletin No. 7,* University of Washington, Seattle, 248p.

Edmondson, W. T., 1972, The present condition of Lake Washington, *Int. Soc. Theor. Appl. Limnol. Proc.* **16:**153–158.

Franklin, J. R., and C. T. Dyrness, 1973, Natural vegetation of Oregon and Washington, *U.S. Department of Agriculture Forest Service General Technical Report* PNW-8, U.S. Department of Agriculture Forest Service, Portland, Oreg., 417p.

Grier, C. C., R. L. Edmonds, D. W. Cole, and R. H. Waring, 1979, Forest management implications of productivity, nutrient cycling and water relations research in western conifers, in Proc. 1978 Annu. Meet., Soc. Am. For. and Can. Inst. of For. St. Louis, Mo. Society of American Foresters, Washington, D.C., pp. 96–106.

Hawk, G. M., J. F. Franklin, W. A. McKee, and R. B. Brown, 1978, H. J. Andrews reference stand system: Establishment and use history, *US/IBP Coniferous Forest Biome Bulletin No. 12,* University of Washington, Seattle, 79p.

Ugolini, F. C., H. Dawson, and J. Zachara, 1977, Direct evidence of particle migration in the soil solution of a Podzol, *Science* **198:**603–605.

Waring, R. H., and J. F. Franklin, 1979, Evergreen forests of the Pacific Northwest, *Science* **204:**1380–1386.

Washington State Department of Ecology, 1975, Reconnaissance data on lakes in Washington, *Water-Supply Bulletin 43,* Vols. 1-4, Olympia, Washington.

2

Relations Between Vegetation and Environment

G. M. Hawk, J. N. Long, and *J. F. Franklin*

INTRODUCTION

The Coniferous Forest Biome program directed much of its early efforts to sampling, ordering, classifying, and describing forest communities. The formulation of hypotheses to explain vegetation diversity resulted, and correlations between environmental and vegetational gradients have emerged.

Most of the work relating vegetational and environmental gradients was conducted at the two intensive study sites (The Cedar River watershed, Washington, and the H. J. Andrews Experimental Forest, Oregon) and is discussed here. The vegetation of the intensive sites is discussed in detail in Chapter 1 so a brief description is sufficient here.

The principal vegetation zones of western Washington are represented in the Cedar River watershed. The *Tsuga heterophylla* zone occurs below about 600 m elevation, the *Abies amabilis* zone between 600 m and 1300 m, and the *Tsuga mertensiana* zone generally above 1300 m elevation.

Most of the lower watershed is covered by second-growth forests that date from logging or fires early in the century. *Pseudotsuga menziesii* is the dominant overstory species on all but the wettest sites; *Alnus rubra* occurs on these sites, the only forest stands not dominated by conifers.

Between 600 and 1000 m in elevation periodic disturbances, primarily fires, have been frequent enough to result in the dominance by *Tsuga heterophylla* on most sites. *Abies amabilis* is the principal species reproducing beneath the canopies of mature stands. At higher elevations *Tsuga heterophylla* disappears, leaving *Abies amabilis* as the principal dominant community.

Subzonal vegetational units on the Cedar River watershed have been identified (Table 2.1) and described by del Moral and Long (1977). Ten different community types were recognized, six of which represent old-growth stands on the upper watershed (above 600 m) and four that represent second-growth stands on the lower watershed (about 180 to 600 m). Extensive descriptions of

TABLE 2.1 *Summary of the major factors characterizing the vegetation types of the Cedar River watershed.[a]*

Group	Community type[b]	Elevation (m)	Aspect	Slope	Age (yr)	Comments
A	Tshe-Abam/Xete	900–1200	W-SE	mod-steep	250	Not wholly homogenous; two groups joined by discriminant analysis
B	Tshe/Vaov	700–900	E-NW	gentle	250–300	Greater Abam dominance than C
C	Tshe/Vaal	600–1000	W-NE	gentle-mod	250	Well-developed Abam regeneration
D	Abam-Tsme/Xete	900–1200	various	mod	150–250	Regeneration mainly Abam
E	Abam/Vame-Vaov	700–900	various	steep	200–250	Strong Abam dominance
F	Abam-Tshe/Vame	900–1200	various	moderate	—	Differs from E in high amounts of Tshe
G	Psme/Gash	190–400	W-S-E	gentle	38–73	Characteristic of xeric habitats within the Tshe zone
H	Psme/Pomu	280–490	various	gentle-mod	31–50	Seral stands, hemlock regeneration
I	Psme/Pomu-Libo	190–550	various	gentle	40	Similar to H except in relatively high abundance of Libo
J	Alru/Pomu	170–520	various	gentle	39–50	Such stands are exceedingly common in Puget Sound Lowlands particularly on moist and recently disturbed sites

[a]From del Moral and Long 1977; *copyright © 1977 by the British Columbia Provincial Museum and the authors.*

[b]See Table 2.2 for identification of abbreviations.

these plant communities are published elsewhere (Long 1973, 1976; del Moral and Long 1977).

Sampling of the H. J. Andrews site in Oregon was based on prior knowledge of general plant communities of the area (Dyrness 1965; Rothacher et al. 1967). Plots represented the majority of closed forest communities on both extreme and moderate sites. Other regional classifications were reviewed and incorporated into the classification of the H. J. Andrews site (Franklin et al. 1972; Dyrness 1973; Hawk and Zobel 1974).

The rationale, in part, for the biome studies of vegetation and community environmental interactions was to direct specific attention to testing hypothesized relations between floristic gradients and climatic gradients in moisture, temperature, snow depth, and snow duration. If community types or vegetation gradients are highly correlated with key environmental factors, the results of detailed process studies can be extrapolated over a much broader area where it would be prohibitively expensive to install instrumentation. The objective of these studies were: (1) to describe the key structural and compositional features of forest ecosystems in order to relate these features to ecosystem function; (2) to ordinate the vegetation sample plots using solely vegetation characteristics; (3) to use the ordination results and environmental data to formulate hypotheses that might explain vegetation–environment interactions; and (4) to test the hypotheses.

The approaches used at the two intensive study sites varied though the same ultimate objectives were reached. On the Washington site, specific plant communities were selected according to the supposition that they represented different portions of the environmental spectrum. The plots were sampled, ordered, and then classified. On the Oregon site, previous classification studies were combined with our own sampling (Franklin et al. 1970) to develop the ordination and classification scheme.

VEGETATION CLASSIFICATION AND ORDINATION

Because of the broad spectrum of community and environmental variation in the study sites, a large number of stands was sampled to stratify the vegetation into relatively homogeneous and easily recognizable units. A rapid reconnaissance method for sampling vegetation was used (Franklin et al. 1970) that enabled data acquisition over a wide range of environments and ensured a reasonable degree of completeness in representing the different forest stand types. A total of forty-three mature and forty-five second-growth forest stands was sampled in the Cedar River watershed. Three hundred plots were sampled in and around the H. J. Andrews Experimental Forest.

In synecological studies, a common objective has been to describe apparently homogeneous vegetation units and to discuss their interrelationships (with regard primarily to floristics); however, ecosystem studies demand clarification not only of the relations between units but also between them and the environment. The approach used to determine these relations was indirect gradient analysis, that is, the use of vegetation ordination to infer environmental gradients (Whittaker 1970). This implies that vegetation gradients such as those generated in Washington and Oregon may or may not always correspond to actual environmental gradients.

A computer routine, SIMORD, was used to ordinate the vegetation data (Dick-Peddie and Moir 1970; Franklin et al. 1970; Hawk and Zobel 1974). The routine is similar to the Wisconsin comparative ordination techniques. SIMORD results in a two-dimensional reference stand ordination with the position of a stand in the ordination plane dependent on that stand's similarity (of vegetation characteristics) to other stands included in the analysis.

Ordination, in this context, is the arrangement of stands into one or more derived vegetation gradients. Floristic characteristics were used to delimit portions of the gradients into relatively homogeneous plant communities. Environmental sampling was done in stands representative of particular community types or location along the vegetational gradient. The results of these investigations were then used to establish relations between vegetational and environmental gradients.

The ordination of plant communities of the H. J. Andrews Experimental Forest resulted in the separation of twenty-three plant communities over the vegetational gradient (Figure 2.1). Of the twenty-three communities, fourteen are in the *Tsuga heterophylla* (Tshe) zone, including the transition zone, and nine are in the *Abies amabilis* (Abam) zone or the lower part of the *Tsuga mertensiana* (Tsme) zone. The *Tsuga heterophylla* zone is at low elevation and dominated by *Pseudotsuga menziesii, Tsuga heterophylla,* and *Thuja plicata.* Past studies and the ordination procedures used made it obvious that *Tsuga heterophylla* zone communities were displayed (Figure 2.1) along a complex moisture gradient with *Tsuga heterophylla* the climax dominant in all but the driest communities. The *Abies amabilis* zone is at high elevation and dominated by *Abies amabilis, Tsuga heterophylla,* and *Tsuga mertensiana* in mature

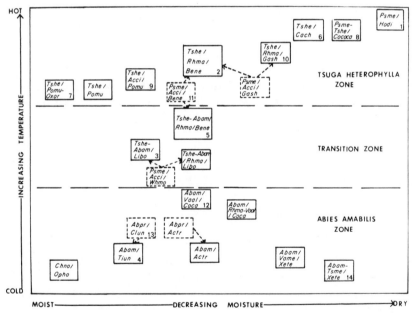

FIGURE 2.1 *Hypothesized relations between forest communities and environment in the central western Cascades (Dyrness et al. 1974). This figure is based on their vegetation ordinations, somewhat modified by the intuition of the investigators. Communities enclosed with dashed borders are considered to be seral, the others to be climax. Communities sampled in this study are identified by the reference stand number in the box.*

climax forest, and *Pseudotsuga menziesii* and *Abies procera* in subclimax stands. These upper elevation forests also appear to be arranged along a moisture gradient.

A large area of forest lies between the *Tsuga heterophylla* and *Abies amabilis* zones, representing a transition zone dominated by mixed young- and old-growth stands of *Pseudotsuga menziesii, Tsuga heterophylla, Thuja plicata,* and *Abies amabilis.* The *Tsuga mertensiana* zone is not a major zone in the Cascades of central western Oregon; therefore its lower elevational components were treated as elements of the *Abies amabilis* zone.

Association tables were constructed as a result of the ordination analysis for stands in the H. J. Andrews Forest and these are presented in Dyrness et al. (1974). The tables illustrate the difficulty of classifying habitat types within an area that includes substantial landscape and species diversity. A diagrammatic display of plant communities over the observed temperature and moisture gradients (Figure 2.1) shows the *Pseudotsuga menziesii/Holodiscus discolor* (Psme/Hodi) community at the warm dry extreme, followed by communities in cooler and moister environments along the gradients. The sword fern communities of lower elevations are at the warm moist extreme. *Rhododendron* communities are mesic in terms of both the temperatures and moisture gradients. Beargrass communities occupy the cool dry areas and herb-rich communities occupy the cool moist extremes at upper elevations.

Ordination of communities resulted in development of community classification keys. Present communities are finer resolution classification units than those defined as habitat types by Pfister et al. (1977) or Daubenmire (1968). Some of our communities include both habitat types and phases that are presently being defined.

DISTRIBUTION OF SPECIES AND COMMUNITIES ALONG ENVIRONMENTAL GRADIENTS

Cedar River Watershed, Washington

Ordination of data from old-growth stands in the *Abies amabilis* zone of the Cedar River watershed suggests that two environmental complexes are primarily responsible for controlling the distribution of these forest communities. It was hypothesized that these factors of the physical environment, correlating with the x- and y-axes of the ordination (Figure 2.2, Table 2.2), are: (1) factor(s) strongly correlated with elevation (x-axis); and (2) available soil moisture (y-axis).

The ordering of the stands along the x-axis indicates that elevation accounts for the distribution of the montane forest communities in the upper Cedar River watershed. For example, on the low end of the x-axis is a *Tsuga heterophylla*–dominated stand at 700 m, while an *Abies amabilis*–dominated stand at 1300 m represents the upper end of this vegetational gradient.

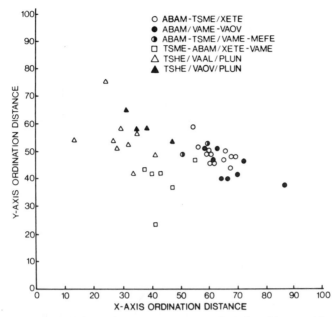

FIGURE 2.2 *Relations between stands in the* Abies amabilis *zone of the Cedar River watershed based on a vegetation ordination (Long 1976). Community classifications follow del Moral and Long (1977); abbreviations for communities are identified in Table 2.2.*

In the western Cascade Mountains of Washington there are several environmental factors strongly associated with elevation (del Moral et al. 1976). Some factors important in the distribution of vegetation include: (1) depth of snowpack; (2) air and soil temperature; and (3) precipitation and available soil moisture.

For community ordination on the Cedar River watershed, precipitation seems to be the least promising of the factors listed. The relation between mean annual precipitation and elevation for the entire watershed is not simple. The difference in precipitation at Seattle and Chester Morse Lake, corresponding approximately to the lower and upper elevational limits of the *Tsuga heterophylla* zone, is large in contrast to the difference in precipitation between Chester Morse Lake and Findley Lake, the elevations of which correspond closely to those of the lower and upper limits of the *Abies amabilis* zone (Figure 2.3). The implication is that within the Cedar River watershed there is a rather steep precipitation gradient associated with the *Tsuga heterophylla* zone and that this gradient is lacking in the *Abies amabilis* zone. The pattern of precipitation over the entire upper watershed is therefore a reflection of the orographic effect of high ridges on either side of the valley floor.

It was hypothesized that the most important environmental factor controlling distribution of forest communities within the *Abies amabilis* zone of the

TABLE 2.2   *Mean cover (percentage) for common species in vegetation types of the Cedar River watershed.*

Species	A	B	C	D	E	F	G	H	I	J	Avg.
Trees											
Abies amabilis (Abam)	25.8	28.0	10.5	41.8	76.2	35.0	0	0	0	0	19.2
Abies procera (Abpr)	17.5	0	0.1	0.8	0.1	1.6	0	0	0	0	1.4
Acer macrophyllum (Acma)	0	0	0	0	0	0	0	0	0.9	6.7	1.0
Alnus rubra (Alru)	0	0	0	0	0	0	0	1.6	0	74.6	10.4
Pseudotsuga menziesii (Psme)	12.7	4.2	17.8	0	0	3.3	76.4	71.4	78.1	3.4	27.4
Tsuga heterophylla (Tshe)	31.2	46.0	65.2	1.6	0.1	25.0	9.6	23.7	18.1	3.6	22.4
Tsuga mertensiana (Tsme)	0	0	0	34.0	9.6	5.3	4.5	0	0	0	6.3
Shrubs											
Acer circinatum (Acci)	4.7	0	3.0	0	0	0	3.6	2.6	2.5	7.8	2.7
Berberis nervosa (Bene)	0.2	0.2	3.9	0	0	0	2.7	0	1.3	3.8	1.6
Gaultheria shallon (Gash)	3.3	0	3.0	0	0	0	56.4	2.1	2.8	1.9	8.5
Menziesia ferruginea (Mefe)	0.2	3.0	1.7	6.9	3.5	17.0	0	0.1	0	0	2.3
Oplopanax horridum (Opho)	0	0	4.7	0.1	0	0	0	1.3	0	1.1	1.1
Vaccinium alaskaense (Vaal)	0.2	0	10.0	7.2	3.8	8.7	0	0	0	0	3.7
Vaccinium deliciosum (Vade)	0	0	0	4.7	0	0	0	0.3	0	0	0.6
Vaccinium membranaceum (Vame)	10.6	2.2	2.7	7.7	11.9	73.3	0.9	0.3	0	0	6.1
Vaccinium ovalifolium (Vaov)	0	46.0	5.0	1.3	9.4	0	0	0	0	0	4.6
Vaccinium parvifolium (Vapa)	1.2	3.2	3.1	0.1	0	0	2.4	2.4	3.4	1.1	1.8
Herbs and ferns											
Achyls triphylla (Actr)	4.5	0	3.2	0.2	0.2	1.6	0	0	0.1	0.6	1.0
Clintonia uniflora (Clun)	2.1	1.6	1.9	2.5	3.0	6.7	0	0	0	0	1.4
Festuca sp. (Fesp)	0	0	0	0	0	0	0	0.1	0.1	4.2	0.6
Linnaea borealis (Libo)	0.3	1.2	2.3	0	0	1.7	6.1	0.1	10.9	0.1	2.4
Polystichum munitum (Pomu)	0	0	0.3	0	0	0	3.7	65.0	23.0	58.3	15.9
Pteridium aquilinum (Ptaq)	0.3	0	0.1	0	0	0	8.0	1.8	1.8	8.4	2.5
Rubus ursinus (Ruur)	0	0	0.1	0	0	0	0	2.7	3.3	2.2	2.2
Tiarella trifoliata (Titr)	0	0.2	0.6	0.2	0.1	0	0	0.1	0	0.5	0.3
Tolmiea menziesii (Tome)	0	0	0	0	0	0	0	0	0	1.3	0.2
Xerophyllum tenax (Xete)	17.8	0.4	1.7	12.9	5.0	0	0	0	0	0.4	3.8
Mosses											
Eurhynchium organum (Euor)	0	0	1.9	0.8	0	2.0	39.1	18.5	27.5	9.3	10.8
Hylocomium splendens (Hysp)	0	0	1.1	0	0	0	3.1	1.0	12.2	1.4	2.0
Mnium insigne (Mnin)	0	0.2	0.1	0	0	0.3	0.5	1.4	0.8	0.8	0.4
Plagiothecium undulatum (Plun)	6.0	44.0	16.5	0.8	0.4	8.3	0	0	0	0	6.2

Note: Letters correspond to community types listed in Table 2.1.

Cedar River watershed is the depth and duration of winter snowpack. While there is apparently no great difference in the amount or timing of precipitation within the *Abies amabilis* zone, the form in which it falls varies considerably. At high elevations (Findley Lake, 1200 m) most precipitation falls as snow. The snowpack may be several meters thick and its duration may exceed seven

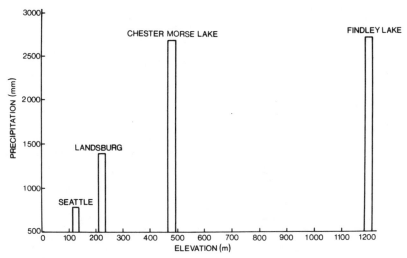

FIGURE 2.3 *Relation between mean annual precipitation and elevation for four locations in western Washington.*

months. In the Chester Morse Lake area the total annual snowfall is generally less than 120 cm, with snow remaining on the ground for less than thirty days.

We hypothesized that the *y*-axis of the Cedar River ordination represents a moisture gradient (this is inferred from the floristic gradient). For example, *Xerophyllum tenax*, a species indicative of dry habitats (Dyrness et al. 1974), is important only in those stands at the middle to lower end of this hypothesized moisture gradient. *Vaccinium ovalifolium*, a presumed mesic site indicator species, is important in stands at the middle to upper end of the moisture gradient.

Indirect gradient analysis thus yields the following hypotheses concerning the distribution of vegetation within the *Abies amabilis* zone on the Cedar River watershed: (1) a gradient in the winter snowpack depth and duration is responsible for much of the variability in the forest vegetation; and (2) a gradient in soil moisture during the growing season accounts for an additional component in the variability of the forests.

Population distribution of particular species along gradients may provide a starting point for determining the nature of particular plant-environment interactions. For example, snow depth, and by inference its duration, can be measured in each of several stands whose *x*-axis position is known. A high degree of correlation between these two variables can provide evidence for the existence of the hypothesized gradient as well as its association with the vegetational gradient. Similarly, correlation between seasonal development of water deficits and position on the *y*-axis may provide evidence of the hypothetical soil moisture gradient.

Limited access to high-elevation sites during the periods of maximum snow accumulation places a practical restriction on the direct measurement of snow depths in any of the sampled stands. Therefore the use of an apparent sensitivity of some epiphytic lichens to snowpack yields an indirect measure of relative snowpack accumulations. Corticolous lichens respond to environmental gradients on the boles of trees (Hale 1965; Gough 1975). Daubenmire (1974) suggests that under some circumstances the minimum height of lichens on tree boles is a function of the depth of winter snowpack. One of the most common of these lichens in the upper Cedar River watershed is *Alectoria sarmentosa*. It occurs from treetops to nearly ground level. Throughout the *Abies amabilis* zone it forms the major component of the epiphytic community. The lower distributional limits of the lichen on the boles is quite distinct; on each of the trees in a given stand the minimum height above ground to which the lichens extend is very nearly the same. It was concluded (Long 1976) that the average minimum height of lichens on the boles of trees in a stand represents a suitable indirect measurement of the maximum depth of the winter snowpack for that particular stand. Figure 2.4 relates the average minimum lichen height for each stand to that stand's x-axis ordination value. The regression of lichen heights, and presumably snow depth, against the x-axis ordination values is significant at the 0.01 level ($r^2 = 0.93$).

Time of snowmelt in the spring is a function of the depth of winter snowpack (Brooke et al. 1970). Data from 1968, 1973, and 1974 from nine weather stations in the western Cascades of Washington were used in an attempt to quantify this relation (Figure 2.5). These particular years were picked as they appear to represent a typical range of snow conditions for that area of the state.

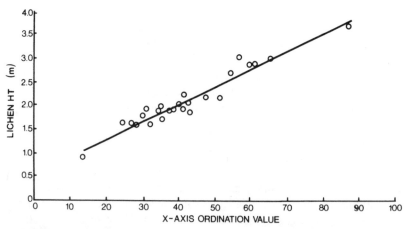

FIGURE 2.4 *Relation between minimum lichen heights on the boles of trees and the x-axis ordination value for individual stands (height = 0.521 + 0.038X, $r^2 = 0.93$).*

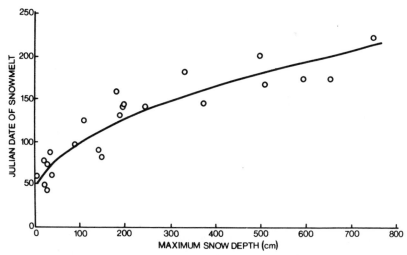

FIGURE 2.5   *Relation between maximum snow depth and the date of snow-melt for nine U.S. Weather Bureau stations in the western Cascade Mountains of Washington. Data are for 1968, 1973, and 1974 (Julian date = 36.33 + 6.39 depth $^{-2}$, $r^2 = 0.86$).*

The correlation of the Julian date for the beginning of the snow-free period against the maximum depth of snow is significant at the 0.01 level ($r^2 = 0.86$).

The hypothesized relation between the vegetational gradient represented by the y-axis of the ordination and available soil moisture was tested using measurements of plant moisture deficit (PMD), termed plant moisture stress (PMS) by Waring and Cleary (1967). Plant moisture deficit is the negative xylem sap pressure potential (Boyer 1967). A total of eight stands, representing various y-axis ordination values, was sampled for predawn PMD (Long 1976). The estimate of maximum seasonal predawn PMD for each stand was regressed against its corresponding y-axis ordination value (Figure 2.6). The regression is significant at the 0.01 level ($r^2 = 0.92$).

H. J. Andrews Experimental Forest, Oregon

The H. J. Andrews Experimental Forest ordinations yielded two primary gradients (Figure 2.1). We hypothesized that the x-axis represents highly divergent conditions along a complex moisture gradient, while the y-axis represents a thermal gradient.

In order to test hypothesized relations between forest community composition and environment, studies were concentrated in near-modal representative forest stands called *reference stands*. Within these stands environmental measurements were made. Sixteen of the twenty-three communities defined by

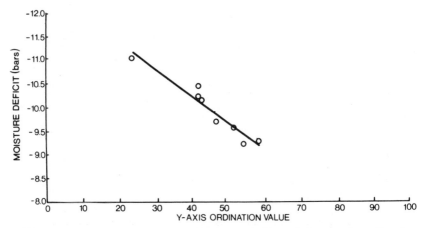

FIGURE 2.6 *Relation between predawn PMD and the y-axis ordination value for individual stands (PMD = 0.057Y - 12.52, r^2 = 0.92).*

ordination were chosen for intense analysis. Environmental measurements were made on small conifers, primarily Douglas-fir, western hemlock, and Pacific silver fir. Air and soil temperatures were recorded continuously for strata occupied by the foliage and roots of the understory trees. The moisture index used was PMD, and the predawn PMD was determined at the end of each growing season.

A temperature index for the growing season, called the *temperature growth index* (TGI), was determined from sapling phenology (Zobel et al. 1976) and a formula provided by Cleary and Waring (1969). The formula weighs temperature through its effect on Douglas-fir seedling production in controlled environments. The index yields a measure of growth conditions regulated by temperature. The TGI was summed up over the growing season for each site, and the growing season was defined as the period from conifer sapling budbreak to the date of the second fall frost. Subsequent studies (Chapter 3) set October 15 as the end of the growing season.

The PMD varied from 1970 to 1972 in response to changes in precipitation. Summers of 1970 and 1972 were dry, leading to high PMD values; however 1971 was relatively wet (Figure 2.7, Table 2.3). This test supported the hypothesis that at least in the lower *Tsuga heterophylla* and transition zones, the x-axis of the vegetation ordination corresponded to a moisture gradient. The PMD values of the *Abies amabilis* zone stands were measured in 1973 and 1974. The correlation of PMD with elevation is similar to that of the lower elevation zone, but the small number of samples resulted in nonsignificant regression coefficients.

The TGI in the reference stands showed considerable variation from 1971 to 1976 (Table 2.4). It was generally highest in 1973, particularly in the cooler stands, which had unusually late fall frosts. The relative positions of stands

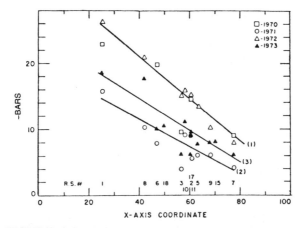

FIGURE 2.7 *Relation of maximum yearly predawn PMD to position of the* Tsuga heterophylla *and transition zone communities on the x-axis of the vegetation ordination of Dyrness et al. (1974). The community represented by each reference stand is listed in Table 2.3.* Linear regressions: *(1) 1970 + 1972$_2$ - Y = -33.96 + 0.319X, r^2 = 0.95; (2) 1971 - Y = -20.00 + 0.207X, r^2 = 0.83; (3) 1973 - Y = -24.31 + 0.241X, r^2 = 0.82 (data from reference stand 3 were excluded from regression equations; from Zobel et al. 1976; copyright © 1976 by the Ecological Society of America).*

from year to year remained similar; for example, correlation analysis yielded a coefficient of determination (r^2) of 0.98 ($n = 12$) for 1972 and r^2 of 0.96 ($n = 14$) for 1973. Communities in different vegetation zones were clearly separated by TGI in all years (Table 2.4). The differences among sites in unweighted temperature data were accentuated by TGI. Thus TGI is significantly correlated with elevation but there is great variation within elevational zones, indicating a temperature index other than that explained by elevation alone. This probably includes the effects of landform and aspect differences of the reference stands.

Distribution of species or communities along TGI and PMD gradients may reveal the fidelity with which either may be used to predict environmental variables if the predictions are made in the area where the correlations were made. Predictive value of some species may differ when they are found in different regions such as the central western Cascades and the Siskiyou Mountains (Zobel et al. 1976).

Most of the variation in community ordination in the H. J. Andrews Experimental Forest is associated with PMD and TGI gradients. Nutrient analysis of understory sapling needles taken in selected stands in early summer suggests that nutritional influences on community composition are important

TABLE 2.3 *Characteristics of reference stands sampled by Zobel et al. (1976). Sample represents a 50- by 50-m area at each stand.*

Zone	Reference stand no.	Community	Elevation (m)	Aspect	Slope (°)	Tree Mature	Tree Reproducing	Shrub	Herb
Tsuga heterophylla	1	Pseudotsuga/Holodiscus	510	SW	35	50	20	46	36
	2	Tsuga/Rhododendron-Berberis	520	NW	20	105	10	30	24
	6	Tsuga/Castanopsis	710	S	40	83	30	123	14
	7	Tsuga/Polystichum-Oxalis	490	NW	18	110	42	17	41
	8	Pseudotsuga-Tsuga/Corylus	500	W	40	81	25	64	27
	9	Tsuga/Acer/Polystichum	490	WNW	45	100	35	72	48
	10	Tsuga/Rhododendron-Gaultheria	670	SSW	5	89	60	118	7
	11	Pseudotsuga/Acer/Berberis	1060	SSE	25	96	35	62	10
	15	Tsuga/Polystichum	720	NW	45	108	43	14	18
	16	Tsuga/Castanopsis	670	SW	40	107	48	108	7
	17	Tsuga/Rhododendron-Berberis	530	NNW	18	102	47	43	37
Transition	3	Tsuga-Abies/Linnaea	950	SW	10	120	88	38	24
	5	Tsuga-Abies/Rhododendron-Berberis	920	N	8	90	27	125	5
	18	Pseudotsuga/Acer/Whipplea	1080	SE	30	81	24	92	23
Abies amabilis	4	Abies/Tiarella	1440	SW	10	116	50	9	39
	12	Abies/Vaccinium-Cornus	1020	W	5	103	31	56	33
	13	Abies/Clintonia	1480	S	15	93	20	12	32
	14	Abies-Tsuga/Xerophyllum	1570	NW	15	100	27	3	33

TABLE 2.4 *Temperature growth index (TGI) for reference stands in 1971 through 1976.*[a]

RD	1971	1972	1973	1974	1975	1976	Mean	SD
1	95	102	107	97	94	98	98.8	4.9
2	74	84	99	85	82	75	83.2	9.0
3	56	67	77	75	—	—	68.7	9.5
4	34	38	52	53	45	50	45.3	7.8
5	60	70	82	71	63	60	67.7	8.5
6	85	93	92	95	—	—	91.3	4.4
7	80	82	88	85	81	71	8.2	5.8
8	90	98	101	—	—	—	96.3	5.7
9	81	87	98	85	—	—	87.7	7.3
10	76	83	91	83	80	77	81.7	5.4
11	73	78	92	89	67	72	78.5	10.0
12	40	49	68	67	—	—	56.0	13.8
13	—	37	52	51	41	42	44.6	6.6
14	—	32	53	46	41	41	42.6	7.7
15	—	—	89	—	—	—	89.0	—
16	—	—	93	95	—	—	94.0	—
17	—	—	88	82	74	68	78.0	8.8
19	—	—	85	—	—	—	—	—

[a]W.H. Emmingham, personal communication.

only in nitrogen-poor sites. The environmental field defined by PMD and TGI (Figure 2.8, Table 2.3) thus separates the plant communities in a useful manner. This illustrates the utility of TGI in separating various zones and PMD in arranging communities within at least the lower elevation and warmer zones. The array of plant communities (stands) generally supports the hypotheses of Dyrness et al. (1974). The major difference is in the lack of sites with high PMD in the *Abies amabilis* zone. Such sites at high elevation are typically not forested, however, and no samples could be included from these sites.

SUMMARY AND CONCLUSIONS

Floristic gradients were constructed from two-dimensional ordination of plant communities in both the Cedar River watershed in Washington and the H. J. Andrews Experimental Forest in Oregon. In both sites there is a strong correlation between floristic gradients and environmental factors associated with elevation. In Washington the floristic gradient is apparently associated with a gradient in depth and duration of winter snowpack while in Oregon it is associated with a gradient in growing season TGI. The second floristic gradient in both the Cedar River watershed and the H. J. Andrews Experimental Forest is associated with a gradient in summer PMD, which was verified by predawn

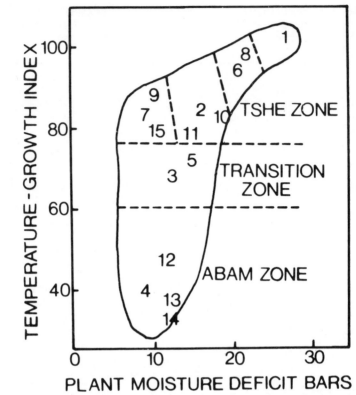

FIGURE 2.8 *Position of reference stands in a two-dimensional environmental field. Temperature is represented by TGI computed by the method of Cleary and Waring (1969). Moisture is assessed as the late-summer predawn PMD of conifer saplings. Most data are for 1972. Psme = Pseudotsuga menziesii, Tshe = Tsuga heterophylla, Abam = Abies amabilis. The community represented by each reference stand number here is listed in Table 2.3 (after Zobel et al. 1976).*

PMD measurements. At the Oregon site differences between vegetation zones are reflected in a temperature index, while within zones communities are distinguished by moisture deficits and to a lesser extent by temperature. In two cases in Oregon, vegetation differences appeared related to low needle nitrogen contents.

In further support of the classification scheme in Oregon, several investigations have provided evidence of gradient effects on producers, consumers, and decomposers; for example, Zobel et al. (1976) found that species diversity (the total number of vascular species) increased and dominance (Simpson's index) decreased toward either warmer–drier or colder communities. They also found that dominance is concentrated in fewer strata of the vegetation on the colder sites. Wiens and Nussbaum (1975) found significant differences in population density and species composition within selected plant communities in their study of model estimation of energy flow in northwestern coniferous forest bird communities. Fogel and Cromack (1977) found significant differences in amounts and rates of decomposition of several size classes of *Pseudotsuga menziesii* litter within different plant communities (Chapter 7). Gholz et al. (1976) describe significant differences in productivity and biomass accumulation within several communities of the H. J. Andrews Experimental Forest. These studies tend to increase the utility of derived predictive models of terrestrial primary producer systems and the diversity of the studies makes interfacing with other major sections of the ecosystem studies more meaningful.

LITERATURE CITED

Boyer, J. S., 1967, Leaf water potentials measured with a pressure chamber, *Plant Physiol.* **42**:133–137.

Brooke, R. C., E. B. Peterson, and V. J. Krajina, 1970, The subalpine mountain hemlock zone, *Ecol. West. North Am.* **2**:147–349.

Cleary, B. D., and R. H. Waring, 1969, Temperature: Collection of data and its analysis for the interpretation of plant growth and distribution, *Can. J. Bot.* **47**:167–173.

Daubenmire, R., 1968, *Plant Communities: A Textbook of Plant Synecology,* Harper & Row, New York, 300p.

Daubenmire, R., 1974, *Plants and Environment,* John Wiley & Sons, New York, 422p.

del Moral, R., and J. N. Long, 1977, Classification of montane forest community types in the Cedar River drainage of western Washington, U.S.A., *Can. J. For. Res.* **7**:217–225.

del Moral, R., A. F. Watson, and R. S. Fleming, 1976, Vegetation structure of the Alpine Lakes region of Washington State: Classification of vegetation on granitic rocks, *Syesis* **9**:291–316.

Dick-Peddie, W. A., and W. H. Moir, 1970, Vegetation of the Organ Mountains, New Mexico, *Range Sci. Dep. Sci. Ser. No. 4,* Colorado State University, Fort Collins, 28p.

Dyrness, C. T., 1965, The effect of logging and slash burning on understory vegetation in the H. J. Andrews Experimental Forest, *U.S. Department of Agriculture Forest Service Research Note PNW-31,* Portland, Oreg., 13p.

Dyrness, C. T., 1973, Early stages of plant succession following logging and burning in the western Cascades of Oregon, *Ecology* **54**:57–69.

Dyrness, C. T., J. F. Franklin, and W. H. Moir, 1974, A preliminary classification of forest communities in the central portion of the western Cascades in Oregon. *US/IBP Coniferous Forest Biome Bulletin No. 4,* University of Washington, Seattle, 123p.

Fogel, R., and K. Cromack, Jr., 1977, Effect of habitat and substrate quality on Douglas-fir litter decomposition in western Oregon, *Can. J. Bot.* **55**:1632–1640.

Franklin, J. F., C. T. Dyrness, and W. H. Moir, 1970, A reconnaissance method for forest site classification, *Shinrin Richi* **12**:1–14.

Franklin, J. F., F. C. Hall, C. T. Dyrness, and C. Maser, 1972, *Federal Research Natural Areas in Oregon and Washington: A Guidebook for Scientists and Educators.* U.S. Department of Agriculture Forest Service, Portland, Oreg., 495p.

Gholz, H. L., F. K. Fitz, and R. H. Waring, 1976, Leaf area differences associated with old-growth forest communities in the western Oregon Cascades, *Can. J. For. Res.* **6**:49–57.

Gough, L. P., 1975, Cryptogram distribution on *Pseudotsuga menziesii* and *Abies lasiocarpa* in the Front Range, Boulder County, Colorado, *Bryologist* **78**: 124–145.

Hale, M. E., Jr., 1965, Vertical distribution of cryptograms in a red maple swamp in Connecticut, *Bryologist* **68**:193–197.

Hawk, G. M., and D. B.Zobel, 1974, Forest succession on alluvial landforms of the McKenzie River valley, Oregon, *Northwest Sci.* **48**:245–265.

Long, J. N., 1973, Initial stages of secondary plant succession in a series of *Pseudotsuga menziesii/Gaultheria shallon* stands in western Washington, M.S. thesis, University of Washington, Seattle, 79p.

Long, J. N., 1976, Forest vegetation dynamics within the *Abies amabilis* zone of a western Cascades watershed, Ph.D. dissertation, University of Washington, Seattle, 175p.

Pfister, R. D., B. L. Kovalchik, S. F. Arno, and R. C. Presby, 1977, Forest habitat types of Montana, *U.S. Department of Agriculture Forest Service General Technical Report INT-34,* Ogden, Utah, 174p.

Rothacher, J., C. T. Dyrness, and R. L. Fredriksen, 1967, Hydrologic and related characteristics of three small watersheds in the Oregon Cascades. *U.S. Department of Agriculture Forest Service Miscellaneous Paper,* U.S. Department of Agriculture Forest Service, Portland, Oreg., 54p.

Waring, R. H., and B. D. Cleary, 1967, Plant moisture stress: Evaluation by pressure bomb. *Science* **155**:1248–1254.

Whittaker, R. H., 1970, *Communities and Ecosystems,* Macmillan, London, 158p.

Wiens, J. A., and R. A. Nussbaum, 1975, Model estimation of energy flow in northwestern coniferous forest bird communities, *Ecology* **56**:547–561.

Zobel, D. B., W. A. McKee, G. M. Hawk, and C. T. Dyrness, 1976, Relationships of environment to composition, structure, and diversity of forest communities of the central western Cascades of Oregon, *Ecol. Monog.* **46**:135–156.

3

Ecological Indexes as a Means of Evaluating Climate, Species Distribution, and Primary Production

W. H. Emmingham

INTRODUCTION

Much of the research conducted in the Coniferous Forest Biome program was directed toward obtaining a deep understanding of one or more ecosystems. This chapter reports on some of the efforts to obtain a broader understanding of how gradients of moisture, temperature, and light across the biome affect ecosystem structure and function.

The diversity of vegetation and environment found in the western coniferous biome (Chapter 1; Whittaker 1961; Waring 1969; Franklin and Dyrness 1973) makes land-use allocation and management difficult. Productivity, for example, is difficult to predict, because trees grow differently in cool moist sites than they do under other conditions. In addition, the number of trees per hectare on dry sites never approaches that found on more moist sites (Wikstrom and Hutchinson 1971; Maclean and Bolsinger 1973). Successful regeneration of cutover land is often difficult because of a great variety of conditions (Cleary et al. 1977).

The natural vegetation types mentioned in Chapter 2 provide a means of identifying ecosystems that behave in a similar manner following disturbance. Ecological indexing methods have now been developed that help determine why each ecosystem behaves differently; they therefore aid in choosing among management options for maximizing desired forest products. These methods involve measuring the climate at representative forest sites and evaluating the climatic data with models of the response of Douglas-fir (Waring et al. 1972). The result is a set of ecological indexes that quantify the climate at each location. This is analogous to planting an individual or clone of one species at each of several locations and measuring the response to that particular environment.

The quantification of environmental factors has helped: (1) to explain species distribution and community composition (Chapter 2; Waring 1969;

Waring et al. 1975; D. B. Zobel and G. M. Hawk, pers. comm.; (2) to explain changes in productivity along environmental gradients (Emmingham and Waring 1977; Reed and Waring 1974); and (3) to predict silvicultural problems and suggest solutions for them (Cleary et al. 1977). Perhaps the most important contribution has been the demonstration of the important link between natural vegetation classification and climate (Dyrness et al. 1974; Zobel et al. 1976).

This chapter compares widely situated coniferous ecosystems using these ecological indexing methods. Emphasis was on determining which climatic factors were responsible for changes in the structure and function of the ecosystems. Structural features were height and basal area of tree stands, while functional analysis centered on primary productivity. Ecological indexes included evaluations of temperature, soil moisture, evaporative demand, and light.

BACKGROUND

The techniques used to compare climates with ecological indexes were the result of over ten years of research into the physiology and ecology of coniferous biome species and ecosystems. The general approach is stated in Waring et al. (1972).

The major steps involved in comparing forest ecosystems include: (1) choosing sites representative of widely occurring forest ecosystems or habitat types; (2) collecting climatic and physiological data from each ecosystem; (3) using Douglas-fir, a widespread dominant plant, as a reference species to develop models of how the physical environment affects important plant processes on a daily basis; (4) evaluating the climate with these models (that is, simulations); (5) summing up the results of the simulations for important time intervals; (6) comparing the ecological indexes with observed structural and functional characteristics of the ecosystem; and (7) using the ecological indexes in a stand growth and succession simulation (see Chapter 4).

Comparison of the environment at different locations required a standard set of plant response models. The models were based on one reference species (coastal Douglas-fir), which, although widespread, does not span the diversity of environments found within the coniferous forest biome. No species does. This technique has the advantage of providing a single set of standards but should not be interpreted as a precise estimate of what the local variety or species could do.

Ecological indexes used were: (1) temperature growth index (TGI)—effect of soil and air temperatures on Douglas-fir growth (Cleary and Waring 1969); (2) moisture stress indexes—(a) maximum predawn plant moisture deficit or xylem water potential during the summer (Waring and Cleary 1967; Waring 1969; Zobel et al. 1976), and (b) sum of deficits during the growing season (Emmingham 1974), where the growing season is the number of days between year days 121 and 288 when soil and air temperatures are above 5°C and –1°C, respectively; (3) the summation of daily simulated photosynthesis indexes—(a) potential, (b) predicted actual, and (c) the ratio of predicted to potential (Emmingham and Waring 1977; these are estimates for coastal Douglas-fir and may be quite different from actual CO_2 fixation by a local conifer species); and (4) transpiration indexes—(a) potential (the summation of the daily product of absolute humidity deficit and maximum leaf conductance), (b) predicted actual (using leaf conductance estimated from moisture deficits), and (c) predicted/potential ratio. This last ratio is well correlated with the maximum height of trees in a variety of coniferous forest ecosystems (Reed and Waring 1974).

The data required to evaluate temperature, light, and moisture regimes were collected by cooperators in each state (see Acknowledgments). Temperature, humidity, and moisture stress observations were taken within each forest stand. Radiation data were recorded in the open. While the temperature, humidity, and radiation data were measurements of the physical conditions taken continuously, the soil moisture condition was evaluated by measuring plant water deficits at night on established one- to two-m-tall trees at two-week intervals. Methods are described in detail in Waring and Cleary (1967), Cleary and Waring (1969), Waring (1969), Zobel et al. (1976), Emmingham and Waring (1977), and Emmingham and Lundberg (1977).

Several measures of site productivity were used because of the difficulty in assessing stands of different ages. Site index (base age 100) was used because it is a conventional measure of site quality (Carmean 1975). Despite its widespread use, however, site index has many disadvantages (Daubenmire 1976). Thus two other measures of productivity were also used: growth basal area (GBA) (F. C. Hall, pers. comm.), and the product of a constant and the height and diameter growth indexes, being a volume index. The GBA method involved estimation of the ability of dominant trees to grow in diameter given the basal area of the surrounding trees as an estimate of competition. The basal area at which trees would grow 2.54 cm in radius in 30 years (GBA_{30}) was chosen as an index because many of these stands were growing at or near that rate.

STUDY AREAS

Study sites in Alaska, Arizona, Colorado, Idaho, Montana, Oregon, Utah, and Washington were selected to cover the geographic, floristic, and climatic ranges found within the coniferous forest biome. For descriptive purposes the study sites were divided into arctic and alpine forests, dry forests, and modal forest types.

In all areas the study plots were chosen to be representative of widespread ecosystems. In Oregon and Idaho the plant communities were described and named according to the dominant climax species after Dyrness et al. (1974) and Daubenmire and Daubenmire (1968). In other areas plant communities were named for the species that dominated the tree stand. In all cases the descriptive data were collected on the study plot. Floristic and physical descriptions are given in Tables 3.1 and 3.2, respectively.

TABLE 3.1 *Floristic description of forest ecosystems studied.*

LOCATION Forest type	Major tree species [a]	Tree layer cover (%)	Major shrub species	Shrub layer cover (%)	Major ground layer plants	Ground layer cover (%)
ALASKA [b]						
Black spruce (Arctic)	*Picea mariana* [a]	55	*Salix scouleriana* *Vaccinium uliginosum* *Vaccinium vitis-idaea*	25	*Geocaulon lividum* *Pleurozium schreberi* *Cladonia* spp.	100
White spruce (Arctic)	*Picea glauca* [a] *Populus tremuloides*	70	*Alnus crispa* *Salix alaxensis* *Viburnum edule*	20	*Hylocomium* sp. *Pleurozium* sp.	50
ARIZONA [c]						
Ponderosa pine (dry)	*Pinus ponderosa* [a]	75	none	0	*Festuca arizonica* *Muhlenbergia montana*	5
COLORADO [d]						
Spruce fir (alpine)	*Picea engelmannii* [a] *Abies lasiocarpa* [a]	70	*Vaccinium scoparium* *Ribes lacustre* *Sambucus pubens*	15	*Carex geyeri* *Arnica cordifolia* Lichens, mosses	75
IDAHO [e]						
Douglas-fir (dry)	*Pinus ponderosa* *Pseudotsuga menziesii* [a] var. *glauca*	80	*Physocarpus malvaceus* *Symphoricarpos albus* *Berberis repens*	30	*Fragaria* spp. *Festuca idahoensis* *Achillea millefolium*	5
Grand fir (modal)	*Pinus ponderosa* *Pseudotsuga menziesii* [a] var. *glauca* *Larix occidentalis* *Pinus contorta* *Abies grandis* [a]	90	*Berberis repens* *Rosa gymnocarpa* *Holodiscus discolor* *Rubus parviflorus* *Pachistima myrsinites*	15	*Calamagrostis rubescens* *Linnaea borealis* *Fragaria* spp. *Clintonia uniflora*	20

Vegetation type	Tree cover %	Tree species	Shrub cover %	Shrub species	Herb cover %	Herb species
Western hemlock (modal)	95	Pseudotsuga menziesii var. glauca, Larix occidentalis, Pinus monticola, Thuja plicata, Abies grandis, Tsuga heterophylla[a]	10	Rubus parviflorus, Rosa gymnocarpa, Lonicera utahensis, Spiraea betulifolia, Pachistima myrsinites	25	Linnaea borealis, Clintonia uniflora, Viola orbiculata, Adenocaulon bicolor, Smilacina stellata
Lodgepole pine (modal)	60	Pinus contorta, Pseudotsuga menziesii var. glauca, Abies lasiocarpa[a], Pinus monticola	10	Vaccinium membranaceum, Pachistima myrsinites, Sorbus sitchensis	40	Xerophyllum tenax, Spiraea betulifolia, Goodyera oblongifolia
Subalpine fir (alpine)	70	Tsuga heterophylla[a], Larix occidentalis, Abies lasiocarpa, Pinus monticola	10	Menziesia ferruginea, Vaccinium membranaceum, Vaccinium scoparium	30	Xerophyllum tenax, Gaultheria humifusa, Goodyera oblongifolia
OREGON[f]						
Sitka spruce (modal)	95	Pseudotsuga menziessi var. menziesii, Picea sitchensis, Tsuga heterophylla[a]	25	Vaccinium parvifolium, Menziesia ferruginea	50	Polystichum munitum, Oxalis oregana, Maianthemum dilatatum, Montia sibirica, Eurhynchium oreganum
Douglas-fir (dry)	50	Psuedotsuga menziesii[a] var. menziesii, Pinus lambertiana	30	Holodiscus discolor, Acer circinatum, Corylus cornuta var. californica, Berberis nervosa	30	Whipplea modesta, Polystichum munitum, Synthyris reniformis, Linnaea borealis
Western hemlock (modal)	100	Pseudotsuga menziesii var. menziesii, Tsuga heterophylla[a]	40	Rhododendron macrophyllum, Berberis nervosa, Acer circinatum	30	Linnaea borealis, Polystichum munitum, Coptis laciniata, Chimaphila umbellata

49

TABLE 3.1 *Continued*

LOCATION Forest type	Major tree species [a]	Tree layer cover (%)	Major shrub species	Shrub layer cover (%)	Major ground layer plants	Ground layer cover (%)
OREGON [f]						
Pacific silver fir (modal)	*Pseudotsuga menziesii* var. *menziesii* / *Abies amabilis* [a] / *Tsuga heterophylla*	100	*Vaccinium membranaceum* / *Acer circinatum*	5	*Tiarella unifoliata* / *Achlys triphylla* / *Cornus canadensis*	40
Mountain hemlock (arctic & alpine)	*Tsuga mertensiana* [a] / *Abies procera* / *Abies amabilis* [a] / *Pinus monticola*	60	*Vaccinium membranaceum*	5	*Xerophyllum tenax* / *Pyrola secunda*	50
MONTANA [c]						
Douglas-fir (modal)	*Pseudotsuga menziesii* [a] / var. *glauca* / *Pinus contorta* / *Larix occidentalis*	60	*Arctostaphylos uva-ursi* / *Berberis repens* / *Spiraea betulifolia*	15	*Calamagrostis rubescens* / *Arnica cordifolia*	5
UTAH [x]						
Douglas-fir (modal)	*Psuedotsuga menziesii* [a] / var. *glauca* / *Pinus flexilis*	80	*Acer glabrum* / *Berberis repens* / *Lonicera utahensis*	10	*Clematis pseudoalpina* / *Arnica cordifolia* / *Goodyera oblongifolia*	5
Englemann spruce-subalpine fir (arctic & alpine)	*Picea engelmannii* / *Abies lasiocarpa* [a]	75	*Pachistima myrsinites* / *Lonicera utahensis*	1	*Osmorhiza chilensis* / *Pedicularis racemosa* / *Aster foliaceus*	15

	Tree species	%	Shrub species	%	Herb species	%
Ponderosa pine-oak (dry)	Pinus ponderosa[a] Quercus garryana Pseudotsuga menziesii[a] var. menziesii	50	Ceanothus integerrimus Amelanchier alnifolia Corylus cornuta	5	Apocynum androsaemifolium var. pumilum Vicia americana var. truncata Lupinus sp. Arenaria macrophylla Gramineae	10
Ponderosa pine (dry)	Pinus ponderosa Pseudotsuga menziesii var. menziesii	80	Purshia tridentata Chrysothamnus viscidiflorus	5	Achillea millefolium Viola nuttallii Osmorhiza chilensis Horkelia fusca Gramineae	90
Pacific silver fir (modal)—	Abies amabilis[a] Abies procera Pseudotsuga menziesii var. menziesii Tsuga heterophylla	90	Vaccinium membranaceum Pachistima myrsinites Acer circinatum	20	Berberis nervosa Xerophyllum tenax Chimaphila umbellata Linnaea borealis	10
Grand fir (modal)	Pseudotsuga menziesii[a] var. menziesii Pinus ponderosa Abies grandis	95	Holodiscus discolor Corylus cornuta Rubus parviflorus Symphoricarpos mollis	5	Berberis nervosa Chimaphila menziesii Pteridium aquilinum Achlys triphylla Trientalis latifolia	10

[a]Designates the major reproducing tree species.
[b]Viereck and Little 1975.
[c]Avery et al. 1976.
[d]J. D. Richards, personal communication.
[e]Hitchcock and Cronquist 1974.
[f]Franklin and Dyrness 1973.
[g]Henderson et al. 1976.
[h]Susan Meyer, under direction of K. L. Reed; James Long and Gordon Swartzman contributed to the study.
[i]Pseudotsuga menziesii was judged to be the climax species in this location although it had been excluded by repeated fires.

TABLE 3.2 *Physical description of reference sites and tree stands.*

LOCATION Forest type	Latitude	Longitude	Elevation (m)	Slope (°)	Aspect	Dominant Tree Means Age (yr)	Diam (cm)	Ht (m)	Stand basal area (m²/ha)
ALASKA									
Black spruce	65°10′	147°53′	490	0	—	68	7	6	6
White spruce	64°51′	148°44′	260	10	SSW	70	37	20	40
ARIZONA									
Ponderosa pine	35°16′	111°45′	2270	0	—	88	41	20	39
COLORADO									
Engelmann spruce- subalpine fir	37°50′	107°30′	3470	15	W	100	24	17	44
IDAHO									
Douglas-fir	48°22′	116°29′	780	27	SSW	82	46	28	31
Grand fir	48°22′	116°29′	730	9	W	71	38	27	41
Western hemlock	48°22′	116°29′	850	6	NW	100	40	32	40
Londgepole pine	48°21′	116°25′	1555	14	WSW	94	24	18	60
Subalpine fir	48°21′	116°25′	1555	6	NE	137	27	20	42
MONTANA									
Douglas-fir	46°52′	113°27′	1470	16	S	175	26	20	45
OREGON									
Sitka spruce	45°04′	123°57′	200	10	W	116	76	48	119
Douglas-fir	44°12′	122°15′	510	35	SW	450	117	49	56
Western hemlock	44°13′	122°14′	530	20	NNW	450	129	75	119
Pacific silver fir	44°16′	112°08′	1310	27	W	350	104	46	109
Mountain hemlock	44°21′	122°04′	1530	15	NW	135	53	37	65
UTAH									
Douglas-fir	41°57′	111°31′	2210	2	E	166	41	27	43
Engelmann spruce- subalpine fir	41°58′	111°25′	2650	32	N	237	67	32	58
WASHINGTON									
Ponderosa pine-oak	45°55′	121°04′	646	1	WNW	83	41	20	41
Ponderosa pine	46°00′	121°19′	572	0	—	139	72	32	46
Pacific silver fir	46°07′	121°37′	1009	19	W	217	63	40	77
Grand fir	46°00′	121°26′	750	1	SE	207	67	40	50

Arctic and Alpine Forest Types

The most northern and severe study site was a diminutive black spruce forest north of Fairbanks, Alaska, where the permafrost layer melted to a depth of only 50 to 60 cm during the growing season (Viereck 1973). A few kilometers west of Fairbanks a white spruce forest was chosen because it, too, experienced the rigors of the central Alaskan winter but was not underlain by permafrost (Van Cleve and Zasada 1976; Zasada 1976).

In Colorado and Utah, Engelmann spruce and subalpine fir forests at high elevation were examined. The composition and basal area of the stands were similar, but the trees in Utah were over 100 years older and 20 m taller than those in Colorado.

The coolest site in northern Idaho was the subalpine fir stand, which had white pine and western larch as seral dominant tree species rather than Engelmann spruce. It was classified as an *Abies lasiocarpa/Menziesia ferruginea* habitat type (Daubenmire and Daubenmire 1968).

A mountain hemlock in the Cascade Mountains of Oregon was at the cool end of the Oregon gradient and had a rich mixture of tree species including seral noble fir, western white pine, and the shade-tolerant Pacific silver fir. This site was representative of the *Tsuga mertensiana—Abies amabilis/Xerophyllum tenax* habitat type of Dyrness et al. (1974).

Modal Forest Types

The modal forest types were those judged to be at neither the cold—moist nor warm–dry extremes in the local area. Three forest sites in Oregon (Sitka spruce, western hemlock, and Pacific silver fir) were chosen. These forests were the tallest (48 to 75 m) and had the greatest basal area (over 100 m^2/ha) found in this study.

Near the Pacific Ocean a forest dominated by Sitka spruce and western hemlock was chosen because of its high productivity (Fujimori 1971). In contrast to all the other study sites, snow is rare at this location.

At the western hemlock forest site in the western Cascades of Oregon, snow is common, but persistent winter snowpack is unusual. Stands are dominated by large, old-growth Douglas-fir that average over 1 m in diameter at breast height (dbh). This site is typical of the *Tsuga heterophylla/Rhododendron macrophyllum/Berberis nervosa* habitat type (Dyrness et al. 1974).

At higher elevations, the Pacific silver fir forest sites of Oregon and Washington contained both Douglas-fir and noble fir as seral dominants. A heavy snowpack is common on these sites and snow often persists until the first of July.

The grand fir site in western Washington occurred in a depression and from climatic records it was evident that frost was frequent and severe. Like the grand fir site in Idaho *(Abies grandis/Pachistima myrsinites* habitat type), it had both Douglas-fir and ponderosa pine as seral dominants in the stand.

The three modal types in Idaho included the grand fir and western hemlock *(Tsuga heterophylla/Pachistima myrsinites* habitat type) sites, and a lodgepole pine stand on an *Abies lasiocarpa/Xerophyllum tenax* habitat type. The grand fir and hemlock sites were similar in elevation, but the fir type was on a more southerly aspect. Lodgepole pine was at higher elevation in a denser stand (60 versus 40 m^2/ha basal area) than the grand fir and hemlock. Despite the greater basal area found in this stand, tree height indicated lower site productivity.

The Douglas-fir site in northern Utah and the lodgepole pine stand in Montana were chosen to represent modal types in their areas. Both stands were at the cool end of the climatic gradient for Douglas-fir. Henderson et al. (1976) classed the Utah site as a *Pseudotsuga menziesii* (var. *glauca*)/*Berberis repens* habitat type, while the Montana site fell into the *Pseudotsuga menziesii* (var. *glauca*)/*Linnaea borealis* habitat type of Pfister et al. (1977).

Dry Forest Types

An open ponderosa pine forest near Flagstaff, Arizona, was the most southern of the sites. It was chosen for comparison with the ponderosa pine stand in Washington. The pine communities in western Washington were in the arid rain shadow of the Cascade Mountains. The driest of the two sites was a ponderosa pine/Oregon white oak community located on rocky, shallow soils. A pure pine stand was located at a lower elevation on a deeper soil. Douglas-fir was judged capable of regenerating, but it had been excluded by repeated wildfires.

The driest of the Idaho sites was typical of the *Pseudotsuga menziesii* (var. *glauca*)/*Physocarpus malvaceus* habitat type. It was chosen for comparison with the *Pseudotsuga menziesii* (var. *menziesii*)/*Holodiscus discolor* habitat type in Oregon, which is the driest conifer-dominated type west of the Cascade Mountains of Oregon. The larger trees on this site were 49 m high and the basal area was 56 m/ha. Thus growth was relatively good compared with that on other dry sites, but considerably less than on other Oregon sites.

COMPARISON OF ECOLOGICAL AND PRODUCTIVITY INDEXES ACROSS THE CONIFEROUS BIOME

Evaluation of the climate at a variety of western coniferous forest sites provided a means to examine functional relations responsible for differences in vegetation composition and productivity. For example, interior western hemlock, Douglas-fir, and ponderosa pine forest sites can be compared with similar forest types nearer the Pacific coast. Arctic and alpine forests also can be compared. Ecological (temperature, moisture, photosynthesis, and transpiration) and productivity indexes are shown in Table 3.3 for each site. Sites were assigned reference numbers.

Temperature Indexes

The TGI ranged from 14 to 115 at the cold and dry extremes, while modal types in Oregon were 80 to 90 (Table 3.3). For the arctic sites (1 and 2) TGI values were less than 25, while on the alpine sites in Colorado (4), and Idaho (9), Oregon (15), and Utah (17), they averaged about 43. Warm dry sites (3, 5, 11, 18, and 19) averaged 89. The Douglas-fir type in Oregon (11) and pine/oak types in Washington (18) had TGI values over 105. Interestingly, the ponderosa pine site in Arizona (3) had a temperature index of only 70, partly because of restriction of the growing season by frost. In general the low-elevation sites in Oregon and Washington had greater temperature indexes than inland areas because they had longer growing seasons.

Moisture Stress Indexes

Both maximum and sum-of-moisture stress measured on small trees at each site confirmed the droughty nature of the sites with Douglas-fir or ponderosa pine as dominant species (sites 3, 5, 6, 11, 16, and 18, Table 3.3). The grand fir type (6) in Idaho was included because Douglas-fir and ponderosa pine dominated the stand. The Douglas-fir/ponderosa pine site in Washington (19) had much lower stress than these dominants indicated, suggesting that repeated fires have excluded more tolerant species. Even relatively moist sites, including the spruce sites in Oregon (12) and Alaska (1 and 2) had maximum moisture deficits of –5 or –6 bars.

Moisture stress sum, which represents accumulated drought during the growing season, was greatest in ponderosa pine types of Arizona (3) and Washington (18) and the Douglas-fir site (11) in Oregon (Table 3.3). Lowest sums were in Alaska (sites 1 and 2) and the Engelmann spruce site (19) in Utah. The spruce site in Utah had a low moisture stress total because summer frosts cut the growing season off before the moisture deficit became severe.

Modal forest types in the Cascades of Washington and Oregon (sites 13, 14, 20, and 21) averaged less than –11 bars maximum moisture deficit at the peak of drought (Table 3.3). In contrast, inland modal sites (7, 8, 10, and 16) averaged around –15 bars. Although all these sites probably start the growing season with soils at field capacity, the inland sites apparently did not have as great a soil water storage capacity to meet evaporative demand.

The western hemlock forests of Oregon have many floristic similarities to those in Idaho, although inland forests were more diverse in both tree and shrub layers. Climatically, the Oregon site (13) was warmer (TGI = 90) than the Idaho site (7; TGI = 65) and more moist (–9.1 versus –15.9 maximum moisture deficit; Table 3.3). The ponderosa pine type in Washington (18) was warmer (TGI = 115 versus 70), but similar in moisture deficit to the analogous pine type in Arizona (3).

TABLE 3.3 *Indexes to reference stand productivity and environment.*

Site No.	LOCATION Forest type	Eco-class[a]	Productivity indexes				Moisture stress (-bars)		Ecological indexes (in growing season)				
									Photosynthesis (mg[CO_2]dm^{-2})			Transpiration (mg[H_2O]cm^{-2})	
			Ht[b]	Diam[c]	Vol[d]	TGI[e]	Max.	Sum.	Poten-tial	Pre-dicted	Ratio	Pre-dicted	Ratio
	ALASKA												
1	Black spruce	A	28[f]	25	10	14	6.1	200	2538	1076	0.42	—	—
2	White spruce	A	86[g]	87	107	24	5.7	316	4870	2801	0.58	274	0.57
	ARIZONA												
3	Ponderosa pine	D	83[h]	175	207	70	22.2	1715	10 196	1296	0.13	107	0.11
	COLORADO												
4	Engelmann spruce-subalpine fir	A	56[i]	—	—	50	13.8	820	9191	3502	0.38	214	0.39
	IDAHO												
5	Douglas-fir	D	98[i]	142	199	80	19.5	1235	11 242	2842	0.25	191	0.25
6	Grand fir	M	101[i]	171	247	64	21.5	1022	10 322	3300	0.32	215	0.31
7	Western hemlock	M	105[i]	161	241	65	15.9	992	11 109	3725	0.34	—	—
8	Lodgepole pine	M	62[i]	200	177	43	15.6	820	7540	2118	0.28	178	0.30
9	Subalpine fir	A	59[i]	165	139	33	12.5	721	6587	1774	0.27	129	0.27
	MONTANA												
10	Lodgepole pine	M	50	164	117	59	10.5	687	9687	5123	0.53	360	0.54

OREGON

No.	Species	Class[a]	Height/growth index[b]								TGI[e]		
11	Sitka spruce	M	150[j]	480	1303	80	5.0	402	13 170	10 296	0.78	—	—
12	Douglas-fir	D	120[j]	210	360	106	25.7	2017	13 116	5190	0.40	460	0.46
13	Western hemlock	M	160[j]	477	1070	90	9.1	758	12 936	8694	0.67	646	0.58
14	Pacific silver fir	M	120[j]	413	708	60	8.1	579	9308	5697	0.61	272	0.51
15	Mountain hemlock	A	110[j]	280	440	47	13.4	629	6559	3546	0.54	216	0.44
	UTAH												
16	Douglas-fir	M	75[k]	167	179	53	18.6	1230	8522	2045	0.24	247	0.33
17	Engelmann spruce-subalpine fir	A	65[k]	290	269	41	13.1	373	4905	4882	0.95	689	0.95
	WASHINGTON												
18	Ponderosa pine-oak	D	70[j]	95	95	115	20.8	1840	13 020	2907	0.22	298	0.19
19	Douglas-fir-ponderosa pine	D	88[i]	390	490	73	7.8	754	9615	3311	0.34	283	0.35
20	Pacific silver fir	M	104[j]	186	276	60	11.0	688	9537	4705	0.49	381	0.52
21	Grand fir	M	108[j]	441	680	69	7.5	630	8508	3791	0.45	361	0.43

[a] Each site was placed in one of the following ecological classes: A = arctic and alpine; D = dry; and M = modal type.

[b] The height/growth index is the height (in feet; 1 ft - 0.305 m) to which dominant and codominant trees grow in 100 years.

[c] The diameter/growth index is the basal area (in square feet per acre; square feet per acre times 0.2296 = square meters per hectare) of surrounding or competing trees when dominant and codominant trees grow by a radius of 0.85 mm/yr or 1 in/30 yr (GBA_{30}).

[d] The volume/growth index is equal to the height index times volume index times 70^{-1}. This approximates cubic volume growth potential of the site.

[e] TGI is the temperature/growth index, which integrates the effect of air and soil temperatures on tree growth (Cleary and Waring 1969; Zobel et al. 1976).

[f] The height/growth index was estimated directly when trees were near 100 years of age (see Table 3.2).

[g] Derived from Farr 1967.

[h] Derived from Minor 1964.

[i] Derived from Meyer 1961.

[j] Derived from McArdle et al. 1961.

[k] From Henderson et al. 1976.

Photosynthesis Indexes

The lowest potential photosynthesis was at the Alaska black spruce perma-frost site, while the highest was in the Oregon Sitka spruce zone (Table 3.3). The potential photosynthesis index was relatively high for the Arizona pon-derosa pine and the warm, low-elevation sites in Idaho, Oregon, and Washing-ton. Surprisingly, there was only about a fivefold difference between photosyn-thesis potentials at all the sites.

Photosynthesis simulations throughout the year for nine representative sites are shown in Figure 3.1. The upper curve is the simulated potential photosynthesis using air temperature and solar radiation. The predicted (actual) photosynthesis is the lower or heavy line, and represents the photosynthesis given moisture deficits, frost, and cold soils. The Oregon sites are characteris-tic of the west coast area, including Oregon and Washington. The other sites shown include the cold extremes in Alaska and Colorado, as well as the interior forests of Utah, Idaho, Arizona, and Montana.

The potential photosynthesis during the summer was between 70 and 90 $mg \cdot dm^{-2} \cdot day^{-1}$ for all sites. There was a general trend toward higher potential with decreasing latitude. The similarity between sites at such wide extremes suggests, however, that temperature and radiant energy are not the most impor-tant limiting factors during the growing season.

There were large differences in photosynthetic potential during the winter months. Interior sites were generally lower than coastal sites. At the coastal sites, the winter potential was near 40 $mg \cdot dm^{-2} \cdot day^{-1}$ (Figure 3, 1f, i) while in the arctic and more severe sites it was zero (Figure 3.1a, b, d). Although classed as an alpine site, the mountain hemlock site in Oregon showed considerable potential because of mild air temperatures ($0°$ to $5°C$) during part of the winter.

In extreme arctic Alaska and the nearly desert environment of Arizona, no more than 50 percent of the photosynthetic potential was captured during any period of the year (Figure 3.1a, g). In all other locations, nearly 100 percent of the potential for photosynthesis was captured at some time during the year. The big difference between the interior sites in Colorado, Idaho, and Montana (Figure 3.1b, e, h) was in the duration of full photosynthetic potential. In the western hemlock (Figure 3.1f) and Douglas-fir types of Oregon (Figure 3.1i), the winter and spring months appear especially important for the capture of the sun's energy. The mountain hemlock site in Oregon (Figure 3.1c) showed a soil temperature restriction during winter and spring and fairly severe reduction from drought during the growing season.

Although western hemlock sites in Idaho (Figure 3.1e) and Oregon (Figure 3.1f) have similar photosynthetic potential, moisture stress at the Idaho site reduced predicted photosynthesis to less than half that in Oregon. This helps explain higher productivity (site index 160 versus 105) of the Oregon sites. Also, wintertime photosynthetic potential was greater in Oregon (Figure 3.1f).

Comparison of Douglas-fir forests of Oregon and Idaho showed a similar trend in temperature and predicted photosynthesis (Table 3.3); however, maximum moisture deficit was greater in Oregon Douglas-fir forests (Table 3.3). Conditions for photosynthesis during winter and spring are considerably more favorable in Oregon than in the Douglas-fir forests of either Idaho or Utah.

On a growing season basis, ponderosa pine forests of Washington were considerably warmer than those in Arizona (Table 3.3). In addition, dry spring conditions in Arizona (Figure 3.1g) induced high moisture deficits reducing predicted photosynthesis to only about 13 percent of the potential. Moisture stress indexes for the growing season were similar for both sites (Table 3.3).

The lowest predicted photosynthesis indexes occurred at the geographic extremes; in Alaska black spruce and Arizona ponderosa pine sites. The highest predicted photosynthesis indexes were at the coastal location and western hemlock site in Oregon. There was a nearly tenfold difference in the index between the black spruce site in Alaska and Sitka spruce site in Oregon.

Comparison of photosynthesis ratio showed the ponderosa pine site in Arizona was at the low extreme with only 13 percent of the potential. In contrast, the spruce-fir site in Utah had 95 percent of the potential. The Sitka spruce site (12) had the highest predicted photosynthesis, but this was only 78 percent of the potential photosynthesis.

Transpiration Indexes

Lowest predicted transpiration occurred in Arizona (3), where, although demand for water was quite high, moisture stress restricted leaf conductance (Table 3.3). Highest transpiration occurred at the western hemlock site in Oregon (13), where demand was high and supply relatively good. Humidity data were not available for the Sitka spruce site and therefore were not included in this comparison. Transpiration ratios were highly correlated with the photosynthesis ratio because both were dependent on moisture deficits and leaf conductance.

Productivity Indexes and Relationships to Ecological Indexes

The relationship between productivity and temperature index is shown in Figure 3.2. Productivity diminished at either end of the temperature scale, indicating that cold temperatures restrict productivity and that high temperatures were generally accompanied by excessive evaporative demand and high respiration costs. The solid curve traces the maximum potential productivity.

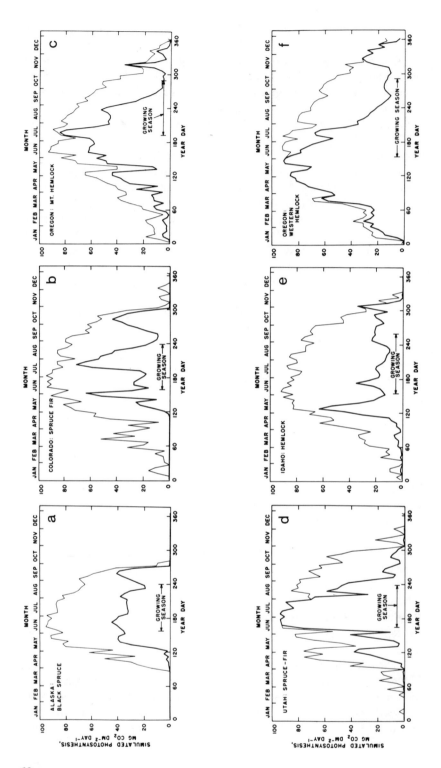

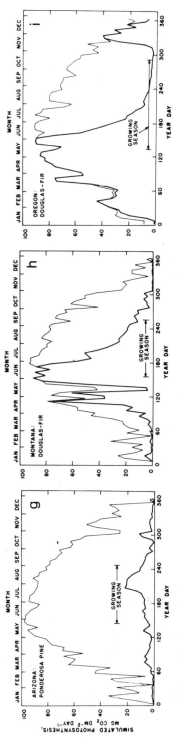

FIGURE 3.1 *Graphs of potential (upper, thin line) and predicted (lower, thick line) photosynthesis are shown for nine representative forest ecosystems for the entire year. Note that the potential during the growing season is similar for all sites. Large differences are evident in the amount of the potential captured as predicted photosynthesis and in the dormant season potential photosynthesis. The photosynthesis indexes are equivalent to area under the curve during the growing season.*

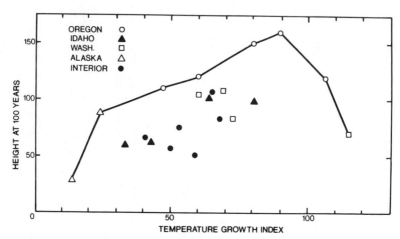

FIGURE 3.2   *The estimated height to which trees would grow in 100 years plotted against the TGI during the growing season. The line represents the maximum possible height growth for sites across the temperature range (see Table 3.3 for units).*

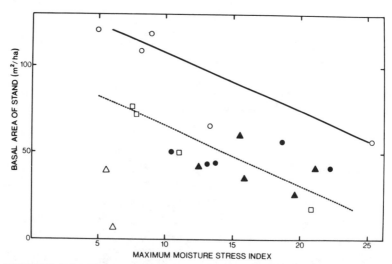

FIGURE 3.3   *The actual basal area of stand plotted over the maximum moisture deficit measured on understory reference trees. The low-elevation Oregon sites (○) apparently had a higher capacity to accumulate basal area at any moisture stress than the sites in Washington (□), Idaho (▲), and the other interior sites (●). Even at low moisture stresses, the Alaska sites (△) had low basal areas. (Moisture stress index is in −bars.)*

In Figure 3.3 total stand basal area is plotted against maximum moisture stress index. Low moisture stresses are required for, but do not guarantee, high productivity. The solid line is an estimate of maximum basal area at moisture stress index levels in areas with a mild winter. The dotted line shows basal area in inland areas where winters are severe. The implication is that stressful conditions during the growing season may be compensated for by photosynthesis during the dormant season. Also, the maximum stress index is most useful in comparing sites in a smaller area with similar macroclimates.

The relation between volume productivity and summer photosynthesis index is shown in Figure 3.4. This is nearly a linear relationship and all indexes of productivity were better correlated with the predicted photosynthesis index than any of the other ecological indexes. Correlation coefficients (r) between the predicted photosynthesis and site index, GBA_{30}, volume index, and accumulated basal area were 0.81, 0.73, 0.86, and 0.73, respectively. Since the model used to compute the predicted photosynthesis index includes evaluation of many of the stress factors affecting primary production, this high correlation could be expected. Between 75 and 85 percent of the variation in site index, volume index, basal area growth, or total basal area was explained in multiple

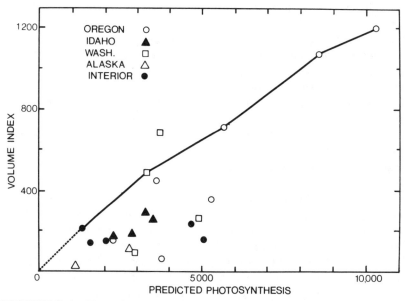

FIGURE 3.4 *The relation between maximum volume index and predicted photosynthesis (during the growing season) was nearly linear. The fact that many of the points fell below the curve indicated that other factors such as nutrition, winter conditions, or respiration have an important bearing on productivity (see Table 3.3 for units).*

regression equations that included up to three of the indexes to environment. The most common second and third terms to enter were the maximum plant moisture stress and transpiration or photosynthesis ratio. The fact that many of the points fall below the line connecting the higher volume index values indicates there are other important factors unaccounted for in this comparison. Preliminary comparisons indicate that an *annual* predicted photosynthesis index accounts for more of these factors.

CONCLUSIONS

Ecological indexes provide a method for evaluating stress in coniferous forest ecosystems. One stress feature that seems to be common to all coniferous forest ecosystems is drought or physiological drought. Even the moist coastal Sitka spruce ecosystem had moisture stress that lasted several weeks and reduced predicted actual photosynthesis to 78 percent of the potential for that site. At the black spruce site in Alaska, moisture stresses of –4 to –6 bars during the growing season were responsible for a 50 percent reduction in carbon fixation. This may be a case of physiological drought induced by the cool temperature in the root system.

The two- to five-times greater productivity of the modal types in western Oregon can be explained in several ways. They had less moisture stress and were warmer than the inland areas. This allowed for more photosynthesis during the summer. Mild winter conditions indicate that a significant portion of the annual carbon uptake may occur during the ''dormant'' period on the coastal and Cascade Mountains.

Results of the photosynthesis simulations support the hypothesis that the rise of the western mountain ranges and resultant summer drought was a primary factor in the elimination of rich hardwood forest ecosystems apparent in the fossil records (Franklin and Dyrness 1973). Evergreen trees can take advantage of the relatively favorable winter conditions when hardwoods are without leaves.

The system of ecological indexes used here provides a systematic way of quantifying the difficult-to-measure environmental differences found among coniferous forest ecosystems. It can be used to quantify test hypotheses about species distribution, ecosystem structure, or functional attributes. For example, the hypothesis that the climate in northern Idaho and western Oregon is similar because forests of western hemlock dominate the landscape was proved false; the Oregon site was both warmer and less droughty.

High correlation between the ecological indexes and productivity demonstrates the link between the ecosystem function and the indexes. The nearly linear relationship between productivity and the predicted photosynthesis index make that index the most promising for future investigation.

LITERATURE CITED

Avery, C. C., F. R. Larson, and G. H. Schubert, 1976, Fifty-year records of virgin stand development in southwestern ponderosa pine, *U.S. Department of Agriculture Forest Service General Technical Report RM-22,* Fort Collins, Colo., 71p.

Carmean, W. H., 1975, Forest site quality evaluation in the United States, *Adv. Agron.* **27**:209–269.

Cleary, B. D., and R. H. Waring, 1969, Temperature: Collection of data and its analysis for the interpretation of plant growth and distribution, *Can. J. Bot.* **47**:167–173.

Cleary, B. D., R. D. Greaves, and R. K. Hermann, 1977, *Regenerating Oregon's Forests,* Oregon State University Extension Service, Corvallis, Oreg., 300p.

Daubenmire, R., 1976, The use of vegetation in assessing the productivity of forest lands, *Bot. Rev.* **42**:115–143.

Daubenmire, R., and J. B. Daubenmire, 1968, Forest vegetation of eastern Washington and northern Idaho, *Washington Agricultural Experimental Station Technical Bulletin 60,* Washington State University, Pullman, Wash., 104p.

Dyrness, C. T., J. F. Franklin, and W. H. Moir, 1974, A preliminary classification of forest communities in the central portion of the western Cascades in Oregon, *US/IBP Coniferous Forest Biome Bulletin 4,* University of Washington, Seattle, 123p.

Emmingham, W. H., 1974, Physiological responses of four Douglas-fir populations in three contrasting field environments, Ph.D. dissertation, Oregon State University, Corvallis, 162p.

Emmingham, W. H., and G. A. Lundburg, 1977, Climatic and physiological data summaries for the H. J. Andrews Reference Stand Network, *US/IBP Coniferous Forest Biome Internal Report 166,* University of Washington, Seattle, 109p.

Emmingham, W. H., and R. H. Waring, 1977, An index of photosynthesis for comparing forest sites in western Oregon, *Can. J. For. Res.* **7**:165–174.

Farr, W. A., 1967, Growth and yield of well-stocked white spruce stands in Alaska, *U.S. Department of Agriculture Forest Service Research Paper PNW-53,* Portland, Oreg., 30p.

Franklin, J. F., and C. T. Dyrness, 1973, Natural vegetation of Oregon and Washington, *U.S. Department of Agriculture Forest Service General Technical Report PNW-8,* Portland, Oreg., 417p.

Fujimori, T., 1971, Primary production of a young *Tsuga heterophylla* stand and some speculations about biomass of forest communities on the Oregon coast, *U.S. Department of Agriculture Forest Service Research Paper PNW-123,* Portland, Oreg., 11p.

Henderson, J. A., R. L. Mauk, D. L. Anderson, R. Ketchie, P. Lawton, S. Simon, R. H. Sperger, R. W. Young, and A. Youngblood, 1976, *Preliminary Forest Habitat Types of Northwest Utah and Adjacent Idaho,* Department of Forestry and Outdoor Recreation, Utah State University Logan, 99p.

Hitchcock, C. L., and A. Cronquist, 1974, *Flora of the Pacific Northwest,* University of Washington Press, Seattle, 730p.

McArdle, R. E., W. H. Meyer, and D. Bruce, 1961, The yield of Douglas-fir in the Pacific Northwest, *U.S. Department of Agriculture Technical Bulletin 201,* U.S. Department of Agriculture, Washington, D.C. 74p.

Maclean, C. D., and C. L. Bolsinger, 1973, Estimating productivity on sites with a low stocking capacity, *U.S. Department of Agriculture Forest Service Research Paper PNW-152,* Portland, Oreg., 18p.

Meyer, W. H., 1961, Yield of even-aged stands of ponderosa pine, (revised) *U.S. Department of Agriculture Technical Bulletin 630,* U.S. Department of Agriculture, Washington, D.C., 59p.

Minor, C. O., 1964, Site index for young growth ponderosa pine in northern Arizona, *U.S. Department of Agriculture Forest Service Research Note RM-37,* Fort Collins, Colo., 8p.

Pfister, R. D., B. L. Kovalchik, S. F. Arno, and R. C. Presby, 1977, Forest habitat types of Montana, *U.S. Department of Agriculture Forest Service General Technical Report INT-34,* Ogden, Utah, 174p.

Reed, K. L., and R. H. Waring, 1974, Coupling of environment to plant response: A simulation model of transpiration, *Ecology* **55:**62–72.

Van Cleve, K., and J. C. Zasada, 1976, Response of 70-year-old white spruce to thinning and fertilization in interior Alaska, *Can. J. For. Res.* **6:**145–152.

Viereck, L. A., 1973, Ecological effects of river flooding and forest fires on permafrost in the taiga of Alaska, in *Permafrost: The North American Contribution to the Second International Conference,* National Academy of Sciences, Washington, D.C., pp. 60–67.

Viereck, L. A., and E. L. Little, Jr., 1975, Atlas of United States trees, 2: Alaska trees and common shrubs, *U.S. Department of Agriculture Forest Service Miscellaneous Publication 1293,* U.S. Department of Agriculture Forest Service, Washington, D.C., 19 p., 105 maps.

Waring, R. H., 1969, Forest plants of the eastern Siskiyous: Their environmental and vegetational distribution, *Northwest Sci.* **43:**1–17.

Waring, R. H., and B. D. Cleary, 1967, Plant moisture stress: Evaluation by pressure bomb, *Science* **155:**1248–1254.

Waring, R. H., K. L. Reed, and W. H. Emmingham, 1972, An environmental grid for classifying coniferous forest ecosystems, in *Proceedings— Research on Coniferous Forest Ecosystems—A Symposium,* J. F. Franklin, L. J. Dempster, and R. H. Waring, eds., U.S. Department of Agriculture Forest Service, Portland, Oreg., pp. 79–91.

Waring, R. H., W. H. Emmingham, and S. W. Running, 1975, Environmental limits of an endemic spruce, *Picea breweriana, Can. J. Bot.* **53:**1599-1613.

Whittaker, R. H., 1961, Vegetation history of the Pacific coast states and the "central" significance of the Klamath region, *Madrono* **16:**5-23.

Wikstrom, J. H., and S. B. Hutchinson, 1971, Stratification of forest land for timber management planning on the western national forests, *U.S. Department of Agriculture Forest Service Research Paper INT-108,* Ogden, Utah, 38p.

Zasada, J. C., 1976, Alaska's interior forests, *J. For.* **74:**333-341.

Zobel, D. B., W. A. McKee, and G. M. Hawk, 1976, Relationships of environment to composition, structure and diversity of forest communities of the central western Cascades of Oregon, *Ecol. Monogr.* **46:**135-156.

4

The Niche and Forest Growth

K. L. Reed and *S. G. Clark*

INTRODUCTION

In the preceding chapters the reader was introduced to the concept of ecological indexes. Hawk et al. (Chapter 2) showed that these indexes are useful for ordinating plant communities along moisture and temperature gradients, and Emmingham (Chapter 3) discussed their relation to productivity.

The strong correlation of community ordinations with measured environment supports the idea that the evironment can in turn be predicted from community ordination, once the relation has been established. For example, in Waring et al. (1972), the distribution of certain trees, shrubs, and forbs was found to be constrained to certain ranges of two moisture indexes and a heat index as measured on numerous plots in southern Oregon. These sensitive species were termed "indicator species." Other plots were selected, and their environment was predicted from the presence of indicator species. Subsequently, the environment was measured on those plots and was found to agree very well with the predicted environment. Reed (1980) discussed this subject from a niche theoretic perspective.

In practice, once an area has been mapped as to community type, the communities can be selectively monitored with respect to environment, and the whole mapped region can be assigned environmental values. The environmental variables can then be used as inputs to models such as the photosynthesis simulator of Emmingham and Waring (1977). They reported that productivity of four forest stands in Oregon was strongly correlated with simulated yearly net photosynthesis. Reed and Waring (1974) demonstrated that height of conifers was strongly related to the heat index and a ratio of simulated seasonal transpiration to potential water loss.

This approach provides a ready means of integrating the disciplines of plant physiology and biometeorology with plant ecology (Reed and Waring 1974; Zobel et al. 1976; Emmingham and Waring 1977; Reed 1980), with implications for prediction of productivity. Further, the ordination of measured environment provides an opportunity to apply Hutchinson's (1957) niche theory to real-world situations. By imposing certain constraints on classical niche definitions, it is possible to propose research for investigation of concepts that have eluded definitive experiments for years, such as competition, succession, adaptive strategies, and the classical concept of niche. Given a working definition of the niche, forest models can be developed based upon ecological and physical principles.

In this chapter we: (1) discuss niche theory and its relation to ecological indexes, illustrated by examples of hypothetical niches for ponderosa pine, western red cedar, and Douglas-fir in the western United States; (2) show how the niche concept can be related to succession; and (3) discuss a model that integrates the concepts of ecological indexing and environmental quantification, niche theory, and succession. This model is a forest stand growth simulator called SUCSIM (SUCession SIMulator).

DEVELOPMENT OF NICHE THEORY

Niche theory goes back to Grinnell (1917), who noted that the California thrasher *(Toxostoma redivivum)* was very restricted in its range, being found almost exclusively in the chaparral association, which in turn was limited by elevation (temperature) and moisture. He suggested that these factors define the niche of the species; however, not until Hutchinson (1957) formalized the concept could mathematical analysis be applied. Hutchinson proposed that environment be expressed as linear coordinates of an abstract space, called "environment space" or "E-space." Each environmental variable forms one dimension of the space. Since there are many possible variables, E is an *n*-dimensional space.

It is difficult to visualize *n*-dimensional space, but it is easily expressed mathematically. For a simple illustration, consider two environmental variables that represent, say, moisture and temperature. The two variables, then, form a plane or "2-space." Any point in the plane can be referenced by the simple Cartesian notation $P(x,y)$. Addition of a third dimension produces a space like a box; a point is referenced by the coordinates $P(x,y,z)$. Likewise, if there are four dimensions the space is called a "hyperspace" and a point in that space is simply $P(w,x,y,z)$.

Hutchinson suggested that with respect to a single variable an upper and lower limit could be found beyond which a given organism cannot survive. Similarly, survival limits can be established with respect to other environmental variables. In 2-space, these limits give four points, $P(x_1,y_1)$, $P(x_1,y_2)$, $P(x_2,y_1)$, and $P(x_2,y_2)$, that delimit the environmental coordinates within which the species can survive (Figure 4.1a). Those basic limits reflect survival without competition—the *fundamental niche*. Hutchinson suggested that competition with other species restricts the niche. This restricted region in E-space is the *realized niche* (shaded area in Figure 4.1a). In three dimensions, the niche will have a three-dimensional shape (Figure 4.1b).

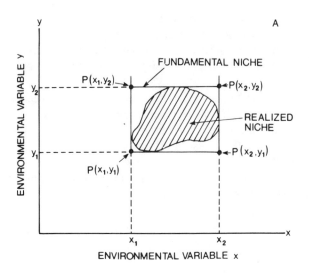

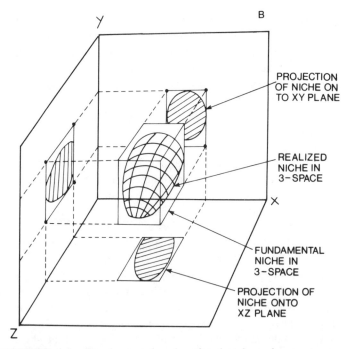

FIGURE 4.1 *Fundamental and realized niches of a species expressed as survival relative to two and three environmental variables (after Hutchinson 1957). (a) 2-dimensional projection of E-space; (b) 3-dimensional projection of E-space with 2-dimensional projections of the niche onto the appropriate planes.*

As this concept, formalized by Hutchinson, was elaborated and expanded by numerous researchers (see Whittaker and Levin 1975), much confusing terminology appeared, and attempts to relate the concept of niche to real-world situations were disappointing (Green 1971; Whittaker et al. 1973). Much of the difficulty has resulted from imprecise distinctions between site characteristics and environment. Some of the quantities that are conveniently measured are not truly sensed by the organism of interest, so attempts to quantify responses to those quantities are correlative at best, and useless at worst.

Because organisms and communities of organisms are systems, it is germane to examine some systems concepts here. In a systems context, environment is described as that which is external to the system but interacting with the system and evoking a response (Bertalanffy 1969; Klir 1969). Environment can be quantified as a set of inputs to the system causing certain behavior in response to those inputs. The responses are quantified as outputs. A central tenet of this perspective is that environment must be sensed by the system; if it is not, there can be no response.

Mason and Langenheim (1957) attempted to apply some semantic concepts to the definition of environment and also concluded that environment must be expressed in terms of the sensing organism. Quantities important to one system may be irrelevant to another. For example, degree of ocean salinity is important to sea organisms and may be included in their environmental specifications, but it is meaningless to a Rocky Mountain pine tree.

Factors commonly measured by foresters and ecologists, such as elevation, slope, and aspect, are not "environment," but instead are correlated with environment. These indirect measures of environment have been useful in ecology and forestry, but, because of their relative nature, they lack predictive power except in the specific locale wherein the data were taken. For example, mountain hemlock, *Tsuga mertensiana,* grows at elevations of 1300 to 1700 m in northern Washington and 1700 to 2000 m in southern Oregon (Franklin and Dyrness 1973). Direct measurement of light, temperature, and moisture status throughout the hemlock zone would probably yield a range of values that would be more consistent from north to south. Therefore a growth model of mountain hemlock based on elevation would be applicable only in a specific locale, but a model based on measured environment should be more general in its applicability.

Green (1971) agreed that proper definition of environment is critical but noted that there exists no generally accepted methodology of measurement and interpretation of environment in forest ecosystems. The approach reported by Waring (1969), Waring et al. (1972), Reed and Waring (1974), Emmingham and Waring (1977), Reed (1980), and Emmingham (Chapter 3) was a central effort of the Coniferous Forest Biome and is consistent with the concepts discussed above: (1) environment must be organism specific; (2) it must be sensed by the organism; and (3) it must evoke a response from the organism. These environmental variables can be used to form axes of an n-dimensional Hutchinsonian environment space. Given such an environmental coordinate system, it is possible to define mathematically a set of responses to environment (Maguire 1973). These responses can be interpreted as a realization of the species' *niche*. Delimitation of the niche by use of our growth model is illustrated in Figure 4.2. We are analyzing data to check these functions at the time of this writing.

Figure 4.2 shows two 2-dimensional projections of E; the contours describe hypothetical niches for three forest species (ponderosa pine, western red cedar, and Douglas-fir) simulated by our growth model. The environmental variables are displayed on the lower and left axes; the species response (simulated) is expressed as height after 50 years on the right axis. Three sites are represented at points e_1, e_2, and e_3. Remember that these points are defined as $P(x,y,z)$ in 3-space, but in our projections $P(x,y,z)$ is illustrated as $P(x,y)$ and $P(x,z)$. The environmental variables used in Figure 4.2 are those discussed in Chapter 3 and by Reed and Waring (1974). One of the axes is the temperature-growth index (TGI), which reflects the influence of air and soil temperature on growth, and the units of which are optimum temperature days (OTD) (Cleary and Waring 1969; Waring 1969). The axis that reflects moisture supply and demand is the transpiration ratio of Reed and Waring (1974). This is a ratio of potential transpiration on a site to "actual" transpiration computed from on-site environmental data. Potential transpiration is the total amount of water that would be lost if there were no stomatal control (an assessment of atmospheric water demand). The transpiration model includes the effect of stomatal closure, which is a function of plant water stress. When the ratio is equal to 1, that site has all the water needed. There is a species-specific lower limit below which that species does not occur; so far as we know, all species will grow where the ratio is 1 if other factors permit. Waring et al. (1972) present numerous examples of species limits to the transpiration ratio. The third axis is simply light expressed as a fraction of full sun.

The trajectory shown for e_1 at time t_1 to e_1t_3 represents changes in environment on a site over a period of years. In Figure 4.2a, the site becomes cooler and wetter as the stand develops. Also, note that the trajectory crosses the niche boundary of Douglas-fir. If other factors (not illustrated) permit, Douglas-fir could become established on the site. Thus a community of ponderosa pine and Douglas-fir would be expected at e_1t_3. Also, both species would be expected to grow more than 30 m in 50 years; however, Figure 4.2b shows that the same site at time t_3 would be too dark for good growth. Growth for Douglas-fir at time t_3 would be much better than that of ponderosa pine. From Figure 4.2b alone it might be expected that western red cedar would occur in the community, but from Figure 4.2a we see that it would be too hot.

THE NICHE AND SUCCESSION

A community is possible only on sites where the environmental loci are within the niche volumes of each species; that is, $e(\theta) \in N_c$, where θ is the set of

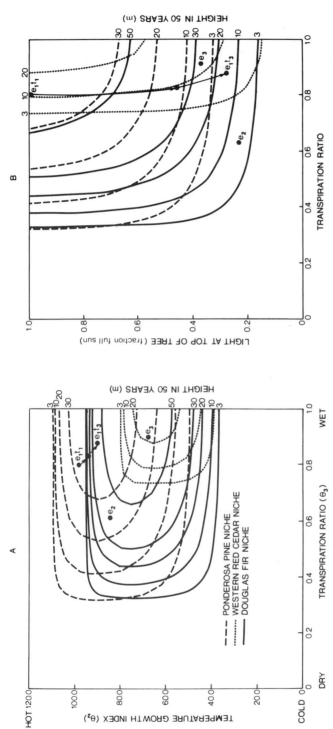

FIGURE 4.2 *Postulated niches of three coniferous species defined in terms of height growth. The points* e_1t_1 *and* e_1t_3 *represent environment on a site at different times;* e_2 *and* e_3 *are environmental conditions on other sites measured at one time only. (a) niches relative to temperature and moisture; (b) the same niches relative to light and moisture.*

environmental variables and N_C is the set of niche volumes of the C species composing the community (Reed 1980). Some factors such as fire, although important for establishment of a species, cannot be conveniently defined along a continuous ordinate. These factors could be called "trigger variables," and can be modeled.

As the site's environment changes, its representation, $e(\theta)$, moves through E-space; as it crosses a niche boundary, a new community is possible. This could be termed a potential community, or $e(\theta) \epsilon N_P$, where N_P is the set of niche hypervolumes that *could* be realized on the site. Given an appropriate trigger, the new species can invade, and N_P becomes equal to N_C if all possible species invade. The *realized* community is defined as N_C. In nature, plant succession can result from environmental changes on a site over time; prediction of the environmental changes could allow prediction of succession. Human activities that result in environmental change can strongly influence forest community structure and succession.

The above theory provides a foundation for the work discussed in Hawk et al. (Chapter 2) and Emmingham (Chapter 3). Because a community can exist only where the site locus e is an element of all the niches N_C, then the converse is also true: The location of e in E-space can be defined as the intersection of the set of niches comprising the community (Reed 1980). If the niches of the major species are known, the environmental coordinates of a particular site can be determined by simply extrapolating from the point of intersection to the ordinates, as did Waring et al. (1972).

A practical application of this theory to land management is possible. If the land were mapped according to vegetation, habitat types, or other plant ordination systems, then the environment or selected community types could be measured and the habitat types could be characterized in terms of their environmental ranges. Land management practices could be based on knowledge of management impact on environment, hence community type and productivity. Models could be developed that use environment as input and more directly and accurately predict ecosystem response to environmental change. Such a model is discussed below.

THE FOREST GROWTH MODEL (SUCSIM)

The work discussed above defines environment space and can delimit community and niche. The time-trajectories of a site reference locus through E-space, and the resulting community response, can be simulated by a forest growth model. To this end, a forest growth and SUCcession SIMulator (SUCSIM) based on the above theory was developed (Reed and Clark 1978). Tree growth is expressed as a function of environment, leaf biomass, and tree size. This growth function can be used to illustrate niche as in Figure 4.2. Natural establishment of the forest is simulated according to niche and trigger variables, and mortality is predicted as a function of slow growth and other trigger variables. These ideas, while expressed differently, do not differ greatly from most forest and tree simulation models (for example, Botkin et al. 1972; Fries 1974; Botkin 1977).

A principal disadvantage of most forest growth models is that they require individual trees to be grown on small plots. This causes two serious problems: (1) the population must be limited to avoid reaching computer time and size limits; and (2) extrapolation from the small plot to more useful units (for example, quantities per hectare) can be difficult. For example, if the simulation plot size is 0.1 ha, each tree on the plot represents 10 trees/ha; it is impossible to "kill" fewer than 10 trees/ha. Consequently, to simulate reality, numerous runs with random mortality functions must be made and averaged. This can be prohibitively expensive.

The problem is avoided in SUCSIM, which is so structured that the plot size can be large. Simulation of a forest requires that the forest be divided into discrete plots. The only criterion for determining plot size is the requirement that environment be relatively homogeneous across the plot. Because the plot size can be specified at 1 ha or greater, conversion to useful units is easy and only one run is required for simulations.

Plots of variable size are simulated easily and efficiently in SUCSIM by growing *cohorts* of trees rather than individuals. A cohort is defined as an *object* with a set of attributes including species (with an associated set of specific parameters for the growth function, and so on), population, height, diameter, leaf biomass, and age. In SUCSIM these attributes are more precisely defined as, for example, "height of trees in cohort i." This can be considered to be the mean height of the trees in the ith cohort. One species of a given age, height, diameter, and the like is defined as a *cohort*. This does not imply that there is only one cohort per species; there can be n different cohorts of species j, each having one or more differences among their attributes. Table 4.1 shows a partial cohort list from a typical SUCSIM run (1-ha plot, 102 years).

The algorithm is simplified and run-time is greatly reduced by use of cohorts. At each step, the program calls each subroutine (GROW, BROWSE [optional], LITTER, DEATH, and so on) once for each cohort. Certain plot attributes, such as light at each level of the stand and fraction of the plot covered by leaves, are computed after the cohort attributes are updated. The seeding subroutine (SEED) decides which species to establish, depending on environment. If the environmental coordinates of the stand are within the niche of a given species, that species can be established. The number of seedlings varies with environment and the number of other species to be established. Once SEED has decided which and how many species with an initial height of 3 cm to seed, the system computes the other cohort attributes.

At present there are two ways for trees to die: slow growth and random mortality. As the canopy closes, certain cohorts receive less light and their growth slows. When diameter growth is reduced below a certain species-

TABLE 4.1 *List of selected cohort attributes from a typical SUCSIM run at year 102 (good Douglas-fir/hemlock site).*

Cohort number[a]	Species	Population (stems/ha)	Age (yr)	Height (m)	DBH (cm)	Leaf biomass (kg)	Diameter increment[b] (cm)	Height increment (cm)	New leaf biomass[c] (kg)	Litterfall (kg)
1	Douglas-fir	367	102	33.3	66.6	40.7	0.26	11.5	2.1	2.1
3	Western hemlock	527	102	22.4	38.9	16.2	0.15	7.15	0.72	0.72
7[d]	Western hemlock	2	92	0.68	0	0.033	0.0015	0.083	0.0002	0.0002
14	Western hemlock	1	92	0.65	0	0.021	0.00089	0.051	0.0001	0.0001
Plot total		958			190[e] m²/ha	23.5 t/ha			1.15 t/ha	1.15 t/ha

[a] Not all cohorts are given here. Cohort identities are retained and not reused. Cohort 6, for example, has died out.
[b] Diameter increment is at the base of the tree.
[c] New leaf biomass and litterfall reach an equilibrium depending on light and growth rates.
[d] Cohort 7, seeded in at year 8, was browsed at some time, creating cohort 14. Both cohorts are doomed.
[e] Basal area of the two dominant cohorts.

specific critical level, a fraction of the cohort is killed. The number of trees killed is given as a function of growth rate. Subroutine DEATH reduces the population of the cohort accordingly. When the population is zero, the system's memory management removes that cohort from the program's allocated core.

The dynamic core allocation keeps the operating space requirements as small as possible. A typical 100-year run requires fewer than 40,000 words (60 bits per word) of central memory of the CDC computer at the University of Washington, and usually runs in less than 5 seconds. Several 500-year runs were tried; run-time ranged from 35 to 40 seconds. Very simple runs (such as the stocking level runs discussed below) required slightly more than 1 second of central processing unit time per 100 years. The system maintains its own files, allows direct access to any function or parameter at any given time, and can be run interactively or batched with equal ease. The syntax is simple and easily learned. The program development required a large effort, and the models themselves are still at a primitive stage.

The program uses the environmental variable TGI as the heat input variable (see Emmingham, Chapter 3); moisture is given by the ratio of seasonal transpiration to potential transpiration (Reed and Waring 1974); and the third variable is light. Complete model documentation is presented in Reed and Clark (1979). Three-dimensional representations of the niche of two species with respect to SUCSIM environment are shown in Figure 4.3.

Space allows only two examples of SUCSIM runs. The simulated effects of different environments on mixed Douglas-fir/ponderosa pine stands after establishment are illustrated in Figure 4.4a to f. Stand development is simulated under two climatic regimes, warm and dry versus warm and wet, conditions that approximate two sites in the Mt. Adams area of Washington. In each case, 500 Douglas-fir and ponderosa pine were seeded (3 cm tall) on a 1-ha plot. The plot was browsed at irregular intervals and no management activity was simulated. In an effort to emphasize the differential effects of environment on establishment of the two species, seed years were restricted to nine-year intervals with no off-year seeding. One of the principal differences between the two species is an assumption that Douglas-fir cannot seed into an area exposed to direct sunlight, while ponderosa pine may. This assumption is based on unpublished observations by K. L. Reed in the Mt. Adams area.

In Figure 4.4a, the population on both plots rapidly declined during the first eight years with a large influx of pine seedling at year 9, but no additional Douglas-fir was added because the light level at the forest floor was excessive. Ultimately, by the third seed year (year 27), Douglas-fir and other species (not illustrated) became established on the dry site, but the wet site was by then fully stocked and too dark at the forest floor for pine and Douglas-fir. The light climate can be inferred from the total leaf biomass curves in Figure 4.4b. Also, because we have set a greater potential for browse of pine, more pine was killed

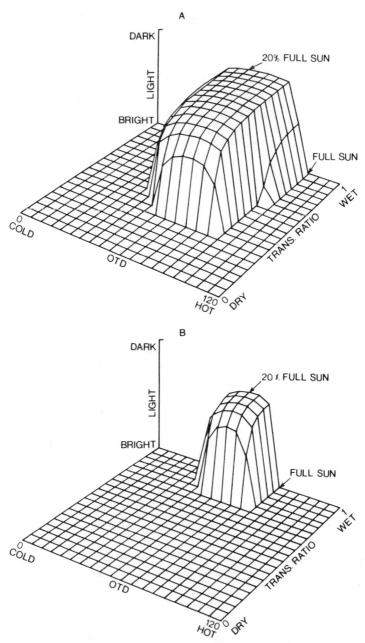

FIGURE 4.3 *Three-dimensional representations of the niches of two species. (a) Douglas-fir niche defined by a minimum height growth of 10 m in 50 years; (b) western red cedar niche defined by the same criteria.*

by browse than was Douglas-fir (Figure 4.4a, years 1 to 9). Browse losses are heavier on dry sites because slower growing trees are more susceptible, given an equivalent population of hungry animals with the same browse preference.

A seeming paradox in Figure 4.4b is evident. In spite of the fact that Douglas-fir makes up only about 17 percent of the "stand" on the wet site at year 50, approximately half the leaf biomass is Douglas-fir. This seeming paradox is explainable by the fact that Figure 4.4a shows the total population of the "stand"; most of the subsequent pine cohorts are small and suppressed. Actually, since Douglas-fir typically carry more leaf biomass than pine; we would expect more Douglas-fir leaf biomass on the wet site. Dissimilarities between Figure 4.4a and typical forestry stocking curves occur because all trees are represented, not just the dominant and codominant trees.

To summarize these results, browse damage causes rapid population drops on both plots. A heavy seed year at year 9 results in a great ponderosa pine population explosion, but the dry site seeding is approximately half that of the wet site because the climate inhibits seedling establishment. On both sites, Douglas-fir establishment is minimal. As the stand ages, the microclimate is modified, and successive seed years are more successful on the dry site until, at approximately year 30, the population curves cross. Mortality is greater on the set site owing to faster growth of the dominant cohorts, which shade out the smaller cohorts. The dense shade prevents establishment of new cohorts, resulting in a steady population decline. The dry site remains open much longer with less leaf biomass (Figure 4.4b). The maximum total leaf biomass of the wet site is reached around 30 years, while the dry site leaf biomass continues to increase slightly from year 45 through year 85. The values appear reasonable (see Turner and Long 1975), although they were higher than observed by Grier and Logan (1977) on old-growth Douglas-fir forests. Comparisons of height, diameter, diameter growth, and bole volume are also shown in Figure 4.4c to f.

The SUCSIM algorithm allows specification of height of seedlings in order to simulate planting of larger seedlings. This is illustrated in Figure 4.5, where we simulated the planting of 500 pine seedlings 30 cm tall and 500 pine seedlings 3 cm tall on the warm, dry site. Only the heights of the tallest pine cohorts are illustrated. The larger seedlings had a head start that produced larger trees and had other minor effects on the stand (not illustrated). These effects included a reduction in pine mortality due to browse, because the bigger seedlings were less vulnerable and volume was greater. Growth of the 3-cm seedlings was progressively less than that of the bigger seedlings, because of direct competition.

The second set of demonstration runs was devised to address the question: What level of stocking will produce the greatest yield of Douglas-fir on good and poor sites? Simulated height, diameter at breast height, diameter growth, leaf biomass, and basal area as a function of time and stocking levels on a good

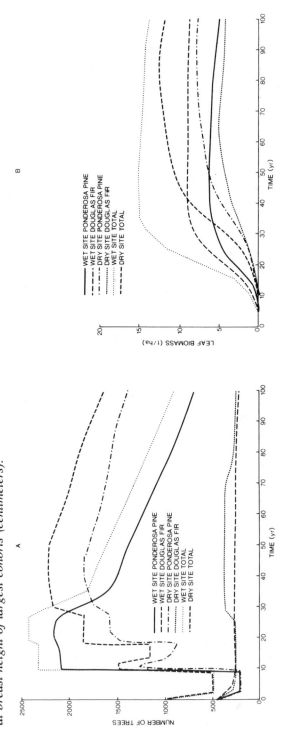

FIGURE 4.4 *Comparisons of simulated growth on two forest plots. The thermal environment on both plots was optimal for ponderosa pine, less so for Douglas-fir. The plots differed only in moisture status, one being wet, the other dry. Douglas-fir and ponderosa pine were "planted"; only these species' results were plotted. (a) population; (b) leaf biomass (tons per hectare); (c) height of tallest cohorts (meters); (d) basal diameter growth of largest cohorts (centimeters per year); (e) volume of boles (cubic meters per hectare); (f) diameter at breast height of largest cohorts (centimeters).*

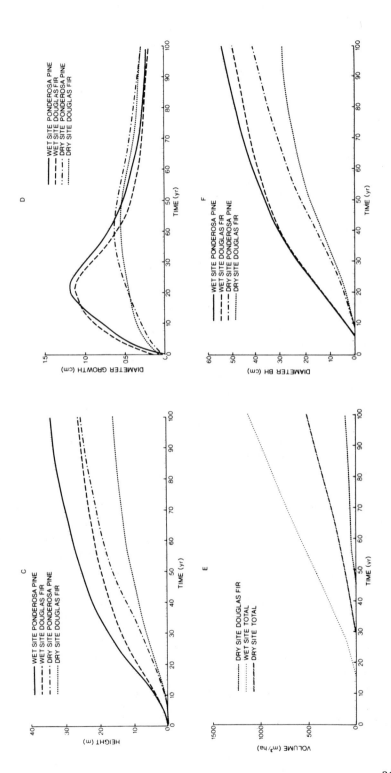

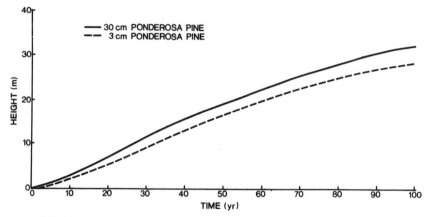

FIGURE 4.5 *Comparison of simulated height of ponderosa pine "planted" at initial heights of 30 cm and 3 cm on an optimal pine site. Only the two tallest cohorts were plotted.*

site are shown in Figure 4.6a to e, respectively. Figure 4.7 compares the impact of stocking levels on cubic volume of the good site and a poor, dry site.

The environmental coordinates of the simulation for the good site were 70 OTD, full sun, and transpiration ratio of 1. These conditions are optimal for Douglas-fir in this version of the model. In these runs, mortality, seeding, and browse routines were turned off; only the growth routine was active. Program SUCSIM keeps track of individual crown area and leaf biomass in twenty strata, which allows simulation of crown closure. Crown closure results in lower available light, which reduces growth, thus allowing comparison of the effects of stocking level.

Four stocking levels are compared, ranging from 240 to 1440 stems/ha. Decreased stocking produces larger trees (mean height, Figure 4.6a), but reduces total basal area per hectare (Figure 4.6e) because of the lower population. Crown closure (indicated by the break in the leaf/biomass curves) in the lowest stocking level is 10 years later than in the highest (Figure 4.6d). The differences between the poor, dry site and the good site are summarized in Table 4.2, and the volume curves are compared in Figure 4.7a and b. Aside from the lower values on the poor site, a significant difference is that the volume curves of the good site cross at year 40, while the poor site curves are just beginning to converge at year 100. The crossing at year 40 suggests that the high site stand should be thinned no later than year 40, if volume is the decision criterion, while the dry site yields more at high stocking.

The examples of SUCSIM runs presented here demonstrate only a few of the simulation experiments possible with the model. Thinning can be simulated using a given set of criteria, and the harvested "wood" can be left on the plot (as input to a decomposition model yet to be developed) or removed. Manage-

TABLE 4.2 *Comparison of simulated production on good and poor, dry Douglas-fir sites.*

Stock level (stems/ha)	DBH (cm)	Height (m)	Basal area (m²/ha)	Leaf biomass (t/ha)
High site: temp. index = 70 OTD, $\tau/\tau_p = 1$				
1440	44.5	23.6	224	24.2
960	52.2	27.1	205	22.8
480	68.2	34.2	175	20.7
240	87.7	42.4	145	18.5
Low site: temp. index = 80 OTD, $\tau/\tau_p = 0.6$				
1440	36.6	19.4	151	19.7
960	42.4	22.2	135	18.2
480	54.6	27.7	112	16.1
240	69.5	34.3	91	15.0

Note: Temperature is expressed in optimum temperature days (OTD); moisture regime is defined in terms of a ratio of transpiration over potential transpiration (τ/τ_p), as discussed in the text.

ment can be simulated by selective planting, thinning, and even pruning. The simulated stand can be clearcut, partially cut, high-graded harvested by species, or some combination thereof. Insect defoliation can be simulated. Natural forest conditions (as in Figure 4.4) or ideal experimental conditions (as in Figures 4.6 and 4.7) can be simulated. Given realistic parameter values, the model can "grow" any species of tree. All parameter values can be easily changed, and modification of submodels is a relatively simple task.

One of the principal goals of modeling work is the development of a model that can be used to generate data for optimization and decision routines. Here a criterion is established ànd the model is exercised to produce results that can be mathematically analyzed to optimize the system with respect to the criterion of interest. Such routines are exceedingly expensive and would require a very efficient model. We believe that the speed and efficiency of SUCSIM, coupled with the considerable degree of biological reality, will make optimization experiments possible.

Further, the theoretical concepts of niche, adaptation, competition, and succession can be studied with a model that is far more complex and realistic than the simple differential equations most often used. Such studies should provide a better understanding of the nature of forest ecosystem dynamics and lead to the clarification of many concepts that are now poorly understood. This better understanding could give rise to land management systems that are more ecologically sound, and would reemphasize the importance of ecology in land management problems.

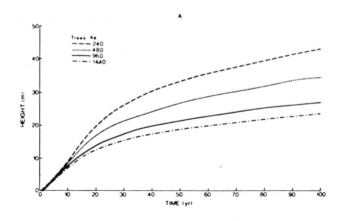

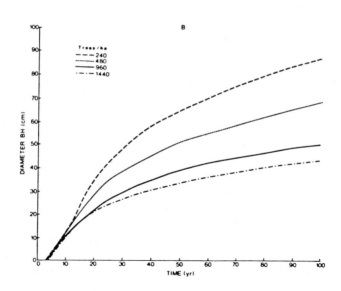

FIGURE 4.6 *Comparison of productivity on a good Douglas-fir site as affected by stocking levels (population density; lines represent numbers of trees per hectare). (a) height (meters); (b) basal diameter (centimeters); (c) basal diameter growth (centimeters per year); (d) leaf biomass (tons per hectare); (e) basal area at breast height (square meters per hectare).*

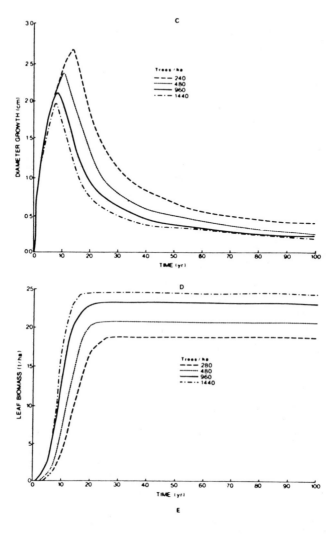

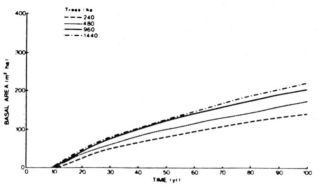

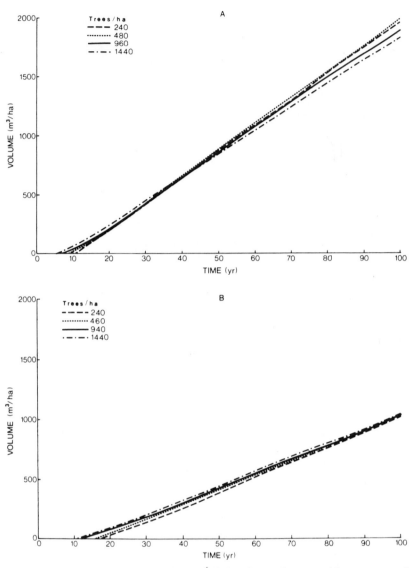

FIGURE 4.7 *Comparison of simulated cubic volume yields on a good Douglas-fir site and a poor site as affected by stocking levels (population density; lines represent numbers of trees per hectare). (a) good site; (b) poor site.*

LITERATURE CITED

Bertalanffy, L. von, 1969, *General System Theory.* Braziller, New York, 289p.

Botkin, D. B., 1977, Life and death in a forest: The computer as an aid to understanding, *Ecosystem Modeling in Theory and Practice,* C. H. S. Hall and J. W. Day, Jr., eds. Wiley-Interscience, New York, pp. 213–233.

Botkin, D. B., J. F. Janek, and J. R. Wallis, 1972, Some ecological consequences of a computer model of forest growth, *J. Ecol.* **60**:849–872.

Cleary, B. D., and R. H. Waring, 1969, Temperature: Collection of data and its analysis for the interpretation of plant growth and distribution, *Can. J. Bot.* **47**:167–173.

Emmingham, W. H., and R. H. Waring, 1977, An index of photosynthesis for comparing forest sites in western Oregon, *Can. J. For. Res.* **7**:165–174.

Franklin, J. F., and C. T. Dyrness, 1973, Natural vegetation of Oregon and Washington, *U.S. Department of Agriculture Forest Service General Technical Report PNW-8,* Portland, Oreg., 417p.

Fries, J., 1974, Growth models for tree and stand simulation. *Royal College Forest Bulletin No. 30,* Stockholm, 379p.

Green, R. H., 1971, A multivariate statistical approach to the Hutchinsonian niche: Bivalve molluscs of central Canada, *Ecology* **52**:543–556.

Grier, C. C., and R. S. Logan, 1977, Old-growth *Pseudotsuga menziesii* communities of a western Oregon watershed: Biomass distribution and production budgets, *Ecol. Monogr.* **47**:373–400.

Grinnell, J., 1917, The niche-relationships of the California thrasher, *Auk* **34**:427–433.

Hutchinson, G. E., 1957, Concluding remarks, *Cold Spring Harbor Symp. Quant. Biol.* **22**:415–427.

Klir, G. J., 1969, *An Approach to General Systems Theory,* Van Nostrand Reinhold, New York, 323p.

Maguire, B., 1973, Niche response structure and the analytical potentials of its relation to the habitat, *Am. Nat.* **107**:213–246.

Mason, H. L., and H. H. Langenheim, 1957, Language analysis and the concept *Environment, Ecology* **38**:392–404.

Reed, K. L., 1980, An ecological approach to modeling growth of forest trees, *For. Sci.* **26**:33–50.

Reed, K. L., and S. G. Clark, 1979, SUCession SIMulator: A coniferous forest simulator, Model documentation, US/IBP *Coniferous Forest Biome Bulletin No. 11,* University of Washington, Seattle, 96p.

Reed, K. L., and R. H. Waring, 1974, Coupling of environment to plant response: A simulation model of transpiration, *Ecology* **55**:62–72.

Turner, J., and J. N. Long, 1975, Accumulation of organic matter in a series of Douglas fir stands, *Can. J. For. Res.* **5**:681-690.

Waring, R. H., 1969, Forest plants of the eastern Siskiyous: Their environmental and vegetational distribution, *Northwest Sci.* **43**:1–17.

Waring, R. H., K. L. Reed, and W. H. Emmingham, 1972. An environmental grid for classifying forest ecosystems, in *Proceedings—Research on Coniferous Forest Ecosystems—A Symposium,* J. F. Franklin, L. V. Dempster, and R. H. Waring, eds., U.S. Department of Agriculture Forest Service, Portland, Oreg., pp. 79-91.

Whittaker, R. H., and S. A. Levin, eds., 1975, *Niche: Theory and Application,* Dowden, Hutchinson & Ross, Stroudsburg, Pa., 464p.

Whittaker, R. H., S. A. Levin, and R. B. Root, 1973, Niche, habitat and ecotype, *Am. Nat.* **107:**321-328.

Zobel, D. B., A. McKee, G. M. Hawk, and C. T. Dyrness, 1976, Relationships of environment to composition, structure, and diversity of forest communities of the central western Cascades of Oregon, *Ecol. Monogr.* **46:**135-156.

5

Productivity of Western Coniferous Forests

J. N. Long

INTRODUCTION

A unique attribute of forests, in contrast with other types of plant communities, is their striking accumulation of biomass. Among the forest types of the world none is more massive than the old-growth coniferous forest of the middle latitudes of western North America (Franklin and Dyrness 1973; Kira 1975; Westman and Whittaker 1975; Fujimori 1977).

The productivity of forest ecosystems worldwide is extremely variable (Kira 1975; Shidei and Kira 1977), but with the exception of the humid tropics, nowhere are found forests more productive than in western Oregon and Washington (Fujimori 1971a; Zavitkovski and Stevens 1972; Grier 1978).

Investigation of the production, accumulation, and distribution of organic matter in these forest ecosystems was a principal pursuit of the Coniferous Forest Biome. While tissue-level study of production-related processes in forest ecosystems has definite value (Chapter 6), it is difficult, if not impossible, to extrapolate such studies to whole trees and stands (Assmann 1970). The understanding of stand productivity and biomass distribution provides an excellent framework for studies of ecosystem-level functions such as water relations (Chapter 6), and nutrient cycling (Chapter 7).

Most of the work on primary production was conducted within Douglas-fir-dominated ecosystems. This widespread species is both ecologically and economically important in the region; it also dominates all but a small part of the Thompson and H. J. Andrews research sites. The studies have for the most part involved destructive sampling and extensive use of allometric correlations (Newbould 1967); inferences concerning changes in productivity and biomass distribution associated with ecosystem development are based on comparisons of different aged stands.

The purpose of this chapter is: (1) to discuss changes in the distribution of organic matter within developing Douglas-fir ecosystems; (2) to indicate trends in production-related processes (such as gross and net primary productivity, respiration) within the same forests; and (3) to discuss ways in which these processes may differ in other types of forest ecosystems. The first part of the chapter, dealing with the accumulation and distribution of organic matter, is divided into sections on the crown, bole, understory, forest floor, and below-ground components of developing Douglas-fir stands.

DEVELOPMENT OF INDIVIDUAL CROWNS AND STAND CANOPIES

Knowledge of crown structure is a prerequisite for detailed ecosystem-level studies related to productivity, microclimatology, and nutrient and organic matter cycling. Crown structure has, for example, been shown to be an important determinant of the photosynthetic productivity of plant canopies (Chapter 6; Monsi et al. 1973). Knowledge derived from such studies provides a link between investigations of stand structure and process-related studies of assimilation and water relations. For example, estimates of foliar distribution in tree crowns are necessary for extrapolation of gas exchange data (Stephens 1969; Kinerson and Fritschen 1971; Walker et al. 1972); however, extrapolation is difficult because of the complexity of canopy structure, arising from both spatial and temporal variations. Without detailed information on these variations, extrapolation of gas-exchange data can be the source of substantial error in estimates of stand primary production (Newbould 1967).

Crown Development

The development of foliar biomass and surface area for many tree species has been shown to be exponentially related to diameter at breast height (dbh) (for example, Assmann 1970; Kira and Shidei 1967). This allometric relationship and the bias introduced by the use of the logarithmic transformation have been the subject of considerable work (Madgwick 1970; Baskerville 1972; Beauchamp and Olson 1973; Mountford and Bunce 1973). The relation between crown weight (foliage and branches) and dbh for Douglas-fir is shown in Figure 5.1.

It has been suggested (Kira and Shidei 1967) that under some circumstances the allometric correlation between diameter and crown weight for a particular species may differ from that which is normal for the species. An example of such a change is the overestimation of foliar biomass for trees with large diameters, for example, greater than 50 cm dbh (Kira and Shidei 1967). It has been shown by Grier and Waring (1974) that for several species of conifers, including Douglas-fir, sapwood cross-sectional area at breast height is a better predictor of foliar biomass than is total basal area, particularly for large trees. The ratio of sapwood cross-sectional area to total area tends to decrease with tree size. The relation between foliage and the water-conducting tissue of the

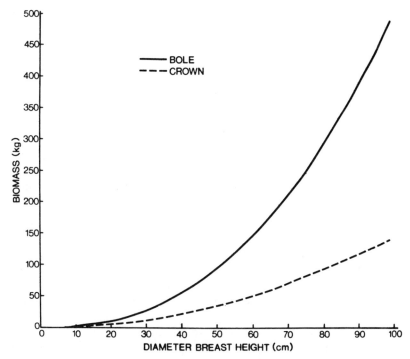

FIGURE 5.1 *Douglas-fir crown and bole weights as a function of breast height diameter (based on equations from Grier and Logan 1977).*

sapwood may provide support for an explanation of stem form based on physiology (Larson 1963; Shinozaki et al. 1964; Assmann 1970; Hinckley et al. 1978).

Distribution of Biomass Within the Crowns of Individual Trees

The distribution of biomass within the crowns of trees has important morphological, ecological, and silvicultural implications. The relation between canopy structure and photosynthesis has been reviewed by Monsi et al. (1973). Much of the forestry literature concerning the relation between crown structure and productivity of forest trees has been synthesized by Assmann (1970). Information concerning the crown structure of Douglas-fir has been incorporated into a stand growth model (Mitchell 1975).

A detailed treatment of crown dynamics is, of course, dependent on an understanding of patterns of individual branch growth. For example, the extension of primary branch internodes is, for Douglas-fir, highly dependent on the position of the branch within the crown of the tree such that internode length decreases with increasing internode number from the bole. While the pattern of internode extension with increasing branch age is similar for the trees on different sites, internode lengths are in general much greater on more productive sites.

The regular pattern of branch extension (that is, the sum of successive branch primary internodes) results in a predictable relation between branch age and total length for trees on a given site. This relation has been used for the prediction of crown structure necessary for modeling of tree growth and stand development (Mitchell 1975). The prediction of crown shape from branch lengths, however, is based on the simplifying assumption that branches develop perpendicular to the bole of the tree and remain horizontal for their entire length. For at least several species of conifers this is not the case (Stiehl 1969; Jensen 1976). The departure of individual branches from a horizontal orientation can, in fact, be considerable. The pattern for Douglas-fir is one of the decreasing branch angle, from the top of the crown, and increasing weight to a point near the base of the live crown. Beneath this point the branches again demonstrate an upward sweep. Branches that depart from the horizontal, either by virtue of their orientation with the bole or by curvature, result in a somewhat reduced crown profile compared with horizontal branches of similar length. The orientation of the branches with respect to the horizontal can be explained in large part on the basis of the distribution of foliar biomass (Jensen 1976). In general, the center of mass for the foliage moves outward on individual branches as they age (Figure 5.2). It is possible, by combining the distribution of foliage along individual branches, to approximate the overall distribution of foliage within the tree crown (Figure 5.3). The contours, representing percentage of maximum foliar weight, indicate that above whorl 11 foliage is concen-

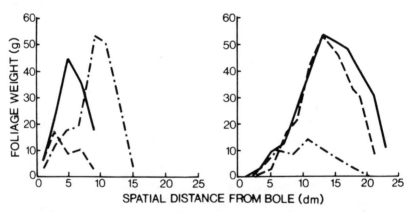

FIGURE 5.2 *Distribution of foliar biomass on individual branches of a codominant Douglas-fir (Jensen 1976). Whorl number equals branch age. Dashed lines = whorls 4 (left) and 14 (right), solid lines = whorls 6 (left) and 17 (right); dot-and-dashed lines = whorls 8 (left) and 22 (right).*

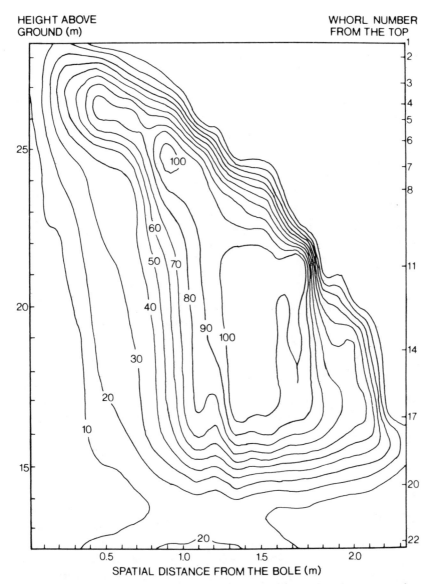

HEIGHT ABOVE
GROUND (m)

WHORL NUMBER
FROM THE TOP

FIGURE 5.3 *Relative distribution of foliar weight within the crown of a codominant Douglas-fir (Jensen 1976); contour intervals represent 10 percent of maximum foliar weight.*

trated near the ends of individual branches. For example, the peak in foliage weight for a branch at whorl 8 is about 1.0 m from the bole. For a branch at whorl 4 the peak is about 0.5 m from the bole. Thus foliage tends to be distributed farther from the bole with increasing distance from the top of the tree. Such an arrangement tends to minimize self-shading and maximize photo-synthetic efficiency (Chapter 6; Monsi et al. 1973). In contrast, there appears to be a great deal of "stacking" of foliage below whorl 11, an arrangement of foliage that undoubtedly increases self-shading of these needles and decreases productivity in that part of the crown.

It has been observed that maximum radial increment along the upper stem of a conifer often occurs at a point above the base of the live crown (Chapter 6; Duff and Nolan 1957; Larson 1963; Dobbs 1966). There are within the crowns, and even within individual branches of Douglas-fir, zones corresponding to different levels of photosynthetic efficiency (Woodman 1968; Kinerson 1971; Leverenz 1974). Not surprisingly, this efficiency decreases from the top of the tree to the base of the live crown. The height, therefore, of the maximum "effective" foliar biomass is not necessarily coincident with the position of the maximum in foliar biomass (Woodman 1968; Kinerson 1971). It has been suggested that the position of maximum radial increment may correspond to the height of the maximum "effective" foliar biomass (Larson 1963; Assmann 1970).

The relation between twig and foliage weights at different heights within the crowns of codominant Douglas-fir (Dice 1970; Jensen 1976) suggests a possible structural link between the distribution of foliage and radial increment along the bole. In the upper portion of the crown, dry weights of foliage and woody branch material are approximately equal (Figure 5.4). Lower in the crown the values diverge, with the weight of woody material increasing more rapidly than the foliage. As can be seen in Figure 5.4, the area of maximum ring width along the bole coincides with the divergence of foliage and twig weights.

The age structure and population dynamics of a tree's needle complement are important in the context of foliar efficiency, nutrient cycling, and crown morphology. Younger age classes of foliage tend to have a higher photosynthetic efficiency (Woodman 1968; Leverenz 1974), and models of needle litter production involve assumptions about the age-class distribution of living needles (Gessel and Turner 1976; Tadaki 1977). The woody material of branches is the supportive tissue of foliage. Older and larger branches are less efficient than younger, smaller branches on the basis of foliage-to-twig weight ratios (Figure 5.4); it seems likely that the maintenance costs associated with large branches in the lower portions of the crown are higher per unit of supported foliage than for smaller branches in the upper crown (Assmann 1970; Jensen 1976).

The age structure of needles within the crowns of Douglas-fir suggests a fairly regular loss of needles across age classes. Silver (1962), working with eight- to ten-year-old Douglas-fir, found the youngest age class of foliage typically accounted for about 23 to 25 percent of the total; the next age class accounted for somewhat less, and so on. Jensen (1976), working with a large codominant tree, found almost exactly the same pattern (Figure 5.5). He found in addition, however, that the age structure of the branch internodes is very similar to that of the foliage (Figure 5.5).

It is apparent from the age-class distributions of needles and internodes

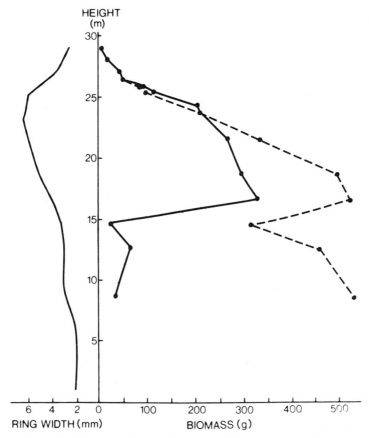

FIGURE 5.4 *Distribution of stem radial increment and crown biomass in a codominant Douglas-fir (Jensen 1976). Dashed line = twig biomass, solid line = foliage biomass.*

(Figure 5.5) that the reduction in older needles results, for the most part, from the death of older internodes. Much of this internode mortality results in turn from the death of both short-lived internodal branches and relatively old branches at the bottom of the crown (Jensen 1976). Within the crown of the tree studied by Jensen significant needle loss from living internodes did not occur until individual internodes and their needles were between five and six years of age.

These data appear to lend support to the concept that the crowns of Douglas-fir may attain a state of dynamic equilibrium in terms of their internode and foliage age-class distributions. Because of its high proportion of one- and two-year-old foliage (approximately 45 percent of total), this particular age distribution is more efficient than one in which older needles are relatively more abundant. The similarity between the foliar age distribution of the eight-

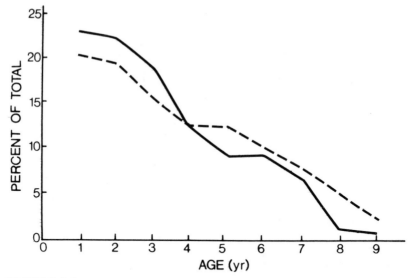

FIGURE 5.5 *Age-class distributions for needles and internodes in the crown of a codominant Douglas-fir (Jensen 1976). Solid line = needles, dashed line = internodes.*

to ten-year-old trees of Silver (1962) and the thirty-seven-year-old tree of Jensen (1976) and the 53-year-old trees of Kay (1978) may indicate that equilibrium of age structure is achieved early in crown development and maintained at least through the stage of canopy closure. In comparison, Pike et al. (1977) found that only about 37 percent of the foliage of a 400-year-old Douglas-fir was one and two years old. They pointed out, however, that this figure is probably an underestimate, since their sample did not include the top several meters of the crown.

Canopy Development

The structural development of forest canopies is a function of the development of many individual trees. Not all trees, of course, develop in the same way. Inter- and intraspecific competition within developing forest communities results in the differentiation of crown classes, which in turn are differentially susceptible to mortality. Crown differentiation is one attribute of vigorous, even-aged forests (Assmann 1970). All of the trees, typically representing a number of different crown classes, together compose the overstory forest canopy.

A number of investigations, primarily within the last decade, dealing with the accumulation of organic matter in forests, have led to the suggestion of an equilibrium or steady state in overstory foliar biomass. Mar:Møller (1947) attributed this suggested upper limit of foliar biomass to the full "occupancy" of the site by the stand. This condition was obtained only following canopy closure. Tadaki et al. (1970) suggest that the timing of canopy closure and thus the timing of a peak or equilibrium in foliar biomass may be related to initial stand density.

The ecological implications of an equilibrium in overstory foliar biomass are considerable. For example, such an equilibrium may be associated with an equilibrium in gross primary production for the stand; this, along with the continued accumulation of respiring biomass, may result in a decline in net primary production. In addition, achievement of an equilibrium in overstory foliage may signal a change in patterns of nutrient cycling by the developing ecosystem to patterns characteristic of mature forests (Chapter 7; Marks and Bormann 1972; Turner 1975; Vitousek and Reiners 1975; Vitousek 1977). The subcanopy environment of a stand's subordinate vegetation must also be influenced by the presence of a relatively constant amount of overstory foliage.

The development of an equilibrium level of overstory foliar biomass (Figure 5.6) has been demonstrated for low-site-quality (III–IV) Douglas-fir stands (Turner and Long 1975). The accumulation of foliar biomass is primarily a function of age but may be rapid or slow depending on initial stand density (Tadaki et al. 1970; Long and Turner 1975). The fact that high initial densities accelerate stand development for such parameters as basal area and volume has been recognized for many years (Assmann 1970); high density also appears to affect such parameters as canopy closure, foliar biomass and, indirectly, understory weight and succession (Long and Turner 1975).

The data used in the analysis of foliar equilibrium represented by Figure 5.6 are from low-site-quality stands, all of which are less than 75 years old. The status of the canopy beyond this stage is important; unfortunately, few comparison data are available from older stands. Data from a 450-year-old stand located in the H. J. Andrews Experimental Forest provide some basis for speculation on the maintenance of foliar biomass in old-growth Douglas-fir. Grier et al. (1974) report that this stand, on a relatively low-quality site, supported an overstory foliar biomass of 8906 kg/ha. It may be argued that this comparatively low figure illustrates a stage of decline in foliar biomass from a previously higher equilibrium level. Alternatively, if the foliage of the subordinate vegetation, which includes trees up to 15 cm dbh, is included as a component of the overstory foliage, the total is 10,510 kg/ha. Thus it might be argued that this stand has maintained a relatively constant foliar biomass by virtue of ingrowth during the stage of overstory deterioration.

It is interesting to speculate on the environmental or physiological factors that might affect an equilibrium in foliar biomass. It is apparent, for example, that there are different upper limits for different species, and much of this variation is attributable to differences in life form and climate (Gholz et al. 1976; Tadaki 1977). Intuitively, it seems as if upper limits of foliar biomass

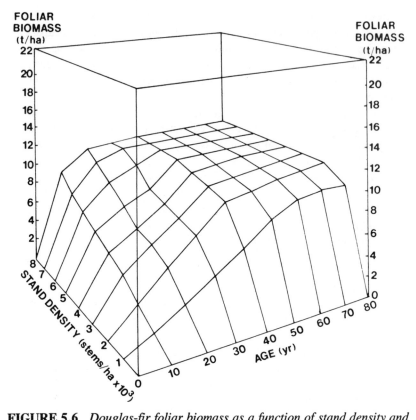

FIGURE 5.6 *Douglas-fir foliar biomass as a function of stand density and age (after Turner and Long 1975). Data are from stands of similar site quality.*

should vary among sites; however, investigations of the foliar carrying capacity of different sites for a given species are limited and conflicting (Mar:Møller 1947; Doucet et al. 1976).

   Environmental factors that may affect an equilibrium level include light, nutrient, and moisture regimes. Equilibrium levels of foliar biomass found for several coniferous forest biome species include: western hemlock 21,000 kg/ha (Fujimori 1971a); Pacific silver fir 18,000 kg/ha (Turner and Singer 1976; Fujimori et al. 1976); and Douglas-fir 11,000 kg/ha (Turner and Long 1975). The differences between species may reflect a light-limited upper limit to foliar biomass; western hemlock is perhaps slightly more tolerant than is Pacific silver fir (Hodges and Scott 1968; Thornburgh 1969), while Douglas-fir is relatively intolerant (Fowells 1965). It has been observed (Kajihara 1977) for plantations of *Cryptomeria japonica* that the crown surface area exposed to sunlight reaches an equilibrium at the same time as foliar biomass.

Nutrient deficiencies in an ecosystem may also act to limit the accumulation of foliage (Chapter 7). While some investigations have shown foliar biomass to be independent of or inversely proportional to site quality, many have shown a positive relationship between these two parameters (Doucet et al. 1976). For example, Heilman (1961) has shown a positive correlation between site quality, foliage, and total crown weight for Douglas-fir. An argument for nutrient-limited foliar biomass is provided by the fact that nitrogen fertilization often results in increased foliage weights (Heilman and Gessel 1963). The increase in weight is a function of the increase in size of individual needles as well as longer rentention of older needles (Gessel and Turner 1976; Turner and Olson 1976). While data of more than several years' duration are few, there is some indication that the increase in stand foliar biomass associated with fertilization may be short-lived, with a return to pretreatment levels occurring in several years (Gessel and Turner 1976).

Moisture is a third factor that may be important in limiting an ecosystem's overstory foliar biomass. For example, there appears to be a strong relation between the total leaf area supported by a coniferous forest community and the water balance of the community (Grier and Running 1797). Leaf area is, of course, strongly related to foliar biomass. It is suggested, therefore, that available soil moisture and evaporative demand may be important determinants of maximum foliar biomass.

STEM DEVELOPMENT

Figure 5.7 illustrates a possible pattern of bole (stemwood plus bark) biomass accumulation with time for relatively low-site-quality Douglas-fir stands. The weight of the boles in the stands appears to increase rapidly for approximately 130 to 150 years, at which time a leveling off occurs. This high level of biomass can be maintained for at least 400 to 500 years. Eventually increasing mortality in the stand begins to offset stemwood increment of the remaining trees such that total bole biomass may decline (Grier and Logan 1977). It is especially noteworthy that much of this striking accumulation of stemwood is associated with a relatively constant amount of foliar biomass.

UNDERSTORY DEVELOPMENT

The development of the overstory canopy in these Douglas-fir-dominated ecosystems is associated with drastic changes in understory composition and structure (Long and Turner 1975). The most dynamic period in the development of the understory is that stage of stand development prior to and immediately following canopy closure. In the first several years following stand initiation the understory is characterized by high levels of diversity (Figure 5.8),

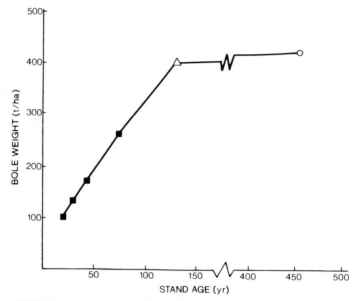

FIGURE 5.7 *Bole weight as a function of age in low-site Douglas-fir stands.* ■ *= Turner and Long (1975);* △ *= C. C. Grier (pers. comm.);* ○ *= Grier and Logan (1977).*

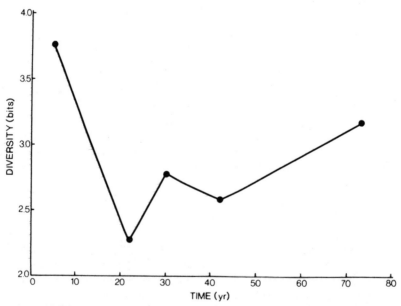

FIGURE 5.8 *Plant species diversity in a series of different-aged Douglas-fir stands (after Long 1977).*

rapid species replacement, and relatively low aboveground biomass (Figure 5.9; Long 1977; Long and Turner 1975; Dyrness 1973; Shugart and Hett 1973). Composition of the understory includes many "residual" species characteristic of mature forests (Mueller-Dombois 1965) as well as "opportunistic" species adapted to recently disturbed habitats (Dyrness 1973). High diversity results from a combination of species richness (that is, many different species) and the absence of strong dominance by any single species (Long 1977).

As low-site-quality Douglas-fir stands continue to grow, another stage of stand development is characterized by a rapid increase in the aboveground biomass of the ericaceous shrub *Gaultheria shallon* (Pursh). The increase in *Gaultheria* biomass may be attributable to the creation of a more favorable environment beneath the still open canopy of the developing overstory (Swank 1972). It is undoubtedly due also in part to the strong vegetative growth of this rhizomatous species (Sabhasri 1961).

As the overstory canopy closes, *Gaultheria* biomass declines. The declining *Gaultheria* biomass results in a reduction of total aboveground understory biomass but is associated with an increase in the understory biomass contributed by those species other than *Gaultheria* (Long and Turner 1975). Various species of moss in particular become increasingly important in the understory

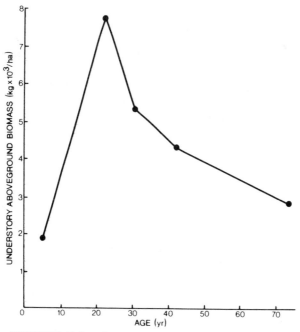

FIGURE 5.9 *The development of understory biomass with time for naturally regenerated stands of Douglas-fir (Long and Turner 1975).*

of the developing stand. For example, Long and Turner (1975) found mosses contributing less than 1 percent of aboveground understory biomass immediately prior to canopy closure, but nearly 60 percent following canopy closure. The increase in the importance of mosses reflects an absolute increase in moss biomass of about 600 percent, as well as a relative increase associated with the decline in *Gaultheria* (Long and Turner 1975).

Many of the changes in understory structure are associated with canopy closure. For example, the aboveground biomass of *Gaultheria* is closely correlated with changes in overstory foliar biomass (Figure 5.10). Similarly, changes in the relative importance of *Gaultheria* are strongly correlated with changes in the diversity of the subordinant herbs and mosses (Figure 5.11).

Prior to and immediately following closure of the Douglas-fir overstory is a period of rapid change in the composition and structure of the understory. Following canopy closure, understory composition and diversity appear to stabilize (Long and Turner 1975, Long 1977). Aboveground understory biomass also appears to stabilize at between 2000 and 3000 kg/ha (Long and Turner 1975, Grier and Logan 1977).

CHANGES IN THE RETURN OF ORGANIC MATTER
TO THE FOREST FLOOR

There are some general trends in litter production for the intensively studied Douglas-fir forests. For example, there is an increase in leaf litter production within the developing stands up to time of canopy closure (Gessel and Turner 1976). The equilibrium in leaf litter production is, not surprisingly, associated with the equilibrium in overstory foliar biomass. Typically, leaf litter produced annually represents approximately 20 percent of the foliar biomass (Gessel and Turner 1976). As can be inferred from the age distribution of needles in the crown of a Douglas-fir (Figure 5.5), the loss is not merely from the oldest age class of needles, but rather represents losses from all age classes.

Total litter production, needles plus woody material, continues to increase after canopy closure because of the increasing contribution of woody material from the crowns of the trees. In the Douglas-fir stands studied by Turner and Long (1975) at the Thompson site, the woody component of tree litter production increased from approximately 6 percent in the twenty-two-year-old stand to over 50 percent in the seventy-three-year-old stand. In old-growth stands the production of woody litter may exceed 60 percent as large logs are added to the forest floor (Grier et al. 1974, Sollins et al. 1980). A similar increase in woody litter production has been observed in overmature stands of *Alnus rubra* (Turner et al. 1976).

The return of organic matter from the understory to the forest floor changes drastically with stand development (Turner and Long 1975). Prior to canopy closure the contribution of the understory to total litter production may exceed

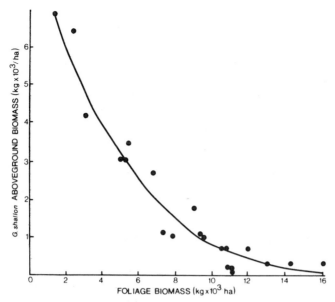

FIGURE 5.10 *Aboveground biomass of the dominant under-story shrub* (Gaultheria shallon) *as a function of overstory foliar biomass (after Long and Turner 1975).*

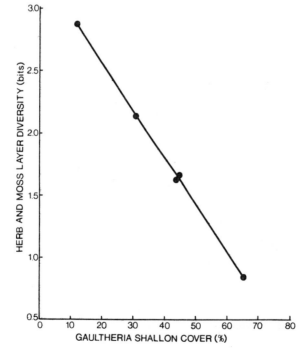

FIGURE 5.11 *Herb and moss layer species diversity as a function of* Gaultheria shallon *cover (after Long 1977).*

40 percent; following canopy closure this component may decline to less than 20 percent. The organic matter returned to the forest floor by the understory changes in character as well as amount as the species composition of the understory changes. For example, the understory return includes increasingly greater proportions of moss. It includes not only discrete pieces of organic matter that fall on the surface of the forest floor but also the portion of the moss layer that has already been partially incorporated into the forest floor (Turner and Long 1975).

A distinct feature of these Douglas-fir ecosystems is the lack of equilibrium in detritus (litter plus large woody matter) even after several hundred years of stand development. Figure 5.12 illustrates the trends in accumulation of organic matter on the forest floor of several Douglas-fir stands. The weight of the forest floor (leaf litter plus woody litter less than 15 cm in diameter) appears to stabilize relatively early in stand development, indicating that the addition of litter is being offset by decomposition. The continuing addition of large logs, however, results in a nearly linear increase in total detritus. The ratio of detritus to total aboveground organic matter increases from less than 10 percent in the 22-year-old stand at the Thompson site to over 27 percent in the 450-year-old stand on watershed 10.

The long-term imbalance between detritus production and decomposition and the resulting buildup of organic matter has important consequences in

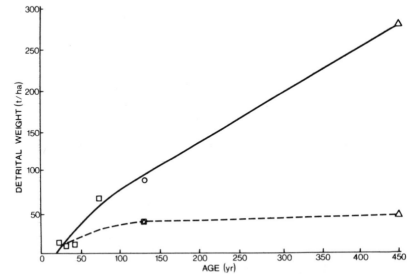

FIGURE 5.12 *Detrital weight as a function of stand age for low-site-quality Douglas-fir. Solid line = forest floor + large woody material; dashed line = forest floor alone; △ = Grier and Logan (1977), □ = Turner and Long (1975); ○ = C.C. Grier, (pers. comm.).*

terms of nutrient cycling and fire ecology. The accumulated dead organic matter represents an important reservoir of nutrients. Natural wildfire may represent an important decomposing agent in temperate coniferous ecosystems (Habeck and Mutch 1973; St. John and Rundel 1976).

ROOT BIOMASS

The physiological and structural importance of roots is unquestioned; however, root systems of plant communities have been neglected in most ecosystem-level studies because of the formidable problems associated with their analysis. Data compiled by Santantonio et al. (1977) for many different tree species demonstrate the existence of a consistent relation between root system biomass and stem diameter (Figure 5.13). The data come from a variety of sources and represent a wide range of methodology, environmental conditions, and diameters. It is noteworthy that within-species variation may be as great as the variation between different species of conifers and angiosperms (Santantonio et al. 1977).

Using regression equations developed for the prediction of biomass of roots larger than 5 mm in diameter and data from Santantonio et al. (1977) for biomass of the smaller roots, Grier and Logan (1977) derived estimates of root biomass for the old-growth forest on watershed 10. Total root biomass was estimated to be 152.5 t/ha or 18 percent of the total biomass for the community. Of this amount, 11.3 t/ha or 1 percent was estimated to be fine roots.

Several investigators have suggested that root system biomass, fine roots in particular, may reach a more or less steady state at some early stage of stand development (Mar:Møller 1947; Tadaki et al. 1970). Santantonio et al. (1977) have suggested that this hypothesized equilibrium in fine root biomass may indicate the existence of a mechanism that controls a "balance between the physiologically most active parts of the belowground and aboveground portions of older woody plants." They estimate, for example, that the old-growth forest of watershed 10 is supporting a fine root biomass of approximately 11.3 t/ha, and is at the same time supporting a foliar biomass of approximately 10.5 t/ha. It is possible that both figures represent equilibrium values, achieved following canopy closure, imposed by environmental conditions and maintained notwithstanding drastic changes in the biomass of stems, branches, and large roots.

STAND PRODUCTIVITY

The accumulation of organic matter in an ecosystem is a function of the balance between the production of organic matter and its removal or decomposition. Biomass is thus an integration of these processes over the entire period of

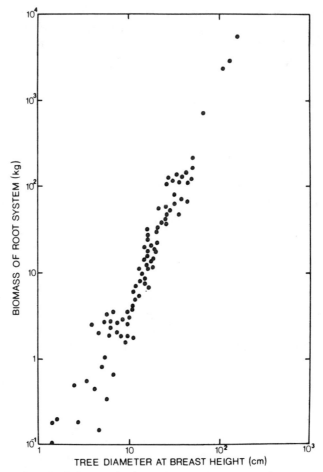

FIGURE 5.13   *Relation between biomass of root systems and tree diameter at breast height for several tree species (after Santantonio et al. 1977).*

stand development. Productivity, in the broad sense, is the rate at which organic matter is produced. Net primary productivity is the rate of accumulation of organic matter in excess of autotrophic respiration (that is, gross primary productivity minus autotrophic respiration). In forest production ecology, productivity is usually estimated in kilograms per hectare per year.

The aboveground productivity of trees can be estimated as follows (Newbould 1967):

$$P_n = P_t + P_d + P_a$$

where P_n is net production, P_t is aboveground production of the trees over a one-year period, P_d is loss by death, and P_a is loss by consumers (this component is commonly ignored). The component P_t can be subdivided for measurement as follows:

$$P_t = P_f + P_b + P_s$$

where P_f is foliar production, P_b is branch production, and P_s is stem production. The total aboveground productivity for a stand is the sum of productivity of the trees plus that of the understory.

Estimates of net aboveground primary productivity for seven stands at the Thompson site are shown in Table 5.1 (Turner and Long 1975). The productivity estimates indicate the importance of the understory in relation to total stand productivity. Within the tree component of the stand, foliar productivity is relatively constant regardless of stand age. Generally, the higher productivities occur in the younger stands, and the greatest total tree productivity that was measured occurred in the lightly stocked forty-two-year-old natural stand. This may indicate that the period of highest productivity in a stand occurs at about the time of canopy closure, independent of age. When the ratio of foliar biomass and leaf litter production is compared, it becomes obvious that there is a rapid turnover of foliage in the twenty-two- and thirty-year-old stands, which indicates a short period of needle retention in these younger, highly competitive stands. There is a tapering off in tree productivity with age, which is to be expected from past volume studies in Douglas-fir as well as in other species (Assmann 1970).

The aboveground productivity of the understory is also greatest before crown closure. The decline in productivity of *Gaultheria,* the dominant understory species, with stand age is associated with increasing canopy biomass (Long and Turner 1975), and there is a similar trend for the rest of the vascular understory. The mosses begin to increase in importance with time in both biomass and productivity, so that at twenty-two years the mosses represent 0.4 percent of the understory aboveground production, but at seventy-three years they represent 82 percent. The understory makes a greater contribution to stand productivity than to accumulated biomass. For example, in the twenty-two-year-old stand the understory provides 17 percent of total aboveground productivity and declines to 10 percent in the seventy-three-year-old stand, while the understory is never more than 5.5 percent of the total aboveground biomass.

Using the annual productivity figure as the current annual increment of the trees and using the standing biomass to calculate mean annual increment, it is found that the time where current and mean annual increments are equal for stem production is about 30 years (Figure 5.14). The estimate is a function of stand stocking, as indicated by the forty-two-year-old sparse stand, but it can be expected that in these relatively low-site-quality stands the productivity will begin the decline at about the time of canopy closure.

Decline in productivity per unit of foliage with increasing structural biomass (Figure 5.15) is undoubtedly due in part to the differentiation of crown classes that accompanies stand development. The dense shade to which inter-

TABLE 5.1 *Estimates of net aboveground productivity ($kg \cdot ha^{-1} \cdot yr^{-1}$) for low-site-quality Douglas-fir stands.*[a]

Stand no.	Stand age (yr)	Tree production				Understory production				Moss understory (%)	Stand total	Understory total (%)
		Leaf	Branch	Stem	Total	Annuals	Salal	Moss	Total			
1	22 nat.[a]	2100	540	6130	8770	1176	806	8	1990	0.4	11560	17
2	30 nat.	3142	527	4763	8432	340	456	151	947	16	9379	10
3	30 plant.[b]	2097	539	4982	8618	—	—	—	—	—	—	—
4	42 nat.	2230	673	6392	9295	254	296	83	633	13	9928	6
5	42 plant.	2443	483	3650	6576	95	218	230	543	42	7119	7
6	49 plant.	2200	420	3300	5920	105	211	210	526	40	6446	8
7	73 nat.	2280	330	2500	5110	2	98	467	567	82	5677	10

[a]Turner and Long 1975.
[a]Naturally established.
[b]Plantation established.

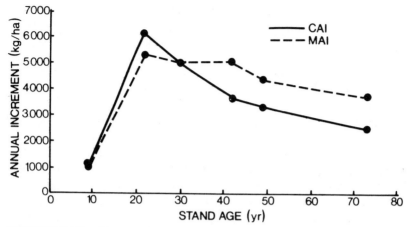

FIGURE 5.14 *Changes in mean and current annual increment in low-site-quality Douglas-fir stands (after Turner and Long 1975).*

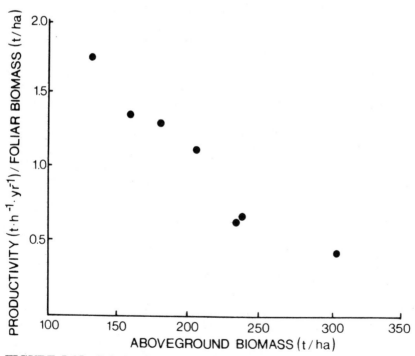

FIGURE 5.15 *Relation between productivity per unit of overstory foliage and aboveground biomass.*

mediate and suppressed trees are subjected is accompanied by reduced growth. In addition, it has long been recognized that, in general, trees with smaller crowns have higher rates of production per unit of ground area covered. This decrease in efficiency of growing space occupancy with increasing crown size has been related to a corresponding increase in nonassimilating shoots and branches relative to foliage (Assmann 1970). It is thus possible that the declining efficiency of the larger crown classes may be in part responsible for the peak in net primary productivity, early in stand development, of even-aged coniferous forests.

Estimates of annual net primary production for the Douglas-fir stands at the Thompson site ranged from a low of 5.7 t/ha to 11.6 t/ha (Cole et al. 1968; Turner and Long 1975). Similar estimates of annual net primary production were obtained in a study of several 450-year-old stands on watershed 10 at the H. J. Andrews site (Grier and Logan 1977). These Douglas-fir-dominated, old-growth stands had annual rates of between 6.3 and 10.1 t/ha. Fujimori et al. (1976), working in a 110-year-old Douglas-fir stand of higher site quality, obtained a net productivity estimate of 13 $t \cdot ha^{-1} \cdot yr^{-1}$.

For areas of similar potential productivity (that is, similar site quality), it is possible that gross production may often be approximately equal for young and old stands. This may follow as a direct consequence of the early attainment and maintenance of an equilibrium in foliar and fine root biomass. It is noteworthy that for coniferous forests foliar respiration may account for between 65 and 70 percent of total autotrophic respiration (Yoda et al. 1965; Grier and Logan 1977).

While foliar biomass and net production for different-aged stands of similar site quality may be similar following canopy closure, there are dramatic differences in the allocation of production. In younger stands (for example, 20 to 40 years old) 70 percent or more of the net production may be accumulated as standing biomass. On the other hand, in mature stands (for example, 450 years old) an amount equal to or greater than net production may be actually converted to detritus (Grier and Logan 1977). This relation helps to explain the rapid accumulation of biomass in young stands and the leveling off or even decline in biomass in old-growth stands even though gross and net production remain relatively high.

COMPARISONS WITH OTHER ENVIRONMENTS AND VEGETATION TYPES

Some of the patterns in production and biomass accumulation observed for Douglas-fir ecosystems appear to parallel those found in some other coniferous forest ecosystems. Differences do exist, of course, depending on the character of the vegetation and its physical environment.

The most productive forest ecosystems in the middle latitudes of North America, and perhaps the world, are included within the western hemlock forests of coastal Oregon and Washington (Fujimori 1971a,b). The moderate maritime climate is characterized by high precipitation, low evaporative demand, and a general lack of temperature extremes (Walter 1973).

Fujimori (1971a) obtained an estimate of net primary productivity for a young (nineteen- to thirty-two-year-old) western hemlock stand of approximately $36 \, t \cdot ha^{-1} \cdot yr^{-1}$. This exceedingly high value is comparable to the highest estimates for the forest ecosystems of the world (Tadaki and Hatiya 1968; Kira 1975). It is noteworthy that this stand was estimated to be supporting in excess of 21 t/ha of overstory foliar biomass. This figure is approximately double the values typical of low-site Douglas-fir stands (Long and Turner 1975; Grier and Logan 1977). The estimate of net primary productivity is approximately three times larger than those for comparably aged Douglas-fir stands (Turner and Long 1975).

Data from a series of western hemlock stands in coastal Oregon, ranging in age from approximately 20 to 120 years, suggest a drastic decrease in productivity following canopy closure. The estimates of productivity for the older stands are, nevertheless, relatively high compared with estimates for deciduous broadleaf forests and are comparable to estimates for evergreen broadleaf forests (Kira 1975). These comparisons serve to support Kira's (1975) conclusion that, in general, evergreen forests are significantly more productive than deciduous ones, and in addition suggest that some coniferous forests, under appropriate environmental conditions, may have productivities comparable even to evergreen broadleaf forests.

Studies of production and biomass accumulation in deciduous forests of this conifer-dominated region are understandably limited. Nevertheless, investigations of forests of the relatively short-lived red alder (*Alnus rubra* Bong) seem to indicate that even deciduous broadleaf forests of this region are unusually productive (Kira 1975).

An estimate of $22.2 \, t \cdot ha^{-1} \cdot yr^{-1}$ for net aboveground productivity has been reported for ten- to fifteen-year-old red alder forests ($26 \, t \cdot ha^{-1} \cdot yr^{-1}$ for total net productivity; Zavitkovski and Stevens 1972). Leaf and litter production were also found to reach a maximum after about 10 years (Gessel and Turner 1974). Foliar production in the red alder stands studied by Zavitkovski and Stevens (1972) was found to represent approximately 25 percent of the total aboveground production. This figure is comparable to similar estimates for other temperate forests, for example, 19 percent for a twenty-six-year-old western hemlock forest (Fujimori 1971a) and 23 percent for a twenty-two-year-old Douglas-fir forest (Turner and Long 1975).

Zavitkovski and Newton (1971) found red alder litter production to be essentially unaffected by tree height, density, or site quality. Similarly, Smith and DeBell (1974) concluded that "stand density is at least as important as site quality in determining yield of fully stocked red alder stands." Gessel and Turner (1974) suggest that symbiotic nitrogen fixation may be responsible for the apparent insensitivity of alder foliar production to differences in site quality. For species not involved in nitrogen fixation, factors (especially those reducing available nitrogen) that lower site quality could be expected to reduce foliar production (Madgwick 1970; Gessel and Turner 1974).

A rapid buildup of nitrogen during the initial stage (zero to five years) of ecosystem development is followed by a more gradual increase as the stand develops further (Van Cleve et al. 1971). Gessel and Turner (1974) suggest that from about five years of age onward red alder stands return at least 80 kg·ha^{-1}·yr^{-1} (and up to 200 kg·ha^{-1}·yr^{-1}) of nitrogen to the forest floor. In contrast, young Douglas-fir stands may have nitrogen returns of between 7 and 22 kg·ha^{-1}·yr^{-1}.

Yield-Density Relations

Data have been presented from a number of even-aged plant communities, including forests, suggesting the existence of a relation between the density and mean weight (or volume) of surviving individuals (Yoda et al. 1963). The relation can be represented in the form:

$$\log \overline{w} = a + b \log \rho$$

where $\overline{w}$ is the mean weight of the surviving plants, b is the slope of the line, equaling -1.5, ρ is density, and a is a constant, the value of which varies depending on the species. In their analysis, Yoda et al. (1963) assume that the plant communities are fully stocked (that is, with closed canopies), even-aged, and monospecific. They conclude that, while site quality differences do not affect the relation, species differences do affect the value of the slope intercept.

A geometric model is proposed by Yoda et al. (1963) to explain the $-3/2$ relation between mean plant weight and stand density. It is assumed that crown shape is uniform and that the reciprocal of mean density and the mean weight are proportional to the square and cube, respectively, of some unspecified linear plant dimension (Ford 1975; Drew and Flewelling 1977).

Evidence has been presented suggesting that populations of two annual species, grown in combination, may also conform to the $-3/2$ law (White and Harper 1970; Bazzaz and Harper 1976). In these cases the dominant species contribute the most to growth and the least to mortality. This differential growth and mortality between the two species results in the maintenance of the expected relation between average plant weight and density when the population is considered collectively.

A plot of mean tree aboveground biomass and density for a number of coniferous biome forests is represented in Figure 5.16. The data range from young, exceedingly dense stands of red alder to mixed coniferous old growth consisting of exceedingly large trees. The slope of the fitted regression line is -1.48, which is not significantly different from the hypothesized value of -1.5. These data suggest that, at least for the northern temperate forests represented here, a general relation between density and biomass does exist.

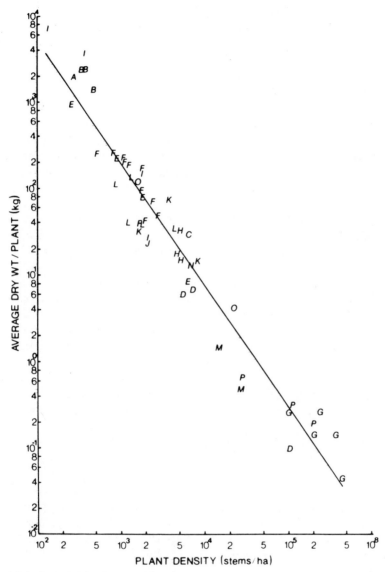

FIGURE 5.16 *Relation between mean aboveground tree dry weight and stand density for a variety of forest stands with closed canopies. (A) Grier et al. (1974); (B) Fujimori et al. (1976); (C) Fujimori (1971a); (D) Van Cleve and Viereck (1972); (E) Zavitovski and Stevens (1972); (F) Long and Turner (1975), Turner and Long (1975); (G) Smith and DeBell (1974); (H) Moore and Verspoor (1973); (I) Long (1976); (J) Elkington and Jones (1974); (K) Moir (1972); (L) Swank (1960); (M) Barney and Van Cleve (1973); (N) Weetman and Harland (1964); (O) Klemmedson (1976); (P) Dawson et al. (1976).*

The relation, which appears to be independent of site quality and species differences, may have important silvicultural applications (Drew and Flewelling 1979).

Leaf Area Differences

Knowledge of leaf area and its spatial distribution within a plant community is essential for understanding of ecosystem processes such as photosynthesis, transpiration, and respiration (Chapter 6; Gholz et al. 1976). The relation between leaf area and these production-related functions is intuitive in that the surface of foliage is the principal interface across which gas exchange occurs.

Leaf areas for the forested communities of the region are exceptionally variable. Reported estimates range from approximately 2 m^2/m^2 for a western juniper *(Juniperus occidentalis)* savanna of eastern Oregon (Gholz 1980) to over 42 m^2/m^2 for a midelevation western hemlock/Pacific silver fir stand in the western Cascade Mountains (Gholz et al. 1976). The latter estimate of total leaf area, when converted to an estimate of projected leaf area, becomes approximately 18.6 m^2/m^2 for the hemlock/fir forest. These figures are near the lowest and highest, respectively, reported for coniferous ecosystems (Tadaki 1977).

Differences in leaf area, precipitation, and elevation for various vegetation zones are shown in Figure 5.17 (Grier and Running 1977). The data came from the major vegetation zones crossed by an east-west transect of central Oregon from the coast *(Picea sitchensis)* to the interior plateau *(Artemesia tridentata)*. Rain-shadow effects are apparent in the distribution of precipitation with elevation.

There is a positive relation between community leaf area and precipitation; nevertheless, the variability is relatively great. Precipitation is, of course, but one part of water balance. Grier and Running (1977) reason that in areas "where atmospheric evaporative demand during the growing season is greater than available water, trees must strike a balance between maximizing photosynthesis and maintaining a suitable internal water status." While an increased leaf area suggests a higher photosynthetic potential, it also results in potentially higher transpirational water loss. Grier and Running (1977) suggest that on

FIGURE 5.17 *Leaf area, precipitation, and elevation for stands representative of several vegetation zones in Oregon (after Grier and Running 1977). The stands form a transect from near the coast to the steppe of central Oregon. PS = Picea sitchensis; TH = Tsuga heterophylla; IV = interior valley; A-T = Abies-Tsuga transition; AA = Abies amabilis; TM = Tsuga mertensiana; MC = mixed conifer, east slope; PP = Pinus ponderosa; P-P = P. ponderosa/Purshia; JO = Juniperus occidentalis; AT = Artemisia tridentata.*

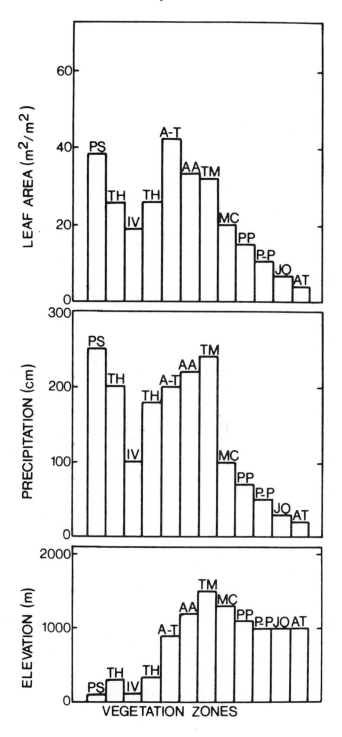

sites where available soil water and stomatal regulation of water loss are insufficient to maintain water potential above critical levels, leaf area is reduced sufficiently to restore an equilibrium with the water balance (Figure 5.18). Major adjustments of leaf area may result from reduction in the amount of foliage supported by the trees or from mortality of less competitive individuals. They further suggest that the observed linear relation between water balance and leaf area may be largely independent of species, at least within the major coniferous forest zones of Oregon.

Waring et al. (1978) present data that suggest that temperature has an influence on community leaf area in the west-central Cascade and Siskiyou mountains of Oregon. In both physiographic regions the highest leaf areas were associated with adequate soil moisture and moderate temperatures. Under similar conditions of moisture and temperature, however, the forests of the Cascades were found to have twice the leaf area supported by the forests in the Siskiyous. The lower leaf area of the forests in the Siskiyous was attributed to generally greater evaporative demand as well as to lower winter temperatures, which cause stomatal closure that in turn results in reduced primary production. Waring et al. (1978) also suggest that under some edaphic conditions, for example, the nutritionally unbalanced ultrabasic soils in the Siskiyou Mountains, reduced leaf areas may result from nutritional stress.

Another environmental factor that reduces leaf area (and biomass) is pruning. Fujimori et al. (1976) and Grier (1978) attribute the unusually low (7.9 t/ha) foliar biomass of a 120-year-old coastal western hemlock/Sitka spruce forest to the "pruning of living foliage by winds associated with winter storms." Pruning by snow limits the foliar biomass and leaf area of some species near the upper limit of their distributions. For example, as much as 30 percent of the foliar biomass of a 130-year-old Douglas-fir stand on the H. J.

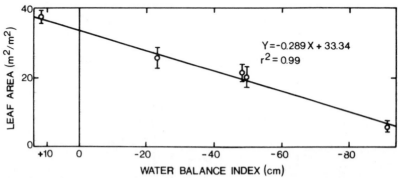

FIGURE 5.18 *Leaf area as a function of water balance (after Grier and Running 1977). Water balance index equals the difference between available water (growing season precipitation plus soil water stored in the rooting zone at the beginning of the growing season) and open-pan evaporation.*

Andrews Experimental Forest may have been lost as a result of pruning during a single, unusually heavy snowfall (C. C. Grier, pers. comm.).

Production Efficiencies

Net production in a plant community is a function of two kinds of ecological efficiency: the efficiency with which solar energy is captured (gross production) and the efficiency with which gross production is used. The efficiency of gross production typically ranges between 2.0 percent and 3.5 percent for forests of all types (Kira 1975). The estimates, based on total shortwave radiation, led Kira to conclude that forest communities are exceedingly efficient in their gross production compared with most terrestrial and aquatic plant communities.

The efficiency with which captured solar energy or gross production is converted to net production can be expressed by the ratio of net primary production (NPP) to gross primary production (GPP). Forest communities with NPP/GPP ratios generally between 0.25 and 0.50 are typically less efficient than perennial herbaceous or annual herbaceous communities with NPP/GPP ratios of 0.50 to 0.55 and 0.55 to 0.70, respectively (Kira 1975; Reichle 1975). This ordering of efficiencies is not surprising when one considers that while GPP efficiency is increased with high levels of leaf biomass, the increased foliage is supported by increasing amounts of branch, stem, and root biomass (Kira 1975). The increase in nonphotosynthetic supportive tissue leads to increased community respiration and smaller NPP/GPP ratios.

Coniferous forests in the Pacific Northwest appear to have higher rates of GPP than are typical for other forest types (Table 5.2). Estimates of GPP for the old-growth stands of watershed 10 are exceedingly high, approximately $160 \, t \cdot ha^{-1} \cdot yr^{-1}$. This value is similar to the highest estimates reported for any forests in the world (Kira 1975); however those biotic and environmental factors that contribute to high GPP (for example, large leaf biomass, relatively mild summer and winter temperatures, and exceptionally large biomass accumulations) also contribute to high levels of autotrophic respiration.

The high efficiency of GPP of these coniferous ecosystems is thus partially offset by NPP/GPP ratios much lower than normal for forest communities. For example, the NPP/GPP ratios estimated by Grier and Logan (1977) for mature Douglas-fir stands on watershed 10 are between 6 and 8 percent. These values are in sharp contrast to estimates of between 42 and 45 percent for NPP/GPP of deciduous forests of eastern North America (Woodwell and Botkin 1970; Sollins et al. 1973; Reichle 1975).

The differences in production efficiency may be accounted for in part by differences in foliar respiration. For the stands of watershed 10 foliar respiration has been estimated to represent 68 percent of total autotrophic respiration (Grier and Logan 1977). Similar proportions have been observed in *Abies*

TABLE 5.2   *Estimates of productivity and respiration for several North American ecosystem types. Values in kilograms carbon per square meter per year. Old-growth Douglas-fir data have been converted from biomass estimates assuming carbon equal to 48 percent of total biomass.*[a]

	Old-growth Douglas-fir forest	Eastern deciduous forest	Eastern oak/pine forest	Prairie	Tundra
Gross primary production (GPP)	7.72	1.62	1.32	0.64	0.24
Autotrophic respiration (R_A)	7.20	0.94	0.68	0.22	0.12
Net primary production (NPP)	0.52	0.68	0.60	0.42	0.12
Heterotrophic respiration (R_H)	0.36	0.52	0.37	0.27	0.11
Net ecosystem production					
($GPP - R_E$)	0.16	0.16	0.27	0.15	0.01
Ecosystem respiration					
($R_E = R_H + R_A$)	7.56	1.47	1.05	0.49	0.23
Production efficiency (R_A/GPP)	0.93	0.57	0.52	0.34	0.50
Effective production (NPP/GPP)	0.07	0.42	0.45	0.66	0.50
Maintenance efficiency (R_A/NPP)	13.80	1.38	1.13	0.51	1.00
Respiration allocation (R_H/R_A)	0.05	0.55	0.54	1.26	0.90
Ecosystem productivity (NEP/GPP)	0.02	0.10	0.20	0.23	0.05

[a]Grier and Logan 1977; all other data are from Reichle 1975.

sachalinensis stands in Japan (Yoda et al. 1965). In contrast, foliar respiration may represent less than 35 percent of total autotrophic respiration for deciduous *Liriodendron* forests in eastern North America (Sollins et al. 1973). These data tend to generalize Kira's (1975) conclusion that in forests of low latitudes a longer growing season, and specifically longer leaf retention, has greater impact on GPP than on NPP (that is, increased respiration may act to largely offset much of the increase in GPP).

Kira (1975) presents data that suggest that 40 $t \cdot ha^{-1} \cdot yr^{-1}$ may be an approximate upper limit of NPP for ordinary (C_3) plant communities. It is noteworthy that despite high respiration rates, some coniferous forests in middle latitudes of western North America may approach this level (Fujimori 1971a; Grier and Logan 1977).

SUMMARY

In Douglas-fir, as in other types of coniferous forest, an equilibrium in overstory foliar biomass is achieved early in stand development, that is, about the time of canopy closure. The rate at which the equilibrium is reached has been shown to be directly related to stand density. The amount of overstory foliar biomass represented by the equilibrium varies with species. Western hemlock stands, for example, may support nearly twice the foliar biomass of

Douglas-fir stands (21 t/ha versus 11 t/ha). Over a broad geographic area the foliage supported by coniferous forest ecosystems has been shown to be related to differences in site water balance.

The relatively stable upper limit in the amount of overstory foliage supported by a coniferous forest ecosystem affects understory composition, structure, and production as well as an equilibrium in gross primary production. An increase in overstory foliage in a developing Douglas-fir stand is associated with up to 60 percent reduction in understory biomass. The species composition of the understory is substantially changed. Productivity of the understory also declines drastically (70 percent) as the overstory canopy reaches its upper weight limit.

Despite equilibria in the amount of foliage and gross primary production, biomass in the form of wood continues to increase over much of the life of the stand. The weight of living boles and branches may, in some old-growth stands, reach spectacular levels, for example, greater than 400 t/ha. While the amount of fine, easily decomposed material in the forest floor probably becomes stable within a few decades following canopy closure, large material continues, in the absence of fire, to accumulate indefinitely.

Factors such as evergreenness, mild winters, and high levels of foliar biomass, which contribute to high (up to 160 $t \cdot ha^{-1} \cdot yr^{-1}$) gross primary productivity also contribute, along with the accumulation of nonphotosynthetic biomass, to high levels of autotrophic respiration. As a result, net primary productivity may represent less than 10 percent of gross primary productivity for old-growth Douglas-fir stands.

The middle latitudes of western North America are unique in that biomass accumulation in old-growth forests of the region surpasses that found in plant communities anywhere else in the world. While productivity of forests in western Oregon and Washington varies considerably with species, environment, and stand age, net primary productivity of young stands on good sites is as great as that of any temperate forests and may even exceed that of many forests in the humid tropics.

LITERATURE CITED

Assmann, E., 1970, *The Principles of Forest Yield Study: Studies in the Organic Production, Structure Increment, and Yield of Forest Stands*, Pergamon Press, Oxford, 506p.

Barney, R. J., and K. van Cleve, 1973, Black spruce fuel weights and biomass in two interior Alaska stands, *Can. J. For. Res.* **3:**304–311.

Baskerville, G. L., 1972, Use of logarithmic regression in the estimation of plant biomass, *Can. J. For. Res.* **2:**49–53.

Bazzaz, F. A., and J. L. Harper, 1976, Relationships between plant weight and numbers in mixed populations of *Sinapsis alba* (L.) Rabenh. and *Lepidium sativum* L., *J. Appl. Ecol.* **13:**211–216.

Beauchamp, J. J., and J. S. Olson, 1973, Corrections for bias in regression estimates after logarithmic transformation, *Ecology* **54**:1403–1407.

Cole, D. W., S. P. Gessel, and S. F. Dice, 1968, Distribution and cycling of nitrogen, phosphorus, potassium and calcium in a second-growth Douglas-fir ecosystem, in *Primary Productivity and Mineral Cycling in Natural Ecosystems,* H. E. Young, ed., University of Maine Press, Orono, pp. 197–233.

Dawson, D. H., J. G. Isebrands, and J. C. Gordon, 1976, Growth, dry weight yields and specific gravity, *U.S. Department of Agriculture Forest Service Research Paper NC-122,* St. Paul, Minnesota, 7p.

Dice, S. F., 1970, The biomass and nutrient flux in a second-growth Douglas-fir ecosystem (a study in quantitative ecology), Ph.D. dissertation, University of Washington, Seattle, 165p.

Dobbs, R. C., 1966, The intraseasonal development of longitudinal growth patterns in Douglas-fir (*Pseudotsuga menziesii* [Mirb.] Franco), Ph.D. dissertation, University of Washington, Seattle, 157p.

Doucet, R., J. V. Berglund, and C. E. Farnsworth, 1976, Dry matter production in 40-year-old *Pinus banksiana* stands in Quebec, *Can. J. For. Res.* **6**:357–367.

Drew, T. J., and J. W. Flewelling, 1977, Some recent Japanese theories of yield-density relationships and their application to Monterey pine plantations, *For. Sci.* **23**:517–534.

Drew, T. J., and J. W. Flewelling, 1979, Stand density management: an alternative approach and its application to Douglas-fir plantations, *For. Sci.* **25**:518–532.

Duff, G. H., and N. J. Nolan, 1957, Growth and morphogensis in the Canadian forest species, II: Specific increments and their relation to the quantity and activity of growth in *Pinus resinosa* Ait, *Can. J. Bot.* **35**:527–572.

Dyrness, C. T., 1973, Early stages of plant succession following logging and burning in the western Cascades of Oregon, *Ecology* **54**:57–69.

Elkington, T. T., and B. M. G. Jones, 1974, Biomass and primary productivity of birch (*Betula pubescens* S. lat.) in south-west Greenland, *J. Ecol.* **62**:821–830.

Ford, E. D., 1975, Competition and stand structure in some even-aged plant monocultures, *J. Ecol.* **63**:311–333.

Fowells, H. A., 1965, Silvics of forest trees of the United States, *U.S. Department of Agriculture Handbook 271,* U.S. Department of Agriculture Forest Service, Washington, D.C., 762p.

Franklin, J. F., and C. T. Dyrness, 1973, Natural vegetation of Washington and Oregon, *U.S. Department of Agriculture Forest Service General Technical Report PNW-8,* Portland, Oreg.; 417p.

Fujimori, T., 1971a, Primary productivity of a young *Tsuga heterophylla* stand and some speculations about biomass of forest communities on the Oregon coast, *U.S. Department of Agriculture Forest Service Research Paper PNW-123,* Portland, Oreg., 11p.

Fujimori, T., 1971b, Analysis of forest canopy on the basis of a *Tsuga heterophylla* forest, *Jap. J. Ecol.* **21**:134–139.

Fujimori, T., 1977, Stem biomass and structure of a mature *Sequoia sempervirens* stand on the Pacific Coast of northern California, *J. Jap. For. Soc.* **59**:435–441.

Fujimori, T., S. Kawanabe, H. Saito, C. C. Grier, and T. Shidei, 1976, Biomass and primary production in forests of three major vegetation zones of the northwestern United States, *J. Jap. For. Soc.* **58**:360–373.

Gessel, S. P., and J. Turner, 1974, Litter production by red alder in western Washington, *For. Sci.* **20**:325–330.

Gessel, S. P., and J. Turner, 1976, Litter production in western Washington Douglas-fir stands, *Forestry* **49**:63–72.

Gholz, H. L., 1980, Structure and productivity of *Juniperus occidentalis* in central Oregon, *Am. Midl. Nat.* **103**:251–261.

Gholz, H. L., F. K. Fitz, and R. H. Waring, 1976, Leaf area differences associated with old-growth forest communities in the western Oregon Cascades, *Can. J. For. Res.* **6**:49–57.

Grier, C. C., 1978, Biomass, productivity and nitrogen-phosphorus cycles in hemlock-spruce stands of the central Oregon coast, in *Western Hemlock Management,* W. A. Atkinson and R. J. Zasoski, eds., Coll. For. Res., Inst. For. Prod. Cont. no. 34, University of Washington, Seattle, pp. 71–81.

Grier, C. C., and R. S. Logan, 1977, Old growth *Pseudotsuga menziesii* communities of a western Oregon watershed: Biomass distribution and production budgets, *Ecol. Monogr.* **47**:373–400.

Grier, C. C., and S. W. Running, 1977, Leaf area of mature northwestern coniferous forests: Relation to site water balance, *Ecology* **58**:893–899.

Grier, C. C., and R. H. Waring, 1974, Conifer foliage mass related to sapwood area, *For. Sci.* **20**:205–206.

Grier, C. C., D. W. Cole, C. T. Dyrness, and R. L. Fredriksen, 1974, Nutrient cycling in 37- and 450-year-old Douglas-fir ecosystems, in *Integrated Research in the Coniferous Forest Biome,* R. H. Waring and R. L. Edmonds, eds., Coniferous Forest Biome Bull. No. 5, University of Washington, Seattle, pp. 21–34.

Habeck, J. R., and R. W. Mutch, 1973, Fire-dependent forests in the northern Rocky Mountains. *Quat. Res.* **3**:408–424.

Heilman, P. E., 1961, Effects of nitrogen fertilization on the growth and nitrogen distribution of low-site Douglas-fir stands, Ph.D. dissertation, University of Washington, Seattle, 214p.

Heilman, P. E., and S. P. Gessel, 1963, Nitrogen requirements and the biological cycling of nitrogen in Douglas-fir stands in relationship to the effects of nitrogen fertilization, *Plant Soil* **18**:386–402.

Hinckley, T.M., J. P. Lassoie, and S. W. Running, 1978, Temporal and spatial variations in the water status of forest trees, *For. Sci. Monogr. 20,* 72p.

Hodges, J. D., and D. R. M. Scott, 1968, Photosynthesis in seedlings of six conifer species under natural environmental conditions, *Ecology* **49:**973–981.

Jensen, E. C., 1976, The crown structure of a single codominant Douglas-fir, M.S. thesis, University of Washington, Seattle, 83p.

Kajihara, M., 1977, Studies on the morphology and dimensions of tree crowns in even-aged stand of Sugi (V). Crown surface area and crown volume, *J. Jap. For. Soc.* **59:**233–240.

Kay, M., 1978, Foliage biomass of Douglas fir in a 53-year-old plantation, *New Zealand J. For. Sci.* **8:**315–326.

Kinerson, R. S., 1971, Selected aspects of gas and energy exchange in a young, mature Douglas-fir stand, Ph.D. dissertation, University of Washington, Seattle, 91p.

Kinerson, R. S., and L. J. Fritschen, 1971, Modeling a coniferous forest canopy, *Agric. Meteorol.* **8:**439–445.

Kira, T., 1975, Primary production of forests, in *Photosynthesis and Productivity in Different Environments*, J. P. Cooper, ed., Cambridge University Press, Cambridge, England, pp. 5–40.

Kira, T., and T. Shidei, 1967, Primary production and turnover of organic matter in different forest ecosystems of the western Pacific, *Jap. J. Ecol.* **17:**30–87.

Klemmedson, J. O., 1976, Effect of thinning and slash burning on nitrogen and carbon in ecosystems of young dense ponderosa pine, *For. Sci.* **22:**45–53.

Larson, P. R., 1963, Stem form development of forest trees, *For. Sci. Monogr.* **5,** 42p.

Leverenz, J. W., 1974, Net photosynthesis as related to shoot hierarchy in a large dominant Douglas-fir tree, M.S. thesis, University of Washington, Seattle, 126p.

Long, J. N., 1976, Forest vegetation dynamics within the *Abies amabilis* zone of a western Cascades watershed, Ph.D. dissertation, University of Washington, Seattle, 175p.

Long, J. N., 1977, Trends in plant species diversity associated with development in a series of *Pseudotsuga menziesii/Gaultheria shallon* stands, *Northwest Sci.* **51:**119–130.

Long, J. N., and J. Turner, 1975, Aboveground biomass of understorey and overstorey in an age sequence of four Douglas-fir stands, *J. Appl. Ecol.* **12:**179–188.

Madgwick, H. A. I., 1970, Biomass and productivity models of forest canopies, in *Analysis of Temperate Forest Ecosystems*, D. E. Reichle, ed., Springer-Verlag, New York, pp. 47–54.

Mar:Møller, C., 1947, The effect of thinning, age, and site on foliage, increment, and loss of dry matter, *J. For.* **45:**393–404.

Marks, P. L., and F. H. Bormann, 1972, Revegetation following forest cutting: Mechanisms for return to steady state nutrient cycling, *Science* **176:**914–915.

Mitchell, K. J., 1975, Dynamics and simulated yield of Douglas-fir, *For. Sci. Monogr. 17,* 39p.

Moir, W. H., 1972, Litter, foliage, branch, and stem production in contrasting lodgepole pine habitats of the Colorado Front Range, in *Proceedings— Research on Coniferous Forest Ecosystems—A Symposium,* J. F. Franklin, L. J. Dempster, and R. H. Waring, eds., U.S. Department of Agriculture Forest Service, Portland, Oreg., pp. 189–198.

Monsi, M., Z. Uchijima, and T. Oikawa, 1973, Structure of foliage canopies and photosynthesis, *Ann. Rev. Ecol. Syst.* **4:**301–327.

Moore, T. R., and E. Verspoor, 1973, Aboveground biomass of black spruce stands in antarctic Quebec, *Can. J. For. Res.* **3:**596–598.

Mountford, M. D., and R. G. H. Bunce, 1973, Regression sampling with allometrically related variables, with particular reference to production studies, *Forestry* **47:**203–212.

Mueller-Dumbois, D., 1965, Initial stages of secondary succession in the coastal Douglas-fir and western hemlock zones, *Ecol. West. North Am.* **1:**38–41.

Newbould, P. J., 1967, *Methods for Estimating the Primary Production of Forests,* IBP Handbook No. 2, Blackwell Scientific, Oxford, England, 62p.

Pike, L. H., R. A. Rydell, and W. C. Denison, 1977, A 400-year-old Douglas-fir tree and its epiphytes: Biomass, surface area, and their distributions, *Can. J. For. Res.* **7:**680–699.

Reichle, D. E., 1975, Advances in ecosystem analysis. *BioScience* **25:**257–264.

Sabhasri, S., 1961, An ecological study of salal, *Gaultheria shallon* Pursh, Ph.D. dissertation, University of Washington, Seattle, 134p.

St. John, T. V., and P. W. Rundel, 1976, The role of fire as a mineralizing agent in a Sierran coniferous forest, *Oecologia* **25:**35–45.

Santantonio, D., R. K. Hermann, and W. S. Overton, 1977, Root biomass studies in forest ecosystems, *Pedobiologia* **17:**1–31.

Shidei, T., and T. Kira, eds., 1977, *Primary Productivity of Japanese Forests,* JIBP Synthesis Volume 16, University of Tokyo Press, Tokyo, 289p.

Shinozaki, K., K. Yoda, K. Hofumi, and R. Kira, 1964, A quantitative analysis of plant form—The pipe model theory, I: Basic analyses. *Jap. J. Ecol.* **14:**97–105.

Shugart, H. H., and J. M. Hett, 1973, Succession: Similarities of species turnover rates, *Science* **180:**1379–1381.

Silver, G. T., 1962, The distribution of Douglas-fir foliage by age. *For. Chron.* **38:**433–438.

Smith, J. H. G., and D. S. DeBell, 1974, Some effects of stand density on biomass of red alder, *Can. J. For. Res.* **4:**335–340.

Sollins, P., D. E. Reichle, and J. S. Olson, 1973, Organic matter budget and model for a southern Appalachian *Liriodendron* forest, ORNL-IBP-73-2., Oak Ridge National Laboratory, Oak Ridge, Tenn, 150p.

Sollins, P., C. C. Grier, F. M. McCorison, K. Cromack, Jr., R. Fogel, and R. L. Fredriksen, 1980, The internal element cycles of an old-growth Douglas-fir ecosystem in Western Oregon. *Ecol. Monogr.* **50**:261–285.

Stephens, G. P., 1969, Productivity of red pine, I: Foliage distribution in tree crowns and stand canopy, *Agric. Meteorol.* **6**:275–282.

Stiehl, W. A., 1969, Crown structure in plantation red pine, *Canadian Department of Fish and Forestry, For. Branch Publ. 1249,* 12p.

Swank, W. T., 1960, A quantitative analysis of vegetation on the Fern Lake watershed, M.S. thesis, University of Washington, Seattle, 90p.

Swank, W. T., 1972, Water balance, interception and transpiration studies on a watershed in the Puget Lowland region of western Washington, Ph.D. dissertation, University of Washington, Seattle, 193p.

Tadaki, Y., 1977, Leaf biomass, in *Primary Productivity of Japanese Forests,* T. Shidei and T. Kira, eds., JIBP Synthesis Volume 16, University of Tokyo Press, Tokyo, pp. 39–44.

Tadaki, Y., and K. Hatiya, 1968, *The Forest Ecosystem and Its Dry Matter Production,* Ringyo Kagaku Gijutsu Shinko-sho, Tokyo, 64p.

Tadaki, Y., K. Hatiya, K. Tochiaki, H. Miyauchi, and U. Matsuda, 1970, Studies on the production structure of forest, 16: Primary productivity of *Abies veitchii* forest in the subalpine zone of Mt. Fuji, *Bull. Gov. For. Exp. Stn., Tokyo* **229**:1–20.

Thornburgh, D. A., 1969, Dynamics of the true fir-hemlock forests of the west slope of the Washington Cascade Range, Ph.D. dissertation, University of Washington, Seattle, 210p.

Turner, J., 1975, Nutrient cycling in a Douglas-fir ecosystem with respect to age and nutrient status, Ph.D. dissertation, University of Washington, Seattle, 191p.

Turner, J., and J. N. Long, 1975, Accumulation of organic matter in a series of Douglas-fir stands, *Can. J. For. Res.* **5**:681–690.

Turner, J., and P. R. Olson, 1976, Nitrogen relations in a Douglas-fir plantation, *Ann. Bot.* **40**:1185–1193.

Turner, J., and M. J. Singer, 1976, Nutrient distribution and cycling in a sub-alpine coniferous forest ecosystem, *J. Appl. Ecol.* **13**:295–301.

Turner, J., D. W. Cole, and S. P. Gessel, 1976, Mineral nutrient accumulation and cycling in a stand of red alder *(Alnus rubra). J. Ecol.* **64**:965–974.

Van Cleve, K., and L. A. Viereck, 1972, Distribution of selected chemical elements in even-aged alder *(Alnus)* ecosystems near Fairbanks, Alaska, *Arct. Alp. Res.* **4**:239–255.

Van Cleve, K., L. A. Viereck, and R. L. Schlentner, 1971, Accumulation of nitrogen in alder *(Alnus)* ecosystems near Fairbanks, Alaska, *Arct. Alp. Res.* **3**:101–114.

Vitousek, P. M., 1977, The regulation of element concentrations in mountain streams in the northeastern United States, *Ecol. Monogr.* **47**:65–87.

Vitousek, P. M., and W. A. Reiners, 1975, Ecosystem succession and nutrient retention: A hypothesis, *BioScience* **25**:376–381.

Walker, R. B., D. R. M. Scott, D. J. Salo, and K. L. Reed, 1972, Terrestrial process studies in conifers: A review, in *Proceedings—Research on Coniferous Forest Ecosystems—A Symposium,* J. F. Franklin, L. J. Dempster, and R. H. Waring, eds., U.S. Department of Agriculture Forest Service, Portland, Oreg., pp. 221–225.

Walter, H., 1973, *Vegetation of the Earth,* English University Press, Ltd., London/Springer-Verlag, New York, 237p.

Waring, R. H., H. L. Gholz, C. C. Grier, and M. L. Plummer, 1977, Evaluating stem conducting tissue as an estimator of leaf area in four woody angiosperms, *Can. J. Bot.* **55:**1474–1477.

Waring, R. H., W. H. Emmingham, H. L. Gholz, and C. C. Grier, 1978, Variation in maximum leaf area of coniferous forests in Oregon and its ecological significance, *For. Sci.* **24:**131–140.

Weetman, G. F., and R. Harland, 1964, Foliage and wood production in unthinned black spruce in northern Quebec, *For. Sci.* **10:**80–88.

Westman, W. E., and R. H. Whittaker, 1975, The pigmy forest region of northern California: Studies on biomass and productivity, *J. Ecol.* **63:**493–520.

White, J., and J. L. Harper, 1970, Correlated changes in plant size and number in plant populations, *J. Ecol.* **58:**467–485.

Woodman, J. N., 1968, The relationship of net photosynthesis to environment within the crown of a large Douglas-fir tree, Ph.D. dissertation, University of Washington, Seattle, 188p.

Woodwell, G. M., and D. B. Botkin, 1970, Metabolism of terrestrial ecosystems by gas exchange techniques: The Brookhaven approach, in *Analysis of Temperate Forest Ecosystems,* D. E. Reichle, ed., Springer-Verlag, New York, pp. 73–85.

Yoda, K., T. Kira, H. Ogawa, and K. Hozumi, 1963, Self-thinning in overcrowded pure stands under cultivated and natural conditions. Intraspecific competition among higher plants XI, *J. Biol. Osaka City Univ.* **14:**107–129.

Yoda, K., K. Shinozaki, H. Ogawa, K. Hozumi, and T. Kira, 1965, Estimation of the total amount of respiration in woody organs of trees and forest communities, *J. Biol. Osaka City Univ.* **16:**15–26.

Zavitkovski, J., and M. Newton, 1971, Litterfall and litter accumulation in red alder stands in western Oregon, *Plant Soil* **35:**267–268.

Zavitkovski, J., and R. D. Stevens, 1972, Primary productivity of red alder ecosystems, *Ecology* **53:**235–242.

6

Physiological Activity in Douglas-Fir

J. P. Lassoie

INTRODUCTION

Primary producers form the cornerstone on which all life is ultimately dependent, since they provide the means by which energy is supplied to drive the biosphere. Therefore, an understanding of those processes related to carbon fixation in green plants is paramount to the overall understanding of the mass and energy transfer within a terrestrial ecosystem.

Trees as stationary terrestrial organisms have adapted in order to tolerate or avoid the rigors imposed by the highly variable atmospheric and edaphic components of the ecosystem. As living interfaces between these two components, trees are controlled by those abiotic factors that regulate their physiological processes and eventually determine the distribution and abundance of species throughout the terrestrial biosphere. Trees, as do all autotrophic plants, utilize water, nutrients, carbon dioxide, and sunlight as the building blocks on which growth, maintenance, defense, reproduction, and, ultimately, survival depend. The biotic and abiotic factors that govern the processing and utilization of these building blocks have always received considerable attention from tree physiologists (for example; Walker et al. 1972; Larcher 1975; Bannister 1977; Kramer and Kozlowski, 1979).

This chapter elucidates the abiotic and biotic control of those tree physiological processes felt to be of major importance to the functioning of the western coniferous forest biome. Specifically, emphasis is on temporal and spatial variations in, and interrelations between, net photosynthesis, tree water relations, meristematic activities, and biomass accumulations. Furthermore, owing to their ecologic and economic dominance throughout the biome, large, field-grown Douglas-fir (*Pseudotsuga menziesii* [Mirb.] Franco) are considered primarily in the following discussion.

Presented here is an integrated view of whole-tree physiological processes in Douglas-fir. The approach is based on a wide variety of interrelated physiological data and is viewed in reference to the functioning of the entire coniferous forest biome. Though there has been continuing interest in tree physiology since the work of Hales (1727), such an approach in the past has been confined primarily to European studies (for example, Ellenberg 1971). Also presented is physiological support for other chapters in this volume (for example, Chapters 3 and 5) and physiological reasoning behind the distribution and abundance of Douglas-fir throughout the coniferous forest biome is illustrated. In addition, voids are identified in the understanding of Douglas-fir physiology and future research needs and directions are suggested.

Numerous techniques were used by investigators at different study sites throughout the U.S. coniferous forest biome in order to produce the data on which this chapter is based. The techniques and approaches are summarized in Table 6.1 and no attempt will be made to discuss the methodologies. Readers needing specific information should consult the references cited in the table.

PHYSIOLOGICAL ACTIVITY AND ITS CONTROL

Physiological activity in forest trees is controlled by certain intrinsic and extrinsic factors. Various physiological steps are involved in the accumulation of tree biomass; specifically, net photosynthesis, the internal flow of carbon and its incorporation into biomass constituents, and the cell growth process. These phenomena are complex and precise quantification currently is not possible. The following presentation should yield at least a qualitative understanding of the physiological connection between carbon dioxide uptake at the needle and biomass accumulation throughout the aboveground portions of conifers, particularly Douglas-fir.

Net Photosynthesis Rates

Higher plants differ in their primary mode of fixing carbon dioxide. All forest trees seem to be C_3 plants, which fix carbon according to the classic Calvin cycle. Maximum net photosynthesis rates for C_3 plants generally range between 15 and 40 mg$\cdot$dm$^{-2}\cdot$h^{-1} and most studies suggest that rates in conifers are generally lower than those in deciduous trees (Jarvis and Jarvis 1964; Larcher 1969, 1975; Black 1973). However, some evidence suggests that photosynthetic capacities in conifers and deciduous trees may be similar but that the needle arrangements on conifer branches promote mutual shading, which lowers total photosynthesis (Krueger and Ferrell 1965; Krueger and Ruth 1969; Ludlow and Jarvis 1971; Norman and Jarvis 1974, 1975).

Limiting Factors

As an outgrowth of Liebig's law of the minimum, the concept of limiting factors states that a biological process (for example, photosynthesis or growth)

TABLE 6.1 *Summary of important techniques used in various investigations of physiological activity in Douglas-fir within the coniferous forest biome.*

Factor	Technique and reference(s)	Investigators[a]	Units	Study locations[b]
Net photosynthesis rate	Infrared gas analysis (Šesták et al. 1971, Zelawski and Walker 1976)	I, N	$mg\ CO_2 \cdot dm^{-2} \cdot h^{-1}$	WA
	Steady-state mathematical model	K	$mg\ CO_2 \cdot dm^{-2} \cdot s^{-1}$	WA
	Curve-fitting model	B	$mg\ CO_2 \cdot dm^{-2} \cdot d^{-1}$	OR
Transpiration rate	Gravimetrically: lysimeter (Fritschen et al. 1973)	C, D, H	$mm\ H_2O$	WA
	Humidity sensors: gas exchange (Salo 1974)	I, N	$g\ H_2O \cdot dm^{-2} \cdot h^{-1}$	WA
	Heat-pulse velocity (Swanson 1967)	F, H	cm/h	WA
	Tritiated water (Kline et al. 1970)	E	liters/h, liters/d	WA, OR
	Low-resolution simulation model	J	$g\ H_2O/cm^2$	OR
Photosynthate translocation	$^{14}CO_2$ labelling (Webb 1977)	O	%C-14 assimilated/d	OR
	$^{14}CO_2$ labelling (Ross 1972)	L	%C-14 assimilated	WA

128

Cambial growth	Automated band dendrometers (Dobbs 1969)	F	mm^2	WA
	Direct measurement (also shoot growth)	A	mm, cm	OR
Stomatal activity	Diffusion porometer (Turner et al. 1969, Kanemasu 1975)	G, M	s/cm	WA, OR
	Infiltration pressures (Fry and Walker 1967)	F, G, H	MPa	WA
	Calculation based on transpiration (Holmgren et al. 1965)	I, N	s/cm	WA
	Regression models	J, M	s/cm	OR
Xylem pressure	Pressure chamber (Ritchie and Hinckley 1975)	B, F, H, I, J, M, N	–MPa	WA, OR

Note: See primary references for information on environmental measurement techniques.

[a] Primary reference: A = Emmingham 1977; B = Emmingham and Waring 1977; C = Fritschen and Doraiswamy 1973; D = Fritschen et al. 1977; E = Kline et al. 1976; F = Lassoie 1973, 1975, 1979; G = Lassoie et al. 1977b; H = Lassoie et al. 1977c; I = Leverenz 1974; J = Reed and Waring 1974; K = Reed et al. 1976; L = Ross 1972; M = Running 1976; N = Salo 1974; L = Webb 1975a b.

[b] Study location: WA = Washington, primarily the A. E. Thompson Research Center; OR = Oregon, primarily the H. J. Andrews Experimental Forest.

is controlled by that factor present in the least amount relative to its minimum requirement (Blackman 1905). The concept has had a tremendous impact on the course of biological studies (Kramer and Kozlowski 1979; Spurr and Barnes 1980). Though this is a relatively simplistic way to examine complex physiological processes, investigations of net photosynthesis lend themselves quite readily to such analysis.

Typically, when net photosynthesis rates (or many other physiological processes) are monitored under field conditions and plotted against a single controlling independent variable, a scatter diagram results (see Figure 6.1). The exact configuration of the diagram depends on the variable involved, but obviously net photosynthesis is not neatly related to any single plant or environmental variable.

Faced with this variability, how can one separate the various factors that control net photosynthesis? Three primary methods exist. Webb (1972) and Jarvis (1976) have suggested the use of boundary-line analysis in interpreting single variable relations. Thus, if an adequate number of measurements are taken in order to fill a variable data space, the upper limit of the scatter diagram will delineate the response of net photosynthesis to a particular independent variable when other factors are not limiting (Figure 6.1). Values below this line, therefore, represent control by other limiting factors. Most commonly such analysis is used with measurement of net photosynthesis under fluctuating ambient environmental conditions (for example, Lassoie and Chambers 1976; Leverenz 1981a).

Under controlled environmental conditions, another type of limiting factor analysis is possible. With some gas exchange systems it is possible to alter one environmental variable artificially while the others are kept at optimal levels

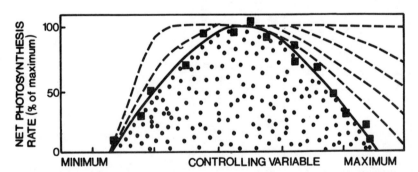

FIGURE 6.1 *Idealized relation between net photosynthesis rate and a controlling plant (for example, leaf conductance of carbon dioxide) or environmental (for example, temperature) factor; actual shape of the curve (dashed lines) depends on the variable involved. The curve represents either a boundary line when data (●) were collected under field conditions or a least-squares fit line when data (■) were collected under controlled environmental conditions.*

(for example, Salo 1974; Dougherty and Hinckley, 1981). A least-squares fit is then used in order to generate the response curve (Figure 6.1).

A third approach to separating the various factors that affect net photosynthesis is available in studies producing large data sets. It is then possible to examine the data in specific temperature, light, vapor pressure deficit, and plant water potential classes, thereby better identifying the control actions of different variables on net photosynthesis (Hallgren 1978; Leverenz 1981b).

Larcher (1969) has listed and discussed numerous variables that can affect net photosynthesis; they include radiation, temperature, ventilation, carbon dioxide concentration, water supply, relative humidity, soil, genetic characteristics, stage of phenological development, types of special adaptations, and chorophyll. However, Reed et al. (1976), used only light, temperature, carbon dioxide concentration, and stomatal resistance in successfully modeling net photosynthesis in yellow poplar *(Liriodendron tulipifera)*. In this model, stomatal resistance integrated the effect of tree water balance on gas exchange at the leaf-air interface. The following discussion concentrates on the controlling functions of these four factors. Other limiting factors are discussed only in relation to their effect on stomatal activity.

Temperature. Temperature response curves for net photosynthesis in conifers generally have seasonal optima between 10° and 20°C (Larcher 1969; Pisek et al. 1973; Bauer et al. 1975). Temperature optima are usually very broad, often spanning 10° to 15°C. For example, with Douglas-fir under controlled environmental conditions, the temperature response curve at near optimal light levels (in excess of 500 μmol $\cdot$m^{-2}$\cdot$s^{-1}; 1 μmol $= 2.37 \times 10^{-1}$ joules) is quite flat between 2° and 25°C; the optimum is 10°C (Figure 6.2). Controlled light and temperature studies under field conditions during the summer support this 10°C optimum (Salo 1974). Field studies by Leverenz (1981a, b), however, suggest that the optimum temperature range is 20°C or below. J. A. Helms (pers. comm.) has found that optimum net photosynthesis in Douglas-fir growing at 1000 m in the Sierra Nevada Mountains of California occurred over a broad temperature range of 15° to 30°C.

The optimum temperature range for maximum net photosynthesis in Douglas-fir of between 10° and 25°C is well supported by the work of others (Pharis et al. 1970; Sorensen and Ferrell 1973). The variability often expressed reflects genetic variability as well as differences due to environmental factors in addition to temperature. For example, temperature optima are light dependent (Figure 6.2; Brix 1967; Webb 1971) and perhaps vapor pressure deficit dependent (Ng 1978).

The high temperature limit for positive net photosynthesis is determined by effects on respiration and the dark reactions of photosynthesis (Bauer et al. 1975). This temperature maximum ranges between 36° and 45°C in Douglas-fir (Helms 1965; Krueger and Ferrell 1965; Salo 1974; Leverenz 1981b).

The rate of photosynthesis is directly reduced by cold temperatures, which lower the activity of enzymes involved in the dark reaction. It is indirectly retarded by mechanical injuries resulting from ice formation and by abnormally low leaf water potentials that follow the freezing of the sapwood (Salo 1974). Minimum temperatures for assimilation activity are generally between $-3°$ and $-5°C$ (Pisek et al. 1973). It is interesting to note that with Douglas-fir, net photosynthesis at $0°C$ is still 70 percent of that occurring at $10°C$ (Figure 6.2).

Light. Solar radiation is probably the single most important environmental factor regulating net photosynthesis. Light is necessary for photosynthetic phosphorylation, stomatal activity, and photorespiration. In Douglas-fir, net photosynthesis rates typically increase rapidly with increasing light levels; high rates occur at about 600 μmol $\cdot m^{-2} \cdot s^{-1}$ (about 3500 ft-c; 1 ft-c = 10.764 lx) with little increase thereafter, under both controlled environmental conditions (Figure 6.2) and in the field (Figure 6.3). This value for the light saturation of the photosynthetic machinery is within the range reported for other conifers (Larcher 1969; Walker et al. 1972). However, because of the mutual shading of needles on and between individual twigs composing a sample (Leverenz and Jarvis 1979), net photosynthetic rates often tend to increase slowly as more

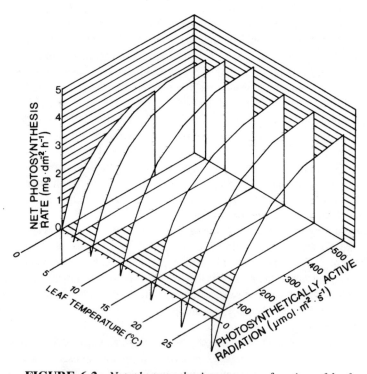

FIGURE 6.2 *Net photosynthesis rate as a function of leaf temperature and photosynthetically active radiation during autumn studies conducted under controlled environmental conditions with ten-year-old, garden-grown Douglas-fir (after Salo 1974).*

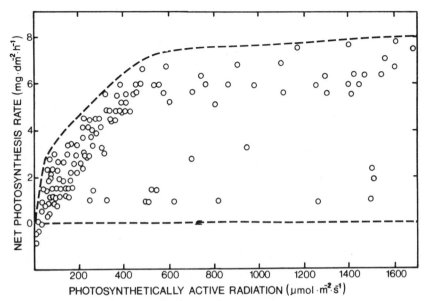

FIGURE 6.3 *Net photosynthesis rate as a function of photosynthetically active radiation for current-year foliage near midcrown in a forty-year-old, twenty-seven-meter, dominant Douglas-fir under a variety of environmental conditions during late summer (after Leverenz 1974).*

needle surfaces become illuminated at light levels above 600 μmol $\cdot m^{-2} \cdot s^{-1}$ (Figure 6.3). Furthermore, because of the three-dimensional nature of tree crowns and the mutual shading between branches, the concept of light saturation cannot be clearly extended to the entire crown.

As mentioned earlier, net photosynthesis rates at light saturation are also temperature-dependent, with rates decreasing on either side of a 10°C optimum (Figure 6.2). Regardless of temperature, maximum rates at saturating light intensities were higher with forest-grown trees (Figure 6.3) than with garden-grown trees (Figure 6.2). The garden-grown trees, however, had a relatively high ratio of leaf surface area to dry weight, which is typical of shade-adapted needles (Drew and Ferrell 1977). When net photosynthesis rates were expressed on a dry weight basis, they were similar to those of field material reported in the same units (for example, about 5 mg $CO_2 \cdot g$ dry wt$^{-1} \cdot h^{-1}$; Salo 1974).

Water and stomatal activity. The influence of water deficits (that is, water stresses) on net photosynthesis rates is exerted primarily through a decrease in stomatal conductance of carbon dioxide (Hsiao 1973). Stomatal activity is complex, however, and is influenced by a variety of factors including light, leaf water potential, soil water potential, vapor pressure difference between leaf and air, leaf temperature, various plant hormones, and internal carbon dioxide concentration (Jarvis 1976; Tan et al. 1977). The following discussion considers the control of stomatal conductances in Douglas-fir by such factors. More inclusive reviews may be found in the works of Jarvis (1976) and Hinckley et al. (1978).

Douglas-fir stomata typically open rapidly with increasing light levels, and maximum leaf conductance is usually reached at about 200 μmol $\cdot m^{-2} \cdot s^{-1}$ or less (Figure 6.4a; Tan et al. 1977; Leverenz 1981a). This light level is about 10 percent of full sunlight, a level causing similar stomatal responses in numerous hardwoods (Davies and Kozlowski 1974; Federer and Gee 1976) and in other conifers (Running 1976). Running noted that leaf conductance maxima differed between eight conifer species but that most were in the range between about 0.2 and 0.4 cm/s, a range similar to that for numerous hardwood trees (Federer 1977; Körner et al. 1979). Douglas-fir had a total range from 0.003 to 0.333 cm/s (Running 1976). Salo (1974) has reported maximum leaf conductances in dominant Douglas-fir to be between 0.20 and 0.33 cm/s, which are similar to maxima reported for seedlings (Drew and Ferrell 1979). Maxima reported by Salo (1974) and Running (1976) were generally higher than those illustrated in Figure 6.4a since the latter accounted for the diffusion coefficient for carbon dioxide (Jarvis 1971).

Stomata are generally closed in the dark. During late fall, winter, and early spring, however, when evaporative demand is low and tree water deficits are minimal, Fry (1965), Hinckley (1971); Running (1976) and Blake and Ferrell (1977) all have observed Douglas-fir stomata staying open all night. Similar results were noted by Hinckley and Ritchie (1973) in Pacific silver fir *(Abies amabilis)* and are also suggested in Figure 6.4a.

The effect of temperature on leaf conductance is difficult to separate from other variables affecting stomatal activity. Specifically, care must be taken in interpreting the effects of temperature on stomata, since increases in leaf temperature lead to larger vapor pressure differences unless compensating changes are made in the ambient humidity (Neilson and Jarvis 1976). In Douglas-fir, leaf conductance for carbon dioxide seems to be maximum at about 20°C, dropping rapidly at higher temperatures (Figure 6.4b). J. A. Helms (pers. comm.) found that optimal leaf conductances for water vapor occurred at 10°C, slowly decreased between 10° and 25°C, and then rapidly decreased as leaf temperatures approached 40°C. The decrease at higher temperature is no doubt also influenced by concurrent changes in vapor pressure gradient between the leaf and the air, which affects mesophyll (Stålfelt 1962) and peristomatal transpiration rates (Lange et al. 1971), which in turn influence guard cell turgor.

In Sitka spruce *(Picea sitchensis)* leaf conductances to water vapor have been observed to drop on either side of 15°C (Neilson and Jarvis 1976). Therefore, though no data are presented in Figure 6.4b below 15°C, lower conductances might be expected as temperatures approach 0°C. Freezing air temperatures do seem to promote stomatal closure in Douglas-fir (Reed 1968; Drew et al. 1972; Salo 1974). Drew and Ferrell (1979) noted a decline in leaf conductances in the winter with Douglas-fir seedlings that was independent of

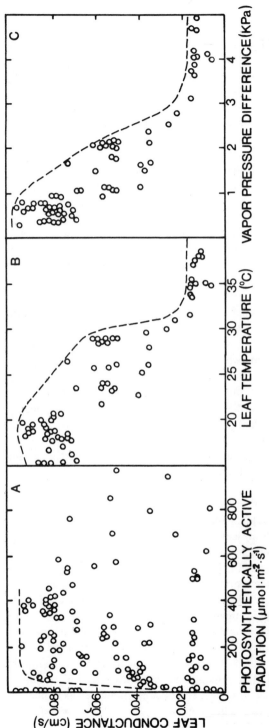

FIGURE 6.4 *Calculated leaf conductance of carbon dioxide as a function of (A) photosynthetically active radiation, (B) leaf temperature, and (C) vapor pressure difference between the leaf and the air at light levels greater than 200 $\mu mol \bullet m^{-2} \bullet s^{-1}$. Measurements were taken on current-year foliage near midcrown in a forty-year-old, twenty-seven-meter, dominant Douglas-fir under a variety of environmental conditions (after Leverenz 1974).*

leaf water potential but simultaneous with the onset of subfreezing air temperatures. In addition, lower than expected conductances following freezing or
chilling have been observed in other conifer species (Kaufmann 1976; Running
1976; Lassoie et al. 1977a; Fahey 1979). Care must be taken when evaluating
the effect of freezing on stomatal activity, however, as the temperature effect
may actually be mediated through its effect on internal water deficits (Salo
1974, Lassoie et al. 1977a).

The impact of humidity on stomatal activity is equally difficult to separate
from those effects associated with temperature. In Douglas-fir, rapid decreases
in leaf conductances occur as leaf-to-air vapor pressure gradients increase to
about 3.5 kPa (Figure 6.4c). Many other studies with both hardwoods and
conifers have noted a leaf conductance to atmospheric humidity relationship
similar to that reported for Douglas-fir (Schulze 1970; Davies and Kozlowski
1974; Hinckley et al. 1975; Kaufmann 1976; Lassoie and Chambers 1976;
Running 1976). Neilson and Jarvis (1976) and Watts et al. (1976) have also
observed a strong correlation between stomatal conductance and vapor pressure
deficit for Sitka spruce. Leverenz (1981b) has reported a synergistic interaction
between the response of stomatal conductance to humidity and temperature.
This probably results in the apparent lack of response of conductances illustrated in Figure 6.4c at vapor pressure differences above 3.5 kPa (Leverenz
1981a). A similar interaction between humidity and temperature has been
shown for Scotch pine *(Pinus sylvestris)* and discussed by Hall et al. (1976).

The exact mechanism by which atmospheric humidity controls stomata is
not yet clear. Some investigators have hypothesized that stomata react primarily
to turgor changes in the bulk leaf (for example, Meidner and Mansfield 1968),
while others feel that the actual transpirational loss of water directly from and
around the guard cells (peristomatal transpiration) reduces their turgor causing
closure (Lange et al. 1971; Hall and Kaufmann 1975; Tyree and Yianoulus
1980; Leverenz 1981b).

Obviously, only turgor pressure differences in guard cells and associated
epidermal cells directly affect stomatal apertures. Most commonly, these turgor pressures are inferred from leaf water potentials measured using thermocouple psychrometers (Brown and Van Haveren 1972) or estimated using the
pressure chamber (Ritchie and Hinckley 1975). Running (1976) and Tan et al.
(1977) have found that an abrupt midday stomatal closure in Douglas-fir saplings was triggered by branch xylem pressure potentials reaching a threshold of
about –2.0 MPa. Waring and Running (1978) reported a threshold of –2.2 MPa
in a 40-m Douglas-fir while closure was initiated near –1.7 MPa in seedlings.
Work by Drew and Ferrell (1979) confirmed this –1.7 MPa threshold for
Douglas-fir seedlings during the fall. However, during the summer the threshold increased to about –1.0 MPa, possibly indicating seasonal osmotic adjust-
ment in order to maintain needle conductances at maximum levels (Cline and
Campbell 1976). In addition, seedlings grown at low light levels had lower
thresholds for stomatal closure, thus making them less drought resistant than
seedlings grown under full sunlight.

Different coniferous species have different thresholds generally ranging between about –1.2 and –2.5 MPa (Lopushinsky 1969; Puritch 1973; Running 1976). However, as suggested above, these thresholds may vary depending on the specific environmental conditions and on the season.

It should be emphasized that if the threshold water potential is not reached by the tree, leaf conductance is then controlled by base (predawn) leaf water potential (Figure 6.5) and/or humidity (Figure 6.4c). When base xylem pressure potentials are very low, stomata are relatively closed all day as hydraulic considerations almost completely override the photoactive response illustrated in Figure 6.4a (Salo 1974; Zobel 1974; Lassoie and Salo 1981; Figure 6.5).

Stomata of some species are reported to be very responsive to the concentration of carbon dioxide near the inner walls of the guard cells (Allaway and Milthorpe 1976). However, several investigators have concluded that the influence of changes in internal carbon dioxide levels on stomatal functioning is often overridden by other limiting factors (for example, Hall and Kaufmann 1975; Schulze et al. 1975). Thus no strong relations have been observed between calculated internal carbon dioxide concentrations and stomatal activity in Douglas-fir (Fry 1965; Leverenz 1974, 1981a) or Sitka spruce (Neilson and Jarvis 1976; Beadle et al. 1979). Such results illustrate the current lack of knowledge concerning the exact control of guard cell movement by both inter-

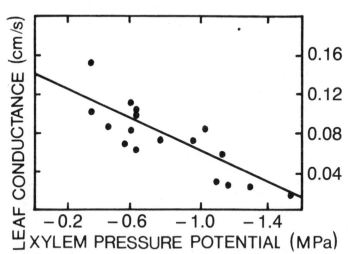

FIGURE 6.5 *Regression of maximum morning leaf conductance of water vapor as a function of base (predawn) xylem pressure potential (coefficient of determination [r^2] = 0.71). Each data point represents the average of at least nine conductance measurements taken before 0900 h in the canopy of various one- to three-m Douglas-fir growing in the field (after Running 1976).*

nal (for example, hormones) and external (for example, carbon dioxide) factors (Burrows and Milthorpe 1976).

Considerable interest has recently been directed toward the possible role of abscisic acid in inhibiting stomatal opening, inducing stomatal closure, and reducing gas exchange rates. Unfortunately, little of this work has examined the dynamics of endogenous abscisic acid levels in tree species (see reviews by Livne and Vaadia 1972; Hsiao 1973; Meidner and Willmer 1975; Wright 1978). In a study with drought-stressed Douglas-fir seedlings, Blake and Ferrell (1977) noted that as the soil dried and xylem pressure potentials decreased (that is, plant water deficits increased), abscisic acid concentrations increased; when a threshold in the abscisic acid level was reached (at about 1700 ng/g dry wt), stomata began to close both in the light and the dark (Figure 6.6). Similar results have been observed in balsam fir *(Abies balsamea)* and white spruce *(Picea glauca)* (Little and Eidt 1968; Little 1975),and suggested by work with transplanted Sitka spruce (Coutts 1980). Therefore there seems to be a possible connection between the diurnal development of internal tree water deficits and the promotion of stomatal closure by enhanced abscisic acid levels; however, this interesting phenomenon has yet to be fully clarified.

Of course, as has been suggested, environmental and biological factors controlling stomatal activity never act independently from one another under

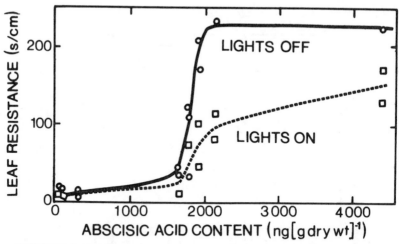

FIGURE 6.6 *The association between leaf resistance (the reciprocal of conductance) and abscisic acid content in progressively stressed two-year-old Douglas-fir seedlings (unwatered for about thirty days with base xylem pressure potentials exceeding –3.0 MPa). The rapid rise in leaf resistance was associated with an abscisic acid content of about 1700 ng/gram dry wt and base xylem pressure potentials between –1.0 and –1.2 MPa. Relation is shown under both light and dark conditions (after Blake and Ferrell 1977).*

field conditions. Though independent relations can be defined using boundary line analyses (for example, Figure 6.4), they do not illustrate how various controlling factors interact to simultaneously influence the stomatal mechanism. For example, it was shown earlier that the maximum conductance attainable during a day by Douglas-fir needles was linearly related to the base xylem pressure potential (Figure 6.5). When similar data are separated based on the absolute humidity deficit, however, a more complex relation results (Figure 6.7; Tan et al. 1977). Thus Douglas-fir stomata will remain relatively closed on days when atmospheric evaporative demand is high even though base xylem pressure potentials are high. The contrast seems true on more humid days, even those marked by low soil moisture levels. Such "fine tuning" to evaporative demand by Douglas-fir stomata may possibly be an adaptation strategy to prevent excessive water loss on days when soil moisture levels might otherwise promote stomatal opening.

The preceding discussion illustrates the need for further studies to identify the controlling influence of multiple factors on leaf conductance. To date it may be best to assume that synergistic interactions do not occur and that limiting factors are simply multiplicative; that is, less than additive (for example, two factors that independently reduce leaf conductance to 80 percent of maximum may, in combination, cause a reduction to 64 percent of maximum; Jarvis 1976). However, there are a few reports of synergistic interactions occurring (for example Ng and Jarvis 1980; Leverenz 1981b) and the preceding remarks may soon need to be revised.

Ambient carbon dioxide concentration. Carbon dioxide at normal ambient concentrations (about 320 μl/liter) is below the level required for maximum net photosynthesis rates in forest trees (Fry 1965; Ludlow and Jarvis 1971; Green and Wright 1977; Dougherty and Hinckley 1979). The slight carbon dioxide gradient between the ambient air and the chloroplasts and the resistances to transport in the leaf-air boundary layer and through the stomata and mesophyll seem to be the regulating forces involved (Larcher 1969; Reed et al. 1976; Leverenz 1981a). With Douglas-fir seedlings maintained at 2400 ft-c (1 ft-c = 10.764 lx; about one-fourth full sunlight), Salo (1969) observed a 100 percent increase in net photosynthesis as the carbon dioxide concentration was increased from 200 to 500 μl/liter. Furthermore, this relation seems to be quite light-dependent, with carbon dioxide concentrations above the ambient level exerting their greatest control at relatively high light intensities (Figure 6.8). Carbon dioxide concentrations may also affect stomatal activity, making the actual relation between net photosynthesis and high carbon dioxide concentrations difficult to assess accurately (Jarvis 1976).

Carbon dioxide concentrations below about 250 μl/liter greatly limit net photosynthesis in Douglas-fir (Figure 6.8). Under normal field conditions, however, where adequate air mixing occurs, ambient carbon dioxide concentrations normally remain between 360 and 380 μl/liter (Woodman 1968; Leverenz 1974; Doraiswamy 1977). Thus, when proper gas exchange tech-

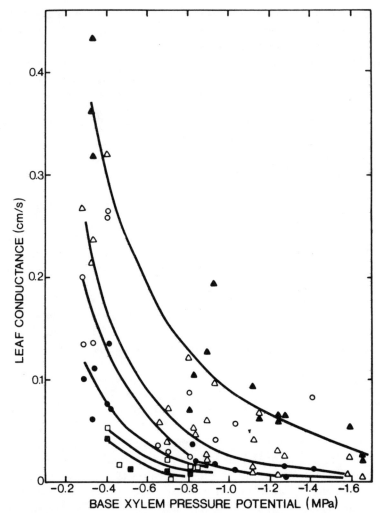

FIGURE 6.7 *Relation between leaf conductance and base (pre-dawn) xylem pressure potential in various Douglas-fir seedlings. The data were separated into six ranges of absolute humidity deficit and were collected on twenty days. Each data point represents the mean of seven to fifteen measurements (after Hallgren 1978). Key: Absolute humidity in grams per cubic meter:* ▲ = 3 to 6, △ = 6 to 9, ○ = 9 to 12, ● = 12 to 15, □ = 15 to 18, ■ = 18 to 21.

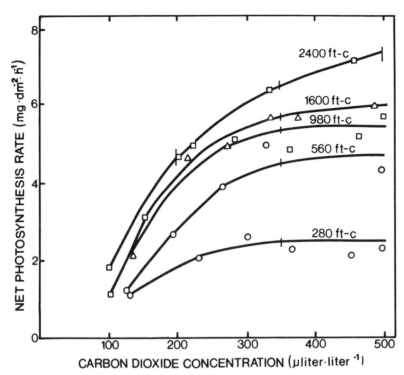

FIGURE 6.8 *The influence of carbon dioxide concentration on net photosynthesis rate in Douglas-fir seedlings at different light intensities (2400 ft-c is about one-fourth full sunlight) under controlled environment conditions (after Fry 1965).*

niques are used in the tree canopy studies, the carbon dioxide concentrations in the ambient air normally need not be considered a limiting factor (Larcher 1969).

Internal Carbon Flow and Incorporation

Understandably, there must be a close relation between carbon fixation and biomass production in forest trees (see Chapters 3 and 5); however, in order to relate net photosynthesis to growth, the distribution of photosynthates to the respective carbon sinks in the tree must be known (Ledig 1969). The relation between carbon uptake and growth involves the translocation of carbohydrates that are intermediates in a number of metabolic pathways. Their concentration in any tissue reflects the balance between the rates of photosynthate influx and efflux, or conversion of storage constituents (lipids) to soluble products. The use of radioactive carbon-14 to label photosynthetic products has greatly advanced the understanding of the pattern and control of photosynthate distribution in Douglas-fir seedlings (Webb 1975a,b) and saplings (Ross 1972). Since the work of Ross (1972) involved an examination of temporal and spatial source-sink relations for photosynthates, such information will be presented later in this chapter.

Webb (1975a,b) examined the accumulation rates of photoassimilated carbon relative to total tissue carbon in various tissues of two-year-old Douglas-fir seedlings just after bud set (Figure 6.9). Results support the source-sink concept; that is, actively growing sites accumulate carbon at the highest rates. Differences in source strengths existed between old and new needles and followed phenological development of these tissues (Gordon and Larson 1968; Ross 1972; Chung and Barnes 1980a,b). The accumulation rates illustrated in Figure 6.9 represent growth and carbon storage in the respective tissue respiration (Webb 1975b). Differences can be attributed to the separate carbon requirements of different tissues for maintenance and tissue construction (Chung and Barnes 1977; 1980a,b) and to differences in accumulation rates due to the lags inherent in the translocation process. Needles all had positive y-intercepts while other tissues had negative values, indicating that a lag was occurring before carbon was translocated into the stem; the lag was intensified for the roots (Figure 6.9). Roots received photoassimilated carbon later than the stem but accumulated carbon faster, which represented a flux of carbon through tissue with a low carbon requirement (the stem) into tissue with a higher requirement (the roots).

In order to estimate the steady rate accumulation of photoassimilated carbon in the various tissues, Webb (1975a) developed a compartment model of carbon flow in Douglas-fir seedlings. The model illustrated the transient condition of carbon flow during the first six days of the experimental period (Figure 6.10). After this point, photoassimilated carbon was increasing at essentially constant rates in all tissues (Figure 6.9, Table 6.2). The constant increase represented the real accumulation of carbon resulting from the uptake and distribution pattern instead of the apparent rates, which were obtained directly from the tracer results (Figure 6.9). Roots received the most carbon per day followed by new needles, old needles, new shoots, and then stems (Table 6.2). These rates were the average accumulation rates for each tissue and reflected the total average carbon in each tissue as well as the demand of each for photoassimilated carbon on a per-unit-of-tissue basis. When accumulation rates were adjusted based on the total amount of carbon present in the various tissues, new and old needles accumulated carbon at the highest rates (that is, milligrams photoassimilated carbon per day per milligram of total tissue carbon), followed by roots, new shoots, and then stems. Generally, the lower rates for roots, stems, and new shoots, compared with needles, reflected the much higher metabolic activity (unit weight basis) in the needles. Thus needles were

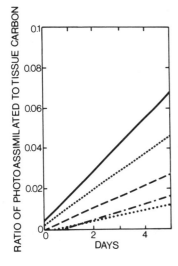

FIGURE 6.9 *The accumulation of photoas-similated carbon relative to tissue carbon in Douglas-fir seedlings (after Webb 1975a).*
Key: *Solid line = new needles; square dotted line = old needles; dashed line = new shoots; dot-and-dashed line = roots; round dotted line = stem.*

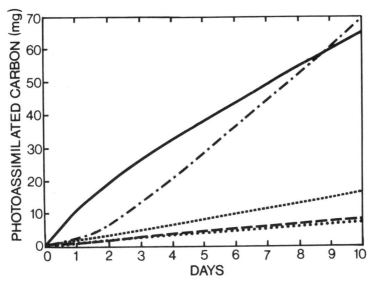

FIGURE 6.10 *Model calculations of accumulated photoassimi-lated carbon in Douglas-fir seedlings (after Webb 1975a).*
Key: *Solid line = new needles; square dotted line = old needles; dashed line = new shoots; dot-and-dashed line = roots; round dotted line = stem.*

TABLE 6.2 *Steady rate increase of photoassimilated carbon in Douglas-fir seedlings.*[a]

Tissue type	Average total carbon (mg)	Increase of photoassimilated carbon (mg/d)	Increase of photoassimilated/ total carbon
New needles	573	5.39	0.0094
Old needles	157	1.79	0.0114
New shoots	192	0.73	0.0038
Stem	445	0.71	0.0016
Roots	1592	7.98	0.0050

[a]From Webb 1975a.

clearly a major sink for photoassimilated carbon as well as the major source. Ross (1972) has presented a similar conclusion for ten-year-old Douglas-fir saplings under field conditions.

Though the source-sink concept seems to explain adequately the internal flow of carbon in forest trees, the relation between carbon dioxide uptake, assimilation, and biomass yield still remains vague for Douglas-fir. In order to address this relation adequately, Chung and Barnes (1977) noted that information is needed in three main areas: (1) the temporal and spatial distribution of biomass formation (Chapter 5); (2) the temporal and phenological fluctuations in biochemical composition of various portions of the tree; and (3) the metabolic pathways involved in, and substrate and energy requirements for, biosynthesis of constituent compounds. Most commonly, ratios of carbon dioxide uptake to biomass production are calculated. Woodwell and Botkin (1970) estimated that this ratio was 1.0:0.614 based on the assumptions that 1 g of carbon dioxide produces 0.682 g of glucose and that 1 g of glucose forms 0.900 g of biomass (that is, anhydroglucose $[C_6H_{10}O_5]_n$). Chung and Barnes (1977), however, have indicated that this assumption is not completely correct as biomass consists of much more than merely hexose polymers; their carbon dioxide-to-biomass ratio for loblolly pine *(Pinus taeda)* was 1.0:0.433. This ratio compared favorably with the 1.0:0.55 ratio derived for balsam fir by Loach and Little (1973).

Shoot and Cambial Growth Processes

The cellular growth process, utilizing photosynthates synthesized in the needles, results in the formation of biomass that is of considerable ecologic and economic importance in the coniferous forest biome (see Chapter 5). Because of the relative magnitudes and the obvious economic implications involved, the greatest amount of interest has been in stemwood production. In this respect, the correlation between total seasonal net photosynthesis and stemwood production is surprisingly close (Chapter 3; Emmingham and Waring 1977).

The meristematic activity responsible for major aboveground biomass accumulation in large Douglas-fir is reviewed briefly here, with particular focus on the processes related to diameter and height growth arising from cellular division occurring in the cambial and apical meristems, respectively. It must be noted, however, that the tree growth process, leading to total stand biomass accumulation, also involves roots, needles, and reproductive structures. Though extremely important, the growth dynamics of these structures are not considered herein, and readers are directed to the texts of Kozlowski (1971a,b) for such information. In addition, a more recent review of tree root structure, distribution, and growth is also available (Hermann 1977).

Shoot Growth

Douglas-fir have preformed shoots; that is, overwintering buds are telescoped shoots that contain the primordia of all the needles that will expand during the next growing season. Thus the growth potentials of shoots are essentially fixed in the apical buds. Shoot growth is also seasonally determinate, meaning that after the terminal shoots elongate, there is a period of inactivity until new terminal buds form and can expand; usually the expansion phase occurs only once a year.

The environment controls shoot growth by influencing the production of new primordia, which will expand the next spring. Since the photosynthetic and growth processes are inseparably linked, the environmental control factors discussed earlier for net photosynthesis also influence the production of new buds and their subsequent growth (Kozlowski 1971a). In general, late-summer environmental stresses do not greatly restrict current-year elongation of preformed, predetermined shoots as they usually complete most of their expansion before that time. Late-season stresses, however, affect shoot growth the following spring by reducing the number of primordia produced in the new, unopened bud. Thus bud size is a prime indicator of shoot growth potential (Clements 1970).

When unusually severe environmental stresses occur during the growing season, the full growth potential of the preformed buds is not realized (Kozlowski 1971a). For example, during the installation of a weighing tree-lysimeter at the Thompson site in the summer of 1971 (Fritschen et al. 1973), the tree was periodically subjected to abnormally severe internal water deficits with base xylem pressure potentials often decreasing below -1.8 MPa (R. B. Walker and D. J. Salo, pers. comm.). Severe water deficits coupled with mineral deficiencies during the elongation growth phase resulted in the 1971 shoots' being uncommonly short but covered with numerous, closely spaced needles. In addition, the 1972 shoots were relatively sparse, presumably because of a reduction in the number of leaf primordia formed in the new buds at the end of the 1971 growing season. These effects strongly suggest "transplanting shock," (Coutts 1980) which became morphologically undetectable by the 1973 growing season.

Cambial Growth

Diameter growth in stems, roots, and branches arises from the meristematic activity of their cambiums and accounts for the major proportion of the standing biomass in Douglas-fir (see Chapter 5). The term "cambium" actually denotes a zone of cells between the secondary xylem and phloem that undergoes periclinal cell divisions. This zone is composed of various types of initiating cells producing an assortment of derivatives. In conifers, fusiform initials give rise to tracheids and various axial parenchymal cells toward the inside and sieve and parenchymal cells to the outside. The width of the cambial zone is greatest in fast-growing trees and hence proportionately greater amounts of phloem and xylem tissue are associated with such individuals (Grillos and Smith 1959).

After their production by xylem mother cells, daughter cells go through three distinct phases before becoming functional tracheids (Wodzicki 1971): (1) radial enlargement, characterized by the uptake of water into the vacuole, increases in turgor pressure, and cell expansion; (2) maturation, which involves secondary wall synthesis and lignification; and (3) cellular differentiation, which often lags considerably behind cell division. New xylem cells, during their enlargement phase, can exchange water with the transpiration stream and fluctuate in size, thereby becoming involved in the internal storage of water and in the reversible stem shrinkage phenomenon (Dobbs and Scott 1971; Lassoie 1973, 1979).

Tree water balance seems to play an important role in the differentiation of xylem derivatives and is therefore involved in the transition from earlywood to latewood within the annual ring of conifers. Variations in tracheid diameter depend upon seasonal fluctuations in the growth rate during the enlargement phase, while the final cell wall thickness is determined by the duration of the maturation phase (Wodzicki 1971). The duration of the latter phase is in turn controlled by the delay in the onset of autolysis of the cytoplasm, which marks its termination. All these processes seem to be greatly influenced by the water relations of the vascular cambium (see review by Zahner 1968); however, the controlling influence of hormonal action should not be neglected (Pharis 1976; Wodzicki and Wodzicki 1980).

The phloem of conifers is composed of conducting tissue, consisting of living, mature sieve cells that lack nuclei and tonoplasts, various types of parenchyma cells, and dead, nonconducting tissue. Typically, sieve cell production and differentiation begin in the spring and continue until fall

(Srivastava 1963). In Douglas-fir, callose plugs form on sieve areas during the middle of July but then dissolve the following year; therefore sieve cells remain alive and functional for most of two growing seasons (Grillos and Smith 1959).

In Douglas-fir phloem, parenchyma cells typically accumulate substances such as resins, tannins, and starches (Grillos and Smith 1959). Fusiform ray initials and resin canals are also common in older individuals. Ray parenchyma and ray cells act as channels for moving materials between the phloem and the xylem. The radial transport of water along these channels has been suggested to be an important aspect of stem water storage (Stewart 1967) and stem dimensional fluctuations (Dobbs and Scott 1971).

Auxin, the traditional cambial stimulus, is generated in the needle primordia contained in the buds and is propagated basipetally in forest trees, affecting cambial activity in a gradient extending downward and inward from the shoot tips. No doubt such activity also involves the balance of several growth regulators (for example, auxin, gibberellins, and cytokinins) and various synergistic effects between them (Kozlowski 1971b, Pharis 1976; Berlyn 1979). In addition, internal gradients of various growth components (for example, water, nutrients, and photosynthates) as well as the various environmental factors that control them are also involved, and all result in longitudinal variations in cambial growth rates along Douglas-fir stems (Dobbs 1966). Thus those factors discussed earlier that affect net photosynthesis also, at least indirectly, affect cambial growth rates (Berlyn 1979); however, the relation is probably confounded in Douglas-fir by the existence and utilization by the cambium of stored photosynthates (Ross 1972).

Tree water balance and internal water deficits seem to have direct influence on cambial cell activity and growth potential. Both division and elongation usually occur only under conditions of relatively high cell turgor (Vaadia et al. 1961). Lassoie (1975, 1979) has reported that positive cambial growth increments in various crown classes of Douglas-fir abruptly terminated at both breast height (1.3 m) and near midcrown when base xylem pressure potentials decreased below about -0.5 MPa. Thus summertime irrigation has been shown to enhance seasonal diameter growth in field-grown Douglas-fir by extending the growing season into late summer (Woodman 1971a). In contrast, Ross (1972) reported that irrigation in midsummer following an extended and severe drought did not influence cambial growth, presumably because of cambial dormancy initiated during the drought period.

Growth Interdependency

The foliage, stems, and roots of forest trees seem to be so hydraulically and biochemically interrelated that their growth dynamics are mutually interdependent (Reich et al. 1980; Hinckley and Lassoie 1981). In Douglas-fir, water flux through a stem is closely related to its sapwood cross-sectional area (Figure

6.11; Huber 1956; Kline et al. 1976), which is in turn linearly related to leaf biomass (Figure 6.12; Grier and Waring 1974) and to leaf area (Chapter 5; Grier and Running 1977). A similar relation between sapwood area and foliar area has been reported for other conifers (Grier and Waring 1974; Running 1980) and for various hardwood trees (Waring et al. 1977; Rogers and Hinckley 1979). Recent results by Long et al. (1981) have extended this relationship to include any point along the stem of a large Douglas-fir. In addition, Santantonio et al. (1977) have found a significant correlation between diameter at 1.3 m and root biomass in mature Douglas-fir trees. Thus it seems that the entire root-sapwood-leaf water transport system maintains a dynamic equilibrium that assures adequate water uptake and transport to foliar surfaces in order to meet transpirational demands (Hinckley et al. 1978).

TEMPORAL AND SPATIAL VARIATIONS IN PHYSIOLOGICAL ACTIVITY

Forest trees are long-lived, three-dimensional organisms that must interface with highly variable soil and atmospheric environments. Hence their physiological activity depends not only on diurnal and seasonal fluctuations in controlling environmental variables but also upon spatial and age-related factors. In this section, temporal variations in certain physiological processes are first discussed, followed by a consideration of within-tree variations, specifically those related to height, aspect, and age.

Temporal Variations

Growing Season Activity

The spring and summer comprise the major portion of the growing season for Douglas-fir. The period is characterized by aboveground meristematic activity and is defined by a seasonally fluctuating set of interrelated environmental variables. These factors are also geographically variable and the timing, trend, and magnitude of various physiological processes in Douglas-fir are different throughout the coniferous forest biome (Campbell and Sugano 1979). For example, the initiation, rate, duration, and total increment of cambial and apical growth in Douglas-fir varies throughout Oregon depending primarily upon the elevation (Table 6.3). The influence of elevation includes such controlling factors as water, temperature, and light, which are generally more favorable for net photosynthesis and growth at lower elevations; thus growing season lengths typically decrease with altitude (Larcher 1975). Work by Emmingham (1977) with Douglas-fir also has shown that growth rate may be

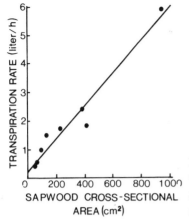

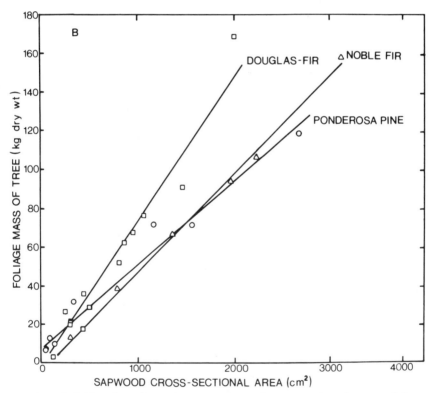

FIGURE 6.11 *The relation between sap-wood cross-sectional area and transpiration rate in various Douglas-fir trees (after Kline et al. 1976).*

FIGURE 6.12 *The relation between sapwood cross-sectional area at 1.3 m and total foliage mass for Douglas-fir (coefficient of determination [r^2] = 0.97), noble fir ($r^2 = 0.98$) and ponderosa pine ($r^2 = 0.97$) (after Grier and Waring 1974).*

TABLE 6.3 *Phenology and growth for cambiums and leaders of sapling Douglas-fir (coastal range—Corvallis, Oregon, seed source) in three western Oregon plantations.*[a]

Location[b]	Bud swell	Bud break	Extension growth 90%	Extension growth 100%	Rate[c] (cm/d)	Duration[d] (d)	Total (cm)	Start of divisions	Start of latewood	Growth (90%)	Rate[c] (mm/d)	Duration[e] (d)	Total (mm)
			Leader growth and phenology (1971)					Cambial growth and phenology (1971)					
CAS	June 1	June 22	Aug. 9	Sept. 8	0.66	135	33	June 4	Aug 9	Aug 20	0.032	77	2.56
COA	Apr 18	May 10	July 26	Aug 18	1.14	100	73	Apr 18	Aug 3	Sept 3	0.047	139	6.45
WIL	Apr 20	May 10	July 4	Sept 3	2.00	87	120	Apr 19	Aug 4	Sept 2	0.071	139	10.38

[a] From Emmingham (1977).

[b] CAS = Cascade Mountains near Molalla, Oreg., at 1050 m; COA = Coast Range Near Corvallis, Oreg., at 570 m; WIL = Willamette Valley near Salem, Oreg., at 70 m.

[c] Growth rates taken from slope of leader and cambium growth curves.

[d] Leader growth duration is time from budbreak to growth cessation.

[e] Cambial growth duration is time from initiation of cell divisions to completion of 90 percent of growth.

equally as important as duration, especially when considering the terminal leader (Table 6.3).

In general, Douglas-fir phenology and growth at low to medium elevations in western Washington varies within the extremes defined by data from the Coast Range and Willamette Valley in Table 6.3 (Dobbs 1966; Woodman 1968; Ross 1972; Lassoie 1975). It seems that the greatest discrepancies between the Washington site and the Oregon sites involve the specific timing of the termination of both cambial and apical meristematic activity. Such differences probably indicate geographic variability in controlling environmental factors as well as possible genetic differences.

Genetic differences within the species Douglas-fir can have an effect on an individual's physiological activity. For example, two distinct varieties are commonly recognized, a coastal form (var. *menziesii*) and a Rocky Mountain or inland form (var. *glauca*), with intergradations occurring in size and phenological traits within their transition zone (Sorensen 1979). Provenance trials have illustrated differences between these two varieties with respect to the timing of budbreak and onset of dormancy and to apical and cambial growth rates (Irgens-Moller 1968; Rehfeldt 1977). In general, adaptation to a maritime environment has genetically fixed the coastal variety with growth potentials superior to the Rocky Mountain variety. In addition, it seems that coastal Douglas-fir seedlings, when compared with those from inland sources, have relatively higher net photosynthesis rates at all light intensities below saturation (Krueger and Ferrell 1965). This superiority is realized only in relatively mild climates, however, as the coastal form typically does not survive the severities of continental climates (Rehfeldt 1977).

There also seem to be marked genetic differences within each of the two Douglas-fir varieties. Hermann and Lavender (1968) and Campbell (1979) have demonstrated altitudinal and topographical differentiations within the coastal form. In general, seedling growth potential decreased with the altitude of the seed source regardless of the testing environment. There was also a shorter growth period and a larger root-to-shoot ratio for the progeny of trees from south-facing slopes compared with those from north-facing locations. These differences were viewed as survival adaptations to the environmental extremes associated with southern exposures. A similar study has examined genetic variations within the inland variety (Rehfeldt 1974, 1979a,b).

Temporal fluctuations in Douglas-fir physiological processes during the growing season can often be separated into three intergrading phases that depend on tree water status: the predrought, drought, and recovery or postdrought periods. In most of the coniferous forest biome, precipitation is normally sparse during July, August, and early September when atmospheric evaporative demand is relatively high; decreasing soil moisture levels throughout this period characterize the summer drought phase (Figure 6.13).

Typically, the predrought period is marked by low evaporative demands, high soil and tree moisture levels, and intense cambial activity (Figure 6.13).

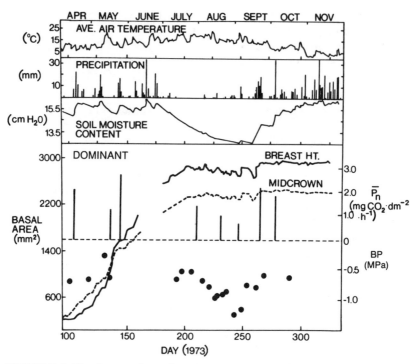

FIGURE 6.13 *Seasonal trends in average daily air temperature, total daily precipitation, soil moisture content in the top meter of soil, basal area increment at breast height (1.3 m) and midcrown (20 m), daylight mean net photosynthesis rate* (P_n), *and base (predawn) xylem pressure potential (BP) for a dominant Douglas-fir (after Salo 1974; Lassoie 1975, 1979).*

Surprisingly, the seasonally greatest stem respiration rates (indicative of cambial activity) are not typically associated with this period, as the formation of springwood uses less carbon per unit increment of radius than summerwood formation (Linder and Troeng 1977). In the early spring, stem growth commences earlier and progresses more rapidly near midcrown than at lower levels, because of the differential initiation of cambial activity starting from the top downward. Interestingly, much of this early growth may not involve actual cell division. Dobbs (1966) has noted that increases in stem circumference in Douglas-fir occur about three to five weeks prior to actual growth because of the rehydration and swelling of the cambial zone before meristematic activity is initiated. The cambial zone can exchange water internally and undergo minor diurnal contractions in size during this period; however, the predrought growth phase is characterized by the continuous increase in stem size arising from nighttime recoveries surpassing daytime shrinkages (Figure 6.14a). In fact, mitotic activity by the cambium during the spring may not seem to be greatly affected by the diurnal contractions of the bole (Wilson 1966); however the expansion phase is most definitely terminated during such shrinkage periods.

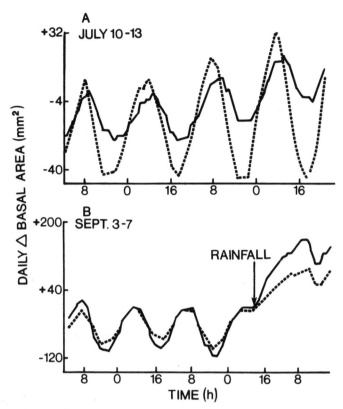

FIGURE 6.14 *Diurnal fluctuations in basal areas at breast height (1.3 m; solid line) and near midcrown (20 m; dotted line) in a forty-year-old, twenty-nine-meter, dominant Douglas-fir during the: (A) predrought, late-growth phase and (B) peak of the summer drought period (after Lassoie 1975, 1979).*

Since water does not seem to be greatly limiting during this period, cambial growth responds primarily to warm, rainless periods (especially in May; Figure 6.13). This fact suggests that light and temperature are probably regulating the growth process (Doley and Leyton 1968).

By midsummer, soil moisture reserves become depleted, thereby causing a comparable decrease in base xylem pressure potentials (Sucoff 1972; Lassoie 1975). At this time, afternoon and evening rehydration (swelling) of cambial tissue fails to completely account for daytime dehydration (shrinking) (Figure 6.14b) and net stem contractions occur (Figure 6.13). The progressive contraction of the stem is periodically interrupted by temporary increases during periods of relatively low evaporative demand, and some actual cell growth may occur (Shepherd 1964; Green 1969). However, such major diurnal shrinkages represent a time of cambial cell dehydration and loss of turgor (Hopkins

1968), and thus cell divisions and expansions during that phase are greatly limited (Wilson 1966; Doley and Leyton 1968). In support, Linder and Troeng (1977) have reported that, with twenty-year-old Scotch pine late in the growing season, the diurnal minimum in stem respiration rates occurred simultaneously with the diurnal minimum in stem radius. These authors cautioned, however, that precise correlations between stem respiration and cambial growth activity are not possible without careful consideration,of the stem shrinkage phenomenon and the seasonal changes occurring in growth ring densities. Additional work is warranted.

Stem shrinkage in the morning and recovery in late afternoon commence up to four hours earlier at a midcrown position compared with breast height (Figure 6.14a,b; Dobbs and Scott 1971; Lassoie 1973, 1979). Such a lag probably results because water reserves nearest the transpiring crown are relatively more sensitive to fluctuating tree water deficits developed at the foliage than those elsewhere along the stem.

Rehydration of the stem during the late afternoon and evening occurs in two recognizable phases (Figure 6.14a,b). First there is a rapid expansion phase that has been attributed to hydraulic recharge (Hinckley et al. 1974), followed by a slower rate of increase that continues until the commencement of shrinkage the next morning and implies actual cell growth (Namken et al. 1969). Similar two-phase increases in leader length have been reported for Douglas-fir seedlings by Zaerr and Holbo (1976).

Daily trends in net photosynthesis vary depending on the progression of various environmental factors that control its functioning. Under adequate light conditions (clear, sunny summer days), net photosynthesis rates depend primarily on the stomatal mechanism and its control by changing soil moisture levels and internal tree water deficits (Figure 6.15; Lassoie and Salo 1981). Under well-watered conditions, net photosynthesis varies with early morning increases and late afternoon decreases in light (Figure 6.15, curve 1). As the soil progressively dries, stomata tend to be less responsive to early morning increases in light (Running 1976) and initiate closure earlier in the day (Figure 6.15, curves 2 to 5) until no opening occurs and net photosynthesis remains negative most of the day (Figure 6.15, curve 6). On cloudy, overcast days when light levels are fluctuating and are often below those saturating the photosynthetic machinery (Figures 6.3 and 6.4a), net photosynthesis rates closely reflect the fluctuations in light (Salo 1974). Leaf temperatures can also modify these general diurnal trends in net photosynthesis but normally only as they approach freezing or exceed about 25°C (Figures 6.3 and 6.4b).

Seasonal trends in net photosynthesis are commonly reported by computing either the total daily net carbon dioxide exchanged or by averaging that value over the daylight period. Since day length varies appreciably over the year, the latter approach is often preferred if comparisons are to be interpreted in relation to other limiting factors. In the spring, average daily net photosynthesis rates are the highest on cool, cloudy days when internal water deficits

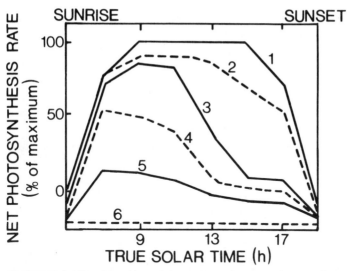

FIGURE 6.15 *Hypothetical diurnal trends in net photosynthesis rates showing the effect of increased soil water deficits (for example, curve 1, base xylem pressure potential equal to about −0.2 MPa; curve 6, about −2.0 MPa) for various sunny spring and summer days (based on data for Douglas-fir; Leverenz 1974, Salo 1974, and selected literature).*

remain low (for example, May 24, Figure 6.13). In contrast, sunny, hot days are marked by reduced assimilation activity (for example, May 15, Figure 6.13) because of either supraoptimal leaf temperatures (Figure 6.3) or hydroactive stomatal closure during the afternoon (Running 1976; Lassoie et al. 1977c; Lassoie and Salo 1981). As soil and tree moisture levels decrease during the summer drought, stomata remain open for progressively shorter times, thereby confining active carbon dioxide uptake to the early morning hours (August and early September, Figure 6.13).

Similar midday depressions in net photosynthesis rates have been reported by others for Douglas-fir (Gentle 1963; Helms 1965; Woodman 1968; Leverenz 1981). In addition, modeling efforts by Emmingham and Waring (1977) have illustrated the impact of such midday stomatal closure on seasonal net photosynthetic trends in Douglas-fir at various locations throughout western Oregon. They found a summertime reduction in potential net photosynthesis due to drought that ranged from 25 percent at a moist coastal site to 65 percent at a dry interior range site (see Chapter 3).

The fall is normally characterized by cool temperatures and frequent rainfall leading to the recharge of soil and tree moisture levels and the rapid enlargement of Douglas-fir stems (Figures 6.13 and 6.14b). Since temperature and tree water deficits are generally moderate, assimilatory activity can be substantial (Figure 6.13). By late October, however, the relatively short day length limits total daily net photosynthesis (Salo 1974).

From the preceding discussion the question remains as to whether Douglas-fir foliage retains the same photosynthetic potential throughout the year. It is well known that different-aged needles have different assimilatory capabilities and that expanding new needles have relatively low net photosynthesis rates because of their growth activity. Such features will be discussed when spatial variabilities are considered; however, does the assimilatory capacity change in a given age class of needles during the year? If so, the change could greatly affect the interpretation of field measurements of net photosynthesis.

Brix (1971) has examined this possibility by measuring net photosynthesis rates under optimal light and temperature conditions in shoots periodically excised from a twenty-four-year-old Douglas-fir. Results indicated that net photosynthesis rates in new needles increased from negative values (that is, net respiration) in the early stages of shoot expansion to a high of about 8.3 mg $CO_2 \cdot dm^{-2} \cdot h^{-1}$ by the end of August (Figure 6.16). During the winter the rate decreased to a low (about 25 percent of maximum) in early February and then increased steadily throughout the next spring. Such data indicate that certain endogenous factors, probably related to biochemical, hormonal, or enzymatic

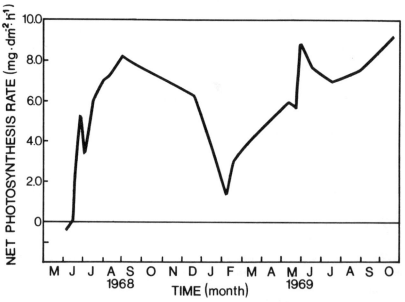

FIGURE 6.16 *Seasonal trend of maximum potential net photosynthesis rate for current-year shoots in 1968 and one-year-old shoots in 1969 excised from twenty-four-year-old Douglas-fir trees and measured under 2500 ft-c and 20°C conditions (after Brix 1971).*

reactions, or all three, or possibly to seasonal changes in the source-sink strength for photosynthates in the needles (Chung and Barnes 1980a,b), may affect net photosynthesis rates. In addition to these rhythms, temperature adjustments over the year in both net photosynthesis and leaf conductance have been noted in Douglas-fir (D. J. Salo, R. G. Amundson, and R. B. Walker, pers. comm.) as well as in Sitka spruce (Watts et al. 1976). Thus a portion of the seasonal variability illustrated in Figure 6.16 may have resulted from maintaining experimental temperatures at an optimal 20°C (Brix 1971) while actual temperature optima in the field changed to reflect changes in ambient temperatures. The adaptive significance of such an occurrence is obvious but has yet to be fully examined for Douglas-fir.

Being able to quantify and interpret temporal fluctuations in net photosynthesis rate and stem growth, based on their controlling biotic and abiotic factors, unfortunately lends little to an understanding of how cells eventually arise from carbon dioxide exchanged at the needles. Quite generally, the translocation and incorporation of carbon once it enters the stomata involve the relative strengths of various sources (primarily the needles) and sinks (primarily meristematic tissues). Simply stated, source-strength is related to needle age and sink-strength is dependent on the growth activity of meristematic tissues (for example, root, stem, and branch cambiums and apical meristems, and new needles); translocation between the sources and the sinks is a function of their proximity to each other and the time of year.

Ross (1972) has examined the source-sink relationship in ten-year-old, field-grown Douglas-fir using the carbon-14 technique. He observed that diurnal assimilation rates were similar to those discussed earlier where light controlled net photosynthesis rates during the morning and late afternoon and increasing tree water deficits became limiting throughout the daylight period (Figure 6.15). There was also a 75 percent reduction in the rate of photosynthate efflux from one-year-old needles toward new shoots during the day, presumably because of a drop in the availability of photophosphorylation energy for vein loading (Plaut and Reinhold 1969), and possibly decreases in respiratory activity associated with cool nighttime temperatures (Hartt and Kortschak 1967).

The observed diurnal differences in the fate of currently assimilated carbon must be interpreted in terms of the changing environmental conditions associated with the light/dark cycle as well as the tree's developmental stage and physiological status on the specific days examined. Environmental conditions that promote high internal tree-water deficits also limit meristematic activity throughout the tree, thereby confining positive increases in shoot length and diameter to evening periods when conditions for growth are more favorable (Figure 6.14; Ross 1972; Lassoie 1975; Zaerr and Holbo 1976). The findings of Ross (1972) indicate that both photosynthesis and the export of photosynthetic products are less affected by high internal water deficits during the day than are cell growth processes. Similar conclusions have been presented by

Boyer (1970) for several herbaceous plants and by Brix (1972) and Leverenz (1981a) for Douglas-fir. Thus, under drought conditions, nocturnal shoot growth in Douglas-fir utilizes current photosynthates accumulated during the day in storage tissues of the old internodes (Ross 1972).

Diurnal and seasonal trends in foliar transpiration can closely resemble those illustrated for net photosynthesis because of the common influence of the stomata (Figure 6.15). The transpiration process is also dependent on the vapor pressure gradient between the leaf mesophyll cells and the atmosphere. Examinations of diurnal transpiration rates in Douglas-fir based on measurements at the foliage (Leverenz 1974, 1981a; Salo 1974) and on estimates for entire trees (Fritschen et al. 1977; Lassoie et al. 1977c) have exemplified the relationship between stomatal activity and evaporative demand in determining water loss rates. In general, such control changes temporally, with transpiration mimicking evaporative demand as long as stomata remain open. Hydroactive stomatal closure during the afternoon reduces water loss rates even though evaporative demands may be high.

Seasonal transpiration patterns have also been examined by modeling both potential and actual transpiration for one- to two-year-old Douglas-fir growing in various environments in southwestern Oregon (Reed and Waring 1974). Striking differences were noted between the predictions of potential and actual water losses depending on the particular location. The ratio of these two factors varied from 1.0, indicating that no measurable stomatal closure was occurring and soil water levels were adequately meeting the transpirational demand, to about 0.3 at drier sites. At such locations hydroactive stomatal closure was exercising a major influence on tree water losses. Similar results have been noted by Hinckley and Ritchie (1973) in noble fir *(Abies procera)* and Pacific silver fir.

More recent studies have indicated that the preceding view that hydroactive stomatal closure and soil moisture are simply and directly related may need to be reevaluated. That is, there now seems to be ample evidence that internal sources of water may be called upon during periods of reduced soil water availability and might postpone hydroactive stomatal closure, thereby maintaining carbon dioxide uptake into the afternoon (Hinckley et al. 1978; Running 1980; Hinckley and Lassoie 1981). Two primary water storage areas exist in tree stems, the living tissues at and near the cambium and the water-conducting sapwood.

The formation of internal tree-water deficits occurs as water content at a particular location decreases due to transpirational losses exceeding supplies and/or water between cells or specific parts of the tree being redistributed (Richter 1973; Jarvis 1976). As water moves from nearby tissues, hydrostatic tensions are transmitted throughout the tree. As tensions increase within elastic tree tissues, their deformation occurs; with the release of internal tensions they recover in size. In tree stems, roots, and branches such dimensional fluctuations occur principally in the living phloem, cambium, and newly derived xylem cells (Dobbs and Scott 1971; Jarvis 1975). These fluctuations are directly related to changes in tissue water content, thereby providing an internal storage area (that is, a source-sink) for water (Oertli 1971). It appears that inelastic stem tissues, the sapwood and heartwood, are also involved as internal water storage areas in large forest trees (Running et al. 1975; Roberts 1976; Waring and Running 1976, 1978). The subject of stem tissue water storage has been reviewed by Jarvis (1975), Hinckley et al. (1978) and Hinckley and Lassoie (1981).

Dimensional contractions are generally equivalent in magnitude to the amount of water lost to the transpiration stream (Jarvis 1975). Thus calculations of volumetric contractions along tree stems (both diurnal and seasonal) would provide estimates of the amount of water exchanged internally between extensible tissues and the conducting xylem. Such calculations indicate that the maximum amount of water stored seasonally in elastic stem tissues of a dominant Douglas-fir between breast height and midcrown is about 2.5 liters (Lassoie 1979). On a seasonal basis, this net amount of water seems insignificant considering the quantity that moves through the tree from the soil reserve (Jarvis 1975; Roberts 1976; Fritschen et al. 1977). Therefore such seasonal water losses are probably more important in that they indicate the gradual depletion of internal water reserves available for daily exchange (Lassoie 1979).

When similar calculations are made based on the maximum diurnal shrinkage and recovery noted during a summer period, it appears that a potential maximum of 1.8 liters of water is available per day (Lassoie 1979). It is presently unknown whether this water is lost daily through transpiration or merely exchanged between elastic and inelastic stem tissues. The value is relatively high considering the amount available seasonally and represents about 5 percent of the maximum total daily water loss from a large Douglas-fir (Fritschen and Doraiswamy 1973; Kline et al. 1976; Fritschen et al. 1977). Obviously the elastic stem tissues near the cambium between breast height and midcrown represent only a small part of the total living tissues capable of undergoing internal water exchange (Jarvis 1975). In addition, R. H. Waring (pers. comm.) has estimated that about 4 percent of the xylem in Douglas-fir stems constitutes living parenchyma cells that are capable of exchanging water with the transpiration stream but that do not contribute to stem dimensional fluctuations (Dobbs and Scott 1971). The impact of such storage in living tissues on net photosynthesis and growth may be significant if the stomatal mechanism is favorably affected but such a phenomenon has yet to be adequately considered.

The contribution of water from nonelastic, sapwood tissues to total tree-water balance has also been examined (Running et al. 1975; Waring and Running 1976, 1978). Initially a water-flux model was developed that included a sapwood compartment from which water was withdrawn daily to meet transpirational demand (Running et al. 1975). For an 80-m Douglas-fir, the model predicted an average transpiration rate of 390 liters/day over a summer marked by seventeen days when water loss was reduced because of hydroactive stomatal closure. The maximum change in volume of water in the sapwood was estimated to represent more than a ten-day supply for transpiration. Whether this water was immediately available for transpiration was not verified, but work by Kline et al. (1976) has shown a daily water loss of 530 liters in a 76-m Douglas-fir, a value close to that of Running et al. (1975) when one considers that their lower average included low transpiration periods. The model indicated that a 2-m sapling lost an average of 4.3 liters of water per day during the summer with actual transpiration falling short of potential for 54 days. Because of its size, this tree had a relatively small sapwood water storage capacity.

In an examination of a 50- to 60-m, old-growth Douglas-fir stand, Waring and Running (1978) have reported that sapwood water represented a storage reservoir of about 268×10^3 liters/ha (26.8 mm) with 75 percent of this residing in the stemwood. The depletion of sapwood storage areas reached 1.25 to 1.70 mm/d on clear days following cloudy or rainy weather.

The internal redistribution of water discussed above is exemplified when foliar transpiration rates are compared with the rates of water movement through the stem (Lassoie et al. 1977c; Waring et al. 1980). Simplistically, they should be equal, but because of internal sources and sinks for water within the tree the relation is often more complex. Though Lassoie et al. (1977c) reported a good correlation between sap velocity at breast height and actual foliar transpiration, time lags often exist between these two phenomena (Waring et al. 1980). For example, during the morning, water loss from Douglas-fir foliage depleted internal reserves and sap velocities lagged behind transpiration (Lassoie et al. 1977c). In the late afternoon, or when evaporative demands otherwise decreased, the reverse was observed, indicating the recharge of those tissues dehydrated during the transpiration period. As tree-water deficits increased due to drying of soil and/or high rates of tree water loss these lags become exaggerated, suggesting a temporary lack of significant water uptake by the roots. The transpirational demand evidently was supplied by water stored in internal reservoirs (Swanson 1972).

Wintertime Activity

During the late fall and winter conifers are often considered to be dormant throughout the coniferous forest biome. This idea arises from the fact that net photosynthesis rates are often limited by light, temperature, water transport, or all three (Gentle 1963; Helms 1965; Salo 1974). Aboveground meristematic activity is negligible. However, recent modeling efforts indicate that Douglas-fir trees may accumulate more than 50 percent of their total annual assimilate between October and May (Chapter 3; Emmingham and Waring 1977). In support, gas exchange studies with Douglas-fir in the Pacific Northwest (Salo

1974; D. J. Salo, R. G. Amundson, and R. B. Walker, pers. comm.) and with eastern red cedar *(Juniperus virginiana)* in mid-Missouri (Lassoie et al. 1977a) have shown that appreciable net photosynthesis rates are possible during periods of the year other than the aboveground growing season. Furthermore, Bradbury and Malcolm (1978) have reported doubling of dry weights of Sitka spruce seedlings between late September and mid-April, an indication of appreciable photosynthetic activity.

Diurnal stem contractions during cold periods (Figure 6.17) are atypical compared with those occurring in the summer (Figure 6.14a) and primarily reflect the freeze/thaw cycle of the foliage (Turner and DeRoo 1974). When temperatures drop below −2°C, the sapwood water freezes (thereby disrupting the water conduction system; Hammel 1967), eventually promoting extremely low xylem pressure potentials, continuously closed stomata, and net respiration rates in the foliage (Figure 6.17). Often there is a reversal of the normal

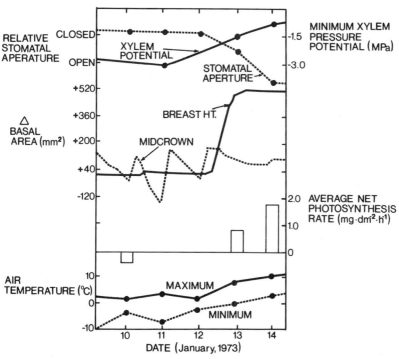

FIGURE 6.17 *The diurnal progress of stem basal area, daylight average net photosynthesis rates, minimum daily xylem pressure potentials, and relative stomatal aperture openings (based on pressure infiltration measurements; Fry and Walker 1967) for a dominant Douglas-fir during a cold winter period. Maximum and minimum daily air temperatures are also shown (after Salo 1974; Lassoie 1975).*

(summertime) pattern of tree-water deficits, with xylem pressure potentials actually increasing during the daylight period after a predawn minimum (Evans 1973; Salo 1974).

Following an increase in temperature and a thawing of the sapwood water, the hydraulic conducting system is re-established, internal tensions relax, and internal water levels increase. This causes an abrupt rehydration and expansion of tree stems, stomatal opening, and subsequent increases in net photosynthesis rates (Figure 6.17). Once again, light becomes a controlling factor, after having been superseded by hydroactive stomatal closure during freezing periods.

Potentially, conifers are physiologically active throughout most of the year. In addition, positive net photosynthesis rates during the winter may have a significant impact on Douglas-fir throughout the coniferous forest biome (Chapter 3; Helms 1964; Salo 1974; Emmingham and Waring 1977). This general subject has yet to be examined in detail, however, especially with respect to photosynthate translocation, storage, and subsequent utilization.

Within-Tree Spatial Variations

Forest trees, whether standing alone or as part of a community, are subject to a temporally fluctuating gradient of different environmental variables including temperature, light, wind, and relative humidity. Vertical gradients of environmental variables have been examined within Douglas-fir communities in relation to canopy carbon dioxide exchange and water vapor loss (Kinerson 1973, 1974; Kinerson and Fritschen 1973; Doraiswamy 1977). Such gradients in environment, in association with biological factors related to tree-tissue age, result in striking physiological heterogeneity within and between trees occupying a forest stand. A tree's three-dimensional nature further complicates the picture (Hinckley and Ritchie 1970; Woodman 1971b; Hinckley et al. 1978; Hinckley and Lassoie 1981). Thus point sampling within a tree canopy in order to characterize physiological activity is difficult since obvious microclimatic variations, differences in tissue age and morphology, internal redistribution of water, nutrients, and photosynthates, and differences in internal resistances to transport all contribute to considerable physiological variability (Richter 1973, 1974).

Height Above the Water Table

Under conditions of no flow (zero transpiration), the water potential at any point in a tree should merely be a function of the density of water, gravity, and the height above the water table (Richter 1973). Theoretically, a negative hydrostatic gradient, approximately equal to 0.01 MPa/m, should then exist from the roots upward. Under conditions of transpirational flux, however, a more negative hydrostatic gradient (0.12 MPa/m in Douglas-fir; Tan et al. 1977) would be expected due to frictional shear forces between the xylem sap and the conduit walls as well as between the torus and the xylem sap in conifer pits (Richter 1973).

The hydrostatic water potential gradient combines with radiation attenuation through the canopy to cause variations in leaf conductance with height. On sunny days, Tan et al. (1977) found stomatal conductance to be highest at the top of a 7- to 9-m Douglas-fir canopy and lowest at the bottom, a trend also found in Sitka spruce (Beardsell et al. 1972; Watts et al. 1976); however, a number of factors may change the pattern. For example, on cloudy days, when diffuse light penetrates the lower canopy, differences in stomatal conductance between the upper and lower canopy are usually much reduced (Beardsell et al. 1972). In addition, Waring and Running (1978) have found that the hydrostatic gradient in a 80-m Douglas-fir may alone cause lower conductances than expected in the upper canopy. Osmotic potentials also change with tree height and season, which can affect stomatal reponse (Hellkvist et al. 1974).

Obviously, vertical gradients in light, water potential, and leaf conductance all potentially affect net photosynthesis. In 1975, D. J. Salo, R. L. Amundson, and R. B. Walker (pers. comm.) investigated spatial variability in net photosynthesis rates with respect to height in large Douglas-fir. Light response curves for net photosynthesis were generated under controlled greenhouse conditions using branches excised in the field from various heights. Results indicated that foliage obtained from the lower part of the canopy (15 m) had a 15 percent lower potential for assimilation than foliage from more sunlit locations in the upper canopy (at twenty-three meters). These data were used to generate simple predictive equations relating net photosynthesis to light intensity at various temperatures. The model was then used to estimate net photosynthesis rates at various canopy heights following field measurements of light and temperature. The estimate indicated that, under a wide variety of climatic conditions, total daily net photosynthesis decreases considerably at canopy levels below 21 m as do total daily light levels (Figure 6.18). Field measurements by Woodman (1968, 1971b), using a multiple cuvette system in a forty-nine-year-old, dominant Douglas-fir crown, support these findings. Kinerson (1973), using the aerodynamic approach to investigate the flux of water vapor and carbon dioxide through a forty-year-old Douglas-fir stand, concluded that leaf area and the attenuation of light were the chief factors controlling the variations in net photosynthesis with canopy height. Therefore it appears that differences between samples, especially with respect to branch water status, light, and leaf temperature, are probably more important in determining maximum assimilatory activity than merely height in the crown. As discussed later, however, foliage age can also be an important consideration when examining photosynthetic differences between branch samples.

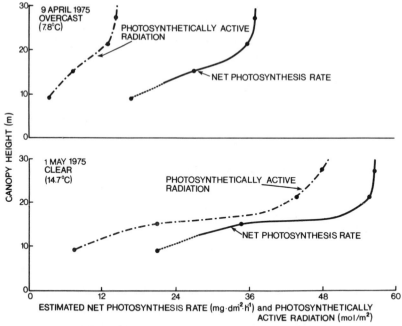

FIGURE 6.18 *Daily totals for estimated net photosynthesis rates and measured photosynthetically active radiation at various heights in the crown of a dominant Douglas-fir on two spring days (overcast versus clear); average air temperature above the canopy is also shown for each day (after D. J. Salo, R. G. Amundson, and R. B. Walker, pers. comm.).*

Crown Aspect

A conifer crown has differential radiation loads impinging upon it, which cause different microclimates and variations in physiological activity with aspect. This seems to be especially true with respect to leaf conductance (Hinckley et al. 1978; Leverenz and Jarvis 1979). Fetcher (1976) found that with large, field-grown lodgepole pine *(Pinus contorta)*, sunlit needles had a mean conductance of water vapor of 0.24 cm/s while shade needles averaged 0.06 cm/s. In contrast, Hinckley and Ritchie (1970), working with Pacific silver fir, have reported more closed stomata (hence lower conductances) on southerly exposed needles compared with more shaded needles, presumably due to induced hydroactive closure arising from high transpiration rates. Though Douglas-fir has a different range of needle conductances (Running 1976), these data indicate the controlling importance of local microclimatic differences in determining the degree of stomatal opening (Leverenz 1981a).

Considerable variation in branch xylem pressure potentials is possible within the crowns of large Douglas-fir, because various plant and environmental factors combine to influence internal water supply and demand at particular locations (Hinckley et al. 1978). Variations one might expect in conifers are summarized in Table 6.4. In general, the greatest variation is associated with days marked by high evaporative demand and moderate soil water deficits. At lower soil water levels, hydroactive stomatal closure reduces water losses throughout the crown and variability in xylem pressure potentials decreases. Furthermore, the greatest variability can be expected to occur within the crown, as such measurements reflect both the variation due to differential radiation loads as well as hydrostatic pressure differences due to height.

When considering net photosynthesis rates in large Douglas-fir, light appears to be the primary factor controlling variability throughout the crown (Salo 1974). For example, Woodman (1971b) has reported that maxima in daily total net photosynthesis occur on the south side of a dominant Douglas-fir crown while minima occur on the north; the east and west sides have similar rates. When these findings are viewed with vertical variations in net photosynthesis rates, the crown can be divided into distinct, three-dimensional zones depending on the maximum daily mean net photosynthesis possible: Zone I is the highest (about 3.0 mg $CO_2 \cdot g^{-1} \cdot h^{-1}$) and is located near midcrown at the boundary between continuous sun and shade conditions; while zone III is the lowest (about 0.5 mg $CO_2 \cdot g^{-1} \cdot h^{-1}$) and is located at the very bottom of the crown. Zone II has maximum daily mean photosynthesis rates of about 1 to 3 mg $CO_2 \cdot g^{-1} \cdot h^{-1}$. It is located at the top of the crown under full sun conditions and in the bottom half of the crown between zones I and III.

Varying microclimates would also be expected to affect transpiration rates

TABLE 6.4 *Expected variation in xylem pressure potential within a branch, between sun- and shade-exposed branches, and within a conifer tree.[a]*

Environmental conditions[b]		Location within conifer ($\pm$MPa)[c]		
Atmospheric evaporative demand	Soil water potential	Within branch	Sun vs. shade	Within tree
Very low	Very high	0.01	0.03	0.04
Low	High	0.04	0.06	0.07
Moderate	Low	0.06	0.11	0.16
High	High	0.06	0.11	0.16
High	Low-medium	0.10	0.19	0.27
High	Medium	0.14	0.20	0.31

[a]From Hinckley et al. 1978.

[b]Atmospheric evaporative demand ranges from less than 0.5 kPa to greater than 3.5 kPa while soil water potential ranges from greater than or equal to −0.03 MPa to less than −1.5 MPa.

[c]Data combined for various conifers under field conditions (Waring and Cleary 1967; Hinckley and Ritchie 1970; Hinckley and Scott 1971; Kotar 1972; Lassoie 1973).

from various portions of a Douglas-fir crown; the controlling factors are primarily those affecting the evaporative gradient between the leaf and the air. Differences in foliar water loss between eastern and western crown sections of a 15-m Pacific silver fir have been noted by Hinckley and Ritchie (1970). In addition, when soil moisture was relatively low, transpiration in Norway spruce *(Picea excelsa)* was found to be greater in the lower portion of the crown than in the upper (Pisek and Tranquillini 1951). When soil moisture was high, the trend was reversed. Similar results have been observed by Beardsell et al. (1972) in Sitka spruce. Furthermore, indirect evidence has been provided by the investigations of Lassoie et al. (1977c), who examined sap velocities in a twenty-year-old, dominant Douglas-fir stem. They found that the highest velocities occurred on the south side of the stem and the lowest on the north. An interrelation between stem aspect and time of day was observed, as the east side had the greatest rates in the morning and the west side had the greatest rates in the late afternoon. It is tempting to suggest that these data indicate the daily progression of differential radiation loads on the crown. This conclusion must be viewed carefully, however, as the sap-ascent pattern in Douglas-fir is actually much more complicated due to the anatomical complexity of the xylem system (Rudinsky and Vité 1959).

Conifers retain their needles for a number of years depending upon species, tree vigor, and environment (see Chapter 5); hence their crowns are composites of needles that differ morphologically and physiologically. Needles throughout a Douglas-fir crown are morphologically different depending on the light conditions occurring during their growth and development (Phillips 1967). In a forty-year-old dominant Douglas-fir, the largest needles are those growing in the full sun. Shade needles in the lower canopy are shorter, narrower, and thinner, and have a greater leaf surface area per unit dry weight than needles growing in the sun. A similar needle condition has been observed in one-year-old Douglas-fir seedlings grown under low light intensities (Drew and Ferrell 1977). Furthermore, the number of stomatal rows and the depth of the stomatal tubes increase with height in the crown but the number of stomata per unit length of a row does not. Stomatal densities per unit needle length (lower epidermis) are about 20,000 for sun and 16,000 for shade needles. The influence of these morphological characteristics on observed spatial differences in gas exchange rates and leaf conductances needs to be examined.

Shade-adapted foliage should be characterized by greater assimilatory efficiencies at relatively lower light levels than sun needles, which are in turn capable of utilizing high light intensities producing a much greater total quantity of photosynthate. Shade needles also have a lower light compensation point (net photosynthesis = 0) than sun needles (Larcher 1969). Leverenz (1974) has observed higher net photosynthesis rates in sun-adapted foliage than in needles growing elsewhere, but the difference seemed readily attributable to differences in leaf conductance, dry weight, and radiation intensity.

Leverenz (1974; 1981b) has also suggested that shoot hierarchy may influence net photosynthesis rates. He observed that net photosynthesis and transpiration rates in current-year terminal and lateral shoots had similar patterns of response, however, on warm and sunny days the absolute rates were generally lower in the laterals. Lateral shoots also had larger specific leaf ratios (that is, the area divided by oven-dry weight) than terminal shoots, a characteristic of shade-adapted Douglas-fir needles (Phillips 1967). Differences in gas exchange rates were not directly attributable to differences in microclimate, water status, or carbon dioxide concentration. Leverenz (1974) hypothesized that the controlling factor might involve differences in hormone concentrations. In partial support, Ross (1972) has found that current-year needles are a strong sink for photosynthates that export little carbon until the following year, thereby suggesting a degree of hormonal control. In addition, terminal shoots are a considerably stronger sink than are lateral shoots, based both on the amount of photosynthate exchanged and on actual growth rates. Terminal shoots typically elongate more than laterals and have higher dry weight to leaf area ratios (Leverenz 1981b).

There is a strong physiological relation between shoot growth and cambial activity along the stem owing to the regulatory influence of foliar-derived auxins and photosynthates (Pharis 1976). Since the physiological activity of the foliage varies throughout the crown, the distribution of cambial growth varies at different heights along the stem (Hinckley and Lassoie 1981). For example, the stem basal area increment added annually to a large Douglas-fir is greater at breast height than near midcrown (Lassoie 1975; see Figure 6.13). Though cambial activity, as exemplified by ring width, is generally greater at midcrown heights in large trees, greater basal area increments commonly occur at bole locations below the live crown (Heger 1965; Dobbs 1966; Hinckley and Lassoie 1981). This is primarily the result of the interaction between cambial growth rates and the size of the initial stem in determining the magnitude of basal area increments.

Studies by Dobbs (1966) have supplied a complete picture of the intraseasonal development of longitudinal growth in field-grown Douglas-fir. He observed that ring width increased from the apex to a point in the crown in the vicinity of the most physiologically active foliage, below which ring width decreased (Figure 6.19). This longitudinal pattern is quite typical of coniferous trees in general (Duff and Nolan 1953; Walters and Soos 1962). Dobbs (1966), however, found the mass increment pattern to increase basipetally (Figure 6.19). Mass increment is the product of volume increment and annual ring density or specific gravity. Hence its distribution along a stem is an estimate of the longitudinal distribution of the metabolite consumption and is the result of the interrelation between patterns of photosynthate production, translocation, storage, and utilization. From such data, Dobbs concluded that the distribution of mass increment along the stem was not significantly influenced by patterns

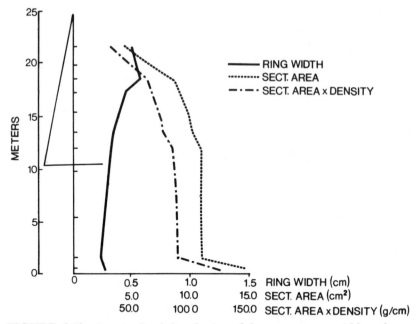

FIGURE 6.19 *Longitudinal distribution of the current-year width, volume increment, and mass increment for a dominant Douglas-fir (after Dobbs 1966).*

of carbohydrates export within the crown. The mass increment distribution is obviously affected by the longitudinal distribution of earlywood and latewood. In Douglas-fir, the maximum width of earlywood generally occurs a short distance from the apex while the maximum latewood occurs below this point, often on the lower bole (Heger 1965). Such patterns indicate the interaction between internal auxin levels and photosynthate production (Kozlowski 1971b).

Tissue Age

Douglas-fir in the humid transition zone usually retain their needles for five to seven years depending on the site and on tree vigor (see Chapter 5). Since the physiological activity of these needles progressively changes as they age, total branch net photosynthesis becomes a component of varying assimilatory rates that depend on needle age as well as local microclimatic factors. Work by Salo (1974), however, suggests that net photosynthesis rates are not affected until the needles are three years old. For example, it appears that the portion of each age class (current-year, one-, and two-years-old) contributing to total branch net photosynthesis closely approximates the fraction contributed to the total branch leaf area (D. J. Salo, pers. comm.). In support, R. G.

Amundson, R. B. Walker, and D. J. Salo (pers. comm.), using excised branches under controlled environmental conditions, have observed that the photosynthetic capacities of second- and third-year needles were, respectively, only 5 percent and 25 percent lower than fully expanded first-year needles. These data are in contrast to those reported for Douglas-fir by other investigators (Woodman 1968; Brix and Ebell 1969; Brix 1971). All these authors noted appreciable decreases in net photosynthesis rates with increasing foliage age (for example, about a 22 percent decrease in maximum net photosynthesis per year of needle age for at least four years).

The impact of foliage age also affects the fate of carbon once it is fixed and involves the relative source-sink strengths of various tree tissues. Ross (1972) has examined the internal dynamics of carbon-14 photoassimilated by different age classes of needles. His results indicated that the relative magnitudes of net photosynthesis measured in foliage of different ages cannot be used as a reliable index for the amount of photosynthate available for growth elsewhere in the tree. The proportion of photosynthate exported from needles was found to be a function of age, with one-year-old needles exporting more than two-year-old needles. Rapidly elongating new needles were observed to be the strongest photosynthetic sinks even after the completion of growth extension, and they exported very little to the rest of the tree compared with older needles. Thus their contribution to stem and branch growth was relatively small. Preferential transport between the sources and sinks depended on the distances and the relative growth rates involved. Both primary and secondary one-year-old needles preferentially translocated photosynthates toward new shoots (acropetally) while two-year-old needles exported more to the stem (basipetally). An exception occurred during periods of active shoot elongation, when two-year-old needles also translocated the bulk of their photosynthates acropetally. It seemed that only the older, less productive, two-year-old needles near the branch base made any significant photosynthate contribution to the stem during its period of rapid diameter growth. Little photosynthate was available from older needles until branch extension growth was near completion. Thus Ross suggested that stored photosynthates possibly play a more important role in cambial growth in Douglas-fir than has been previously recognized.

Age-related effects on net photosynthesis rates seem to be closely tied to the progressive loss of stomatal reactivity to light, which occurs as a leaf ages (Turner 1974). A variety of suggestions have been proposed for this loss of reactivity but the exact causative agent or agents have yet to be clearly identified (Hinckley et al. 1978).

Conductances in western white pine *(Pinus monticola)* needles appear to increase during the first year following emergence (Cline and Campbell 1976). Waggoner and Turner (1971) cited maximum daily leaf conductances for red pine *(Pinus resinosa)* of 0.091, 0.059, 0.045, 0.043, and 0.036 cm/s for newly emerged to four-year-old needles. With Sitka spruce, Watts et al. (1976) reported that recently emerged needles had lower conductances than one-year-old needles, but following complete shoot expansion conductances were similar in both age classes. Contrary to these findings, Running (1976) has detected no differences in leaf conductances of current to three-year-old ponderosa pine *(Pinus ponderosa)* needles. In Douglas-fir saplings he observed a complex relationship between conductance, needle age, and the local environment. Maximum conductances were often higher in older foliage than in current-year foliage but daily averages were usually comparable for all age classes. On a mild day, however, when hydroactive stomatal closure did not occur, average daily leaf conductances were 0.078, 0.066, 0.051, and 0.041 cm/s for current-year to four-year-old foliage. From these and other data, Running suggests that atmospheric humidity has a differential impact depending on needle age while midday xylem pressure potential affects all needle ages equally. Such data might help explain the variable effects that different needle ages seem to have on net photosynthesis in Douglas-fir compared with other species.

SUMMARY

The coastal variety of Douglas-fir (var. *menziesii*) is well adapted physiologically to the mesic, maritime climate (that is, relatively wet, warm winters and dry summers) that characterizes the coniferous forest biome. Douglas-fir abounds throughout the biome, surviving on a variety of sites, living for centuries, and accumulating a tremendous amount of biomass (see Chapter 5). Its longevity is no doubt genetically based but also reflects the relatively low occurrence of major windstorms within the biome (Waring and Franklin 1979).

Douglas-fir is considered intermediate with respect to shade tolerance but is a hearty pioneer species thriving in openings created by glaciation, fires, and logging operations (Fowells 1965). General physiological responses in Douglas-fir to certain environmental factors are not extremely different from those exhibited by other western conifers or even by deciduous trees in other biomes. Net photosynthesis is controlled by such limiting factors as temperature, light, carbon dioxide, and water, which are often mediated through their influence on the stomatal mechanism. In addition, stomatal activity is regulated by the vapor pressure gradient between the leaf and the air and probably by the hormone abscisic acid. These specific responses in combination give Douglas-fir a unique set of physiological characteristics that accounts for its ecological success.

Douglas-fir stomata open very rapidly with increasing light levels and typically reach their maximum aperture at less than 10 percent of full sunlight. Furthermore, the photosynthetic process light-saturates near 25 percent of full sunlight and exhibits a broad temperature optimum between about 2° and 25°C. Therefore, high net photosynthesis rates can occur in Douglas-fir during springs typically marked by relatively cool, overcast climatic conditions. Such relatively high rates occur during the time when photosynthates are needed for the production of new foliage and assure large photosynthetic areas in the future.

Summers in the coniferous forest biome are characterized by limited amounts of water (Waring and Franklin 1979). Throughout much of July, August, and early September precipitation is infrequent and soil moisture levels rapidly decrease while atmospheric evaporative demands remain high. Douglas-fir stomata respond to such conditions and reduce excessive water loss via hydroactive closure. A number of interrelated reactions seem to be involved.

First, maximum stomatal opening during the day is closely regulated by the amount of water in the rhizosphere such that maximum daily needle conductances decrease with decreasing base (predawn) xylem pressure potentials. Second, a threshold xylem pressure potential initiates stomatal closure during the day. This threshold varies between different species and also seems to depend on tree size. For example, Douglas-fir seedlings initiate closure at higher xylem pressure potentials (-1.7 MPa) than saplings (-2.0 MPa) or very large, old-growth trees (-2.2 MPa). These differences may reflect variations in the extent of root development (hence the ability to utilize larger and deeper soil masses), osmotic potential differences, and/or differences in evaporative severities within the respective crowns. In addition, the hydrostatic gradient (0.01 MPa per meter of height) alone can regulate the extent of stomatal opening in very large trees, thereby possibly placing some limit on maximum tree height and water loss from tall, exposed crowns. Third, if threshold water deficits are not reached, needle conductances can be controlled by the atmospheric evaporative demand occurring at the leaf-air interface. Thus high vapor pressure gradients (which include the influence of leaf temperature) can override either base or threshold xylem pressure potentials and the photoactive stomatal response, in order to promote closure or limit aperture size. Therefore Douglas-fir stomata seem capable of fine-tuning their activity to atmospheric conditions, thereby preventing excessive rates of water loss during those times when soil and internal water levels might otherwise promote stomatal opening. Such conditions in the coniferous forest biome would probably exist during the late spring or early summer before a major amount of soil drying had occurred.

It seems definite that low soil moisture levels and high evaporative demands promote hydroactive stomatal closure and reduced carbon dioxide uptake throughout much of the summer in Douglas-fir (see Chapter 3). This species, however, as well as other conifers within the coniferous forest biome and elsewhere, is capable of active net photosynthesis during those periods of the year when its meristems are dormant. Specifically, Douglas-fir can fix a major amount of carbon between October and May owing to its active assimilation at temperatures near freezing and the fact that wintertime environmental conditions are relatively mild throughout the coniferous forest biome (Waring and Franklin 1979).

Douglas-fir needles may be held for five or more years and seem to be a photosynthetic asset for at least three years. During their first year, however, most of their photosynthates go directly into their own growth and development. Once the needles are fully developed, photosynthates are then supplied to other growth centers (for example, buds, cambial and apical meristems, and fruits) and to storage areas, which are utilized at a later date. A large foliar area (that is, small root-to-shoot ratio) can be a liability when water becomes limiting, as it represents the major site for tree water loss. Thus an important tradeoff is necessary between maximizing photosynthate production and maintaining an adequate internal water balance. Such a tradeoff also involves root production and maintenance but these important aspects of tree-water relations were not directly addressed in this chapter.

There are also other features associated with holding multiple age classes of needles that are important to a tree's water balance. Not only are old needles less efficient at fixing carbon dioxide, they also lose relatively less water because of the reduced photoactivity of their stomata. Thus needles progressively become less of a liability as they age. Furthermore, a large amount of foliar biomass promotes selfshading in and between separate branches throughout the crown. This lowers needle temperatures, which in turn reduces vapor pressure gradients and water loss rates. Even though shaded, the needles probably maintain open stomata and high net photosynthesis rates owing to the relatively low light requirements necessary for these processes.

While maintaining a large amount of foliage, Douglas-fir similarly amasses a great quantity of conducting tissue, as the two seem to be hydraulically interrelated. Undoubtedly, the amount of root surface area maintained is similarly interrelated in order to supply the transpiring surfaces adequately. The living tissues and the conducting sapwood in large trees act as internal reservoirs for water and probably nutrients and carbohydrates. Such internal storage of water could be critical to large trees if this source is used to retard hydroactive stomatal closure and to allow for more carbon dioxide uptake than would be possible based only on water supplied by the soil.

Though a qualitative picture of the control of net photosynthesis and tree growth has yielded an understanding of the distribution and abundance of Douglas-fir within the coniferous forest biome, there remain areas of uncertainty and voids in our quantitative understanding of certain physiological processes. Additional effort is needed before a precise interpretation of the abiotic and biotic control of the stomatal mechanism emerges. This is especially true concerning the possibility of synergistic interactions between such factors as vapor pressure gradient, water, temperature, carbon dioxide, and endogenous abscisic acid. The photosynthate translocation process and the biochemical conversion to specific biomass constituents remains vague. This is especially true concerning the carbon dioxide fixed during the growth dormancy period. The intriguing question of storage during this period and mobilization and utilization at a later time needs quantification. In addition, the impact of internal water storage and the possibility of concurrent nutrient storage in portions of large tree stems needs to be tied more closely to stomatal activity, photosynthesis, and tree growth. Furthermore, the water storage phenomenon associated with living tissues near, and including, the cambial zone needs to be more closely related to cambial meristematic activity (both division and elongation), diurnal and seasonal contractions in size, and translocation processes in the phloem (Hinckley et al. 1978). Finally, though not directly addressed in this chapter, there is a need to incorporate root physiological activity into the aboveground phenomena discussed herein.

Faced with the temporal and spatial complexities and variabilities typical of tree physiological processes under field conditions, it is not surprising that many areas remain vague even after years of intense investigation. Such unknowns encourage continued and refined research activities. The research accomplished within the coniferous forest biome under the auspices of the International Biological Program has sharpened our understanding of many physiological processes and has revealed specific voids in our understanding. Perhaps a major value of such studies is not so much what was discovered but what was not. Such identification is, and will remain, the basis on which scientific discipline evolve in order to continually address questions of increasing complexity and importance, thereby enhancing our understanding and appreciation of the ecosystems of the world.

LITERATURE CITED

Allaway, W. G., and F. L. Milthorpe, 1976, Structure and functioning of stomata, in *Water Deficits and Plant Growth, IV: Soil Water Measurement, Plant Responses and Breeding for Drought Resistance,* T. T. Kozlowski, ed., Academic Press, New York, pp. 57–102.

Bauer, H., W. Larcher, and R. B. Walker, 1975, Influence of temperature stress on CO_2-gas exchange, in *Photosynthesis and Productivity in Different Environments,* J. P. Cooper, ed., Cambridge University Press, New York, pp. 557–586.

Bannister, P., 1977, *Introduction to Physiological Plant Ecology,* Halstead Press, New York, 273p.

Beadle, C. L., P. G. Jarvis, and R. E. Neilson, 1979, Leaf conductance as related to xylem water potential and carbon dioxide concentration in Sitka spruce, *Physiol. Plant.* **45:**158–166.

Beardsell, M. F., P. G. Jarvis, and B. Davidson, 1972, A null-balance diffusion porometer suitable for use with leaves of many shapes, *J. Appl. Ecol.* **9:**677–690.

Berlyn, G. P., 1979, Physiological control of differentiation of xylem elements, *Wood and Fiber* **11:**109–126.

Black, C. D., 1973, Photosynthetic carbon fixation in relation to net CO_2 uptake, *Ann. Rev. Plant Physiol.* **24:**253–286.

Blackman, F. F., 1905, Optima and limiting factors, *Ann. Bot.* **19:**281–295.

Blake, J., and W. K. Ferrell, 1977, The association between soil and xylem water potential, leaf resistance and abscisic acid content in droughted seedlings of Douglas-fir *(Pseudotsuga menziesii)*, *Physiol. Plant.* **39**:106–109.

Boyer, W. D., 1970, Shoot growth patterns of young loblolly pine, *For. Sci.* **16**:473–482.

Bradbury, I. K., and D. C. Malcolm, 1978, Dry matter accumulation by *Picea sitchensis* seedlings during winter, *Can. J. For. Res.* **8**:207–213.

Brix, H., 1967, An analysis of dry matter production in Douglas-fir seedlings in relation to temperature and light intensity, *Can. J. Bot.* **45**:2063–2072.

Brix, H., 1971, Effects of nitrogen fertilization on photosynthesis and respiration in Douglas-fir, *For. Sci.* **17**:407–414.

Brix, H., 1972, Nitrogen fertilization and water effects on photosynthesis and earlywood-latewood production in Douglas-fir, *Can. J. For. Res.* **2**:467–478.

Brix, H., and L. F. Ebell, 1969, Effects of nitrogen fertilization on growth, leaf area, and photosynthesis rate in Douglas-fir, *For. Sci.* **15**:189–195.

Brown, R. W., and B. P. Van Haveren, eds., 1972, Psychrometry in water relations research, *Proceedings of the Symposium on Thermocouple Psychrometers,* Utah State University, 17–19 March 1971, Utah Agricultural Experimental Station, Logan, Utah, 342p.

Burrows, F. J., and F. L. Milthorpe, 1976, Stomatal conductance in the control of gas exchange, in *Water Deficits and Plant Growth, IV: Soil Water Measurement, Plant Responses, and Breeding for Drought Resistance,* T. T. Kozlowski, ed., Academic Press, New York, pp. 103–152.

Campbell, R. K., 1979, Genecology of Douglas-fir in a watershed in the Oregon Cascades, *Ecology* **60**:1036–1050.

Campbell, R. K., and A. I. Sugano, 1979, Genecology of bud-burst phenology in Douglas-fir: Response to flushing temperature and chilling, *Bot. Gaz.* **140**:223–231.

Chung, H.-H., and R. L. Barnes, 1977, Photosynthate allocation in *Pinus taeda,* I: Substrate requirements for synthesis of shoot biomass, *Can. J. For. Res.* **7**:106–111.

Chung, H.-H., and R. L. Barnes, 1980a, Photosynthate allocation in *Pinus taeda,* II: Seasonal aspects of photosynthate allocation to different biochemical fractions in shoots, *Can. J. For. Res.* **10**:338–347.

Chung, H.-H., and R. L. Barnes, 1980b, Photosynthate allocation in *Pinus taeda,* III: Photosynthate economy: Its production, consumption and balance in shoots during the growing season, *Can. J. For. Res.* **10**:348–356.

Clements, J. R., 1970, Shoot responses of young red pine to watering applied over two seasons, *Can. J. Bot.* **48**:75–80.

Cline, R. G., and G. S. Campbell, 1976, Seasonal and diurnal water relations of selected forest species, *Ecology* **57**:367–373.

Coutts, M. P., 1980, Control of water loss by actively growing Sitka spruce seedlings after transplanting, *J. Exper. Bot.* **31**:1587–1597.

Davies, W. J., and T. T. Kozlowski, 1974, Stomatal responses of five woody angiosperms to light intensity and humidity, *Can. J. Bot.* **52**:1525–1534.

Dobbs, R. C., 1966, The intraseasonal development of longitudinal growth patterns in Douglas-fir *(Pseudotsuga menziesii* [Mirb.] Franco.), Ph.D. dissertation, University of Washington, Seattle, 157p.

Dobbs, R. C., 1969, An electrical device for recording small fluctuations and accumulated increment of tree stem circumference, *For. Chron.* **45**:187–189.

Dobbs, R. C., and D. R. M. Scott, 1971, Distribution of diurnal fluctuations in stem circumference of Douglas-fir, *Can. J. For. Res.* **1**:80–83.

Doley, D., and L. Leyton, 1968, Effects of growth regulating substances and water potential on the development of secondary xylem in Fraxinus, *New Phytol.* **67**:579-594.

Doraiswamy, P. C., 1977, The radiation budget and evapotranspiration of a Douglas-fir stand. Ph.D. dissertation, Univ. Washington, Seattle, 164p.

Dougherty, P. M., and T. M. Hinckley, 1979, Net photosynthesis and early growth trends of a dominant white oak, *Plant Physiol.* **64**:930–935.

Dougherty, P. M., and T. M. Hinckley, 1981, The influence of a severe drought on net photosynthesis of white oak, *Can. J. Bot.* **59**:335–341.

Drew, A. P., and W. K. Ferrell, 1977, Morphological acclimation to light intensity in Douglas-fir seedlings, *Can. J. Bot.* **55**:2033–2042.

Drew, A. P., and W. K. Ferrell, 1979, Seasonal changes in the water balance of Douglas-fir *(Pseudotsuga menziesii)* seedlings grown under different light intensities, *Can. J. Bot.* **57**:666–674.

Drew, A. P., L. G. Drew, and H. C. Fitts, 1972, Environmental control of stomata activity in mature semiarid ponderosa pine, *Ariz. Acad. Sci.* **7**:85–93.

Duff, G. H., and N. J. Nolan, 1953, Growth and morphogenesis in the Canadian forest species, I: The controls of cambial and apical activity in *Pinus resinosa* Ait, *Can. J. Bot.* **31**:471–513.

Ellenberg, H., ed., 1971, *Integrated Experimental Ecology: Methods and Results of Ecosystem Research in the German Solling Project,* Ecological Studies, Vol. 2, Springer-Verlag, New York, 214p.

Emmingham, W. H., 1977, Comparison of selected Douglas-fir seed sources for cambial and leader growth patterns in four western Oregon environments, *Can. J. For. Res.* **7**:154–164.

Emmingham, W. H., and R. H. Waring, 1977, An index of photosynthesis for comparing forest sites in western Oregon, *Can. J. For. Res.* **7**:165–174.

Evans, A. K., 1973, Patterns of water stress in Engelmann spruce, M.S. thesis, Colorado State University, Fort Collins, 57p.

Fahey, T. J., 1979, The effect of night frost on the transpiration of *Pinus contorta* ssp. *latifolia, Oecol. Plant.* **14**:483–490.

Federer, C. A., 1977, Leaf resistance and xylem potential differ among broadleaved species, *For. Sci.* **23**:411-419.

Federer, C. A., and G. W. Gee, 1976, Diffusion resistance and xylem potential in stressed and unstressed northern hardwood trees, *Ecology* **57**:975-984.

Fetcher, N., 1976, Patterns of leaf resistance to lodgepole pine transpiration in Wyoming, *Ecology* **57**:339-345.

Fowells, H., 1965, Silvics of forest trees of the United States, *U.S. Department of Agriculture Handbook No. 271,* U.S. Department of Agriculture Forest Service, Washington, D.C., 762p.

Fritschen, L. J., and P. Doraiswamy, 1973, Dew: An addition to the hydraulic balance of Douglas-fir, *Water Resour. Res.* **9**:891-894.

Fritschen, L. J., L. Cox, and R. Kinerson, 1973, A 28-meter Douglas-fir in a weighing lysimeter, *For. Sci.* **19**:256-261.

Fritschen, L. J., J. Hsia, and P. Doraiswamy, 1977, Evapotranspiration of a Douglas-fir determined with a weighing lysimeter, *Water Resour. Res.* **13**:145-148.

Fry, K. E., 1965, A study of transpiration and photosynthesis in relation to the stomatal resistance and internal water potential in Douglas-fir, Ph.D. dissertation, University of Washington, Seattle, 192p.

Fry, K. E., and R. B. Walker, 1967, A pressure-infiltration method for estimating stomatal opening in conifers, *Ecology* **48**:155-157.

Gentle, S. W., 1963, The effect of local weather conditions on the assimilation of carbon dioxide by Douglas-fir in western Washington, Ph.D. dissertation, University of Washington, Seattle, 122p.

Gordon, J. C., and P. R. Larson, 1968, Seasonal course of photosynthesis, respiration, and distribution of C in young *Pinus resinosa* trees as related to wood formation, *Plant Physiol.* **43**:1617-1624.

Green, J. W., 1969, Continuous measurements of radial variation in *Eucalyptus pauciflora* (Sieb.) ex spreng, *Aust. J. Bot.* **17**:191-198.

Green, K., and R. Wright, 1977, Field response of photosynthesis to CO_2 enhancement in ponderosa pine, *Ecology* **55**:687-692.

Grier, C. C., and S. W. Running, 1977, Leaf area of mature northwestern coniferous forests: Relation to site water balance, *Ecology* **58**:893-899.

Grier, C. C., and R. H. Waring, 1974, Conifer foliage mass related to sapwood area, *For. Sci.* **20**:205-206.

Grillos, S. J., and F. H. Smith, 1959, The secondary phloem of Douglas-fir, *For. Sci.* **5**:377-388.

Hales, S., 1727, *Vegetable Statics,* W. and J. Innys and T. Woodward, London, 111p.

Hall, A. E., and M. R. Kaufmann, 1975, Regulation of water transport in the soil-plant-atmosphere continuum, in *Perspectives of Biophysical Ecology,* D. M. Gates and R. B. Schmerl, eds., Ecological Studies Vol. 12, Springer-Verlag, New York, pp. 187-202.

Hall, A. E., E. D. Shutze, and O. L. Lange, 1976, Current perspectives of steady-state stomatal responses to environment, in *Water and Plant Life—*

Problems of Modern Approaches, O. L. Lange, L. Kappen, and E. D. Shutze, eds., Ecological Studies Vol. 19, Springer-Verlag, New York, pp. 169–188.

Hallgren, S. W., 1978, Plant water relations in Douglas-fir seedlings and screening sepected families for drought resistance, M.S. thesis, Oregon State University, Corvallis, 68p.

Hammel, H. T., 1967, Freezing of xylem sap without cavitation, *Plant Physiol.* **42:**55–66.

Hartt, C. E., and H. P. Kortschak, 1967, Translocation of C^{14} in the sugar cane plant during day and night, *Plant Physiol.* **42:**89–94.

Heger, L., 1965, Morphogenesis of stems of Douglas-fir *(Pseudotsuga menziesii* [Mirb.] Franco.), Ph.D. dissertation, University of British Columbia, Vancouver, 176p.

Hellkvist, J., G. P. Richards, and P. G. Jarvis, 1974, Vertical gradients of water potential and tissue water relations in Sitka spruce trees measured with the pressure chamber, *J. Appl. Ecol.* **11:**637–668.

Helms, J. A., 1964, Apparent photosynthesis of Douglas-fir in relation to silviculture treatment, *For. Sci.* **10:**432–442.

Helms, J. A., 1965, Diurnal and seasonal patterns of net assimilation in Douglas-fir, *Pseudotsuga menziesii* (Mirb.) Franco, *Ecology* **46:**698–708.

Hermann, R. K., 1977, Growth and production of tree roots: A review, in *The Belowground Ecosystem: A Synthesis of Plant-Associated Processes,* J. K. Marshall, ed., Range Sci. Dep. Sci. Ser. 26, Colorado State University, Fort Collins, pp. 7–28.

Hermann, R. K., and D. P. Lavender, 1968, Early growth of Douglas-fir from various altitudes and aspects in southern Oregon, *Silvae Genet.* **17:**143–151.

Hinckley, T. M., 1971, Estimate of water flow in Douglas-fir seedlings, *Ecology,* **52:**525–528.

Hinckley, T. M., and J. P. Lassoie, 1981, Radial growth in conifers and deciduous trees: A comparison, in *Proceedings of the I.U.F.R.O. Symposium on Radial Growth in Trees,* W. Tranquillini, ed., Innsbruck, Austria, Sept. 1980 (in press).

Hinckley, T. M., and G. A. Ritchie, 1970, Within-crown patterns of transpiration, water stress, and stomatal activity in *Abies amabilis, For. Sci.* **16:**490–492.

Hinckley, T. M., and G. A. Ritchie, 1973, A theoretical model for calculation of xylem sap pressures from climatological data, *Am. Midl. Nat.* **90:**56–69.

Hinckley, T. M., and D. R. M. Scott, 1971, Estimates of water loss and its relation to environmental parameters in Douglas-fir saplings, *Ecology* **52:**520–524.

Hinckley, T. M., J. P. Lassoie, and S. W. Running, 1978, Temporal and spatial variations in the water status of forest trees, *For. Sci. Monogr. No. 20,* 72p.

Hinckley, T. M., J. L. Chambers, D. N. Bruckerhoff, J. E. Roberts, and J. Turner, 1974, Effect of mid-day shading on net assimilation rate, leaf surface resistance, branch diameter, and xylem potential in a white oak sapling, *Can. J. For. Res.* **4:**296–300.

Hinckley, T. M., M. O. Schroeder, J. E. Roberts, and D. N. Bruckerhoff, 1975, Effect of several environmental variables and xylem pressure potential on leaf surface resistance in white oak, *For. Sci.* **21:**201–211.

Holmgren, P., P. G. Jarvis, and M. S. Jarvis, 1965, Resistances to carbon dioxide and water vapor transfer in leaves of different plant species, *Physiol. Plant.* **18:**557–573.

Hopkins, E. R., 1968, Fluctuations in the girth of regrowth eucalypt stems, *Aust. For.* **32:**95–110.

Hsiao, T. C., 1973, Plant responses to water stress, *Ann. Rev. Plant Physiol.* **24:**519–570.

Huber, B., 1956, Die Gefassleitung, in *Handbuch der Pflanzen physiologie,* W. Ruhland, ed., vol. III, Springer-Verlag, Berlin, pp. 841–852.

Irgens-Moller, H., 1968, Geographical variation in growth patterns of Douglas-fir, *Silvae Genet.* **17:**106–110.

Jarvis, P. G., 1971, The estimation of resistance to carbon dioxide transfer, in *Plant photosynthetic production: Manual of methods,* Z. Šesták, J. Čatsky, and P. G. Jarvis, eds., Dr. W. Junk N. V. Publishers, The Hague, pp. 556–631.

Jarvis, P. G., 1975, Water transfer in plants, in *Heat and Mass Transfer in the Environment of Biosphere, I: Transfer Processes in the Plant Environment,* D. A. de Vries and N. H. Afyan, eds., 1974 Seminar of the International Centre for Heat and Mass Transfer, Dubrovnik, Scripta Book Co., Washington, D. C., pp. 369–394.

Jarvis, P. G., 1976, The interpretation of the variations in leaf water potential and stomatal conductance found in canopies in the field, *Phil. Trans. Royal Soc., London, Ser. B,* **273:**593–610.

Jarvis, P. G., and M. S. Jarvis, 1964, Growth rates of woody plants, *Physiol. Plant.* **17:**654–666.

Kanemasu, E. T., ed., 1975, Measurement of stomatal aperture and diffusive resistance. *College of Agricultural Research Center Bull. No. 809,* Washington State University, Pullman, 38p.

Kaufmann, M. R., 1976, Stomatal response of Engelmann spruce to humidity, light and water stress, *Plant Physiol.* **57:**898–901.

Kinerson, R. S., 1973, Fluxes of visible and net radiation within a forest canopy, *J. Appl. Ecol.* **10:**657–660.

Kinerson, R. S., 1974, Selected aspects of CO_2 and H_2O exchange in a Douglas-fir stand, *Am. Midl. Nat.* **91:**170–181.

Kinerson, R. S., and L. J. Fritschen, 1973, Modeling air flow through vegetation, *Agric. Meteorol.* **12:**95–104.

Kline, J. R., J. R. Martin, C. F. Jordan, and J. J. Koranda, 1970, Measurement of transpiration in tropical trees using tritiated water, *Ecology* **51:**1068–1073.

Kline, J. R., K. L. Reed, R. H. Waring, and M. L. Stewart, 1976, Field measurement of transpiration in Douglas-fir. *J. Appl. Ecol.* **13:**273–283.

Körner, Ch., J. A. Scheel, and H. Baver, 1979, Maximum leaf conductance in vascular plants, *Photosynthetica* **13:**45–82.

Kotar, J., 1972, Ecology of *Abies amabilis* in relation to its altitudinal distribution and in contrast to its common associate *Tsuga heterophylla,* Ph.D. dissertation, University of Washington, Seattle, 172p.

Kozlowski, T. T., 1971a, *Growth and Development of Trees; 1: Seed Germination, Ontogeny, and Shoot Growth,* Academic Press, New York, 443p.

Kozlowski, T. T., 1971b, *Growth and Development of Trees, II: Cambial Growth, Root Growth, and Reproductive Growth,* Academic Press, New York, 514p.

Kramer, P. J., and T. T. Kozlowski, 1979, *Physiology of Woody Plants,* Academic Press, New York, 811p.

Krueger, K. W., and W. K. Ferrell, 1965, Comparative photosynthesis and respiratory response to temperature and light by *Pseudotsuga menziesii* var. *menziesii* and var. *glauca* seedlings, *Ecology* **46:**794–801.

Krueger, K. W., and R. H. Ruth, 1969, Comparative photosynthesis of red alder, Douglas-fir, Sitka spruce and western hemlock seedlings, *Can. J. Bot.* **47:**519–527.

Lange, O. L., R. Losch, E. D. Schulze, and L. Kappen, 1971, Response of stomata to changes in humidity, *Planta* **100:**76–86.

Larcher, W., 1969, The effect of environmental and physiological variables on the carbon dioxide gas exchange of trees, Photosynthetica **3:**167–198.

Larcher, W., 1975, *Physiological Plant Ecology,* Springer-Verlag, New York, 252p.

Lassoie, J. P., 1973, Diurnal dimensional fluctuations in a Douglas-fir stem in response to tree water status, *For. Sci.* **19:**251–255.

Lassoie, J. P., 1975, Diurnal and seasonal basal area fluctuations in Douglas-fir tree stems of different crown classes in response to tree water status, Ph.D. dissertation, University of Washington, Seattle, 301p.

Lassoie, J. P., 1979, Stem dimensional fluctuations in Douglas-fir of different crown classes, *For. Sci.* **25:**132–144.

Lassoie, J. P., and J. L. Chambers, 1976, The effects of an extreme drought on tree water status and net assimilation rates of northern red oak under greenhouse conditions, in *Central Hardwood Forest Conference Proceedings,* J. S. Fralish, G. T. Weaver, and R. C. Schlesinger, eds., Southern Illinois University, Carbondale, pp. 269–283.

Lassoie, J. P., and D. J. Salo, 1981, Physiological response of large Douglas-fir to natural and induced soil water deficits, *Can. J. For. Res.* **11:**139–144.

Lassoie, J. P., P. M. Dougherty, and T. M. Hinckley, 1977a, Fall and winter gas exchange rates in *Juniperus virginiana* L., *Bull. Ecol. Soc. Am.* (Abstr.) **58:**43.

Lassoie, J. P., N. Fetcher, and D. J. Salo, 1977b, Stomatal infiltration pressures versus diffusion porometer measurements of needle resistance in Douglas-fir and lodgepole pine, *Can. J. For. Res.* **7:**192–196.

Lassoie, J. P., D. R. M. Scott, and L. J. Fritschen, 1977c, Stem sap velocity studies of transpiration in Douglas-fir using the heat pulse technique, *For. Sci.* **23:**377–390.

Ledig, F. T., 1969, A growth model for tree seedlings based on the rate of photosynthesis and the distribution of photosynthate, *Photosynthetica* **3:**263–275.

Leverenz, J. W., 1974, Net photosynthesis as related to shoot hierarchy in a large dominant Douglas-fir tree, M.S. thesis, University of Washington, Seattle, 126p.

Leverenz, J. W., 1981a, Photosynthesis and transpiration in large forest-grown Douglas-fir: Diurnal variation, *Can. J. Bot.* **59:**349–356.

Leverenz, J. W., 1981b, Photosynthesis and transpiration in large forest-grown Douglas-fir: Interactions with apical control, *Can. J. Bot.* (in press).

Leverenz, J. W., and P. G. Jarvis, 1979, Photosynthesis in Sitka spruce, VIII: The effects of light flux density and direction on the rate of net photosynthesis of the stomatal conductance of needles, *J. Appl. Ecol.* **16:**919–932.

Linder, S., and E. Troeng, 1977, Gas exchange in a 20-year-old stand of Scots pine, *Swedish Coniferous Forest Project, Int. Rep. 57,* Uppsala, Sweden, 14p.

Little, C. H. A., 1975, Inhibition of cambial activity in *Abies balsemea* by internal water stress: Role of abscisic acid, *Can. J. Bot.* **53:**3041–3050.

Little, C. H. A., and D. C. Eidt, 1968, Effects of abscisic acid on bud break and transpiration in woody species, *Nature* **220:**498–499.

Livne, A., and Y. Vaadia, 1972, Water deficits and hormone relations, in *Water Relations and Plant Growth, III: Plant Responses and Control of Water Balance,* T. T. Kozlowski, ed., Academic Press, New York, pp. 255–275.

Loach, K., and C. H. A. Little, 1973, Production, storage, and use of photosynthate during shoot elongation in balsam fir, *Can. J. Bot.* **51:**1161–1168.

Long, J. N., F. W. Smith, and D. R. M. Scott, 1981, The role of stem sapwood and heartwood in the mechanical and physiological support of Douglas-fir crowns, *Can. J. For. Res.* **11:**459–464.

Lopushinsky, W., 1969, Stomatal closure in conifer seedlings in response to leaf moisture stress, *Bot. Gaz.* **130:**258–263.

Ludlow, M. M., and P. G. Jarvis, 1971, Photosynthesis in Sitka spruce (*Picea sitchensis* [Bong.] Carr.), *J. Appl. Ecol.* **8:**925–953.

Meidner, H., and T. A. Mansfield, 1968, *Physiology of Stomata,* McGraw-Hill, New York, 179p.

Meidner, H., and C. Willmer, 1975, Mechanics and metabolism of guard cells, *Comment. Plant Sci.* **17:**1–15.

Namken, L. N., J. F. Bartholic, and J. R. Runkles, 1969, Monitoring cotton plant stem radius as an indication of water stress, *Agron. J.* **61:**891–893.

Neilson, R. E., and P. G. Jarvis, 1976, Photosynthesis in Sitka spruce (*Picea sitchensis* [Bong.] Carr.), VI: Response of stomata to temperature, *J. Appl. Ecol.* **12:**879–891.

Ng, P. A. P., 1978, Response of stomata to environmental variables in *Pinus sylvestris* L., Ph. D. dissertation, University of Edinburgh, Edinburgh, Scotland, 200p.

Ng, P. A. P., and P. G. Jarvis, 1980, Hystersis in the response of stomatal conductance in *Pinus sylvestris* L. needles to light: Observations and a hypothesis, *Plant Cell Environ.* **3:**207–216.

Norman, J. M., and P. G. Jarvis, 1974, Photosynthesis in Sitka spruce (*Picea sitchensis* [Bong.] Carr.), III: Measurement of canopy structure and interception of radiation, *J. Appl. Ecol.* **11:**375–398.

Norman, J. M., and P. G. Jarvis, 1975, Photosynthesis in Sitka spruce (*Picea sitchensis* [Bong.] Carr.), IV: Radiation penetration theory and a test case, *J. Appl. Ecol.* **12:**839–878.

Oertli, J. J., 1971, A whole-system approach to water physiology in plants, *Adv. Front. Plant Sci.* **27:**1–283.

Pharis, R. P., 1976, Probable roles of plant hormones in regulating shoot elongation, diameter and crown form of coniferous trees, in *Tree Physiology and Tree Improvement,* M. G. R. Cannell and F. T. Last, eds., Academic Press, New York, pp. 291–306.

Pharis, R. P., H. Hellmers, and E. Schuurmans, 1970, Effects of subfreezing temperatures on photosynthesis of evergreen conifers under controlled environment conditions, *Photosynthetica* **4:**273–279.

Phillips, R. A., 1967, Stomatal characteristics through a tree crown, M.S. thesis, University of Washington, Seattle, 67p.

Pisek, A., and W. Tranquillini, 1951, Transpiration und Wasserhaushalt der Fichte *(Picea excelsa)* bei zunehmender Luft- und Bodentrochenheit, *Physiol. Plant.* **4:**1–26.

Pisek, A., W. Larcher, A. Vegis, and K. Napp-Zinn, 1973, The normal temperature ranges, *Temperature and Life,* H. Precht, J. Christophersen, H. Hensel, and W. Larcher, eds., Springer-Verlag, New York, pp. 102–194.

Plaut, Z., and L. Reinhold, 1969, Concomitant photosynthesis implicated in the light effect on translocation in bean plants, *Aust. J. Biol. Sci.* **22:**1105–1111.

Puritch, G. S., 1973, Effect of water stress on photosynthesis, respiration, and transpiration of four *Abies* species, *Can. J. For. Res.* **3:**293–298.

Reed, K. L., 1968, The effects of sub-zero temperatures on the stomata of Douglas-fir, M.S. thesis, University of Washington, Seattle, 79p.

Reed, K. L., and R. H. Waring, 1974, Coupling of the environment to plant response: A simulation model of transpiration, *Ecology* **55**:62–72.

Reed, K. L., E. R. Hamerly, B. E. Dinger, and P. G. Jarvis, 1976. An analytical model for field measurement of photosynthesis, *J. Appl. Ecol.* **13**:925–942.

Rehfeldt, G. E., 1974, Local differentiation of populations of Rocky Mountain Douglas-fir, *Can. J. For. Res.* **4**:399–406.

Rehfeldt, G. E., 1977, Growth and cold hardiness of intervarietal hybrids of Douglas-fir, *Theor. Appl. Genet.* **50**:3–15.

Rehfeldt, G. E., 1979a, Ecological adaptations in Douglas-fir *(Pseudotsuga menziesii* var. *glauca)* populations, I: Northern Idaho and north-east Washington, *Heredity* **43**:383–397.

Rehfeldt, G. E., 1979b, Genetic differentiation of Douglas-fir populations from the northern Rocky Mountains, *Ecology* **59**:1264–1270.

Reich, P. B., R. O. Teskey, P. S. Johnson, and T. M. Hinckley, 1980, Periodic root and shoot growth in oak, *For. Sci.* **26**:590–598.

Richter, H., 1973, Frictional potential losses and total water potential in plants: A re-evaluation, *J. Exp. Bot.* **24**:983–994.

Richter, H., 1974, Erhohte Saugspannungswerte und morphologische Veranderungen durch transversale Einschnitte in einem *Taxus*—Stamm, *Flora* **163**:291–309.

Ritchie, G. A., and T. M. Hinckley, 1975, The pressure chamber as an instrument for ecological research, *Adv. Ecol. Res.* **9**:165–254.

Roberts, J., 1976, An examination of the quantity of water in mature *Pinus sylvestris* L., *J. Exp. Bot.* **27**:473–479.

Rogers, R., and T. M. Hinckley, 1979, Foliar mass and area related to current sapwood area in oak, *For. Sci.* **25**:298–303.

Ross, S. D., 1972, The seasonal and diurnal source-sink relationships for photo-assimilated ^{14}C in the Douglas-fir branch, Ph.D. dissertation, University of Washington, Seattle, 99p.

Rudinsky, J. A., and J. P. Vité, 1959, Certain ecological and phylogenetic aspects of the pattern of water conduction in conifers, *For. Sci.* **5**:259–266.

Running, S. W., 1976, Environmental control of leaf water conductance in conifers, *Can. J. For. Res.* **6**:104–112.

Running, S. W., 1980, Relating plant capacitance to the water relations of *Pinus contorta, For. Ecol. Man.* **2**:237–252.

Running, S. W., R. H. Waring, and R. A. Rydell, 1975, Physiological control of water flux in conifers—A computer simulation model, *Oecologia* **18**:1–16.

Salo, D. J., 1969, A study of the exchange of O_2 and CO_2 in plants, M.S. thesis, University of Washington, Seattle, 75p.

Salo, D. J., 1974, Factors affecting photosynthesis in Douglas-fir, Ph.D. dissertation, University of Washington, Seattle, 150p.

Santantonio, D., R. K. Hermann, and W. S. Overton, 1977, Root biomass studies in forest ecosystems, *Pedogiologia* **17**:1–31.

Schulze, E.-D., 1970, Der CO_2-Gaswechsel der buche *(Fagus silvatica* L.) in Abhangigkeit von den klimafaktoren im Freiland, *Flora* **159:**177–232.

Schulze, E.-D., O. L. Lange, M. Evenari, L. Kappen, and U. Buschbom, 1975, The role of air humidity and temperature in controlling stomatal resistance of *Prunus armeniace* L. under desert conditions, *Oecologia* **19:**303–314.

Šesták, Z. J. Čatský, and P. G. Jarvis, eds., 1971, *Plant Photosynthetic Production: Manual of Methods,* Dr. W. Junk N. V. Publishers, The Hague, 818p.

Shepherd, K. R., 1964, Some observations on the effect of drought on the growth of *Pinus radiata* D. Don., *Aust. For.* **28:**7–22.

Sorensen, F. C., 1979, Provenance variation in *Pseudotsuga menziesii* seedlings from the var. *menziesii*-var. *glauca* transition zone in Oregon, *Silvae Genet.* **28:**96–103.

Sorensen, F. C., and W. K. Ferrell, 1973, Photosynthesis and growth of Douglas-fir seedlings when grown in different environments, *Can. J. Bot.* **51:**1689–1698.

Spurr, S. H., and B. V. Barnes, 1980, *Forest Ecology,* 3rd ed., John Wiley and Sons, New York, 687p.

Srivastava, L. M., 1963, *Secondary Phloem in the* Pinaceae, University of California Press, Berkeley, 141p.

Stålfelt, M. G., 1962, The effects of temperature on opening of the stomatal cells, *Physiol. Plant.* **15:**772–779.

Stewart, C. M., 1967, Moisture content in living trees, *Nature* **214:** 138–140.

Sucoff, E., 1972, Water potential in red pine: Soil moisture, evapotranspiration, crown position, *Ecology* **53:**681–686.

Swanson, R. H., 1967, Seasonal course of transpiration of lodgepole pine and Engelmann spruce, in *Proceedings of the International Symposium of Forest Hydrology* W. E. Sopper and H. W. Lull, eds., Pergamon Press, Oxford, pp. 417–432.

Swanson, R. H., 1972, Water transpired by trees is indicated by heat pulse velocity, *Agric. Meteorol.* **10:**277–281.

Tan. C. S., T. A. Black, and J. U. Nnyamah, 1977, Characteristics of stomatal diffusion resistance in a Douglas-fir forest exposed to soil water deficits, *Can. J. For. Res.* **7:**595–604.

Turner, N. C., 1974, Stomatal response to light and water under field conditions, in *Mechanisms of Regulation of Plant Growth,* R. L. Bieleski, A. R. Ferguson, and M. M. Cresswell, eds., Bull. 12, The Royal Society of New Zealand, Wellington, pp. 423–432.

Turner, N. C., and H. C. DeRoo, 1974, Hydration of eastern hemlock as influenced by waxing and weather, *For. Sci.* **20:**19–24.

Turner, N. C., F. C. C. Pedersen, and W. H. Wright, 1969, An aspirated diffusion porometer for field use. *Connecticut Agricultural Experimental Station Special Soils Bull. No. 29,* New Haven, Conn., 12p.

Tyree, M. T., and P. Yianoulis, 1980, The site of water evaporation from sub-stomatal cavities, liquid path resistance and hydroactive and stomatal closure, *Ann. Bot.* **46:**175–193.

Vaadia, Y., F. C. Raney, and R. M. Hagan, 1961, Plant water deficits and physiological processes, *Ann. Rev. Plant Physiol.* **12:**265–292.

Waggoner, P. E., and N. C. Turner, 1971, Transpiration and its control by stomata in a pine forest, *Connecticut Agricultural Experimental Station Bulletin No. 726,* New Haven, Conn., 87p.

Walker, R. B., D. R. M. Scott, D. J. Salo, and K. L. Reed, 1972, Terrestrial process studies in conifers—A review, in *Proceedings—Research on Coniferous Forest Ecosystems—A Symposium,* J. F. Franklin, L. J. Dempster, and R. H. Waring, eds., U.S. Department of Agriculture Forest Service, Portland, Oreg., pp. 211–225.

Walters, J., and J. Soos, 1962, The vertical and horizontal organization of growth in some conifers of British Columbia, *Faculty of Forestry, University of British Columbia Research Paper 51,* Vancouver, B.C., 11p.

Waring, R. H., and B. D. Cleary, 1967, Plant moisture stress: Evaluation by pressure bomb, *Science* **155:**1248–1254.

Waring, R. H., and J. F. Franklin, 1979, Evergreen forests of the Pacific Northwest. *Science* 204:1380–1386.

Waring, R. H., and S. W. Running, 1976, Water uptake, storage and transpiration by conifers: A physiological model, in *Water and Plant Life,* O. L. Lange, L. Kappen, and E. D. Schulz, eds., Ecological Studies vol. 19, Springer-Verlag, New York, pp. 189–202.

Waring, R. H., and S. W. Running, 1978, Sapwood water storage: Its contribution to transpiration and effect upon water conductance through the stems of old growth Douglas-fir, *Plant Cell Environ.* **1:**131–140.

Waring, R. H., D. Whitehead, and P. G. Jarvis, 1980, Comparison of an isotropic method and the Penman-Monteith equation for estimating transpiration from Scots pine, *Can. J. For. Res.* **10:**555–558.

Waring, R. H., H. L. Gholz, C. C. Grier, and M. L. Plummer, 1977, Evaluating stem conducting tissue as an estimator of leaf area in four woody angiosperms, *Can. J. Bot.* **55:**1474–1477.

Watts, W. R., R. E. Neilson, and P. G. Jarvis, 1976, Photosynthesis in Sitka spruce *(Picea sitchensis* [Bong.] Carr), VII: Measurement of stomatal conductance and $^{14}CO_2$ uptake in a forest canopy, *J. Appl. Ecol.* **13:**623–639.

Webb, R. A., 1972, Use of the boundary line in the analysis of biological data, *J. Hortic. Sci.* **47:**309–319.

Webb, W. L., 1971, Photosynthetic models for a terrestrial plant community, Ph.D. dissertation, Oregon State University, Corvallis. 79p.

Webb, W. L. 1975a, Dynamics of photoassimilated carbon in Douglas-fir seedlings, *Plant Physiol.* **56:**455–459.

Webb, W. L., 1975b, The distribution of photoassimilated carbon and the growth of Douglas-fir seedlings, *Can. J. For. Res.* **5:**68–72.

Webb, W. L., 1977, Rates of current photosynthate accumulation in roots of Douglas-fir seedlings: Seasonal variation, in *The Belowground Ecosystem: A Synthesis of Plant Associated Processes,* J. K. Marshall, ed., Range Science Department, Science Series 26, Colorado State University, Fort Collins, pp. 149–152.

Wilson, B. F., 1966, Mitotic activity in the cambium zone of *Pinus strobus, Am. J. Bot.* **53:**364–372.

Wodzicki, T. J., 1971, Mechanisms of xylem differentiation in *Pinus sylvestris* L., *J. Exp. Bot.* **22:**670–687.

Wodzicki, T. J., and A. B. Wodzicki, 1980, Seasonal abscisic acid accumulation in stem cambial regions of *Pinus sylvestris* and its contribution to the hypothesis of latewood control system in conifers, *Physiol. Plant.* **48:**443–447.

Woodman, J. N., 1968, The relationship of net photosynthesis to environment within the crown of a large Douglas-fir, Ph. D. dissertation, University of Washington, Seattle, 188p.

Woodman, J. N., 1971a, Is there a future for irrigation in the management of forests? Paper presented at the 1971 annual meeting A.S.A.E., Washington State University, Pullman, Paper No. 71-179, 12p.

Woodman, J. N., 1979b, Variation of net photosynthesis within the crown of a large forest-grown conifer, *Photosynthetica* **5:**50–54.

Woodwell, G. M., and D. B. Botkin, 1970, Metabolism of terrestrial ecosystems by gas exchange techniques: The Brookhaven approach, in *Analysis of Temperate Forest Ecosystems,* Ecological Studies, vol. 1, D. E. Reichle, ed., Springer-Verlag, New York, pp. 73–85.

Wright, S. T. C., 1978, Phytohormones and stress phenomena, in *Phytohormones and Related Compounds—A Comprehensive Treatise,* vol. II, D. S. Letham, P. G. Goodwin, and T. J. V. Higgins, eds., Elsevier/North Holland, New York, pp. 495–536.

Zaerr, J. B., and R. Holbo, 1976, Measuring short-term shoot elongation of Douglas-fir seedlings in relation to increasing water potential, *For. Sci.* **22:**378–382.

Zahner, R., 1968, Water deficits and growth of trees, in *Water Deficits and Plant Growth, II: Plant Water Consumption and Response,* T. T. Kozlowski, ed., Academic Press, New York, pp. 191–254.

Zelawski, W., and R. B. Walker, 1976, Photosynthesis, respiration, and dry matter production, in *Modern Methods in Forest Genetics,* J. P. Miksche, ed., Springer-Verlag, New York, pp. 89–119.

Zobel, D., 1974, Local variation in intergrading *Abies grandis—A. concolor* populations in the central Oregon Cascades, II: Stomatal reaction to moisture stress, *Bot. Gaz.* **135:**200–210.

7

Nutrient Cycling in Forests of the Pacific Northwest

D. W. Johnson, D. W. Cole, C. S. Bledsoe, K. Cromack, R. L. Edmonds, S. P. Gessel, C. C. Grier, B. N. Richards, and *K. A. Vogt*

INTRODUCTION

Ecosystem analysis has established nutrient cycling as an important area of ecology involving biological, chemical, and geological interactions. Studying the flow of elements through ecosystems provides us with a tool for understanding the functioning of ecosystems. For example, if an ecosystem component has a rapid flux of elements through it, or if it stores large amounts of an element, that component is clearly important in ecosystem function. Nutrient cycling strongly influences ecosystem productivity since nutrient flows are closely linked with transfers of carbon and water. In addition nutrient cycling may also affect succession and evolution in forest ecosystems.

Various distinct processes are involved in nutrient cycling, such as decomposition, weathering, uptake, leaching, and so on. Each is a precursor to another and the flow of nutrients follows a set of interconnected steps. Although the basic nutrient cycling processes are common to all ecosystems, the rates of the processes vary from one forest ecosystem to another. This variation plays an important role in forest succession and evolution. For example, long-term foliage retention by conifers may allow a species to exist where only a marginal nutrient supply is available from the soil. Nitrogen-fixing species, on the other hand, can occupy sites where nitrogen availability is low because they can provide their own nitrogen. An understanding of nutrient cycling is thus essential for the rational management of forest ecosystems.

Nitrogen is recognized as the most limiting element for forest growth in the Pacific Northwest, particularly in Douglas-fir *(Pseudotsuga menziesii)* ecosystems (Gessel and Walker 1956; Gessel et al. 1969). For this reason this chapter focuses largely on nitrogen cycling. Cycling of other elements such as potassium and calcium are compared with that of nitrogen, where contrasting behavior may provide insight into nutrient-cycling processes.

The objectives of this chapter are to (1) briefly describe the important nutrient cycling processes; (2) contrast nutrient cycles in different forest ecosystems; (3) contrast nutrient cycles in relation to stand development; and (4) assess the impact of forest-management practices on nutrient cycling.

KEY PROCESSES IN FOREST NUTRIENT CYCLES

Study of nutrient cycles in forest ecosystems requires a basic conceptual framework to organize the nutrient capitals and transfer processes. Diagrams of nutrient cycles in forests have been presented before, for example, by Duvigneaud and Denaeyer-DeSmet (1970). The scheme followed by coniferous forest biome researchers is similar (Figure 7.1). As Figure 7.1 shows, there are many important biological and physical processes involved. In particular the importance of belowground processes is recognized. In this section nutrient inputs, nutrient transfers within ecosystems, and nutrient outputs are briefly discussed. More detailed discussions of the processes controlling nutrient availability and conservation follow.

Inputs

Input of mineral nutrients by dry particulate deposition, precipitation, and gaseous fixation can be an important source of new nutrient elements for ecosystems. This and release of nutrients by weathering of soil parent material constitute the only two sources of new nutrients for forest ecosystems. These sources must replace any losses that occur as well as provide for nutrient accumulation.

Atmospheric Inputs

Inputs by dust, dry aerosol impaction, and precipitation are generally low in the coniferous biome compared with those in the eastern United States. For example, inputs of nitrogen are generally less than 3 kg·ha^{-1}yr^{-1} throughout much of western Oregon and Washington. In contrast nitrogen inputs in excess of 6 kg·ha^{-1}yr^{-1} are routinely reported for northeastern hardwood forests (Likens et al. 1977). One exception to the low atmospheric nutrient inputs for northwestern forests is coastal ecosystems. In these, nutrient input originating as sea spray contributes up to 10 kg·ha^{-1}yr^{-1} of nitrogen and large amounts of other nutrients (Grier 1978a).

Nitrogen Fixation

Nitrogen fixation occurs throughout the coniferous biome by free-living algae and bacteria, by canopy epiphytes, and by symbiotic associations with

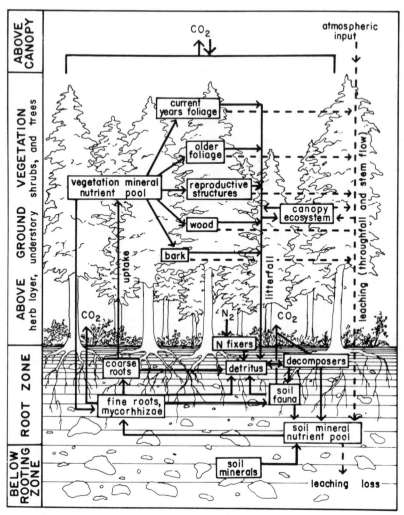

FIGURE 7.1 *Conceptual model of nutrient transfers in coniferous forests.*

roots of plants such as red alder *(Alnus rubra).* Red alder is a widespread deciduous tree species in the Pacific Northwest. It has been known for many years that symbionts associated with red alder roots fix nitrogen (Bond 1954) and that an alder sere can improve site fertility for succeeding nonnitrogen-fixing species (Tarrant and Miller 1963; Newton et al. 1968).

Organic matter production and nitrogen fixation by red alder appear to be correlated. Maximums in both occur at a stand age of about twenty years. Estimates of the amounts of nitrogen fixed by alder stands vary considerably. Tarrant and Miller (1963) calculated an average nitrogen accretion of $41 \text{ kg} \cdot \text{ha}^{-1} \cdot \text{yr}^{-1}$ during thirty years of site occupancy by red alder, while Newton et al. (1968) reported an extremely high accumulation of up to 321 $kg \cdot ha^{-1} \cdot yr^{-1}$ over fifteen years of alder occupancy on sites near the Oregon coast.

In a study conducted by the coniferous forest biome researchers, Cole et al. (1978) estimated an average annual fixation rate of 85 $kg \cdot ha^{-1} yr^{-1}$ over thirty-five years. These values were obtained by comparing nitrogen capitals of thirty-five-year-old red alder and Douglas-fir stands on the same soil series at the Thompson site in Washington.

Another northwestern species known to host nitrogen-fixing symbionts is snowbush *(Ceanothus velutinus)*. This species occupies drier sites than alder and typically grows from buried seed activated by fire. Youngberg and Wollum (1976) found nitrogen accretion of about 1080 kg/ha over ten years of snowbush occupation of a burned clearcut in Douglas-fir and 715 kg/ha for ten years in a burned ponderosa pine clearcut in the Oregon Cascades. At these rates of fixation, they calculate that the nitrogen lost during burning is replaced in about seven years. Other *Ceanothus* species may also host nitrogen-fixing symbionts.

Contributions to ecosystem nitrogen capital by free-living microbes in the soil were not examined by coniferous forest biome researchers. However, microbe contribution is thought to be less than that of nitrogen-fixing organisms hosted by green plants.

In-depth studies on nitrogen fixation in forest canopies as well as other nutrient-cycling aspects of canopy-dwelling organisms were conducted in old-growth Douglas-fir forests in Oregon (Denison 1973). Significant fixation was found to occur in at least one species of epiphytic lichen, *Lobaria oregana*. A conservative nitrogen fixation rate of 3.8 $kg \cdot ha^{-1} \cdot yr^{-1}$ was estimated using acetylene reduction methods. Fixation rates were positively correlated with moisture content of the lichen thallus. This was in turn related to precipitation and atmospheric vapor pressure deficit.

Another possible site for nitrogen fixation in the coniferous biome is in decaying logs. Several studies (Grier 1978b; Cromack, pers. comm.) showed nitrogen accumulation occurring in fallen trees both in coastal and Douglas-fir forests. Some evidence suggests this may result, in part, from nitrogen fixation. Specific nitrogen-fixing organisms residing in fallen logs are unknown. But, Aho et al. (1974) have shown that nitrogen-fixing bacteria do inhabit decaying heartwood of white fir *(Abies concolor)* in southwestern Oregon. The same or similar organisms may account for nitrogen accumulation in fallen logs.

Soil Weathering

Weathering of soil parent material is a major source of new cation nutrients and can often be the major source of new phosphorus and sulphur in an ecosystem. Weathering of soil primary minerals and other soil-forming processes were studied within the biome program; a large part of the effort going into a study of podzolization processes in a mature *Abies amabilis* stand at Findley Lake (Singer and Ugolini 1974; Ugolini et al. 1977a, b; Singer et al. 1978).

The term "weathering" is used here to describe nutrient release from primary soil minerals. This release constitutes a functional nutrient input to the ecosystem, since it adds previously unavailable nutrients to the available nutrient pool. Rates of nutrient release are difficult to measure *in situ* because of the masking effects of nutrient uptake by vegetation and microorganisms. Release rates can be calculated as the normally small difference between other major nutrient transfers, but the accuracy of such measurements is questionable in view of the errors associated with the other measurements.

Rough estimates of mineral weathering in one soil were obtained as a result of long-term plot studies conducted in young Douglas-fir stands at the Thompson site. Measurements of nutrient-cycling processes in a second growth Douglas-fir stand at the Thompson research site were initiated in 1962. Remeasurements of exchangeable cations in 1976 indicated that soil weathering input to exchangeable nutrient pools was not keeping pace with immobilization of cations in living biomass or their loss by leaching (Table 7.1). In the surface horizons there was a general decrease in amounts of exchangeable calcium, potassium and magnesium over the fourteen-year span of this study. But, in this interval, cation-exchange capacity remained the same. These data indicate that an assumption of steady state in soil exchangeable cations may not be justifiable. Thus weathering rate calculations based on this assumption (Duvigneaud and Denaeyer-DeSmet 1970, Likens et al. 1977) may be in error.

Nutrient Transfers Within Coniferous Ecosystems

Once nutrients have entered an ecosystem they are subject to transfer by a large number of processes. Clearly, all the steps involved, that is, litterfall, decomposition, uptake, and internal translocation, are highly interdependent. In the following sections we consider these processes individually and discuss how they interact to regulate nutrient cycling in stands subjected to very different climatic conditions.

Litterfall and Crownwash

Litterfall and its components are part of a spectrum of organic matter and nutrient return to the forest floor ranging from nutrients in small particles returned in canopy wash to those returned in logs and other large woody material. The different components of this spectrum vary widely in nutrient concentration and, when they reach the forest floor, also vary in the amount of time required for decomposition and nutrient mineralization to occur. Nutrients dissolved in canopy wash may be in immediately available ionic form whereas

TABLE 7.1 *Cation exchange capacity and exchangeable cations in the Everett soil at the Thompson Research Center, Washington, in 1962 and 1976. Standard deviations are in parentheses.*[a]

Horizon and depth (cm)	Cation exchange capacity			CA^{2+}			Mg^{2+}			K$^+$		
	1962a[b]	1962b[c]	1976[d]	1962a	1962b	1976	1962a	1962b	1976	1962a	1962b	1976
						meq/100 g soil						
A (0 to 15)	9.78 (0.556)	—	9.50 (0.995)	1.33 (0.192)	—	0.90 (0.20)	0.26 (0.48)	—	0.12 (0.022)	0.17 (0.011)	—	0.11 (0.016)
B21 (15 to 30)	6.99 (2.912)	6.23	6.21 (0.613)	0.44 (0.213)	0.43	0.30 (0.042)	0.13 (0.052)	0.10	0.06 (0.005)	0.08 (0.018)	0.08	0.05 (0.002)
B21 (30 to 45)	6.52 (0.979)	5.01	4.43 (0.578)	0.32 (0.114)	0.22 (0.100)	0.18 (0.081)	0.09 (0.025)	0.05 (0.010)	0.04 (0.015)	0.06 (0.006)	0.05 (0.005)	0.03 (0.008)
B22 (45 to 60)	3.15 (1.223)	2.56 (0.769)	3.64 (0.591)	0.15 (0.033)	0.90 (0.015)	0.17 (0.044)	0.04 (0.019)	0.03 (0.010)	0.04 (0.003)	0.04 (0.026)	0.03 (0.016)	0.03 (0.005)

[a] D. W. Cole and R. L. Lamon, unpublished data.

[b] 1962a: sampled and measured in 1962.

[c] 1962b: sampled in 1962, measured in 1976.

[d] 1976: sampled and measured in 1976.

nutrients incorporated in woody material may require prolonged decomposition before they are available for uptake.

The proportion of a given nutrient returned along various pathways is different for different elements (Will 1959; Cole et al. 1968). For example, Cole et al. found that after canopy closure, 8 to 12 percent of the nitrogen, 65 to 85 percent of the potassium, and 15 to 20 percent of the calcium moved to the forest floor from the canopy by way of crown leaching and stemflow. The remainder was returned in litterfall.

Detailed studies were conducted on nutrient dynamics within the canopy of old-growth Douglas-fir forests (Denison 1973). Entire ecosystems occupy niches within old-growth canopies. These ecosystems contain all the major elements of the larger ecosystem including primary producers, such as lichens, mosses, and occasional ferns, decomposers, and consumers, mainly microarthropods. These microecosystems also have many of the same properties as larger ecosystems; they cycle and conserve nutrients and thus exert a strong influence on nutrient return via crownwash and, to a lesser extent, litterfall. A full discussion of this intricate system is well beyond the scope of this chapter, but a summary diagram of the canopy ecosystem is presented in Figure 7.2. The diagram is largely self-explanatory, but the point to be stressed is that neither crownwash nor litterfall can be considered as a process solely regulated by the trees. What the researcher observes in ground-level collectors is the output of complex microecosystems that thrive within many forest canopies. Unfortunately, it is difficult to measure these intricate fluxes and few of them have been directly quantified as yet.

Decomposition Processes

Organic-matter decomposition and subsequent nutrient release are key processes in forest ecosystems, and the rate at which carbon and nutrients flow through the forest floor can play a large role in regulating ecosystem productivity. This regulatory role is particularly important in systems that operate on a very low nutrient capital and in those where decomposition processes are limited by environmental extremes.

Factors known to influence decomposition and mineralization rates of litter components are: (1) environmental factors (temperature, moisture); (2) litter nutrient content, particularly N; (3) C/N ratio; and (4) lignin content. These factors and nutrient release from decomposing litter are discussed in more detail in later sections along with the role of mycorrhizae.

Uptake and Internal Translocation

Uptake processes were studied in the biome program from both short- and long-term perspectives. Long-term information can be gleaned from nutrient

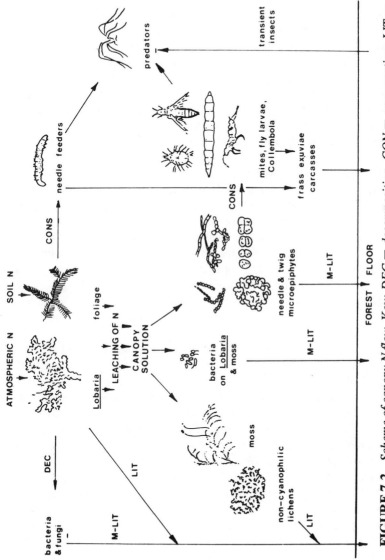

FIGURE 7.2 *Scheme of canopy N flow. Key: DEC = decomposition, CON = consumption, LIT = macrolitterfall, M-LIT = microlitterfall (after G. C. Carroll, pers. comm.).*

budgets in stands of various ages and this approach is pursued later in this chapter. Highlights of the short-term studies are reported here.

Most attention was paid to the uptake of nitrogen since it plays such an important role in the functioning of ecosystems in the biome. Nitrogen-uptake processes, however, are not well understood. Trees can utilize either ammonium or nitrate, but there is still some controversy over which is the preferred form. In the biome program nutrient uptake was studied using nonmycorrhizal Douglas-fir seedlings in solution culture.

These solution-culture studies revealed that nutrient-uptake rates increased with increasing ion concentrations until a plateau was reached (Cole and Bledsoe 1976). Nitrogen, either in NH_4^+ or NO_3^- form, was taken up more rapidly than other nutrients. Ammonium was taken up more rapidly than NO_3^-. Uptake of NH_4^+ temporarily depressed or precluded the uptake of other cation nutrients (presumably by ion competition), whereas NO_3^- uptake occurred simultaneously with cation uptake. In addition, it was shown that the seedlings were efficient at removing nitrogen at low levels, since nitrogen uptake rates decreased little even as concentration decreased.

Preferences for NH_4^+ or NO_3^-, however, may be different in soils than in solution culture. Van den Driessche and Dangerfield (1975) reported that Douglas-fir seedlings grew well in sand culture in both NH_4^+ and NO_3^-. However, well-irrigated seedlings favored NH_4^+ as the nitrogen source, while less irrigated seedlings favored NO_3^-, apparently because NH_4^+ is less mobile than NO_3^- in soils. In addition mycorrhizae in soils may influence nitrogen preference because of their ability to produce extensive hyphal networks in the soil. Uptake of organic nitrogen by forest trees is also possible but we know very little about this process.

In the solution-culture studies, the form of nitrogen supplied to Douglas-fir seedlings had a significant effect on final distribution of mineral nutrients. Figure 7.3 illustrates the concentrations of N, P, Ca, K, and Mg in parts of harvested seedlings. Although seedlings grown in $NH_4^+ - N$ accumulate considerably more nitrogen than do those grown in NO_3^--N, the accumulation of cations in the former is usually lower. This may be because of the charge-balance problem presented to seedlings that are taking up nitrogen as a cation (NH_4^+) and therefore have to limit their uptake of K^+, Ca^{2+}, and Mg^{2+}.

Analyses of xylem sap from roots of decapitated seedlings suggested that nitrate reduction occurred in the root tissues (Riekerk 1977). When nitrate was supplied in solution culture to seedling roots, ammonium predominated in the sap. Concentrations of potassium in xylem sap were also high, presumably because of the use of K^+ for carbohydrate and anion transfer through the xylem.

In addition to nutrient uptake by roots, internal translocation, or the withdrawal of nutrients from older tissues for use in production of new tissues, also constitutes a mechanism by which trees obtain nutrients for growth. It is also an important mechanism for nutrient conservation by trees. Nutrient requirements thus can be met in part by internal translocation. This partially short-circuits the more tortuous and less certain route of litterfall return, decomposition, and

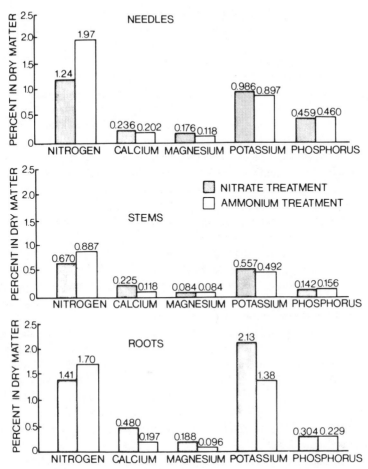

FIGURE 7.3 *Nutrient distribution in Douglas-fir seedlings given NH_4^+ and NO_3^- sources of N from solution culture (after C. S. Bledsoe, pers. comm.). Values are significantly different at the 99 percent level.*

uptake. Internal translocation is discussed in more detail later in the section on nutrient conservation mechanisms.

Outputs

Soil Leaching Processes

Soil-leaching processes were studied in some detail during the biome program. These processes are important for a number of reasons: (1) leaching is important in regulating nutrient losses from the rooting zone; (2) leaching and exchange reactions make nutrients available for plant uptake by bringing them into solution; (3) soil leaching processes play a large role in regulating the chemistry of water entering aquatic ecosystems.

Conceptually, the rate of soil leaching can be viewed as a function of the level of mobile anions in soil solution (Shilova 1959; McColl and Cole 1968). The cation-exchange capacity of most soils is greater than their anion exchange capacity. Because of this, cation leaching is restricted by exchange reactions and since total cations must equal total anions in solution, it is usually more convenient to consider factors affecting the level of anions in the soil. Shilova (1959) and McColl and Cole (1968) showed that bicarbonate was the major anion involved in soil leaching at their temperate forest sites and deduced that carbonic acid was the major leaching agent.

Carbonic-acid leaching operates as shown in Figure 7.4. Because of respiration and reduced CO_2 diffusivity in the soil, CO_2 pressure builds up relative to the ambient atmosphere. An incoming wetting front encounters this higher CO_2 pressure and may increase it by further reducing CO_2 diffusivity. Carbonic acid forms as CO_2 dissolves. Carbonic acid in turn dissociates into hydrogen (H^+) and bicarbonate ions (HCO_3^-), H^+ displaces cations from exchange sites, and a bicarbonate-cation solution leaves the system.

Soil-leaching processes were investigated at three sites within the coniferous biome and at a tropical site near La Selva, Costa Rica (Johnson et al. 1977). The temperate forest site, the A. E. Thompson site where McColl and Cole (1968) worked, was used as a basis of comparison with a subalpine site at Findley Lake, a high latitude, low-elevation site near Petersburg, Alaska, and the tropical site. At each site, all major anions in solution were balanced against major cations so that the relative roles of various leaching agents could be deduced (Figure 7.5).

Bicarbonate dominated soil solutions at the tropical (La Selva) and temperate (Thompson) sites (Figure 7.5). Because of high soil respiration and CO_2 pressure, soil solution bicarbonate concentrations were greatest at the tropical site (Johnson et al. 1975, 1977). Precipitation was acid (pH 4.5 to 4.8) at the La Selva and Thompson sites, presumably because of inputs of sulfuric acid from nearby SO_2 sources (volcanic at the La Selva site and industrial at the Thompson site).

The pH of solutions rose as they passed through the forest canopy and soil (pH 5.5 to 6.0) presumably by H^+ exchange processes. Increased pH allowed bicarbonate to dominate soil solutions at both sites (Figure 7.5).

Precipitation pH was near normal (5.7) for atmospheric CO_2 levels at the subalpine (Findley Lake) and northern (Alaska) sites, but was reduced to 4.1 to 4.8 in passing through the canopy and forest floor. Coincident with pH lowering, solution color increased and an anion deficit (total cations minus total anions) developed (Figure 7.5). These observations imply that organic acids leaching from the forest canopy and forest floor lower pH and bicarbonate

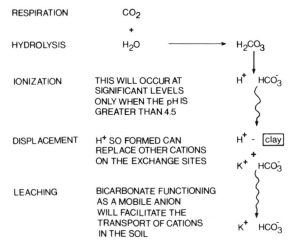

FIGURE 7.4 *Schematic representation of soil carbonic acid leaching (after Cole et al. 1975).*

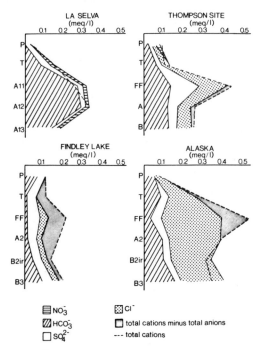

FIGURE 7.5 *Anion and total cation concentrations of solutions from four forest ecosystems (from Johnson et al. 1977). Key: P = precipitation, T = throughfall, FF = forest floor; soil horizons are indicated.*

levels and thus account for the anion deficit (Shilova 1959, Johnson et al. 1977). In and below the B2ir soil horizon, where organic acids and their chelated cation associates precipitate (Kononova 1966), pH and bicarbonate concentrations rise. Thus organic acids appear to play a significant role in throughfall and upper soil horizons at these cold sites, both in cation transport and in reducing pH and the role of bicarbonate. In fact, it appears that organic anions dominated upper horizon soil solutions at the subalpine site. Ugolini et al. (1977b) verified the presence of fulvic acids in soil solutions from upper horizons at Findley Lake. Moreover, fulvic-acid concentrations were reduced 60 to 70 percent as soil solutions passed through the B2 soil horizon. The chloride ion dominated solutions at the Alaskan site, presumably because of its proximity to salt water (4 km).

In total, the intensity of carbonic-acid leaching corresponded with the intensity of biological activity at the various sites. In cold forest ecosystems, the production of organic acids served to conserve nutrients by suppressing carbonic-acid leaching within the rooting zone. This is particularly important in cold forest soils since CO_2 pressures can build to very high levels beneath melting snowpacks, creating a great potential for carbonic-acid leaching if pH conditions were to allow it (Marakov 1966, Johnson et al. 1977).

Other Nutrient Outputs

Gaseous inputs and outputs can be very important to the cycling of nitrogen and sulfur in forest ecosystems (Likens et al. 1977; Shriner and Henderson 1978). Unfortunately, these outputs are extremely difficult to measure and quantify, and little is known about their importance in forests of the Pacific Northwest. This is an area that clearly deserves further research.

Another area worthy of more research is migration of particulate matter through soils. A major finding of Ugolini et al. (1977a), working at Findley Lake, was that suspended material in soil solutions reflected the same trends as the dissolved material. They demonstrated that soil leachates in upper horizons contained organic particles associated with aluminum, iron, silicon, and sulfur. The downward transport of these particles was arrested in the B2hir horizon, below which phyllosilicates, quartz, and silicate minerals dominated suspended materials. Their results provided direct evidence for the mechanism of podzolization. They demonstrated the crucial importance of the B2hir horizon as an illuvial horizon for suspended organics and their complexed metals, and as an eluvial horizon for silicates.

Erosion is also an important process in terms of nutrient output from terrestrial systems and input to aquatic ecosystems. Unlike the other processes discussed in this section, erosion is primarily episodic in nature in forest ecosystems and its study must be approached in unique ways. Because of its episodic nature, erosional nutrient losses are difficult to quantify and express on a yearly basis as other nutrient transfers traditionally are. Researchers at Oregon State University spent a great deal of effort studying erosional processes and their impacts on aquatic ecosystems. This subject is discussed in Chapter 9, which deals with terrestrial/aquatic interface studies.

NUTRIENT CYCLES IN DIFFERENT FOREST ECOSYSTEMS IN THE BIOME IN CONTRASTING ENVIRONMENTS

General Nutrient Cycles in Various Ecosystems in the Biome

Coniferous forests tend to dominate in the biome. These forests occupy a wide range of habitats including wet warm coastal, wet cold subalpine, boreal, and dry hot interior. Moreover, there are also significant areas supporting deciduous forest species such as red alder in the biome, and the nutrient cycles in these ecosystems provide an interesting contrast with those of coniferous ecosystems.

As previously indicated, nutrient-cycling processes are broadly similar in most northwestern ecosystems, but the rates of these processes vary considerably from one ecosystem to another. These variations produce different nutrient distributions among the compartments indicated in Figure 7.1. Also, because nutrient and carbon pools are closely linked, organic matter pools tend to vary from one ecosystem to another.

The abiotic environment an ecosystem occupies has a great influence on the processes controlling nutrient availability to trees and thus will also have a great influence on tree growth. Belowground processes, including decomposition, mineralization and the presence of mycorrhizae, are particularly important in controlling nutrient availability. These are relatively sensitive to differences in abiotic environments. Many ecosystems have developed nutrient-conservation mechanisms, particularly fungal nutrient immobilization and nutrient redistribution inside trees.

We will first examine some contrasting ecosystems. Table 7.2 shows organic-matter and nitrogen distributions for two Douglas-fir ecosystems, a coastal western hemlock/Sitka spruce ecosystem and a subalpine Pacific silver fir ecosystem. Additional data from other ecosystems in the biome are presented in Cole and Rapp (1980). It is immediately apparent that the distribution of organic matter and nitrogen in these ecosystems differs considerably. Although the old- and young-growth Douglas-fir ecosystems have similar foliar biomasses the old-growth ecosystem has considerably more organic matter and nitrogen, particularly in the forest floor and soil. This is largely due to age differences. The other two ecosystems have even greater accumulations of organic matter and nitrogen than the Douglas-fir ecosystems, again with large

TABLE 7.2 *Organic matter and N (in parentheses) distribution (kg/ha) for young- and old-growth Douglas-fir, western hemlock/Sitka spruce, and Pacific silver fir ecosystems.*

	Ecosystem			
Component	36-year-old Douglas-fir (Thompson site)[a]	450-year-old Douglas-fir (H. J. Andrews)[a]	121-year-old western hemlock/Sitka spruce (Cascade Head)[b]	170-year-old Pacific silver fir (Findley Lake)[c]
OVERSTORY				
Foliage	9,097	8,906	8,100	15,700
	(102)	(75)	(85)	(173)
Branches	22,031	48,543	50,600	17,710
	(61)	(49)	(91)	(18)
Stemwood	121,687	472,593	856,900	265,010
	(77)	(189)	(589)	(116)
Bark	18,728	472,593	856,900	38,710
	(48)	(189)	(589)	(13)
Roots	32,986	74,328	186,700	—
	(32)	(162)	(157)	
Total Overstory	204,529	604,370	1,102,300	337,130
	(320)	(375)	(922)	(320)

SUBORDINATE VEGETATION (including lichens)	1,010 (6)	9,864 (58)	4,300 (15)	3,670 (28)
FOREST FLOOR				
Wood	6,345 (14)	55,200 (132)	24,700 (180)	137,710 (104)
Litter and humus	16,427 (161)	43,350 (434)	34,000 (265)	43,520 (571)
SOIL	111,552 (2,809)	79,250 (4,300)	776,000 (34,900)	243,960 (15,855)
TOTAL ECOSYSTEM	339,863 (3,310)	792,034 (5,300)	2,128,300 (36,282)	765,990 (16,878)

[a] Grier et al., 1974.
[b] Grier, 1976.
[c] Turner and Singer, 1976.

accumulations in the soil. The reasons for these similar accumulations, however, are different in the coastal hemlock/spruce ecosystem than in the subalpine ecosystem. The coastal forest is considerably more productive than the subalpine forest and as a result the overstory biomass accumulation is greater. This, of course, results in a greater litterfall (Table 7.3) and significant litter accumulation in spite of higher decomposition rates. Dead roots also contribute a considerable amount of organic matter, especially to the soil. Once on the forest floor, the litter is subject to decomposition and mineralization and this critical process determines the rate of accumulation of organic matter and nitrogen in the soil. Although decomposition rates are faster in the western hemlock ecosystem than the Pacific silver fir ecosystem the greater productivity in the hemlock system offsets this, resulting in large soil accumulations. Nitrogen accumulations in the hemlock soil are about an order of magnitude higher than those in the Douglas-fir soils.

Contrasts between the red alder and Douglas-fir ecosystems are interesting because these species occupy similar habitats and soils. Table 7.2 and 7.4 compare nutrient distributions in adjacent alder and Douglas-fir stands. While the Douglas-fir ecosystem is of similar age to the red alder ecosystem, it has accumulated only half the nitrogen and slightly less organic matter than the red alder ecosystem. The additional nitrogen in the red alder stand appears to result from nitrogen fixation by symbionts associated with alder roots. Nitrogen returned to the forest floor via litterfall is considerably greater in the red alder ecosystem, as are losses from the forest floor (Tables 7.3 and 7.4).

Nitrogen cycling strategies are thus different in the red alder and Douglas-fir ecosystems and also among coniferous ecosystems. This implies that the critical belowground processes influencing nutrient availability, including N inputs, decomposition, mineralization, nutrient immobilization, mycorrhizal uptake, and redistribution within trees also vary from ecosystem to ecosystem.

Critical Processes Influencing Nutrient Availability

Nitrogen fixation was discussed previously and will not be elaborated upon. Rates of litter decomposition and nitrogen mineralization in coniferous biome ecosystems, however, do need further discussion. Decomposition rates of various litter components including needles, leaves, twigs, cones, roots, and wood, and the factors controlling them, were assessed in various ecosystems.

After two years of decomposition, k values (decomposition constants based on the equation $x = x_o e^{-kt}$; Olson 1963) were 0.44 for red alder leaves and 0.42 and 0.38 for Douglas-fir and western hemlock needles, respectively, at the Thompson research site (Edmonds 1980). In a variety of Douglas-fir ecosystems in Oregon and Washington, k values for needles ranged from 0.22 to 0.56 (Fogel and Cromack 1977; Edmonds 1979) with highest values on

TABLE 7.3 *Nitrogen transfers (kg·ha⁻¹·yr⁻¹ in young- and old-growth Douglas-fir, mature western hemlock/Sitka spruce and mature Pacific silver fir ecosystems.*

	Ecosystem			
Component	42-year-old Douglas-fir (Thompson site)[a]	450-year-old Douglas-fir (H. J. Andrews)[b]	121-year-old western hemlock/Sitka spruce (Cascade Head)[c]	170-year-old Pacific silver fir (Findley Lake)[d]
INPUT (precipitation and dry fall)	1.67	2.0	5.5	1.3
RETURN TO FOREST FLOOR				
Throughfall plus stemflow	0.53	3.4	—	1.3
Litterfall	25.4	25.6	—	16.3
Total	25.93	29.0	35.8	17.6
WITHIN VEGETATION				
Requirement	45.8	33.3	39.9	23.1
Redistribution	20.7	18.5	0.0	12.4
Uptake	25.1	14.8	39.9	11.9
SOIL TRANSFERS				
Loss from forest floor	7.3	4.7	—	10.3
Loss from rooting zone	3.4	1.5	1.5-2.5	2.7

[a]Turner 1975.
[b]Sollins et al. 1980.
[c]Grier 1976.
[d]Turner and Singer 1976.

TABLE 7.4　*Organic matter and N budgets and N transfers in a 34-year-old red alder ecosystem at the Thompson site.*

Component	Budgets (kg/ha)	
	Dry Weight	N
OVERSTORY		
Foliage	4,060	100
Branches	20,530	23
Stemwood	135,150	144
Bark	23,550	165
Roots	35,230	176
Total Overstory	209,800	589
SUBORDINATE VEGETATION	9,530	103
FOREST FLOOR		
Wood	27,740	264
Leaves	13,040	195
Humus	21,220	361
Fern Branch	4,350	57
Total Forest Floor	66,350	877
SOIL	158,520	5,450
TOTAL ECOSYSTEM	444,200	7,019

	N Transfers ($kg \cdot ha^{-1} \cdot yr^{-1}$)
LITTERFALL	
Tree: Foliage	61
Wood	18
Stem	8
Understory	24
Total Litterfall	111
LEACHING	
Precipitation	1.7
Stemflow	0.1
Throughfall	8.8
Total Return to Forest Floor	122.0

moister sites. Decomposition of Douglas-fir needles was also studied in differing habitats in four communities dominated by an overstory of old-growth Douglas-fir at the Andrews site (Fogel and Cromack 1977). Rates of needle decomposition shown in Table 7.5 were greatest in the cool moist habitat ($k = 0.28$) and least in the warm-dry habitat ($k = 0.22$). Slow decomposition rates were also observed for Pacific silver fir needles at the cold Findley Lake site ($k = 0.31$), but decomposition did occur under snow (Vogt et al. 1980; Edmonds 1980).

TABLE 7.4 *Continued.*

	N Transfers $(kg \cdot ha^{-1} \cdot yr^{-1})$
LEACHED FROM FOREST FLOOR	15.0
REQUIREMENT	
Uptake: Foliage	78.8
Branches	0.8
Wood	5.3
Bark	7.1
Understory	21.8
Total Uptake	113.8
REDISTRIBUTION	
Tree: Foliage	29.9
Branches	1.7
Wood	10.7
Bark	13.5
Understory	12.2
Total Redistribution	68.0
TOTAL REQUIREMENT	
Foliage	99.9
Branches	2.5
Wood	16.0
Bark	20.6
Understory	34.0
Total Stand Requirement	173.0

TABLE 7.5 *Decomposition constants (k, yr^{-1}) for Douglas-fir litter components in different environments in the H. J. Andrews Forest, Oregon, 1973–1975.*[a]

	Site and community[b]			
	——Increasingly warmer and drier——►			
	Tshe/[c] Pomu- Oxor	Tshe/ Rhma- Bene	Tshe/ Cach	Psme/ Hodi
Needles	0.28	0.28	0.24	0.22
Branches	0.07	0.09	0.06	0.08
Cones	0.06	0.07	0.06	0.08
Bark	0.03	0.04	0.03	0.01

[a]After Fogel and Cromack 1977; based on 2 years' cumulative weight loss.
[b]Means of two sites per community except for Psme/Hodi.
[c]Tshe = *Tsuga heterophylla;* Pomu = *Polystichum munitum;* Oxor = *Oxalis oregena;* Rhma = *Rhododendron macrophyllum;* Cach = *Castanopsis chrysophylla;* Psme = *Pseudotsuga menziesii;* Hodi = *Holodisus discolor.*

Both temperature and moisture were found to regulate litter decomposition rates. Moisture was particularly limiting in Douglas-fir ecosystems, with the effect being more pronounced in Oregon than Washington. Temperature plays a more important role in cold high-altitude ecosystems. Little decomposition occurred in the summer in many ecosystems in the biome due to dry conditions.

The chemical constituents of litter also influence decomposition rates, particularly lignin content. As lignin values increase, k values decrease. This is illustrated in Table 7.5 for Douglas-fir branches, cones, and bark. Initial lignin content appeared to be better related to woody litter decomposition rates than C/N ratios (Fogel and Cromack 1977). Edmonds (1980), however, found that needle and leaf decomposition rates were better related to initial C/N ratios than lignin content.

Data on the decomposition rates of fine roots and logs in the biome were also obtained. The decomposition rate for Douglas-fir fine roots was similar to that for needles ($k = 0.24$). For Douglas-fir logs at the Andrews site, decomposition rates were very slow, with k values ranging from 0.008 to 0.043 depending on the state of log decay. These values are similar to those found by Grier (1978b), who found an average k value of 0.012 for western hemlock logs in a coastal site at Cascade Head in Oregon. Logs, of course, have a high lignin content.

Since litter-decomposition rates varied from one ecosystem to another it is not surprising that nitrogen mineralization rates also varied (Table 7.6). Nitrogen was most rapidly released from red alder leaves, with next most rapid release occurring from Douglas-fir needles. On the other hand, nitrogen accumulated in western hemlock and Pacific silver fir needles during two years of decomposition. Nitrogen mineralization rates were related to C/N ratios, with mineralization occurring when ratios fell below about 25.0 to 30.1 (Edmonds 1979; 1980). Above this ratio microbial immobilization occurred. The nitrogen content of decaying western hemlock logs also increased with time (Grier 1978b). Even after forty years, log nitrogen contents were higher than those of freshly fallen logs. This increase may result from nitrogen fixation (Cornaby and Waide 1973; Aho et al. 1974); from translocation of nitrogen from adjacent litter by fungi inhabiting the fallen logs; or from inputs to log surfaces through litterfall and throughfall.

Fungal immobilization by decomposer and mycorrhizal fungi and nutrient redistribution within the tree are important processes in retaining nutrients within ecosystems as discussed below.

Critical Processes Influencing Nutrient Retention in Ecosystems

Fungi dominate the microflora in coniferous forests and they play important roles in cycling and conserving nutrients. Fungal immobilization of nutri-

TABLE 7.6   *Carbon-to-nitrogen ratios and percentage of initial N remaining in red alder leaves and Douglas-fir and western hemlock needles at the Thompson Research Center, in Pacific silver fir needles at Findley Lake, and in Douglas-fir needles at the H. J. Andrews Forest after 1 and 2 years in litterbags.*

Site	Community[a]	Litter species	C/N ratio after 1 yr	C/N ratio after 2 yr	Percent of initial N remaining after 1 yr	Percent of initial N remaining after 2 yr
A. E. Thompson, Wash.[b]	Alru/Pomu	Red alder	19	20	74	67
	Psme/Gash	Douglas-fir	25	24	108	83
	Tshe/Pomu	Western hemlock	51	37	103	103
Findley Lake, Wash.[b]	Abam-Tsme/ Vade	Pacific silver fir	34	28	106	126
H. J. Andrews, Oreg.[c]	Tshe/Rhma- Bene	Douglas-fir	42	37	110	100

[a]Alru = *Alnus rubra;* Gash = *Gaultheria shallon;* Abam = *Abies amabilis;* Tsme = *Tsuga mertensiana;* Vade = *Vaccinum deliciosum;* Bene = *Berberis nervosa;* for other abbreviations see Table 7.5.
[b]Edmonds, 1980.
[c]K. Cromack, unpublished data.

ents varies from ecosystem to ecosystem in the biome. Immobilization occurs when nutrients are incorporated into fungal biomass, as during periods of active growth. Vogt and Edmonds (1980) found greater fungal immobilization of nitrogen, phosphorus, calcium, and potassium occurring in lowland western hemlock and subalpine Pacific silver fir ecosystems than in lowland Douglas-fir and red alder ecosystems. Maximum immobilization occurred in winter and spring and appeared to correlate with active fungal growth. Immobilization in these seasons may serve to prevent leaching losses during the wet period of the year, particularly during snowmelt. Phosphorus may also be conserved in terrestrial ecosystems as a result of calcium oxalate production by fungi (Graustein et al. 1977).

Although mycorrhizae received only limited attention from biome researchers, their importance and the importance of the belowground ecosystem should not be underestimated. Mycorrhizae are important in nutrient immobilization and tree uptake. Fogel and Hunt (1979) recently pointed out their importance in Douglas-fir ecosystems.

Another method that trees use to conserve nutrients is internal translocation. This was amply demonstrated by Turner (1977), who observed the effects of soil nitrogen availability on nitrogen transfers in a low-site-quality, forty-two-year-old Douglas-fir stand. He used a number of treatments to vary nitrogen availability. The five treatments consisted of 0 (control), 220, and 880 kg/ha of urea-N; a sugar and sawdust application; and a sugar, sawdust, phosphorus, potassium, sulfur, and calcium treatment. The last two treatments were intended to stress the nitrogen supply by stimulating microorganism activity and possibly inducing growth responses to other nutrients.

In the 880 kg/ha nitrogen treatment, growth requirements were entirely met by uptake and internal translocation became negative. Nitrogen uptake exceeded growth requirement thus nitrogen accumulated in older tissue. In the 220 kg/ha nitrogen treatment, growth nutrient requirement was greater than uptake and the difference was provided by translocation. The difference between requirement and uptake increased in the control and carbohydrate treatments. This study indicates that internal translocation provides a mechanism by which trees can maximize growth under nutrient-poor conditions.

On a broader, long-term scale, one might expect that forests in habitats where nitrogen mineralization is slow might slowly accumulate large foliar nitrogen reserves. These reserves would provide for within-tree translocation during periods of low nitrogen availability, for example, during unusually dry or cold growing seasons, when decomposition and nitrogen mineralization rates are very slow. The absolute values of foliar nitrogen pools, however, may not be controlled by forest floor nitrogen availability. Grier and Running (1977) showed that leaf-area index is strongly related to site water balance for a variety of ecosystems in Oregon. Since foliar biomass is closely related to leaf-area index, and since foliar nitrogen concentration varies much less than biomass, it would seem that foliage nitrogen content is dictated by site water balance.

Some of Grier and Running's data are shown in Figure 7.6 in the form of a transect from the wet Oregon coast to the very dry eastern slope of the Cascade Mountains. Foliar biomass and nitrogen content are quite high on the coast, but they drop off in the drier Willamette Valley, which lies in the rain shadow of the Coast Range. In the wetter, west slopes of the Cascades, foliar biomass and nitrogen content increase again and then rapidly drop on the dry, east slopes of the Cascades.

To properly assess foliar nitrogen reserves, however, total foliage nitrogen content must be viewed in terms of the flux into and out of that pool. One way to approach this is to calculate mean residence times (MRT) in years as indexes of relative foliar reserves. This is done by dividing total foliage content by litter plus throughfall transfer. Similarly, forest floor MRT values (calculated in a similar way) can serve as indexes of decomposition and nitrogen mineralization.

Forest floor MRT is not exclusively regulated by climatic conditions. Lignin content and nitrogen status have a strong effect on decomposition rate, as shown earlier. For instance nitrogen MRT values are different in the Douglas-fir and red alder stands at the Thompson site (6.5 and 1.5 years, respectively) even though the stands are adjacent to each other and are subject to the same climatic conditions. While it is obvious that climatic conditions

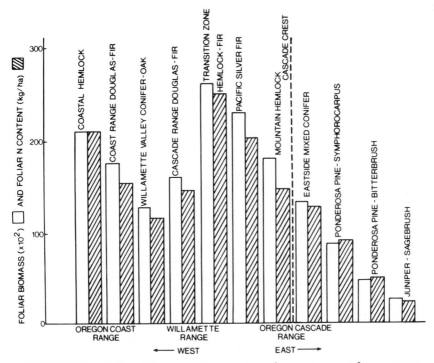

FIGURE 7.6 *Foliage biomass and N content along a transect from eastern Oregon to the Oregon coast (after Grier and Running 1977).*

affect decomposition and N mineralization rates, neither forest floor nor foliar MRT was well correlated with mean annual temperature or precipitation ($r^2 < 0.5$ in both cases). Thus, in this exercise, we view forest floor MRT as an independent variable (influenced by climatic conditions and species differences) and hypothesize that foliar MRT is correlated with it. Both nitrogen and forest floor MRT values for all the forest ecosystems studied in the coniferous forest biome are plotted in Figure 7.7. Although these ecosystems encompass a wide range of species and climatic conditions (deciduous and coniferous, subalpine to coastal), it is clear that good correlations exist. This does not prove cause and effect, but it supports the hypothesis that forest floor nitrogen availability affects the way trees handle foliar nitrogen reserves.

NUTRIENT ACCUMULATION AND CYCLING DURING STAND DEVELOPMENT

Douglas-Fir Ecosystems

It is clearly not feasible to measure productivity and nutrient cycling during the development of a single stand without the devotion of many generations of

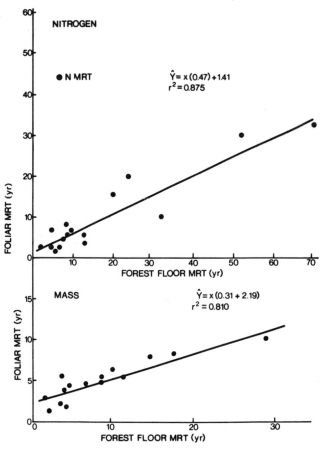

FIGURE 7.7 *Relation between foliar and forest floor mean residence time (MRT) among various deciduous and coniferous stands in a climatic-geographic gradient in the coniferous forest biome.*

researchers. Alternatively, stand development patterns can be inferred by studying stands of different ages within the same geographic, edaphic, and physiographic setting. Such an analysis was conducted in a series of low-site-quality Douglas-fir stands at the Thompson site (Long and Turner 1975, Turner and Long 1975, Cole and Rapp 1980). This analysis revealed many parallels between organic matter and nutrient accumulation patterns during Douglas-fir stand development.

A full discussion of organic matter production and accumulation during stand development is given in Chapter 5. Here accumulation of nutrients during stand development is compared with that of organic matter. Emphasis is on nitrogen, potassium, and calcium. Also considered are changes in key processes during this development sequence.

The accumulation of nitrogen and potassium within the foliage (Figure 7.8a) closely follows biomass accumulation described in Chapter 5, indicating that for more mobile elements (in this case nitrogen and potassium) a steady-state condition parallel to that found for biomass is achieved. Mobility of these two elements originates from two quite separate processes. Nitrogen is extensively translocated within the tree from older to current foliage while potassium is leached from foliage by throughfall. In the case of the immobile nutrient calcium, accumulation continues for at least the first seventy-five years of development.

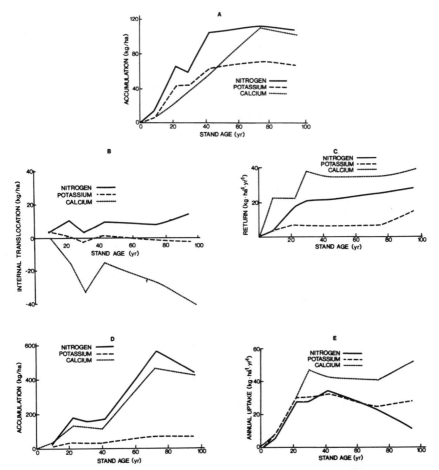

FIGURE 7.8   *(A) Accumulation in foliage; (B) internal translocation; (C) return to the forest floor by both litterfall and crown leaching; (D) accumulation in the forest floor; and (E) annual uptake of N, K and Ca during Douglas-fir stand development (from Cole et al. 1968). Internal translocation was calculated using current tissue N concentrations minus N concentration in older tissue. Corrections were made for leaching losses.*

There appears to be an increase in translocation of nitrogen with age, at least in low productivity, nitrogen-poor Douglas-fir ecosystems (Figure 7.8b). From these data it can be hypothesized that the Douglas-fir forest becomes significantly more efficient in nitrogen utilization as it matures. In that nitrogen is systematically being withdrawn from the cycling process and stored in such tissue as the bole and the bark, this increased efficiency could be of real nutritional importance to the trees in nitrogen-limited ecosystems.

Internal translocation of potassium and calcium is less than that for nitrogen. Large quantities of potassium are leached from the foliage by precipitation before translocation from the older to current tissue has occurred. Thus potassium requirements appear to be met mainly by uptake. Calcium, on the other hand, is largely incorporated in cell wall material. Thus there is no calcium transfer from older to younger foliage.

The increased amount of calcium in foliage of older stands appears to be related to an increase in needle retention time as stands age, thus allowing more time for calcium accumulation to occur in older foliage. Evidence for this increase in needle retention shows up in the leaf litter/standing foliar biomass ratio, which is low for younger stands and high for older ones. The twenty-two-year-old stand appears to retain needles for only two to three years while the ninety-five-year-old stand's retention time is nearer to six years.

The rate of litterfall and crownwash return in a Douglas-fir age sequence follows canopy development, reaching a maximum with crown closure, then remaining at nearly this level (Figure 7.8c).

There is a general pattern of high nutrient return by understory vegetation during the initial twenty to twenty-five years of the stand, which corresponds to the period when this part of the vegetation plays its most dominant role in the structure of the ecosystem (Chapter 5). With the closure of the forest canopy and corresponding decrease in the biomass of the understory species, there is a corresponding decrease in return from the understory species.

As the stand matures, the amount of woody litterfall increases even though leaf litter may remain relatively constant. Up to 90 percent of annual litterfall in a 450-year-old stand in Oregon consisted of wood, including tree stems (Grier and Logan 1977) while about 50 and 25 percent of total litterfall was woody in the 95- and 22-year-old stands at the Thompson site. Since wood has a low nutrient content, total nutrient return should not increase as rapidly as total organic matter return to the forest floor. This widens the C:N ratio and slows nutrient mineralization.

Needle decomposition rates increase until canopy closure and then slowly decrease (Table 7.7; Edmonds 1979). The k values determined after one year were statistically different at the 95 percent level among stands, but there were no differences in decomposition rates based on two years' data. This trend for decomposition rates is closely related to the annual ecosystem productivity in these stands as determined by Turner and Long (1975). The stands with the highest annual productivity also had the largest k values.

As shown in Chapter 5, biomass of woody tissue increases with time and

TABLE 7.7 *Decomposition rates of Douglas-fir needles in relation to stand age at the A. E. Thompson Research Center, Washington.*

Stand Age (yr)	Decomposition constant, k^a (yr^{-1})	
	1 year	2 year
11	0.48	0.41
22	0.69	0.56
44	0.57	0.49
75	0.53	0.53
97	0.56	0.40

[a]Based on the exponential model $x = x_0 e^{-kt}$ (Olson 1963)

will presumably continue to do so for at least several hundred years (Grier et al. 1974). Nutrient accumulation in the forest also increases as the total forest floor biomass increases (Figure 7.8d). One would expect this since the release of nitrogen and calcium is dependent on the decomposition of the forest floor. The accumulation rate for potassium is markedly lower, primarily because potassium is present in ionic form, not as part of organic structures. Thus its retention is dependent on ion exchange, not decomposition. These data suggest that a nitrogen deficiency could be progressively induced with time due to accumulation in the forest floor.

Since forest floor biomass and nutrient content increase during Douglas-fir stand development, it is interesting to speculate as to whether the forest floor is a source or sink of nutrients. Gessel and Balci (1965) speculated that the forest floor is a significant source of nitrogen for tree uptake in this region.

Calculations were made to estimate the proportion of nitrogen uptake derived from forest floor. This was done by assembling nutrient budgets from measured fluxes and changes in nutrient content in the age-sequence of Douglas-fir stands studied at the Thompson site. The results of this calculation suggest that an increasing proportion of uptake is being derived from the forest floor as stand age increases. Up to age 20, 55 percent of the nitrogen taken up is derived from the forest floor, but at age 70 almost 100 percent is taken up from the forest floor. Douglas-fir seems to become less and less dependent on the mineral soil for nutrient requirements as the stand matures and relies more on internal cycling processes and uptake from the forest floor.

The maximum annual uptakes of nitrogen, calcium, and potassium correspond closely to maximum development of the crown (Figure 7.8e). The annual uptake of nitrogen begins to decrease, however, at approximately forty years. By the time the stand is ninety-five years old, annual nitrogen uptake has decreased from a maximum of 40 kg/ha (at forty years) to 17 kg/ha. It is not known whether this reduced uptake pattern is due to decreased nutrient demands or decreased soil supply. In either case, the stand must continue to meet its requirements. This is accomplished in two ways: by an increase in needle retention time and by a significant increase in internal translocation.

The accumulation patterns for the three nutrient elements within the understory closely follow that of understory biomass. Maximum nutrient accumulation is reached between ten and twenty-two years in age and then rapidly decreases as the tree canopy closes (Figure 7.9). A second period of biomass and nutrient accumulation occurs in the understory vegetation when the canopy begins to open in later years. Understory biomass in the 450-year-old Douglas-fir forests of watershed 10 was actually greater in some habitats than that found in young stands (Grier and Logan 1977).

Extrapolation to Other Forest Types

The patterns observed in the Douglas-fir age sequence analysis can be used as a model for other ecosystems as well. It is obvious, however, that two stands of the same age can be at very different stages of stand development. For example, Turner et al. (1976) compared nutrient distribution and transfers in a thirty-four-year-old red alder stand with those in a nearby thirty-six-year-old Douglas-fir stand. They found that tree biomass was comparable in the two stands at this age, but the nitrogen content of the alder was higher, presumably because of its nitrogen-fixing capabilities. The understory component was greater in the thirty-four-year-old alder stand than in the thirty-six-year-old Douglas-fir stand because the two stands appear to be in different stages of development. A thirty-four-year-old alder stand in this region is fully mature and possibly overmature. In contrast, Douglas-fir stands of this age are in their period of most rapid growth. The fact that alder is deciduous whereas Douglas-fir is evergreen may account for some understory differences, but comparisons with understory measurements made in 1963 (at age twenty-four) on the same stand (Balci 1964) indicate that the understory biomass at that time was smaller, more nearly comparable with that of the then twenty-six-year-old Douglas-fir stand. The authors postulate that the thirty-four-year-old red alder stand is at a stage of development somewhat analogous to that of the 450-year-old Douglas-fir stand. Since the life span of alder is about one-tenth that of Douglas-fir, a thirty-four-year-old alder stand might be compared to a 340-year-old Douglas-fir stand. Viewed this way, the development of these two stand types would proceed as shown in Figure 7.10.

EFFECTS OF SITE DISTURBANCE ON NUTRIENT CYCLING AND ITS MANAGEMENT IMPLICATIONS

To evaluate and attempt to predict the effects of various site manipulations on nutrient cycling, we must consider the processes involved in nutrient trans-

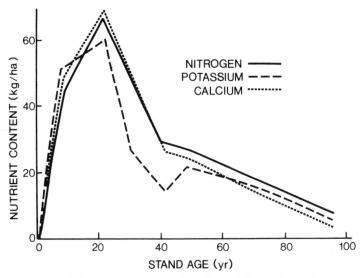

FIGURE 7.9 *Accumulation of N, K, and Ca in the understory vegetation of various aged stands of Douglas-fir (after Cole and Rapp 1980).*

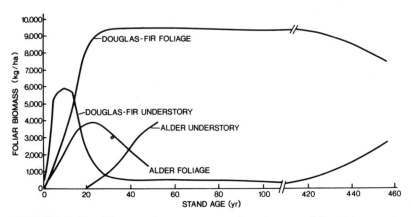

FIGURE 7.10 *Changes in overstory and understory foliar biomass for Douglas-fir and red alder during stand development (after Turner et al. 1976).*

fer. Very seldom are considerations of pool sizes and nutrient budgets useful in themselves in predicting or evaluating the effects of manipulations. An exception to this generality is clearcutting, where a nutrient pool, the tree bole, is removed from the site directly. Thus the following discussion focuses on the processes described previously and the way they are affected by manipulations.

Effect of Harvesting on the Nutrient Capital
of an Ecosystem

The most obvious immediate effect of clearcutting on nutrient distribution is the removal of part of one of the nutrient pools, that is, the trees. Assuming that all of the foliage is left on a site, clearcutting results in the removal of only a small percentage of the nutrient capital of a site, provided the site isn't burned. This is clearly illustrated in Table 7.8 for nitrogen for seventeen ecosystems in Washington and Oregon.

There is a further increase in net losses of nitrogen when the entire above-ground portion of the tree is removed, such as is done in some logging opera-

TABLE 7.8   *Ecosystem nitrogen capital remaining after bole only, whole tree and total vegetation removal in forest ecosystems in Washington and Oregon.*

				% Remaining		
Age (yr)	Ecosystem Species	State	Ecosystem Total (kg/ha)	Bole only removal[a]	Whole tree removal[b]	Vegetation removal[c]
9	Douglas-fir	WA	3017	99.6	98.9	97.4
22	Douglas-fir	WA	3281	95.6	93.1	91.0
30	Douglas-fir	WA	3232	95.6	93.2	91.7
30	Douglas-fir	WA	3477	95.1	90.9	90.1
42	Douglas-fir	WA	3366	93.3	89.4	88.3
49	Douglas-fir	WA	3538	95.3	90.6	89.9
73	Douglas-fir	WA	3751	95.4	90.7	90.2
95	Douglas-fir	WA	3686	92.5	87.9	87.7
95	Douglas-fir	OR	10805	97.5	95.2	95.1
130	Douglas-fir	OR	8775	97.9	95.6	95.5
450	Douglas-fir	OR	5725	93.9	90.1	89.9
30	Western hemlock/ Sitka spruce	OR	33781	99.5	98.6	98.6
121	Western hemlock/ Sitka spruce	OR	36315	98.4	98.0	97.9
130	Noble fir	OR	15500	97.5	96.0	96.0
130	Mountain hemlock/ silver fir	OR	6529	97.2	94.0	93.7
23	Pacific silver fir	WA	2868	99.0	94.1	93.1
170	Pacific silver fir/ Mountain and western hemlock	WA	4895	96.9	93.1	92.8

[a]Tree stems removed to a minimum top diameter inside bark of 10 cm.
[b]Tree stems, branches, foliage and reproductive structures removed from site for all trees greater than 5-cm-diameter breast height (1.4 m above soil surface).
[c]All living vegetation removed to surface of litter layer.

tions in the Pacific Northwest where "whole-tree yarding" is conducted so that tops and limbs may be more efficiently removed at a central landing. Almost 10 percent of the ecosystem nitrogen capital may be removed in some cases (Table 7.8). Only a small further increase is incurred if all living vegetation is removed to the surface of the litter layer.

The concept of whole-tree logging and almost total utilization of logging residues will, if adopted, have some impact on future forest growth, especially on those forest soils with a relatively low supply of essential elements. The reduced site fertility resulting from removal of forest litter for farm-use purposes is still observable in European forests.

In some soil systems this loss can be replaced by weathering or atmospheric input but in others alternative additions may need to be considered. Total loss from the system is determined not only by removal in a given harvest but also by frequency of harvest. Therefore areas managed under a so-called energy plantation concept may have more serious problems than those under less intensive management schemes.

It can be concluded that net loss from the system due to harvesting is nearly independent of the rotation period but highly dependent on degree of utilization of the trees. In general, extending the rotation period does not proportionally increase total elemental loss; however, increasing harvest removal from bole only to whole tree typically increases removals to the point where they become a significant portion of the total nitrogen capital of the ecosystem.

Calculations can be made for any stand where nutrient distribution data are available. These data are available for most major timber species in the biome. For example, in the subalpine area of the state of Washington, harvesting of the 170-year-old Pacific silver fir *(Abies amabilis)* studied at Findley Lake would result in a nitrogen loss of 130 kg/ha if only the boles were removed (Turner and Singer 1976). This is similar to removals estimated for Douglas-fir. With a rotation of one hundred years for these sites and a net annual addition from precipitation of 1 kg/ha, nitrogen loss from harvesting would nearly balance annual additions.

Total tree removal from these higher elevation sites would result in greater loss. These losses would also be greater than estimated for lower elevation Douglas-fir stands since nutrient-rich foliage biomass is appreciably greater. Total tree removal in Pacific silver fir stands would cause a total nitrogen loss of 330 kg/ha (Turner and Singer 1976), an annual net loss from the ecosystem over a 100-year rotation of 2.3 kg/ha. Thus total tree harvesting at these sites should result in a significant increase in nitrogen loss.

Similar calculations can be made for other nutrient elements. For Douglas-fir stands the losses of calcium, magnesium, and potassium are greater than those for nitrogen. Whether or not these ecosystems actually lose these quantities of nutrients from the available pool is largely dependent on the rate of soil mineral weathering. While the stands do not currently display any deficiency symptoms, losses of these nutrients, resulting from harvesting, could result in deficiencies in future rotations. This is especially true in the case of potassium, where exchangeable potassium appears to be at a minimal level to meet uptake requirements and in view of the fact that weathering is apparently not keeping pace with uptake and leaching (see Table 7.1).

Effect of Harvesting on Soil Leaching

The input of foliage and branches to the forest floor compartment dramatically increases the carbon and nutrient content of that compartment. Coupled with an increase in surface temperature, this usually leads to accelerated decomposition (Gessel and Cole 1965). This, in turn, should lead to increased CO_2 evolution and carbonic acid production in soil solution. Experience showed, however, that increased ion leaching occurred only in the upper few centimeters of the soil (Gessel and Cole 1965). This was due to the more acid lower soil horizons donating hydrogen ions to solution, reducing bicarbonate concentration, and causing associated cations to occupy exchange sites (Cole et al. 1975).

Results to date from an experimental clearcut in the H. J. Andrews Forest indicate that immediately following cutting the total loss of nitrogen from the terrestrial system increased by a factor of 4.5. Particulate nitrogen, however, accounted for 72 percent of the loss, dissolved organic nitrogen accounted for 26 percent, and nitrate accounted for only 2 percent. Researchers in Oregon postulate that particulate nitrogen loss will rapidly diminish as the site stabilizes, but that dissolved organic nitrogen loss may remain high for longer periods (up to five years, according to studies by R. L. Fredriksen).

The patterns of dissolved nitrogen loss are interesting in themselves. It was found that losses varied considerably from site to site within the watershed (Figure 7.11). The greatest loss occurred from a toe slope with relatively sparse postlogging vegetative cover, but in the riparian zone between this site and the seep waters entering the stream a great deal of the nitrogen was reabsorbed. As a result, the riparian zone at the Andrews site has received intensive study. Results are presented in Chapter 9.

In a study on the effects of clearcutting, Likens et al. (1969) found large cation fluxes associated with nitrification and nitrate leaching in the Hubbard Brook watershed in New Hampshire. Leaching losses in both the Washington and Oregon studies reported here were much less dramatic. Factors affecting nitrification clearly deserve further study, however, especially in regard to clearcutting.

Effects of Fire

Fire, whether it be a wildfire or a slash burn used in forest management, has a strong influence on nutrient losses from an ecosystem. These losses are

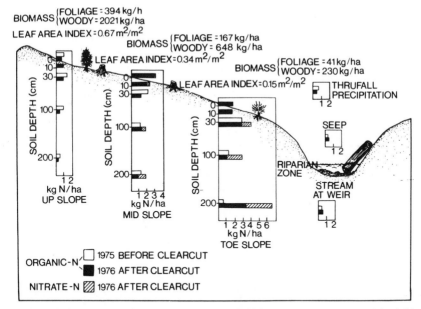

FIGURE 7.11 *Profile of N content in a hillslope transect in watershed 10 and in throughfall precipitation, seep water, and stream water at the weir. Biomass and leaf area index data pertain to postlogging residual vegetation (F. M. McCorison pers. comm.).*

largely due to volatilization, particularly in the case of nitrogen, and increased leaching losses.

Table 7.9 shows nitrogen losses from Douglas-fir ecosystems due to slash burning and wildfire. Also included for comparison are nitrogen losses in undisturbed and clearcut-only ecosystems. There is no nitrogen loss from the undisturbed old-growth ecosystem; in fact nitrogen is accumulating. There is an increasing loss of nitrogen in the progression from a clearcut-only ecosystem (3.8 percent of the ecosystem total nitrogen) to a clearcut and slash-burned ecosystem (9.5 percent loss) to an ecosystem that has experienced an intense wildfire (27 percent loss).

Fire is an important decomposition agent in natural ecosystems and it results in considerably more nitrogen loss from an ecosystem than clearcutting alone. The practice of using fire as a management tool for slash burning needs to be closely examined in relation to its impact on nitrogen losses and tree productivity.

Urea-N Fertilization

The effects of urea fertilization have been studied in some detail prior to and during the IBP. Douglas-fir growth responses to nitrogen have been docu-

TABLE 7.9 *Total annual N losses from undisturbed, clearcut only, and clearcut and slash-burned Douglas-fir ecosystems, and a ponderosa pine/Douglas-fir ecosystem subjected to intense wildfire.*

Treatment and forest type	Age (yr)	Total N loss (kg· ha⁻¹·yr⁻¹)	N loss (% of ecosys- tem total)	Mechanism of loss (in descending order of importance)
Undisturbed[a] Douglas-fir	450	-0.5	—	Accumulation; no loss
Clearcut only [b] Douglas-fir	42	123	3.8	Tree stem removal
Clearcut and slash-burned[c] Douglas-fir	42	299	9.5	Volatilization, tree stem removal, leaching
Intense wildfire[d] ponderosa pine/ Douglas-fir	> 150	736	27	Volatilization, leaching

[a]Fredriksen 1975.
[b]Cole and Gessel 1965; Cole et al. 1968.
[c]Cole et al. 1968.
[d]Grier 1976.

mented for much of the region (Gessel and Walker 1956) and forest fertilization is rapidly becoming an accepted management practice (Gessel et al. 1969, 1973). In an initial effort to evaluate the effects of fertilization on nitrogen cycling in the region, Heilman and Gessel (1963) found that they could account for nearly all of the applied nitrogen in the vegetation and forest floor after two to ten years. They further concluded that the effect of fertilization on Douglas-fir growth response was long-lasting because of increased nitrogen cycling. Following this work, emphasis began to shift toward process-level research in an effort to characterize the mechanisms of nitrogen retention in these ecosystems.

Crane (1972) and Cole et al. (1975) examined the immediate effects of urea fertilization on soil leaching and nitrogen volatilization processes. Volatilization losses were small, but urea fertilization had profound effects on cation transfer in upper soil horizons. Urea is a highly soluble, nonionic, polar organic compound, and it is therefore readily leached if applied during rainy periods. Urea, however, hydrolyzes to ammonium bicarbonate through an enzymatic reaction involving urease, an enzyme common in soils. As the ammonium bicarbonate solution moves through the soil profile, NH_4^+ displaces native cations such as K^+, Ca^{2+}, Mg^{2+}, and H^+ from the exchange sites by mass action. Thus urea fertilization makes many cation nutrients available for uptake in addition to NH_4^+. Displaced H^+ combines with HCO_3^- to form H_2CO_3, so bicarbonate as well as ammonium concentrations decrease as solutions pass deeper into the soil.

Johnson (1979) found rapid immobilization of fertilizer-applied NH_4^+ by microorganisms. He also found that NH_4^+ levels dropped to near those of unfertilized plots within four months of urea fertilization in soils similar to those studied by Crane and Cole (Figure 7.12). At four months most fertilizer nitrogen could be accounted for in the humus fraction of soil nitrogen, but there was evidence for a continual re-release of fertilizer nitrogen during the growing season for up to seven years (Johnson 1979).

Nitrification did not occur following urea fertilization in any of these studies. This is fortunate in terms of nitrogen retention, since nitrate is a mobile anion in the soil and readily leaches from the rooting zone. Laboratory experiments conducted by Heilman (1974) indicated that some forest soils produced considerable nitrate, and that urea treatment increased nitrate production in most cases. Further work is needed to determine the effects of widespread urea application on nitrification in a variety of forest soils.

Douglas-fir has a remarkable array of internal mechanisms that allow it to respond rapidly to changes in soil nitrogen availability. In a nitrogen manipulation study Turner (1977) found that the rate of nitrogen uptake was related to apparent soil nitrogen availability (Figure 7.13). Uptake was high when soil-available nitrogen was high, allowing the trees to increase foliar nitrogen reserves (Figure 7.14). On the other hand, when soil nitrogen availability was reduced by carbohydrate additions, uptake was low (Figure 7.12) and the trees were forced to rely heavily on internal translocation to meet growth requirements (Figure 7.14). As a result, foliar biomass increased and litterfall decreased in urea-treated stands, whereas foliar biomass decreased and litterfall increased in carbohydrate-treated stands. Thus, even though soil nitrogen availability may decrease rapidly after fertilization, trees may continue to benefit from enhanced nitrogen status and grow more rapidly for many years by conserving the fertilizer nitrogen they have stored internally.

Acid Rainfall and Sulfate Deposition

Acid rainfall resulting from increased sulfur dioxide and nitrous oxides from industrial sources has caused concern in recent years in terms of potential effects on both terrestrial and aquatic ecosystems (Dochinger and Seliga 1976). With respect to forest nutrition, it is feared that sulfuric or nitric acid precipitation may leach soil nutrient cations over and above rates occurring in natural systems. This has been observed particularly in Norway (Abrahamsen et al. 1976) and in the eastern United States (Likens and Bormann 1974). Records at the Thompson site show that this area has been subject to acid rainfall for the last ten years, since records of rainfall pH were begun. Analysis shows that sulfuric acid is responsible for the acidity though nitric acid is occasionally

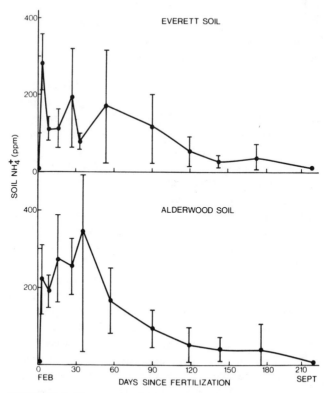

FIGURE 7.12 *Soil NH$_4^+$ levels after fertilization with 200 kg/ha urea-N (from Johnson 1979). Bars represent standard errors of the mean.*

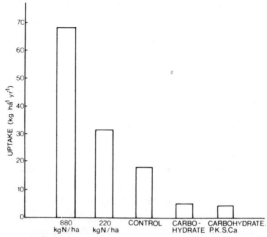

FIGURE 7.13 *Nitrogen uptake as a function of soil N availability (after Turner 1977).*

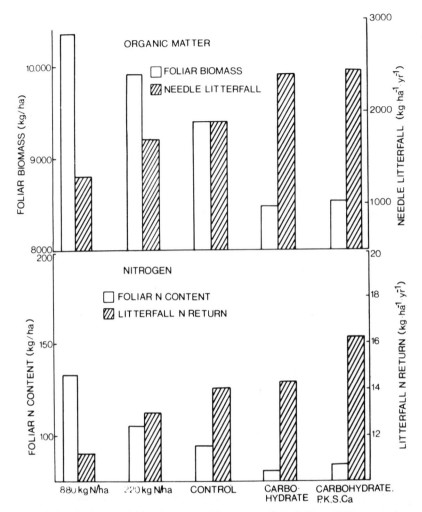

FIGURE 7.14 *Foliar biomass, N content, litterfall, and N return in Douglas-fir stands subjected to different soil N availabilities (after Turner 1977).*

present. At present levels, acid rainfall and sulfate deposition are responsible for about 20 percent of the cations removed from the rooting zone at this site (Table 7.10; Cole and Johnson 1977). This loss may not be critical to maintenance or productivity. However, should sulfuric acid in rainfall increase as anticipated use of high-sulfur coal or large quantities of low-sulfur coal (that is, Great Plains coal) increases, the situation may change.

In order for increased sulfuric acid addition to take a toll on nutrient reserves, the sulfate anion must be mobile in the soil, as is the bicarbonate anion. Two simple experiments have shown that the mobility of sulfate is

TABLE 7.10   *Annual transfers of water (cm), H^+, SO_4^{2-}, HCO_3^-, and cations (eq/ha) at the Thompson Research Center, Washington*[a]

Sample station	Water	H^+	SO_4^{2-}	HCO_3^-	Cations
Precipitation	140	240	260	420	1070
Throughfall	110	70	320	570	1080
Forest floor	90	10	1000	990	2370
A horizon	80	0	400	950	1760
B horizon	70	0	380	840	1570

Note: Average of two years from February 1973 to February 1975 calculated by converting volume fluxes at each station to a per-hectare basis. All measures except those for cations are rounded to the nearest ten units.
[a]Cole and Johnson 1977.

TABLE 7.11   *H^+, SO_4^{2-}, and total cation budgets (eq/ha) after sulfuric acid application to the soil at the Thompson Research Center, Washington.*[a]

	Input			Output			Storage		
Horizon	H^+	SO_4^{2-}	Total cations[b]	H^+	SO_4^{2-}	Total cations	H^+	SO_4^{2-}	Total cations
Forest floor	17,760	17,760	0	0.2	16,000	10,000	17,760	1,760	−10,000
Forest floor +A	35,520	35,520	0	0.2	15,000	11,200	35,520	20,000	−11,200
B (50 cm)	0.2	15,000	11,200	0.0	200	200	0.2	14,800	11,000

[a]Johnson and Cole 1977.
[b]Ca^{2+}, Mg^{2+}, Mn^{2+}, Na^+, and K^+ only.

limited in the Everett soil at the Thompson site (Johnson and Cole 1977). Applications of sulfuric acid ranging from 10^{-3} to 10^{-1} normal resulted in almost no change in cation-sulfate leaching past 50 cm in the soil (Table 7.11). Soil extractions with potassium phosphate solutions showed that the input sulfate was accounted for as absorbed sulfate. Laboratory studies confirmed that the Everett soil has a strong sulfate adsorption capacity, as do many other soils with appreciable sesquioxide contents (Howard and Reisenauer 1966).

This study showed that the Everett series soil at the Thompson site has appreciable sulfur adsorption capacity and temporarily buffers out high acid inputs. Mobility of sulfur in these systems over long periods is now known. It should be recalled that sulfate is an essential nutrient and elimination of the sources of its input may cause sulfur deficiencies (Tabatabai and Bremner 1972). In fact, Turner et al. (1977) have shown that some stands in the northwest that did not respond to nitrogen fertilization have very low foliar sulfate concentrations, implying that they are sulfur-deficient.

CONCLUSIONS

Nutrient cycling research in the coniferous biome program has unquestionably made a large contribution to the body of knowledge on this subject. Coniferous forests of this region contain efficient mechanisms for capitalizing on and conserving critical nutrients, especially nitrogen. Nutrients influence forest productivity because many nutrient cycling pathways are intertwined with carbon pathways.

Although some studies during the biome program suggested actual or potential deficiencies in potassium, magnesium, calcium, or sulfur, the over-riding importance of nitrogen is clearly evident. The fact that nitrogen is the most critically limiting nutrient in forests of the northwest is not new, but biome research has illuminated various coupled mechanisms that allow these forests to efficiently utilize and conserve this critical nutrient.

Atmospheric inputs, nitrogen fixation, soil weathering, internal translocation, litterfall and crownwash, litter decomposition, uptake, and soil leaching are the key processes regulating nutrient cycling. Particulate deposition plays a role in nutrient inputs close to the coast; however, foliage leaching tends to modify atmospheric inputs such that soluble inputs to the forest floor are similar no matter where stands are located.

Nitrogen fixation is obviously the most important source of nitrogen input into coniferous forests. The principal nitrogen fixers in the biome, at least in terms of biomass, are red alder *(Alnus rubra)* and snowbush *(Ceanothus velutinus)*. In old-growth stands, the canopy dwelling foliose lichen *(Lobaria oregana)* is also important. Another site of fixation is downed logs, and estimates of greater than $5 \text{ kg} \cdot \text{ha}^{-1} \cdot \text{yr}^{-1}$ have been made. Estimates of nitrogen fixation by red alder range from 15 to 321 $\text{kg} \cdot \text{ha}^{-1} \cdot \text{yr}^{-1}$ with a maximum at about age 20. Snowbush has fixation rates ranging from 72 to 108 kg $\cdot \text{ha}^{-1} \cdot \text{yr}^{-1}$. Canopy fixation by lichens is relatively small (approximately 5 $\text{kg} \cdot \text{hg}^{-1} \cdot \text{yr}^{-1}$).

Very little accurate information is available on elemental inputs from weathering. It appears, however, that weathering rates for elements at the Thompson site may be unable to keep pace with cation removal by uptake or leaching, and the assumption of steady state in soil-exchangeable cations may not be justifiable.

Internal translocation or withdrawal of nutrients from foliage prior to abscission is an important mechanism of nutrient conservation, particularly for nitrogen. The litterfall/decomposition cycle can be short-circuited in this manner. There appears to be an increase in internal translocation of nitrogen in Douglas-fir stands as they age, particularly in nitrogen-limited ecosystems. On the other hand, potassium and calcium are not internally translocated to the degree noted for nitrogen. Nitrogen transfers via litterfall and internal translocation are very much attuned to available nitrogen in the soil such that in urea-treated stands foliar biomass increases and litterfall decreases.

Litter decomposition is limited more by moisture than temperature in the biome, particularly in lowland ecosystems, and is more pronounced in southern than in northern areas. Temperature plays a more important role in high-altitude ecosystems although considerable decomposition occurs under snowpacks. Decomposition rates generally decrease along age and altitudinal gradients. Litter fungi, both decomposers and mycorrhizae, play an important role in nitrogen conservation and immobilization.

Once nitrogen is released as a result of decomposition it is available to the trees. Studies with Douglas-fir seedlings indicate that the form of nitrogen available influences nitrogen uptake in that $NH_4^+ - N$ is taken up more rapidly than $NO_3^- - N$. Interestingly, although seedlings grown in $NH_4^+ - N$ in solution culture accumulate considerably more N than those grown in $NO_3^- - N$, the accumulation of cations in the latter is lower, probably because of a charge balance problem. In general, nitrogen is taken up more rapidly than other nutrients.

On a stand basis, uptake of nutrients changes significantly with stand age. For example, in Douglas-fir the maximum annual uptake of nitrogen, calcium, and potassium closely corresponds to maximum crown development, which is also the time of maximum decomposition. This is between twenty and thirty years, depending on stand density.

Cations are leached through soil in many temperate forest ecosystems by the carbonic acid or bicarbonate mechanism where H^+ ions associated with bicarbonate ions displace cations from the soil exchange sites. This mechanism, however, does not operate in all forest ecosystems. Although it dominates in tropical and lowland temperate ecosystems, organic acids dominate in subalpine and more northerly sites. For example, in Alaska organic acids dominate, mainly because of low soil pH values and the fact that carbonic acid does not dissociate appreciably below pH 4.5. Cold forest ecosystems thus conserve nutrients by suppressing carbonic acid leaching within the rooting zone. This is important because CO_2 pressures build to very high levels beneath melting snowpacks, and if pH conditions allowed it, carbonic acid leaching would be great. Erosion is also an important process in terms of nutrient output; however, it is episodic in nature. Nitrogen accumulation is a direct expression of the various inputs and outputs during the total age of the ecosystem. In the geologically young Puget Sound lowland soils, only 3000 to 5000 kg nitrogen/ha have accumulated since the glaciers receded approximately 12,000 years ago. This represents an accumulation rate of 0.2 to 0.4 $kg \cdot ha^{-1}$. This seems to be a very low average rate; however, if a site were occupied by red alder, nitrogen accumulation could be as high as $320 \cdot ha^{-1} \cdot yr^{-1}$. Such large inputs are partially balanced by fire and more recently by logging. A fire in a second-growth forest, for example, could consume up to 400 kg/ha of nitrogen. Fire thus plays an important ecological and nutritional role in western coniferous forests.

There are many similarities between organic matter and nutrient accumulation patterns during Douglas-fir stand development. Accumulation of nitrogen and potassium within foliage follows that of foliar biomass (that is, near steady state after canopy closure) but for different reasons. Nitrogen is translocated from older to current foliage while potassium is leached from foliage. Calcium accumulates at least for the first seventy-five years, largely because needle retention time increases as stands age.

Accumulation patterns for nitrogen, potassium, and calcium within the understory closely follow that for understory biomass, reaching a maximum between ten and twenty years in age and then decreasing. A second period of understory nutrient accumulation may occur as the canopy begins to break up in old-growth ecosystems.

Nitrogen and calcium accumulate in the forest floor as stand age increases and nitrogen deficiency can be induced with time because of this accumulation. On the other hand, the accumulation rate for potassium is markedly lower because its retention is not totally dependent on litter decomposition.

Ecosystems with slow nitrogen litter mineralization apparently keep larger foliar reserves; however, some evidence suggests that foliar biomass may not be determined by nutrient status but rather by site water balance, since trees on drier sites retain less foliage. Analysis of MRT of nitrogen in foliage and the forest floor shows that as MRT of the forest floor increases so does foliage retention time, suggesting that nutrient status does control the amount of foliar biomass.

There are large gaps in our knowledge of nitrogen cycling, however. The processes of nitrogen fixation, nitrification, and denitrification are poorly understood and each deserves further study. As nitrogen fertilization becomes more widespread in these forests, information on potential deficiencies of other nutrients and the interactions of nitrogen with them will become increasingly necessary. Biome research has set a direction for future research in this area in terms of weathering release of cations and the relations between acid rain, soil sulfur status, and stand sulfur deficiencies.

In a more general vein, these biome studies have demonstrated the value of a systems approach to the study of nutrient cycling, which integrates long-term budget studies with short-term process studies. Comparisons of state variables such as nutrient content of the soil and foliage are of limited value without complementary information on nutrient transfer processes. State variables such as nutrient pool sizes are no more than a result of several transfer processes integrated over time. We are not yet able to develop a model that numerically integrates all the short-term processes into long-term nutrient accumulations, but we can conceptualize this, as in Figure 7.1. Of the processes depicted in Figure 7.1, biome research has dealt with each at various levels of intensity, but more information is needed, especially for belowground processes. It is to be hoped that post-IBP research will address some of these needs.

LITERATURE CITED

Abrahamsen, G., R. Hornvedt, and B. Tveite, 1976, Impacts of acid precipitation on coniferous forest ecosystems, in *First International Symposium on Acid Precipitation and the Forest Ecosystem Proc.*, L. S. Dochinger and T. A. Seliga, eds., U.S. Department of Agriculture Forest Service General Technical Report NE-23, U.S. Department of Agriculture Forest Service, Upper Darby, Penna., pp. 991–1009.

Aho, P. E., R. J. Seidler, H. J. Evans, and R. N. Raju, 1974, Distribution, enumeration, and identification of nitrogen-fixing bacteria associated with decay in living white fir trees, *Phytopathology* **64:**1413–1420.

Balci, A. N., 1964, Physical, chemical and hydrological properties of certain western Washington forest floor types, Ph.D. dissertation, University of Washington, Seattle, 192p.

Bond, G., 1954, An isotopic study of nitrogen fixation associated with nodulated plants of *Alnus, Myrica,* and *Hippophae, J. Exp. Bot.* **6:**303–311.

Cole, D. W., and C. Bledsoe, 1976, Nutrient dynamics of Douglas-fir, *14th IUFRO World Congr. Proc.*, Div II, 21–25 June 1976, Oslo, Norway, pp. 53–64.

Cole, D. W., and S. P. Gessel, 1965, Movement of elements through a forest soil as influenced by tree removal and fertilizer additions, in *Forest-Soil Relationships in North America,* C. T. Youngberg, ed., Oregon State University Press, Corvallis, pp. 95–104.

Cole, D. W., and D. W. Johnson, 1977, Atmospheric sulfate additions and cation leaching in a Douglas-fir ecosystem, *Water Resour. Res.* **13:**313–317.

Cole, D. W., and M. Rapp, 1980, Elemental cycling in forest ecosystems, in *Dynamic Properties of Forest Ecosystems,* D. E. Reichle, ed., Cambridge University Press, Cambridge, pp. 341–409.

Cole, D. W., S. P. Gessel, and S. F. Dice, 1968, Distribution and cycling of nitrogen, phosphorus, potassium, and calcium in a second-growth Douglas-fir ecosystem, in *Primary Productivity and Mineral Cycling in Natural Ecosystems,* H. E. Young, ed., University of Maine Press, Orono, pp. 197–233.

Cole, D. W., W. J. B. Crane, and C. C. Grier, 1975, The effect of forest management practices on water chemistry in a second-growth Douglas-fir ecosystem, in *Forest Soils and Land Management,* B. Bernier and C. H. Winget, eds., 4th North American Forest Soils Conf. Proc., Les Presses de l'Universite Laval, Quebec, pp. 195–208.

Cole, D. W., S. P. Gessel, and J. Turner, 1978, Comparative mineral cycling in red alder and Douglas-fir, in *Utilization and Management of Alder,* D. G. Briggs, D. S. DeBell, and W. A. Atkinson, compilers, U.S. Department of Agriculture Forest Service General Technical Report PNW-70, U.S.

Department of Agriculture Forest Service, Portland, Oreg., pp. 327–336.

Cornaby, B. W., and J. B. Waide, 1973, Nitrogen fixation in decaying chestnut logs, *Plant Soil* **39**:445–448.

Crane, W. J. B., 1972, Urea-nitrogen transformations, soil reactions and elemental movement via leaching and volatilization in a coniferous forest ecosystem following fertilization, Ph.D. dissertation, University of Washington, Seattle, 285p.

Denison, W. C., 1973, Life in tall trees, *Sci. Am.* **288**:74–80.

Dochinger, L. S. and T. A. Seliga, eds., 1976, *Proceedings of the First International Symposium on Acid Precipitation and the Forest Ecosystem,* U.S. Department of Agriculture Forest Service General Technical Report NE-23, Upper Darby, Pennsylvania, 1074p.

Duvigneaud, P., and S. Denaeyer-DeSmet, 1970, Biological cycling of minerals in temperate deciduous forests, in *Analysis of Temperate Forest Ecosystems,* D. E. Reichle, ed., Springer-Verlag., New York, pp. 199–225.

Edmonds, R. L., 1979, Decomposition and nutrient release in Douglas-fir needle litter in relation to stand development, *Can. J. For. Res.* **9**:132–140.

Edmonds, R. L., 1980, Litter decomposition and nutrient release in Douglas-fir, red alder, western hemlock and Pacific silver fir ecosystems in western Washington, *Can. J. For. Res.* **10**:327–337.

Fogel, R., and K. Cromack, Jr., 1977, Effect of habitat and substrate quality on Douglas-fir litter decomposition in western Oregon. *Can. J. Bot.* **55**:1632–1640.

Fogel, R., and G. Hunt, 1979, Fungal and arboreal biomass in a western Oregon Douglas-fir ecosystem: Distribution patterns and turnover, *Can. J. For. Res.* **9**:245–256.

Fredriksen, R. L., 1975, Nitrogen, phosphorus and particulate matter budgets of five coniferous forest ecosystems in the western Cascades Range, Oregon, Ph.D. dissertation, University of Oregon, Corvallis, 127p.

Gessel, S. P., and A. N. Balci, 1965, Amount and composition of forest floors under Washington coniferous forests, in *Forest-Soil Relationships in North America,* C. T. Youngberg, ed., Oregon State University Press, Corvallis, pp. 11–23.

Gessel, S. P., and D. W. Cole, 1965, Influence of removal of forest cover on movement of water and associated elements through soil, *J. Am. Water Works Assoc.* **57**:1301–1310.

Gessel, S. P., and R. B. Walker, 1956, Height growth response of Douglas-fir to nitrogen fertilization, *Soil Sci. Soc. Am. Proc.* **20**:97–100.

Gessel, S. P., T. N. Stoate, and K. J. Turnbull, 1969, The growth and behavior of Douglas-fir with nitrogenous fertilizer in western Washington, *Institute of Forest Products Contrib. No. 7,* University of Washington, Seattle, 119p.

Gessel, S. P., D. W. Cole, and E. C. Steinbrenner, 1973, Nitrogen balances in forest ecosystems of the Pacific Northwest, *Soil Biol. Biochem.* **5**:19–34.

Graustein, W. C., K. Cromack, and P. Sollins, 1977, Calcium oxalate: Occurrence in soils and effect on nutrient and geochemical cycles, *Science* **198**:1252–1254.

Grier, C. C., 1972, Effects of fire on the movement and distribution of elements within a forest ecosystem, Ph.D. dissertation, University of Washington, Seattle, 167p.

Grier, C. C., 1976, Wildfire effects on nutrient distribution and leaching in a coniferous ecosystem, *Can. J. For. Res.* **5**:599–607.

Grier, C. C., 1978a, Biomass, productivity and nitrogen-phosphorus cycles in hemlock-spruce stands of the central Oregon coast, in *Western Hemlock Management,* R. J. Zasoski and W. A. Atkinson, eds., Institute of Forest Products Contribution No. 34, College of Forest Resources, University of Washington, Seattle, pp. 71–81.

Grier, C. C., 1978b, A *Tsuga heterophylla–Picea sitchensis* ecosystem of coastal Oregon: Decomposition and nutrient balances of fallen logs, *Can. J. For. Res.* **8**:198–206.

Grier, C. C. and R. S. Logan, 1977, Old-growth *Pseudotsuga menziesii* communities of a western Oregon watershed: Biomass distribution and production budgets, *Ecol. Monogr.* **47**:373–400.

Grier, C. C., and S. Running, 1977, Leaf area of mature northwestern coniferous forests: Relation to site water balance, *Ecology* **58**:893–899.

Grier, C. C., D. W. Cole, C. T. Dyrness, and R. L. Fredriksen, 1974, Nutrient cycling in 37- and 450-year-old Douglas-fir ecosystems, in *Integrated Research in the Coniferous Forest Biome,* R. H. Waring and R. L. Edmonds, eds., Coniferous Forest Biome Bulletin No. 5, University of Washington, Seattle, pp. 21–34.

Howard, M. E., and H. M. Reisenauer, 1966, Movement and reactions of inorganic soil sulfur, *Soil Sci.* **101**:326–333.

Heilman, P. E., 1974, Effect of urea fertilization on nitrification in forest soils of the Pacific Northwest, *Soil Sci. Soc. Am. Proc.* **38**:664–667.

Heilman, P. E., and S. P. Gessel, 1963, Nitrogen requirement and the biological cycling of nitrogen in Douglas-fir stands in relationship to the effects of nitrogen fertilization, *Plant Soil* **18**:386–402.

Johnson, D. W., 1979, Some nitrogen fractions in two forest soils and their changes in response to urea fertilization, *Northwest Sci.* **53**:22–32.

Johnson, D. W., and D. W. Cole, 1977, Sulfate mobility in an outwash soil in western Washington, *Water Air Soil Pollut.* **7**:489–495.

Johnson, D. W., D. W. Cole, and S. P. Gessel, 1975, Processes of nutrient transfer in a tropical rain forest, *Biotropica* **7**:208–215.

Johnson, D. W., D. W. Cole, S. P. Gessel, M. J. Singer, and R. V. Minden, 1977, Carbonic acid leaching in a tropical, temperate, subalpine and northern forest soil, *Arct. Alp. Res.* **9**:329–343.

Kononova, M., 1966, *Soil Organic Matter: Its Nature, Its Role in Soil Formation and Soil Fertility,* Pergamon Press, New York, 306p.

Likens, G. E., and F. H. Bormann, 1974, Acid rain: A serious regional environmental problem, *Science* **184:**1176.

Likens, G. E., F. H. Bormann, and N. M. Johnson, 1969, Nitrification: Importance to nutrient losses from a cut-over forest ecosystem, *Science* **163:**1205–1206.

Likens, G. E., F. H. Bormann, R. S. Pierce, J. S. Eaton, and N. M. Johnson, 1977, *Biogeochemistry of a Forested Ecosystem,* Springer-Verlag, New York, 146p.

Long, J. N., and J. Turner, 1975, Aboveground biomass of understory and overstory in an age sequence of four Douglas-fir stands, *J. Appl. Ecol.* **12:**179–188.

McColl, J. G., and D. W. Cole, 1968, A mechanism of cation transport in a forest soil, *Northwest Sci.* **42:**134–140.

Marakov, B. N., 1966, Air regime of a sod-podzolic soil, *Soviet Soil Sci.* (1966):1289–1297.

Newton, M., B. A. El Hassen, and J. Zavitovski, 1968, Role of alder in western Oregon forest succession, in *Biology of Alder,* J. M. Trappe, J. F. Franklin, R. F. Tarrant, and G. M. Hansen, eds., U.S. Department of Agriculture Forest Service, Portland, Oreg., pp. 73–84.

Olson, J. S., 1963, Energy storage and the balance of producers and decomposers in ecological systems, *Ecology* **44:**322–331.

Riekerk, H., 1977, Utilization of a root pressure chamber for nutrient uptake studies, *Plant Soil* **46:**279–282.

Shilova, Ye I. 1959, Five-year observations of qualitative composition of lysimeter water in various types of virgin and cultivated podzolic soils, *Soviet Soil Sci.* (1959):76–86.

Shriner, D. W., and G. S. Henderson, 1978, Sulfur distribution and cycling in a deciduous forest watershed, *J. Environ. Qual.* **7:**392–397.

Singer, M. J., and F. C. Ugolini, 1974, Genetic history of two well-drained subalpine soils formed on complex parent materials, *Can. J. Soil Sci.* **54:**475–489.

Singer, M. J., F. C. Ugolini, and J. Zachara, 1978, *In situ* study of podzolization on tephra and bedrock, *Soil Sci. Soc. Am. J.* **42:**105–111.

Sollins, P., C. C. Grier, F. M. McCorison, K. Cromack, Jr., R. Fogel, and R. L. Fredriksen, 1980, The internal element cycles of an old-growth Douglas-fir ecosystem in western Oregon, *Ecol. Monogr.* **50:**261–285.

Tabatabai, M. A., and J. M. Bremner, 1972, Distribution of total and available sulfur in selected soil profiles, *Agron. J.* **64:**40–44.

Tarrant, R. F., and R. F. Miller, 1963, Accumulation of organic matter and soil nitrogen beneath a plantation of red alder and Douglas-fir, *Soil Sci. Soc. Am. Proc.* **27:**231–234.

Turner, J., 1975, Nutrient cycling in a Douglas-fir ecosystem with respect to age and nutrient status, Ph.D. dissertation, University of Washington, Seattle, 190p.

Turner, J., 1977, Effect of nitrogen availability on nitrogen cycling in a Douglas-fir stand, *For. Sci.* **23**:307–316.

Turner, J., and J. Long, 1975, Accumulation of organic matter in a series of Douglas-fir stands, *Can. J. For. Res.* **5**:681–690.

Turner, J., and M. J. Singer, 1976, Nutrient cycling and distribution in a subalpine forest ecosystem, *J. Appl. Ecol.* **13**:295–301.

Turner, J., D. W. Cole, and S. P. Gessel, 1976, Nutrient accumulation and cycling in a red alder (*Alnus rubra* Bong.) ecosystem, *J. Ecol.* **64**:965–974.

Turner, J., M. J. Lambert, and S. P. Gessel, 1977, Use of foliage sulphate concentrations to predict response to urea application in Douglas-fir, *Can. J. For. Res.* **7**:476–480.

Ugolini, F. C., H. Dawson, and J. Zachara, 1977a, Direct evidence of particle migration in the soil solution of a podzol, *Science* **198**:603–605.

Ugolini, F. C., R. V. Minden, H. Dawson, and J. Zachara, 1977b, An example of soil processes in the *Abies amabilis* zone of central Cascades, Washington, *Soil Sci.* **124**:291–302.

Van den Driessche, R. and J. Dangerfield, 1975, Responses of Douglas-fir seedlings to nitrate and annomium sources under various environmental conditions, *Plant Soil* **42**:685–702.

Vogt, K. A., and R. L. Edmonds, 1980, Patterns of nutrient concentration in basidiocarps in western Washington, *Can. J. Bot.* **58**:694–698.

Vogt, K. A., R. L. Edmonds, G. C. Antos, and D. J. Vogt, 1980, Relationships between carbon dioxide evolution, ATP concentrations and decomposition in red alder, Douglas-fir, western hemlock and Pacific silver fir ecosystems in western Washington, *Oikos* **35**:72–79.

Will, G. M., 1959, Nutrient return in litter and rainfall under some exotic conifer stands in New Zealand, *New Zealand J. Agric. Res.* **2**:719–734.

Youngberg, C. T., and A. G. Wollum, 1976, Nitrogen accretion in developing *Ceanothus velutinus* stands, *Soil Sci. Soc. Am. J.* **40**:109–111.

8

Material Transfer in a Western Oregon Forested Watershed

F. J. Swanson, R. L. Fredriksen, and *F. M. McCorison*

INTRODUCTION

Abiotic transfer of organic and inorganic materials by a diverse family of processes is an essential part of all natural, large-scale ecosystems. Physical processes of material transfer are particularly important in the coniferous forest biome, which contains many geologically youthful and geomorphically active landscapes. High-relief, steep hillslope and channel gradients, dense vegetation, massive trees, and heavy precipitation result in a complex relationship among material transfer processes and vegetation.

In a strict sense, material transfer involves erosion, transport, and deposition. This is equivalent to current usage of the term "sedimentation," which geologists and engineers use to describe transfer of predominantly inorganic material. In a system with significant depositional sites, material transfer includes routing of material through a variety of storage compartments. In this study, which deals mainly with a small, steep watershed where storage opportunities are limited, we emphasize annual material transfer rates and roles of vegetation but do not attempt to quantify deposition and storage.

Material transfer has several important roles in the functioning of forest-stream ecosystems. It is an important mechanism for nutrient redistribution and particularly nutrient export from ecosystems. Erosion and deposition create landforms that offer contrasting habitat opportunities for terrestrial and aquatic organisms on a variety of temporal and spatial scales. Erosion may also determine rates and patterns of succession following or during either erosion disturbances (for example, landslide) or disturbance of vegetation alone (for example, wildfire or insect infestation). These effects may be localized to the scales of root-throw mounds and landslide scars (generally <2000 m^2) or they may extend over broad areas covering many hectares.

There is also a variety of ways in which vegetation regulates rates of erosion processes. These influences of vegetation may result in reduced erosion by the effects of ground cover and rooting strength, or in increased erosion, as in the case of trees serving as a medium for transfer of wind stress to the soil mantle.

233

The great temporal and spatial variability of erosion processes operating on a single landscape and their complex relationships with vegetation have discouraged attempts to quantify erosion on a process-by-process basis in temperate forest ecosystems. Most comprehensive erosion research has been restricted to semiarid lands (Leopold et al. 1966) and alpine and subalpine environments (Jäckli 1957; Rapp 1960; Benedict 1970; Marchand 1971, 1974, Caine 1976). Temperate forest geomorphology was studied on a broad scale in the central Appalachians (Hack and Goodlett 1960), in the Redwood Creek basin, northern California (Janda et al. 1975), and in a drainage basin on the Oregon coast (Dietrich and Dunne 1978). Numerous studies have dealt with material transfer at the scales of individual processes and small watersheds. Recent work on material transfer in forest ecosystems has centered on elemental and particulate matter input/output budgets for small watersheds (Bormann et al. 1969, 1974; Cleaves et al. 1970; Fredriksen 1970, 1971, 1972, 1975; Likens et al. 1977). In none of these small watershed studies was material transfer examined at the process level over an entire watershed.

The purpose of this chapter is to describe the nature of material transfer in a coniferous forest stream ecosystem in terms of: (1) characteristics of the important transfer processes; (2) relations among them; (3) transfer process/vegetation relations; (4) the relative importance of individual processes and process groupings; and (5) the effects of vegetation disturbance on material transfer in a historical context.

DEFINITION OF PROCESSES

Material transfer processes operating in a watershed are broadly grouped into those affecting hillslopes and those operating in stream channels (Figure 8.1). The hillslope processes supply dissolved and particulate organic and inorganic material to the channel, where channel processes take over to break down the material and transport it downstream and out of the watershed. Significant transfer processes both on hillslopes and in channels include infrequent, localized, high-magnitude events and continuous, widely distributed, low-magnitude processes (Table 8.1).

Hillslope Processes

Solution transport results from leaching from vegetation, soil, and weathering bedrock or input from atmospheric sources and occurs in the dissolved state in subsurface water or, rarely, as overland flow. *Litterfall* is the transfer of organic matter as the final step in the sequence of events: nutrient uptake by roots, translocation to and incorporation in aboveground biomass, abscission

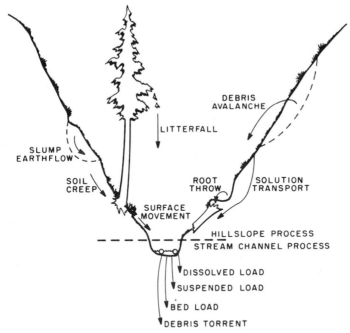

FIGURE 8.1 *Processes that transfer organic and inorganic material in a steep forest watershed ecosystem.*

or breakage, litterfall to the forest floor or stream. In steep terrain, downhill lean of large trees and canopy closure over small streams result in a net downslope displacement of organic matter.

Surface erosion is the particle-by-particle transfer of material over the ground surface by overland flow, raindrop impact, and ice- and snow-induced particle movement and dry ravel, which occurs during dry periods (Anderson et al. 1959). *Creep* is here considered "continuous" creep (Terzaghi 1950); that is, slow, downslope deformation of soil and weathered bedrock. This is a more restrictive definition than that applied by Leopold et al. (1964) and others who include root throw, needle ice, and other processes as part of creep. *Root throw* occurs as movement of organic and inorganic matter by the uprooting and downhill sliding of trees. *Debris avalanches* are rapid, shallow (generally one- to two-meter soil depth) soil mass movements. *Slump and earthflow* are slow, deep-seated (generally five- to ten-meter depth to failure plane) rotational (slump) and translational (earthflow) displacements of soil, rock, and covering vegetation.

TABLE 8.1 *Material transfer process characteristics for watershed 10 in old-growth forest condition.*

Process	Downslope movement rate[a]	Frequency	Watershed area influenced	Landforms
Hillslope processes				
Solution	1	continuous	total	
Litterfall	1	continuous, seasonal	total	
Surface erosion	1	continuous	total	small terracettes
Creep	2	seasonal	total	
Root throw	3	~1/yr	0.10%[b]	pit & mound topography
Debris avalanche	4	~1/370 yr	1 to 2%[b]	shallow, linear down-slope depressions
Slump/earthflow	5[c]	seasonal[c]	5 to 8%	scraps, benches
Channel processes				
Solution	3	continuous	1%	
Suspension	3	continuous, storm	~1%	
Bedload	3	storm	~1%	channel bedforms
Debris torrent	4	~1/580 yr	~1%	incised, U-shaped channel cross section

[a] 1 = cm to m/yr, 2 = mm/yr, 3 = m/s, 4 = 10 m/s, 5 = mm to cm/yr.
[b] Area influenced by one event.
[c] Inactive in past century in watershed 10.

Channel Processes

Solution transport is movement of material dissolved in stream water. *Suspended sediment transport* is movement of material in colloidal to sand size carried in suspension in flowing water. *Bedload transport* is movement of material approximately coarse sand size and larger by tractive forces imparted by streamflow. *Debris torrent* is the rapid, turbulent movement down stream channels of masses that may exceed 10,000 m^3 of soil, alluvium, and living and dead organic matter. Whole trees may be included. *Streambank erosion* occurs as lateral cutting by a stream as it entrains material such as older alluvium or colluvium moved to the streamside area by creep, surface erosion, or other processes.

Relations Among Processes

The movement of a single particle of material through a watershed is accomplished by a series of steps involving numerous material transfer processes. There are in-series, or chain-reaction, relations among processes and there may be superposition of processes operating simultaneously on a particular piece of material. Principal driving variables and sequential relations among erosion processes are shown in Figure 8.2.

Possible types of sequential interactions are varied. Surface erosion rate may be increased by other processes such as root throw and debris avalanche, which expose bare mineral soil and/or locally increase slope steepness. Debris avalanches may be triggered by root throw, and debris avalanche probability is increased by local slope steepening in response to creep, slump, and earthflow activity (Figure 8.2). Probability of root throw is increased by the tipping of trees by creep, slump, and earthflow activity. Creep may be a precursor of debris avalanche, slump, and earthflow movement (Terzaghi 1950), because when strain by creep deformation exceeds a threshold value, discrete, macroscopic failure occurs and translocational or rotational displacement begins.

Hillslope processes supply material to the channel, making it available for transport by channel processes. In the case of debris torrents the debris avalanche, a hillslope process, is a principal triggering mechanism of the channel process. Within the stream environment, chemical and physical processes break down larger particles to smaller ones, and thereby change the relative importance of bed, suspended, and dissolved modes of transport.

In addition to sequential relations, processes work together. A typical column of soil on a steep, forested slope is likely to experience surface erosion, creep, solution transport, and nutrient uptake/litterfall processes simultaneously. The same block of soil may also be subject to slump or earthflow movement.

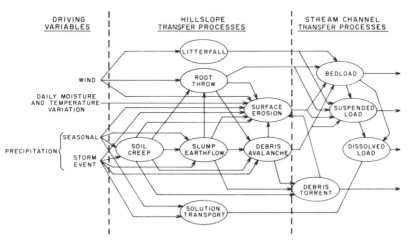

FIGURE 8.2 *Relations among mass transfer processes and principal driving variables. Arrows indicate that one process influences another by supplying material for transfer or creating instability that culminates in the occurrence of the second process.*

Influences of Vegetation on Material Transfer

Vegetation factors regulate rates of transfer processes in a variety of ways (Table 8.2). These factors may either increase or decrease the rate of continuous processes or the probability of episodic events. Knowledge of vegetation-transfer process relations ranges from the obvious (for example, aboveground biomass is the source of litterfall) to the speculative (for example, the effect of windshaking of trees on creep rate). Relations in Table 8.2 are a summary based on inference, direct field observation, modeling studies, and experimentation by many workers.

The mass of living and dead vegetation on hillslopes affects the probability of or rate of hillslope mass erosion by increasing the downslope component of mass, thereby increasing the tendency for movement, and increasing the effective force perpendicular to the slope, which increases friction within the soil mass and decreases movement potential. Although these forces affect slope stability in opposite senses, their net effect is generally believed to increase

TABLE 8.2 *Roles of vegetation in regulating hillslope transfer process rates.*

Vegetation component and fraction	Process						
	Solution	Litter-fall	Surface erosion	Creep	Root throw	Debris avalanche	Slump/ earthflow
Total biomass							
Loading of slope	0	0	0	+	0	+	-,0,+
Living vegetation							
Water uptake	–	0	0	--	0	0	--
Nutrient uptake	---	0	0	0	0	0	0
Regulation of snow- melt hydrology	0	0	0	-,0,+	0	++,0,--	+,0,-
Aboveground biomass							
Medium for transfer of wind stress	0	0	0	0,+	+++	++	0,+
Source of litterfall	0	+++	0	0	0	0	0
Roots							
Vertical anchoring	0	0	0	--	---	---	0
Lateral anchoring	0	0	0	--	---	---	–
Living & dead groundcover							
Surface obstruction	0	0	---	0	0	0	0

Note: Vegetation function: increases (+) or decreases (–) transfer process rate.
Significance of vegetation function: questionable or slight (+,-), significant (++,--), substantial (+++,---).

mass movement potential on slopes steeper than 30° (Bishop and Stevens 1964; Swanston 1970; D. H. Gray, pers. comm.). The magnitude of this effect differs as a function of many variables, the principal one being soil depth.

Living vegetation takes up water and nutrients and regulates snow accumulation and melt. Evapotranspiration by plants decreases annual water yield from a watershed (for example, Harr 1976) and shortens the annual period of high soil moisture conditions (Gray 1970). Reduced water yield may decrease solution export from a watershed, and decreased quantities of subsurface water may reduce creep, slump, and earthflow activity. Nutrient uptake by vegetation reduces export of material in solution (for example, Bormann et al. 1969). Regulation of snow hydrology by vegetation may result in either increased or decreased soil moisture peaks during snowmelt events (for example, Anderson 1969; Rothacher and Glazebrook 1968; Harr and McCorison 1979). In the Pacific Northwest rain-on-snow events result in very high soil moisture conditions that trigger debris avalanches (Rothacher and Glazebrook 1968; Day and Megahan 1975) and may cause periods of accelerated creep, slump, and earthflow movement.

Aboveground biomass serves as a medium for transfer of wind stress to the soil mantle. This effect is most conspicuous in the case of blowdown, where uprooted trees may transport both organic and inorganic matter downslope. Blowdown may contribute to the initiation of debris avalanches (Swanston 1969), and Brown and Sheu (1975) have hypothesized that wind stress on the soil mantle may accelerate creep, slump, and earthflow activity. Living and dead organic matter on the ground surface may intercept and temporarily store material moved downslope by surface erosion processes (Mersereau and Dyrness 1972).

Roots may play an important role in stabilizing the soil mantle by vertical and lateral anchoring across potential failure surfaces (for example, Swanston 1970; Nakano 1971). The effectiveness of roots in stabilizing slopes depends on position of the root network relative to potential zones of movement. Roots are most important in stabilizing potential mass failures where failure surfaces are within the rooting zone.

Large organic debris derived from vegetation on adjacent hillslopes controls channel morphology and routing of sediment and water through the stream (Bormann et al. 1969; Swanson et al. 1976; Keller and Swanson 1979). The principal effects of vegetation on channel processes are to physically retard the downchannel transfer of particulate matter, to buttress streambanks, to cause channel deflection, which can increase bank cutting, and to serve as a substrate for biological activity that involves the interchange of dissolved nutrients with stream water (see Chapter 9). Although total sediment yield is largely controlled by input of hillslope processes, the timing of export from a stream may be regulated by large debris in the channel. The presence of debris and temporarily stored sediment may also reduce the rate of channel downcutting, which may, in turn, slow the rate of sediment input by hillslope processes.

Decomposing organic matter and living vegetation may remove certain nutrients from solution in stream water by plant and decomposer organism uptake. There may also be a net input of certain other dissolved nutrients by leaching and decomposition of particulate organic matter. All of this material is eventually exported from a watershed, but whether it is delivered to the gauging site as dissolved or particulate matter may depend on the uptake and dissolution processes.

MATERIAL TRANSFER IN AN OLD-GROWTH FOREST

In order to compare individual and groups of transfer processes, data on transfer rate by each process have been compiled from research results of the coniferous forest biome program, and the Pacific Northwest Forest and Range Experiment Station, USDA Forest Service. This collaborative research has centered on watershed 10 and in the adjacent H. J. Andrews Experimental Forest (see Figure 1.4). This area is located in deeply dissected Tertiary lava flows, dikes, and volcaniclastic rocks in the central western Cascade Mountains (Peck et al. 1964; Swanson and James 1975).

The area of watershed 10 above the sediment basin and gauging flume is 10.2 ha, of which 767 m^2 or about one percent is considered to be stream channel subject to perennial or intermittent surface flow. Gradients of the hillslopes and lower channel average 65 percent and 18 percent, respectively (Figure 8.3). Soils are shallow, only slightly cohesive, and highly permeable,

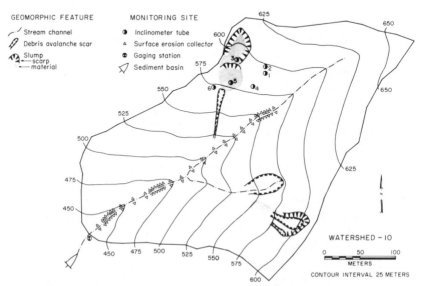

FIGURE 8.3 *Geomorphic features and monitoring sites on watershed 10.*

and they exhibit weakly developed profiles (Harr 1977). Before clearcutting in the summer of 1975, vegetation in the watershed was predominantly *Pseudotsuga menziesii* ranging in age from 400 to 500 years, with younger understory tree canopy composed of *Tsuga heterophylla* on moist sites and *Castanopsis chrysophylla* on dry sites as well as young *Pseudotsuga menziesii*. The dominant old-growth age class appeared to have developed after a disturbance, probably wildfire, about 1475. Portions of the area were again disturbed in about 1800 by a fire that had minor impact on the canopy, but did result in extensive regeneration of *Pseudotsuga menziesii, Tsuga heterophylla,* and *Castanopsis chrysophylla* in the understory. Characteristics of vegetation in the watershed are discussed in detail by Grier and Logan (1977).

The climate of the area is characterized by mild, wet winters and warm, dry summers (Rothacher et al. 1967). Annual precipitation averages between 230 and 250 cm, depending on elevation. At the base of watershed 10 at 440 m elevation more than 90 percent of the annual precipitation falls as rain; snow seldom persists for more than several weeks. Rain-induced snowmelt has resulted in many of the major runoff and hillslope erosion events in the history of the area (Fredriksen 1965).

Many transfer processes are appropriately studied on the spatial scale of watershed 10. These include frequent or continuous processes such as litterfall and surface erosion, as well as less frequent, episodic processes that leave a record of numerous, datable events such as root throw. Processes such as debris avalanches and torrents, which are scattered in time and space, can be viewed better from a wider geographic perspective.

With these constraints in mind, we summarize below available data on transfer of organic and inorganic material by processes operating in a 10-ha, old-growth *Pseudotsuga menziesii* forest. Organic matter is here considered to include all particulate matter made up of carbon (C) compounds plus dissolved organic nitrogen (N) and C. Organic particulate matter includes approximately 1 to 2 percent cations, predominately calcium (Ca), potassium (K), and magnesium (Mg), derived from bedrock and atmospheric inputs. Inorganic matter includes all other material derived from bedrock, volcanic ash fall, and atmospheric sources.

Hillslope Processes

Solution transport of material from hillslopes occurs as water carries dissolved constituents leached from vegetation, soil, and weathering bedrock. There are also atmospheric sources of dissolved mineral material that must be omitted from the total solution export to determine the amount derived from a watershed. Movement of dissolved materials is a pervasive process, operating over the entire watershed and through all strata of the vegetation and soil. Solution transport operates continuously as long as water movement occurs, but variations exist in response to seasonal and storm event fluctuations in moisture availability, flow-through rate, biological activity, and availability of exchangeable cations and anions. Long-term trends in solution export are controlled by the efficiency of nutrient cycling within an ecosystem and by weathering rate, which is determined by bedrock characteristics, climate, and biological processes.

Input and output of dissolved material have been measured for watershed 10 during water year (WY) 1969 (1 October 1968–30 September 1969) through WY 1973 (Table 8.3). Methods of sample collection and analysis are described by Fredriksen (1972, 1975). Samples were collected at a stream gauging station at the base of the watershed. Since we are attempting to calculate only solution export from hillslopes, it is necessary to assume that the total quantity of dissolved material does not change while water flows from the base of the hillslope through the stream to the flume. Comparison of analyses of

TABLE 8.3 *Input and output of water and dissolved inorganic material (kg/ha) for watershed 10, water years 1969–1973.*

Year	H₂O (cm)	Ortho-P	Na	K	Ca	Mg	SiO₃	Total
1969								
In	253.0	0.01	1.54	0.25	8.77	0.73	—	
Out	169.0	0.42	33.74	1.36	53.62	12.67	—	
Net		−0.41	−32.30	−1.11	−44.85	−11.94	−199.91[a]	−290.42
1970								
In	215.9	0.02	2.62	0.16	2.36	1.53	0.28	
Out	134.6	0.44	25.85	2.26	50.60	12.51	213.57	
Net		−0.42	−23.23	−2.10	−48.24	−10.98	−213.29	−298.26
1971								
In	272.1	0.28	6.64	0.32	3.21	2.78	11.45	
Out	172.3	0.71	37.64	0.98	60.91	17.96	211.43	
Net		−0.43	−31.00	−0.66	−57.70	−15.18	−199.98	−304.95
1972								
In	286.3	0.02	3.98	0.33	4.92	0.82	9.87	
Out	228.52	0.85	43.48	3.25	70.20	16.76	303.75	
Net		−0.83	−39.50	−2.92	−65.28	−15.94	−293.88	−418.35
1973								
In	167.8	0.08	2.59	0.59	0.13	1.07	6.12	
Out	80.16	0.31	13.94	1.46	23.24	6.64	80.01	
Net		−0.23	−11.35	−0.87	−23.11	−5.57	−73.89	−115.02
Average net export		0.46	27.46	1.53	47.84	11.92	196.19	285.40

[a]Not measured. Values assigned from 1971 observations; runoff for 1969 and 1971 were approximately equal.

water samples collected at seeps and at the flume indicates that the concentrations of mineral elements do not change significantly between seep and flume sample sites. Similar analyses for N, however, suggest that there may be 10 to 20 percent uptake because of primary production and decomposition processes in the stream (S. V. Gregory, pers. comm.). Other components of the dissolved organic load do not appear to be significantly altered in the stream environment. Because this is a relatively small change based on preliminary data, we will assume that dissolved organic export measured at the gauging station equals the input to the stream from hillslope areas.

Estimation of dissolved inorganic export is based on analyses for Na (sodium), K, Ca, Mg, and orthophosphate (ortho-P) over the entire five-year period. Analyses for silica (SiO_2) were conducted in WY 1970 through WY 1973 only. Based on these data, annual net transfer is 2.9 t/yr of dissolved inorganic material from hillslope areas.

Dissolved organic matter export was estimated using the following algorithm: based on ten measurements of dissolved organic carbon in water samples collected at the gauging station (S. V. Gregory, pers. comm.), a concentration of 2.0 mg C/liter was applied to total discharge during the initial twenty-four-hour period of fall storms (1 October through 31 December) when flow exceeded 1 cfs (28.3 liters/s). For the remainder of the year a concentration of 0.9 mg C/liter was used. This method was applied to WY 1969 through WY 1973 and the annual estimates were multiplied by two to convert from dissolved carbon to dissolved organic matter. The average of these annual estimates of dissolved organic matter export is 0.3 t/yr, which we assume equals the input to the stream.

Litterfall is the final transfer in a chain of processes involving nutrient uptake by roots, translocation to biomass in the aboveground portion of vegetation, and the fall of litter to the forest floor. Even in predominantly evergreen coniferous forests, litterfall is strongly seasonal, coming mainly in the autumn and early winter months with storm winds, needle and leaf abscission, and snow breakage.

Fall of fine litter into the channel area was directly measured at 0.18 t/yr based on three years of collections in standard 1-m^2 traps along the watershed 10 stream (F. J. Triska, pers. comm.). An estimated 0.15 t/yr of log material is input to the stream, assuming that the standing crop (Froehlich et al. 1972) represents 150 years of input. Total organic matter input to the stream by litterfall is 0.33 t/yr.

Surface erosion of organic and inorganic particulate matter occurs throughout the year in response to wind; diel, storm event, and seasonal variations in moisture and temperature; snow creep, needle ice, and other snow- and ice-driven processes; impact of large pieces of falling litter; and movement of scientists and animals, principally deer, elk, and rodents. Much erosion from steep, bare, mineral soil surfaces results from particle-by-particle movement during dry periods (dry ravel) and by needle ice and the impact of rain and throughfall drops during wet periods. Mersereau and Dyrness (1972) report that the highest surface erosion rate at a study site in the Oregon Cascades occurred during periods of dry ravel. Areas covered with forest litter often experience movement of surface particles when drying takes place in the spring and early summer. At this time leaves and other litter dry, curl up, and become more susceptible to downslope movement. Overland flow is observed only rarely and very locally in the study area. No evidence of rill formation exists in most forested watersheds in western Oregon except on some debris avalanche scars, road cuts, and other disturbed sites.

Organic and inorganic material moved by surface processes was collected in sixty-four fifty-cm-long erosion boxes along the perimeter of the watershed 10 stream. The rate of surface movement into the total length of boxes may be extrapolated to the entire perimeter of the stream to estimate total annual surface movement transfer from hillslopes to the stream. Based on two years of observations, 0.30 t of organic material and 0.53 t of inorganic matter were transferred annually into the stream channel.

Soil creep is the slow deformation within and between individual soil particles in response to gravitational stress but without the development of discrete failure planes. Creep grades into more rapid mass movement processes that do have well-developed failure planes, however, and distinction among these processes is somewhat arbitrary (Terzaghi 1950).

Soil creep is difficult to monitor, because it affects virtually all sloping soil masses and movement is slow, generally less than 1 cm/yr. Although precise measurements are required, it is difficult to establish stable reference points. Creep measurement in watershed 10 and at nearby sites have been made with a set of inclinometer installations (D. H. Gray, pers. comm.).

Annual measurement with an inclinometer revealed downslope deflection occurring at soil depths (measured vertically) of up to 4 m. The net downslope deflection was used to calculate an average creep rate for each inclinometer tube (Table 8.4). Displacement ranged from 0.25 to 0.46 mm for four of the tubes, but the other two tubes, which were located on a bench, experienced no significant movement. Because this landform is of limited areal extent (Figure 8.3), creep rates observed for tubes on steeper sites are considered more typical of the watershed. The variability and maximum values of creep rates observed in watershed 10 are comparable to creep rates measured in similar topographic and geologic settings (D. H. Gray, pers. comm.; D. N. Swanston, pers. comm.).

There are certain limitations on the usefulness of the data in Table 8.4. Using a cumulative five-year record of creep observations to calculate annual movement minimizes the analytical problem that at certain depths and in certain tubes annual movement is less than the resolution of the instrument, approximately 0.6 mm (D. N. Swanston, pers. comm.). An additional consideration in evaluating these data is that the bases of the inclinometer tubes may not be fixed to stable bedrock. Therefore additional movement may be taking place

TABLE 8.4 *Creep measurements with inclinometer installation.*[a]

Tube number	Hillslope angle (degrees)	Depth (m)	Annual surface displacement (mm/yr)	Average displacement over entire depth of tube (mm/yr)	Period of record
1	32	3.96	0.60	0.25	1969–1974
2	35	2.44	0.93	0.46	1969–1974
3	27	4.27	0.17	<0.01	1969–1974
4	34	3.96	1.57	0.32	1969–1974
5	27	3.66	0.34	0.04	1969–1973
6	41	3.96	0.73	0.40	1969–1974

[a]D.H. Gray, personal communication.

that is not recorded by these installations. Despite these limitations, we make a minimum estimate of creep transfer of material to the channel by assuming that a block of soil 2.65 m thick, the average thickness for the watershed (R. D. Harr, pers. comm.), crosses the 1150 m of channel perimeter at a rate of 0.35 mm/yr, the depth-integrated average creep rate of tubes 1, 2, 4, and 6. Based on these assumptions and an average bulk density of 1.0 t/m^3 (R. L. Fredriksen, pers. comm.), creep supplies 1.1 t/yr of inorganic material to the channel.

Organic matter transfer by creep may be estimated by creep rate (0.35 mm/yr) $\times$ channel perimeter (1150 m) $\times$ cosine of slope angle (33°) $\times$ biomass per m^2 of watershed (0.125 t/m^2; Grier and Logan 1977). Estimated organic matter transfer to the channel by creep is 0.04 t/yr.

Root throw by living and recently dead trees downed by strong winds generally move organic and inorganic material downslope. When root systems undergo extensive decay before a tree falls, binding between soil and roots is lost and little soil is moved. Pit and mound microrelief due to root throw has been well described in the gentle topography of the eastern United States, where root throw is an important soil disturbance factor (for example, Denny and Goodlett 1956; Stone 1975). In stands of large, old-growth forests on steep slopes erosion by root throw is accentuated by massive root wads and their tendency to slide downslope. Such events are episodic, occurring in windstorms that have a return period of several years to decades. Deep-seated earth movement by slump, earthflow, and creep processes can lead to tipping and even splitting of trees, thereby increasing their susceptibility to blowdown.

Root throw is such a sporadic phenomenon that a long-term historical record is necessary to validly estimate its occurrence. Fortunately, root wads, soil mounds, and pits from which roots and soil were removed are clearly recognizable and their features are datable for more than a century following the event. Events are dated by counting rings of trees growing on the pit, soil mound, or the downed tree. The persistence of pits and mounds attests to slow rates of surface erosion and creep.

In watershed 10, 112 mapped root-throw sites have abundant root and bole material still present. Dendrochronologic observations and the stage of decay of residual organic matter (P. Sollins, pers. comm.) suggest that the inventoried root-throw occurred to large, old-growth trees in the past 150 years. Root-throw sites are distributed rather uniformly over most of the watershed with some concentration along the lower slopes, particularly along the north side of the stream. Direction of fall was predominantly downslope.

The annual quantity of sediment supplied to the stream is difficult to determine, because most root wads in the stream slid >10 m down to the channel, loosening soil along the way. Eight of the inventoried root wads reached the stream. If we assume that these events occurred over the past 150 years, that each one transported or pushed 2 m^3 of soil to the stream, and that soil bulk density was 1.0 t/m^3, annual transfer to the channel would be 0.1 t of inorganic material. The organic matter in roots of <5 cm diameter in the root wad of a 120-cm-dbh old-growth Douglas-fir is estimated to be about 2 t (Santantonio et al. 1977; D. Santantonio pers. comm.), which would result in 0.1 t/yr of annual organic matter transfer to the channel.

Debris avalanche is used here as a general term for rapid, shallow soil mass movements, including events that have been classed by other workers as debris flows, slides, and rapid earthflows (Varnes 1958). These mass movements commonly occur as a result of periods of intense rain or rain plus snowmelt while the soil is already very moist (Fredriksen 1965; Dyrness 1967). Occurrence of debris avalanches are scattered in both time and space. In the H. J. Andrews Experimental Forest, for example, it has taken storms of about a seven-year return period to trigger debris avalanches in forested areas (F. J. Swanson, pers. comm.).

Debris avalanches are commonly believed to be a dominant erosion process in landscapes such as watershed 10 and similar terrains in the H. J. Andrews Experimental Forest (Fredriksen et al. 1975; Swanson and Dyrness 1975); however no debris avalanches of larger than 75 m^3 occurred in the watershed during at least the past century. Their earlier occurrence is suggested by landforms interpretable as avalanche scars (Figure 8.3). The oldest trees growing on these features range in age from 200 to more than 400 years.

Because a 10-ha watershed offers a limited record of its debris avalanche history, examination of a larger area of similar terrain that would contain more recent, datable events for study is useful. A record of all debris avalanches greater than 75 m^3 has been compiled for the period from 1950 to 1975 in the H. J. Andrews Experimental Forest (Dyrness 1967; Swanson and Dyrness 1975). In this twenty-six-year period fourteen debris avalanches occurred in the 20-km^2 portion of the forest that is similar to watershed 10 in terms of soil, topography, and forest cover. The annual frequency of debris avalanches was 0.27 event$\cdot km^{-2}\cdot yr^{-1}$, or 0.0027 event/yr in 10 ha, the area of watershed 10.

The return period for a single event, the inverse of event frequency, is 370 years in a 10-ha area, assuming equal probability of occurrence over the inventoried area.

The fourteen debris avalanches in the terrain similar to watershed 10 transported a total of 30,870 m^3 of soil, an average of 2205 m^3 per event (for a description of field methods see Swanson and Dyrness 1975). The dimensions of mapped debris avalanche scars in watershed 10 indicate that this is a reasonable estimate of the volume of recent, significant (greater than 75 m^3) debris avalanches in the watershed.

Twelve inventoried events entered streams and 99 percent of the volume of material transported was readily available to perennial or intermittent streams. The straight, steep slopes of watershed 10 present no impediments to debris avalanches on their way to the stream. Assuming that all of the debris avalanches move soil from hillslopes to stream channels, and that soil bulk density is 1.0 t/m^3 (R. L. Fredriksen, pers. comm.), transfer of inorganic particulate matter occurs at a rate of 6.0 t/yr.

Debris avalanches also transport organic matter to the stream. The average plan view area of the fourteen inventoried debris avalanches is about 1200 m^2, calculated from average volume, assuming average soil depth of 1.5 m and a slope of 36°. Assuming 0.125 t/m^2 of terrestrial biomass (Grier and Logan 1977), such a debris avalanche would transport 150 t of biomass. If one average-sized event occurred in the watershed in 370 years annual biomass transfer would be 0.41 t/yr.

Slump and earthflow landforms are developed where masses of earth undergo rotational or translational movement along discrete failure planes or zones of failure (Varnes 1958). In the western Cascades these features range in size from less than 1 ha to hundreds of hectares (Swanson and James 1975). Increased rates of slump and earthflow may occur in response to periods of heavy precipitation (R. D. Harr, pers. comm.; F. J. Swanson pers. comm.). In other instances, slump and earthflow features appear to have been inactive for hundreds or thousands of years. Where slumps and earthflows encroach on streams, the channel cross-section is progressively constricted and banks are oversteepened (Swanson and Swanston 1977).

Rotational and translational slump and earthflow movement has produced landforms covering approximately 6 percent of the area of watershed 10 (Figure 8.3). Field observations suggest that the slumps have been dormant for decades or perhaps centuries. Trees growing on the slump benches and deposits exhibit no signs of having experienced splitting, tilting, or periods of eccentric growth typical of vegetation growing on moving ground (Swanson and Swanston 1977). In areas of the Andrews Experimental Forest where differential movement is occurring at rates greater than 1 cm/yr, open tension and shear cracks are formed. Since none of these features has been observed in the slump areas of watershed 10, we conclude that during the past century slump movement in watershed 10 has been negligible.

Stream Channel Processes

Solution transport is a persistent process, operating under all streamflow conditions. Dissolved material in stream water is derived from the dissolved load of groundwater, direct atmospheric inputs, throughfall, and leaching of particulate matter weathering or decomposing in the channel. Values of dissolved inorganic and organic material determined for watershed 10, were 2.9 and 0.3 t/hr, respectively.

Suspended sediment is made available to the stream by all hillslope processes that transport particulate matter and by lateral and vertical cutting of the streambanks and bed. Small amounts of suspended sediment are carried by streams throughout the year, but most of the total annual load is transported during a few large storms. During stormflow fine particulate matter is scoured from streambed and bank deposits of alluvium and colluvium; it is produced by the breakdown of larger particles, and released from temporary storage in coarse alluvium when bedload movement commences.

The input and output of fine particulate matter at watershed 10 have been measured over a five-year period by Fredriksen (1975). Inputs come primarily as atmospheric fallout of particles greater than 0.05 mm in size. Particulate matter was filtered from precipitation collected in birdproof precipitation collectors. The relative contributions of natural and man-influenced and distant and local sources of atmospheric particulate matter are not known (Fredriksen 1975). Aeolian entrainment of organic particulates has not been quantified in ecosystem studies, although several mechanisms for entrainment have been suggested (Fish 1972).

Suspended sediment export was sampled at the flume with a pumping proportional water sampler (Fredriksen 1969, 1975). Both the suspended sediment and atmospheric input samples for WY 1972 and WY 1973 were analyzed for carbon (Fredriksen 1975) and the total organic component was calculated assuming that it is twice the amount of carbon.

Because of the ambiguous status of fine particulate inputs to the watershed, we report export of suspended sediment both with and without subtracting apparent atmospheric inputs. Suspended organic matter export from the watershed was 0.12 t/yr, or 0.07 t/yr when apparent atmospheric input is subtracted. Suspended inorganic matter export amounted to a gross value of 0.78 t/yr, and 0.56 t/yr when atmospheric dust input is subtracted.

For purposes of comparison, we have also examined data for gross organic plus inorganic suspended sediment export from four nearby experimental watersheds with soil, forest cover, and geomorphic conditions similar to watershed 10. The average annual fine particulate export for these watersheds ($98 \text{ kg} \cdot \text{ha}^{-1} \cdot \text{yr}^{-1}$) is in close agreement with the five-year average for watershed 10 ($90 \text{ kg} \cdot \text{ha}^{-1} \cdot \text{yr}^{-1}$).

Bedload transport commonly occurs during only a few major runoff events each year. Material available for bedload transport is temporarily stored in the stream channel, commonly behind large pieces of organic debris, boulders, or outcrops of resistant bedrock. Concentrations of large organic debris in a channel greatly influence its sediment storage capacity. Therefore, on a time scale of years or decades, bedload transport is regulated by changes in channel storage capacity, rates of sediment supply from hillslopes, and hydraulic forces tending to move sediment out of the channel.

Bedload export from watershed 10 was monitored for only two years before logging. The record is inadequate to characterize this erosion process for the basin, so we use the longer record available for experimental watersheds with generally similar forest cover, topography, soil, and geomorphic conditions.

A total of twenty-nine watershed years of bedload data is available for watersheds 1, 2, 3, 9, and 10 in and adjacent to the H. J. Andrews Experimental Forest (Table 8.5; Fredriksen 1970, pers. comm.).

Bedload from watershed 10 was collected in large nets placed at the downstream end of the flume. Sampling was done on a continuous basis during low flow using a 80 μm net and periodically during high flow using a 1 mm net. Bedload export from other watersheds was measured by annual surveys of settling basins at the bottom of each watershed. In all cases reported values are minimum estimates of the true value, because trapping efficiencies of the basins are probably less than 100 percent particularly during peak periods of bedload transport.

Bedload export for all watersheds has been 93 kg·ha⁻¹·yr⁻¹. For the four watershed years at watersheds 9 and 10, 65 percent of total bedload was com-

TABLE 8.5 *Average annual bedload and suspended load export from forested watersheds in the H. J. Andrews Experimental Forest.* [a]

Watershed	Period of record (water year)	(yr)	Bedload (kg·ha⁻¹·yr⁻¹)	Suspended load (kg·ha⁻¹·yr⁻¹)
1	1957–1962	6	61	78[b]
2	1957–1972	16	122[c]	—
	1957–1967	11	—	134[b,c]
3	1957–1959	3	95	130[b]
9	1974–1975	2	21	—
	1969–1973	5	—	31[d]
10	1973–1974	2	32	—
	1969–1973	5	—	90[d]

[a]Bedload average for 29 watershed years = 93 kg·ha⁻¹·yr⁻¹. Suspended sediment average for 30 watershed years = 98 kg·ha⁻¹·yr⁻¹.
[b]Based on depth integrated hand sample at flume.
[c]Includes two highest floods on record in December 1964 and January 1965.
[d]Based on integrated samples collected with a pumping proportional sampler.

posed of inorganic material. Therefore the estimated inorganic matter export from watershed 10 is 0.60 t/yr, and coarse particulate organic matter export is 0.33 t/yr.

Debris torrents are commonly triggered by debris avalanches entering the channel from adjacent hillslopes (Swanson et al. 1976). A debris avalanche may maintain its momentum, becoming a debris torrent as it moves directly down the channel, scouring the streambanks and bed. Debris torrents are also initiated by mobilization of debris that had previously entered the channel by a variety of processes such as debris avalanches, windthrow, and bank cutting. Debris torrents are infrequent events, occurring in response to major storms. Most torrents in small streams are in part regulated by the debris avalanche potential of hillslopes in the basin. Most small basins experience a torrent less frequently than once in a century.

As in the case of debris avalanches, debris torrent history is not adequately represented in a small area the size of watershed 10. This analysis is based on debris torrent activity in the H. J. Andrews Experimental Forest from 1950 through 1975. Nine debris torrents occurred in 20 km^2 of terrain with geomorphic and forest conditions similar to those of watershed 10. It follows that there were 0.017 debris torrents $\cdot km^{-2} \cdot yr^{-1}$, which is an annual probability of 0.0017 that an event will occur in an area the size of watershed 10, or an estimated average return period of one event in 580 years.

Eight of the nine inventoried events were triggered by debris avalanches. Debris avalanches also appear to be the dominant triggering mechanism of debris torrents in watershed 10 where steep, smooth slopes lead directly from debris avalanche-prone areas to the stream channel (Figure 8.3). The average length of inventoried events was 370 m. In watershed 10 the two most prominent debris avalanche sites would initiate torrents at points about 260 m upstream from the flume.

If the entire mass of an average debris avalanche (2205 t inorganic matter and 150 t organic) were to move through the channel and past the flume as a debris torrent, it would involve 5.3 t/yr export of inorganic matter and 0.26 t/yr export of organic material, based on the occurrence of a single event during the estimated 580-year return period. This hypothetical debris torrent would also entrain alluvium, organic debris, and soil from the channel and adjacent banks. Of course the volume of material in a channel varies greatly with recent history of storms, vegetation, and geomorphic processes. The prelogging concentrations of organic and inorganic material in the channel of watershed 10 represented a moderate level of channel loading relative to observations made in other streams (Froehlich et al. 1972; Froehlich 1973). Before logging, approximately 40 t of organic matter was in a four-meter-wide strip along the 260 m of the channel between the most likely point of introduction and the flume (Froehlich et al. 1972). Inorganic matter in this strip along the channel is estimated to be 470 t, assuming a 0.3 m average depth of alluvium and soil with bulk density of 1.0 t/m^3 and a six-meter-wide torrent track. If all of this material were entrained by a debris torrent, total debris torrent export from the watershed (entrained material plus debris avalanche material) would be 4.6 t/yr of inorganic matter and 0.33 t/yr organic matter.

Accuracy and Limitations of Estimates

The usefulness of erosion process rate estimates summarized in Table 8.6 is directly related to their accuracy. Unfortunately, in most cases it is impossible to calculate an estimate of accuracy objectively owing to lack of data to quantify some of the key assumptions used to make the erosion rate estimate. Accuracy of estimates is a particular problem in the cases of debris avalanches, torrents, and bedload transport, which occur mainly during infrequent, large storms. A few storms can dominate even a record of more than 25 years such as that available for mass movement processes. This period of record contained only three of the top ten annual peak flows recorded in the fifty-nine-year record for the McKenzie River at McKenzie Bridge, the nearest long-term gauging site (Dalrymple 1965). The highest peak flow of the entire fifty-nine-year record, however, occurred in December 1964, and on Lookout Creek in the H. J. Andrews Forest it was 27 percent higher than the estimated fifty-year recurrence interval event (Waananen et al. 1971). Because the return period of this event was much greater than the length of record, these rates of debris avalanches, torrents, and bedload transport may be overestimated. The available record is too brief to characterize these episodic processes accurately. Furthermore, transfer rates for the mass-movement processes are based on small sample sizes. Therefore we estimate that the measures of debris avalanche and debris torrent rates have an accuracy of no better than +60 percent to −100 percent. As a result of more frequent occurrence of bedload transport and sampling inefficiencies, we estimate accuracy of bedload transfer rate to be ±60 percent.

The more frequent or continuous processes are better characterized by the available data. Rates of solution transport and to some extent creep and suspended sediment are related to total annual water yield. Analysis of long-term streamflow records suggests that the transfer estimates for solution transport, creep, and suspended sediment are good representations of the past twenty-five years, but may overestimate rates for the past sixty-five years, which includes some drier periods earlier this century. Estimated accuracy of transfer rates for these processes is about ±30 percent. For all other process rates, we estimate an accuracy of approximately ±50 percent.

It is important to note that these estimates of transfer rates apply to old-growth forest conditions; some process rates vary significantly for different stand conditions on the same landscape. This is particularly true immediately following ecosystem disturbances such as wildfire or clearcutting. These factors are considered further in a later section.

EROSION UNDER FORESTED CONDITIONS

Material transfer data may be examined in terms of total watershed-ecosystem export, contrast of total hillslope and channel transfer, and comparisons among processes. In each case we compare the roles of episodic and the more frequent or continuous processes, the relative importance of organic versus inorganic transfer, and dissolved versus particulate material export.

Watershed-Ecosystem Export

Total watershed-ecosystem export by channel processes is 0.99 t·ha^{-1}·yr^{-1} (Table 8.6). This figure includes debris torrents, which account for an estimated 50 percent of the total, even though it is assumed that only one event occurs in 580 years. Total export by the commonly measured processes of dissolved, suspended, and bedload sediment transport is 0.5 t·ha^{-1}·yr^{-1}. Par-

TABLE 8.6 *Transfer of organic and inorganic material to the channel by hillslope processes (t/yr) and export from the channel by channel processes (t/yr) for watershed 10.*

Process	Inorganic matter	Organic matter
Hillslope processes		
Solution transfer	3	0.3
Litterfall	0	0.3
Surface erosion	0.5	0.3
Creep	1.1	0.04
Root throw	0.1	0.1
Debris avalanche	6	0.4
Slump/earthflow	0	0
Total	10.7	1.4
Total particulate		
Including debris avalanche	7.7	1.1
Excluding debris avalanche	1.7	0.7
Channel processes		
Solution transfer	3.0	0.3
Gross suspended sediment	0.8	0.1
Net suspended sediment	0.6	0.1
Bedload	0.6	0.3
Debris torrent	4.6	0.3
Total	8.9	1.0
Total particulate		
Including debris torrent	5.9	0.7
Excluding debris torrent	1.3	0.4

ticulate matter composes 34 percent of this total. Organic matter makes up 24 percent of the particulate matter export (excluding debris torrents) and 9 percent of total dissolved export.

Values for organic and inorganic, particulate and dissolved materials are summarized in Table 8.7 along with similar data from Hubbard Brook, New Hampshire, the only site for which complete comparable data exist. Characteristics of these two watershed ecosystems (Table 8.8), are the basis for contrasting the two systems.

In the cases of all four constituents, export values for watershed 10 (even excluding debris torrents) exceed those for watershed 6, Hubbard Brook, by a factor of at least 2. Some of the apparent contrasts may arise from differences in methods and efficiencies of sample collection and analysis, from possible differences in the relative magnitude of major storms (in terms of return period) that occurred within the respective sampling periods, and possibly from differences in magnitudes of storms of comparable return period. Contrasts in estimated export from the two watersheds is so great for each of the variety of forms of export, however, that much of the difference may be due to real differences in system behavior.

Systems may differ in terms of the availability of material to be transported and the energy available to transport material. Export of dissolved constituents

TABLE 8.7 *Export of dissolved and particulate organic and inorganic material ($kg \cdot ha^{-1} \cdot yr^{-1}$) from watershed 10, H. J. Andrews Experimental Forest, Oregon, and watershed 6, Hubbard Brook, New Hampshire.*[a]

	Watershed 10 H. J. Andrews Experimental Forest		Watershed 6 Hubbard Brook
	Excluding debris torrents	Including debris torrents	
Dissolved			
Organic	30	30	15
Inorganic	300	300	58
Total	330	330	73
Particulate			
Organic	40	70	10
Inorganic	130	590	15
Total	170	660	25
Total			
Organic	70	100	25
Inorganic	430	890	73
Total	500	990	98

[a]Bormann et al. 1974.

tends to be directly related to total annual discharge, while particulate matter export is controlled by high discharge events (Bormann et al. 1974). Availability of particulate material for transport from a channel depends on the input rate of material from adjacent hillslopes and stream power, a function of discharge and channel gradient. Availability of material for transport in solution is determined in part by the ability of the biota to immobilize nutrients in living vegetation and detritus. In the case of inorganic material, rates of weathering and decomposition also determine availability of dissolved material.

Dissolved organic matter export from watershed 10 is twice that of watershed 6, which may largely reflect the higher annual runoff from the Oregon site (Table 8.8). The five times greater standing crop of organic matter in watershed 10 also results in more material available for leaching from the ecosystem. The contrast is especially striking considering that dead biomass in watershed 10 equals total biomass reported for the Hubbard Brook site.

The condition of greater biomass available for export from watershed 10 doubtless contributes to its fourfold higher particulate organic matter export. Availability of material for export from watershed 10 is also affected by the much steeper hillslopes, which result in greater rate of particulate matter transfer to the channel. The much higher litterfall rate in watershed 10 also contributes to greater particulate organic matter export. These factors must more than compensate for slightly higher gradient in the lower 100 m of channel and

TABLE 8.8 *Characteristics of watershed 10, H. J. Andrews Experimental Forest, Oregon, and watershed 6, Hubbard Brook, N.H.*

		Slope				Runoff			
Water-shed no.	Area (ha)	Total water-shed (%)	Channel lower 100 m (%)	Av (1/sec^{-1}/ ha^{-1})	Peak (1/sec^{-1}/ ha^{-1})	Av annual peak (1/sec^{-1}/ ha^{-1})	Av annual (cm)	Av annual air temp (°C)	Dominant tree species
10	10.2	60	18	0.5	19	12	156	9.5[a]	*Pseudotsuga menziesii, Tsuga heterophylla*
6	13.2[d]	26[c]	21[c]	0.3[c]	25[c]	15[c]	80[c]	4.3[f]	*Acer saccarum, Fagus grandifolia, Betula alleghaniensis*[d]

[a]Waring et al. 1978.
[b]Grier and Logan 1977.
[c]P. Sollins, personal communication.
[d]Bormann et al. 1970.

higher average annual peak discharge for the five-year periods of record at the Hubbard Brook site.

Particulate organic matter export from small watersheds may also be regulated by retentiveness or roughness of the channel system. Boulders and living and dead vegetation in and adjacent to the channel slow downstream routing of particulate matter, providing more opportunity for biological processing and export from the system by respiration and leaching. In streams at Hubbard Brook boulders are the dominant elements of bed roughness, whereas large woody debris is the major controller of particulate matter routing through a small Oregon stream. Both systems appear to have high roughness and therefore a tendency to retain organic detritus until it is processed by aquatic organisms (Bormann et al. 1969; Sedell and Triska 1977).

The export of dissolved inorganic matter from watershed 10 exceeds that of watershed 6 by about sixfold (Table 8.7). Part of this difference is accounted for by higher total runoff from watershed 10, but a more important factor is the greater weathering rate of soils and bedrock at the Oregon site. The higher weathering rate at the Oregon site is due to higher temperatures and precipitation and the mineralogy of altered volcanic rocks. Hydrothermal alteration of these volcanic breccias resulted in formation of readily weathered secondary minerals and amorphous materials even before the rocks were subjected to the modern weathering environment. Weathering of bedrock and the compact till that blankets the Hubbard Brook watershed proceeds at a slower pace in response to mineralogic properties and the weathering environment of the soil.

Age (yr)	Biomass (watershed) (kg/m^2) Live	Dead	Litterfall incl. stems (kg/m^2)	Bedrock	Soil
100 to 150 and 400 to 500	86[b]	38[b]	1.1[b,c]	volcanic breccias, tuffaceous sediments propylitically altered	Dystrochrept, poor horizon development
55[g]	16[g]	22[g]	0.57[g]	Quartz-biotite gneiss, sillimanite-zone metamorphism[f]	Spodosols (Haplorthods), moderate profile development[f]

[c]Bormann et al. 1974.
[f]Federer 1973.
[g]Gosz et al. 1976.

Differences in ability of the biota to immobilize cations and thereby regulate dissolved inorganic matter export from the two watersheds are probably minor, because 70 to 80 percent of this export component is made up of SiO_2 and Na, which are not significantly accumulated in the plant or microbial biomass of these ecosystems.

Estimated particulate inorganic matter export from watershed 10, excluding debris torrents, is about nine times greater than that of watershed 6 (Table 8.7). As described in the case of particulate organic matter, in their lower reaches the two channel systems appear to have similar transport capability, except in the case of debris torrents. Therefore, marked differences in particulate inorganic matter export probably arise from a more rapid rate of sediment input to the channel from steeper hillslopes of watershed 10.

Comparison of Hillslope and Channel Material Transfer

Estimated total particulate organic and inorganic inputs to the watershed 10 channel are greater than comparable output values. Much of the input/output difference for particulate organic matter is due to biological utilization (see Tables 10.3 and 10.4), whereas the difference for particulate inorganic matter is within the error of input and output estimations. If input generally exceeds output, the streambed should experience net aggradation. Actually the watershed 10 stream is at the bottom of a steep-sided, V-notch valley, indicating a long history of downcutting. Short-term watershed budget studies and examination of sediment routing function and history of large woody debris in streams (Swanson et al. 1976) suggest, however, that channel systems may be sites of net increase in storage for long periods of time interrupted by infrequent, major flushing events. Consequently, such forested streams may be aggrading on the time scale of years and decades, while experiencing degradation on a broader time scale.

Comparison of Processes

The material transfer data may also be evaluated in terms of relative roles of various processes. Rates of processes accounting for inorganic matter transfer vary over a broad range (Table 8.6). The most infrequently occurring processes, debris avalanches and torrents, appear to be dominant, although only one event occurs every few centuries on the average. Solution transfer, one of the most continuous processes, is the second most important mechanism of inorganic matter transport. Processes of secondary importance include creep, surface erosion, and root throw on hillslopes and suspended sediment and bedload transport in the channel. Litterfall, slump, and earthflow processes are presently insignificant in terms of transporting inorganic matter.

In the case of organic matter transport there is much less variation in the relative importance of most processes (Table 8.7). Among hillslope processes debris avalanche, surface erosion, litterfall, solution, and root throw each supplies material to the channel at rates of about 0.1 to 0.4 t/yr. Particulate organic matter transfer by creep is about an order of magnitude lower, and slump and earthflow processes are presently negligible. Estimated organic matter export rate for each channel process is in the range of 0.1 to 0.3 t/hr. Episodic processes are relatively less important than more continuous ones in transporting organic matter.

EFFECTS OF ECOSYSTEM DISTURBANCE

As a result of numerous interactions between vegetation and material transfer processes in forests, severe disturbances of vegetation affect transfer processes throughout forested watershed ecosystems. This fact has been amply demonstrated in terms of sediment yield from paired forested and manipulated watersheds in areas of diverse climate, vegetation, and geomorphic setting (for example, Fredriksen 1970; Brown and Krygier 1971; Bormann et al. 1974; Fredriksen et al. 1975). Results of watershed manipulation experiments in the Pacific Northwest have been highly varied, depending on treatment, terrain, and history of past disturbances. Effects of timber harvest on sediment yield range from negligible in the case of two watersheds of low slope (7 to 12 percent) that were 25 percent clearcut (Fredriksen et al. 1975) to a twenty-three-fold increase in suspended sediment export over a fourteen-year period from watershed 3 in the H. J. Andrews Experimental Forest, which was 25 percent clearcut and 6 percent roaded (Fredriksen 1970; pers. comm.). Watershed 10 was clearcut and cable yarded in summer 1975 and early stages of postlogging erosion are being examined.

Initial observations in watershed 10 and other experimental watersheds suggest that postclearcut watershed export comes from three sources, each associated with a specific time frame: (1) material input to the channel during falling and yarding operations, consisting of mainly fine, green organic matter and some mineral soil; (2) material that had entered the channel by natural processes and was in temporary storage behind debris obstructions before logging, but is released from storage when large pieces of organic debris are removed from the channel during logging; and (3) material input to the channel by hillslope erosion processes following logging. A general phasing of watershed export of materials from these three sources may occur with material from source 1 mainly leaving the watershed in the first one to three years following cutting, source 2 gaining importance in the latter part of this period, and the postlogging hillslope erosion (source 3) becoming a dominant source several years after cutting. This phasing or routing of material through a watershed is an important element of ecosystem response to disturbance and it is relevant to interpretation of sediment yield data. Sediment yield from manipulated watersheds is commonly interpreted in terms of hillslope transfer processes, where in some cases it may result from changes in channel storage.

Ultimately, postcutting studies in watershed 10 will test hypotheses concerning the role of revegetation in returning individual process rates to levels characteristic of forested conditions. Each process has a different magnitude and timing of response to deforestation due to differences in interactions between transfer processes and vegetation. Hypothetical trajectories of several hillslope process rates following cutting are shown in Figure 8.4. The timing of change in debris avalanche potential is partly a response to the timing of decay of root systems from the precutting vegetation and the buildup of root systems in the postcutting stand. The net effect of this and possibly other factors in areas of the H. J. Andrews Experimental Forest similar to watershed 10 has been a 2.8 times increase in debris avalanche erosion over about a twelve-year period following clearcutting (Swanson and Dyrness 1975). Surface erosion involves a pulse of material transfer during and soon after the logging operation followed by a period of recovery. Timing of recovery is controlled by the rate of reestablishment of ground cover or development of a residual armor layer of coarse soil particles. Soil solution transport is regulated by nutrient and water uptake by vegetation. With recovery of leaf area and rates of primary production, a proportion of available nutrients is incorporated into biomass and a smaller amount is flushed from the system. Additionally, recovery of vegeta-

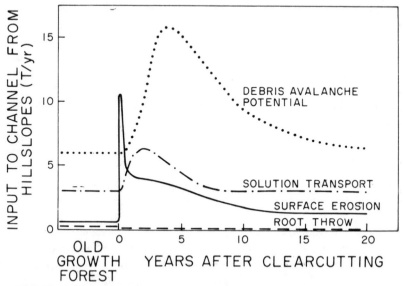

FIGURE 8.4 *Hypothetical trajectories of potential rates of selected hillslope transfer processes after clearcutting of watershed 10.*

tion reduces annual water yield to predeforestation levels over a period of a decade or more. Root throw within the deforested watershed is eliminated as a significant process for several decades until regeneration trees are large enough to be subject to blowdown. Rates of other hillslope and channel processes and channel storage conditions may all vary somewhat out of phase with one another, although there is some degree of interdependence since hillslope processes supply material for transport by channel processes.

To fully assess effects of ecosystem disturbance on material transfer, a broad historical perspective is needed. Typically in the assessment of management impacts, manipulated systems are compared with forested reference or benchmark watersheds; however, most natural, unmanaged watersheds are subject to periodic severe disturbance. Consequently material transfer history under both managed and natural conditions is composed of periods with transfer rates characteristic of established forest conditions interspersed with periods of accelerated transfer spanning up to several decades following severe disturbance of the ecosystem.

In many Pacific Northwest *Pseudotsuga menziesii* forests, natural premanagement disturbances during the past 1000 years have been predominantly major crown fires with a return period of several centuries. Erosional consequences of this type of disturbance are doubtless great, but unknown in steep landscapes. Timber harvest in this area is expected to recur at 80 to 100-year intervals, and its consequence in terms of material transfer is understood in only a preliminary fashion. Based on these assumptions and data, we construct a hypothetical variation in sediment yield from watershed 10 relative to a 500-year history of wildfire and a projected pattern of future management activities and related accelerated material transfer (Figure 8.5). Clear understanding of timber management impact in such a long-term perspective will require knowledge of frequency and consequences of both management and natural premanagement disturbances of the ecosystem.

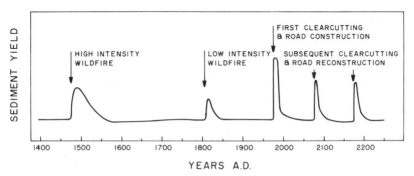

FIGURE 8.5 *Hypothetical history of sediment yield in response to vegetation disturbances on watershed 10.*

SUMMARY

Physical transfer of organic and inorganic matter is an important part of ecosystem behavior. At the system level, physical processes of material transfer account for principal nutrient cycling fluxes. From the standpoint of vegetation distribution, erosion and deposition create constrasting habitat opportunities for aquatic and terrestrial organisms. Erosion also reduces the nutrient capital of a site and affects the course of succession.

Material transfer in steep, forested watersheds of the coniferous forest biome is accomplished by processes that interact with one another and with various components of vegetation. The principal hillslope processes are solution transfer, litterfall, surface erosion, debris avalanche, creep, root throw, slump, and earthflow. These processes supply organic and inorganic material to the channel where downstream transport then occurs as dissolved and suspended material, bedloads, and debris torrents.

These processes operate on a variety of scales in time and space. At one extreme, debris avalanches and torrents may occur in a small watershed only once every few centuries under forested conditions and an event affects only a small percentage of the landscape. On the other hand, creep, litterfall, and solution transfer operate continually over the entire watershed.

These processes are highly interactive. Some events may directly trigger other processes, as in the case of root throw, which may instantaneously initiate a debris avalanche. One process may also set the stage for the occurrence or acceleration of another process, such as the baring of mineral soil by root throw and debris avalanche, which leads to a period of increased surface erosion. Processes also supply material for transport by other processes, so that transfer of a particular particle of soil through a watershed occurs as a series of steps in a variety of modes of transport.

Vegetation increases the rates of some transfer processes while decreasing others. Rooting strength, the mass of vegetation on a hillslope, and hydrologic effects of vegetation regulate rates of debris avalanche, creep, slump, and earthflow activity. Root throw occurs because standing trees serve as a medium for transfer of wind stress to the soil mantle. Nutrient uptake by plants and other processes regulate export of dissolved material. Litterfall results in a net downslope transfer of particulate organic matter as a result of nutrient uptake, incorporation into biomass, and subsequent abscission or pruning by wind or other means. Large woody debris forms retention structures in streams and regulates particulate matter transport by stream processes.

Studies in a small (10-ha) western Oregon watershed and adjacent areas have quantified transfer process rates in an example of an old-growth *Pseudotsuga menziesii/Tsuga heterophylla* ecosystem. Excluding debris torrents, total export is estimated to be 500 kg·ha^{-1}·yr^{-1}, of which 6 percent is dissolved organic matter, 60 percent dissolved inorganic matter, 8 percent particulate organic matter, and 26 percent particulate inorganic matter. Total export including debris torrents is 990 kg·ha⁻¹·yr⁻¹.

Even excluding from consideration debris torrents, the values for each of these forms of export exceed similar estimates for watershed 6 in the fifty-five-year-old hardwood forest at Hubbard Brook, New Hampshire. Higher export values from the Oregon watershed are mainly a result of its higher annual runoff, more readily weathered bedrock and soil, warmer environments for weathering and decomposition, steeper hillslopes, higher litterfall rates, and greater standing crop of living and dead biomass.

Transfer of inorganic matter appears to be dominated by episodic processes, debris avalanches, and torrents. Solution transfer of inorganic matter is second in importance, followed by suspended sediment and bedload transport in the channel and creep, surface erosion, and root throw from hillslopes.

The relative importance of processes in organic matter transport is less varied. The magnitude of importance of episodic processes suggests that nutrient cycling studies based on short-term records may lead to misleading conclusions concerning long-term ecosystem behavior.

The rate of each process varies in response to ecosystem perturbations as a result of numerous interactions between vegetation and transfer processes. The magnitude and duration of rate increases or decreases vary widely from process to process, depending on the type of ecosystem disturbance. For example, clearcutting eliminates root throw while increasing debris avalanche occurrence by several times over a period of one to two decades. Timing of recovery of various process rates to levels typical of forested conditions is dependent on rates of recovery of key components of vegetation.

Short-term comparisons of transfer rates under clearcut conditions with forested conditions may not yield realistic estimates of management impacts on long-term soil loss. In forests of the Pacific Northwest, long-term erosion history under both natural and human-influenced conditions involves long periods with only minor year-to-year fluctuations interrupted by periods of severe ecosystem disturbance and resulting pulses of accelerated material transfer. Clearcutting and road construction have replaced wildfire as major disturbances of these forests and landscapes. Therefore assessment of management impacts requires knowledge of the frequency and consequences of both management and premanagement disturbances.

LITERATURE CITED

Anderson, H. W., 1969, Snowpack management, in *Snow,* Seminar of Oregon Water Resources Research Institute, Oregon State University, Corvallis, pp. 27–40.

Anderson, H. W., G. B. Coleman, and P. J. Zinke, 1959, Summer slides and winter scour—Dry-wet erosion in southern California mountains, *U.S. Department of Agriculture Forest Service Technical Paper PSW-36,* Berkeley, Calif., 12p.

Benedict, J. B., 1970, Downslope soil movement in a Colorado alpine region: Rates, processes and climatic significance, *Arct. and Alpine Res.* **2:**165–226.

Bishop, D. M., and M. E. Stevens, 1964, Landslides on logged areas in southeast Alaska, *U.S. Department of Agriculture Forest Service Research Paper NOR-1,* Juneau, Alaska, 18p.

Bormann, F. H., G. E. Likens, and J. S. Eaton, 1969, Biotic regulation of particulate and solution losses from a forest ecosystem, *BioScience* **19:**600–610.

Bormann, F. H., T. G. Siccama, G. E. Likens, and R. H. Whittaker, 1970, The Hubbard Brook ecosystem study: Composition and dynamics of the tree stratum, *Ecol. Monogr.* **40:**373–388.

Bormann, F. H., G. E. Likens, T. G. Siccama, R. S. Pierce, and J. S. Eaton, 1974, The export of nutrients and recovery of stable conditions following deforestation at Hubbard Brook, *Ecol. Monogr.* **44:**255–277.

Brown, C. B., and M. S. Sheu, 1975, Effects of deforestation on slopes, *J. Geotech. Eng. Div., Am. Soc. Eng.* **101:**147–165.

Brown, G. W., and J. T. Krygier, 1971, Clear-cut logging and sediment production in the Oregon Coast Range, *Water Resour. Res.* **7:**1189–1198.

Caine, N., 1976, A uniform measure of subaerial erosion, *Geol. Soc. Am. Bull.* **87:**137–140.

Cleaves, E. T., A. E. Godfrey, and O. P. Bricker, 1970, Geochemical balance of a small watershed and its geochemical implications, *Geol. Soc. Am. Bull.* **81:**3015–3032.

Dalrymple, T., 1965, Flood peak runoff and associated precipitation in selected drainage basins in the United States, *U.S. Geological Survey Water-Supply Paper 1813,* Washington, D.C., 406p.

Day, N. F., and W. F. Megahan, 1975, Landslide occurrence on the Clearwater National Forest, 1974, *Geol. Soc. Am. Abstr. with Prog.* **7:**602–603.

Denny, C. S., and J. C. Goodlett, 1956, Microrelief resulting from fallen trees, in *Surficial Geology and Geomorphology of Potter County, Pennsylvania,* C. S. Denny, ed., U.S. Geological Survey Professional Paper 288, Washington, D.C., pp. 59–72.

Dietrich, W. E., and T. Dunne, 1978, Sediment budget for a small catchment in mountainous terrain, *Zeit. Geomorph. Suppl.* **29:**191–206.

Dyrness, C. T., 1967, Mass soil movements in the H. J. Andrews Experimental Forest, *U.S. Department of Agriculture Forest Service Research Paper PNW-42,* 12p.

Federer, C. A., 1973, Annual cycles of soil and water temperatures at Hubbard Brook, *U.S. Department of Agriculture Forest Service Research Note NE-167,* Portland, Oreg., 7p.

Fish, B. R., 1972, Electric generation of natural aerosols from vegetation, *Science* **175**:1239–1240.

Fredriksen, R. L., 1965, Christmas storm damage on the H. J. Andrews Experimental Forest, *U.S. Department of Agriculture Forest Service Research Note PNW-29*, Portland, Oreg., 11p.

Fredriksen, R. L., 1969, A battery-powered proportional stream water sampler, *Water Resour. Res.* **5**:1410–1413.

Fredriksen, R. L., 1970, Erosion and sedimentation following road construction and timber harvest on unstable soils in three small western Oregon watersheds, *U.S. Department of Agriculture Forest Service Research Paper PNW-104*, Portland, Oreg., 15p.

Fredriksen, R. L., 1971, Comparative chemical quality—Natural and disturbed streams following logging and slash burning, in *Forest Land Uses and Stream Environment,* J. T. Krygier and J. D. Hall, eds., Continuing Education, Oregon State University, Corvallis, pp. 125–137.

Fredriksen, R. L., 1972, Nutrient budget for a Douglas-fir forest on an experimental watershed in western Oregon, in *Proceedings—Research on Coniferous Forest Ecosystems—A Symposium,* J. F. Franklin, L. J. Dempster, and R. H. Waring, eds., U.S. Department of Agriculture Forest Service, Portland, Oreg., pp. 115–131.

Fredriksen, R. L., 1975, Nitrogen, phosphorous and particulate matter budgets of five coniferous forest ecosystems in the western Cascades Range, Oregon, Ph.D. dissertation, Oregon State University, Corvallis, 127p.

Fredriksen, R. L., D. G. Moore, and L. A. Norris, 1975, The impact of timber harvest, fertilization and herbicide treatment on streamwater quality in western Oregon and Washington, in *Forest Soils and Forest Land Management,* B. Bernier and C. H. Winget, eds., Les Presses de l'Université Laval, Quebec, pp. 283–313.

Froehlich, H. A., 1973, Natural and man-caused slash in headwater streams, *Loggers Handb.* **33**:15–17, 66–70, 82–86.

Froehlich, H. A., D. McGreer, and J. R. Sedell, 1972, Natural debris within the stream environment, *US/IBP Coniferous Forest Biome Internal Report No. 96,* University of Washington, Seattle, 7p.

Gosz, J. R., G. E. Likens, and F. H. Bormann, 1976, Organic matter and nutrient dynamics of the forest and forest floor in the Hubbard Brook forest, *Oecologia* **22**:305–320.

Gray, D. H., 1970, Effects of forest clearcutting on the stability of natural slopes, *Assoc. Eng. Geol. Bull.* **7**:45–77.

Grier, C. C., and R. S. Logan, 1977, Old-growth *Pseudotsuga menziesii* communities of a western Oregon watershed: Biomass distribution and production budgets, *Ecol. Monogr.* **47**:373–400.

Hack, J. T., and J. C. Goodlett, 1960, Geomorphology and forest ecology of a mountain region in the central Appalachians, *U.S. Geological Survey Professional Paper 347,* Washington, D.C., 66p.

Harr, R. D., 1976, Forest practices and stream flow in western Oregon, *U.S. Department of Agriculture Forest Service General Technical Report PNW-49,* Portland, Oreg., 18p.

Harr, R. D., 1977, Water flux in soil and subsoil on a steep forested slope, *J. Hydrol.* **33:**37–58.

Harr, R. D., and F. M. McCorison, 1979, Initial effects of clearcut logging on size and timing of peak flows in a small watershed in western Oregon, *Water Resour. Res.* **15:**90–94.

Jäckli, H., 1957, Gegenwartsgeologie des bundnerischen Rheingebietes-ein Beitrag sur exogenen dynamik alpiner gebirgslandschaften. Beiträge zur geologie der Schweiz, *Geotechnische serie Leiferung 36,* 126p.

Janda, R. J., K. M. Nolan, D. R. Harden, and S. M. Colman, 1975, Watershed conditions in the drainage basin of Redwood Creek, Humboldt County, California, *U.S. Geological Survey Open-File Report 75-568,* Menlo Park, Calif., 266p.

Keller, E. M., and F. J. Swanson, 1979, Effects of large organic material on channel form and fluvial processes, *Earth Surface Process.* **4:**361–380.

Leopold, L. B., M. G. Wolman, and J. P. Miller, 1964, *Fluvial Processes in Geomorphology,* W. H. Freeman, San Francisco, 522p.

Leopold, L. B., W. W. Emmett, and R. M. Myrick, 1966, Channel and hillslope processes in a semiarid area, New Mexico, *U.S. Geological Survey Professional Paper 352-G,* Washington, D.C., 61p.

Likens, G. E., F. H. Bormann, R. S. Pierce, J. S. Eaton, and N. M. Johnson, 1977, *Biogeochemistry of a Forested Ecosystem,* Springer-Verlag, New York, 146p.

Marchand, D. E., 1971, Rates and modes of denudation, White Mountains, eastern California, *Am. J. Sci.* **270:**109–135.

Marchand, D. E., 1974, Chemical weathering, soil development and geochemical fractionation in a part of the White Mountains, Mono and Inyo Counties, California, *U.S. Geological Survey Professional Paper 352-J,* Washington, D.C., 46p.

Mersereau, R. C., and C. T. Dyrness, 1972, Accelerated mass wasting after logging and slash burning in western Oregon, *J. Soil Water Conserv.* **27:**112–114.

Nakano, H., 1971, *Soil and Water Conservation Functions of Forest on Mountainous Lands,* Report of Forest Influences Division, Government Forest Experiment Station, Japan, 66p.

Peck, D. L., A. B. Griggs, H. G. Schlicker, F. G. Wells, and H. M. Dole, 1964, Geology of the central and northern parts of the western Cascade Range in Oregon, *U.S. Geological Survey Professional Paper 449,* Washington, D.C., 56p.

Rapp, A., 1960, Recent development of mountain slopes in Karkevagge and surrounding, northern Scandinavia, *Geogr. Ann.* **42:**71–200.

Rothacher, J., and T. B. Glazebrook, 1968, Flood damage in the national forests of Region 6, *U.S. Department of Agriculture Forest Service,* Portland, Oreg. 20p.

Rothacher, J., C. T. Dyrness, and R. L. Fredriksen, 1967, Hydrologic and related characteristics of three small watersheds in the Oregon Cascades, *U.S. Department of Agriculture Forest Service Miscellaneous Publication,* U.S. Department of Agriculture Forest Service, Portland, Oreg., 54p.

Santantonio, D., R. K. Hermann, and W. S. Overton, 1977, Root biomass studies in forest ecosystems, *Pedobiologia* **17:**1–31.

Sedell, J. R., and F. J. Triska, 1977, Biological consequences of large organic debris in Northwest streams, in *Logging Debris in Streams, II: Forestry Extension Workshop,* G. D. Wingate, compiler, 21–22 March 1977, Oregon State University, Corvallis, Oreg., 10p.

Stone, E. L., 1975, Windthrow influences on spatial heterogeneity in a forest soil, *Mitt. Eidg. Anst. Forstl. Versuchswes.* **51:**77–87.

Swanson, F. J., and C. T. Dyrness, 1975, Impact of clearcutting and road construction on soil erosion by landslides in the western Cascade Range, Oregon, *Geology* **3:**393–396.

Swanson, F. J., and M. E. James, 1975, Geology and geomorphology of the H. J. Andrews Experimental Forest, western Cascades, Oregon, *U.S. Department of Agriculture Forest Service Research Paper PNW-188,* Portland, Oreg., 14p.

Swanson, F. J., and D. N. Swanston, 1977, Complex mass-movement terrains in the western Cascade Range, Oregon, *Rev. Eng. Geol.* **3:**113–124.

Swanson, F. J., G. W. Lienkaemper, and J. R. Sedell, 1976, History, physical effects and management implications of large organic debris in western Oregon streams, *U.S. Department of Agriculture Forest Service General Technical Report PNW-56,* Portland, Oreg., 15p.

Swanston, D. N., 1969, Mass wasting in coastal Alaska, *U.S. Department of Agriculture Forest Service Research Paper PNW-83,* Portland, Oreg., 15p.

Swanston, D. N., 1970, Mechanics of debris avalanching in shallow till soils of southeast Alaska, *U.S. Department of Agriculture Forest Service Research Paper PNW-103,* Portland, Oreg., 17p.

Terzaghi, K., 1950, Mechanism of landslides, in *Application of Geology to Engineering Practice,* S. Paige, ed., Berkey Volume, Geological Society of America, Boulder, Colo., pp. 83–123.

Varnes, D. J., 1958, Landslide types and processes, in *Landslides and Engineering Practice,* E. B. Eckel, ed., Highway Research Board Special Publication 29, Washington, D.C., pp. 20–47.

Waananen, A. O., D. D. Harris, and R. C. Williams, 1971, Floods of December 1964 and January 1965 in the far western states, Part 1: Description, *U.S. Geological Survey Water-Supply Paper 1866-A,* Washington, D.C., 265p.

Waring, R. H., H. R. Holbo, R. P. Bueb, and R. L. Fredriksen, 1978, Documentation of meteorological data from the Coniferous Forest Biome primary station in Oregon, *U.S. Department of Agriculture Forest Service General Technical Report PNW-73*, Portland, Oreg., 23p.

9

Land–Water Interactions: The Riparian Zone

F. J. Swanson, S. V. Gregory, J. R. Sedell, and *A. G. Campbell*

INTRODUCTION

The interface between aquatic and terrestrial environments in coniferous forests forms a narrow riparian zone. Until recently, structure, composition, and function of the riparian zone had received little consideration in ecosystem level research, because this zone forms the interface between scientific disciplines as well as ecosystem components. In some climate-vegetation zones particular aspects of riparian zones have received much study. The conspicuous riparian plant communities in arid lands have been studied extensively, primarily in terms of wildlife habitat (Johnson and Jones 1977; Thomas et al. 1979). Research on riparian vegetation along major rivers has dealt mainly with forest composition and dynamics (for example, Lindsey et al. 1961; Sigafoos 1964; Bell 1974; Johnson et al. 1976). Riparian vegetation research has been largely neglected in forested mountain land, where it tends to have smaller areal extent and economic value than upslope vegetation. From an ecosystem perspective, however, the riparian zone is an integral part of the forest/stream ecosystem complex.

This chapter synthesizes general concepts about the riparian zone in northwest coniferous forests and the results of coniferous forest biome research on: (1) structure and composition of riparian vegetation and its variation in time and space; and (2) functional aspects of the riparian zone in terms of physical, biological, and chemical terrestrial/aquatic interactions. We emphasize conditions observed in mountain streams and small rivers.

The riparian zone may be defined in a variety of ways, based on factors such as vegetation type, groundwater and surface water hydrology, topography, and ecosystem function. These factors have so many complex interactions that defining the riparian zone in one sense integrates elements of the other factors. We prefer to define the riparian zone functionally as that zone of direct interaction between terrestrial and aquatic environments. Vegetation, hydrology, and topography all determine the type, magnitude, and direction of functional relationships. The direction of riparian interactions refers to the notion that the terrestrial system may affect the aquatic or vice versa. In arid land systems, where streams may recharge groundwater, as well as in floodplain situations, streams and rivers are often viewed as exercising important control over streamside vegetation. Steep terrain and massive forests in the Pacific Northwest emphasize effects of forests on streams.

The riparian zone can be viewed on three distinct scales. In the strictest sense the zone of direct interaction could be considered the water's edge. This restricted zone is preferentially occupied by bank and large wood-dwelling beetle adults, *Diptera* larvae, Collembola, and hydrophilic plants. Such a narrowly defined, linear view of terrestrial/aquatic interactions ignores many important characteristics of the riparian zone.

In a slightly broader sense, the aquatic/terrestrial interface includes the areas of the streambed, banks, and floodplain that may be submerged only part of the year. At different times of the year these sites may be subjected to processes and be habitats for species that are typical of either terrestrial or aquatic environments or some mix of the two. This type of interface occurs as a result of both headward and lateral expansion and contraction of stream area on the time scales of storms and seasons. This planar view of the riparian zone accounts for only limited aspects of aquatic/terrestrial interactions.

The third and largest scale on which we view riparian vegetation is more three-dimensional and incorporates the concept that at any point in time a forested stream is directly influenced biologically, physically, and chemically by aboveground and belowground components of streamside vegetation. If the riparian zone is defined functionally in terms of the area of direct interaction between aquatic and terrestrial environment, then it forms a zone of interaction extending upward and outward from the stream through the overhanging canopy. In the Pacific Northwest, structure and composition of riparian vegetation include herbaceous groundcover, understory shrubby vegetation (commonly deciduous), overstory trees on the floodplain (generally a mix of deciduous and coniferous), and possibly the upper parts of trees rooted at the base of adjacent hillslopes (generally coniferous). Each of these components of riparian vegetation is involved in a variety of terrestrial/aquatic interactions, many of which are summarized in Table 9.1.

We choose to consider the land/stream interface on this broad scale and in terms of compositional, structural, and functional aspects of riparian vegetation. This perspective offers a conceptual basis for examining the full range of terrestrial/aquatic interactions. Discussion of the riparian zone begins with composition and structure of the vegetation, because these two factors determine the character of functional relationships.

STRUCTURE AND COMPOSITION OF RIPARIAN VEGETATION

Hydrologic, climatic, and substrate factors determine the composition and therefore the structure and function of riparian vegetation. Relative to upslope

TABLE 9.1   *Function of riparian vegetation with respect to aquatic ecosystems.*

Site	Component	Function
Aboveground/ above channel	Canopy and stems	1. Shade controls temperature and in stream primary production 2. Source of large and fine plant detritus 3. Wildlife habitat
In channel	Large debris derived from riparian vegetation	1. Control routing of water and sediment 2. Shape habitat—pools, riffles, cover 3. Substrate for biological activity
Streambanks	Roots	1. Increase bank stability 2. Create overhanging banks—cover 3. Nutrient uptake from ground and streamwater
Floodplain	Stems and low-lying canopy	1. Retard movement of sediment, water and floated organic debris in flood flows

sites, the riparian environment is protected from high winds and extremes of summer drought. It is subjected to periodic flooding, however, that causes inundation, destruction of some vegetation, and creation of fresh sites for establishment of vegetation. These physical factors result in some distinctive structural and compositional attributes of riparian vegetation.

Riparian-zone vegetation in the Douglas-fir region has been characterized in terms of: (1) stream/stand relations in a variety of forest age classes and stream sizes; and (2) types of riparian plant communities along streams of different sizes and disturbance histories. Much of the descriptive ecology and geomorphology dealing with riparian vegetation in the Pacific Northwest has been carried out in the H. J. Andrews Experimental Forest, the primary site for the IBP stream ecology research (Sedell et al. 1974, 1975; Sedell and Triska 1977; Swanson et al. 1976; Swanson and Lienkaemper 1978; Anderson et al. 1978; Campbell and Franklin 1979). Mack Creek, a principal study stream, offers examples of riparian vegetation structure and composition in steep, intermediate-sized streams of this region.

Maps of large shrub and small tree (Figure 9.1A) and small shrub and herb (Figure 9.1B) vegetation and a vegetation valley bottom cross profile (Figure 9.2) portray the distribution of plants along a section of Mack Creek. Here the streams flow over boulders and large organic debris through a 450- to 500-year-old *Pseudotsuga menziesii/Tsuga heterophylla* forest.

Vegetation along Mack Creek and other small and intermediate-sized streams has a pronounced stratification from low-lying herbs and shrubs to

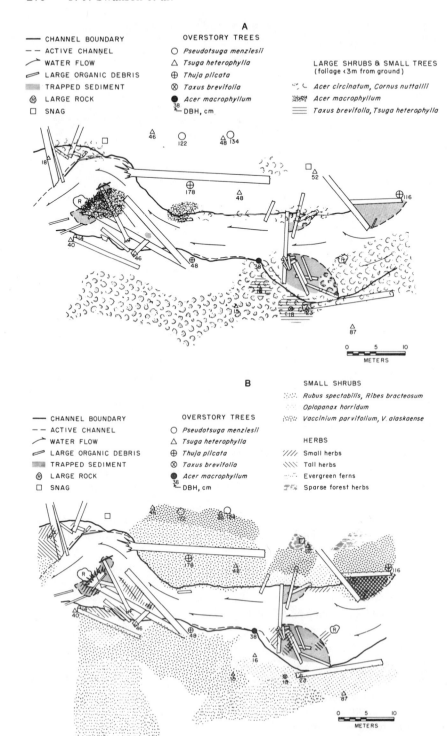

A

CHANNEL BOUNDARY
ACTIVE CHANNEL
WATER FLOW
LARGE ORGANIC DEBRIS
TRAPPED SEDIMENT
LARGE ROCK
SNAG

OVERSTORY TREES

○ *Pseudotsuga menziesii*
△ *Tsuga heterophylla*
⊕ *Thuja plicata*
⊗ *Taxus brevifolia*
● *Acer macrophyllum*
DBH, cm

LARGE SHRUBS & SMALL TREES
(foliage <3m from ground)

Acer circinatum, Cornus nuttallii
Acer macrophyllum
Taxus brevifolia, Tsuga heterophylla

B

CHANNEL BOUNDARY
ACTIVE CHANNEL
WATER FLOW
LARGE ORGANIC DEBRIS
TRAPPED SEDIMENT
LARGE ROCK
SNAG

OVERSTORY TREES

○ *Pseudotsuga menziesii*
△ *Tsuga heterophylla*
⊕ *Thuja plicata*
⊗ *Taxus brevifolia*
● *Acer macrophyllum*
DBH, cm

SMALL SHRUBS

Rubus spectabilis, Ribes bracteosum
Oplopanax horridum
Vaccinium parvifolium, V. alaskaense

HERBS

Small herbs
Tall herbs
Evergreen ferns
Sparse forest herbs

small trees, and large overstory trees. Large trees that shade streams are predominantly *Pseudotsuga menziesii*, *Thuja plicata*, and *Tsuga heterophylla*, which may be rooted adjacent to the channel or well away from it, and lean out over the stream. Development of small trees along a stream may be greater than in upslope areas in response to greater light availability where streams are wide enough to have at least partially broken canopy above the channel. In old-growth forests of the H. J. Andrews Forest this lower-tree stratum is mainly composed of deciduous trees that lean over the stream into the light. In the western Cascade Mountains, streamside herb and shrub communities also typically have greater biomass per unit area than the same vegetation strata in upslope areas (C. C. Grier, pers. comm.). This may be due to lower plant moisture stress in the streamside area.

In a broad sense, streamside vegetation is composed of generalist species that inhabit upslope areas as well as specialists whose range is restricted to the very moist streamside habitats. For example, generalists in the Mack Creek area include *Acer circinatum*, *Acer macrophyllum*, *Vaccinium parvifolium*, and *Oxalis oregana*, whereas *Oplopanax horridum* and *Rubus spectabilis* are specialists restricted to the streamside area and other very wet sites (Figure 9.1). Plants that are specialists along Mack Creek may be widely distributed on hillslope areas in other climatic settings.

A variety of site factors such as substrate type, frequency and intensity of scouring, light availability, and site area constrain the types and distributions of riparian zone plant communities. On small, steep, first-order streams riparian habitats are so restricted in area that only fragments of synusiae may form, while full-scale forests are found on floodplains of larger streams and rivers. The amount of sunlight reaching the vicinity of a stream also influences the type and degree of development of herb, shrub, and small tree components of riparian vegetation. Aspect, stream width, and stand crown condition all regulate light penetration to the stream and adjacent areas.

Riparian plant associations within the herb and shrub layers are commonly limited by substrate type. For example, in the central western Cascade Range of Oregon clans of seed-disseminated herbs such as *Circaea alpina* and *Montia sibirica* are common on fresh deposits of sand and fine gravel. Other species, such as *Petasites frigidus* and *Stachys cooleyea*, sustain themselves by spreading their root systems below the level of frequent scour among small boulders in sunny areas. Wet cliff faces may support communities dominated by *Adiantum pedantum*, *Tolmiea menziesii*, and mosses. *Oplopanax horridum* or *Ribes bracteosum* and *Rubus spectabilis* are common components of the shrub layer

FIGURE 9.1 *Components of riparian vegetation along a third-order section of Mack Creek, H. J. Andrews Experimental Forest. Watershed area is 600 ha; channel gradient is about 10 percent. (A) Map of large shrubs (>2 m high) and low-lying canopy (<3 m) of small-tree strata. (B) Map of herb and small-shrub (50 cm to 2 m high) strata.*

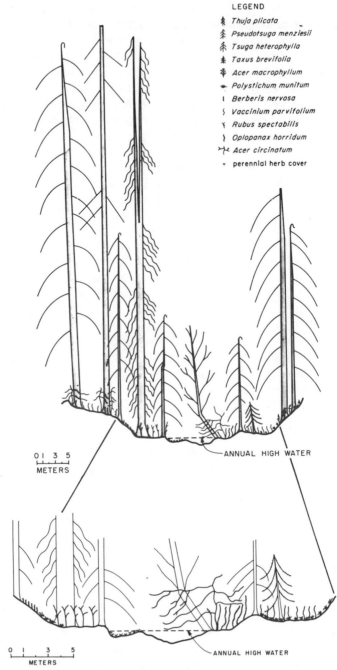

LEGEND

🌲 *Thuja plicata*
🌲 *Pseudotsuga menziesii*
🌲 *Tsuga heterophylla*
🌲 *Taxus brevifolia*
🌿 *Acer macrophyllum*
🌿 *Polystichum munitum*
| *Berberis nervosa*
) *Vaccinium parvifolium*
γ *Rubus spectabilis*
) *Oplopanax horridum*
⋋⋌ *Acer circinatum*
⌄ perennial herb cover

ANNUAL HIGH WATER

0 1 3 5
METERS

ANNUAL HIGH WATER

0 1   3   5
METERS

FIGURE 9.2 *Generalized vegetation/valley bottom cross profile of Mack Creek, H. J. Andrews Experimental Forest.*

where subsoil remains wet and scouring is not a problem. Farther from the stream, the understory is dominated by the same synusiae found in the wettest of typical forest plant communities—*Vaccinium parvifolium, Oxalis oregana, Polystichum munitum,* and others (Zobel et al. 1976).

The effects of variation in substrate type, availability of sunlight, and scouring history on riparian plant community development are evident in surveys of community types on nine first- through third-order streams in the H. J. Andrews Experimental Forest and vicinity, summarized in Table 9.2 by stratigraphic groups of riparian plants. Communities dominated by shrubs, *Acer circinatum,* and other small trees increase in percentage of cover with increasing stream size. This trend appears to be a response to greater sunlight penetration to middle strata of the forest where stream width is sufficient to cause opening of the overstory canopy. The small and large herb classes show no consistent change in cover over the three stream orders, possibly because the increased light availability in larger streams is utilized by higher vegetation strata. Plant cover conditions along the watershed 2 stream are very different from those of the other inventoried streams. High herb layer cover reflects the abundance of bedrock and very small, localized pockets of soil along the stream. A debris torrent scoured this channel in the late 1940s, leaving a steep-sided bedrock notch in the second-order portion of this watershed. Opportunity for rooting by larger plants is severely limited.

Several features of the riparian zone tend to retard development of streamside vegetation. As in the case of the watershed 2 stream, erosion along small

TABLE 9.2   *Percent cover of stratigraphic classes of riparian communities in small tree, shrub, and herb strata along four first-order, three second-order, and one third-order stream with predominantly gravel, boulder, and substrates, and along watershed 2 stream, a second-order bedrock-dominated channel.[a]*

	Percent cover			
	Stream order			Watershed 2
Stratigraphic class[b]	1	2	3	(second-order)
Small herb	6	6	2	23
Large herb	5	14	9	39
Shrub	2	19	25	
Large shrub/small tree		3	13	
Acer circinatum	26	31	37	9

[a]Campbell and Franklin 1979.
[b]Small herbs are up to 30 cm tall, for example, *Tolmiea menziesii;* large herbs, 30 cm to 2 m tall, for example, *Aralia californica;* small shrubs, 50 cm to 2 m, for example, *Oplopanax horridum;* large shrubs/small trees, 2 to 6 m tall, for example, *Osmaronia cerasiformis.*

and intermediate-sized streams may leave a channel bordered by steep bedrock slopes with soil cover sufficient to support only patchy herbaceous vegetation. Large woody debris in channels is also an unsuitable substrate for establishment of many plant species, so it may suppress development of riparian vegetation where it is heavily concentrated, particularly in logged or burned areas. Streamside vegetation subject to periodic wetting is also vulnerable to partial or complete destruction during major floods when stream-transported debris, ice, or both may severely batter plants along streams and rivers. Therefore a riparian plant community at a particular time reflects both long- and short-term histories of channel changes.

FUNCTIONS OF THE RIPARIAN ZONE

Discussion of terrestrial/aquatic interactions proceeds from physical to biological to chemical factors. The physical environment forms a template on which the biota develops and both physical and biological factors determine the type and rates of changes in soil-water and stream-water chemistry that occur across the terrestrial/aquatic interface.

Physical Terrestrial/Aquatic Interactions

Much of the classic work on physical characteristics of the stream environment has been concerned with the shaping of channel pattern and bedforms by flowing water (Leopold et al. 1964). Most of this work has dealt with meandering, low-gradient streams and rivers where sediment type and hydraulic forces clearly control fluvial morphology. Mountain streams and small rivers in the coniferous forests of the Pacific Northwest, however, are primarily shaped by external factors—hillslope erosion processes, bedrock control of channel position and geometry, channel stabilization by riparian vegetation, and large organic material derived from terrestrial vegetation.

Hillslope erosion processes determine the rate of supply of sediment and large organic debris to the channel, frequency of catastrophic flushing by debris torrents, and rates of channel constriction (see Chapter 8). These factors control channel geometry, streambed substrate, and the character of riparian vegetation in a variety of ways. Abundance and size distribution of alluvium in a channel reflect, in part, the balance between sediment supply by hillslope processes and removal by channel processes. Sediment type determines the channel bedforms, bed roughness, bed stability (frequency and depth of scour and fill), and habitat for benthic organisms. In addition to supplying sediment to a channel, slow, deep-seated mass-erosion processes also disrupt riparian zone vegetation by tipping big trees and contributing to the occurrence of small streamside slides that destroy established riparian vegetation and create an opportunity for the development of new plant communities. Over the course of years, these processes of creep, slump, and earthflow progressively close channels until they are reopened by floods (Swanson and Swanston 1977). Rapid mass erosion events from hillslope areas have the potential for greater, more immediate impact on streams and the riparian zone. Debris avalanches may completely destroy riparian vegetation at the base of a slope, and they are the prime triggering mechanism of debris torrents (Swanson et al. 1976). Movement of debris torrents down steep channels often completely obliterates streamside vegetation.

Channel erosion and downstream transport of organic and inorganic detritus are also influenced by streamside vegetation. Studies in agricultural systems indicate that vegetation in shallow channels reduces sediment transport (Karr and Schlosser 1978). Smith (1976) and others argue that root networks of streamside plants retard bank erosion, and, in the Colorado River system, Graf (1978) documents reduced channel width due to sediment entrapment and stabilization by invading *Tamarix chinensis*. Channel geometry differs for forest and pasture vegetation along several small streams in northern Vermont (Zimmerman et al. 1967). During floods, streamside vegetation is both a source of transportable woody debris and a device for trapping transported material. Large amounts of leaves, twigs, and small limbs trapped in riparian vegetation are evidence that floating organic matter is combed from floodwaters by streamside brush. Streamside vegetation also reduces water velocity and therefore erosive capability by increasing roughness (Petryk and Bosmajian 1975).

The input of large organic debris to streams from the surrounding forest is a complex and important link between terrestrial and aquatic components of the forest ecosystem. The quantity of large organic debris in a stream at any specific time is a result of the balance between input and output processes over the previous several centuries (Figure 9.3). Debris input is regulated by the dynamics of the surrounding forest and landscape, which involve biotic factors such as episodes of stand thinning and the abiotic processes of blowdown, debris avalanche, and streambank cutting. Debris input processes interact in several ways (Figure 9.3), such as wind stress on the tree canopy that may trigger streamside debris avalanches. Debris avalanching may also occur in response to bank cutting by the stream or by debris torrents. Undercutting of streamside trees makes them more susceptible to being blown down.

Large woody debris may be moved out of a channel section by: (1) flotation of individual pieces or "rafts" of debris during floods; (2) debris torrents involving rapid, turbulent movement of masses of soil, alluvium, and organic matter down stream channels; and (3) transport of dissolved and fine particulate matter following decomposition, leaching, and processing by aquatic invertebrates.

Standing crops of coarse woody debris (> 10-cm diameter) in western Oregon streams have been measured by Froehlich (1973) and J. R. Sedell and

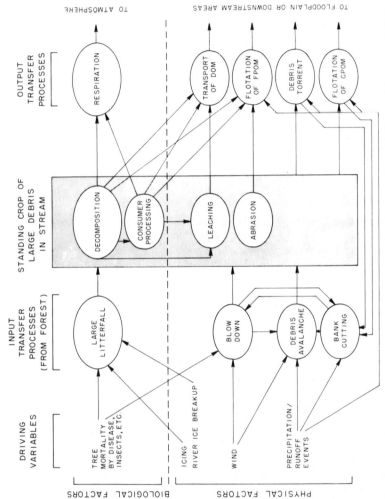

FIGURE 9.3 *Dynamics of large woody debris in streams (from Keller and Swanson 1979).*

G. W. Lienkaemper (pers. comm.). Eleven small streams flowing through old-growth forests and draining areas of 3 to about 50 ha contain coarse debris ranging from 2.8 kg/m^2 in a channel recently flushed by a debris torrent to 90.2 kg/m^2. These figures include both the channel and bank areas immediately adjacent to the stream. Average standing crop of debris, excluding the recently cleared channel, was 50.4 kg/m^2.

The standing crop of coarse debris in channels decreases downstream due to increased stream transport capability and reduced influence of adjacent forests on progressively wider streams. Standing crop of coarse debris decreases systematically in a series of samples taken along a gradient of stream sizes from first to sixth order in the upper McKenzie River system (Table 9.3). Coarse organic debris levels exceed 30 kg/m^2 at sample sites on first- through third-order stream reaches, but the sixth-order McKenzie River site at Rainbow, Oregon, has only about 1 percent of the standing crop of the first-order channel.

The spatial distribution of coarse debris also varies systematically from small streams to large rivers (Keller and Swanson, 1979). Maps of stream channels (Figures 9.1, 9.4, and 9.5) reveal the generally lower debris concentrations and greater clumping of debris pieces in larger streams. The distribution of debris reflects in part the balance between stream size and debris size. Debris in small streams is large relative to channel dimensions and volume of flood flows, so it cannot be floated and redistributed (Figure 9.4). Consequently, the debris is randomly distributed and located where it initially fell; however these small channels are in the steepest part of the drainage network, and are most prone to catastrophic flushing by debris torrents. Intermediate-sized streams are large enough to redistribute coarse woody debris but narrow enough that debris accumulations crossing the entire channel are common

TABLE 9.3   *Coarse (> 10 cm diam) debris loading sampled in sections of five streams flowing through old-growth Douglas-fir forests in McKenzie River system, western Oregon. Specific gravity of wood assumed to be 0.50 g/cm^3.[a]*

Stream	Coarse debris loading (kg/m)	Length of sampled station (m)	Channel width (m)	Channel gradient (%)	Stream order	Watershed area (km^2)
Devil's Club Creek	43.5	90	1	40	1	0.2
Watershed 2 Creek	38.0	135	2.6	26	2	0.8
Mack Creek	28.5	300	12	13	3	6.0
Lookout Creek	11.6	300	24	3	5	60.5
McKenzie River at Rainbow	0.5	800	40	0.6	7	1024

[a]From Keller and Swanson 1979.

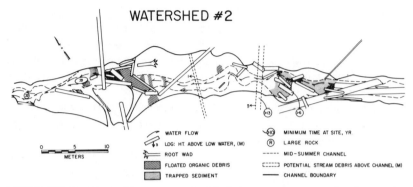

FIGURE 9.4 *Map of large organic debris in an upper second-order section of watershed 2 stream (mapped by G. W. Lienkaemper).*

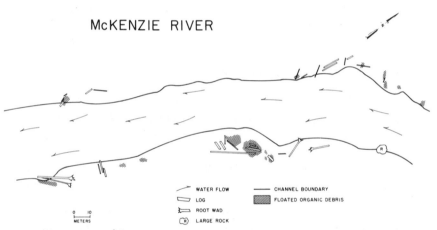

FIGURE 9.5 *Map of large organic debris in a sixth-order section of McKenzie River (mapped by G. W. Lienkaemper).*

(Figure 9.1). The debris tends to be concentrated in distinct accumulations spaced several channel widths apart along the stream. In large rivers, debris is commonly collected in scattered, distinct accumulations at high water (Figure 9.5) and particularly on upstream ends of islands and at bends in the river.

Large debris in streams controls channel morphology as well as sediment and water routing (Keller and Swanson 1979). Debris helps form a stepped gradient in streams up to about the third order (Heede 1972). The streambed is made up of long, low gradient sections separated by relatively short, steep falls or cascades. Therefore much of the streambed may have gradient less than the overall gradient of the valley bottom, because much of the stream drop, or decrease in potential energy, takes place in the short, steep reaches. This pattern of energy dissipation in short stream reaches results in less erosion of bed and banks, more sediment storage in the channel, slower routing of organic detritus, and greater habitat diversity than in straight, even gradient channels.

Comparison of volumes of stored sediment and volume of annual sediment export suggests that small forested streams annually export only a small fraction of sediment in storage in the channel system. In the case of the 60-ha watershed 2 in the H. J. Andrews Experimental Forest, average bedload export measured in a sediment basin for 1957 through 1976 has been 3.8 m^3/yr (R. L. Fredriksen, pers. comm.). In a 100-m channel section upstream of the basin, 20.1 m^3 of sediment is stored behind organic debris. The entire length of perennial and intermittent channel is about 1700 m, so in this watershed annual sediment yield is probably much less than 10 percent of material in storage. Megahan and Nowlin (1976) have made similar observations in several small, forested watersheds in central Idaho where sediment yield was only about 10 percent of sediment stored in the channel systems. Woody materials made up 75 to 85 percent of the obstructions that trapped sediment in the Idaho streams.

Unfilled storage capacity serves to buffer the sedimentation impacts on downstream areas when pulses of sediment enter channels. Scattered debris in channels reduces the rate of sediment movement and routes sediment through the stream ecosystem more slowly, except in cases of catastrophic flushing events.

Debris has both positive and negative effects on bank stability, on the lateral mobility of channels, and on stability of aquatic habitats. Debris-related bank stability problems in steep-sided, bedrock-controlled streams result from undercutting of the soil mantle on hillslopes by debris torrents. Undercut slopes are subject to progressive failure by surface erosion and small-scale (< 100-m^3) mass erosion over a period of years. Both bank instability and lateral channel migration may be facilitated by debris accumulations in channels with abundant alluvium and minimal bedrock influence. Change in channel conditions and position often occurs as a stream bypasses a debris accumulation and cuts a new channel. Where channels flow through massive depositional areas behind and through debris accumulations, streamflow may be subsurface much of the year. In areas of active creep and earthflows, lateral stream cutting may undermine banks and encourage further hillslope failure and accelerated sediment supply to the channel. On balance, however, large debris generally stabilizes small streams by its roles in stream energy dissipation and bank protection.

Large organic debris may be the principal factor in determining characteristics of aquatic habitats in small and intermediate-sized mountain streams in the northwest. In classic meandering channels, hydraulic factors regulate the formation of pools and riffles, which are the major contrasting habitat components of low-gradient streams and rivers. Large organic debris, however, may regulate the distribution of fast-water areas and slow-water depositional sites in steep forested streams. Logs and riparian vegetation in all types of forest streams provide cover and offer other benefits as well as negative effects for fish habitat (Narver 1971; Hall and Baker 1977). Wood itself also serves as a

habitat or substrate for a great deal of biological activity by microbial, invertebrate, and other aquatic organisms (Anderson et al. 1978; Sedell and Triska
1977).

The influence of wood on aquatic habitats has been measured in several
streams in the H. J. Andrews Experiment Forest. Along a third-order stretch of
Mack Creek flowing through old-growth forest, 11 percent of the stream area is
covered with wood, 16 percent is wood-created habitat (primarily depositional
sites), and 73 percent is nonwood habitat, mainly boulder-dominated areas of
fast water. Wood composes 25 percent of the stream area and another 21 percent
is habitat-influenced by wood in Devil's Club Creek, a first-order stream.
Much of the biological activity by detritus processing and other consumer
organisms is concentrated in the areas of wood and wood-related habitat.

Biological Terrestrial/Aquatic Interactions

Riparian vegetation controls both the energy base and physical structure of
low-order streams in coniferous forests. In addition, this vegetation may influence the chemistry of soil solution and stream water. Composition of riparian
communities determines both the quantity and food quality of organic matter
contributed to the aquatic environment. Through these influences the riparian
zone also regulates the composition of the aquatic community in terms of
relative importance of functional groups (Cummins 1974).

Biotic communities in streams are supported by dual energy sources, autochthonous primary production and allochthonous detritus. Both energy
sources are always present but their relative magnitudes are determined largely
by conditions of surrounding vegetation and landscape. Inputs of allochthonous
detritus to small streams flowing through old-growth forests account for more
than 95 percent of organic matter inputs (see Tables 10.3 and 10.4). Shading by
riparian vegetation restricts the amount of primary production in a stream by
reducing the amount of sunlight reaching the streambed. Sunlight is the energy
base for photosynthesis and a source of energy for warming stream water
(Brown and Krygier 1970). Both of these factors enhance primary production.
Primary production by algae and diatoms in open streams contributes greatly to
the energy base of the stream and may well be a more important source of
organic matter than streamside vegetation.

Allochthonous detrital inputs range from rapidly-processed, fine particulate inputs, such as leaves, needles, and twigs, to large, slowly-processed,
woody debris. Though woody material has lower food quality than nonwoody
detritus, the high standing crop and physical stability of logs and branches in
Pacific Northwest streams make wood an important and relatively reliable food
source for stream organisms over the long term. The energy base of the stream
is constantly supplied with refractory fine organic material from wood. This
process provides a buffer for the energy base of the biota during periods when
few leaves or needles are available.

The function of large organic debris to provide retention structures and longer residence time for fine detritus benefits aquatic organisms by increasing opportunity for detritus processing. Adequate time for detritus processing is critical in headwater streams because microbial conditioning of important food sources such as conifer needles may take more than one hundred days (Sedell et al. 1975).

The species composition of riparian vegetation affects the timing and quality of food resources of aquatic systems. Deciduous vegetation has a more seasonally pulsed and readily decomposed litter input to streams than coniferous trees (Sedell et al. 1974; F. J. Triska pers. comm.). Decomposition of woody debris from the dominant coniferous species in the region is also slower than that of wood of common riparian deciduous species. Therefore, the diversity of food resources, both heterotrophic and autotrophic, reflect a variety of characteristics of the riparian zone.

The position of riparian zones in watersheds makes them potentially effective in modifying the chemistry of groundwater as it approaches streams. The shallow position of bedrock in many mountain streams of the Pacific Northwest results in flow of groundwater through the rooting zone of streamside vegetation. Nutrients that have either escaped the rooting zone of upslope vegetation or entered solution as a result of mineral weathering below the rooting zone may be incorporated into this last terrestrial site for nutrient retention. Additionally, the extensive contact between riparian zone soils and groundwater and stream water accommodates leaching of chemicals into the water. Thus riparian zones have high potential for regulating nutrient fluxes.

The physical environment of riparian zones is well suited for vigorous extended plant growth and nutrient uptake. The position of the riparian zone along streams ensures adequate soil moisture for plant utilization throughout the most of the year. During summer, it is buffered against evapotranspiration stress because of relatively higher humidity and lower temperature in the area along streams. The streamside corridor does not experience the high temperatures of upslope areas, because of cooling by evaporation along the stream. During winter it is not exposed to the winds more prevalent at higher elevations of watersheds. The combination of these factors makes the riparian zone one of the best suited portions of watersheds for seasonally prolonged metabolic activity. Longer periods of growth increase the potential for retention of nutrients from groundwater.

Riparian vegetation dominated by *Alnus rubra* can provide nitrogen to nitrogen-poor aquatic ecosystems of the Pacific Northwest as a result of nitrogen fixation and nitrogen-rich litter. *Alnus rubra,* a common component of riparian stands, converts atmospheric nitrogen gas to reduced or organic nitrogen forms. This species competes best on wet, disturbed sites and thus is often found in the wet bottom areas at the bases of steep slopes in the Cascade and Coast ranges (Newton et al. 1968). Its litter contains approximately 2 percent nitrogen (dry weight) while most other deciduous or coniferous litter contains approximately 0.5 percent to 1 percent nitrogen.

These and other factors, including the high rate of *Alnus rubra* litter production, result in greater standing crop of nitrogen in litter and soil and much faster rates of nutrient cycling in *Alnus rubra* stands contrasted with *Pseudotsuga menziesii* stands (Bollen and Lu 1968). Cole et al. (1978) observed these patterns in thirty- to fifty-year-old *A. rubra* and *P. menziesii* stands on level ground in the Washington Cascades. Zavitkovski and Newton (1971) measured even higher rates of leaf litterfall in younger *A. rubra* stands on more mesic sites in western Oregon.

The high nutrient quality of this litter affects its rate of processing. Since microbial processing of litter is limited by the nitrogen content of the organic matter (Alexander 1961), the higher nitrogen content of *Alnus*-dominated riparian litter results in faster turnover of organic matter within this zone (Cole et al. 1978). In addition, the nitrogen quality of leaf litter in streams has been shown to limit the decomposition by the litter microbes (Kaushik and Hynes 1971). In view of the fact that aquatic invertebrate utilization of leaf litter depends on microbial conditioning (Barlocher and Kendrick 1973), the quality of litter from the riparian zone has a significant impact on dynamics of the stream ecosystem.

Food resources and physical habitat opportunities, which we have suggested are controlled by riparian vegetation, determine much of the structure of aquatic invertebrate communities. Particular functional groups of organisms are adapted to processing specific materials under certain habitat conditions (Chapter 10; Cummins 1974). For example, "gougers," such as beetle larvae, utilize large woody debris (Anderson et al. 1978), "shredders" consume leaves and needles, and "scrapers" eat algae on the surfaces of rocks. Consequently, changes in relative proportions of these food and substrate types in a stream trigger shifts in aquatic communities. Compositional, structural, and functional changes in riparian vegetation trigger changes in structure and composition of stream communities. Biological consequences of terrestrial/aquatic interactions are described in greater detail in Chapter 10.

SPATIAL VARIATION OF TERRESTRIAL/AQUATIC INTERFACES

The character of the terrestrial/aquatic interface changes systematically with variation in stream size. The forest dominates small headwater streams and suppresses development of herb, shrub, and small tree components of the riparian community. The canopy is partially open over intermediate-sized streams (third through fourth or fifth order), permitting greater expression of deciduous riparian plants. Larger rivers in western Oregon are bordered by stands dominated by deciduous trees, principally *Alnus rubra* and *Populus trichocarpa*, developed on fresh substrates prepared by major floods. Although the transition is gradual and varies with regional physiography and vegetation, the energy base shifts from heterotrophy in small streams to autotrophy in rivers because of reduced shading and litter input by riparian vegetation. In western Oregon this energy base shift occurs in the range of third- to fourth-order streams.

In general, the intensity of terrestrial/aquatic interactions under flow conditions up to bank-full diminishes with increasing stream size. Wider streams receive less litter input per unit of stream surface area and less shading by streamside vegetation and have greater capability for transporting large organic material.

TEMPORAL VARIATION IN THE RIPARIAN ZONE

Temporal variation in the riparian zone occurs on time scales of storm and seasonal changes of water level and successional response to severe disturbance of streamside and upslope vegetation. These sources of variation are common under the general climatic conditions of the Pacific Northwest, which are characterized by mild, wet winters and warm, dry summers. Large floods occur rather commonly in response to heavy rains and warm rain on snow cover. Consequently, small forested watersheds in the H. J. Andrews Experimental Forest, such as the 60-ha watershed 2, have an average August streamflow of only about 2.5 percent of average January runoff. Peak discharge of a 10-year return period flood in watershed 2 is more than one hundred times larger than average August runoff (R. D. Harr, pers. comm.).

In order to contrast the wet and dry seasons of an active stream area, we surveyed the 6400-ha Lookout Creek drainage, H. J. Andrews Experimental Forest, at two streamflow levels. The stream network was mapped and channel widths were measured in the spring when discharge at the Lookout Creek gauging station was 2.26 m³/sec (80 cfs) to characterize winter baseflow, which is typical minimum flow for the wettest six to eight months of the year. (G. W. Leinkaemper pers. comm.) Remapping of the network and measuring of channel widths was done in late summer when discharge of Lookout Creek was 0.71 m³/sec (25 cfs) to characterize summer baseflow conditions. This fifth-order drainage network experiences a 28 percent reduction in total length between winter and summer baseflow (Figure 9.6). Decrease in average width ranges from 60 percent for first-order streams to 16 percent for the fifth-order stream segment. Total wetted stream area is reduced 45 percent between early spring and late summer. Of course, maximum annual change in stream area is much greater; in the 19 year period of record on Lookout Creek maximum and minimum discharges have been 189 m³/sec (6660 cfs) and 0.18 m³/sec (6.4 cfs).

Extremes of climate and runoff contribute to occurrence of a variety of disturbance mechanisms that affect streamside areas and/or upslope vegetation. During floods on large and intermediate-sized rivers, large, floating or-

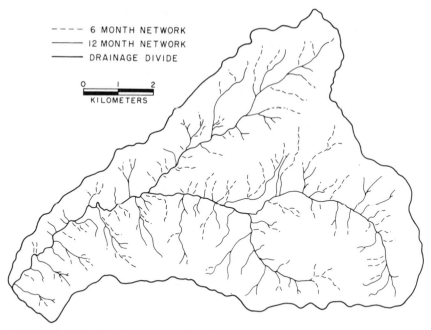

FIGURE 9.6 *Drainage networks of Lookout Creek watershed for six- and twelve-month periods in a year (mapped by G. W. Lienkaemper).*

ganic debris and ice may trim, batter, and destroy vegetation along the riparian corridor, thereby initiating sprouting from many species of damaged residual trees and shrubs (Sigafoos 1964). Lateral cutting by streams and rivers wipes out existing riparian communities and sets the stage for development of new ones by invading plants. Summer drought contributes to the occurrence of wildfire that may destroy vegetation in both riparian and upslope areas. In the steep terrain of the western Cascade Mountains, however, wildfire commonly leaves natural streamside buffer strips (F. J. Swanson, pers. comm.), apparently because of more moist conditions along streams and the natural tendency for fires to burn upslope. These conditions reduce the impact of a severe disturbance of the forest on the stream environment. Similarly, current forest practice rules call for buffer strips along third-order and larger streams.

Severe disturbances of riparian vegetation initiate successional redevelopment of the plant communities. Both streamside and upslope vegetation in many situations in western Oregon have been disturbed simultaneously and equally. Riparian and upslope communities in these cases follow successional sequences with contrasting compositional and structural development. Field observations of stands up to forty years in age after clearcutting have led to the following conceptual model or relative riparian and upslope vegetation development (Figure 9.7) that is now being tested quantitatively. We hypothesize that in the first five to ten years following disturbance, deciduous riparian species, notably *Alnus rubra* and *Salix* spp., may develop more rapidly than

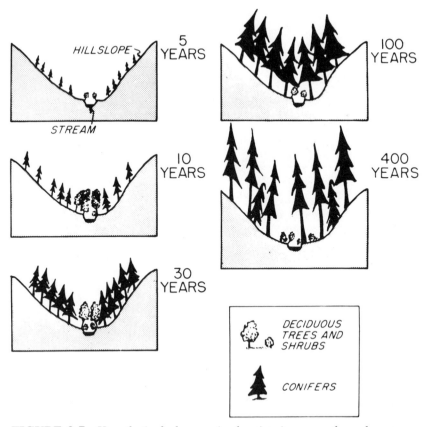

FIGURE 9.7 *Hypothetical changes in the riparian zone through succession.*

shrubs and conifer seedlings and saplings on upslope sites. This rapid expansion of riparian vegetation would return the aquatic ecosystem to a detrital energy base typical of forested streams more quickly than it would if the stream were solely dependent on upslope vegetation communities for shading and detrital inputs. As a stand reaches an age of about thirty to sixty years, upslope conifers close canopy over small streams, shade out lower strata of streamside vegetation, and gradually suppress this component of riparian zone vegetation. Establishment of shade-tolerant conifers may also occur at this stage, further enhancing the switch from deciduous to coniferous dominance along streams. Blowdown and other mortality may open the canopy in old-growth stands, permitting greater development of riparian vegetation than in intermediate-age stands.

This hypothetical phasing of deciduous and coniferous dominance during successional development of riparian zone vegetation would result in progressive changes in the quality, quantity, and seasonal timing of litter inputs to the stream. Figure 9.8 schematically depicts temporal variation of organic matter

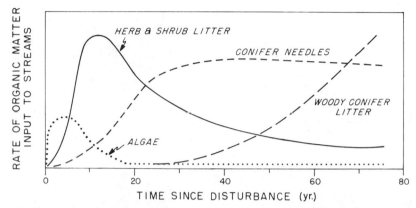

FIGURE 9.8 *Hypothetical phasing of organic matter inputs into a small stream following removal of riparian and upslope vegetation (after Turner and Long 1975; S. V. Gregory pers. comm.; F. J. Triska pers. comm.).*

inputs to a small stream during eighty years of stand development. The initial pulse of algae is a response to high light levels, which are quickly reduced by shading of herbaceous and shrubby vegetation. Herbs and shrubs dominate litter production in the second decade following disturbance; then conifer needles, followed in time by conifer woody litter, are major types of organic matter inputs (Turner and Long 1975).

The pattern and timing of response of the riparian zone to disturbance depends both on the type of disturbance and the rate of recovery of various components and related functions of riparian zone vegetation (Table 9.1). Events such as debris torrents primarily damage the lower strata of riparian vegetation, reducing shade and litter inputs from deciduous and annual components of streamside vegetation for five to fifteen years, but the role of undamaged overstory conifers in performing the same functions may be unaltered.

If upslope vegetation is removed by wildfire or clearcutting, its role as a source of large debris may be reduced or eliminated for decades. Large debris, however, commonly has sufficient residence time in a channel to continue controlling structure of the stream environment until the postdisturbance stand begins to contribute large organic material. Based on dendrochronologic dating of downed logs, we have commonly observed pieces of debris that have been in channels from twenty to more than a hundred years (Swanson et al. 1976). *Thuja plicata* is particularly long-lasting, followed by *Pseudotsuga menziesii, Tsuga heterophylla,* and *Alnus rubra* in order of increasing rate of breakdown (Anderson et al. 1978).

The postwildfire phasing of debris loading has been studied in small streams flowing through a chronosequence of stands ranging from 75 to 135 years in age (Swanson and Lienkaemper 1978). Debris from prefire and postfire stands may be distinguished by evaluating debris size, residence time in channel, and other factors. Some of these relations are evident in Figure 9.9,

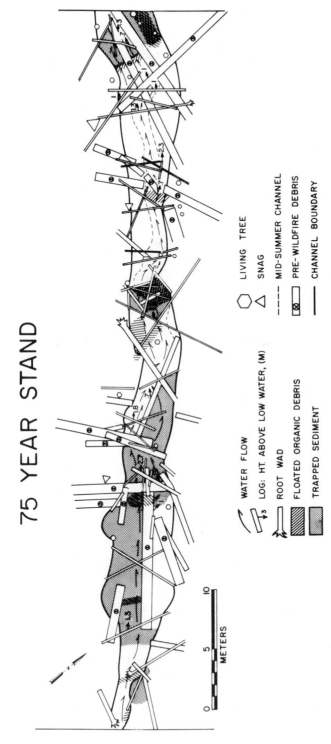

75 YEAR STAND

LIVING TREE

SNAG

LOG: HT. ABOVE LOW WATER, (M)

WATER FLOW

ROOT WAD

FLOATED ORGANIC DEBRIS

TRAPPED SEDIMENT

MID-SUMMER CHANNEL

PRE-WILDFIRE DEBRIS

CHANNEL BOUNDARY

METERS

0   5   10

FIGURE 9.9 *Map of large organic debris in a first-order stream flowing through a seventy-five-year-old postwildfire stand (mapped by G. W. Lienkaemper).*

which shows debris in a stream section in a seventy-five-year-old stand. The large-diameter pieces were introduced from the prefire, old-growth stand, and the small pieces were derived from the postfire stand. Observations in streams such as this indicate that the change in dominance of debris of prefire and postfire origin is gradual, occurring over more than a century.

Although this discussion emphasizes infrequent, catastrophic disturbances and subsequent succession, numerous small-scale disturbances are more common in streamside areas. This frequent mortality of individual and small groups of trees results in complex, mixed-age-class stands of streamside vegetation.

SUMMARY

The riparian zone is subject to many definitions. Based on a functional rather than vegetative or topographic definition, the riparian zone is the area of direct interaction between aquatic and terrestrial environments. This zone includes low-lying vegetation in and adjacent to channels as well as higher vegetation strata forming the overhanging canopy. Riparian zone vegetation in coniferous forests of the Pacific Northwest is typically composed of low strata of herbs and deciduous shrubs and small trees beneath a canopy of large conifers.

The composition and structure of riparian plant communities are largely determined by light availability; substrate conditions such as wetness, frequency and intensity of scouring; and availability of sites for rooting. Specific plant associations are adapted to fresh alluvial deposits, wet cliffs, wet flat subsoil conditions, and other types of sites. In a sampling of first- through third-order sites, larger streams have higher cover of shrub, and large shrub/ small tree strata, apparently in response to greater light availability due to opening of the overstory. Variation in the small and large herb strata is particularly sensitive to substrate type and disturbance history.

Vegetation along small and intermediate-sized streams (up to about fourth-order) exercises important controls over physical conditions in the stream environment. Rooting by herbaceous and woody vegetation tends to stabilize streambanks, retard erosion, and determine bank morphology. Aboveground riparian vegetation is an obstruction to highwater streamflow and sediment and detritus movement and is a source of large organic debris for streams. Large pieces of woody debris in streams: (1) control routing of sediment and water through channel systems; (2) dissipate stream energy; (3) define habitat opportunities; and (4) serve as substrates for biological activity by microbial and invertebrate organisms.

Riparian vegetation regulates the energy base of the aquatic ecosystem by shading and supplying plant and animal detritus to streams. Shading affects both stream temperature and light availability to drive primary production. Thus multiple functions of riparian vegetation determine the balance between autotrophy and heterotrophy in aquatic ecosystems. By controlling this balance and the quantity, food quality, and seasonal timing of litter inputs, riparian vegetation also influences the composition of the aquatic community in terms of relative importance of functional groups.

Riparian vegetation and organic detritus derived from it may also alter the chemical composition of water as it moves through the aquatic/terrestrial interface and as it flows through the stream ecosystem. The forest/stream interface is a zone of numerous interactions. Living vegetation takes up nutrients from stream-adjacent soil solution and, in the case of hydrophytic roots, from stream water itself. Nutrients are released from dead organic matter by leaching and decomposition. Decomposition also involves nutrient uptake.

All of these functions of riparian vegetation vary in time and space. Temporal variation occurs on the time scale of vegetative succession following major disturbances such as wildfire, clearcutting, and floods. Spatial variation of riparian characteristics takes place along the continuum of increasing stream size from small headwater streams to large rivers.

The forest/stream interface is a zone of numerous interactions important to both terrestrial and aquatic components of watershed ecosystems. Understanding of this ecosystem should not be viewed as the sum of strictly aquatic and strictly terrestrial components that meet in an abrupt interface. The transfer of materials and energy between these two components is mediated by a riparian zone distinctive in composition and structure from upslope vegetation.

LITERATURE CITED

Alexander, M., 1961, *Introduction to Soil Microbiology,* Wiley-Interscience, New York, 472p.

Anderson, N. H., J. R. Sedell, L. M. Roberts, and F. J. Triska, 1978, The role of aquatic invertebrates in processing of wood debris in coniferous forest streams, *Am. Midl. Nat.* **100:**64–82.

Barlocher, F., and B. Kendrick, 1973, Fungi and food preferences of *Gammarus pseudolimnaeus, Arch. Hydrobiol.* **72:**501–516.

Bell, D. M., 1974, Tree stratum composition and distribution in the streamside forest, *Am. Midl. Nat.* **92:**35–46.

Bollen, W. B., and K. C. Lu, 1968, Nitrogen transformations in soils beneath red alder and conifers, in *Biology of Alder,* J. M. Trappe, J. F. Franklin, R. F. Tarrant, and G. M. Hansen, eds., U.S. Department of Agriculture Forest Service, Portland, Oreg., pp. 141–148.

Brown, G. W., and J. T. Krygier, 1970, Effects of clear-cutting on stream temperature, *Water Resour. Res.* **6:**1133–1139.

Campbell, A. G., and J. F. Franklin, 1979, Riparian vegetation in Oregon's western Cascade Mountains: Composition, biomass, and autumn phenology, US/IBP *Coniferous Forest Biome Bull. No. 14,* University of Washington, Seattle, 90p.

Cole, D. W., S.P. Gessel, and J. Turner, 1978, Comparative mineral cycling in red alder and Douglas-fir, in *Utilization and Management of Alder,* D. G. Briggs, D. S. DeBell, and W. A. Atkinson, compilers, U.S. Department of Agriculture Forest Service General Technical Report PNW-70, Portland, Oreg., pp. 327–336.

Cummins, K. W., 1974, Structure and function in stream ecosystems, *BioScience* **24:**631–641.

Froehlich, H. A., 1973, Natural and man-caused slash in headwater streams, *Loggers Handb.* **33:**15–17, 66–70, 82–86.

Graf, W. L., 1978, Fluvial adjustments to the spread of tamarisk in the Colorado Plateau region, *Geol. Soc. Am. Bull.* **89:**1491–1501.

Hall, J. D., and C. O. Baker, 1977, Biological impacts of organic debris in Pacific Northwest streams, in *Logging Debris in Streams Workshop,* Oregon State University, Corvallis, 13p.

Heede, B. H., 1972, Flow channel characteristics of two high mountain streams, *U.S. Department of Agriculture Forest Service Research Paper RM-96,* Fort Collins, Colo., 12p.

Johnson, R. R., and D. A. Jones eds., 1977, Importance, preservation and management of riparian habitat: A symposium, *U.S. Department of Agriculture Forest Service General Technical Report RM-43,* Fort Collins, Colo. 217p.

Johnson, W. C., R. L. Burgess, and W. R. Keammerer, 1976, Forest overstory vegetation and environment on the Missouri River floodplain in North Dakota, *Ecol. Monogr.* **46:**59–84.

Karr, J. R., and I. J. Schlosser, 1978, Water resources and the landwater interface, *Science* **201:**229–234.

Kaushik, N. K., and H. B. N. Hynes, 1971, The fate of the dead leaves that fall into streams, *Arch. Hydrobiol.* **68:**465–515.

Keller, E. M., and F. J. Swanson, 1979, Effects of large organic material on channel form and fluvial processes, *Earth Surface Process.* **4:**361–380.

Leopold, L. B., M. G. Wolman, and J. P. Miller, 1964, *Fluvial Processes in Geomorphology,* W. H. Freeman, San Francisco, 522p.

Lindsey, A. A., R. O. Petty, D. K. Sterling, and W. Van Asdall, 1961, Vegetation and environment along the Wabash and Tippecanoe Rivers, *Ecol. Monogr.* **31:**105–156.

Megahan, W. F., and R. A. Nowlin, 1976, Sediment storage in channels draining small forested watersheds in the mountains of central Idaho, in *3rd Fed. Interagric. Sedimentation Conf. Proc.,* Denver, Colo., pp. 4-115-4-126.

Narver, D. W., 1971, Effects of logging debris on fish production, in *Forest Land Uses and Streams Environment,* J. T. Krygier and J. D. Hall, eds., Continuing Education Publication, Oregon State University, Corvallis, Oreg., pp. 100–111.

Newton, M., B. A. El Hassen, and J. Zavitkovski, 1968, Role of red alder in western Oregon forest succession, in *Biology of Alder,* J. M. Trappe, J. F.

Franklin, R. F. Tarrant, and G. M. Hansen, eds., U.S. Department of Agriculture Forest Service, Portland, Oreg., pp. 73–84.

Petryk, S., and G. Bosmajian, 1975, Analysis of flow through vegetation, *ASCE J. Hydraul. Div.* **101**:871–882.

Sedell, J. R., and F. J. Triska, 1977, Biological consequences of large organic debris in Northwest streams, In *Logging Debris in Streams, II:* Forest Extension Workshop, 21–22 March 1977, Oregon State University, Corvallis, 10p.

Sedell, J. R., F. J. Triska, J. D. Hall, N. H. Anderson, and J. H. Lyford, 1974, Sources and fates of organic inputs in coniferous forest streams, in *Integrated Research in the Coniferous Forest Biome,* R. H. Waring and R. L. Edmonds, eds., Coniferous Forest Biome Bull. 5, University of Washington, Seattle, pp. 57–69.

Sedell, J. R., F. J. Triska, and N. S. Triska, 1975, The processing of conifer and hardwood leaves in two coniferous forest streams, I: Weight loss and associated invertebrates, *Verh. Int. Verein. Limnol.* **19**:1617–1627.

Sigafoos, R. S., 1964, Botanical evidence of floods and flood-plain deposition, *Geological Survey Professional Paper 485-A,* Washington, D.C., 35p.

Smith, D. G., 1976, Effect of vegetation on lateral migration of a glacier meltwater river, *Geol. Soc. Am. Bull.* **87**:857–860.

Swanson, F. J., and G. W. Lienkaemper, 1978, Physical consequences of large organic debris in Pacific Northwest streams, *U.S. Department of Agriculture Forest Service General Technical Report PNW-69,* 12p.

Swanson, F. J., and D. N. Swanston, 1977, Complex mass-movement terrains in the western Cascade Range, Oregon, *Rev. Eng. Geol.* **3**:113–124.

Swanson, F. J., G. W. Lienkaemper, and J. R. Sedell, 1976, History, physical effects, and management implications of large organic debris in western Oregon streams, *U.S. Department of Agriculture Forest Service General Technical Report PNW-56,* Portland, Oreg., 15p.

Thomas, J. W., C. Maser, and J. E. Rodick, 1979, Riparian zones—their importance to wildlife and their management, In *Forest-Wildlife Relationships in the Blue Mountains of Washington and Oregon,* U.S. Department of Agriculture Forest Service, Agric. Handbook 553, Washington, D.C., 512p.

Turner, J., and J. N. Long, 1975, Accumulation of organic matter in a series of Douglas-fir stands, *Can. J. For.* **5**:681–690.

Zimmerman, R. C., J. C. Goodlett, and G. H. Comer, 1967, The influence of vegetation on channel form of small streams, in *Symposium on River Morphology,* Int. Assoc. Sci. Hydrol. Publ. No. 75, pp. 255–275.

Zavitkovski, J., and M. Newton, 1971, Litterfall and litter accumulation in red alder stands in western Oregon, *Plant Soil* **35**:257–268.

Zobel, D. B., A. McKee, G. M. Hawk, and C. T. Dyrness, 1976, Relationships of environment to composition, structure, and diversity of forest communities of the central western Cascades of Oregon., *Ecol. Monogr.* **46**:135–156.

10

Coniferous Forest Streams

F. J. Triska, J. R. Sedell, and *S. V. Gregory*

INTRODUCTION

Forest streams have long been used to integrate physical and chemical processes on a watershed; however, measurements of processes such as water flux, erosional yield, and nutrient loss consider only the transport function of streams. Streams, in addition to their transport function, also serve as temporary pools for particulate and dissolved materials lost from the surrounding forest. Watershed topography concentrates these particulate and dissolved materials into an area composing less than 1 percent of the watershed and permits establishment of a distinctive biological community. The stream program in the coniferous forest biome program has attempted to examine holistically the processing efficiency and capability for energy flow and nutrient cycling by this separate biological system and its relation to canopy density, retention capacity, and carbon and nutrient quality of particulate inputs within a stream reach. The relation of biological structure and function with physical and chemical structure of streams was examined, as well as their variations through time and space. This chapter is a synthesis of research dealing with stream structure and function, organic matter budgets, spatial and temporal aspects of the coniferous forest stream, and forest land-use impacts. Most data presented here were collected at five sites in or adjacent to the H. J. Andrews Environmental Forest, Oregon: watershed (WS) 10 stream, Devil's Club Creek, Mack Creek, Lookout Creek, and the McKenzie River (see Figure 1.4 for stream locations and Table 1.5 for physical characteristics).

The stream on WS 10 is first order (Strahler 1964; see Table 1.4), drains 10.24 ha, and rises from 430 m at the outlet stream gauging station at 670 m at its highest elevation. The overall slope of the stream channel is 45 percent. Side slopes, however, range up to 90 percent. Stream discharge varies from around 0.23 liter/s in summer to about 140 liters/s during winter freshets. The uppermost reaches are intermittent during summer. Mean annual precipitation on the watershed is 240 cm. Mean width of the stream channel ranges from 0.25 m in the upper reaches to 1.0 to 1.5 m at the base of the watershed. The streambed is a "stairstep" series of small pools connected by free-fall zones or riffles running on bedrock. Pools are usually formed behind accumulations of wood debris. The substrate consists of loose rocks and gravel from tuff and breccia bedrock.

Devil's Club Creek is also a first-order stream channel with large accumulations of coarse organic debris derived from the surrounding old-growth (>400 years) forest. Debris consists of large logs of Douglas-fir and western hemlock and leaf litter (primarily huckleberry, devil's club, maple leaves, and Douglas-fir needles). Autochthonous production is nearly zero in this heavily shaded tributary of Mack Creek.

Mack Creek is one of three major drainages of the Andrews Forest (see Figure 1.6). Morphology of this third-order stream is a stairstep of pools, free-fall zones, and turbulent water around boulders. Woody debris is an important morphological feature but is found in lower concentrations than in Devil's Club Creek. The forest canopy is open slightly because of tree mortality, blowdown, and a wider stream channel. This allows some light to reach the stream. Benthic primary production occurs but is not the major organic input. Leaf fall from maple and Douglas-fir, some windfall, and upstream input from tributaries are the principal inputs. Mack Creek is a major tributary of Lookout Creek.

Lookout Creek, receives runoff from the entire Andrews Forest (see Figure 1.4). Morphology of this fifth-order stream is extensive shallow riffles interspersed with pools. Substrate is either large cobble or bedrock. Smaller amounts of wood debris are present here than in Mack Creek. The canopy is open and there is an extensive periphyton (attached algal) community.

The McKenzie River is a major sixth-order stream draining the western Cascade Mountains (see Table 1.5). Morphologically it is 85 percent riffle with a few calm water areas. Substrate is cobble and large boulders. Woody debris is not important to this river either morphologically or biologically. Inputs are primarily from upstream transport and benthic primary production. A small amount of allochthonous input occurs from alder and Douglas-fir along the river banks. Autochthonous input occurs from a zone of moss (*Fontinalis* sp.) that extends out 5 m from both banks and from a moderate to dense periphyton community that colonizes the entire substrate.

STREAM STRUCTURE AND FUNCTION

If an aerial photograph of an old-growth watershed containing a third-order stream were examined, determination of drainage patterns would have to be made from topographic features since the actual watercourses would be obscured by forest canopy. This dense vegetation ties the stream both morphologically and biologically to the adjacent landscape.

Morphologically, first- and second-order streams in the Cascades are characterized as high gradient with some areas of exposed bedrock. Inputs of old-growth boles and large limbs lie where they fall, trap sediments, and create habitats for various aquatic organisms. As the stream becomes larger (third- and fourth-order), high storm flows build enough hydrologic force to clump debris into larger accumulations. These debris dams constitute important morphological features that retain finer organic debris. In addition to its physical role, wood also functions biologically as a refractory carbon source, processed abiotically by water movement and biologically by microbes and invertebrates (Figure 10.1).

A second biologically available input from the terrestrial landscape is forest litter. Input and processing of leaf litter has attracted considerable attention by stream researchers over the past ten years. In fact, leaf litter often constitutes the energy base of small forest streams on an annual basis. Within a day after it enters the stream, leaf litter has been divided into two components: a dissolved fraction that enters the dissolved organic material (DOM) pool and a residue processed slowly by the microbial community (Figure 10.1). Once conditioned by microbial colonization this residue forms a readily available food source for invertebrates called "shredders" (Cummins 1973). While some of the conditioned litter is used by invertebrates for tissue synthesis and maintenance, most is egested and enters the fine particulate organic matter (FPOM) pool. The FPOM pool consists of organic particulates less than 1 mm but greater than 0.45 μm in size. Fine organic particles, whether derived from physical, chemical, or biological processes, serve as a food source for collector invertebrates.

Thus, in heavily shaded first-order streams where primary production is minimal, two major organic substrates, wood and leaf litter, constitute the

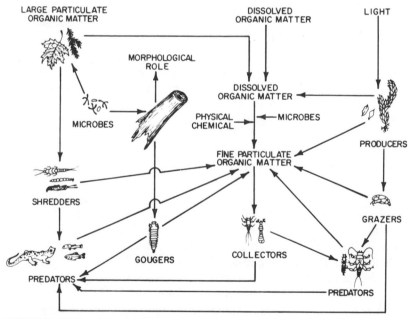

FIGURE 10.1 *A generalized view of biotic structure and function in a coniferous forest stream (after Cummins 1973).*

energy base. These respective substrates differ greatly in terms of amount and time required for processing (Table 10.1). Although it may vary by season, less than 5 percent of particulate organic matter in the benthic standing crop is in the form of leaves and needles; greater than 60 percent is in the form of small, woody substrates (cones, branches, twigs, bark). This does not include large boles, which dominate small streams. Leaf inputs occur primarily during autumn. Wood inputs, on the other hand, occur erratically, particularly blowdown during major windstorms. Since leaf litter has a higher nitrogen (N) and lower fiber content than wood, it is utilized more rapidly by the microbial and invertebrate community but has little morphological impact on the stream. Of the two detrital inputs, the smaller pool of leaf litter is characterized by a rapid turnover dominated by microbial processes and shredding, and the extremely large wood pool by a long turnover time dominated by microbial processes and gouging. The product of both pools (FPOM) is further processed by collector organisms. As a refractory pool, wood effectively buffers the system physically and to a lesser extent metabolically. On the other hand, FPOM buffers the system metabolically but not physically, since it is readily exported. In fact, FPOM constitutes the major fraction of particulate organic matter exported to downstream reaches.

In addition to large inputs of terrestrial litter, primary production occurs where sunlight penetrates the canopy and reaches the stream bottom. In small streams with extreme canopy cover, primary production is undertaken almost exclusively by mosses. Where the canopy is open, however, an attached algal community, primarily diatoms, colonizes bottom mineral substrates. This periphyton is consumed by grazer invertebrates. Feces from both shredders and grazers enter the FPOM pool and become available to the collector community. Finally, all three invertebrate functional groups may in turn be consumed by predators, primarily insects, salamanders, and cutthroat trout.

Heterotrophic Function

Biological functioning in streams (that is, energy flow and nutrient cycling) through the heterotrophic pathway is a complex series of events dependent on interactions between various biological components. One good example of such an interaction is microbial colonization (conditioning) of leaf litter prior to shredder consumption. Leaf litter is processed by the microbial community at a continuum of rates dependent on biochemical composition. Figure 10.2 illustrates such a continuum of decay rates from various species of leaf litter from Mack Creek, H. J. Andrews Forest, and from Augusta Creek, Michigan. In each stream various leaf species exhibit differential rates for leaf processing. This processing is a function of the time required for leaf tissue to be colonized and metabolically utilized by the microbial community (Triska 1970).

TABLE 10.1 *Comparison of leaves and wood debris as components of small coniferous forest stream ecosystems.*[a]

Substrate	Standing crop (% of particulate matter)	Seasonality of inputs	Impact on stream morphology	Carbon/nitrogen ratio	Total fiber (%)	Degradation time	Microbial colonization pattern	Invertebrate component	Invertebrate utilization
Leaves	<5	Pulsed autumnal	Minor	25 to 100:1	20 to 40	2 to 12 mo	Surface and matrix	High (mg/g)	Food, shelter
Wood debris	>60 (excluding boles)	Erratic	Major (stabilize and destabilize)	300 to 1000:1	70 to 80	5 to 200 yr	Primarily surface	Low (mg/kg)	Shelter, substrate, oviposition, pupation, emergence, food (direct and indirect)

[a]From Anderson et al. 1978.

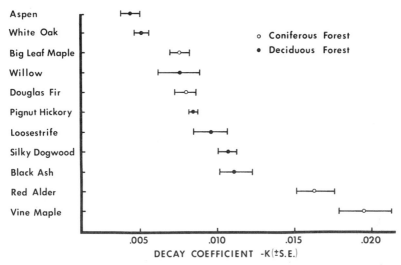

FIGURE 10.2 *Decay rates for major litter inputs to a coniferous forest stream (Mack Creek) and a deciduous forest stream (Augusta Creek, Michigan).*

Although the mechanism of conditioning is unknown, its occurrence has been verified by both field and laboratory studies. In a laboratory experiment Anderson and Grafius (1975) used leaf litter of red alder *(Alnus rubra),* a common riparian species. Alder is low in fiber and high in N, and hence decomposes rapidly. It was conditioned for periods up to fifty days and then presented to larvae of the caddis fly *(Lepidostoma quercina).* Consumption rate was very low on leaves of less than thirty days' conditioning time. After about thirty days litter was readily consumed at a rate related to length of conditioning time (Figure 10.3). A similar pattern, but with much longer conditioning times, was also observed for needle litter of Douglas-fir conditioned up to three hundred days prior to ingestion by larvae of *Lepidostoma unicolor* (Anderson and Grafius 1975).

Long-term microbial conditioning of refractory litter was also demonstrated in field studies at Mack Creek (Figure 10.4). There Douglas-fir litter was ignored by invertebrate larvae for approximately one hundred and fifty days. After that period, litter was readily consumed, as demonstrated by dramatic weight loss of leaf packs and weight gain by shredders. Most needle consumption occurred during spring as temperature warmed, larvae reached their final instar, and after most deciduous litter had decomposed. Although riparian species vary from stream to stream, the continuum of processing rates required for diverse allochthonous inputs mitigates the effect of large autumnal input and guarantees the availability of conditioned detritus at all seasons. In this way invertebrate life cycles can be geared to quality of litter inputs and activity of the microbial community.

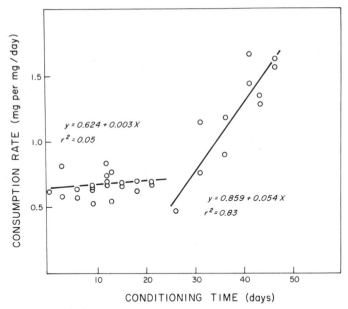

FIGURE 10.3 *Consumption rates of leaf litter of red alder (Alnus rubra) fed to larvae of the caddis fly (Lepidostoma quercina) after being conditioned for periods of 0 to 50 days in a laboratory stream (Anderson and Grafius 1975).*

One major benefit of microbial conditioning for the shredder community is the increase in protein content, first demonstrated by Kaushik and Hynes (1968). This factor may be particularly important for litter with an extremely high carbon/nitrogen ratio such as Douglas-fir needles (C/N = 93). Data from six streams in Oregon and Washington (Triska and Buckley 1978) illustrate change in absolute N content of needle litter based on leaf packs with a normalized starting weight of 10 g (Figure 10.5). Such a 10-g leaf pack had a N capital of about 59 mg prior to incubation. Leaching lowered the N capital to approximately 20 mg during the first few days. Thus, while total weight loss due to leaching amounted to 20 percent, loss of N capital exceeded 50 percent. From this base of approximately 20 mg, N capital increased rapidly as decomposition proceeded. Nitrogen content was greatest between the periods of 30 to 60 percent weight loss. At some state of decomposition, an absolute increase in N capital was observed in all six streams. After peaking, N capital declined steadily as C was mineralized. Similar gains in absolute N content have previously been reported for lotic ecosystems (Mathews and Kowalczewski 1969; Iverson 1973; Hodkinson 1975; Triska and Sedell 1976). Although the mechanism is complex and not well established, the gain in N capital does demonstrate how particulate organic matter and associated microflora serve as an N pool for stream biota.

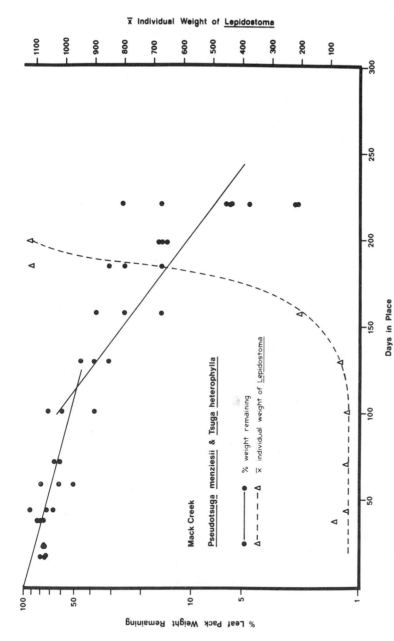

FIGURE 10.4 *Leaf-pack weight loss and mean individual weight of larvae of Lepidostoma unicolor, as leaf litter of Douglas-fir underwent decomposition in Mack Creek (Sedell et al. 1975).*

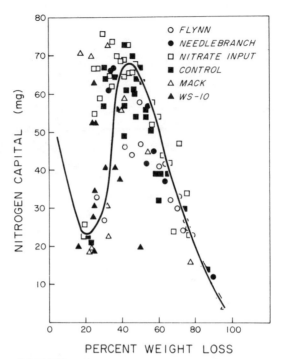

FIGURE 10.5 *Nitrogen capital of Douglas-fir needle litter as decomposition proceeds in six streams of the Pacific Northwest. Data are based on a normalized starting weight of 10 g.*

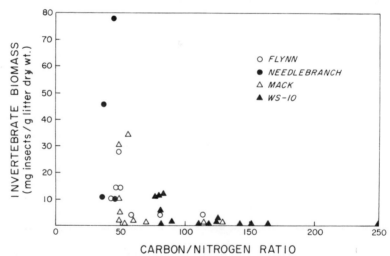

FIGURE 10.6 *Invertebrate biomass associated with decomposing needle litter of Douglas-fir as a function of C/N ratio from four streams in the Pacific Northwest.*

If N content is a major factor in conditioning, then utilization of organic matter by invertebrates should be maximum near the lowest C/N ratio (Figure 10.6). Watershed 10, which had the least gain in N concentration and the highest C/N ratio, also had least invertebrate biomass associated with needle packs. Maximum invertebrate biomass (11.2 mg/g leaf pack) was found at the time of lowest C/N ratio (80). In Mack Creek, the lowest C/N ratio was approximately 50 and occurred about three weeks before maximum inverte-brate biomass was observed on the litter. Once discovered by the invertebrate community, a maximum of 35 mg invertebrate biomass occurred per gram of needle pack. This compares favorably with data for Flynn Creek, where a maximum of 28 mg invertebrate biomass/g needle pack was collected at a C/N ratio of 49. Higher invertebrate biomass was associated with litter packs at Needle Branch Creek, which also reached the lowest C/N ratio (42). In that stream highest invertebrate biomass was 76 mg invertebrates/g of needle pack, on a sample with a C/N ratio of 50. This overall invertebrate response suggests how a simple trophic function such as consumption of litter by invertebrates is a complex interaction between quality, quantity, and timing of terrestrial inputs; physical processes; nutrient regime; microbial community; and invertebrate shredders. It is through a large series of such complex interactions at each level of processing that the heterotrophic component of the stream functions as an ecological unit.

Autotrophic Function

Besides allochthonous detritus, autochthonous primary producers such as attached algae, mosses, and vascular plants constitute the second source of organic matter processed by stream invertebrates. In heavily shaded streams, primary production is dominated by bryophytes with a slight contribution by attached diatoms. In larger, unshaded streams most primary production shifts to benthic diatoms with seasonal inputs by filamentous green algae. Thus community structure of primary producers in Pacific Northwest streams varies depending on both season and canopy density (Table 10.2). The seasonality of green algae and diatom communities results from increased photoperiod and light intensity in early spring and subsequent senescence and sloughing of algae during late autumn periods of high flow. The drought year of 1976 demon-strated the role of high discharge in controlling community structure. Since no storms occurred until March 1977, an abundance of filamentous or thallus algal forms persisted until March, whereas this community is normally depleted by scouring between October and December (J. Rounick, pers. comm.).

Shading by terrestrial vegetation influences both autotrophic community structure and the rate of primary production. Gross primary production gener-ally increased in the McKenzie River drainage from headwater to higher order

TABLE 10.2   *Community characteristics and patterns of growth of the periphyton communities at four study sites in three streams of the Cascade Mountains, Oregon.*

Community type	Characteristic plant	Location	Pattern of growth
Pennate diatom	*Achnanthes*	Upper Mack Creek Lower Mack Creek Lookout Creek Watershed 10	Year-round
Thallus green algae	*Prasiola*	Upper Mack Creek Lower Mack Creek	March to August
Filamentous green algae	*Ulothrix zygnema*	Lower Mack Creek Lookout Creek	April to July June to November
Centric diatom	*Melosira*	Lookout Creek	July to January

rivers with maximum production in the fifth-order stream (Figure 10.7). The role of light in this progression is shown by the substantial increase in primary production in the open third-order site in contrast to the forested third-order site. One complicating factor in this trend, however, is low concentration of inorganic N in headwater streams, which might account for low production rates. In fact, during summer, inorganic N is undetectable in first-order streams while concentrations of 30 to 100 μg/liter NO_3-N occur in higher orders.

To test the hypothesis that light rather than nutrients limited primary production, a section of a first-order, old-growth forest stream was artificially lighted (Gregory 1980). Halfway through the lighted section NO_3-N was added to achieve a concentration of 100 μg NO_3N/liter. Four treatments resulted: (1) natural light; (2) increased light; (3) increased light plus nitrate; and (4) natural light plus nitrate. After twenty-eight days, gross primary production, community respiration, and diatom community structure were measured. Gross primary production was lowest in the natural light and natural light-plus-nitrate section and no difference was detected between the two (Figure 10.8). Only in the light sections did gross primary production approach a balance with community respiration. Primary production was appreciably greater than respiration in the light-plus-nitrate section. In the natural light sections, primary production was far less than respiration. This does not imply that algae were not compensating for their own respiration in these sections, but rather that algae were not able to supply all the energy needed to support the epilithic communities of algae, bacteria, and fungi. In lighted sections, however, autotrophs were able to produce enough energy to account for respiration of the entire epilithic community.

As a result of this experiment, it is evident that light rather than nutrients is limiting primary production in headwater streams of coniferous forests. Once streams are sufficiently lighted, nutrient inputs become a critical factor in

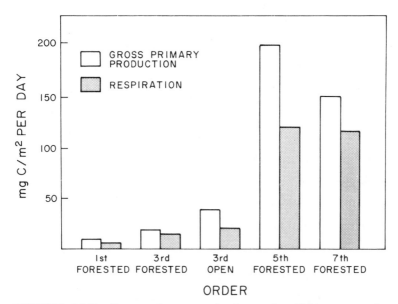

FIGURE 10.7 *Gross primary production and epilithic community respiration (mg $C \cdot m^{-2} \cdot day^{-1}$) in selected first- through seventh-order streams of the McKenzie River drainage.*

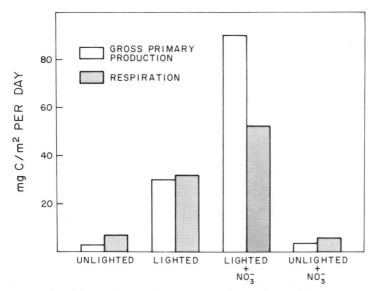

FIGURE 10.8 *Gross primary production and epilithic community respiration (mg $C \cdot m^{-2} \cdot day$) in watershed 10, resulting from experimental manipulation of light and nitrate input.*

primary production. This explains the greater production rate found in fifth-order streams, which are richer in inorganic N than less productive but unshaded third-order streams (Figure 10.7). Influence by the surrounding terrestrial ecosystems is demonstrated by regulating not only detrital inputs but also solar energy for driving primary production within the stream ecosystem.

Besides changes in primary production with light addition, changes in relative abundance of individual species of algae were observed. *Achnanthes lanceolata, Cocconeis placentula lineata, Eunotia pectinalis,* and *Meridion circulare* were dominant species in lighted areas but were found in small concentrations in natural lighted sections. *Diatoma heimale mesodon, Gomphonema intricatum pumila, G. parvulum, G. subclavatum,* and *Navicula radiosa tenella* were the most abundant of those taxa in unlighted areas and showed little response to increased light intensity. Diatom community structure in the light-plus-nitrate section was similar to that in the lighted section. Therefore there appears to be no species response to added nitrate after increased lighting.

Not only can nutrients affect primary production in open streams, but primary production affects the nutrient regime of streams. Stream chemistry has been traditionally interpreted as a function of bedrock-soil geochemistry and terrestrial nutrient cycling of the watershed, but under certain conditions stream biota may also alter stream water chemistry. Primary production creates a demand for critical elements, particularly inorganic N. Therefore, as primary production increases, the potential for alteration of stream chemistry also increases. Nitrate concentration was monitored throughout a day for a series of streams ranging from a forested, first-order stream to a fifth-order stream. Midday reduction of nitrate was greatest for the fifth-order, the most productive stream (Figure 10.9). No significant nitrate reduction was observed in the first-order stream. The open section of the third-order stream, however, had a significant reduction of nitrate, though not as great as the more productive fifth-order stream. Further evidence to relate observed changes in nitrate concentrations to primary production was provided by concentrations of inorganic C throughout the day in these same streams (Figure 10.10). Essentially the same relation was found for inorganic C as for nitrate concentrations, the fifth-order stream displaying greatest diel variation and the first-order stream showing least. Therefore the biota of stream systems are not merely existing within their ecosystems but rather interacting extensively to affect the chemical nature of streams.

PARTICULATE ORGANIC MATTER BUDGETS

One tool used by stream ecologists to view overall ecosystem function has been calculation of material or energy balance. Most often the budget process has been used to examine patterns of energy flow (Odum 1957; Mann et al.

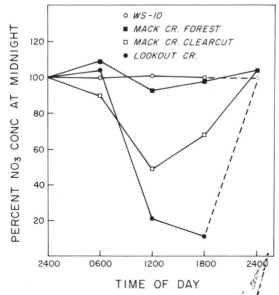

FIGURE 10.9 *Percentage change from midnight concentration of nitrate in a summer-derived sample from first-order (watershed 10), third-order (Mack Creek), and fifth-order (Lookout Creek) streams.*

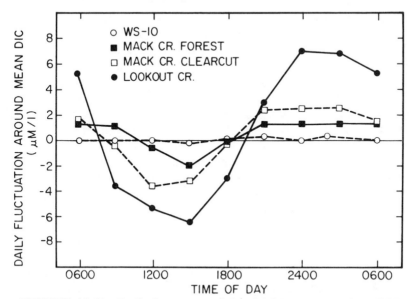

FIGURE 10.10 *Daily fluctuation of dissolved inorganic carbon (DIC) concentration in a first-, third-, and fifth-order stream.*

1972; Hall 1972; Fisher and Likens 1973; Sedell et al. 1974), although patterns of N cycling (Triska et al. in press) also provide a suitable base. The budget process encourages a holistic view of the stream ecosystem by defining the relative importance of various fluxes and pools. Extension of the budget process over more than one year also helps define variation in ecosystem behavior. Through examination of internal fluxes, organic matter and nutrient budgets provide significant insight into processing capabilities of small streams on an annual basis and their contribution to downstream communities. Measurement of these same parameters also provides an index to quantity and quality of the energy base in small streams. Measurement of production/ respiration (P/R) ratios indicates allochthonous versus autochthonous influences and indexes a stream reach as either autotrophic or heterotrophic. Comparison of amount and quality of litter inputs with exports provides an index of the stream's ability to process organic debris. Estimates of detrital standing crop provide an index of retention capacity and identify physical and metabolic buffers operating in streams. Budgets allow a comparison of particulates with the dissolved components passing through the system. Once a holistic view is achieved and the importance of various fluxes is determined, budgets help set priorities for future research effort.

Organic matter budgets were constructed for WS 10 to estimate nutrient and energy flow in a small coniferous forest stream. The organic matter fluxes and standing crop were measured for a dry year 1973 (160 cm precipitation) and a wet year 1974 (300 cm precipitation). The approach was to construct a material balance budget by tallying hydrological and biological (terrestrial and aquatic) inputs minus hydrological and biological export and changes in particulate organic storage. For the C budget the major hydrological and meterological input was dissolved organic C, which entered in groundwater. Samples were taken at sites where major seeps drain into the stream and were compared with export samples taken at a gauging station at the bottom of the watershed. Terrestrial biological inputs were throughfall, litterfall, and lateral movement of particulate organic matter along the ground from the adjacent terrestrial forest (Sedell et al. 1974). The "in-stream" biological input was primary production. Since the stream was small, export was measured by collecting all particulate organic matter in excess of 80 μm during 1973 and 1 mm in 1974 in a net located at the base of the watershed. Export of particles between 80 μm and 0.45 μm was not estimated. Standing crop was determined monthly by coring, using a 15-cm pipe sampler. A Gilson respirometer was used to determine microbial respiration of benthic organic matter.

Once major inputs, outputs, and standing crops had been measured, organic budgets for 1973 and 1974 were calculated (Tables 10.3 and 10.4). Total organic input was 490 kg/yr for the dry year 1973 and 789 kg/yr during the wet year 1974. Total litterfall and lateral movement dominated inputs for both years at 361 kg/yr or 75 percent of inputs in 1973 and 503 kg/yr or 65 percent in 1974. Throughfall, both particulate and dissolved, constituted less than 10 percent of

TABLE 10.3 *An annual organic budget for watershed 10, H. J. Andrews Experimental Forest, for water year 1973 (1 Oct 1972 to 30 Sept 1973).*

	Inputs		Standing crop			Outputs		
	(kg/yr)	(%)		(kg)	(%)		(kg/yr)	(%)
Litterfall	161	33	Large detritus (>10 cm diam)	8698	83	Particulate organic	37	11
Throughfall	41	8	Small detritus (<10 cm to 1 mm diam)	1382	13	Microbial respiration	186	55
Lateral movement	200	41	Fine particulate organic matter (FPOM) (<1 mm to 75 µm)	87	1	Macroinvertebrate respiration	2	1
			Ultrafine detritus (>75 µm to 0.45 µ)	233	2	Primary producer respiration:		
Gross primary production:						Algae	<1	0.3
Algae	<1	0.2				Moss	15	4
Moss	23	5	Primary producer biomass	31	0.3	Dissolved organic matter	96	28
Dissolved organic matter	64	13	Macroinvertebrates	1				
Total	490		Total	10,432		Total	337	

307

TABLE 10.4 *An annual organic budget for watershed 10, H. J. Andrews Experimental Forest, for water year 1974 (1 Oct 1973 to 30 Sept 1974).*

Inputs	(kg/yr)	(%)	Standing crop	(kg)	(%)	Outputs	(kg/yr)	(%)
Litterfall	170	22	Large detritus (>10 cm)	8692	82	Particulate organic	245	32
Throughfall	57	7	Small detritus (<10 cm to 1 mm)	1535	15	Microbial respiration	183	24
Lateral movement	333	43	Fine particulate organic matter (FPOM) (<1 mm to 75 μm)	87	1	Macroinvertebrate	2	0.3
Gross primary production:			Ultrafine detritus (<75 μm to 0.45 μm)	233	2	Primary producer respiration:		
Algae	<1	0.1				Algae	<1	0.1
Moss	23	3	Primary producer biomass	31	0.3	Moss	15	2
Dissolved organic matter	206	26	Macroinvertebrates	0.8		Dissolved organic matter	310	41
Total	790		Total	10585		Total	756	

308

the budget in both years. Input of dissolved organic matter constituted about 13 percent of organic output in 1973 and 26 percent in 1974.

Massive accumulations of large detritus, primarily boles, dominated the stream and constituted 85 percent of standing crop. Small detritus, which includes leaf litter, was dominated by fine wood debris since leaf material was easily mineralized by the microbial community and lost via microbial respiration and conversion to FPOM. In fact, more than half the estimated output of WS 10 in 1973 (56 percent) occurred as microbial respiration. The large pool of fine detritus (87 kg/yr) was especially significant since it is a degradation product of large detritus and constitutes a refractory pool available to collector invertebrates. The size of the fine detritus pool was underestimated by absence of measurements for ultrafine detritus ($< 75 \mu$m). Subsequent estimates during 1974 and 1975 indicate the ultrafine detritus pool is 2.5 times as large as the fine detritus pool on WS 10. This ultrafine detritus is the product of both breakdown of large organic debris and flocculation of dissolved organic matter (Lush and Hynes 1973; C. H. Dahm, pers. comm.).

Capacity of large debris to retain detritus and permit litter processing by biota was established in several ways: (1) during 1973 less than 10 percent of the particulate organic input was exported; (2) respirometry measurements estimated some 186 kg/yr of particulate organic matter could be accounted for by microbial respiration due to retention within the reach; and (3) existence of a large pool of fine detritus verifies an extensive processing capability since the pool itself (particularly in the 250-μm to 1-mm size class) is a residue of that process.

The budget also reflects the paucity of primary production in these small forested streams. Gross primary production was low at 24 kg/yr, less than 1 kg/yr of which was by algae. Of the 24 kg/yr of gross primary production about 8 kg/yr was calculated as net primary production; the remainder was lost as plant respiration. As a result, net primary production provided only about 2 percent of the organic budget, indicating the heterotrophic nature of these first-order streams.

The refractory nature of many inputs prevented microbial degradation within one year. In addition, low streamflow during 1973 and retention structures in WS 10 effectively prevented export of detritus. The result was a large storage of small detritus (Table 10.4). Comparison of the amount and quality of debris input with export indicates that labile litter such as leaves and needles were effectively retained and only a minor proportion was exported in a recognizable state in either year (Figure 10.11).

Although water year 1974 had twice as much precipitation as 1973, overall conclusions remained the same. The largest budget difference was a threefold increase in DOM. Even during the wet year the organic budget was still dominated by particulate organic matter, which constituted 65 percent of organic inputs. A major change was also observed in particulate export, which was dominated by woody debris not effectively transported the preceding year

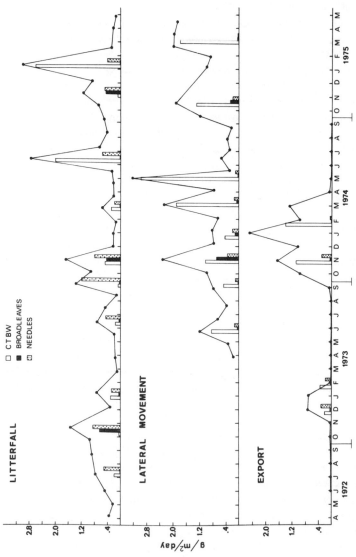

FIGURE 10.11 *Three-year record of total particulate organic input and export (solid line) in g/m⁻²/day⁻¹. Histograms are provided for major litter components. The designation CTBW is combined input of wood litter (cones, twigs, bark and wood). Data from watershed 10, H. J. Andrews Experimental Forest.*

(Figure 10.11). The role of the microbial community was reduced from 56 percent of organic output to 25 percent, because of increased transport. Despite increased transport relative to retention, significant particulate storage was observed during both years, 136 kg/yr in 1973 and 75 kg/yr in 1974. Particulate storage was derived by difference between particulate inputs (litterfall + lateral movement) minus outputs (respiration + particulate). Some storage was observed despite massive increase in particulate export, partially because of a 65 percent increase in lateral movement. Although not measured directly, loss of 0.45- to 75-μm particles (Frederiksen 1975) would not significantly affect the organic budget of 1973. As data from 1974 are analyzed, ultrafines may prove to be a significant export component.

Construction of the organic budgets provided insight into the functioning of a small stream as an ecosystem. It provided estimates of the magnitude, type, quality, and timing of various inputs to a small coniferous forest stream. It led to elucidation of the role of large debris as retaining structures. Finally, the organic budget resulted in discovery of a large pool of fine detritus, which is the product of debris processing and flocculation and quantified the role of FPOM as a major export and a refractory organic pool for the biota. The capacity of biota to mineralize debris was also quantified. Construction of budgets for two very different years allowed observations of various shifts in outputs, and introduced a temporal perspective to the inputs and overall functioning of a stream ecosystem.

TEMPORAL ASPECTS

Lake and terrestrial ecologists are often able to place their systems in historical perspective, to view the current state of their systems as a result of past events. Sediments in lakes and annual rings in trees both provide a historical record. Because history is not neatly recorded for streams, past events rarely have been considered in studies of stream ecosystem behavior. Stream ecosystem energetics are greatly dependent on recent flood event history, long-term variation in runoff, and adjacent vegetation. Storage and export values measured today reflect past and present annual runoff, flood size and frequency patterns, vegetation, and erosional conditions of a watershed. If organic budgets are not placed in a historical context, their usefulness in terms of comparing other sites, understanding processes at a site, or deriving relationships among photosynthesis, respiration, and input/export ratio is subject to serious question. Unfortunately, data are not available to directly evaluate the magnitude of historical variation in organic matter storage or transport; however a number of sources of information may be used to assess long-term variation indirectly and to evaluate the magnitude of short-term variation.

One indirect measure of export and long-term storage capacity of a stream channel is discharge, which has largely been ignored by biologists. As much as

80 percent of particulate organic matter exported annually is discharged during one or two storms (Bormann et al. 1969, 1974; Hobbie and Likens 1973; Fisher and Likens 1973; J. R. Sedell, pers. comm.). The history of sediment movement into and through a stream community has yet to be determined. Presently there are no published studies in which field sampling for organic matter budgets has been placed in the context of either annual flood cycles or long-term discharge patterns. It is important to know if study periods involved a major flood and, if not, what effect such a flood would have. At a minimum, material or energy budget measurements should be placed in a general perspective of flood return frequencies of the preceding year and the year of the measurements. Otherwise, there is no basis on which to determine if outputs of a given hydrologic year are related to inputs for the same year or different years.

Within the past century there have been periods of distinctly higher- and lower-than-average precipitation, mean annual discharge, and peak annual discharge. The record of discharge for the McKenzie River at McKenzie Bridge, Oregon, offers an indication of the historical variations in mean and peak annual flow in the Pacific Northwest (Figure 10.12). Occurrence of major floods is not restricted to generally wet periods. The flood of December 1964, the largest well-documented historic flood of a regional scale in the Pacific Northwest and California, occurred during a year of otherwise average discharge.

In Figure 10.12 the record of annual discharge at McKenzie Bridge is also plotted as cumulative departure from the mean of the mean annual discharges for a sixty-two-year period. A negative slope, such as shown for the period from 1928 to 1945, reflects a period of lower-than-average mean discharge; a positive slope, like that between 1947 and 1958, indicates above-average run-off. Annual mean discharge during the dry period was 14 percent less than mean conditions and exhibited average peak annual discharges only 69 percent of peak flow of the wet period. Thus, during dry seasons, flushing capacity of a stream would be considerably reduced. Although there are no organic budgets for these early periods, it is likely that storage of refractory organic materials in the stream occurred during dry years, with annual net loss or reduced net accumulation during wet periods.

Importance of discharge history can be seen in the two annual organic budgets presented earlier. Figure 10.13 presents return frequencies of peak discharge for twenty-five years of record at WS 2, H. J. Andrews Forest. The year prior to initiation of the budget study (1972) had three of the ten highest storm flows recorded (second, seventh, and ninth). As a result, these budgets were initiated at a time when storage of organic materials should have been low. Wet-year organic inputs by litterfall and lateral (surface) movement exceeded dry-year inputs by 5 percent and 65 percent, respectively. Clearly, inputs change significantly with the pattern of precipitation and discharge. The dissolved organic matter (DOM) loss was 323 percent higher in 1974 since solution loss is related to mean annual discharge. Although annual mean discharge

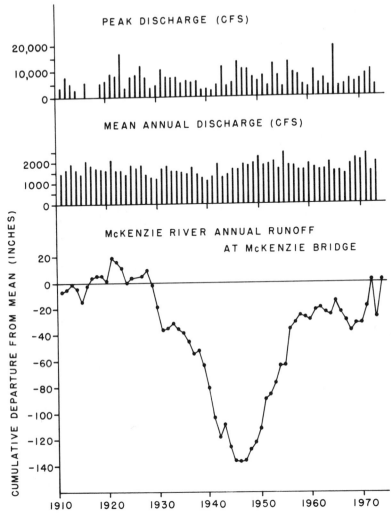

FIGURE 10.12 *Sixty-year discharge record of the McKenzie River measured at a gauging station at McKenzie Bridge, Oregon.*

for 1974 was second highest in the sixty-three-year discharge record of the upper McKenzie drainage, peak discharge had a one-year return period, and, on that basis, capability to export particulate organic matter could be considered average. Thus parameters measured to construct an organic budget for streams are extremely responsive to magnitude and frequency of storms. Storage, export, and biological process rates must be evaluated in terms of mean discharge and flood return frequency for temporal understanding of interaction between processes at the ecosystem level.

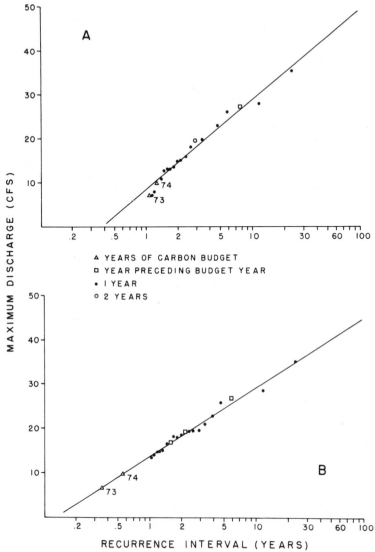

FIGURE 10.13 *Return frequencies of peak discharge (A) and partial return frequencies (B) from a twenty-five-year discharge record at watershed 2, H. J. Andrews Forest.*

A SPATIAL PERSPECTIVE

With the exception of arid regions, streams generally increase in size and discharge as they flow into higher order streams. As streams become larger, influence of the terrestrial system diminishes (Figure 10.14; Vannote et al.

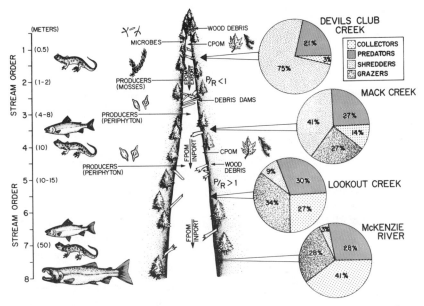

FIGURE 10.14 *A simplified schematic diagram of a river network reflecting the response of biotic community structure to modified input of water, particulate organic matter, and light.*

1980, Cummins 1976, 1977). A natural river system, from headwaters to mouth, can be considered a gradient of process zones ranging from a strongly detrital system in headwater streams to an annual autotrophic regime in moderate-sized streams, followed by a gradual return to predominantly heterotrophic processes in 'large river systems. Biotic structure shifts from a system dominated by shredder and collector processes to one where shredder functions are diminished and grazer functions increase. As streams flow into larger rivers, benthic algae are often replaced by more planktonic forms. Collector organisms shift from a major component of insects to a system dominated by such organisms as sponges, mussels, and worms. These patterns of change in both the hydraulic geometry of streams and nature of organic inputs appear predictable throughout natural river systems. As a result a spatial perspective can be obtained by examination of parameters related to physical structure, stream chemistry, and biological processing capabilities down a river system. Chemical and biological parameters measured in the McKenzie River drainage include: (1) heterogeneity of soluble organic matter; (2) amounts and ratio of coarse particulate organic matter to fine particulate organic matter on the stream bottom (CPOM/FPOM); (3) spatial aspects of retention and transport; (4) ratio of primary productivity to total community respiration; and (5) shifts in invertebrate functional groups.

Heterogeneity of Soluble Organic Matter

A river continuum hypothesis outlined by Vannote et al. (1980) predicts that the composition of DOM undergoes change in a downstream direction. As water passes through the lotic network, DOM becomes available for biotic uptake, as well as for physical-chemical processes such as flocculation or ultraviolet degradation. As a result, DOM transport exhibits a fractionation pattern reflecting loss of the most labile components and a decrease in heterogeneity of DOM through a spatial continuum.

In the McKenzie River system, total DOC concentration in our small headwater stream was always higher than in third-, fifth-, or seventh-order streams and also showed a difference in fractionation pattern.

Table 10.5 summarizes some data obtained from Sephadex G-25 analyses conducted by R. Larson, Stroud Water Research Center (pers. comm). Residual "humic acid" was low in all streams. This is to be expected in streams of low color; some southeastern streams of high color have 1 to 10 mg humic acid/liter (Martin and Pierce 1971). The bulk of colored material in the four systems appeared to be similar to fulvic acid, as shown by the Sephadex patterns. Total color decreased downstream from first- to third-order sites. Analyses of dissolved carbohydrate showed the highest concentration in first- and third-order streams, as had been observed previously in other river systems (R. Larson, pers. comm.). In each system, the percentage of DOC that could be classified as carbohydrate, phenolics, or amino acid generally decreased from first- to sixth-order streams.

If stream microorganisms degrade low-molecular-weight organic fractions in preference to those of larger size, Sephadex fractionation patterns for a stream system should show progressive decreases in the size of later eluting peaks (small molecular size) relative to those eluting earlier (large molecular size) as stream order increases. This decrease was observed spatially at the

TABLE 10.5 *Stream water concentration of total dissolved organic matter (DOM) fractionated into major organic subcomponents in four Oregon streams.[a]*

Stream system	Humic acid content (mg/l)	Total color	TOC (mg/l)	Carbo-hydrate (mg/l) C	Phenol (mg/l) C	Amino acid (mg/l) C	Σ last 3 as % of TOC
Devil's Club Creek	—	4.14	2.87	0.81	0.22	0.02	37
Mack Creek	0.25	0.68	1.81	0.47	0.06	0	29
Lookout Creek	0.90	0.52	1.20	0.64	0.05	0	58
McKenzie River	0.08	0.28	1.70	0.27	0.05	0	19

[a] R. Larson, personal communication.

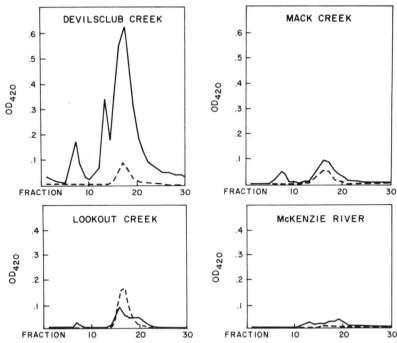

FIGURE 10.15 *Sephadex fraction pattern of dissolved organic matter from four streams of increasing size: Devil's Club Creek (first-order); Mack Creek (third-order); Lookout Creek (fifth-order); and McKenzie River (sixth-order): Solid line = color, dashed line = fluorescence (data from R. Larson, pers. comm.).*

Oregon sites (Figure 10.15); DOM in Devil's Club Creek displayed greater color maxima than other sites, with a large contribution of medium-sized polymers. At Mack Creek and Lookout Creek sites, most colored DOM had disappeared. McKenzie River DOM was virtually free of colored or fluorescent material. R. Larson (pers. comm.) suggests that DOM from different watersheds will have characteristic fluorescence distributions, probably related to principal leaf and wood litter, soil constituents, or both, supplied to the stream in each area. Although data at hand are very limited, it appears that much processing of DOM in Cascade river systems occurs rapidly in very small streams.

Total Amounts and CPOM/FPOM Ratios of Benthic Organic Material

Old-growth western Cascades forests (>400 years) have trees that are large (> 50 cm diam) and often infected with heartrot, which increases susceptibility for windthrow into streams. The result is episodic input of large wood debris. Accumulation of debris in dams is less likely to occur in large channels than in small streams, regardless of gradient. Instead, larger streams deposit bole wood on bends and flood terraces inundated only briefly during the year. Debris in these larger streams functions as food or habitat to only a limited extent. In smaller streams, large boles are not moved by water except during debris torrents. Debris clumped into dams traps small organic debris and sediments and helps shape and stabilize the channel. Because of forest age, large tree size, and resistance to decomposition and export, bole wood overwhelms the amount of small wood in Cascade streams (Table 10.6). Table 10.7 reflects the influence of bole wood (> 10 cm diam) in benthic standing crop. Even if bole wood is excluded, Devil's Club Creek and the stream at watershed 10 have a greater year-round standing crop of detritus than Lookout Creek or the McKenzie River because of capture of fine organic particles by large debris dams. Neither the fifth-order section of Lookout Creek nor of McKenzie River has significant accumulations of large woody debris, because of the transport capacity of these larger streams. Consequently, detritus standing crops are

TABLE 10.6   *Estimated quantities and surface areas of wood debris in four Oregon streams.*[a]

Stream system	Large branch and bole wood			Small branch wood[b]	
	(> 10 cm diam.)			(< 10 cm diam.)	
	Biomass (kg/m^2)	Surface area (m^2/m^2)	Surface to vol ratio (m^2/m^2)	Biomass (kg/m^2)	area (m^2/m^2)
Devil's Club Creek	140.89	0.43	8.62	1.11	0.14
Mack Creek	28.50	0.16	9.94	0.61	0.08
Lookout Creek	11.65	0.04	5.37	0.08	0.01
McKenzie River	0.08	0.003	19.28	0.08	0.01

[a]From Anderson et al. 1978.
[b]Surface:volume ratio of small branch wood measured only for Lookout Creek = 27.96.

TABLE 10.7   *Mean standing crop of benthic organic matter (g ash free dry weight · m^{-2}). Estimates exclude large woody debris (>10 cm dia.).*

	Winter	Spring	Summer	Autumn
Devil's Club Creek	3242	1640	2296	1040
Mack Creek	173	564	1706	87
Lookout Creek	62	285	85	58
McKenzie River	128	76	52	79

[a]Anderson et al., 1978 and Naiman and Sedell, 1979.

TABLE 10.8 *Percent composition of benthic detritus by size class and season from a spatial continuum of four Oregon streams.*[a]

Stream system	Season	Percentage of total organic storage[b]		
		>1 mm	1 mm to 53 μm	53 μm to 0.45 μm
Devil's Club Creek	Winter	96.9	3.1	—
	Spring	66.8	29.7	3.5
	Summer	59.4	26.2	19.2
	Autumn	38.2	37.6	24.1
	Mean	65.3	24.2	15.6
Mack Creek	Winter	74.2	25.8	—
	Spring	67.2	26.7	6.1
	Summer	62.3	32.4	5.3
	Autumn	41.9	47.0	11.1
	Mean	61.4	32.9	7.5
Lookout Creek	Winter	41.8	18.5	38.7
	Spring	69.2	29.7	1.1
	Summer	47.8	41.7	7.2
	Autumn	41.2	45.3	13.5
	Mean	50.0	33.8	15.4
McKenzie River	Winter	50.4	13.8	39.7
	Spring	52.9	43.4	4.0
	Summer	26.2	61.3	12.5
	Autumn	31.9	56.9	11.1
	Mean	40.4	43.7	16.8

[a]From Naiman and Sedell, 1979.
[b]Does not include large woody debris >10 cm diameter.

relatively low, ranging from 62 to 285 ash-free dry g/m^2 in Lookout Creek and from 52 to 128 ash-free dry g/m^2 in the McKenzie River.

Excluding bole wood, there is a progressive decrease in percentage of total organic storage contributed by the >1-mm fraction as stream order increases (Table 10.8). Mean percentage of the >1-mm size class ranges from 65 percent in Devil's Club Creek down to 40 percent in the McKenzie River. Correspondingly, importance of the 1-mm to 53-μm fraction increases as stream order increases. This fraction composes a mean of 24 percent in Devil's Club Creek and 43 percent in the McKenzie River. The 53-μm to 0.45-μm fraction is generally a minor component of benthic standing crop, although at Lookout Creek and the McKenzie River it constitutes 39 and 40 percent, respectively, of detritus during winter. In smaller streams the percentage remains nearly constant (8 to 17 percent range) with no discernible trends in response to stream order.

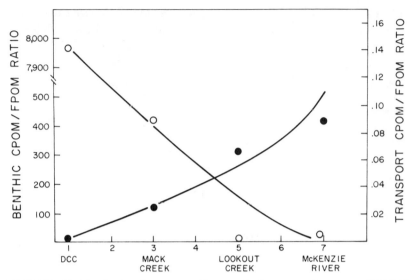

FIGURE 10.16 *Ratio of coarse to fine particulate organic matter (CPOM/FPOM) in benthic standing crop (○), and transport (●) in the first through seventh orders of a stream system.*

In Devil's Club Creek the CPOM/FPOM ratio in benthic standing crop ranged annually from approximately 95:1 to 6500:1 (Figure 10.16). The amount of coarse particulates remained nearly constant but fine particulates varied enough during the year to cause the wide range. In Mack Creek the ratio ranged seasonally from less than 96 to about 477. Again, most variation was caused by fluctuations in the standing crop of fine particulates. In both Lookout Creek and the McKenzie River the CPOM/FPOM ratio was always less than 10 and nearly constant throughout the year.

The general downstream decrease in the ratio of CPOM to FPOM is due to decreased quantity of large woody debris (Table 10.6), while fine particulates < 1 mm become a dominant component of benthic detritus (Table 10.8). Although the percentage of FPOM as a component of benthic standing crop increases in the downstream direction, the amount decreases, because in very small streams such as Devil's Club Creek retention structures effectively trap fine detritus. These small streams can be envisioned as a transition between terrestrial and aquatic ecosystems, which are efficient in retaining and processing organic inputs (Fisher and Likens 1973; Sedell et al. 1974; Naiman 1976; Webster and Patten 1979). When stream order increases, as in Mack Creek, storm flows become sufficient to overcome some retention structures and transport fine particles downstream, but not powerful enough during normal years to move large woody debris. Hence the capacity for retention and time for biological processing within a reach decreases in a downstream direction as the capacity for transport increases in large stream orders.

Spatial Consideration in Material Transport

The decrease in wood-generated habitat at each step in the continuum varies the amount and composition of small organic residue. As retention capacities decrease, transport mechanisms previously buffered by organic debris begin to operate. The resultant capacity to move particulate organic material is reflected in the quality and quantity of organic transport. Initially, one might suspect coarse materials from first-order streams, with most intimate terrestrial interaction, would supply more productive third- to fifth-order streams with large quantities of leaf litter. In fact, the findings were the opposite. First-order streams, as shown by organic budgets, are extremely retentive and primarily transport materials previously processed to FPOM. Only in larger streams, where formation of rentention structures is prevented by the hydraulic capacity to move debris, is coarse particulate material such as leaf litter effectively transported (Figure 10.16). As a result the CPOM/FPOM ratio for transport increases in a downstream direction. The transport ratio indicates that first-order streams supply downstream reaches primarily through input of FPOM to collector invertebrates rather than input of intact leaf litter to shredders. In fact, 75 to 90 percent of the organic particles in transport were between 0.5 and 50 μm in diameter at all four sites in the McKenzie drainage (Sedell et al. 1978). Large wood in small streams dissipates the energy of flow and retains coarse organic particulates, while in larger streams channel morphology dissipates energy but permits transport of larger organic particles.

**Ratio of Primary Production to Total Community
Respiration Rates (P/R)**

The ratio of gross primary production to community respiration has been used to assess the degree to which a stream reach is basically autotrophic or heterotrophic (Fisher and Likens 1973). A P/R ratio of less than 1.0 generally indicates a heterotrophic energy base while a ratio greater than 1.0 indicates a basically autotrophic stream reach. In the McKenzie drainage, P/R ratio increases through the first six orders of the river system. Devil's Club Creek is most heterotrophic, followed by Mack Creek, which also has a P/R < 1. Lookout Creek has a P/R > 1 but less than the McKenzie River.

Devil's Club Creek may attain a fairly high P/R seasonally but never reaches 1.0, since it is dominated by microbial activity that increases community respiration. Mack Creek has a P/R ratio greater than 1.0 for every season except winter, but it still has a considerable amount of detritus (Table 10.8), which depresses the P/R ratio. Mack Creek has both algae and detritus as an energy base. During spring Mack Creek approaches conditions of an algal-driven, autotrophic stream, but is heterotrophic on an annual basis. Lookout Creek is autotrophic during all seasons. The standing crop of detritus is relatively small and the leaf litter component is biologically available primarily during winter. In Lookout Creek microbial activity on detritus does not depress the P/R ratio to < 1. The benthic algal community of the McKenzie River has the highest P/R ratio. Thus this river is definitely autotrophic at all seasons. The macrophyte community along the shores of this river has a P/R ratio between 0.7 and 0.9, which partially reduces the overall ratio; however, boulders and cobbles free of macrophytes constitute about 85 percent of the benthic area. Since both light input and P/R ratio increase in a downstream direction, the data reinforce the hypothesis of canopy control of P/R ratio over the first six stream orders.

Functional Group Shifts

The relative dominance of invertebrate functional groups also shifts spatially in response to changes in particulate organic inputs (both algal and detrital), substrate conditions, and materials in transport.

Functional groups shift in response to organic input at sites along the McKenzie River drainage (Figure 10.14). Data were from benthic samples collected in gravel areas for invertebrates larger than 500 μm. As a result the smallest invertebrates (chironimids and copepods) were not included. The diagram is based on a percentage by numbers of samples collected during summer 1976 (C. L. Hawkins, pers. comm.). In the small, first-order stream (Devil's Club Creek), with a completely closed canopy, wood retention devices, and low P/R ratio, 75 percent of collected invertebrates were classified as shredders. Only about 3 percent were classified as fine particle feeders; none of the sampled invertebrates were grazers. At the third-order stream (Mack Creek), with partial canopy and less retention capacity, the role of shredders was reduced while the grazing functional group increased significantly. In Mack Creek collectors also exhibited a far more significant role. In samples from the fifth-order stream, Lookout Creek, shredders decreased to only a minor role. With its open canopy and greater primary production, grazers represented 34 percent of sampled invertebrate organisms. The proportion of collectors also increased. In the sixth-order river, grazers continued to be important; however, collectors dominated the community. Numbers of invertebrate predators varied only between 20 and 30 percent at all four sites. Thus the downstream continuum characterized by canopy opening, decreased terrestrial inputs per square meter, and input of preprocessed fine organic material by transport results in a definite response in biotic structure and function.

In areas dominated by wood debris, the resultant habitat also influences composition of the invertebrate community (Figure 10.17). In very small streams approximately 25 percent of the stream area is wood, and a second 25 percent is organic debris and sediments stored behind wood residues. As a result, half the stream habitat is either wood or wood-created. The remainder is either bedrock or mineral sediment. In third- to fourth-order streams in the H. J.

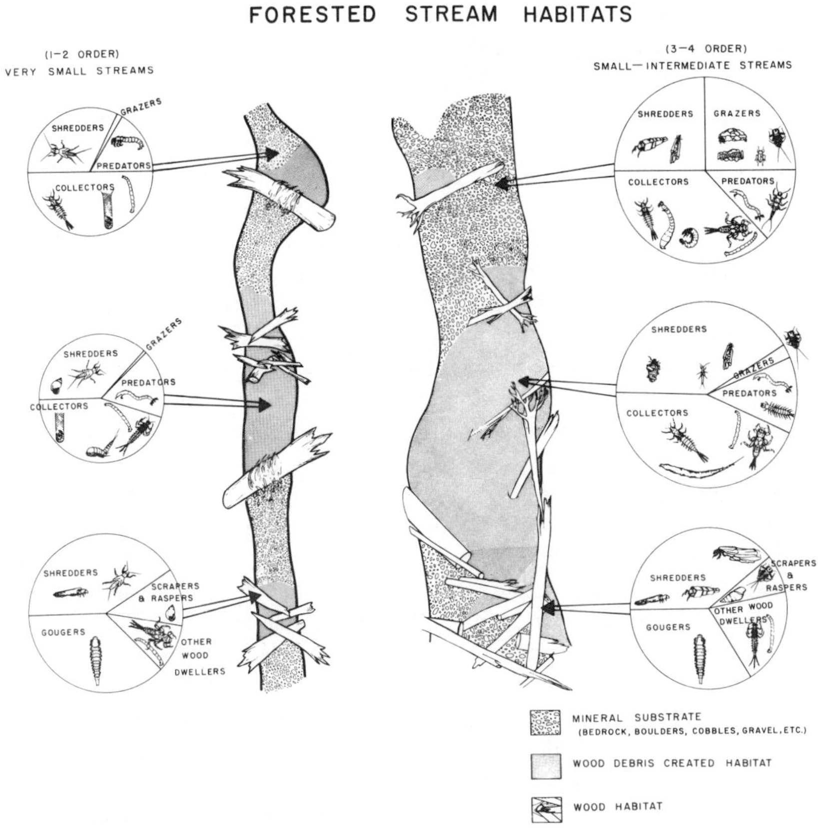

FORESTED   STREAM   HABITATS

FIGURE 10.17   *Schematic diagram illustrating the role of large wood debris in modifying stream habitat in large and small streams, and its influence on invertebrate biota.*

Andrews Forest, only about 12 percent of the area is occupied by wood with nearly equal amounts in wood-created habitat, while 75 percent of the stream is mineral substrate. As noted previously, wood in fifth-order streams is found along or on the banks depending on flow conditions. Although the smallest streams have the greatest wood-created habitat, invertebrate biomass is lowest in the smallest streams. The smallest streams also have a large proportion of small invertebrates. In larger streams, particularly those with an algal and detrital base, there is greater biomass diversity of functional groups and species of invertebrates.

FOREST LAND-USE IMPLICATIONS

Knowledge of the stream's basic physical-biological structure through time and space can form a basis for evaluating response of lotic systems to land-use practice. In the Oregon Cascades, and indeed in much of the coniferous forest biome, timber harvest is a major land use. Therefore response of streams to typical logging practices through time has become a critical land-use consideration. As stated previously, small forest streams in old-growth forests are completely dominated by forest vegetation. This domination includes shading, input of organic litter for the biota, large debris inputs that partially regulate channel morphology, and contribution of the riparian zone (Chapter 9). Therefore, removal of forest canopy either naturally by fire or by timber harvesting critically affects the adjacent stream.

One hypothetical scenario is that canopy opening will result in a significant increase in primary production and an attendant shift in biotic structure as a result of shifting from heterotrophic to autotrophic energy pathways. This open canopy would be transient, however, since the riparian zone responds rapidly to canopy removal (Chapter 9). Within ten to fifteen years a thicket of alder and willow would occupy the riparian zone and reshade the stream. We hypothesize this would result in a decline of the temporary autotrophic base and a return to heterotrophic conditions. Quality of allochthonous inputs, primarily litter of alder and willow, is much higher (more labile) than coniferous litter of old-growth forests and is processed more rapidly by the biotic community. As the coniferous canopy recovers, shrub species in the riparian zone would be slowly shaded out and the alder/willow component of the riparian zone would die out. Mortality in the riparian zone would reintroduce wood debris to the stream. Since hardwoods are processed more rapidly, however, debris dams would not be as persistent. As alder and willow litter declined in amount, return to coniferous litter would signal a general decline in food quality for biota and overall production would decline rapidly. Finally, after about 125 years, coniferous tree mortality would increase, and debris dams capable of stabilizing the streambed would be formed. At this time, coniferous mortality in the adjacent forest would reintroduce some direct lighting and the community of the old-growth forest stream would become reestablished.

Although evidence to support this hypothetical scenario is part of our current research, shaded and unshaded sections of streams were previously examined to determine algal, insect, and fishery response to canopy removal. Aho (1976) conducted a study of cutthroat trout *(Salmo clarki clarki)* in an unshaded and a shaded section of Mack Creek. The objective of this study was to test the hypothesis that no differences existed between trout populations in the two stream sections. Periodic sampling and tagging were used to determine population levels, growth rates, and production. Movement, diet, and prey-size selection were also investigated.

Aho found the unshaded section supported higher trout biomass than the shaded section. Trout up to three years old were as numerous in the unshaded as the shaded area, but biomass (wet weight) of all trout was 12.2 g/m^2 in the unshaded and 6.2 g/m^2 in the shaded section. Mean length by year class was also greater for trout from the unshaded habitat. From 1973 to 1974, estimated production was 7.5 g/m^2 in the unshaded and 2.6 g/m^2 in the shaded section.

Higher level of trout production in the unshaded section probably resulted from a combination of factors including the differences in diet, abundance of prey, and water temperature. A more productive food resource in the unshaded habitat was indicated by a greater abundance of multivoltine insects and grazers in the diet of trout from this area. In the unshaded section, emergence traps captured approximately twice the combined biomass of several insect groups important in the trout diet. Because of higher water temperatures, trout fry emerged earlier in the unshaded section. Earlier emergence probably provided an initial growth advantage that was maintained throughout the life of the trout.

Primary production rates in the clearcut reach were more than twice as high as in the forest reach of Mack Creek (Figure 10.18). This increase in algal material has potential advantages for consumers. Algae have low C/N ratios (6 to 12) and are therefore high-quality food for collectors and grazers. Algae have fast turnover rates and therefore can support high standing crops of consumers relative to their own standing crop. This was evidenced both by simulation modeling (McIntire 1973), which showed algae could support fifteen times their own standing crop of consumers, and by experiments on grazers in laboratory streams. In an experiment using four densities of snails, only the heaviest density resulted in decreased production of algae (Figure 10.19). Thus algae can sustain heavy rates of cropping and still maintain uniform standing crop. Another advantage of the autotrophic food base is that the major insect forms that graze algae in Northwest streams are Ephemeroptera, some of which are multivoltine and have fast turnover rates. These insects are also more prone to drift than most detrital feeders, and would therefore be more available for trout consumption. Thus increased algal production has many attributes that would favor higher production on invertebrates and trout.

Relative increase in autochthonous inputs is a function of shading prior to canopy removal since the degree of canopy openness determines the level of primary production in streams. We examined algal colonization rates in eight pairs of old-growth forest and clearcut sections of streams. Relative difference in colonization rates between forested and clearcut sections was strongly related to stream width, an indirect measure of canopy openness (Figure 10.20). Thus change in stream productivity as a result of deforestation is greatly dependent on physical parameters of the stream such as solar radiation and temperature, both of which are determined by canopy openness.

These observations suggest that clearcutting can potentially lead to enhancement of trout production if the stream channel is maintained physically (debris dams, lack of significant erosion, lack of large temperature increases). On a long-term basis (25 to 175 years), however, there may be no net enhancement in stream production due to rapid revegetation of the riparian zone.

Trout populations in small streams (old-growth, clearcut, second-growth) in the western Cascades were inventoried to assess logging impacts on trout abundance (Murphy 1979). Cutthroat trout *(Salmo clarki)* was the only salmonid present in sites with gradients higher than 2 percent. Trout biomass (g/m^2 wet wt) varied according to density of forest canopy (Figure 10.21). The same

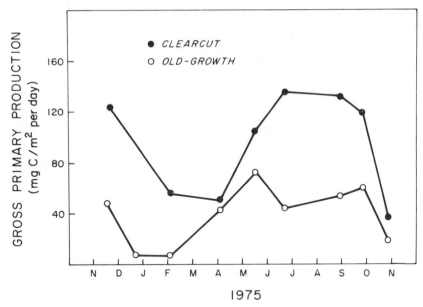

FIGURE 10.18 *Pattern of annual gross primary production in an open ten-year-old clearcut and a forested old-growth section of Mack Creek.*

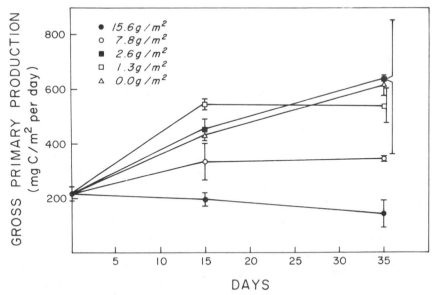

FIGURE 10.19 *Laboratory determination of gross primary production in experimental channels subjected to four levels of grazing pressure by snails. The levels of grazers' biomass (ash-free dry wt) were: 15.6 g/m² (●); 7.8 g/m² (○); 2.6 g/m² (■); 1.3 g/m² (□); and ungrazed control (△).*

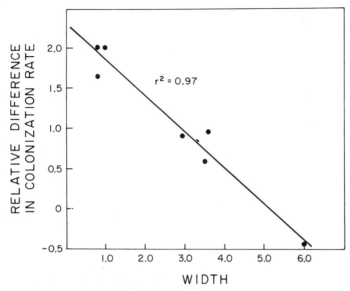

FIGURE 10.20 *Relative difference in algal colonization rate on clay tiles incubated in seven streams of the H. J. Andrews Forest in relation to stream width (m).*

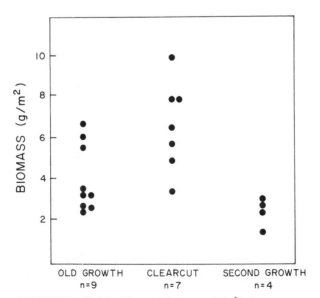

FIGURE 10.21 *Trout biomass (g/m²) in twenty streams draining old-growth, clearcut, and second-growth forests of the western Cascades.*

response was also found for insect predators (Murphy 1979). Biomass and diversity tended to be greatest in young clearcut (< 10 years) sites, intermediate in old-growth (> 450 years) sites, and least in second-growth (> 15 years) sites. After fifteen to twenty-five years the riparian zone in the western Cascades gradually switches from deciduous to coniferous species. Although only a few stands have been studied to date, data indicate only a temporary enhancement of biological production in streams by opening the canopy, and perhaps a long-term reduction of biological production because of heavy shading by second-growth stands. With eighty-year rotations intense shading of second-growth could become a proportionally greater part of stream history than natural rotations, which include long periods of moderate shading characteristic of old-growth stands.

Another aspect that should be considered in a recovery perspective is the potential shift in functional groups as a result of clearcutting. Insect functional groups described previously have specialist roles in the ecosystem, that is, grazing, gouging, and shredding. In the coast range of Oregon most streams have a significant component of snails, which are best described as generalists. That is, snails can consume leaves (shredding), graze on the surface of mineral substrate (scraping), and even consume fine particulate organic matter (collecting). Although data are scant, they indicate a shift to the generalist snail following clearcutting in the coast range (Figure 10.22). As the canopy closes again in second growth, generalists begin to decline and are replaced by inver-

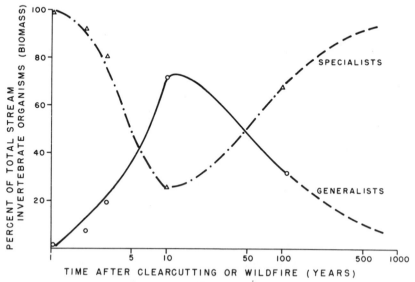

FIGURE 10.22 *Comparison of specialist and generalist compositions of the invertebrate community in five streams of the Coast Range of Oregon draining stands of different ages.*

tebrate specialists. The cause of this shift and its long-term influence on the diversity of biota of streams is unknown. To answer a question such as this, however, requires an appreciation for the biotic structure of streams and its interaction with the terrestrial environment through time.

A third aspect to be considered in land management decisions is the geomorphological role of wood on the biota. Streams adjust to changes in timing and amounts of water and sediment by changing width, depth, gradient, hydraulic roughness, and amount of sediment in transport. For streams in the northwest, wood greatly influences channel morphology. In terms of routing of water and sediment, wood (boles) is every bit as important to streams as the timing and quantity of sediment and water. The consequences of ignoring this third element are becoming more obvious when one considers the "historical" role of wood and how we are currently managing land and streams.

Under current management practice, extensive stream cleanup is required after logging, which results in removal of wood debris. Yet without stable wood debris in the highest gradient streams, retention of gravel and organic material for biotic habitat could not occur. The result is removal of retention mechanisms that are characteristically present and that allow the biological component of the stream to function effectively.

In the natural stream, loading with large wood debris occurs more or less evenly through time. With short-rotation timber harvesting this important morphological component may be permanently removed. Furthermore, as the last old-growth timber lands are cut, wood may diminish as a significant organic input. Eighty-year rotations, in conjunction with precommercial and commercial thinning, could gradually eliminate debris dams as a morphological feature of streams. The highest gradient streams may then erode to bedrock and become functionally depauperate in a biological sense. Sediments could be routed more rapidly and sediment load formerly retained as habitat may impact downstream fisheries. Removal of debris dams, which formerly dissipated energy of water in high gradient streams, may in the future allow high water to erode banks, promote siltation, and speed discharge to lower gradient streams with resultant flooding.

Under current land-use practices, we are effectively channeling our mountain streams and managing land to keep them so. In channeled high-gradient streams, normal sediment and organic loads are routed more quickly than under natural conditions. Retention of sediments and organics is neither large in amount or long in time. If the stream does not retain organic material and maintain a diversity of physical habitats then, biologically, it may be unable to process organic matter from the adjacent forest and large, functional and structural components in the stream ecosystem could disappear.

Wise management of streams and watersheds can prevent these problems and preserve biological functioning in streams. The development of future management strategies will best result from a basic knowledge of the biotic structure and function of streams and their interaction with physical and chemical components of stream ecosystems. Once developed, effective application of management strategies will depend on a basic knowledge of the stream ecosystem and how it functions through time and space.

LITERATURE CITED

Aho, R. S., 1976, A population study of the cutthroat trout in an unshaded and shaded section of streams, M.S. thesis, Oregon State University, Corvallis, 87p.

Anderson, N. H., and E. Grafius, 1975, Utilization and processing of allochthonous materials by stream Trichoptera, *Verh. Int. Verein. Limnol.* **19**:3082–3088.

Anderson, N. H., J. R. Sedell, L. M. Roberts, and F. J. Triska, 1978, Role of aquatic invertebrates in processing wood debris in coniferous forest streams, *Am. Midl. Nat.* **100**:64–82.

Bormann, F. H., G. E. Likens, and J. S. Eaton, 1969, Biotic regulation of particulate and solution losses from a forest ecosystem, *BioScience* **19**:600–610.

Bormann, F. H., G. E. Likens, T. G. Siccama, R. S. Pierce, and J. S. Eaton, 1974, The export of nutrients and recovery of stable conditions following deforestation at Hubbard Brook, *Ecol. Monogr.* **44**:255–277.

Cummins, K. W., 1973, Trophic relations of aquatic insects, *Ann. Rev. Entomol.* **18**:183–206.

Cummins, K. W., 1976, The ecology of running waters: Theory and practice, in *Sandusky River Basin Symp. Proc.,* D. B. Baker, W. B. Jackson, and B. L. Prater, eds., Int. Joint Comm. Great Lakes, Washington, D.C., pp. 277–293.

Cummins, K. W., 1977, From headwater streams to rivers, *Am. Biol. Teach.* **39**:305–312.

Fisher, S. G., and G. E. Likens, 1973, Energy flow in Bear Brook, New Hampshire: An integrative approach to stream ecosystem metabolism, *Ecol. Monogr.* **43**:421–439.

Fredriksen, R. L., 1975, Nitrogen, phosphorus and particulate matter budgets of five coniferous forest ecosystems in the Western Cascades Range, Oregon, Ph.D. dissertation, Oregon State University, Corvallis, 127p.

Gregory, S. V., 1979, Primary production in Pacific Northwest streams, Ph.D. dissertation, Oregon State University, Corvallis, 98p.

Hall, C. A. S., 1972, Migration and metabolism in a temperate stream ecosystem, *Ecology* **53**:585–604.

Hobbie, J. W., and G. E. Likens, 1973, The output of phosphorus, dissolved organic carbon, and fine particulate carbon from Hubbard Brook watersheds, *Limnol. Oceanogr.* **18**:734–742.

Hodkinson, I. D., 1975, Dry weight loss and chemical changes in vascular plant litter of terrestrial origin occurring in a beaver pond ecosystem, *J. Ecol.* **63:**131–142.

Iverson, T. M., 1973, Decomposition of autumn shed beech leaves in a springbrook and its significance to the fauna, *Arch. Hydrobiol.* **73:**305–312.

Kaushik, N. K., and H. B. N. Hynes, 1968, Experimental study on the role of autumn shed leaves in aquatic environments, *J. Ecol.* **52:**229–243.

Lush, D. L., and H. B. N. Hynes, 1973, The formation of particles in freshwater leachates of dead leaves, *Limnol. and Oceanogr.* **18:**968–977.

McIntire, C. D., 1973, Periphyton dynamics in laboratory streams: A simulation model and its implications, *Ecol. Monogr.* **43:**399–420.

McIntire, C. D., J. A. Colby, and J. D. Hall, 1975, The dynamics of small lotic ecosystems: A modeling approach, *Verh. Int. Verein. Limnol.* **19:**1599–1609.

Mann, K. H., R. H. Britton, A. Kowalczewski, T. J. Lack, C. P. Mathews, and I. McDonald, 1972, Productivity and energy flow at all trophic levels and the River Thames, England, in *Proceedings of the IBP-UNESCO Symposium on Productivity Problems of Freshwater,* Z. Kajak and A. Hillbricht-Ilkowska, eds., Polish Scientific Publications, Warsaw-Krakow, pp. 579-596.

Martin, D. F., and R. H. Pierce, 1971, A convenient method of analysis of humic acid in freshwater, *Environ. Lett.* **1:**49–52.

Mathews, C. P., and A. Kowalczewski, 1969, The disappearance of leaf litter and its contribution to production in the River Thames, *J. Ecol.* **57:**543–552.

Murphy, M., 1979, Determinants of community structure and impacts of logging on predator communities in streams of the Western Cascades, M.S. thesis, Oregon State University, Corvallis, 73p.

Naiman, R. J., 1976, Primary production, standing stock and export of organic matter in a Mohave Desert thermal stream, *Limnol. and Oceanogr.* **21:**60–73.

Naiman, R. J., and J. R. Sedell, 1979, A study of benthic organic matter as a function of stream order, *Archiv. Hydrobiol.* **87:**404–472.

Odum, H. T., 1957, Trophic structure and productivity of Silver Springs, Florida, *Ecol. Monogr.* **27:**55–112.

Sedell, J. R., F. J. Triska, J. D. Hall, N. H. Anderson, and J. H. Lyford, 1974, Sources and fates of organic inputs in coniferous forest streams, in *Integrated Research in the Coniferous forest Biome,* R. H. Waring and R. L. Edmonds, eds., Coniferous Forest Biome Bull. 5., University of Washington, Seattle, pp. 57–69.

Sedell, J. R., F. J. Triska, and B. M. Buckley, 1975, The processing of coniferous and hardwood leaves in two coniferous forest streams, 1: Weight loss and associated invertebrates, *Verh. Int. Verein. Limnol.* **19:**617–627.

Sedell, J. R., R. J. Naiman, K. R. Cummins, G. W. Minshall, and R. L. Vannote, 1978, Transport of particulate organic material in streams as a function of physical processes, *Verh. Int. Verein. Limnol.* **20**:1366–1375.

Strahler, A. N., 1964, Quantitative geomorphology of drainage basins and channel networks, in *Handbook of Applied Hydrology*, V. T. Chow, ed., McGraw-Hill, New York, Sections 4–11.

Triska, F. J., 1970, Seasonal distribution of aquatic hypomycetes in relation to disappearance of leaf litter from a woodland stream, Ph.D. dissertation, University of Pittsburgh, Pittsburgh, Pa., 189p.

Triska, F. J., and B. M. Buckley, 1978, Patterns of nitrogen uptake and loss in relation to litter disappearance and associated invertebrate biomass in six streams of the Pacific Northwest, U.S.A., *Verh. Int. Verein. Limnol.* **20**:1324–1332.

Triska, F. J., and J. R. Sedell, 1976, Decomposition of four species of leaf litter in response to nitrate manipulation, *Ecology* **57**:783–792.

Triska, F. J., J. R. Sedell, K. Cromack, Jr., and F. M. McCorison, in press, Nitrogen budget of a small watershed stream: Influence of allochthonous organic inputs and associated biological processes, *Ecol. Monogr.*

Vannote, R. L., G. W. Minshall, K. W. Cummins, J. R. Sedell and C. E. Cushing, 1980, The river continuum concept, *Can. J. Fish. Aquat. Sci.* **37**:130–137.

Webster, J. R., and B. C. Patten, 1979, Effects of watershed perturbation on stream potassium and calcium dynamics, *Ecol. Monogr.* **49**:51–72.

11

Lake Ecosystems of the Lake Washington Drainage Basin

R. C. Wissmar, J. E. Richey, A. H. Devol, and *D. M. Eggers*

INTRODUCTION

Lakes are closely coupled to terrestrial systems, and the trophic state of a particular body of water reflects carbon and nutrient inputs from its entire watershed (Fisher 1970; Hutchinson et al. 1970; Fisher and Likens 1973; Likens and Davis 1975). This is particularly true in the Pacific Northwest, where the surrounding coniferous forests are among the most productive in the world, and are characterized by large accumulations of biomass and detritus (Sedell 1972; Taub et al. 1972).

One of the major objectives of the lakes program was to study these terrestrial influences in an effort to better understand their impact on lake metabolism. Four lakes in the Lake Washington drainage basin were studied. They ranged from high-altitude lakes surrounded by forests (Findley and Chester Morse lakes) to low-altitude lakes in more urban environments (Sammamish and Washington lakes). A progression from oligotrophy to mesotrophy exists in the order Findley Lake, Chester Morse Lake, Lake Sammamish, and Lake Washington (Table 11.1). More detailed physical descriptions of these lakes are provided in Chapter 1.

Here we evaluate the production and community structure of the four lakes in relation to terrestrial inputs of nutrients and carbon. The processes that control nutrient and organic matter cycling in soils and terrestrial vegetation of an ecosystem adjacent to a lake are addressed briefly to provide background. Subsequently, material pathways within the lakes are discussed. Findley Lake and Lake Sammamish are considered in terms of the behavior of primary nutrients and production of biological communities. The next section discusses the response of plankton metabolism and physiology to varying environmental conditions. Finally, the relations between forage base and fish production in Lake Washington are discussed.

Our research shows that the metabolic pathways and community structure of lakes in coniferous forests are influenced and, in certain cases, dominated by terrestrial inputs. Carbon budgets calculated for Findley Lake show that annual terrestrial inputs of particulate carbon in the lake causes the production of

333

TABLE 11.1 *Comparison of trophic status of four lakes in the Lake Washington drainage basin (average yearly rates, nutrient values as prebloom concentrations).*

Lake	PO_4-P ($\mu g/\ell$)	NO_3-N ($\mu g/\ell$)	Phytoplankton productivity ($mg\ C \cdot m^{-2} \cdot d^{-1}$)	ETS ($mg\ O_2 \cdot m^{-2} \cdot h^{-1}$)	Maximum growth rate (h^{-1})	K, (PO_4)	Zooplankton production (mg dry $wt \cdot m^{-2} \cdot d^{-1}$)	Zooplankton biomass (mg dry wt/m^2)
Findley	1.3	40.0	220	9	0.011	0.17	0.4	13.3
Chester Morse	2.1	107.0	262	13	0.007	0.36	0.5	12.5
Sammamish	14.7	467.0	499	62	0.008	0.42	0.9	22.5
Washington	16.3	290.0	1070	55	0.131	2.84	2.0	—

detritivorous insects equivalent to the production of herbivorous zooplankton. Interestingly, even in Lake Washington, a large lake recently rehabilitated by sewage diversion, benthic fish communities and detrital food chains are more productive than are limnetic communities and autotrophic food chains. A comparison of the annual production and respiration for aquatic environments in different biomes further supports our hypothesis that terrestrial organic production in coniferous forests is very important in determining the patterns of metabolism in adjacent aquatic ecosystems.

Our research has also shown that primary energetic processes of lakes can be better understood through the use of physiological stress or "metabolic" indicators. These indicators include production/respiration (P/R) and carbon/adenosine triphosphate (C/ATP) ratios, and estimates of nitrate reductase activity and $^{32}PO_4$ flux. In the lakes we studied, these indicators reflect such processes as microplankton production and nutrient cycling. Changes in these parameters were due to phosphorus stress, which resulted in increased maintenance costs and a decoupling of carbon and nutrient cycles in the phytoplankton. We believe that the use of these indicators can increase our ability to assess the response of lake ecosystems to various lake restorative practices and manipulations such as fertilization for enhancement of fish production.

ELEMENTAL CYCLES IN LAKES OF THE LAKE WASHINGTON DRAINAGE BASIN

Influence of Terrestrial Ecosystems on Elemental Inputs to Lakes

The major pathways through which terrestrially-derived materials enter lake systems are leaching, weathering, erosion, and litterfall. The type of forest ecosystem surrounding the lake strongly affects the chemical characteristics of these inputs. The discussion here focuses on inputs from leaching and weathering. Litterfall is discussed specifically in a later section. Erosion is dealt with more fully in Chapters 8 and 9.

Nutrient distribution and transfer in the mature Pacific silver fir ecosystem at Findley Lake and in younger Douglas-fir ecosystems at the Thompson site in the lower drainage have been determined by Turner and Singer (1976). Inputs and losses of these nutrients below the rooting zone are shown in Table 11.2. The old-growth Pacific silver fir at Findley Lake is more conservative of nutrients than the young-growth ecosystem at the Thompson site. Also, there is relatively little loss of nitrogen (N) and phosphorus (P) from either of these ecosystems, with annual inputs almost balancing outputs. Differences in inputs and outputs of N are probably balanced by biological fixation, while losses of the other elements were assumed to be made up by weathering.

TABLE 11.2   *Anual input (I) and losses (L) from the rooting zone (kg/ha)*
of N, P, K, Ca, and Mg at the Thompson site[a] and
Findley Lake.[b]

Site		N	P	K	Ca	Mg
Thompson site	I	1.4	0.3	2.3	2.2	0.5
	L	3.4	0.6	13.4	12.1	3.6
Findley Lake	I	1.3	0.4	0.8	0.6	1.7
	L	2.7	0.5	2.1	7.3	1.1

[a]Turner 1975.
[b]Turner and Singer 1976.

The mechanisms involved in cation leaching below the soil rooting zone were examined at Findley Lake and the Thompson site (Chapter 7). Bicarbonate is the major anion in soil solutions at the Thompson site, while at Findley Lake organic anions dominate. However, most of the cations that reach Findley Lake probably come from bedrock weathering rather than leaching from the upper soil horizons. This phenomenon is illustrated in Table 11.3. Concentrations of cations and bicarbonate ions in talus groundwater are higher than in streams and precipitation.

Predominance of bedrock weathering in upland sites is suggested by high calcium losses, typical at both Findley Lake (Turner and Singer 1976) and the Andrews Forest (Grier et al. 1974). These upland sites have similar bedrock and soils of andesite origin whereas the Thompson site is mainly granitic and metamorphic rock. Weathering of hornblende and plagioclase feldspars in the andesite appears to be the primary source of calcium in waters at Findley Lake. The principal weathering mechanisms in the Cascade Mountains are carbonation and oxidation. These processes are controlled mainly by supplies of water and hydrogen ions from the atmosphere (Reynolds and Johnson 1972).

In summary, weathering appears as the primary source of most inorganic elements for subalpine Findley Lake. Other important terrestrial influences on the lake include interflow of water, which is coupled to soil respiration and supplies dissolved inorganic carbon, and leaching, which supplies dissolved organics. The importance of dissolved elements, particulate matter from litterfall, and surface flow in the nutrient budgets of the lakes is discussed in a later section (Elemental Transfers Within Lakes).

Elemental Contents of Lakes

Weathering, leaching, and other nutrient inputs can vary according to the relative degree of forestation or urbanization of the shoreline. The four study lakes reflect these differences in their surface water and sediment chemistry. The order of abundance of the major cations in surface waters is similar in the

TABLE 11.3 *Chemical characteristics of different waters in the Findley Lake watershed. Concentrations represent average annual values (mg/liter) except for conductivity and alkalinity.*

Water from	pH	Conductivity (μmho/cm)	HCO_3-C	Alkalinity (meq/ℓ)	Kjel-N	NO_3-N	NH_4-N	Total P	Na	K	Ca	Mg
Precipitation	5.8	21.7	—	0.095	0.37	0.438	0.163	0.016	0.80	0.11	0.30	0.06
Inlet creeks	6.0	18.2	1.38	0.137	0.17	0.012	0.020	0.015	1.27	0.02	1.80	0.22
Forest groundwater	5.3	22.3	0.71	0.055	0.23	0.012	0.053	0.017	1.30	0.27	0.75	0.21
Talus groundwater	6.5	—	3.86	—	0.20	0.112	0.076	0.169	2.13	0.40	2.42	0.51
Lake outlet	6.4	20.3	1.40	0.170	0.09	0.012	0.006	0.004	1.28	0.10	2.50	0.27

upper drainage lakes, Findley and Chester Morse, where calcium (Ca) exceeds sodium (Na) exceeds magnesium (Mg) exceeds potassium (K) (Figure 11.1; Barnes 1976). It is slightly different in Lakes Washington and Lake Sammamish (Ca $\simeq$ Na > Mg > K). There is a general increase in nutrient levels from Findley Lake to the lower, more urbanized Lake Washington and Lake Sammamish (Table 11.1).

The Ca:Mg ratio decreases from 10:1 to 20:1 in the upper lakes to about 3:1 in lowland waters. This increase in Mg relative to Ca in the lower drainage lakes is due partly to the proximity of Puget Sound to these lakes. Sea-salt aerosols are enriched in Na and Mg relative to Ca. Based on elemental ratios in seawater, however, and assuming that most of the Na increase from about 1 mg/liter to about 8 mg/liter is due to sea-salt inputs, only 0.8 to 0.9 mg/liter of the observed 3.0 mg/liter increase in Mg can be accounted for. Accordingly, we assume that most of the observed increase in Mg and other cations from the upper lakes to the lowland lakes is due to increased lithospheric contact through weathering and groundwater inputs. Levels of copper (Cu) and lead (Pb) in all four lakes were similar despite the degree of urbanization in the lower drainage basin. Zinc (Zn) showed a pattern similar to Cu and Pb.

The pattern of higher elemental concentrations in the sediments from the high- to low-elevation lakes was similar to increases observed in the water column, though total concentrations were much higher than the ionic forms in water (Figure 11.2). In general, K, manganese (Mn), and heavy metals (Zn, Cu, Pb) increased from parts-per-billion levels in water to parts-per-million values in sediments. Other elements (Ca, Na, and Mg) showed increases of similar magnitude from parts per million to parts per thousand. The largest increase for an element in the sediments relative to the water was for iron (Fe). The high concentrations of major cations, Fe and Mn, in the Chester Morse sediments reflect the large amount of inorganic material carried into the lake during periods of high runoff and increased erosion from logging activity.

The higher levels of trace metals in the sediments of the large urban lakes may be indicative of anthropogenic enrichment. Further examination of Lake Washington sediment cores for mercury (Hg), Pb, Zn, Cu, chromium (Cr), arsenic (As), and antimony (Sb) showed substantial enrichment over pre-1916 levels (Barnes 1976). The level of Pb in cores appeared to be primarily a reflection of the quantity of automobile emissions (Figure 11.3); As and Sb in sediments can be attributed directly to the Tacoma smelter, which is located upwind from the lake (Crecelius 1974).

Analyses of total C, N, and P contents of surface sediments for the four lakes suggest the importance of terrestrial matter as an energy supplement (Table 11.4). Higher C contents and C:N ratios in sediments of Findley Lake and Chester Morse Lake, compared with those in the lower drainage lakes, were attributed to relative differences in allochthonous (exogenous) and autochthonous (endogenous) C inputs. In the upper drainage lakes, most of the organic C in sediments is derived from terrestrial vegetation (Birch 1976). This

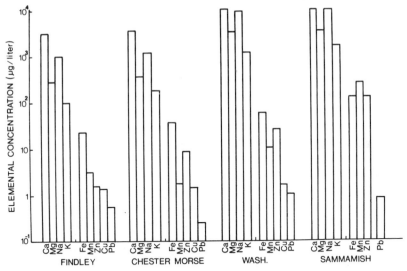

FIGURE 11.1 *Average elemental concentrations in surface waters of lakes in the Lake Washington drainage.*

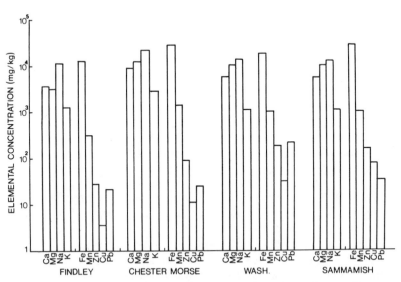

FIGURE 11.2 *Average elemental concentrations in surface sediments of lakes in the Lake Washington drainage (after Horton 1972 and R. S. Barnes pers. comm., 1976).*

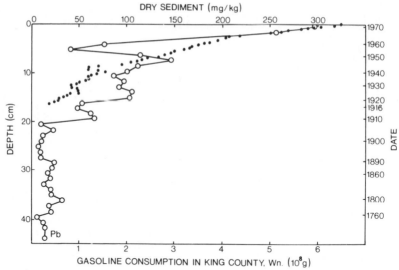

FIGURE 11.3 *Lead in Lake Washington cores (●) compared with gasoline consumption (○) (after Barnes 1976).*

TABLE 11.4 *Average C, N, and P contents of surface sediments from the Lake Washington drainage basin lakes.[a]*

Lake	C[b] (%)	N (mg/kg)	P (mg/kg)	C/N ratio	N/P ratio
Findley	11.50	5.55	1.09	16.18	5.14
Chester Morse	6.08	3.71	1.56	16.41	2.37
Sammamish	4.13	4.82	1.32	10.60	3.65
Washington	4.62	3.71	2.13	11.37	1.74

Note: Values are in terms of oven-dried (104°C) sediment.
[a]Bauer 1971; Horton 1972.
[b]The sediments from all four lakes contain less than 0.1 percent $CO_3^=$ - C on an oven-dried basis.

material is relatively resistant to mineralization, partly as a result of low N content. The phenomenon is also evident in streams (Chapters 9 and 10) and some rivers in coniferous forests (Malick 1977). The high C:N ratios in the sediments of all four lakes (>10) were similar to those in the sediments of English lakes (Dean and Gorham 1976), which also receive considerable amounts of terrestrial material. In the lake sediments in the lower Lake Washington drainage, however, the importance of autochthonous sources was reflected by the higher P content in the upper lake sediments. Total P concentrations for sediments in lakes suggest that P is mainly retained in the sediments in association with inorganic materials such as Fe (Figure 11.2).

ELEMENTAL TRANSFERS WITHIN LAKES

Although concentrations of nutrient elements in lake water and sediments are of interest as a reflection of inputs from the terrestrial environment, C and nutrient transfers within a lake are of greater importance in understanding total lake function. Construction of material budgets for a lake (Bormann and Likens 1967) has facilitated the examination of patterns of accumulation, distribution, and loss and development of insights into the relative importance of alternate material pathways.

We hypothesized that among the Lake Washington drainage basin lakes Findley Lake would be influenced most by terrestrial inputs because of its small size and heavily forested shoreline (Wissmar et al. 1977). In the follow-up sections this hypothesis is examined in some detail. Nutrient regimes have also been studied in Lake Washington and Lake Sammamish. Nutrient budgets of Lake Washington are not discussed in this chapter since its response to eutrophication and its subsequent recovery following sewage diversion have been documented elsewhere (Edmondson 1972, 1974, 1977). A brief description of nutrient budgets of Lake Sammamish is provided both as a contrast to Findley Lake and to examine the failure of a nutrient diversion in this lake to produce a change in trophic state similar to that of Lake Washington.

Findley Lake

The importance of terrestrial inputs to small lakes in the form of organic litter (Gasith and Hasler 1976; Rau 1976) and nutrient loading (Dillon 1975; Devol and Wissmar 1978) have been well documented. The benthic zones of these lakes serve as the principal receiving areas where decomposers and consumers process particulate allochthonous inputs (Wetzel and Rich 1973; Pieczynska 1975; Odum and Prentki 1978; Rich and Devol 1978; Wissmar and Wetzel 1978). Previous workers have linked fates of dissolved nutrients in lakes to hydrologic retention times and subsequent autotrophic production (Devol and Wissmar 1978; Johnson et al. 1978; Likens and Loucks 1978; Wetzel and Richey 1978). While there is a reasonable understanding of autotrophic C pathways in temperate lakes, little information is available on the role of detrital-C-based metabolism and mineral cycling in lakes that have high levels of terrestrial detritus inputs and rapid flushing rates. These conditions are characteristic of Findley Lake.

Research on the Findley Lake watershed was oriented toward determining the structure, productivity, and nutrient cycles of both terrestrial and aquatic ecosystems. It included specific studies of water column processes (Taub et al. 1972; Welch and Spyridakis 1972; Hendrey 1973; Stoll 1973; Bissonnette 1974; Hendrey and Welch 1974; Pederson 1974; Rau 1974, 1976, 1978; Johnson 1975; Pederson and Litt 1976; Pederson et al. 1976; Tison et al. 1977; Richey 1979; A. H. Devol, pers. comm.); sediments (Bauer 1971; Horton 1972; Lanich 1972; Adams 1973; Wekell 1975; Barnes 1976); soils (Singer and Ugolini 1974; Johnson 1975; Ugolini et al. 1977a,b); and vegetation (del Moral 1973; Turner and Singer 1976).

Much of the information from these studies has been synthesized by considering the hypothesis that the major supply of nutrients and C, including both dissolved and particulate matter, for Findley Lake originate in the adjacent forest. Detrital inputs and outputs were measured as particulate and dissolved organic carbon (DOC) and nutrients, inorganic nitrogen (NH_4-N and NO_3-N), and soluble reactive phosphorus (SRP). Lake ecosystem budgets for these inputs and outputs included the influences of internal cycling, phytoplankton uptake, and regeneration by zooplankton.

In 1974 and 1975, allochthonous inputs to Findley Lake supplied 85 percent of the particulate P, 65 percent of the particulate C, 51 to 66 percent of the SRP, and 83 to 89 percent of the dissolved inorganic N (DIN) to the water column (Figure 11.4). Dominant pathways for particulate loss were fluvial outflow and sedimentation. Phytoplankton nutrient requirements for P were supplied by fluvial sources early in the growing season and later by zooplankton excretion. Excess DIN was present throughout the growing season. Allochthonous supplies of DOC and P apparently were not utilized in the water column.

An important feature of the budgets was that sedimentation of allochthonous particulate carbon (~ 4 to 8 g $C \cdot m^{-2} \cdot yr^{-1}$) indicated a major supply of energy for benthic consumers. The subsequent distribution patterns of carbon and nutrients in the sediments as well as the magnitude of insect production reflected the influence of this terrestrial input on the benthic environment. A comparison of the average C, N, and P contents of the surface sediments for Findley Lake with the other lakes of the Lake Washington drainage basin illustrates the high levels of terrestrial matter in the Findley Lake sediments (Table 11.4). The response of the benthic consumers to allochthonous inputs was shown by the detritivorous insect production (0.65 g $C \cdot m^{-2} \cdot yr^{-1}$), which was similar to that of herbivorous zooplankton (0.50 g $C \cdot m^{-2} \cdot yr^{-1}$). A more detailed discussion of Figure 11.4 can be found in Richey and Wissmar (1979).

Additional studies of plankton and inorganic carbon in Findley Lake provided dramatic evidence of the influence of terrestrial environment on a lake. Although atmospheric CO_2 is the primary source for organic C production in both terrestrial and aquatic ecosystems, a large part of the dissolved inorganic carbon (DIC) used for phytoplankton production in Findley Lake has been previously reduced and then oxidized. This carbon flux was identified by the ^{13}C-depleted character of the water column DIC and plankton C ($\delta^{13}C$ of -44 to

−47 per mil). This ^{13}C depletion, coupled with the DIC pool, suggests that benthic metabolism and soil respiration provide important C sources for plankton production in Findley Lake and by analogy other mountain lakes in dense coniferous forests (Rau 1978).

Benthic Nitrogen Cycling

Anomalies in the nutrient budgets support the idea that elemental cycling within the benthic region is important. For example, seasonal N and P budgets did not fully account for observed losses of DIN in summer and fall and for SRP in winter and spring. Here we discuss these anomalies and offer several hypotheses to explain nutrient cycling in benthic environments of lakes such as Findley.

Levels of inorganic N in the water column begin to drop during the phytoplankton bloom and remain low through the fall (Hendrey and Welch 1974; Welch et al. 1975). Seasonal N budgets show that a significant storage, or an unknown sink, of lake N occurs in both summer and fall when total inorganic N levels in the lake are low. Phytoplankton uptake of N and subsequent loss through sedimentation appear to account for only a small portion of the N accumulation. The greatest N storage (October and November) occurs when fluvial and precipitation inputs of N to the lake increase. During this period, however, plankton production decreases and inorganic N concentrations of the water column remain low.

A possible explanation for N depletion during the latter half of the growing season may be uptake by benthic algae and N immobilization by the bacterial and fungal communities associated with allochthonous litter. Paerl (1973, 1975) has shown that microbial attachment to detrital particles occurs in Lake Tahoe and that active heterotrophic metabolism is associated with these particles. Kaushik and Hynes (1968) found that increased N content (primarily protein N) was associated with decomposition of elm leaves. These increases were related to microbial and fungal growth. Similar patterns for N increase have been observed in Oregon streams in decomposing conifer needles (Triska and Sedell 1976) and for P in decomposing leaves (Howarth and Fisher 1976).

Investigations of N accumulation by microflora on coniferous detritus in benthic regions of Findley Lake suggest that similar processes occur in this lake. Changes in N, C, ATP contents, and electron transport system (ETS) activity of decomposing detritus in the benthic environment were measured (R. C. Wissmar, pers. comm.). Results suggest that the microbial-detrital complexes immobilize N and that chemical binding (absorption and complexes) of N is also important. The importance of such binding by detrital residues has been suggested by Iverson (1973), Triska et al. (1975), F. J. Triska (pers. comm.), and Suberkropp et al. (1976).

Regression analyses of the above data from Findley Lake indicate that

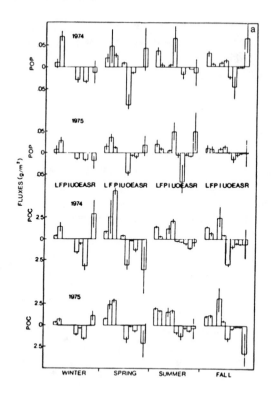

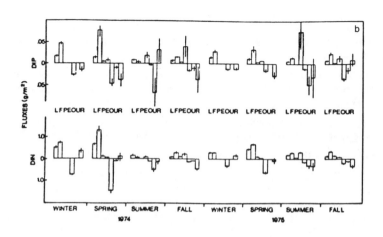

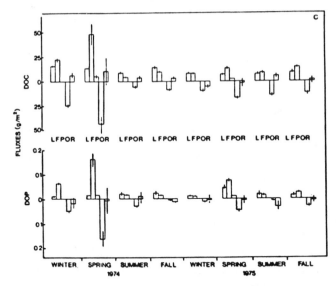

FIGURE 11.4 *Seasonal budgets (A, POC & POP; B, DIN & DIP; C, DOP & DOC) for Findley Lake, 1974–1975, with inputs above and outputs below the horizontal axis. Vertical bar indicates one σ. Key: A = allochthonous sedimentation; E = zooplankton regeneration (b), zooplankton regeneration from POP (a), and respiration from POC (a); F = fluvial inputs; L = lake concentration; O = outflow; P = snowpack plus rainfall precipitation; R = residual; S = autochthonous sedimentation; U = phytoplankton uptake.*

increases in ATP content and decreases in ETS activity of detrital microbes are significantly related to decreases in concentrations of NO_3-N and lake temperature. Microbiota associated with conifer material that has high initial C:N ratios are apparently N-limited. The organisms assimilate most of the available DIN from the surrounding water. The processes involved may be similar to those that occur in soils with high C:N ratios (Alexander 1961).

The initial accumulation of N by microflora on detritus tends to be accompanied by high C loss via mineralization. Subsequent to these primary stages of decomposition, the microbiota apparently die. The processes of autolysis and decomposition result in a release of inorganic N. Some portion of this regenerated inorganic N is assimilated by secondary microbial growth and the cycle is repeated. This process results in more C than N mineralization, thus lowering the C:N ratio of the decomposing detritus. The cycle continues, resulting in the mineralization and release into the sediments and overlying water of both C and N.

In addition to the N inputs already discussed, the other potential biological input of N to Findley Lake is N fixation; however this source is small. Nitrogen fixation (acetylene reduction) by phytoplankton was less than 1 percent of the total annual N income to the lake in 1972 (Tison et al. 1977).

Nitrogen losses other than through outflows and permanent sedimentation appear to be minimal. Denitrification is considered unlikely in these waters because of their well-oxygenated character (Goering and Dugdale 1966, A. H. Devol, pers. comm.).

The fate of N in the sediments of Findley Lake is complicated. The surface sediments have C:N ratios ranging from 12 to 19, suggesting that much of the sediment comes from outside the lake (Dean and Gorham 1976). The percentage of organic N (0.3 to 0.7 percent), E_h values of greater than $+0.200$ volts, low pH, and moisture content (60 to 90 percent) are similar to the values in a mountain lake in Virginia (Obeng-Asamoa 1976), which also receives high levels of allochthonous matter. Given these conditions, and from chemical studies by Obeng-Asamoa (1976), it can be postulated that slow rates of nitrification in surface sediments probably permit some NO_3^- to diffuse into overlying waters. Increased levels of NH_4^+ with depth in the sediment layers imply microbial activity that might be accompanied by decreases in organic N with depth. In addition, the importance of irrigation in deeper sediment layers by macroinvertebrates residing in surface sediments cannot be discounted and could influence the N cycling in the sediments (Bender et al. 1977; Grundmanis and Murray 1977; Vanderborght et al. 1977a, b).

Benthic Phosphorus Cycling

Attempts to balance water column SRP budgets in spring 1974 and winter and spring 1975 indicate that inputs exceeded losses, and suggest an unknown sink for SRP. Several possibilities might explain the result: (1) Bacterial or phytoplankton uptake and storage as polyphosphate seem unlikely, since plankton biomass and activity are extremely low at this time, and polyphosphate has not been detected in Findley Lake; (2) Dissolved inorganic P from streams enters the shallow, nearshore regions of the lake and is utilized by benthic algae and detrital microbes. Perkins (1976) demonstrated that periphyton in small streams could store phosphate as polyphosphate; (3) Some phosphate might be complexed with the iron-rich organic acids that constitute the dissolved organic pool.

During the large and sudden phytoplankton bloom in summer, inputs of SRP to the lake exceed outputs. This suggests that the phosphate required to support the bloom is not accounted for by the measured sources. There are several other possible phosphate sources. Planktonic extracellular products of DOP may be utilized through the enzyme alkaline phosphatase (Lean 1973; Richey 1977); however, Richey (1979) found only monophasic uptake kinetics of $^{32}PO_4$ and no indication of [^{32}P] DOP in Sephadex chromatography experiments, suggesting that this source is almost negligible in Findley Lake. A more likely source of phosphate is from sediment regeneration.

The role of sediments in P cycling pathways has often been considered minimal (Mortimer 1971; Schindler et al. 1973; Richey 1974). This has been justified on the grounds that the oxidized sediments act as a P sink, in the fashion outlined by Mortimer (1941, 1942). Others have stressed the role of sediments as a buffer for P concentrations in the overlying water (Stumm and Leckie 1971). Interstitial sediment P concentrations are much higher than in overlying waters. The forms of P in the sediments and rates of exchange between these pools have been the subject of extensive experimentation. For example, different fractionation techniques have been used in attempts to separate the P species, but the kinetic and equilibrium relations between them are complex and remain poorly understood (Chang and Jackson 1957; Williams et al. 1967; Stumm and Morgan 1970; Sommers et al. 1970, 1972; Williams et al. 1971a, b; Syers et al. 1973). In view of sediment P interchange with the overlying waters, sorption and desorption mechanisms are important and have received much study (for example, Carritt and Goodgal 1954; MacPherson et al. 1958; Golterman 1967; Harter 1968; Shukla et al. 1971). These mechanisms are pH-dependent, and involve solubility relations of phosphate with Fe^{3+}, Al^{3+}, and Ca^{2+} complexes. In undisturbed sediment/water interfaces, the rate-determining step is diffusion transport through the interstitial water (Stumm and Leckie 1971); however bacteria and especially macroinvertebrate irrigation of sediments may accelerate the release processes (Neame 1975).

The mobility of sediment P is dependent on its form. Adsorbed and free inorganic phosphate is more readily available for incorporation into nutrient cycles than P tightly bound in mineral phases. The physical and biological stirring phenomena previously discussed can make the interstitital dissolved P and the loosely adsorbed phosphate available to the entire system. The direction of net P movement across the interface depends on the size of the P pools in the system. Kamp-Nielsen (1974) found that P release from the sediments occurred when the concentration in the overlying water was < 30 μg/liter, and that the subsequent rate of release in an oligotrophic lake amounted to approximately 200 μg $P \cdot m^{-2} \cdot day^{-1}$. Neame (1975) found phosphate release rates of 650 μg $\cdot m^{-2} \cdot day^{-1}$ in Castle Lake, California (a lake similar to Findley Lake), in sediments having high porosity and containing large populations of benthic macroinvertebrates. Neame also suggested that the oxidized zone, normally thought to impede phosphate release from aerobic sediments, may be ineffective when these other conditions coincide. This confirmed the results of Williams and Meyer (1972). Thus it seems possible that phosphate release from the sediments could be a phosphate source for the overlying water column.

Further indirect evidence suggests that P release from the sediments may be occurring in Findley Lake. In the summer and fall growing season there is an increase in P in epilimnetic waters. Such conditions may be due to rapid decomposition of terrestrial detritus and subsequent liberation of phosphate in shallow nearshore sediments during warm weather. Death and autolysis of algal periphyton and heterotrophs may release soluble phosphate. Once released, phosphate may be taken up rapidly by benthic microflora and phytoplankton, precluding detection of changes in ambient phosphate concentrations. In fact, peak phytoplankton biomass and production occurred within several meters of the bottom. This was previously attributed to light inhibition (Hendrey 1973), but it may also be due to proximity to nutrients from the sediments. Rate constants of $^{32}PO_4$ uptake were also generally greater close to the sediments than higher in the water column (Richey 1979).

Summary of Elemental Processing in Findley Lake

The data and discussion presented above suggest a scenario explaining the nature of elemental processing in Findley Lake. A major energy source available to the ecosystem is terrestrial detritus. Most detritus enters the lake through fluvial inputs when the snowpack melts in the spring. Other sources are summer and autumn litter and fluvial inputs. The highest inputs of inorganic P and N are from spring fluvial sources. The availability of these inorganic nutrients may enhance the growth of littoral periphyton and of microbes on detritus. Nevertheless, most nutrients pass through the lake untouched because of the high flushing rate of the lake's volume (7.8 X/yr).

The sequestering of nutrients serves to enrich the nutritional value of detritus as a forage base for benthic detritivores. Benthic detrital deposits and within-sediment accumulation of organics and nutrients suggest the potential importance of nutrient regeneration to overlying waters and to heterotrophic and autotrophic growth on surface sediments. This explanation supports the hypothesis that terrestrial inputs to sediments, and the subsequent cycling of nutrients in the sediments, have a major influence on biological activity in both benthic and water-column environments during most of the growing season. These pathways may be particularly important in years of heavy snowpack followed by rapid melting, when increased flushing rates of nutrients reduce phytoplankton production.

Lake Sammamish

The nutrient regime in Lake Sammamish is very different from that in Findley Lake. The difference is due primarily to the slower flushing rate, the larger size of Lake Sammamish, and, to a lesser extent, to anthropogenic influences. Secondary effluent from a sewage treatment plant was diverted from Lake Sammamish in the mid 1960s, with a reduction in P loading from

$1.02 \text{ g} \cdot \text{m}^{-2} \cdot \text{yr}^{-1}$ to $0.67 \text{ g} \cdot \text{m}^{-2} \cdot \text{yr}^{-1}$. As yet no response in the trophic state of the lake has been observed (Welch 1977).

Lake Sammamish can be divided into distinct trophogenic (0 to 9 m) and tropholytic zones (9 to 24 m). Data from the trophogenic zone in the spring suggest that N and P recycling is fairly efficient, and that a depletion of dissolved N and P pools occurs (Figure 11.5; Birch 1976). This is the net result of a number of factors. Phytoplankton photosynthesis is fairly high during the spring diatom bloom. In early spring it is coupled with a rapid sinking rate, low solubilization rates, and relatively high sedimentation rates when the diatom bloom is at peak. In the tropholytic zone there is a decrease in concentration of particulate N, dissolved N, and particulate P, and an increase in dissolved P. The particulate P and N pools appear to be depleted, because of the combined effects of sedimentation and solubilization. Dissolved P increases due to the solubilization flux and a slight net gain from inflow. The dissolved N pool would probably increase during this period due to the same influences except for losses due to denitrification.

A somewhat different picture is presented during summer in the trophogenic zone (Figure 11.6). Solubilization is very efficient owing to the combined effect of high dissolution rates and slower sinking velocities. It appears that almost as much N and P is solubilized as is transformed into particulate form via photosynthesis. Since the sedimentation flux is rather small there is a slight increase in particulate N and P with a corresponding slight decrease in the dissolved pools. The decreases are much smaller than those observed during spring. It should be noted that there may be increases in dissolved P in the trophogenic zone in late summer as the thermocline erodes and hypolimnetic P is mixed into the epilimnion.

In the tropholytic zone, there are net increases in all the N and P pools. The measured increases in dissolved N and P can be attributed to measured fluxes to a greater extent than can increases in particulate N and P. Dissolved pools increase because of combined influxes from solubilization and sediment release. Since there is a net loss to the particulate pools due to sedimentation into the bottom sediments plus a further loss due to solubilization, the only way an increase in particulate N and P could occur is from fluxes from other pools. One possibility is heterotrophic utilization and subsequent biomass increase in particulate N and P. A second possibility is coprecipitation of P released from the sediments with Fe in contact with the more oxygenated upper hypolimnetic waters. Iron and P could also be precipitating on the surface of *Metallogenium* sp., a bacterium observed in hypolimnetic waters in late summer.

The external loading of P was reduced 30 percent after diversion. This loading of $0.62 \text{ g} \cdot \text{m}^{-2} \cdot \text{yr}^{-1}$ was about twice the internal loading from anoxic sediment release ($0.3 \text{ g} \cdot \text{m}^{-2} \cdot \text{yr}^{-1}$; Birch 1976). Horton (1972) and Rock (1974) have shown, however, that since sediment P release occurs during the stratified period, most of the released P is trapped in the hypolimnion and is not available for algal nutrition until fall overturn. At that time, about 80 percent of this P is

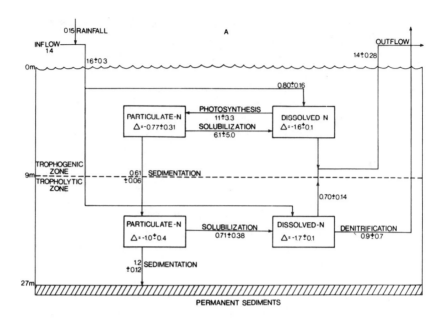

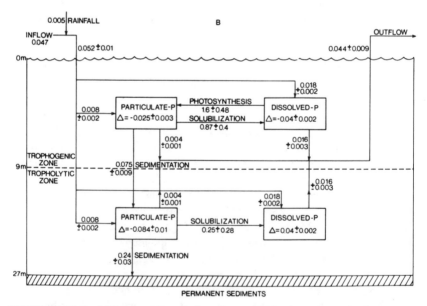

FIGURE 11.5 *Nitrogen (A) and phosphorus (B) budgets for Lake Sammamish, spring period (26 March 1975 to 21 June 1975; in grams per square meter).*

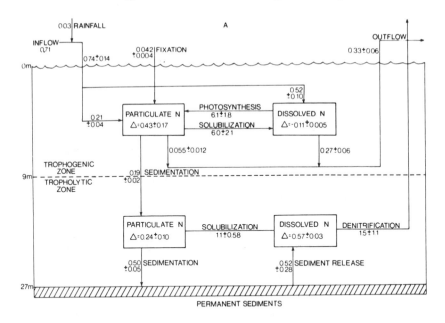

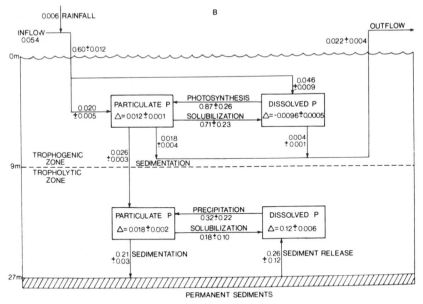

FIGURE 11.6 *Nitrogen (A) and phosphorus (B) budgets for Lake Sammamish, summer period (25 June 1974 to 1 October 1974; in grams per square meter).*

reprecipitated with Fe. Thus internal loading is of minor importance, and the lack of response is presumed due to rapid nutrient recycling during late spring and summer.

PHYTOPLANKTON PHYSIOLOGICAL RESPONSES TO CHANGING NUTRIENT REGIMES

In an attempt to further the understanding of nutrient cycling in lake ecosystems, phytoplankton were studied in some detail. Since phytoplankton metabolism is closely coupled to nutrient regimes in the water column, emphasis was placed on physiological responses of phytoplankton to varying environmental conditions.

Phytoplankton react to changes in their environment by modifications of their biochemical pathways, resulting in altered cell structure and physiology. In recent years investigators have attempted to relate changes in phytoplankton growth to physiological state through the use of biotic parameters (Sakshaug and Holm-Hansen 1977). These parameters are derived from studies of the chemical composition of phytoplankton under various types of limitations, primarily degrees of nutrient limitation. For example, it has been found that: (1) the *in vivo* fluorescence:chlorophyll-*a* ratio increases with increasing N and P limitation (Loftus and Seliger 1975); (2) the C:ATP ratio increases with increasing P deficiency (Cavari 1976; Perry 1976); and (3) the C:N and C:P ratios of phytoplankton increase under N and P limitation (Fuhs et al. 1972; Sakshaug and Holm-Hansen 1977). Other examples of relations between biotic parameters and physiological state can be found in Sakshaug and Holm-Hansen (1977) and Caperon and Meyer (1972).

The goal of such studies is to describe whether or not growth limitation is present in a given situation and, if so, to evaluate the limiting factor. The potential of this approach is indicated by the fact that in chemostat studies it has been possible to relate the chemical composition, or biotic parameters, directly to growth rate (Fuhs et al. 1972; Droop 1974; Perry 1976). At present, however, application of these investigations to field studies of aquatic ecosystems is difficult, because, in contrast to natural populations, nearly all previous studies are species-specific. Therefore they contain neither the detrital component of natural systems, which complicates the interpretation of C, N, and P measurements, nor the changing population structure characteristic of natural systems. In spite of these difficulties, it has been possible to relate biotic parameters to physiological state in some cases (Haug et al. 1973). Furthermore, as pointed out by Sakshaug and Holm-Hansen (1977), even though biotic parameters may have different ranges for field and laboratory populations, the direction of change in chemical composition is probably the same for corresponding alterations in growth conditions in both the field and in the laboratory.

Our research indicates that the biotic parameters, P:R, C:ATP, nitrate reductase activity:chlorophyll (NR:Chl), and $^{32}PO_4$ flux, undergo significant changes soon after the peak of the phytoplankton bloom. These parameters are presumed to be related to changes in the physiology of the phytoplankton community and are described as follows in relation to the chemical and physical environment in the lake.

The seasonal cycles of SRP, inorganic nitrate, temperature, carbon-14 productivity, and chlorophyll-*a* in Lake Washington during 1974 are shown in Figure 11.7. The data are presented on an areal basis integrated over the top 10 m. About 95 percent of the carbon-14 production takes place in that depth interval during all seasons (Devol and Packard 1978; Richey 1979). Furthermore, the 1975 seasonal cycle of these variables was similar to the 1974 cycle shown in Figure 11.7, with only minor changes in the timing of events and the absolute values of the parameters (Richey 1979). Lake Washington is typical of monomictic, temperate lakes with maximum nutrient concentrations and mini-

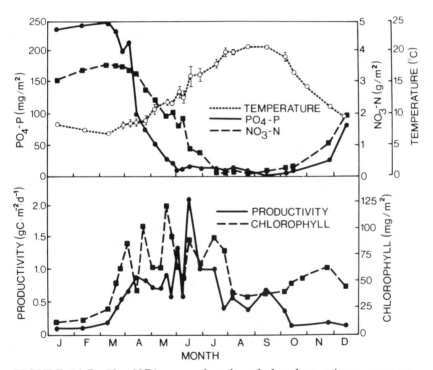

FIGURE 11.7 *The 1974 seasonal cycles of phosphate, nitrate, temperature, productivity, and chlorophyll-*a *in Lake Washington. All data have been integrated over the upper 10 m except temperature, for which the average and range in the upper 10 m are given (after Devol and Packard 1978).*

mum temperatures during the winter isothermal period. In 1974, surface water temperatures increased in early March, which coincided with the onset of the spring bloom as measured by productivity and chlorophyll. Nitrate and phosphate levels began to decrease as a result of biological activity. Nutrient stocks became depleted and increased temperatures resulted in thermal stratification. Low phosphate levels (10 mg/m^2) were reached in early June while low nitrate levels did not occur until mid-July. Maximum phytoplankton production occurred in mid-June and continued at reduced levels through early October. High levels of phytoplankton production and chlorophyll coincided with the period of maximum thermal stratification (deep convective overturn began in November).

The Photosynthesis:Respiration (P:R) Ratio

Steele (1965) has suggested that the P:R ratio is "the main single measure we can obtain of the physiological state of the [phytoplankton] populations." Despite its potential importance, the P:R ratio has not been well investigated. Reported values range from < 1 to 60 and vary with growth phase (Humphrey and Subba Rao 1967), depth in the water column (Yentsch 1975), light (Bunt 1965), nutrient concentration (McAllister et al. 1964), and temperature (Bunt 1965). Only a few studies of seasonal variation in the P:R ratio have been made.

Measurements of ETS activity were used in conjunction with the carbon-14 productivity data presented in Figure 11.8 to calculate two types of P:R ratios for the euphotic zone of Lake Washington (Devol and Packard 1978). The curve labeled $(P:R)_m$ in Figure 11.8 was calculated from hourly data taken at the depth of the maximum assimilation ratio (carbon-14 uptake/Chl), whereas the curve labeled $(P:R)_e$ was calculated from daily data integrated over the depth of the euphotic zone. The P:R ratio is essentially the ratio of net C production during the day to C respired at night. The values of $(P:R)_m$ range from 46 to 2.2 and are within the range reported in the literature (see Devol and Packard 1978). When calculated on a percentage basis, $(P:R)_e$ values indicate that a range of 7 to 142 percent of carbon-14 production is consumed by respiration at night.

Both $(P:R)_m$ and $(P:R)_e$ were high early in the growing season and decreased to lowest values during the thermally-stratified, low-nutrient summer period (Figure 11.8). Devol and Packard (1978) have suggested that this trend is due to increased P limitation as the summer progressed, increased respiration as the lake warmed, or a combination of both factors. Increased temperatures, however, should also result in increased production if other factors are not limiting (Eppley 1972; Goldman and Carpenter 1974). Production:respiration ratios were also calculated for Findley Lake (Figure 11.9) and for Lake Sammamish (not shown). The same trend of decreasing P:R ratios through the growing season was observed also in these lakes.

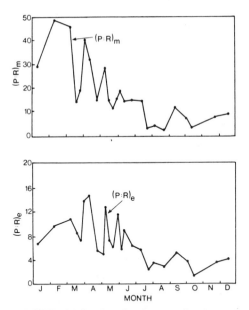

FIGURE 11.8 *Production:respiration ratios for the upper 10 m of Lake Washington during 1974. A detailed description is given in the text (after Devol and Packard 1978).*

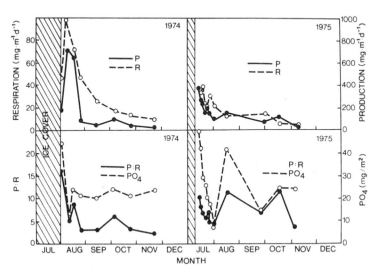

FIGURE 11.9 *Production, respiration, phosphate, and P:R ratio in Findley Lake during 1974 (left) and 1975 (right) growing seasons. All data have been integrated over the entire 25-m euphotic zone.*

Our interpretation of pooled data from Lake Washington and Lake Sammamish taken during the latter half of the spring bloom and the summer stratification period lends support to the proposed mechanism of nutrient stress. Figure 11.10 suggests that production decreases with decreasing concentrations of PO_4, and that chlorophyll-specific respiration increases with increasing temperature. In Findley Lake much of the water column productivity occurs below the thermocline (Wissmar et al. 1977). Thus fluctuations in the P:R ratio as a function of temperature can be eliminated. A regression analysis of data presented in Figure 11.10 indicates that in this region of the water column 81 percent of variation in the P:R ratio can be attributed to ambient phosphate concentration (that is, $r^2 = 0.81$).

The Carbon:Adenosine Triphosphate (C:ATP) Ratio

It is assumed generally that in viable cells ATP occurs in a constant ratio to C (C:ATP = 250:1). When C:ATP ratios were calculated for Lake Washington phytoplankton populations from algal cell volume C (using the method of Strathman 1967) and microplankton ($<75 \ \mu$m) ATP data, however, ratios as

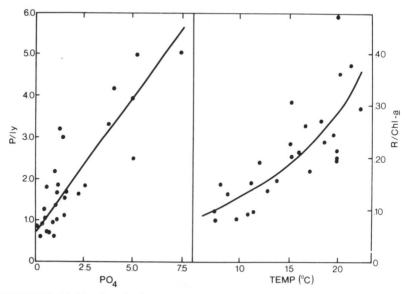

FIGURE 11.10 *Production per langley (P/ly) vs. average euphotic zone phosphate concentration (μg/liter) and respiration per unit chlorophyll-a (R/Chl-a) versus average euphotic zone temperature for plankton from lakes Washington and Sammamish. Data were collected from the latter half of the bloom and during the summer stratification. Values given for P/ly and R/Chl-a have been integrated over the depth of the euphotic zone.*

large as 750 to 1000 (Figure 11.11) were observed. There are two possible explanations for these high ratios: (1) there may have been a significant bacterial contribution to microplankton ATP; and (2) the C:ATP ratio may not have been constant. Although bacterial ATP certainly was present in all our microplankton samples, it is doubtful if it could have accounted for the observed ratios. Bacterial biomass would have had to be three times algal biomass to account for a C:ATP ratio of 1000. Estimates of bacterial biomass by the direct count and the Acridine Orange epifluorescence methods (Daly and Hobbie 1975) showed that bacterial biomass was far too low to explain the observed change.

Variations in C:ATP ratios as great as those we observed have also been reported by Holm-Hansen (1970) and Holm-Hansen and Paerl (1972). Their data indicate that cellular ATP levels decrease during periods of severe nutrient limitation to as little as 16 percent, and more commonly 30 percent, of levels found in healthy cells. This is equivalent to an increase in the C:ATP ratio from 250 to 750. Commensurate with these changes, they found changes in the

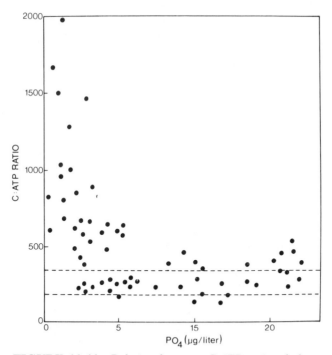

FIGURE 11.11   *Relation between C:ATP ratio of phytoplankton and concentration of inorganic PO_4-P in Lake Washington. The C:ATP ratios have been integrated over the top 10 m and PO_4-P values are averages for the same depth interval. Dashed lines indicate 30 percent confidence levels around C:ATP = 250.*

cellular C:P ratio from about 50 (w/w) for healthy cells to about 250:1 for nutrient-starved cells. The authors questioned, however, whether nutrient starvation to this extent exists in nature. Other workers have also reported high C:ATP ratios (Cavari 1976; Perry 1976; Sakshaug and Holm-Hansen 1977). These high ratios are usually attributed to nutrient limitation.

Our data for natural microplankton communities indicate that C:ATP ratios do increase with diminishing phosphate concentration (Figure 11.11), although the entire range of C:ATP ratios was observed at very low phosphate concentrations. High C:ATP ratios coincided in time with lower P:R ratios. There are several factors, both real and artificial, that could cause this shift. First, microscopic phytoplankton enumeration may include a significant number of dead algal cells; however a ratio of 1000 would require that 75 percent of the counted cells be dead. This would lead to unrealistically high assimilation rates and to phytoplankton turnover rates (production/biomass) on the order of 5/day during the summer low-nutrient period, which was not seen. Second, as cells become nutrient-limited, organic matter synthesis may shift from compounds used for active growth to storage compounds such as carbohydrates (Haug et al. 1973). Then as carbohydrates accumulate in the cell, the C:ATP ratio may increase (Fuhs et al. 1972; Khul 1974). Finally, increases in the C:ATP ratio may result from a shift in the biochemical equilibrium of the adenylate system.

Nitrate Reductase (NR) Activity

A preliminary survey of NR activity (as measured by the method of Eppley et al. 1969) was conducted on Lake Washington plankton (Figure 11.12). Although data are few, NR activity increased through the first half of the spring bloom and then decreased abruptly. When normalized to chlorophyll, NR activity remained relatively constant during the spring and then decreased to nearly zero by mid-June. The data in Figure 11.12 also show the amount of N required to support the observed carbon-14 primary production (assuming a C:N uptake ratio of 106:16, by atoms). Nitrogen requirements in February and March are almost the same as during the summer stratification, but the chlorophyll-specific NR activity is dramatically different. Although there are several potential explanations for the data (Packard et al. 1971), it is noteworthy that the decrease in NR activity takes place in the same time during which the P:R and C:ATP ratios change.

[^{32}P]Phosphate Flux

Phosphorus is the major inorganic nutrient limiting phytoplankton production in both Lake Washington and Lake Findley (Edmondson 1972; Hendrey

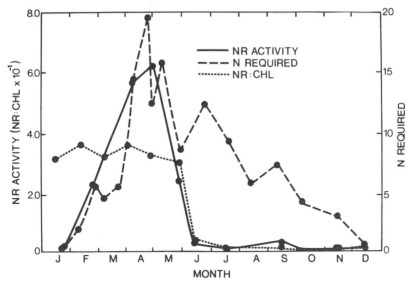

FIGURE 11.12 *Nitrate reductase activity (mmol NO₃ reduced·m⁻²·h⁻¹) and NR:chl (mmol NO₃ reduced ·mg chl⁻¹·h⁻¹) as a function of season in Lake Washington. Also shown is the amount of N (mmol/m²) required to support the observed Carbon-14 productivity as calculated from stoichiometric ratios. All data have been integrated over the depth of the euphotic zone.*

1973). Its availability appears to affect P:R and C:ATP ratios. Phosphorus dynamics were investigated in detail, using $^{32}PO_4$ tracer, organic partitioning, and nutrient addition techniques (Richey et al. 1975; Richey 1977; Richey 1979).

Phosphorus-uptake rate constants measured using $^{32}PO_4$ were compared with the theoretical rate constants required to support photosynthesis, as calculated from carbon-14 uptake and stoichiometric ratios (Richey 1979). Observed and expected rate constants matched well from overturn (November) through the peak of the spring bloom in Lake Washington (Figure 11.13). Thereafter, observed rate constants exceeded those calculated from photosynthetic demand. Through the summer the difference between observed and expected rate constants increased by up to two orders of magnitude. In Findley Lake, the measured constants were always greater than those calculated from production. Possible explanations for the consistent divergence between observed and expected rate constants include: (1) the molybdate blue method for measuring available PO_4 provided a vast overestimate at low concentration; (2) bacterial uptake of PO_4 provided the difference; and (3) the ratio of C:P uptake decreased. Although (1) and (2) undoubtedly explain some of the variance, changes in the C:P uptake are probably of greater importance (Richey 1979). Sakshaug and Holm-Hansen (1977) determined that cellular C:P ratios in-

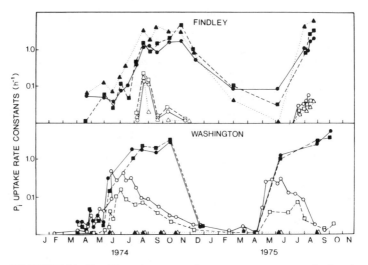

FIGURE 11.13 *Phosphorus uptake rate constants as calculated from ^{32}P uptake (solid points) and carbon-14 uptake (open points) as averages over the following depth intervals: Findley Lake 0 to 10 m (○), 10 to 20 m (□), and 20 to 25 m (△); Lake Washington 0 to 5 m (○), 5 to 10 m (□), and 10 to 58 m (△) (after Richey 1979).*

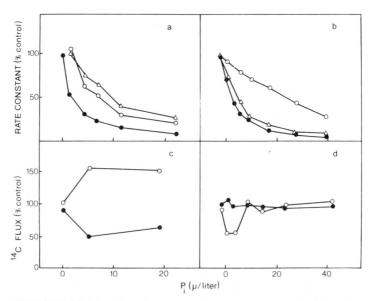

FIGURE 11.14 *Phosphorus uptake rate constants (a, May; b, August) and carbon-14 flux (c, May; d, August) as a function of phosphate addition. In (a) and (b) are shown k_{con} (●), k_i (○), and k_f (△). In (c) and (d) are shown carbon-14 incorporation (○) and extracellular release (●).*

360

creased by about a factor of 10 in phosphorous-deficient cultures of both *Skeleteonema* sp. and *Pavlovia* sp. Similar results have been presented by Fuhs et al. (1972) and others. Such changes in the C:P uptake ratio would drastically alter the P-uptake rate constants calculated from carbon-14-uptake rates.

Short-term bioassay experiments were conducted on Lake Washington plankton to consider the effect of PO_4 addition on P-uptake kinetics and carbon-14 flux. Results from two experiments conducted in May 1975, soon after the bloom peak, and in August 1975, during the thermally stratified, low-nutrient period, are shown in Figure 11.14. If added P does not result in increased uptake velocity, such as would occur under nutrient-sufficient conditions, then the rate constants calculated from concentrations, k_{con}, would decrease proportionately: for example, if phosphate concentration were doubled over a control, k_{con} would be 50 percent of the control. For both experiments the initial rate constants, k_i, measured immediately after P addition, increased over k_{con} by the amount predicted from the respective k_s (half saturation constant) values (Richey 1979). The final rate constant, k_f, however, remained comparable to k_i in the May experiment, but decreased to k_{con} values in the August experiment.

Patterns of carbon-14 flux also differed between the two experiments. In the May experiment incorporation was increased by 50 percent over the control after thirty hours, while extracellular release decreased by 50 percent. In August there was no response to additions with the exception of two low values for incorporation at low addition levels. These results suggest that PO_4 added in May was indeed incorporated by plankton and resulted in increased primary production, whereas in August added PO_4 was initially taken up, but could not be incorporated, and was released.

Physiological Responses: Explanations for Change

We attribute the changes observed in the biotic parameters of the lakes in the Lake Washington drainage to altered algal physiology, primarily as a response to P stress. Thus knowledge of the values of these biotic parameters and their direction of change through time could be a useful indicator of the physiological state of natural plankton populations. Possible explanations for the observed changes in these biotic parameters follow.

Production:respiration.   Decreases in the P:R ratio are the result of a decrease in production , and/or an increase in respiration per unit biomass. It is well known that phosphorus limitation decreases algal specific growth rates and therefore, presumably, carbon-14 production. On the other hand, dark respiration is required to supply energy for cell maintenance and thus, on a per-unit-biomass basis, may not decrease or increase from one production period to another. An additional or alternate explanation of decreasing P:R ratios during summer stratification is that increasing temperatures result in increased respiration rates.

Carbon:adenosine triphosphate.   The increase in the C:ATP ratio may be due to a relative increase in the synthesis of energy storage compounds during periods of P stress. This results in increased C:P and C:N ratios. An alternative explanation is that increased C:ATP ratios may be the result of a decrease in the adenylate energy charge. If the latter explanation is true the total cell adenylate concentration (A_t) would be a better estimator of viable C than ATP (that is, $C:A_t$ = constant).

Carbon:phosphorus.   The divergence between observed and expected P-uptake rate constants can be related to P stress through changes in the C:P uptake ratio. Increases in the C:P uptake ratio under P deficiency would directly decrease the rate constant calculated from carbon-14 uptake; however, it has been found that nutrient uptake and algal growth are not necessarily coupled over short time scales (Dugdale 1976). Thus the high rate constants estimated from ^{32}P during the summer stagnation may represent exchange between external PO_4 and an internal P pool (Taft et al. 1975). Since it has been proposed that the number of P uptake sites per cell increases under P stress (that is, V_{max} increases; Perry 1976), this type of exchange would inflate the values of rate constants estimated from ^{32}P-uptake experiments done during the summer stratification.

Nitrate reductase.   Sufficient data are not available to make any strong statements on the changes in NR activity. The decrease may be due to: (1) changes in the C:N ratio commensurate with changes in the C:P ratio caused by P stress; (2) changes in the biochemical pathways of NO_3 assimilation; or (3) shifts to other sources of N such as NH_3, NO_2, or nitrification.

DETERMINANTS OF CONSUMER COMMUNITY STRUCTURE AND PRODUCTION IN LAKE WASHINGTON

An understanding of lake ecosystems is far from complete without consideration of the trophic dynamics of higher consumers. The major objective of our fisheries research was to provide insight into the response of consumers to changes in lake trophic state and to identify specific determinants of fish community structure (Eggers et al. 1978). Our discussion focuses on consumer dynamics in the Lake Washington ecosystem from the dual perspective of total fish community production and the respective contributions of the fish forage bases, namely zooplankton, mysids, benthos, and fish. Lake Washington is well suited for this investigation because of its unique perturbation history of eutrophication and subsequent recovery (Edmondson 1972).

Twenty-nine species of fish are found in Lake Washington (R. S. Wydoski pers. comm.); twelve are resident species: prickly sculpin *(Cottus asper),* juvenile sockeye salmon *(Oncorhynchus nerka),* peamouth *(Mylocheilus caurinus),* northern squawfish *(Ptychocheilus oregonensis),* yellow perch *(Perca flavescens),* longfin smelt *(Spirinchus thaleichthys),* threespine stickleback *(Gasterosteus aculeatus)*, largescale sucker *(Catostomus macro-cheilus)*, brown bullhead *(Ictalurus nebulosus)*, black crappie *(Pomoxis ni-gromaculatus)*, largemouth bass *(Micropterus salmoides)*, and carp *(Cyprinus carpio)*. The first seven species mentioned are the most common and their annual production and diet are discussed below. The last four are restricted to weedy bays and undeveloped shoreline areas that constitute only a small portion of the total fish habitat of Lake Washington because of urbanization and shoreline development (Hockett 1975). Data sources for limnetic fish populations were Dryfoos (1965), Woodey (1971), Dawson (1972), Traynor (1973), Doble (1974), and Moulton (1974); and for benthic-littoral fish were Bartoo (1972), Nishimoto (1973), Olney (1975), Nelson (1977), and N. A. Rickard (pers. comm.).

Fish Production and Forage Bases

Annual fish production and dietary components were estimated to relate the Lake Washington fish community to the trophic dynamics of the lake. Annual patterns of abundance, growth, and diet for each major fish species and its respective age class were determined. Mean annual biomass and production of the limnetic species were computed for the period 1 January 1972 through 31 December 1972. The estimates included the growth of 1970 and 1971 year classes of juvenile sockeye salmon; 1971 and 1972 year classes of threespine stickleback; and 1970, 1971, and 1972 year classes of longfin smelt. Data on abundance, growth, and diet of the benthic-littoral fish species were collected from 1972 through 1975. Monthly and seasonal population abundances were essentially point estimates. Such data are considered acceptable for annual estimates since most benthic species are long-lived and show no extensive variation in year class strength. Annual production (kilograms wet weight per year) and mean annual biomass (kilograms wet weight) for each species are shown in Table 11.5. Most of the production and biomass of fish in Lake

TABLE 11.5 *Annual production and mean annual biomass of Lake Washington fishes.*[a]

Species	Annual production (kg wet wt/yr)	Percent of total production	Mean annual biomass (kg wet wt)	Percent of total biomass	Turnover rate P/B
Prickly sculpin	9.39×10^5	88.1	6.65×10^5	74.9	1.41
Juvenile sockeye salmon	4.88×10^4	4.6	4.07×10^4	4.6	1.19
Peamouth	2.65×10^4	2.5	1.98×10^4	2.2	1.34
Longfin smelt	2.68×10^4	2.5	3.07×10^4	3.5	0.87
Northern squawfish	1.55×10^4	1.3	1.16×10^5	13.1	0.13
Yellow perch	5.51×10^3	0.5	1.14×10^4	1.3	0.48
Threespine stickleback	3.42×10^3	0.3	4.53×10^3	0.5	0.75

[a]Eggers et al. 1978.

Washington is made up of prickly sculpin.

Since a tremendous number of prey items are available to Lake Washington fishes, a simple grouping system was used to describe carbon flow through both the water column and benthic communities. The prey items in the diet were grouped as zooplankton, benthos, mysids, and fish. The relative contribution of each prey group to limnetic and benthic fish production is presented in Table 11.6. Of the prey groups, benthos was the most important contributor to fish production (74.3 percent), while fish was the least important (6.4 percent).

Limnetic and Benthic Food Chains and Predator-Prey Interactions

A carbon budget was constructed to examine relations between fish and forage organisms in the Lake Washington ecosystem (Table 11.7). Details of the budget may be found in Eggers et al. (1978). The most significant feature of this budget, and of the production estimates in Tables 11.5 and 11.6, is that fish community production appears to be dominated by benthic-feeding fish. Interestingly, the magnitudes of benthos and zooplankton production are comparable. This implies that either zooplankton are not fully exploited as a food resource, or that the benthic forage production is large because an ample energy supply necessary for benthos probably exists in detritus from autochthonous and terrestrial sources. Apparently, decreases in phytoplankton primary production due to sewage (nutrient) diversion did not significantly reduce primary forage bases for consumer organisms. Also phytoplankton production may have been offset by established detrital food chains that have ample supplies of organic matter from littoral plants (periphyton and macrophytes) and terrestrial inputs. Such characteristics suggest that prey resources are not limiting the fish populations and therefore any response in fish production to eutrophication and recovery periods in Lake Washington was dampened.

The most evident change in forage-base organism availability in Lake Washington after recovery from eutrophication has been an increased abundance in *Daphnia* and a concurrent decline in *Neomysis*. Otherwise there has been no overall consistent change in abundance and species composition of the limnetic zooplankton community (copepods and cladocerans) during the post-eutrophication period (Edmondson 1972). The most probable reason for the increase in *Daphnia* is the decline in abundance of its primary predator, *Neomysis*. Evidently the nocturnal *Neomysis* population increased its residence time in the more aphotic benthic environment. This behavioral change is probably a response to the expanded photic zone caused by diversion of sewage in 1966 and subsequent lower algal densities. As a consequence the *Neomysis* population now confines its vertical migratory pattern to deep waters where it experiences large predatory losses to benthic fish. As shown in Table 11.6 *Neomysis* constitutes the major forage base of benthic sculpins.

TABLE 11.6 *Annual fish production and biomass and estimates of fish production attributable to specific forage items. Numbers in parentheses are percentage total production.[a]*

| Fish feeding groups | Representative fish | Fish biomass (kg wet wt) | Fish production (kg wet wt/yr) | Fish production due to forage items | | | |
				Zooplankton	Benthos	Mysids	Fish
Obligate planktivores	Sockeye Stickleback	45,200	52,200	47,640 (91.3)	4,110 (7.9)	450 (0.9)	0 (0)
Facultative planktivores	Smelt	30,680	26,800	9,740 (36.3)	4,200 (15.7)	12,530 (46.8)	3.30 (1.2)
Facultative benthic	Sculpin	19,610	24,460	12,000 (40.0)	11,890 (48.6)	580 (2.4)	0 (0)
Obligate benthic	Peamouth Sculpin	671,980	942,100	0 (0)	768,600 (81.5)	120,700 (13.0)	53,200 (5.5)
Facultative piscivores	Yellow perch Squawfish	127,700	19,420	0 (0)	2,790 (14.4)	2,060 (10.5)	14,570 (75.0)
Total		895,170	1,158,780	69,380 (6.5)	791,590 (74.3)	136,320 (12.8)	68,100 (6.4)

[a]Modified after Eggers et al. 1978.

TABLE 11.7 *Particulate organic carbon budget for Lake Washington (all values are given in* $g \cdot cm^{-2} \cdot yr^{-1}$)[a]

	Water column		Benthic-littoral	
	Value	Source	Value	Source
INPUTS				
Allochthonous			**INPUTS**	
Fluvial	20.0	1	*Water column*	
Precipitation	ND		Sedimentation	53.0	3
Litter	ND			
Autochthonous			*Autochthonous*	
Phytoplankton production	157.0	2	Periphyton	ND	—
			Macrophytes	ND	—
Total inputs	177.0		*Total inputs*	53.0	
LOSSES			**LOSSES**	
Outflow	0.5	1	Benthic respiration	52.0	8
Sedimentation	53.0	3	Fish respiration	3.4	6
Microplankton respiration	75.0	4	Burial	35.0	9
Zooplankton respiration	48.0	5	Emergence	ND	—
Neomysis respiration	ND (2.4)	7	Macrophyte and periphyton respiration	ND	—
Planktivorous fish respiration	0.73	6		
Piscivorous fish respiration	0.03	6		
Total losses	187.26		*Total losses*	104.9	

366

INTERNAL TRANSFORMATIONS

Ingestion

Material ingested by zooplankton	97.0	5
Material ingested by *Neomysis*	ND (4.70)	7
Zooplankton ingested by fish	0.33	6
Neomysis ingested by fish	0.94	6
Fish ingested by fish	0.4	6

Production

Microbial	ND	—
Zooplankton	19.0	5
Neomysis	ND (0.94)	7
Fish production supported by zooplankton	0.10	6
Fish production supported by *Neomysis*	0.19	6
Fish production supported by fish	0.01	6

INTERNAL TRANSFORMATIONS

Ingestion

Material ingested by macroinvertebrates	113.0	10
Macroinvertebrates ingested by fish	5.6	6
Fish ingested by fish	0.5	6

Production

Microbial	ND	—
Macroinvertebrates	16.9	0
Fish production supported by macroinvertebrates	1.1	6
Fish production supported by fish	0.1	6

*Eggers et al. 1978, sources defined therein.

367

As suggested above, this lack of response of fish communities in composition, abundance, and growth conditions is likely due to the buffering capacity of the tremendously diverse and productive forage bases, especially the benthic-detrital forage base. In addition, predatory/prey interactions and conditions in spawning environments have tended to regulate the various fish populations. Bryant (1976) observed that, at low planktivore abundance (primarily juvenile sockeye salmon), predaceous squawfish were predominantly benthic feeders, whereas at high planktivore abundance they consumed mainly planktivores. During the study period, however, planktivores never reached densities that would have satiated the squawfish population. Thus depensatory mortality due to squawfish predation probably prevents planktivore abundance from reaching levels that would in turn deplete zooplankton populations.

The balance of population size among the squawfish, planktivores, and zooplankton was interpreted as the result of complex feeding behavior patterns displayed by the planktivores (Eggers 1976). The planktivores engage in schooling behavior, which has the dual effect of minimizing vulnerability to squawfish predation, and of reducing its foraging efficiency for zooplankton. Predator avoidance by planktivores is also accomplished by a reduction in forage time, which also results in a limitation in feeding efficiency (Eggers 1978).

Piscivorous predation had an impact on benthic-littoral fishes in Lake Washington. Mature benthic-littoral fishes exploited prey items much larger than zooplankton; consequently, these predators were found to have larger body sizes than planktivores. This factor reduced their own losses to piscivorous predation. Larval and juvenile benthic-littoral fishes were extremely vulnerable to three predators: Northern squawfish, yellow perch, and prickly sculpin.

The influence of spawning environment on fish abundance was implied for both sockeye and stickleback populations. Sockeye abundance was related inversely to winter flow conditions in the Cedar River. Stickleback abundance appeared to be related to the improvement of spawning conditions in littoral areas that followed sewage diversion. The other principal fish species were affected only minimally by changes in spawning habitat due to consistently favorable benthic-littoral conditions.

In summary, detritus-based fish production in Lake Washington was much greater than grazer-based fish production. This observation implies that the benthic fish communities and detrital food chains are extremely important in Lake Washington. Community structure was influenced by the fact that limnetic-feeding fish populations were more vulnerable to control by piscivorous predators than were benthic-littoral-feeding fish populations. During the posteutrophication period, mysids became an increasingly important source of fish forage; hence declining mysid predation on zooplankton may have contributed to the recent increase in *Daphnia* populations in the Lake Washington zooplankton community. Given the above observations, the response of the fish community to trophic change in Lake Washington has been slight because of the tremendously diverse and productive forage base.

COMPARISON OF AQUATIC ECOSYSTEMS IN DIFFERENT BIOMES

Knowledge of ecosystem behavior can be enhanced by comparing ecosystems in different biomes. The following comparison considers nine aquatic ecosystems and their associated terrestrial ecosystems in North America. These ecosystems can be considered as representative of four biomes: the western coniferous forest; eastern deciduous and mixed hardwood/coniferous forest; prairie or grassland; and tundra. For terrestrial ecosystems the data source is Chapter 5, and for aquatic ecosystems, the following: the watershed 10 stream, Oregon (Chapter 10), Findley Lake (Wissmar et al. 1977; Richey and Wissmar 1979), Lake Washington (Eggers et al. 1978), Marion Lake, British Columbia, Canada (Hargrave 1969), tundra ponds, Alaska (Hobbie 1972; Stanley 1972), Char Lake, Northwest Territories, Canada (Kalff and Welch 1974; Welch and Kalff 1974), Lawrence Lake, Michigan (Wetzel et al. 1972; Wetzel 1975), Lake Wingra, Wisconsin (Gasith 1974), and Mirror Lake, New Hampshire (Jordan and Likens 1975). Comparisons of Findley, Marion, Lawrence, Wingra, and Mirror lakes are given in Devol and Wissmar (1978), Odum and Prentki (1978), Rich and Devol (1978), and Wetzel and Richey (1978).

These ecosystems are compared on the basis of gross and net production. Terms for terrestrial ecosystems are defined as

$$NPP = GPP - R_A$$
$$NEP = GPP - R_E \quad \text{(where GPP = GEP)}$$
$$R_E = R_A + R_H$$

where GPP = gross primary production, NPP = net primary production, GEP = gross ecosystem production, NEP = net ecosystem production, R_E = ecosystem respiration, R_A = autotrophic respiration, and R_H = heterotrophic respiration. See Chapter 5 for further explanation.

The terminology for aquatic ecosystems is similar except that in aquatic systems GEP includes GPP plus carbon inputs from terrestrial environments. An understanding of these energetics is an integral part of assessing the productive potential of both aquatic and terrestrial ecosystems. The following discussion emphasizes ecosystem energy flux as the flow of organic C (g C·m^{-2}·yr^{-1}) through autotrophic respiration (R_A) and heterotrophic respiration (R_H), and through storage as net ecosystem production (NEP).

In general, in both aquatic and terrestrial ecosystems, an increase in GEP results in an equivalent increase in total ecosystem respiration R_E (Figure 11.15). The gross ecosystem productivity values compared here are greater in

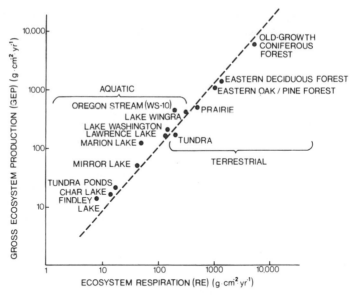

FIGURE 11.15 *Differences in gross ecosystem production for aquatic ecosystems and their associated terrestrial environments.*

the terrestrial ecosystems than in the aquatic and appear to reflect a dependence on climate. The high GEP and respiration (maintenance) levels found in coniferous forests are due mainly to the sustained growth of long-lived coniferous trees. Large evergreens are well adapted to the moisture, temperature, and nutrient regimes of the Pacific Northwest, and primary production benefits from the moist, warm, maritime climate. The vegetation is extremely conservative of its acquired nutrients. In contrast the terrestrial ecosystems of other biomes tend to have lower GEP values. This is assumed to be a function of extreme temperature conditions in which winters are colder and summers hotter than in the Pacific Northwest. Favorable interactions of wind, rain, and evaporation can constitute an energy subsidy in most temperate forests and thus enhance GEP in comparison with areas subject to harsher weather conditions— for example, the tundra.

The highest GEPs for the aquatic ecosystems considered in this comparison are found in the watershed 10 stream in H. J. Andrews Forest in Oregon and in eutrophic Lake Wingra in Wisconsin. These high values are largely the result of energy subsidies unique to their particular watershed. Specifically, watershed 10 receives large inputs of terrestrial C and Lake Wingra receives excessive nutrient loads. Such energy subsidies are especially evident in forested areas where inputs to aquatic ecosystems are related directly to the gross production of the surrounding terrestrial ecosystem. For example, the amount of terrestrial input, relative to aquatic GEP, is highest for the Oregon stream,

Findley Lake, and Marion Lake in the coniferous forest, and lowest for the tundra pond and Lake Char in the tundra (Figure 11.16). The impact of these allochthonous energy subsidies are particularly important in coniferous forest regions where aquatic primary production is usually low and energy supplements increase consumer production (Wissmar et al. 1977).

The relation between production in aquatic ecosystems and their respective terrestrial environments can be described further by the ratio NEP:GEP, termed here *effective ecosystem production*. The NEP:GEP ratios of the aquatic systems tend to be inversely related to the NEP:GEP of their respective terrestrial ecosystems (Figure 11.17). The effective ecosystem production for the aquatic ecosystems shows that relative NEP is much higher in aquatic than in terrestrial systems. Such differences in the rates of net organic matter storage (NEP) and in the rates of respiration (R_A and R_H) are indicative of energy partitioning by different aquatic and terrestrial ecosystems into components of structure, storage, and growth, and into costs of maintenance (R_A) and to consumers (R_H). In both types of ecosystems the carbohydrates synthesized by photosynthesis are utilized only partially in direct respiration processes. Portions of the carbohydrate pool serve as raw material for a variety of chemical transformations, primarily polymerization and amination. Some of the products (celluloses and lignin) become permanent structural parts of the terrestrial system while other products (for example, lipids and starch) serve as storage material in both aquatic and terrestrial systems. Ultimately, all compounds are respired (or degraded) back to CO_2 and H_2O, either during metabolic processes (R_A) or in decomposition after death, or other heterotrophic uses (R_H).

In considering the differences in NEP for aquatic and terrestrial ecosystems, terrestrial NEP is usually low, because, in contrast to aquatic plants, land plants invest a large portion of their productive energy in supportive tissue. This is necessary because the air environment has a much lower density and hence lower supporting capacity than water. In addition, the rate of metabolism of terrestrial plants, per unit of weight, is much less than that of aquatic plants. This concept can be expressed as turnover rate, the ratio of production:biomass (time^{-1}), in that aquatic plants can have turnover rates several hundred times higher than do terrestrial plants. The turnover rate is especially low in coniferous forests where NEP is very low (2 percent of GEP) and massive amounts of supportive tissue exist as wood. In coniferous forests the energetics of production and maintenance (R_A) of structural matter result in the accumulation of large forest stands (biomass) and a detrital material that consists mainly of cellulose and lignin. Although this woody material constitutes a large supply of detritus for consumers in the ecosystem, its refractory nature results in slow rates of decomposition, the principal component of R_H (Figure 11.18). In contrast, the other terrestrial ecosystems considered here tend to have higher rates of NEP (10 to 23 percent of GEP) or storage. These systems usually tie up less energy in woody structures and produce more labile organic matter (that is, leaves and grasses) that can be used readily by decomposers and other con-

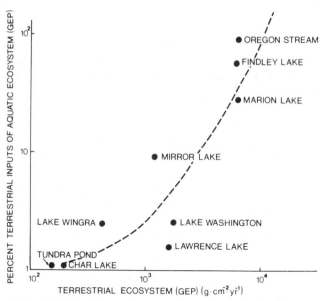

FIGURE 11.16 *Percentages of terrestrial inputs of aquatic ecosystem gross ecosystem production (GEP) in terrestrial ecosystems with varying GEP values.*

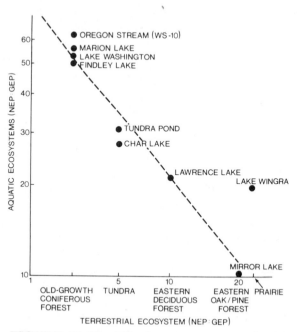

FIGURE 11.17 *Effective ecosystem production (NEP:GEP) of aquatic ecosystems and their associated terrestrial environments.*

sumers. This phenomenon is reflected by higher heterotrophic respiration rates (R_H). An extreme example is the tundra ecosystem. This system uses almost all of its gross primary production in respiration, approximately 50 percent going to R_A and 50 percent to R_H, and thus NEP is only 5 percent of GEP.

The major difference between aquatic and terrestrial NEP is the partitioning of the respiration component. In terrestrial systems, structural maintenance requires expenditure of more energy for autotrophic respiration than for heterotrophic respiration. In contrast, most of the aquatic ecosystems show a greater percentage of respiration as heterotrophic. Thus most of the available energy is utilized by decomposers and higher consumers (Figure 11.18).

The most likely explanation for the observed higher percentage of heterotrophic respiration in aquatic systems, besides minimal structural maintenance (R_A), is that a large portion of total available energy enters the system as a subsidy from terrestrial inputs of carbon and nutrients. In the case of carbon,

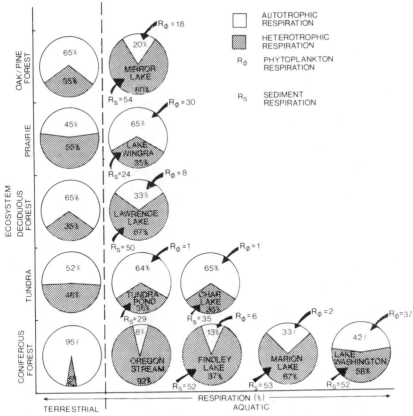

FIGURE 11.18 *Respiration components of aquatic and terrestrial ecosystems. Respiration expressed as percent of total ecosystem respiration (R_E).*

this feature is related to the occurrence of higher primary production levels in terrestrial ecosystems. For example, the terrestrial systems with the highest gross production levels (the coniferous forests, eastern deciduous, and oak/pine forests) yielded large amounts of carbon to their associated aquatic environments, which in turn showed higher percentages of heterotrophic respiration. Such relations are also evident in the fact that heterotrophic sediment respiration (R_s) in aquatic ecosystems was always greater than 50 percent of the total ecosystem respiration (R_E). Autotrophic respiration (R_A) in these aquatic systems was partitioned into three components—phytoplankton, macrophytes, and algal periphyton. Phytoplankton respiration was important only in the more productive Wingra (30 percent), Mirror (18 percent), and Washington (37 percent) lakes. In Lawrence Lake, macrophytes constituted the most important component of autotrophic respiration; macrophytes and periphyton were most important in Wingra and Marion lakes; sedges in the tundra pond; and periphyton in Char Lake. The partitioning of autotrophic respiration can be viewed as the ecosystem adaptation to constraints imposed by lake morphometry, water retention time, and light and nutrient regimes.

SUMMARY

Carbon and nutrient budgets indicate that the principal inputs of particulate carbon, phosphate, and inorganic nitrogen to Findley Lake come from terrestrial and fluvial sources. Most of the annual inputs are lost through high rates of flushing, which eliminate winter nutrient storage and minimize spring plankton blooms. The terrestrial influence on Findley Lake is reflected in the fact that the main sites of element cycling in this ecosystem are associated with benthic processing of allochthonous detritus.

Less-detailed budgets of carbon in Lake Washington and phosphorus and nitrogen in Lake Sammamish demonstrate the relative importance of exogenous and endogenous material pathways in lakes of the lower drainage basin. Element cycling in these systems appears to be dominated by endogenous processes. Phytoplankton blooms in Lake Washington and Lake Sammamish are coupled to internal winter storage of loaded nutrients. Productivity in Lake Sammamish is buffered by the anaerobic release of phosphate from sediments that are regulated by Fe-P precipitation.

The physiological state of algal populations changes with changes in environment. These alterations are primarily a response to phosphorus stress, and indicate an increase in maintenance costs and a decoupling of carbon and nutrient cycles within the cells.

The importance of detritus-based community structure was seen in the benthic regions of Findley Lake and in the fish community of Lake Washington. Detritus-based fish production in Lake Washington was much greater than grazer-based fish production. This observation implies that the benthic fish communities and detrital food chains are extremely important in the lake eco-systems of this region. Community structure was influenced by the greater vulnerability of limnetic-feeding fish populations to control by piscivorous predators than of benthic-littoral feeding fish populations. During the study period, mysids became an increasingly important source of fish forage; hence declining mysid predation on zooplankton may have contributed to the recent increase in *Daphnia* populations in the Lake Washington zooplankton commu-nity. The response of the fish community to trophic change in Lake Washington has been slight because of the tremendously diverse and productive forage base.

Considerations of other ecosystems demonstrates the relation of terrestrial energy subsidies to lakes. This comparison also highlights the partitioning of energy within particular systems.

LITERATURE CITED

Adams, D., 1973, The paleoecology of two lakes in western Washington, M.S. thesis, University of Washington, Seattle, 58p.

Alexander, M., 1961, *Introduction to Soil Microbiology,* Wiley-Interscience, New York, 472p.

Barnes, R. S., 1976, A trace element survey of selected waters, sediments, and biota of the Lake Washington drainage, M.S. thesis, University of Washington, Seattle, 169p.

Bartoo, N. W., 1972, The vertical and horizontal distributions of northern squawfish *(Ptychocheilus oregonensis),* peamouth *(Mylocheilus caurinus),* yellow perch *(Perca flavescens),* and adult sockeye salmon *(Oncorhynchus nerka)* in Lake Washington, M.S. thesis, University of Washington, Seattle, 60p.

Bauer, D. H., 1971, Carbon and nitrogen in the sediments of selected lakes in the Lake Washington drainage, M.S. thesis, University of Washington, Seattle, 91p.

Bender, M. L., K. A. Fanning, P. N. Froelich, G. R. Heath, and V. Maynard, 1977, Interstitial nitrate profiles and oxidation of sedimentary organic matter in the eastern equatorial Atlantic, *Science* **198:**605–609.

Birch, P. B., 1974, Sedimentation of C, N, P and Fe in four lakes of the Lake Washington drainage basin, M.S. thesis, University of Washington, Seattle, 163p.

Birch, P. B., 1976, The relationship of sedimentation and nutrient cycling to the trophic status of four lakes in the Lake Washington drainage basin, Ph.D. dissertation, University of Washington, Seattle, 200p.

Bissonnette, P. A., 1974, Extent of mercury and lead uptake from lake sediments by Chironomidae, M.S. thesis, University of Washington, Seattle, 96p.

Bormann, F. H., and G. E. Likens, 1967, Nutrient cycling, *Science* **155**:424–429.

Bryant, M. D., 1976, Lake Washington sockeye salmon: Biological production, and a simulated harvest by three fisheries, Ph.D. dissertation, University of Washington, Seattle, 159p.

Bunt, J. S., 1965, Measurement of photosynthesis and respiration in a marine diatom with the mass spectrophotometer and with carbon-14, *Nature* **207**:1373–1375.

Caperon, J., and J. Meyer, 1972, Nitrogen-limited growth of marine phytoplankton, 1: Changes in population characteristics with steady-state growth rate, *Deep-Sea Res.* **19**:601–618.

Carritt, D. E., and S. Goodgal, 1954, Sorption reactions and some ecological implications, *Deep-Sea Res.* **1**:224–243.

Cavari, B., 1976, ATP in Lake Kinneret: Indicator of microbial biomass or of phosphorus deficiency? *Limnol. Oceanogr.* **21**:231–236.

Chang, S. C., and M. L. Jackson, 1957, Fractionation of soil phosphorus, *Soil Sci.* **84**:133–144.

Cole, D. W., 1968, A system for measuring conductivity, acidity and rate of flow in a forest soil, *Water Resour. Res.* **4**:1127–1136.

Crecelius, E. A., 1974, The geochemistry of arsenic and antimony in Puget Sound and Lake Washington, Washington, Ph.D. dissertation, University of Washington, Seattle, 133p.

Daly, R. J., and J. E. Hobbie, 1975, Direct counts of aquatic bacteria by a modified epifluorescence technique, *Limnol. Oceanogr.* **20**:775–782.

Dawson, H. J., 1972, Determination of seasonal distribution of juvenile sockeye salmon in Lake Washington by means of acoustics, M.S. thesis, Univ. Washington, Seattle, 112p.

Dean, W. E., and E. Gorham, 1976, Major chemical and mineral components of profundal sediments in Minnesota lakes, *Limnol. Oceanogr.* **21**:259–284.

del Moral, R., 1973, The vegetation of Findley Lake basin, *Am. Midl. Nat.* **89**:26–40.

Devol, A. H., and T. T. Packard, 1978, Seasonal changes in respiratory enzyme activity and productivity in Lake Washington microplankton, *Limnol. Oceanogr.* **23**:104–111.

Devol, A. H., and R. C. Wissmar, 1978, Analysis of five North American lake ecosystems, V: Primary production and community structure, *Verh. Int. Verein Limnol.* **20**:581–586.

Dillon, P. J., 1975, The phosphorus budget of Cameron Lake, Ontario: The importance of flushing rate to the degree of eutrophy of lakes, *Limnol. Oceanogr.* **20**:28–39.

Doble, B. D., 1974, Diel feeding periodicity, instantaneous rate of gastric evacuation and daily zooplankton ration of juvenile sockeye salmon

(Oncorhynchus nerka) in Lake Washington, M.S. thesis, University of Washington, Seattle, 79p.

Droop, M. R., 1974, The nutrient status of algal cells in continuous culture, *J. Mar. Biol. Ass. U.K.* **54**:825–855.

Dryfoos, R. L., 1965, The life history and ecology of the longfin smelt in Lake Washington, Ph.D. dissertation, University of Washington, Seattle, 229p.

Dugdale, R. C., 1976, Nutrient modeling, in *The Sea*, vol. 6., E. D. Goldberg, I. N. McCave, J. J. O'Brien, and J. H. Steele, eds., John Wiley and Sons, New York, pp. 789–806.

Edmondson, W. T., 1972, The present condition of Lake Washington, *Verh. Int. Verein. Limnol.* **18**:284–291.

Edmondson, W. T., 1974, The sedimentary record of the eutrophication of Lake Washington, *Proc. Natl. Acad. Sci. USA* **71**:5093–5095.

Edmondson, W. T., 1977, The recovery of Lake Washington from eutrophication, *Recovery and Restoration of Damaged Ecosystems*, J. Cairns, Jr., K. L. Dickson, and E. E. Herrick eds., University of Virginia Press, Charlottesville, pp. 102–109.

Eggers, D. M., 1976, Theoretical effect of schooling by planktivorous fish predators on rate of prey consumption, *J. Fish. Res. Board Can.* **33**:1964–1971.

Eggers, D. M., 1978, Limnetic feeding behavior of juvenile sockeye salmon in Lake Washington and predator avoidance, *Limnol. Oceanogr.* **23**:1114–1125.

Eggers, D. M., N. W. Bartoo, N. A. Rickard, R. E. Nelson, R. C. Wissmar, R. L. Burgner, and A. H. Devol, 1978, The Lake Washington ecosystem: The perspective from fish community production and forage base, *J. Fish Res. Board Can.* **35**:1553–1571.

Eppley, R. W., 1972, Temperature and phytoplankton growth in the sea, *Fish. Bull.* **70**:1063–1085.

Eppley, R. W., J. L. Coatsworth, and L. Solorzano, 1969, Studies of nitrate reductase in marine phytoplankton, *Limnol. Oceanogr.* **12**:196–206.

Fisher, S. G., 1970, Annual energy budget of a small stream ecosystem: Bear Brook, West Thorton, New Hampshire, Ph.D. dissertation, Dartmouth College, Hanover, N.H., 97p.

Fisher, S. G., and G. E. Likens, 1973, Energy flow in Bear Brook, New Hampshire: An integrative approach to stream ecosystem metabolism, *Ecol. Monogr.* **43**:421–439.

Fuhs, C. W., S. D. Demmerle, E. Canelli, and M. Chen, 1972, Characterization of phosphorus-limited plankton algae (with reflections on the limiting nutrient concept), in *Nutrients and Eutrophication*, No. 1, G. E. Likens, ed., American Society for Limnology and Oceanography, Ann Arbor, Mich., pp. 113–132.

Gasith, A., 1974, Allochthonous organic matter and organic matter dynamics in Lake Wingra, Wisconsin, Ph.D. dissertation, University of Wisconsin, Madison, 209p.

Gasith, A., and A. D. Hasler, 1976, Airborne litterfall as a source of organic matter in lakes, *Limnol. Oceanogr.* **21**:253–258.

Goering, J. S., and V. A. Dugdale, 1966, Estimates of the rates of denitrification in a subarctic lake, *Limnol. Oceanogr.* **11**:113–117.

Goldman, C. R., and R. G. Wetzel, 1963, A study of the primary productivity of Clear Lake, Lake County, California, *Ecology* **44**:283–294.

Goldman, J. C., and E. J. Carpenter, 1974, A kinetic approach to the effect of temperature on algal growth, *Limnol. Oceanogr.* **19**:756–766.

Golterman, H. L., 1967, Influence of the mud on the chemistry of water in relation to productivity, in *Chemical Environment in the Aquatic Habitat,* H. L. Golterman and R. C. Clymo, eds., Proc. IBP Symposium, Amsterdam, pp. 297–313.

Grier, C. C., D. W. Cole, C. T. Dyrness, and R. L. Fredriksen, 1974, Nutrient cycling in 37- and 450-year-old Douglas-fir ecosystems, in *Integrated Research in the Coniferous Forest Biome,* R. H. Waring and R. L. Edmonds, eds., Coniferous Forest Biome Bulletin 5, University of Washington, Seattle, pp. 21–34.

Grundmanis, V., and J. W. Murray, 1977, Nitrification and denitrification in marine sediments from Puget Sound, *Limnol. Oceanogr.* **22**:804–813.

Hargrave, B. T., 1969, Epibenthic algal production and community respiration in the sediments of Marion Lake, *J. Fish. Res. Board Can.* **26**:2003–2026.

Harter, R. D., 1968, Adsorption of phosphorus by lake sediment, *Soil Sci. Soc. Am. Proc.* **32**:514–518.

Haug, A., S. Mykelstad, and E. Sakshaug, 1973, Studies on the phytoplankton ecology of the Trondheim's Fjord, I: The chemical composition of phytoplankton populations, *J. Exp. Mar. Biol. Ecol.* **11**:15–26.

Hendrey, G. R., 1973, Productivity and growth kinetics of natural phytoplankton communities in four lakes of contrasting trophic state, Ph.D. dissertation, University of Washington, Seattle, 263p.

Hendrey, G. R., and E. B. Welch, 1974, Phytoplankton productivity in Findley Lake, *Hydrobiologia* **45**:45–63.

Hobbie, J. E., 1972, Carbon flux through a tundra pond ecosystem at Barrow, Alaska, in *Proceedings, 1972 Tundra Biome Symposium,* 3-5 April 1972, Lake Wilderness Center, University of Washington, Seattle, pp. 206–208.

Hockett, C. A., 1975, Urbanization aspects of the environmental impacts of piers, fill, bulkheads, and related activities in Lake Washington, M.S. thesis, University of Washington, Seattle, 210p.

Holm-Hansen, O., 1970, ATP levels in algal cells as influenced by environmental conditions, *Plant Cell Physiol.* **11**:639–700.

Holm-Hansen, O., and H. W. Paerl, 1972, The applicability of ATP determination for estimation of microbial biomass and metabolic activity, *Mem. Inst. Ital. Idrobiol.* **29**(Suppl.):149–168.

Horton, M. A., 1972, The chemistry of phosphorus in Lake Sammamish, M.S. thesis, University of Washington, Seattle, 220p.

Howarth, R., and S. Fisher, 1976, Carbon, nitrogen and phosphorus dynamics during leaf decay in nutrient-enriched stream ecosystem, *Freshwater Biol.* **6**:221–228.

Humphrey, G. F., and D. V. Subba Rao, 1967, Photosynthetic rate of the marine diatom *Cylindrotheca closterium, Aust. J. Mar. Freshwater Res.* **18**:123–127.

Hutchinson, G. E., E. Bonatti, U. M. Cowgill, C. E. Goulden, E. A. Leventhal, M. E. Mallet, F. Margaritora, R. Patrick, A. Racek, W. A. Robak, E. Stella, J. B. Wart-Perkens, and T. R. Wellman, 1970, Ianula: An account of the history and development of the Lago di Monterosi, Latium, Italy, *Trans. Am. Phil. Soc.* **60**:1–178.

Iverson, T. M., 1973, Decomposition of autumn-shed beech leaves in a spring brook and its significance for the fauna, *Arch. Hydrobiol.* **72**:305–312.

Johnson, D. W., 1975, Processes of elemental transfer in some tropical, temperate, alpine, and northern forest soil: Factors influencing the availability and mobility of major leading agents, Ph.D. dissertation, University of Washington, Seattle, 169p.

Johnson, N. M., J. S. Eaton, and J. E. Richey, 1978, Analysis of five North American lake ecosystems, II: Thermal energy and mechanical stability, *Verh. Int. Verein. Limnol.* **20**:562–567.

Jordan, M., and G. E. Likens, 1975, An organic carbon budget for an oligotrophic lake in New Hampshire, U.S.A., *Verh. Int. Verein. Limnol.* **19**:994–1003.

Kalff, J., and H. E. Welch, 1974, Phytoplankton production in Char Lake, a natural polar lake and in Meretta Lake, a polluted polar lake, Cornwallis Island, Northwest Territories, *J. Fish. Res. Board Can.* **31**:621–636.

Kamp-Nielsen, L., 1974, Mud-water exchange of phosphate and other ions in undisturbed sediment cores and factors affecting the exchange rates, *Arch. Hydrobiol.* **73**:218–237.

Kaushik, N. K., and H. B. N. H ynes, 1968, Experimental study on the role of autumn-shed leaves in aquatic environments, *J. Ecol.* **52**:229–243.

Khul, A., 1974, Phosphorus, in *Algal Physiology and Biochemistry,* W. D. P. Steward, ed., University of California Press, Berkeley, pp. 636–654.

Lanich, J. S., 1972, Mineralogy and cation exchange capacity of surface sediments from selected lakes of the Lake Washington drainage, M.S. thesis, University of Washington, Seattle, 104p.

Lean, D. R. S., 1973, Phosphorus dynamics in lake water, *Science* **179**:678–680.

Likens, G. E., and M. B. Davis, 1975, Post-glacial history of Mirror Lake and its watershed in New Hampshire, U.S.A.: An initial report, *Verh. Int. Verein. Limnol.* **19**:982–993.

Likens, G. E., and O. L. Loucks, 1978, Analysis of five North American lake ecosystems, III: Sources, loading, and fate of nitrogen and phosphorus, *Verh. Int. Verein. Limnol.* **20**:568–573.

Loftus, M. E., and H. H. Seliger, 1975, Some limitations of the *in vivo* fluorescence technique, *Chesapeake Sci.* **16**:79–92.

McAllister, C. D., N. Shaw, and J. D. H. Strickland, 1964, Marine phytoplankton photosynthesis as a function of light intensity: A comparison of methods, *J. Fish. Res. Board Can.* **21**:159–181.

MacPherson, L. B., N. R. Sinclair, and F. R. Hayes, 1958, Lake water and sediment, III: The effect of pH on the partition of inorganic phosphate between water and oxidized mud or its ash, *Limnol. Oceanogr.* **3**:318–326.

Malick, J. E., 1977, Ecology of benthic insects of the Cedar River, Washington, Ph.D. dissertation, University of Washington, Seattle, 188p.

Mortimer, C. H., 1941, The exchange of dissolved substances between mud and water in lakes, II, *J. Ecol.* **29**:280–329.

Mortimer, C. H., 1942, The exchange of dissolved substances between mud and water in lakes, *J. Ecol.* **30**:147–201.

Mortimer, C. H., 1971, Chemical exchanges between sediments and water in the Great Lakes—Speculation on probable regulatory mechanisms, *Limnol. Oceanogr.* **16**:387–404.

Moulton, L. L., 1974, Abundance, growth, and spawning of the longfin smelt in Lake Washington, *Trans. Am. Fish. Soc.* **103**:46–52.

Neame, P. A., 1975, Benthic oxygen and phosphorus dynamics, Ph.D. dissertation, University of California, Davis, 234p.

Nelson, R. E., 1977, Life history of the yellow perch, *Perca flavescens* (Mitchill), in Lake Washington, M.S. thesis, University of Washington, Seattle, 83p.

Nishimoto, M. L., 1973, Life history of the peamouth *(Mylocheilus caurinus)* in Lake Washington, M.S. thesis, University of Washington, Seattle, 73p.

Obeng-Asamoa, E. K., 1976, Nutrient regeneration in the sediment of an oligotrophic lake, *Arch. Hydrobiol.* **78**:526–536.

Odum, W., and R. T. Prentki, 1978, Analysis of five North American lake ecosystems, IV: Allochthonous carbon inputs, *Verh. Int. Verein. Limnol.* **20**:574–580.

Olney, F. E., 1975, Life history and ecology of the northern squawfish *Ptychocheilus oregonensus* (Richardson), in Lake Washington, M.S. thesis, University of Washington, Seattle, 75p.

Packard, T. T., D. Blasco, J. J. McIsaac, and R. C. Dugdale, 1971, Variations of nitrate reductase activity in marine phytoplankton, *Inv. Pesq.* **35**:209–219.

Paerl, H. W., 1973, Detritus in Lake Tahoe: Structural modification by attached microflora, *Science* **180**:496–498.

Paerl, H. W., 1975, Microbial attachment to particles in marine and freshwater ecosystems, *Microb. Ecol.* **2**:73–83.

Pederson, G. L., 1974, Plankton secondary production and biomass: Seasonality and relation to trophic state in three lakes, Ph.D. dissertation, University of Washington, Seattle, 106p.

Pederson, G. L., and A. H. Litt, 1976, A classic example of congeneric occurrence of *Diaptomus* species, *Hydrobiologia* **50**:255–258.

Pederson, G. L., E. B. Welch, and A. H. Litt, 1976, Plankton secondary production and biomass: Their relation to lake trophic state, *Hydrobiologia* **50**:129–144.

Perkins, M. A., 1976, The influence of epilithic periphyton upon phosphorus flow in a subalpine stream, Ph.D. dissertation, University of California, Davis, 187p.

Perry, M. J., 1976, Phosphate utilization by an oceanic diatom in phosphorus-limited chemostat culture and in the oligotrophic waters of the central North Pacific, *Limnol. Oceanogr.* **21**:88–107.

Pieczynska, E., 1975, Ecological interactions between land and the littoral zones of lakes (Masurian Lakeland, Poland), in *Coupling of Land and Water Systems,* A. D. Hasler, ed., Springer-Verlag, New York, pp. 263–276.

Rau, G. H., 1974, The natural dispersal of plant and insect litter into and around a subalpine lake, M.S. thesis, University of Washington, Seattle, 78p.

Rau, G. H., 1976, Dispersal of terrestrial plant litter into a subalpine lake, *Oikos* **27**:153–160.

Rau, G. H., 1978, Carbon-13 depletion in a subalpine lake: Carbon flow implications, *Science* **201**:901–902.

Reynolds, R. C., Jr., and N. M. Johnson, 1972, Chemical weathering in the temperate glacial environment of the northern Cascade Mountains, *Geochim. Cosmochim. Acta* **36**:537–554.

Rich, R., and A. H. Devol, 1978, Analysis of five North American lake ecosystems, VII: Sediment processing, *Verh. Int. Verein. Limnol.* **20**:598–604.

Richey, J. E., 1974, Phosphorus dynamics in Castle Lake, California, Ph.D. dissertation, University of California, Davis, 162p.

Richey, J. E., 1977, An empirical and mathematical approach toward the development of a phosphorus model of Castle Lake, California, in *Ecosystem Modeling in Theory and Practice: An Introduction with Case Histories,* C. A. S. Hall and J. W. Day, Jr., eds., John Wiley and Sons, New York, pp. 268–287.

Richey, J. E., 1979, Patterns of phosphorus supply and utilization in Lake Washington and Findley Lake, *Limnol. Oceanogr.* **24**:906–916.

Richey, J. E., and R. C. Wissmar, 1979, Sources and influences of allochthonous inputs on the productivity of a subalpine lake, *Ecology.* **60**:318–328.

Richey, J. E., M. A. Perkins, and C. R. Goldman, 1975, Effects of kokanee salmon *(Oncorhynchus nerka)* decomposition on the ecology of a subalpine stream, *J. Fish. Res. Board Can.* **32**:817–820.

Rock, C. A., 1974, The trophic status of Lake Sammamish and its relationship to nutrient income, Ph.D. dissertation, University of Washington, Seattle, 129p.

Sakshaug, E., O. Holm-Hansen, 1977, Chemical composition of *Skeletonema costatus* (Greve) Cleve and *Pavlovia (monochrysis) lutheri* (Droop) Green as a function of nitrate-, phosphate-, and iron-limited growth, *J. Exp. Mar. Biol. Ecol.* **29**:1–34.

Schindler, D. W., V. E. Frost, and R. V. Schmidt, 1973, Production of epilithiphyton in two lakes of the Experimental Lakes area, northwestern Ontario, *J. Fish. Res. Board Can.* **30**:1511–1524.

Sedell, J. R., 1972, Studying streams as a biological unit, in *Proceedings—Research on Coniferous Forest Ecosystems—A Symposium,* J. F. Franklin, L. J. Dempster, and R. H. Waring, eds., U.S. Dept. Agriculture Forest Service, Portland, Oreg., pp. 281–287.

Shukla, S. S., J. K. Syers, J. D. H. Williams, D. E. Armstrong, and R. F. Harris, 1971, Sorption of inorganic phosphate by lake sediments, *Soil Sci. Soc. Am. Proc.* **35**:244–249.

Singer, M. J., and F. C. Ugolini, 1974, Genetic history of two well-drained subalpine soils formed on complex parent materials, *Can. J. Soil Sci.* **54**:475–489.

Sommers, L. E., R. F. Harris, J. D. H. Williams, D. E. Armstrong, and J. K. Syers, 1970, Determination of total organic phosphorus in lake sediments, *Limnol. Oceanogr.* **15**:301–304.

Sommers, L. E., R. F. Harris, J. D. H. Williams, D. E. Armstrong, and J. K. Syers, 1972, Fractionation of organic phosphorus in lake sediments, *Soil Sci. Soc. Am. Proc.* **36**:51–54.

Stanley, D. W., 1972, Benthic algae productivity in tundra ponds and lakes, in *Proceedings, 1972 Tundra Biome Symposium,* 3–5 April 1972, Lake Wilderness Center, University of Washington, Seattle, pp. 174–177.

Steele, J. H., 1965, Notes on some theoretical problems in production ecology, *Mem. Inst. Ital. Idrobiol.* **18**(suppl.):383–398.

Stoll, R. K., 1973, Size selective algal grazing of zooplankton using a radioactive tracer, M.S. thesis, University of Washington, Seattle, 57p.

Strathman, R. R., 1967, Estimating the organic carbon content of phytoplankton from cell volume or plasmic volume, *Limnol. Oceanogr.* **21**:411–418.

Stumm, W., and J. O. Leckie, 1971, Phosphate exchange with sediments: Its role in the productivity of surface waters, *5th Int. Water Pollut. Res. Conf. Proc.,* vol. 2, pp. 111–121.

Stumm, W., and J. J. Morgan, 1970, *Aquatic Chemistry,* Wiley-Interscience, New York, 583p.

Suberkropp, R., G. L. Godschalk, and M. Klug, 1976, Changes in the chemical composition of leaves during processing in a woodland stream, *Ecology* **57:**720–729.

Syers, J. K., R. F. Harris, and D. E. Armstrong, 1973, Phosphate chemistry in lake sediments, *J. Environ. Qual.* **2:**1–14.

Taft, J. L., W. R. Taylor, and J. J. McCarthy, 1975, Uptake and release of phosphorus by phytoplankton in the Chesapeake Bay estuary, U.S.A., *Mar. Biol.* **33:**21–32.

Taub, F. B., R. L. Burgner, E. B. Welch, and D. E. Spyridakis, 1972, A comparative study of four lakes, in *Proceedings—Research on Coniferous Forest Ecosystems—A Symposium,* J. F. Franklin, L. J. Dempster, and R. H. Waring, eds., U.S. Department of Agriculture Forest Service, Portland, Oreg., pp. 21–32.

Tison, D. L., F. E. Palmer, and J. T. Staley, 1977, Nitrogen fixation in lakes of the Lake Washington drainage basin, *Water Res.* **11:**843–847.

Traynor, J. J., 1973, Seasonal changes in the abundance, size, biomass, production and distribution of the pelagic fish species in Lake Washington, M.S. thesis, University of Washington, Seattle, 91p.

Triska, F. J., and J. R. Sedell, 1976, Decomposition of four species of leaf litter in response to nitrate manipulation, *Ecology* **57:**783–792.

Triska, F. J., J. R. Sedell, and B. Buckley, 1975, The processing of conifer and hardwood leaves in two coniferous forest streams, II: Biochemical and nutrient changes, *Verh. Int. Verein. Limnol.* **19:**1628–1639.

Turner, J., 1975, Nutrient cycling in a Douglas-fir ecosystem with respect to age and nutrient status, Ph.D. dissertation, University of Washington, Seattle, 190p.

Turner, J., and M. Singer, 1976, Nutrient cycling and distributions in a subalpine coniferous ecosystem, *J. Appl. Ecol.* **13:**295–301.

Ugolini, F. C., H. Dawson, and J. Zachara, 1977a, Direct evidence of particle migration in the soil solution of a podzol, *Science* **198:**603–605.

Ugolini, F. C., R. V. Minden, H. Dawson, and J. Zachara, 1977b, An example of soil processes in the *Abies amabilis* zone of the central Cascades, Washington, *Soil Sci.* **124:**291–302.

Vanderborght, J. P., R. Wollast, and G. Billen, 1977a, Kinetic models of diagenesis in disturbed sediments, 1: Mass transfer properties and silica diagenesis, *Limnol. Oceanogr.* **22:**787–793.

Vanderborght, J. P., R. Wollast, and G. Billen, 1977b, Kinetic models of diagenesis in disturbed sediments, 2: Nitrogen diagenesis, *Limnol. Oceanogr.* **22:**794–804.

Wekell, M. M. B., 1975, Glucose mineralization and chitin hydrolysis by bacteria associated with the sediment in four lakes in the Lake Washington drainage basin, Ph. D. dissertation, University of Washington, Seattle, 306p.

Welch, E. B., 1977, Nutrient Diversion: Resulting Lake Trophic State and Phosphorous Dynamics, EPA-600/3-77-003, Ecol. Res. Ser. U.S. Environmental Protection Agency, Corvallis, Oreg., 91p.

Welch, E. B., and D. W. Spyridakis, 1972, Dynamics of nutrient supply and primary production in Lake Sammamish, Washington, in Proceedings—Research on Coniferous Forest Ecosystems—A Symposium, J. F. Franklin, L. J. Dempster, and R. H. Waring, eds., U.S. Department of Agriculture Forest Service, Portland, Oreg., pp. 301–315.

Welch, H. E., and J. Kalff, 1974, Benthic photosynthesis and respiration in Char Lake, J. Fish. Res. Board Can. 31:609–620.

Welch, E. B., G. R. Hendry, and R. K. Stoll, 1975, Nutrient supply and the production and biomass of algae in four Washington lakes, Oikos 26:47–54.

Wetzel, R. G., 1975, Limnology, W. B. Saunders, Philadelphia, 743p.

Wetzel, R. G., and P. H. Rich, 1973, Carbon in freshwater systems, in Carbon and the Biosphere, G. M. Woodwell and E. V. Pecan, eds., U.S. Atomic Energy Commission Conference 720510, pp. 241–263.

Wetzel, R., and J. E. Richey, 1978, Analysis of five North American lake ecosystems, VIII: Control mechanisms and regulation, Verh. Int. Verein. Limnol. 20:605–608.

Wetzel, R. G., P. H. Rich, M. C. Miller, and H. L. Allen, 1972, Metabolism of dissolved and particulate carbon in a temperate hardwater lake, Mem. Inst. Ital. Idrobiol. 29(suppl.):185–243.

Williams, J. D. H., and T. Meyer, 1972, Effects of sediment diagenesis and regeneration of phosphorus with special reference to lakes Erie and Ontario, in Nutrients in Natural Waters, H. E. Allen and J. R. Kramer, eds., Wiley-Interscience, New York, pp. 280–315.

Williams, J. D. H., J. K. Syers, and T. W. Walker, 1967, Fractionation of soil inorganic phosphate by a modification of Chang and Jackson's procedure, Soil Sci. Soc. Am. Proc. 31:736–739.

Williams, J. D. H., J. K. Syers, D. E. Armstrong, and R. F. Harris, 1971a, Characterization of inorganic phosphate in noncalcareous lake sediments, Soil Sci. Soc. Am. Proc. 35:556–561.

Williams, J. D. H., J. K. Syers, R. F. Harris, and D. E. Armstrong, 1971b, Fractionation of inorganic phosphate in calcareous lake sediments, Soil Sci. Soc. Am. Proc. 35:250–255.

Wissmar, R. C., and R. G. Wetzel, 1978, Analysis of five North American lake ecosystems, VI: Consumer community structure and production, Verh. Int. Verein. Limnol. 20:587–597.

Wissmar, R. C., J. E. Richey, and D. E. Spyridakis, 1977, The importance of allochthonous particulate carbon pathways in a subalpine lake, *J. Fish. Res. Board Can.* **34:**1410–1418.

Woodey, J. C., 1971, Distribution, feeding, and growth of juvenile sockeye salmon in Lake Washington, Ph. D. dissertation, University of Washington, Seattle, 207p.

Yentsch, C. S., 1975, Critical mixing depth, in *Respiration of Marine Organisms,* J. J. Cech, Jr., D. W. Bridges, and D. B. Horton, eds., Proc. Mar. Sect., 1st Marine Biomed. Sci. Symposium, pp. 1–10.

Appendix

CONIFEROUS FOREST BIOME
PROGRAM PUBLICATIONS

Abee, A., and D. P. Lavender, 1972, Nutrient cycling in throughfall and litterfall in 450-year-old Douglas-fir stands, in *Proceedings—Research on Coniferous Forest Ecosystems—A Symposium,* J. F. Franklin, L. J. Dempster, and R. H. Waring, eds., U.S. Department of Agriculture Forest Service, Portland, Oreg., pp. 133–143.

Addor, E. E., 1972, Theodolite surveying for nondestructive biomass sampling, in *Proceedings—Research on Coniferous Forest Ecosystems—A Symposium,* J. F. Franklin, L. J. Dempster, and R. H. Waring, eds., U.S. Department of Agriculture Forest Service, Portland, Oreg., pp. 167–176.

Anderson, N. H., 1976, Carnivory by an aquatic detritivore. *Clistoronia magnifica* (Trichoptera:Limnephilidae), *Ecology* **57:**1081–1085.

Anderson, N. H. 1976, The distribution and biology of the Oregon Trichoptera, *Oregon Agricultural Experiment Station Technical Bulletin 134,* Oregon State University, Corvallis, Oreg., 152p.

Anderson, N. H., 1978, Continuous rearing of the limnephid caddisfly *Clistoronia magnifica* (Banks), in *2d. Int. Sym. on Trichoptera, Proc.* 25–29 July 1977, Junk, The Hague, pp. 317–329.

Anderson, N. H., and K. W. Cummins, 1979, The influences of diet on the life histories of aquatic insects, *J. Fish. Res. Board Can.* **36:**335–342.

Anderson, N. H., and E. Grafius, 1975, Utilization and processing of allochthonous material by stream Trichoptera, *Verh. Int. Verein. Limnol.* **19:**3083–3088.

Anderson, N. H., and J. R. Sedell, 1979, Detritus processing by macroinvertebrates in stream ecosystems, *Ann. Rev. Entomol.* **24:**351–377.

Anderson, N. H., J. R. Sedell, L. M. Roberts, and F. J. Triska, 1978, The role of aquatic invertebrates in processing of wood debris in coniferous forest streams, *Am. Midl. Nat.* **100:**64–82.

Avery, C. C., F. R. Larson, and G. H. Schubert, 1976, Fifty-year records of virgin stand development in southwestern ponderosa pine, *U.S. Department of Agriculture Forest Service Technical Report RM-22,* Fort Collins, Colo., 71p.

Barney, R. J., and K. Van Cleve, 1973, Black spruce fuel weights and biomass in two interior Alaska stands, *Can. J. For. Res.* **3:**304–311.

Bartoo, N. W., R. G. Hansen, and R. S. Wydoski, 1973, A portable verticle gill net system, *Progressive Fish Culturist* **35:**231–233.

Bernstein, M. E., and G. C. Carroll, 1977, Internal fungi in old-growth Douglas-fir foliage. *Can. J. Bot.* **55:**644–653.

Bernstein, M. E., and G. C. Carroll, 1977, Microbial populations on Douglas-fir needle surfaces, *Microbial Ecol.* **4:**41–52.

Bernstein, M. E., H. M. Howard, and G. C. Carroll, 1973, Fluorescence microscopy of Douglas-fir foliage epiflora, *Can. J. Microbiol.* **19:**1129–1130.

Billings, R. F., and R. I. Gara, 1975, Rhythmic emergence of *Dendroctonus ponderosae* (Coleoptera:Scolytidae) from two host species, *Ann. Entomol. Soc. Am.* **68:**1033–1036.

Billings, R. F., R. I. Gara, and B. F. Hrutfiord, 1976, Influence of ponderosa pine resin volatiles on the response of *Dendroctonus ponderosae* to synthetic trans-Verbenol, *Environ. Entomol.* **5:**171–179.

Birch, P. B., and D. E. Spyridakis, in press, Nitrogen and phosphorus recycling in Lake Sammamish, a temperate mesotrophic lake, *Hydrobiologia.*

Birch, P. B., R. S. Barnes, and D. E. Spyridakis, 1980, Sedimentation and its relationship with primary productivity in western Washington Lakes, *Limnol. Oceanogr.* **25:**240–247.

Black, H. C., and R. D. Taber, 1977, Mammals in western coniferous forest ecosystems: An annotated bibliography, *Coniferous Forest Biome Bulletin No. 2,* University of Washington, Seattle, 199p.

Bledsoe, C. S., and D. W. Rains, in press, Cation uptake by Douglas-fir seedlings grown in solution culture, *Can. J. For. Res.*

Brown, G. W., R. H. Burgy, R. D. Harr, and J. P. Riley, 1972, Hydrologic modeling in the Coniferous Forest Biome, in *Proceedings—Research on Coniferous Forest Ecosystems—A Symposium,* J. F. Franklin, J. J. Dempster, and R. H. Waring, eds., U.S. Department of Agriculture Forest Service, Portland, Oreg., pp. 49–70.

Buckley, B. M., and F. J. Triska, 1978, The presence and ecological role of nitrogen-fixing bacteria associated with wood decay in streams, *Verh. Int. Verein. Limnol.* **20:**1333–1339.

Campbell, A. G., and J. F. Franklin, 1979, Riparian vegetation in Oregon's western Cascade Mountains: Composition, biomass, and autumn phenology, *Coniferous Forest Biome Bulletin No. 14,* University of Washington, Seattle, 90p.

Carroll, F. E., and G. C. Carroll, 1973, Senescence and death of conidiogenous cell in *Stemphylium botryosum* Wallroth, *Arch. Mikrobiol.* **94:**109–124.

Carroll, G. C., 1981, Mycological inputs to ecosystem analysis, in *The Fungal Community: Its Organization and Role in the Ecosystem*, D. T. Wicklow and G. C. Carroll, eds., Marcel Dekker, New York, pp. 25–35.

Carroll, G. C., L. H. Pike, J. R. Perkins, and M. Sherwood, in press, Biomass and distribution patterns of conifer twigs microepiphypes in a Douglas-fir forest, *Can. J. Bot.*

Cole, D. W., 1978, Ecosystem research in the natural managed forest with regard to new problems in tending, *Tending in Multiple Use Forestry, IUFRO Proceedings,* Div. I, September 1977, Ossiach, Austria, pp. 75–91.

Cole, D. W., and C. S. Bledsoe, 1976, Nutrient dynamics of Douglas-fir, *16th IUFRO World Congress Proceedings,* Div. II, Norwegian Forestry Research Institute, Oslo, Norway, pp. 53–64.

Cole, D. W., and S. P. Gessel, 1974, Water quality considerations needed for forest planning, in *Foresters in Land-Use Planning*, Proc. Soc. Am. For. 1973 National Convention, Portland, Oreg., pp. 254–263.

Cole, D. W., and D. W. Johnson, 1977, Atmospheric sulfate additions and cation leaching in a Douglas-fir ecosystem, *Water Resour. Res.* **13:**313–317.

Cole, D. W., and D. W. Johnson, 1979, The cycling of elements within forests of the Douglas-fir region, in *Forest Soils of the Douglas-fir Region*, P. E. Heilman, H. W. Anderson, and D. A. Baumgartner, eds., Northwest Forest Soils Council, Washington State University, Pullman, pp. 185–198.

Cole, D. W., and M. Rapp, 1980, Elemental cycling in forest ecosystems, in *Dynamic Properties of Forest Ecosystems*, D. E. Reichle, ed., Cambridge University Press, Cambridge, pp. 341–409.

Cole, D. W., W. J. B. Crane, and C. C. Grier, 1975, The effect of forest management practices on water in a second-growth Douglas-fir ecosystem, in *Forest Soils and Forest Land Management*, B. Bernier and C. H. Winget, eds., 4th North American Forest Soils Conference Proceedings, Les Presses de l'Universite, Laval, Quebec, pp. 195–207.

Cole, D. W., J. Turner, and C. Bledsoe, 1977, Requirement and uptake of mineral nutrients in coniferous ecosystems, in *The Belowground Ecosystem: A Synthesis of Plant-Associated Processes*, J. K. Marshall, ed., Range Sci. Dept., Sci. Ser. No. 26, Colorado State University, Fort Collins, pp. 171–176.

Cole, D. W., S. P. Gessel, and J. Turner, 1978, Comparative mineral cycling in red alder and Douglas-fir, in *Utilization and Management of Alder*, D. C. Briggs, D. S. DeBell, and W. A. Atkinson, compilers, U.S. Department of Agriculture Forest Service General Technical Report PNW-70, Portland, Oreg., pp. 327–336.

Cole, D. W., P. J. Riggan, J. Turner, D. W. Johnson, and D. Breuer, 1978, Factors affecting nitrogen cycling in some Douglas-fir ecosystems of the Pacific Northwest, in *Environmental Chemistry and Cycling Processes,* D. C. Adriano and I. L. Brisban, eds., Technical Information Center, U.S. Department of Energy, CONF-760429, Springfield, Va., pp. 72–94.

Coniferous Forest Biome Modeling Group, 1977, Conifer: A model of carbon and water flow through a coniferous forest: Documentation, *Coniferous Forest Biome Bulletin No. 8,* University of Washington, Seattle, 160p.

Cromack, K., Jr., and C. D. Monk, 1975, Litter production, decomposition and nutrient cycling in a mixed hardwood watershed and a white pine watershed, in *Mineral Cycling in Southeastern Ecosystems,* F. G. Howell, J. B. Gentry, and M. H. Smith, eds., ERDA Sym. Series (CONF-740513), Springfield, Va., pp. 609–624.

Cromack, K., Jr., R. L. Todd, and C. D. Monk, 1975, Patterns of basidiomycete nutrient accumulation in deciduous forest litter, *Soil Biol. Biochem.* **7:**265–268.

Cromack, K., Jr., P. Sollins, R. L. Todd, D. A. Crossley, Jr., W. M. Fender, R. Fogel, and A. W. Todd, 1977, Soil microorganism-arthropod interaction: Fungi as major calcium and sodium sources, in *The Role of Arthropods in Forest Ecosystems,* W. J. Mattson, ed., Springer-Verlag, New York, pp. 78–84.

Cromack, K., Jr., P. Sollins, R. L. Todd, R. Fogel, A. W. Todd, W. M. Fender, M. E. Crossley, and D. A. Crossley, Jr., 1978, The role of oxalic acid and bicarbonate in calcium cycling by fungi and bacteria: Some possible implications for soil analysis, in *6th Int. Soil Zool. Coll. Proc.,* T. Persson and U. Lohm, eds., Int. Soc. Soil Sci., Ecol. Bull. No. 25, Stockholm, Sweden, pp. 246–252.

Cromack, K., Jr., P. Sollins, W. C. Graustein, K. Speidel, A. W. Todd, G. Spycher, C. Y. Li, and R. L. Todd, 1979, Calcium oxalate accumulation and soil weathering in mats of the hypogeous fungus *Hysterangium crassum, Soil Biol. Biochem.* **11:**463–468.

Dawson, H. J., F. C. Ugolini, B. F. Hrutfiord, and J. Zachara, 1978, Role of soluble organics in the soil processes of a podzol, central Cascades, Washington, *Soil Sci.* **126:**290–296.

del Moral, R., 1973, The vegetation of Findley Lake basin, *Am. Midl. Nat.* **89:**26–40.

del Moral, R., and J. N. Long, 1977, Classification of montane forest community types in the Cedar River drainage of western Washington, U.S.A., *Can. J. For. Res.* **7:**217–225.

del Moral, R., and L. A. Standley, 1979, Pollination of angiosperms in contrasting coniferous forests, *Am. J. Bot.* **66:**26–35.

del Moral, R., and A. F. Watson, 1978, Gradient structure of forest vegetation in the central Washington Cascades, *Vegetatio* **38**:29–48.

Denison, W. C., 1973, Life in tall trees, *Sci. Am.* **228**:74–80.

Denison, W. C., D. M. Tracy, F. M. Rhoades, and M. Sherwood, 1972, Direct, nondestructive measurement of biomass and structure in living old-growth Douglas-fir, *Proceedings—Research on Coniferous Forest Ecosystems—A Symposium*, J. F. Franklin, L. J. Dempster, and R. H. Waring, eds., U.S. Department of Agriculture Forest Service, Portland, Oreg., pp. 147–158.

Devol, A. H., 1979, Zooplankton respiration and its relation to plankton dynamics in two lakes of contrasting trophic state, *Limnol. Oceanogr.* **24**:893–905.

Devol, A. H., and T. T. Packard, 1978, Seasonal changes in respiratory and enzyme activity and productivity in Lake Washington microplankton, *Limnol. Oceanogr.* **23**:104–111.

Deyrup, M. A., 1975, The insect community of dead and dying Douglas-fir, I: The Hymenoptera, *Coniferous Forest Biome Bulletin No. 6*, University of Washington, Seattle, 104p.

Deyrup, M. A., in press, The insect community of dead and dying Douglas-fir, II: Diptera, Coleoptera, and Neuroptera, *Coniferous Forest Biome Bulletin No. 10*, University of Washington, Seattle.

Deyrup, M. A., and R. I. Gara, 1978, Insects associated with Scolytidae (Coleoptera) in western Washington, *Pan-Pacific Entomol.* **54**:270–282.

Doble, B. D., and D. M. Eggers, 1978, Diel feeding chronology, rate of gastric evacuation, daily ration, and prey selectivity in Lake Washington juvenile sockeye salmon *(Oncorhyncus nerka)*, *Trans Am. Fish. Soc.* **107**:36–45.

Dyrness, C. T., J. F. Franklin, and W. H. Moir, 1974, A preliminary classification of forest communities in the central portion of the western Cascades in Oregon, *Coniferous Forest Biome Bulletin No. 4*, University of Washington, Seattle, 123p.

Edmonds, R. L., ed., 1974, An initial synthesis of results in the Coniferous Forest Biome, 1970–1973, *Coniferous Forest Biome Bulletin No. 7*, University of Washington, Seattle, 248p.

Edmonds, R. L., 1976, Effects of cold- and warm- water extractives from decayed and nondecayed western hemlock heartwood on growth of *Fomes annosus*, *Can. J. For. Res.* **6**:1–5.

Edmonds, R. L., 1978, The changing nature of western coniferous forests, *Frontiers* **42**:24–47.

Edmonds, R. L., 1979, Decomposition and nutrient release in Douglas-fir needle litter in relation to stand development, *Can. J. For. Res.* **9**:132–140.

Edmonds, R. L., 1979, Western coniferous forests: How forest management has changed them, *Biology Digest* **5**:13–23.

Edmonds, R. L., 1980, Litter decomposition and nutrient release in Douglas-fir, red alder, western hemlock and Pacific silver fir ecosystems in western Washington, *Can. J. For. Res.* **10:**327–337.

Edmonds, R. L., and P. Sollins, 1974, The impact of forest diseases on energy and nutrient cycling and succession in coniferous forest ecosystems, *Am. Phytopathol. Soc. Proc.* **1:**175–180.

Eggers, D. M., 1976, Theoretical effect of schooling by planktivorous fish predators on rate of prey consumption, *J. Fish. Res. Board Can.* **33:**1964–1971.

Eggers, D. M., 1977, Factors in interpreting data obtained by diel sampling of fish stomachs, *J. Fish. Res. Board Can.* **34:**290–294.

Eggers, D. M., 1977, The nature of prey selection by planktivorous fish, *Ecology* **58:**46–59.

Eggers, D. M., 1978, Limnetic feeding behavior of juvenile sockeye salmon in Lake Washington and predator avoidance, *Limnol. Oceanogr.* **23:**1114–1125.

Eggers, D. M., and L. M. Hale, 1972, The modeling process relating to questions about coniferous lake ecosystems, in *Proceedings—Research on Coniferous Forest Ecosystems—A Symposium,* J. F. Franklin, L. J. Dempster, and R. H. Waring, eds., U.S. Department of Agriculture Forest Service, Portland, Oreg., pp. 33–36.

Eggers, D. M., N. W. Bartoo, N. A. Rickard, R. E. Nelson, R. C. Wissmar, R. L. Burgner, and A. H. Devol, 1978, The Lake Washington ecosystem: The perspective from the fish community production and forage base, *J. Fish. Res. Board Can.* **35:**1553–1571.

Emery, R. M., C. E. Moon, and E. B. Welch, 1973, Enriching effects of urban runoff on the productivity of a mesotrophic lake, *Water Res.* **7:**1505–1516.

Emery, R. M., C. E. Moon, and E. B. Welch, 1973, Delayed recovery in a mesotrophic lake after nutrient diversion, *J. Water Pollut. Control Fed.* **45:**913–925.

Emmingham, W., 1977, Comparison of selected Douglas-fir seed sources for cambial and leader growth patterns in four western Oregon environments, *Can. J. For. Res.* **7:**154–164.

Emmingham, W., and R. H. Waring, 1977, An index of photosynthesis for comparing forest sites in western Oregon, *Can. J. For. Res.* **7:**165–174.

Fogel, R., 1975, Insect mycophagy: A preliminary bibliography, Parts I and II, *U.S. Department of Agriculture Forest Service General Technical Report PNW-36,* Portland, Oreg., 21p.

Fogel, R., 1976, Ecological studies of hypogeous fungi, II: Sporocarp phenology in a western Oregon Douglas-fir stand, *Can. J. Bot* **54:**1152–1162.

Fogel, R., 1976, Notes on distribution and spore ornamentation of *Mycolevis siccigleba* (Basidiomycetes, Cribbeaceae), *Mycologia* **68:**1097–1103.

Fogel, R., and K. Cromack, Jr., 1977, Effect of habitat and substrate quality on Douglas-fir litter decomposition in western Oregon, *Can. J. Bot.* **55:**1632–1640.

Fogel, R., and S. B. Peck, 1975, Ecological studies of hypogeous fungi, I: Coleoptera associated with sporocarps, *Mycologia* **67:**741–747.

Fogel, R., and J. M. Trappe, 1978, Fungus consumption (Mycophagy) by small mammals, *Northwest Sci.* **52:**1–31.

Franklin, J. F., 1972, Why a Coniferous Forest Biome? in *Proceedings— Research on Coniferous Forest Ecosystems—A Symposium*, J. J. Franklin, L. J. Dempster, and R. H. Waring, eds., U.S. Department of Agriculture Forest Service, Portland, Oreg., pp. 3–6.

Franklin, J. F., and C. T. Dyrness, 1971, A checklist of vascular plants on the H. J. Andrews Experimental Forest, western Oregon, *U.S. Department of Agriculture Forest Service Research Note PNW-138,* Portland, Oreg., 37p.

Franklin, J. F., and C. T. Dyrness, 1973, Natural vegetation of Oregon and Washington, *U.S. Department of Agriculture Forest Service General Technical Report PNW-8,* Portland, Oreg., 417p.

Franklin, J. F., K. Cromack, Jr., W. C. Denison, A. McKee, C. Maser, J. R. Sedell, F. J. Swanson, and G. Juday, 1981, Ecological characteristics of old-growth forest ecosystems in the Douglas-fir regions, *U.S. Department of Agriculture Forest Service General Technical Report PNW-118,* Portland, Oreg., 48p.

Fredriksen, R. L., 1972, Nutrient budget of a Douglas-fir forest on an experimental watershed in western Oregon, in *Proceedings—Research on Coniferous Forest Ecosystems—A Symposium,* J. F. Franklin, L. J. Dempster, and R. H. Waring, eds., U.S. Department of Agriculture Forest Service, Portland, Oreg., pp. 115–125.

Fritschen, L. J., 1972, The lysimeter installation on the Cedar River watershed, in *Proceedings—Research on Coniferous Forest Ecosystems—A Symposium* J. F. Franklin, L. J. Dempster, and R. H. Waring, eds., U.S. Department of Agriculture Forest Service, Portland, Oreg., pp. 225–260.

Fritschen, L. J., 1977, A milivolt-to-volt and pulse-to-volt integrator for meteorological purposes, *Agric. Meteorol.* **18:**321–325.

Fritschen, L. J., and P. Doraiswamy, 1973, Dew: An addition to the hydrologic balance of Douglas-fir, *Water Resour. Res.* **9:**891–894.

Fritschen, L. J., L. M. Cox, and R. Kinerson, 1973, A 28-meter Douglas-fir in a weighing lysimeter, *For. Sci.* **19:**256–261.

Fritschen, L. J., L. W. Gay, and H. R. Holbo, 1974, Estimating evapotranspiration from forests by meteorological and lysimetric methods, in *Integrated Research in the Coniferous Forest Biome,* R. H. Waring and R. L. Edmonds, eds., Coniferous Forest Biome Bulletin No. 5, University of Washington, Seattle, pp. 35–40.

Fritschen, L. J., J. Hsia, and P. Doraiswamy, 1977, Evapotranspiration of a Douglas-fir determined with a weighing lysimeter, *Water Resour. Res.* **13:**145–148.

Fujimori, T., 1977, Stem biomass and structure of a mature *Sequoia sempervirens* stand on the Pacific Coast of northern California, *J. Jap. For. Soc.* **59:**435–441.

Fujimori, T., S. Kawanabe, H. Saito, C. C. Grier, and T. Shidei, 1976, Biomass and primary production in forests of three major vegetation zones of the Northwestern United States, *J. Jap. For. Soc.* **58:**360–373.

Gara, R. I., and E. H. Holsten, 1975, Preliminary studies on arctic bark beetles (Coleoptera:Scolytidae) of the Noatak River drainage, *Z. angewandte Entomol.* **78:**248–254.

Gay, L. W., 1972, Energy flux studies in a coniferous forest ecosystem, in *Proceedings—Research on Coniferous Forest Ecosystems—A Symposium,* J. F. Franklin, L. J. Dempster, and R. H. Waring, eds., U.S. Department of Agriculture Forest Service, Portland, Oreg., pp. 243–253.

Gay, L. W., and H. R. Holbo, 1974, *Studies of the Forest Energy Budget,* Water Resour. Res. Inst., Oregon State University, Corvallis, 47p.

Gessel, S. P., 1972, Organization and research program of the Coniferous Forest Biome (an integrated research component of the IBP), in *Proceedings—Research on Coniferous Forest Ecosystems—A Symposium,* J. F. Franklin, L. J. Dempster, and R. H. Waring, eds., U.S. Department of Agriculture Forest Service, Portland, Oreg., pp. 7–14.

Gessel, S. P., and J. Turner, 1974, Litter production by red alder in western Washington, *For. Sci.* **20:**325–330.

Gessel, S. P., and J. Turner, 1976, Litter production in western Washington Douglas-fir stands, *Forestry* **49:**63–72.

Gessel, S. P., D. W. Cole, D. W. Johnson, and J. Turner, 1980, The nutrient cycles of two Costa Rican forests, *Prog. Ecol.* **3:**23–44.

Gholz, H. L., 1978, Assessing stress in *Rhododendron macrophyllum* through an analysis of leaf physical and chemical characteristics, *Can. J. Bot.* **56:**546–556.

Gholz, H., 1980, Structure and productivity of *Juniperus occidentalis* in central Oregon, *Am. Midl. Nat.* **103:**251–261.

Gholz, H., in press, Environmental limits on aboveground net primary production, biomass, and leaf area in vegetation zones in the Pacific Northwest, *Ecology.*

Gholz, H. L., F. K. Fitz, and R. H. Waring, 1976, Leaf area differences associated with old-growth forest communities in the western Oregon Cascades, *Can. J. For. Res.* **6:**49–57.

Gholz, H. L., C. C. Grier, A. G. Campbell, and A. T. Brown, 1979, Equations for estimating biomass and leaf area of plants in the Pacific Northwest, *Forest Science Laboratory Research Paper No. 41,* School of Forestry, Oregon State University, Corvallis, 39p.

Grafius, E., and N. H. Anderson, 1979, Population dynamics, bioenergetics, and role of *Lepidostoma quercina* Ross (Trichoptera:Lepidostomatidae) in an Oregon woodland stream, *Ecology* **60**:433–441.

Grafius, E., and N. H. Anderson, 1980, Population dynamics and role of two species of *Lepidostoma (Trichoptera: Lepidostomatidae)* in an Oregon coniferous forest stream, *Ecology* **61**:808–816.

Graustein, W. C., K. Cromack, Jr., and P. Sollins, 1977, Calcium oxalate: Its occurrence in soils and effect on nutrient and geochemical cycles, *Science* **198**:1252–1254.

Gregory, S. V., 1977, Phosphorus dynamics in organic and inorganic substrates in streams, *Verh. Int. Verein. Limnol.* **20**:1340–1346.

Grier, C. C., 1973, Organic matter and nitrogen distribution in some mountain-heath communities of the Source Lake basin, Washington, *Arct. Alp. Res. Part I* **5**:261–267.

Grier, C. C., 1975, Wildfire effects on nutrient distribution and leaching in a coniferous ecosystem, *Can. J. For. Res.* **5**:599–607.

Grier, C. C., 1978, A *Tsuga heterophylla-Picea sitchensis* ecosystem of coastal Oregon: Decomposition and nutrient balances of fallen logs, *Can. J. For. Res.* **8**:198–206.

Grier, C. C., 1978, Biomass, productivity, and nitrogen-phosphorus cycles in hemlock-spruce stands of the central Oregon coast, in *Western Hemlock Management,* W. A. Atkinson and R. J. Zasoski, eds., Coll. For Resour., Inst. For. Prod. Contrib. No. 34, University of Washington, Seattle, pp. 71–81.

Grier, C. C., and D. W. Cole, 1972, Elemental transport changes occurring during development of a second-growth Douglas-fir ecosystem, in *Proceedings—Research on Coniferous Forest Ecosystems—A Symposium,* J. F. Franklin, L. J. Dempster, and R. H. Waring, eds., U.S. Department of Agriculture Forest Service, Portland, Oreg., pp. 103–114.

Grier, C. C., and R. S. Logan, 1977, Old-growth *Pseudotsuga menziesii* communities of a western Oregon watershed: Biomass distribution and production budgets, *Ecol. Monogr.* **47**:373–400.

Grier, C. C., and S. W. Running, 1977, Leaf area of mature northwestern coniferous forests: Relation to site water balance, *Ecology* **58**:893–899.

Grier, C. C., and R. H. Waring, 1974, Conifer foliage mass related to sapwood area, *For. Sci.* **20**:205–206.

Grier, C. C., D. W. Cole, C. T. Dyrness, and R. L. Fredriksen, 1974, Nutrient cycling in 37- and 450-year-old Douglas-fir ecosystems, in *Integrated Research in the Coniferous Forest Biome,* R. H. Waring and R. L. Edmonds, eds., Coniferous Forest Biome Bulletin No. 5, University of Washington, Seattle, pp. 21–34.

Grier, C. C., R. L. Edmonds, R. H. Waring, and D. W. Cole, 1979, Forest management implications of productivity, nutrient cycling, and water relations research in western conifers, in *North America's Forests: Gateway to Opportunity,* Proc. 1978 Joint Convention of Soc. Am. For. and Can. Inst. For. S.A.F., Washington, D.C., pp. 96–106.

Hall, J. D., M. Murphy, and R. Aho, 1978, An improved design for assessing impacts of watershed practices on streams, *Verh. Int. Verein. Limnol.* **20:**1359–1365.

Hatheway, W. H., P. Machno, and E. Hamerly, 1972, Modeling water movement within the upper rooting zone of a Cedar River soil, in *Proceedings—Research on Coniferous Forest Ecosystems—A Symposium,* J. F. Franklin, L. J. Dempster, and R. H. Waring, eds., U.S. Department of Agriculture Forest Service, Portland, Oreg., pp. 95–101.

Hansen, R. G., 1974, Effect of different filament diameters on the selective action of monofilament gill nets, *Am. Fish. Soc. Trans.* **102:**386–387.

Harr, R. D., 1973, Field transport of the neutron soil-moisture meter in steep terrain, *J. Soil Water Cons.* **28:**181–182.

Harr, R. D., 1977, Water flux in soil and subsoil on a steep forested slope, *J. Hydrol.* **33:**37–58.

Harr, R. D., and C. C. Grier, 1976, Methylene bromide as a manometer liquid for tensiometers, *Soil Sci. Soc. Am. J.* **40:**333–334.

Harr, R. D., and F. M.McCorison, 1979, Initial effects of clearcut logging on size and timing of peak flows in a small watershed in western Oregon, *Water Resour. Res.* **15:**90–94.

Hawk, G. M., 1979, Vegetation mapping and community description of a small western Cascade watershed, *Northwest Sci.* **53:**200–212.

Hawk, G. M., and D. B. Zobel, 1974, Forest succession on alluvial land forms of the McKenzie River Valley, Oregon, *Northwest Sci.* **48:**245–265.

Hawk, G. M., J. F. Franklin, W. A. McKee, and R. B. Brown, 1978, H. J. Andrews Experimental Forest reference stand system: Establishment and use history, *Coniferous Forest Biome Bulletin No. 12,* University of Washington, Seattle, 79p.

Hedden, R. L., Jr., and R. I. Gara, 1976, Spatial attack pattern of a western Washington Douglas-fir beetle population, *For. Sci.* **22:**100–102.

Helms, J. A., R. B. Walker, and K. L. Reed, 1974, Photosynthesis in relation to ecosystem studies, in *3rd North American Forest Biology Workshop,* C. P. P. Reid and G. H. Fechner, eds., Colorado State University, Fort Collins, pp. 77–94.

Henderson, G. S., W. T. Swank, J. B. Waide, and C. C. Grier, 1978, Nutrient budgets of Appalachian and Cascade region watersheds: A comparison, *For. Sci.* **24:**385–397.

Hendrey, G. R., and E. B. Welch, 1974, Phytoplankton productivity in Findley Lake, *Hydrobiologia* **45:**45–63.

Hermann, R. K., 1977, Growth and production of tree roots: A review, in *The Belowground Ecosystem: A Synthesis of Plant-Associated Processes,* J. K. Marshall, ed., Range Sci. Dep., Sci. Ser. No. 26, Colorado State University, Fort Collins, pp. 7–28.

Hett, J. M., and O. L. Loucks, 1976, Age structure models of balsam fir and eastern hemlock, *J. Ecol.* **64:**1029–1044.

Hett, J. M., and R. V. O'Neill, 1974, Systems analysis of the Aleut ecosystem, *Arct. Anthropol.* **11**:31–40.

Hett, J. M., R. D. Taber, J. N. Long, and J. Schoen, 1978, Forest management policies and elk summer carrying capacity in the *Abies amabilis* forest, western Washington, *Environ. Manag.* **2**:561–566.

Hinckley, T. M., J. P. Lassoie, and S. W. Running, 1978, Selected aspects of water relations of forest trees, *For. Sci. Monogr. 20,* Society of American Foresters, Washington, D.C., 72p.

Holbo, H. R., R. D. Harr, and J. D. Hyde, 1975, A multiple-well water-level measuring and recording system, *J. Hydrol.* **27:** 199–206.

Jarvis, P. G., 1975, Water transfer in plants, in *Heat and Mass Transfer in the Biosphere, Part I: Transfer Processes in the Plant Environment,* D. A. deVries and N. H. Afgan, eds., Scripta, Washington, D.C., pp. 369–394.

Johnson, D. W., 1979, Some nitrogen fractions in two forest soils and their changes in response to urea fertilization, *Northwest Sci.* **53**:22–32.

Johnson, D. W., and D. W. Cole, 1977, Sulfate mobility in an outwash soil in western Washington, *Water, Air and Soil Poll.* **7**:489–495.

Johnson, D. W., D. W. Cole, and S. P. Gessel, 1975, Processes of nutrient transfer in a tropical rain forest, *Biotropica* **7**:208–215.

Johnson, D. W., D. W. Cole, and S. P. Gessel, 1979, Acid precipitation and soil surface adsorption properties in a tropical and in a temperate forest soil, *Biotropica* **11**:38–42.

Johnson, D. W., D. W. Cole, S. P. Gessel, M. J. Singer, and R. V. Minden, 1977, Carbonic acid leaching in a tropical, temperate, subalpine and northern forest soil, *Arct. Alp. Res.* **9**:329–343.

Jones, W. G. S., J. O. Whitaker, Jr., and C. Maser, 1978, Food habits of jumping mice *(Zapous trinatatus* and *Z. prinzeps)* in western North America, *Northwest Sci.* **52**:57–60.

Keller, E. A., and F. J. Swanson, 1979, Effects of large organic material on channel form and fluvial processes, *Earth Surface Processes* **4**:361–380.

Kickert, R. N., A. R. Taylor, D. H. Firmage, and M. J. Behan, 1974, Fire ecology research needs identified by research scientists and land managers, *Ann. Tall Timbers Fire Ecol. Conf. Proc.* **14**:217–256.

Kline, J. R., M. L. Stewart, and C. F. Jordan, 1972, Estimation of biomass and transpiration in coniferous forests using tritiated water, in *Proceedings—Research on Coniferous Forest Ecosystems—A Symposium,* J. F. Franklin, L. J. Dempster, and R. H. Waring, eds., U.S. Department of Agriculture Forest Service, Portland, Oreg., pp. 154–166.

Kline, J. R., K. L. Reed, R. H. Waring, and M. L. Stewart, 1976, Measurement of transpiration, *J. Appl. Ecol.* **13**:273–283.

Lassoie, J. P., 1973, Diurnal dimensional fluctuations in a Douglas-fir stem in response to tree water status, *For. Sci.* **19**:251–255.

Lassoie, J. P., 1979, Stem dimensional fluctuations in Douglas-fir of different crown classes, *For. Sci.* **25**:132–144.

Lassoie, J. P., and D. J. Salo, 1981, Physiological response of large Douglas-fir to natural and induced soil water deficits, *Can. J. For. Res.* **11**:139–144.

Lassoie, J. P., and D. R. M. Scott, 1972, Seasonal and diurnal patterns of water status in *Acer circinatum, Proceedings—Research on Coniferous Forest Ecosystems—A Symposium,* J. F. Franklin, L. J. Dempster, and R. H. Waring, eds., U.S. Department of Agriculture Forest Service, Portland, Oreg., pp. 265–272.

Lassoie, J. P., and D. R. M. Scott, 1976, Water relations of vine maple in a Douglas-fir stand, in *Proceedings of the Symposium on Terrestrial and Aquatic Ecological Studies of the Northwest,* Eastern Washington State College Press, Cheney, Wash., pp. 23–37.

Lassoie, J. P., N. Fetcher, and D. J. Salo, 1977, Stomatal infiltration pressures versus diffusion porometer measurements of needle resistance in Douglas-fir and lodgepole pine foliage, *Can. J. For. Res.* **7**:192–196.

Lassoie, J. P., D. R. M. Scott, and L. J. Fritschen, 1977, Transpiration studies in Douglas-fir using the heat pulse technique, *For. Sci.* **23**:377–390.

Lettenmaier, D. P., 1976, Detection of trends in water quality data from records with dependent observations, *Water Resour. Res.* **12**:1037–1046.

Lettenmaier, D. P., 1978, Design considerations for ambient stream quality monitoring, *Water Resour. Bull.* **14**:884–902.

Lettenmaier, D. P., and S. J. Burges, 1976, Use of state estimation techniques in water resource system modeling, *Water Resour. Bull.* **12**:83–89.

Lettenmaier, D. P., and S. J. Burges, 1977, An operational approach to preserving skew in hydrologic models of long-term persistence, *Water Resour. Res.* **13**:281–290.

Lettenmaier, D. P., and S. J. Burges, 1977, Operational assessment of hydrologic models of long-term persistence, *Water Resour. Res.* **13**:113–124.

Lettenmaier, D. P., and S. J. Burges, 1978, Climate change: Detection and its impact on hydrologic design, *Water Resour. Res.* **14**:679–687.

Leverenz, J. W., 1981, Photosynthesis and transpiration in large forest-grown Douglas-fir: Diurnal variation, *Can. J. Botany* **59**:349–356.

Leverenz, J. W., in press, Photosynthesis and transpiration in large forest-grown Douglas-fir: Interaction with apical control, *Can. J. Botany.*

Lighthart, B., and P. E. Tieges, 1972, Exploring the aquatic carbon web, in *Proceedings—Research on Coniferous Forest Ecosystems—A Symposium,* J. F. Franklin, L. J. Dempster, and R. H. Waring, eds., U.S. Department of Agriculture Forest Service, Portland, Oreg., pp. 289–300.

Long, J., and J. Turner, 1975, Aboveground biomass of understorey and overstorey in an age sequence of four Douglas-fir stands, *J. Appl. Ecol.* **12**:179–188.

Long, J. N., 1977, Trends in plant species diversity associated with development in a series of *Pseudotsuga menziesii/Gaultheria shallon* stands, *Northwest Sci.* **51**:119–130.

Long. J. N., E. G. Schreiner, and N. J. Manuwal, 1979, The role of actively moving sand dunes in the maintenance of an azonal juniper-dominated community, *Northwest Sci.* **53:**170–179.

Lyford, J. H., Jr., and S. V. Gregory, 1975, The dynamics and structure of periphyton communities in three Cascade mountain streams, *Verh. Int. Verein. Limnol.* **19:**1610–1616.

McBrayer, J. F., J. M. Ferris, L. J. Metz, C. S. Gist, B. W. Cornaby, Y. Kitazawa, T. Kitazawa, J. G. Wernz, G. W. Krantz, and H. J. Jensen, 1977, Decomposer invertebrate populations in U.S. forest biomes, *Pedobiologia* **17:**89–96.

McIntire, C. D., 1973, Periphyton dynamics in laboratory streams: A simulation model and its implications, *Ecol. Monogr.* **43:**399–420.

McIntire, C. D., 1975, Periphyton assemblages in laboratory streams, in *River Ecology: Studies in Ecology,* B. A. Whitton, ed., vol. II, Blackwell Scientific, London, pp. 403–430.

McIntire, C. D., and J. A. Colby, 1978, A hierarchial model of lotic ecosystems, *Ecol. Monogr.* **48:**167–190.

McIntire, C. D., J. A. Colby, and J. D. Hall, 1975, The dynamics of small lotic ecosystems: A modeling approach, *Verh. Int. Verein. Limnol.* **19:**1599–1609.

Male, L. M., 1973, A temporal-spatial model for studying nutrient cycling dynamics of a phytoplankton production system, Part I: Development of model, *Quant. Sci. Pap. No. 35,* University of Washington, Seattle, 29p.

Mandzak, J. M., G. R. Thompson, and M. Behan, 1976, A thermostatically controlled apparatus for the progressive extraction of soils, *Soil Sci.* **121:**256–257.

Maser, C., J. M. Trappe, and R. A. Nussbaum, 1978, Fungal-small mammal interrelationships with emphasis on Oregon coniferous forests, *Ecology* **59:**799–809.

Maser, C., J. M. Trappe, and D. C. Ure, 1978, Implications of small mammal mycophagy to the management of western coniferous forests, *N. Am. Wildlife Nat. Resour. Conv. Trans.,* **43:**78–88.

Maser, C., R. R. Anderson, K. Cromack, Jr., J. T. Williams, and R. E. Martin, 1979, Dead and down woody material, in *Wildlife Habitats in Managed Forests: The Blue Mountains of Oregon and Washington,* U.S. Department of Agriculture Handbook 553, Portland, Oreg., pp. 78–95.

Mathis, W., 1973, A review of the genus *Boroboropsis (Diptera: Heleomyzidae), Pan-Pacific Entomol.* **49:**373–377.

Meehan, W. R., F. J. Swanson, and J. R. Sedell, 1978, Influence of riparian vegetation on aquatic ecosystems with particular reference to salmonids and their food supplies, *Proceedings of the Symposium on the Importance, Preservation, and Management of Riparian Habitat,* U.S. Department of Agriculture Forest Service General Technical Report RM-43, Fort Collins, Colo., pp. 137–145.

Miller, R. E., D. P. Lavender, and C. C. Grier, 1976, Nutrient cycling in the Douglas-fir type—Silvicultural implications, *Soc. Am. For. 1975 Ann. Conv. Proc.*, Washington, D.C., pp. 359–390.

Miller, S. C., W. Erickson, R. D. Taber, and C. H. Nellis, 1972, Small mammal and bird populations on Thompson site, Cedar River: Parameters for modeling, in *Proceedings—Research on Coniferous Forest Ecosystems—A Symposium*, J. F. Franklin, L. J. Dempster, and R. H. Waring, eds., U.S. Department of Agriculture Forest Service, Portland, Oreg., pp. 199–207.

Minyard, P. L., and C. H. Driver, 1972, Initial steps in decomposition of Douglas-fir needles under forest conditions, in *Proceedings—Research on Coniferous Forest Ecosystems—A Symposium*, J. F. Franklin, L. J. Dempster, and R. H. Waring, eds., U.S. Department of Agriculture Forest Service, Portland, Oreg., pp. 201–263.

Mispagel, M. E., and S. D. Rose, 1978, Arthropods associated with various age stands of Douglas-fir from foliar, ground, and aerial strata, *Coniferous Forest Biome Bulletin No. 13*, University of Washington, Seattle, 55p.

Moir, W. H., 1972, Litter, foliage, branch, and stem production in contrasting lodgepole pine habitats of the Colorado [Front] Range, in *Proceedings—Research on Coniferous Forest Ecosystems—A Symposium*, J. F. Franklin, L. J. Dempster, and R. H. Waring, eds., U.S. Department of Agriculture Forest Service, Portland, Oreg., pp. 184–198.

Murphy, M. L., and J. D. Hall, 1981, Varied effects of clear-cut logging on predators and their habitat in small streams of the Cascade Mountains, Oregon, *Can. J. Fish Aquatic Sci.* **38:**137–145.

Nussbaum, R. A., and G. W. Clothier, 1973, Population structure, growth, and size of larval *Dicamptodon ensatus* (Eschscholtz), *Northwest Sci.* **47:**218–227.

Nussbaum, R. A., and C. Maser, 1975, Food habits of the bobcat, *(Lynx rufus)*, in the Coast and Cascade ranges of western Oregon in relation to present management policies, *Northwest Sci.* **49:**261–266.

Nussbaum, R. A., and C. Tait, 1977, Reproductive biology of the Olympic salamander *(Rhyacotriton olympicus)*, *Am. Midl. Nat.* **98:**176–199.

Olsen, S., and D. Chapman, 1972, Ecological dynamics of watersheds, *Bioscience* **22:**158–161.

Olson, P. R., D. W. Cole, and R. Whitney, 1972, Findley Lake—Study of a terrestrial-aquatic interface, in *Proceedings—Research on Coniferous Forest Ecosystems—A Symposium*, J. F. Franklin, L. J. Dempster, and R. H. Waring, eds., U.S. Department of Agriculture Forest Service, Portland, Oreg., pp. 15–20.

Overton, W. S., 1972, Toward a general model structure for a forest ecosystem, in *Proceedings—Research on Coniferous Forest Ecosystems—A Symposium*, J. F. Franklin, L. J. Dempster, and R. H. Waring, eds., U.S.

Department of Agriculture Forest Service, Portland, Oreg., pp. 37–47.

Overton, W. S., 1975, The ecosystem modeling approach in the Coniferous Forest Biome, in *Systems Analysis and Simulation in Ecology,* vol. III, B. C. Patten, ed., Academic Press, New York, pp. 47–138.

Overton, W. S., and C. White, 1979, Evolution of a hydrology model—an exercise in modelling strategy, *Int. J. Gen. Syst.* **4:**89–104.

Overton, W. S., D. P. Lavender, and R. K. Hermann, 1973, Estimation of biomass and nutrient capital in stands of old-growth Douglas-fir, in *IU-FRO Biomass Studies, S4.01 Mensuration, Growth, and Yield,* Nancy, France, and Vancouver, B.C., Canada, University of Maine, Orono, pp. 91–103.

Palmer, F. E., R. D. Methot, Jr., and J. T. Staley, 1976, Patchiness in the distribution of planktonic heterotrophic bacteria in lakes, *Appl. Environ. Microbiol.* **31:**1003–1005.

Pamatmat, M. M., and A. M. Bhagwat, 1973, Anaerobic metabolism in Lake Washington sediments, *Limnol. Oceanogr.* **18:**611–627.

Peacock, R. L., and R. A. Nussbaum, 1973, Reproductive biology and population structure of the western red-backed salamander, *Plethodon vehiculum* (Cooper), *J. Herpetol.* **7:**215–224.

Pederson, G. L., and A. H. Litt, 1976, A classic example of congeneric occurrence of *Diaptomus* species, *Hydrobiologia* **50:**255–258.

Pederson, G. L., E. B. Welch, and A. H. Litt, 1976, Plankton secondary productivity and biomass: Their relation to lake trophic state, *Hydrobiologia* **50:**129–144.

Pike, L. H., 1972, *Tholurna dissimilis* in Oregon, *Bryologist* **75:**578–580.

Pike, L. H., 1981, Estimation of lichen biomass and production with special reference to the use of ratios, in *The Fungal Community: Its Organization and Role in the Ecosystem,* D. T. Wicklow and G. C. Carroll, eds., Marcel Dekker, New York, pp. 533–552.

Pike, L. H., R. A. Rydell, and W. C. Denison, 1977, A 400-year-old Douglas-fir and its epiphytes—biomass, surface area, and their distributions, *Can. J. For. Res.* **7:**680–699.

Pike, L. H., D. M. Tracy, M. A. Sherwood, and D. Nielsen, 1972, Estimates of biomass and fixed nitrogen of epiphytes from old-growth Douglas-fir, in *Proceedings—Research on Coniferous Forest Ecosystems—A Symposium,* J. F. Franklin, L. J. Dempster, and R. H. Waring, eds., U.S. Department of Agriculture Forest Service, Portland, Oreg., pp. 117–187.

Pike, L. H., W. C. Denison, D. M. Tracy, M. A. Sherwood, and F. M. Rhoades, 1975, Floristic survey of epiphytic lichens and bryophytes growing on old-growth conifers in western Oregon, *Bryologist* **78:**389–402.

Rains, D. W., and C. S. Bledsoe, 1976, The effect of Douglas-fir seedlings on the transfer of nutrients through soil columns, *Plant and Soil* **44:**97–112.

Rapp, M., and D. W. Cole, 1973, Évolution des éléments minéraux dissous dans les précipitations et les percolats du sol a travers un écosystème forestier, *Ann. Sci. For.* **39**:175–190.

Rau, G. H., 1976, Dispersal of terrestrial plant litter into a subalpine lake, *Oikos* **27**:153–160.

Rau, G. H., 1978, Carbon-13 depletion in a subalpine lake: Carbon flow implications, *Science* **201**:901–902.

Rau, G. H., 1978, Conifer needle processing in a subalpine lake, *Limnol. Oceanogr.* **23**:356–358.

Rau, G. H., 1980, Carbon 13–12 variation in subalpine lake aquatic insects: Food source implications, *Can J. Fish. Aquatic Sci.* **37**:742–746.

Rausch, R. L., 1975, Cestodes of the genus *Hymenolepis* Weinland, 1858 (sensu lato) from bats in North America and Hawaii, *Can. J. Zool.* **53**:1537–1551.

Reed, K. L., 1980, An ecological approach to modeling growth of forest trees, *For. Sci.* **26**:33–50.

Reed, K. L., and S. G. Clark, 1979, SUCcession SIMulator: A coniferous forest simulator: Model documentation, *Coniferous Forest Biome Bulletin No. 11,* University of Washington, Seattle, 96p.

Reed, K. L., and R. H. Waring, 1974, Coupling of environment to plant response: A simulation model of transpiration, *Ecology* **55**:62–72.

Reed, K. L., and W. L. Webb, 1972, Criteria for selecting an optimal model: Terrestrial photosynthesis, in *Proceedings—Research on Coniferous Forest Ecosystems—A Symposium,* J. F. Franklin, L. J. Dempster, and R. H. Waring, eds., U.S. Department of Agriculture Forest Service, Portland, Oreg., pp. 227–326.

Reed, K. L., E. R. Hamerly, B. E. Dinger, and P. G. Jarvis, 1976, An analytical model for field measurement of photosynthesis, *J. Appl. Ecol.* **13**:925–942.

Rhodes, R. M., 1977, Growth rates in the lichen *Lobaria oregana* as determined from sequential photographs, *Can. J. Bot.* **55**:2226–2233.

Richey, J. E., 1977, An empirical and mathematical approach toward the development of a phosphorus model of Castle Lake California, in *Ecological Models as Tools: Theory and Case Histories,* C. A. S. Hall and J. W. Day, Jr. eds., John Wiley and Sons, New York, pp. 268–287.

Richey, J. E., 1979, Patterns of phosphorus supply and utilization in Lake Washington and Findley Lake, *Limnol. Oceanogr.* **24**:906–916.

Richey, J. E., and R. C. Wissmar, 1979, Sources and influences of allochthonous inputs on the productivity of a subalpine lake, *Ecology.* **60**:318–328.

Richey, J. E., A. H. Devol, and M. Perkins, 1975, Diel phosphate flux in Lake Washington, U.S.A., *Verh. Int. Verein. Limnol.* **19**:222–228.

Richey, J. E., M. A. Perkins, and C. R. Goldman, 1975, Effects of Kokanee salmon *(Oncorhynchus nerka)* decomposition on the ecology of a subalpine stream, *J. Fish. Res. Board Can.* **32**:817–820.

Richey, J. E., R. C. Wissmar, A. H. Devol, G. E. Likens, J. S. Eaton, R. G. Wetzel, W. E. Odum, N. M. Johnson, O. L. Loucks, R. T. Prentki, and P. N. Rich, 1978, Carbon flow in four lake ecosystems: A structured approach, *Science* **202**:1183-1186.

Richter, K. O., 1973, Freeze-branding for individually marking the banana slug: *Ariolimax columbianus* G., *Northwest Science* **47**:109-113.

Richter, K. O., 1976, A method for individually marking slugs, *J. Molluskan Studies* **42**:146-151.

Richter, K. O., 1979, Aspects of nutrient cycling by *Ariolimax columbianus*, G. (Mollusca:Arionidae) in Pacific Northwest coniferous forests, *Pedobiologia* **19**:60-74.

Richter, K. O., 1980, Aerial locomotion, predator defense and other adaptive functions of the caudal mucus slug *Ariolimax columbianus, The Veliger.* **23**:43-47.

Richter, K. O., 1980, Evolutionary aspects of mycophagy in *Ariolimax columbianus* G. and other slugs, *7th International Colloquium on Soil Zoology Proceedings,* EPA-560/13-80-038, Office of Pesticide and Toxic Substances, Environmental Protection Agency, Washington, D.C., pp. 616-636.

Riekerk, H., 1977, Utilization of a root pressure chamber for nutrient uptake studies, *Plant and Soil* **46**:279-282.

Riggan, P., 1976, Simulation of growth and nitrogen dynamics in a Douglas-fir forest ecosystem, in *Proceedings of the Symposium on Terrestrial and Aquatic Ecological Studies of the Northwest,* Eastern Washington State College Press, Cheney, Wash., pp. 145-157.

Rohrmann, G. F., 1978, The origin, structure, and nutritional importance of the comb in two species of Macroterminitinae (Insecta, Isoptera), *Pedobiologia* **18**:89-98.

Rose, S., B. A. Daniels, and J. M. Trappe, 1979, *Glomus gerdemannii* sp. nov., *Mycotaxon* **8**:297-301.

Rounick, J. S., and S. V. Gregory, 1981, Temporal changes in periphyton standing crop during an unusually dry winter in streams of the western Cascades, Oregon, *Hydrobiologia* **83**:197-205.

Running, S. W., 1976, Environmental control of leaf water conductance in conifers, *Can. J. For. Res.* **6**:104-112.

Running, S. W., R. H. Waring, and R. A. Rydell, 1975, Physiological control of water flux in conifers: A computer simulation model, *Oecologia* **18**:1-16.

Salo, D. J., J. A. Ringo, J. H. Nishitani, and R. B. Walker, 1972, Development and testing of an inexpensive thermoelectrically controlled cuvette, in *Proceedings—Research on Coniferous Forest Ecosystems—A Symposium,* J. F. Franklin, L. J. Dempster, and R. H. Waring, eds., U.S. Department of Agriculture Forest Service, Portland, Oreg., pp. 273-277.

Santantonio, D., R. K. Hermann, and W. S. Overton, 1977, Root biomass studies in forest ecosystems, *Pedobiologia* **17**:1-31.

Scott, D. R. M., J. N. Long, and J. Kotar, 1978, Comparative ecological behavior of western hemlock in the Washington Cascades, in *Western Hemlock Management*, W. A. Atkinson and R. J. Zasoski, eds., Coll. For. Resour., Inst. For. Prod., Contrib. No. 34, University of Washington, Seattle, pp. 26–33.

Scott, D. W., and R. I. Gara, 1975, Antennal sensory organs of two *Melanophila* species (Coleoptera:Buprestidae), *Ann. Entomol. Soc. Am.* **68:**842–846.

Sedell, J., 1972, Studying streams as a biological unit, in *Proceedings— Research on Coniferous Forest Ecosystems—A Symposium*, J. F. Franklin, L. J. Dempster, and R. H. Waring, eds., U.S. Department of Agriculture Forest Service, Portland, Oreg., pp. 281–287.

Sedell, J. R., F. J. Triska, and N. S. Triska, 1975, The processing of conifer and hardwood leaves in two coniferous forest streams, I: Weight loss and associated invertebrates, *Verh. Int. Verein. Limnol.* **19:**1617–1627.

Sedell, J. R., F. J. Triska, J. D. Hall, N. H. Anderson, and J. H. Lyford, 1974, Sources and fates of organic inputs in coniferous forest streams, in *Integrated Research in the Coniferous Forest Biome*, R. H. Waring and R. L. Edmonds, eds., Coniferous Forest Biome Bulletin No. 5, University of Washington, Seattle, pp. 57–69.

Sharpe, D. M., K. Cromack, Jr., W. C. Johnson, and B. S. Ausmus, 1980, A regional approach to litter dynamics in southern Appalachian forests, *Can. J. For. Res.* **10:**395–404.

Sherk, T. E., 1977, Development of the compound eyes of dragonflies (Odonata), Part I: Larval compound eyes, *J. Exp. Zool.* **201:**391–416.

Sherk, T. E., 1978, Development of the compound eyes of dragonflies (Odonata), Part II: Development of the larval compound eyes, *J. Exp. Zool.* **203:**47–60.

Sherk, T. E., 1978, Development of the compound eyes of dragonflies (Odonata), Part III: Adult compound eyes, *J. Exp. Zool.* **203:**61–80.

Sherk, T. E., 1978, Development of the compound eyes of dragonflies (Odonata), Part IV: Development of the adult compound eyes, *J. Exp. Zool.* **203:**183–200.

Sherwood, M., and G. C. Carroll, 1974, Fungal succession on needles and young twigs of old-growth Douglas-fir, *Mycologia* **66:**499–506.

Singer, M. J., and F. C. Ugolini, 1974, Genetic history of two well-drained subalpine soils formed on complex parent materials, *Can. J. Soil Sci.* **54:**475–489.

Singer, M. J., and F. C. Ugolini, 1976, Hydrophobicity in the soils of Findley Lake, Washington, *For. Sci.* **22:**54–58.

Singer, M. J., F. C. Ugolini, and J. Zachara, 1978, *In situ* study of podzolization on tephra and bedrock, *Soil Sci. Soc. Am. J.* **42:**105–111.

Sollins, P., and F. M. McCorison, in press, Nitrogen and carbon solution chemistry on an old-growth coniferous forest watershed before and after cutting, *Water Resour. Res.*

Sollins, P., R. H. Waring, and D. W. Cole, 1974, A systematic framework for modeling and studying the physiology of a coniferous forest ecosystem, in *Integrated research in the Coniferous Forest Biome,* R. H. Waring and R. L. Edmonds, eds., Coniferous Forest Biome Bulletin No. 5, University of Washington, Seattle, pp. 7–20.

Sollins, P., A. T. Brown, and G. L. Swartzman, 1979, A model of carbon and waterflow through a coniferous forest: A revised documentation, *Coniferous Forest Biome Bulletin No. 15,* University of Washington, Seattle, 152p.

Sollins, P., K. Cromack, Jr., R. Fogel, and C. Y. Li, 1980, Role of low molecular weight organic acids in the inorganic nutrition of fungi and higher plants, in *The Fungal Community: Its Organization and Role in the Ecosystem,* D. T. Wicklow and G. C. Carroll, eds., Marcel Dekker, New York, pp. 607–619.

Sollins, P., K. Cromack, Jr., F. M. McCorison, R. H. Waring, and R. D. Harr, 1980, Changes in nitrogen cycling at an old-growth Douglas-fir site after disturbance, *J. Environ. Qual.* **10:**37–42.

Sollins, P., R. A. Goldstein, J. B. Mankin, C. E. Murphy, and G. L. Swartzman, 1980, Effects of defoliation on forest growth and water balance: A case study of the applicability of complex ecosystem models, In *Dynamic Properties of Forest Ecosystems,* D. E. Reichle, ed., Cambridge University Press, Cambridge, pp. 537–565.

Sollins, P., C. C. Grier, F. M. McCorison, Jr., K. Cromack, Jr., R. Fogel, and R. L. Fredriksen, 1980, The internal element cycles of an old-growth Douglas-fir ecosystem in western Oregon, *Ecol. Monogr.* **50:**261–285.

Speir, J. A., 1979, Energy transfer in an autotrophic-based ecosystem with special reference to effects of fertilizer nitrogen additions, *Coniferous Forest Biome Bulletin No. 9,* University of Washington, Seattle, 75p.

Speir, J. A., and N. H. Anderson, 1974, Use of emergence data for estimating aquatic insect production, *Limnol. Oceanogr.* **19:**154–156.

Stettler, R. F., and J. C. Cummings, 1973, A guide to forest-tree collections of known source or parentage in the western United States and Canada, *Coniferous Forest Biome Bulletin No. 3,* University of Washington, Seattle, 59p.

Strand, M. A., 1974, Canopy food chain in a coniferous forest watershed, in *Integrated Research in the Coniferous Forest Biome,* R. H. Waring and R. L. Edmonds, eds., Coniferous Forest Biome Bulletin No. 5, University of Washington, Seattle, pp. 41–47.

Strand, M. A., and W. P. Nagel, 1972, Preliminary considerations of the forest canopy consumer subsystem, in *Proceedings—Research on Coniferous Forest Ecosystems—A Symposium,* J. F. Franklin, L. J. Dempster, and R. H. Waring, eds., U.S. Department of Agriculture Forest Service, Portland, Oreg., pp. 71–77.

Swanson, F. J., 1981, Fire, geomorphic processes and land forms, in *Fire Regime and Ecosystem Properties,* H. A. Mooney, P. M. Bonnicksen, N.

L. Christensen, J. E. Lotan, and W. A. Reiners, eds., U.S. Department of Agriculture Forest Service General Technical Report WO-26, Portland, Oreg., pp. 401–420.

Swanson, F. J., and C. T. Dyrness, 1975, Impact of clearcutting and road construction on soil erosion by landslides in the Western Cascade Range, Oregon, *Geology* **3:**393–396.

Swanson, F. J., and M. E. James, 1975, Geology and geomorphology of the H. J. Andrews Experimental Forest, western Cascades, Oregon, *U.S. Department of Agriculture Forest Service Research Paper PNW-188,* Portland, Oreg. 14p.

Swanson, F. J., and M. E. James, 1975, Geomorphic history of the lower Blue River-Lookout Creek area, western Cascades, Oregon, *Northwest Sci.* **49:**1–11.

Swanson, F. J., and G. W. Lienkaemper, 1978, Physical consequences of large organic debris in Pacific Northwest streams, *U.S. Department of Agriculture Forest Service General Technical Report PNW-69,* Portland, Oreg., 12p.

Swanson, F. J., and J. R. Sedell, 1979, Use of watershed and stream research in the Coniferous Biome for forest management, in *North America's Forests: Gateway to Opportunity,* Proc. 1978 Ann. Meeting Soc. Am. For. and Can. Inst. For., Society of American Foresters, Washington, D.C. pp. 107–113.

Swanson, F. J., and D. N. Swanson, 1977, Complex mass-movement terrains in the western Cascade Range, Oregon, *Rev. Eng. Geol.* **3:**113–124.

Swanson, F. J., G. W. Lienkaemper, and J. R. Sedell, 1976, History, physical effects and management implications of large organic debris in western Oregon streams, *U.S. Department of Agriculture Forest Service General Technical Report PNW-56,* Portland, Oreg., 15p.

Swanston, D. N., and F. J. Swanson, 1976, Timber harvesting, mass erosion, and steep land forest geomorphology in the Pacific Northwest, in *Geomorphology and Engineering,* D. R. Coates, ed., Dowden, Hutchinson, & Ross, Stroudsburg, Pa., pp. 119–221.

Swanston, D. N., and F. J. Swanson, 1980, Soil mass movement, in *An Approach to Water Resource Evaluation of Non-Point Silvicultural Sources (A Procedural Handbook),* EPA-60018-80-012, USDA Forest Service and EPA, Washington, D.C., pp. v-1-v-49.

Swartzman, G. L., 1979, Simulation modeling of material and energy flow through an ecosystem: Methods and documentation, *Ecol. Modeling* **7:**55–81.

Taub, F. B., 1974, Closed ecological systems, *Ann. Review Ecol. System,* **5:**139–160.

Taub, F. B., 1980, Relationships between inorganic nutrient input, algal density, herbivore density, and residual inorganic nutrient, in *The Functioning of Freshwater Ecosystems,* Cambridge Univ. Press, pp. 405–410.

Taub F. B., and D. H. Mckenzie, 1973, Continuous cultures of an alga and its grazer, in *Modern methods in microbial ecology*, T. Rosswall, ed., Bull. Ecol. Res. Comm. NFR (Stockholm) No. 17, Ecological Resources Commission, Stockholm, pp. 371–377.

Taub, F. B., R. L. Burgner, E. B. Welch, and D. E Spyridakis, 1972, A comparative study of four lakes, in *Proceedings—Research on Coniferous Forest Ecosystems—A Symposium*, J. F. Franklin, L. J. Dempster, and R. H. Waring, eds., U.S. Department of Agriculture Forest Service, Portland, Oreg., pp. 21–32.

Taylor, A. R., R. N. Kickert, D. H. Firmage, and M. J. Behan, 1975, Fire ecology question survey: Candid expressions of research needs by land managers and scientists in western North America, *U.S. Department of Agriculture Forest Service General Technical Report INT-18*, Ogden, Utah, 122p.

Terry, C. J., 1978, Food habits of three sympatric species of Insectivora in western Washington, *Can. Field Nat.* **92:**38–44.

Terry, C. J., 1981, Habitat differentiation among three species of *Sorex* and *Neurotrichus gibbsi* in Washington, *Am. Mid. Nat.* **106:**119–125.

Thompson, G. R., M. J. Behan, J. M. Mandzak, and C. W. Bowen, 1977, On the evaluation of nutrient pools of forest soils, *Clays and Clay Min.* **25:**411–416.

Thorne, R. E., 1972, Hydroacoustic assessment of limnetic-feeding fishes, in *Proceedings—Research on Coniferous Forest Ecosystems—A Symposium*, J. F. Franklin, L. J. Dempster, and R. H. Waring, eds., U.S. Department of Agriculture Forest Service, Portland, Oreg., pp. 317–322.

Thorne, R. E., J. J. Dawson, J. J. Traynor, and R. L. Burgner, 1975, Population studies of juvenile sockeye salmon in Lake Washington with the use of acoustic assessment techniques, in *Symposium on the Methodology for Surveying, Monitoring, and Appraisal of Fishery Resources in Lakes and Large Rivers, Panel Review and Related Papers*, R. L. Welcomme, ed., EIFAC Technical Paper 23, supplement 1, vol. 1, F.A.O., Rome, pp. 328–345.

Tison, D. L., F. E. Palmer, and J. T. Staley, 1977, Nitrogen fixation in lakes of the Lake Washington drainage basin, *Water Res.* **2:**843–847.

Trappe, J. M., and R. Fogel, 1977, Ecosystematic functions of mycorrhizae, in *The Belowground Ecosystem: A Synthesis of Plant-Associated Processes*, J. K. Marshall, ed., Range Sci. Dept., Sci. Ser. No. 26, Colorado State University, Fort Collins, pp. 205–214.

Triska, F. J., and B. M. Buckley, 1978, Patterns of nitrogen uptake and loss in relation to litter disappearance and associated invertebrate biomass in six streams of the Pacific Northwest, U.S.A., *Verh. Int. Verein. Limnol.* **20:**1324–1332.

Triska, F. J., and J. R. Sedell, 1976, Decomposition of four species of leaf litter in response to nitrate manipulation, *Ecology* **57:**783–792.

Triska, F. J., J. R. Sedell, and B. Buckley, 1975, The processing of conifer and hardwood leaves in two coniferous forest streams, 11: Biochemical and nutrient changes, *Verh. Int. Verein. Limnol.* **19:**1628–1639.

Tucker, G. S., and W. H. Emmingham, 1977, Morphology changes in leaves of residual western hemlock after clear and shelterwood cutting, *For. Sci.* **23:**195–203.

·Turner, J., 1977, Effect of nitrogen availability on nitrogen cycling in a Douglas-fir stand, *For. Sci.* **23:**307–316.

Turner, J., 1981, Nutrient cycling in an age sequence in western Washington Douglas-fir stands, *Annals Bot.* **48:**159–169.

Turner, J., and J. N. Long, 1975, Accumulation of organic matter in a series of Douglas-fir stands, *Can. J. For. Res.* **5:**681–690.

Turner, J., and P. R. Olson, 1976, Nitrogen relations in a Douglas-fir plantation, *Ann. Bot.* **40:**1185–1193.

Turner, J., and M. J. Singer, 1976, Nutrient distribution and cycling in a subalpine coniferous forest ecosystem, *J. Appl. Ecol.* **13:**295–301.

Turner, J., D. W. Cole, and S. P. Gessel, 1977, Mineral nutrient accumulation and cycling in a stand of red alder *(Alnus rubra), J. Ecol.* **64:**965–974.

Turner, J., D. W. Johnson, and M. J. Lambert, 1980, Sulphur cycling in a Douglas-fir forest and its modification by nitrogen applications, *Oecol. Plant.* **15:**27–35.

Turner, J., M. J. Lambert, and S. P. Gessel, 1977, Use of foliage sulfate concentrations to predict response to area application by Douglas-fir, *Can. J. For. Res.* **7:**476–480.

Turner, J., J. N. Long, and A. Backiel, 1978, Under-storey nutrient content in an age sequence of Douglas-fir stands, *Ann. Bot.* **42:**1045–1055.

Ugolini, F. C., H. Dawson, and J. Zachara, 1977, Direct evidence of particle migration in the soil solution of a podzol, *Science* **198:**603–605.

Ugolini, F. C., R. Minden, H. Dawson, and J. Zachara, 1977, An example of soil processes in the *Abies amabilis* zone of central Cascades, Washington, *Soil Sci.* **124:**291–302.

Van Cleve, K., 1973, Energy and biomass relationships in alder ecosystems developing on the Tanana River Floodplain near Fairbanks, Alaska, *Arct. Alp. Res.,* P. 1, **5:**253–260.

Van Cleve, K., and J. C. Zasada, 1976, Response of 70-year-old white spruce to thinning and fertilization in interior Alaska, *Can. J. For. Res.* **6:**145–152.

Vogt, K. A., and R. L. Edmonds, 1980, Patterns of nutrient concentration in basidiocarps in western Washington, *Can. J. Bot.* **58:**694–698.

Vogt, K. A., R. L. Edmonds, G. C. Antos, and D. J. Vogt, 1980, Relationships between carbon dioxide evolution, ATP concentrations and decomposition in red alder, Douglas-fir, western hemlock and Pacific silver fir ecosystems in western Washington, *Oikos* **35:**72–79.

Walker, R. B., 1975, Measurement of primary productivity by gas exchange studies in the IBP, in *Productivity of World Ecosystems,* D. E. Reichle, J. F. Franklin, and D. W. Goodall, eds., U.S. Natl. Acad. Sci., Washington, D.C., pp. 60–63.

Walker, R. B., D. R. M. Scott, D. J. Salo, and K. L. Reed, 1972, Terrestrial process studies in conifers: A review, in *Proceedings—Research on Coniferous Forest Ecosystems—A Symposium,* J. F. Franklin, L. J. Dempster, and R. H. Waring, eds., U.S. Department of Agriculture Forest Service, Portland, Oreg., pp. 211–215.

Waring, R. H., 1974, Structure and function of the Coniferous Forest Biome organization, in *Integrated Research in the Coniferous Forest Biome,* R. H. Waring and R. L. Edmonds, eds., Coniferous Forest Biome Bulletin No. 5, University of Washington, Seattle, pp. 1–6.

Waring, R. H., 1976, Reafforestation in the Pacific Northwest, *Environ. Cons.* **3:**269–272.

Waring, R. H., and J. F. Franklin, 1979, Evergreen coniferous forests of the Pacific Northwest, *Science* **204:**1380–1386.

Waring, R. H., and S. W. Running, 1976, Water uptake, storage, and transpiration by conifers: A physiological model, in *Water and Plant Life, Ecological Studies: Analysis and Synthesis,* O. L. Lange, L. Kappen, and E. D. Schulze, eds., vol. 19, Springer-Verlag, Berlin, pp. 189–202.

Waring, R. H., and S. W. Running, 1978, Sapwood water storage: Its contribution to transpiration and effect upon water conductance through the stems of old-growth Douglas-fir, *Plant Cell Environ.* **1:**131–140.

Waring, R. H., K. L. Reed, and W. H. Emmingham, 1972, An environmental grid for classifying coniferous forest ecosystems, in *Proceedings—Research on Coniferous Forest Ecosystems— A Symposium,* J. F. Franklin, L. J. Dempster, and R. H. Waring, eds., U.S. Department of Agriculture Forest Service, Portland, Oreg. pp. 79–90.

Waring, R. H., W. H. Emmingham, and S. W. Running, 1975, Environmental limits of an endemic spruce, *Picea breweriana, Can. J. Bot.* **53:**1599–1613.

Waring, R. H., J. R. Rogers, and W. T. Swank, 1980, Water relations and hydrologic cycles, in *Dynamic Properties of Forest Ecosystems,* D. E. Reichle, ed., Cambridge University Press, Cambridge, pp. 205–264.

Waring, R. H., H. L. Gholz, C. C. Grier, and M. L. Plummer, 1977, Evaluating stem conducting tissue as an estimator of leaf area in four woody angiosperms, *Can. J. Bot.* **55:**1474–1477.

Waring, R. H., W. H. Emmingham, H. L. Gholz, and C. C. Grier, 1978, Variation in maximum leaf area of coniferous forests in Oregon and its ecological significance, *For. Sci.* **24:**131–140.

Waring, R. H., H. R. Holbo, R. P. Bueb, and R. L. Fredriksen, 1978, Meteorological data from the Coniferous Forest Biome primary station in Oregon, *U.S. Department of Agriculture Forest Service General Technical Report PNW-73,* 23p.

Warren, C. E., and G. E. Davis, 1971, Laboratory stream research: Objectives, possibilities, and constraints, *Ann. Rev. Ecol. Syst.* **2:**111–144.

Webb, W. L., 1972, A model of light and temperature controlled net photosynthesis rates for terrestrial plants, in *Proceedings—Research on Coniferous Forest Ecosystems—A Symposium,* J. F. Franklin, L. J. Dempster, and R. H. Waring, eds., U.S. Department of Agriculture Forest Service, Portland, Oreg., pp. 237–242.

Webb, W. L., 1975, Dynamics of photoassimilated carbon in Douglas-fir seedlings, *Plant Physiol.* **56:**455–459.

Webb, W. L., 1975, The distribution of photoassimilated carbon and the growth of Douglas-fir seedlings, *Can. J. For. Res.* **5:**68–72.

Webb, W. L., 1977, Rates of current photosynthate accumulation in roots of Douglas-fir seedlings: Seasonal variation, in *The Belowground Ecosystem: A Synthesis of Plant-Associated Processes,* J. K. Marshall, ed., Range Sci. Dept., Sci. Ser. No. 26, Colorado State University, Fort Collins, pp. 149–158.

Webb, W. L., and J. B. Zaerr, 1976, Carbon dioxide efflux of Douglas-fir seedlings in light and dark, *Photosynthetica* **10:**388–393.

Welch, E. B., 1977, Nutrient diversion: Resulting lake trophic state and phosphorus dynamics, *Ecol. Res. Series, EPA-600/3-77-003,* U.S. Environmental Protection Agency, Corvallis, Oreg., 91p.

Welch, E. B., and D. E. Spyridakis, 1972, Dynamics of nutrient supply and primary production in Lake Sammamish, Washington, in *Proceedings—Research on Coniferous Forest Ecosystems—A Symposium,* J. F. Franklin, L. J. Dempster, and R. H. Waring, eds., U.S. Department of Agriculture Forest Service, Portland, Oreg., pp. 301–315.

Welch, E. B., C. A. Rock, and J. D. Krull, 1974, Long-term lake recovery related to available phorphorus, in *Proc. Conf. Modeling Eutrophication,* Utah State University, Logan, Utah, pp. 5–13.

Welch, E. B, and G. R. Hendrey, and R. K. Stoll, 1975, Nutrient supply and the production and biomass of algae in four Washington lakes, *Oikos* **26:**47–54.

Welch, E. B., P. Sturtevant, and M. A. Perkins, 1978, Dominance of phosphorus over nitrogen as the limiter to phytoplankton growth rate, *Hydrobiologia* **57:**209–215.

Whitaker, J. O., Jr., and C. Maser, 1976, Food habits of five western Oregon shrews, *Northwest Sci.* **50:**102–107.

Whitaker, J. O., C. Maser, and L. E. Keller, 1977, Food habits of bats of western Oregon, *Northwest Sci.* **51:**46–55.

Wiederholm, T., 1976, A survey of the bottom fauna of Lake Sammamish, *Northwest Sci.* **50:**23–31.

Wiens, J. A., and R. A. Nussbaum, 1975, Estimation of energy flow in northwestern coniferous forest bird communities, *Ecology* **56:**547–561.

Wissmar, R. C., D. M. Eggers, and N. W. Bartoo, 1974, Analysis of lake ecosystems: Lake Washington drainage basin, in *Integrated Research in the Coniferous Forest Biome,* R. H. Waring and R. L. Edmonds, eds., Coniferous Forest Biome Bulletin No. 5, University of Washington, Seattle, pp. 70–96.

Wissmar, R. C., J. E. Richey, and D. E. Spyridakis, 1977, The importance of allocthonous particulate carbon pathways in a subalpine lake, *J. Fish. Res. Board Can.* **34:**1410–1418.

Wydoski, R. S., 1972, Annotated bibliography on the ecology of the Lake Washington drainage, *Coniferous Forest Biome Bulletin No. 1,* University of Washington, Seattle, 102p.

Zobel, D. B., N. A. McKee, G. M. Hawk, and C. T. Dyrness, 1974, Correlation of forest communities with environment and phenology on the H. J. Andrews Experimental Forest, Oregon, in *Integrated Research in the Coniferous Forest Biome,* R. H. Waring and R. L. Edmonds, eds., Coniferous Forest Biome Bulletin No. 5, University of Washington, Seattle, pp. 48–56.

Zobel, D. B., A. McKee, G. M. Hawk, and C. T. Dyrness, 1976, Relationships of environment to composition, structure, and diversity of forest communities of the central western Cascades of Oregon, *Ecol. Monogr.* **46:**135–156.

Index

Abies amabilis. *See* Pacific silver fir
Acid rain, 221
Alder, red
  biomass, 204, 215
  decomposition of leaves
    in forests, 202
    in streams, 297
  litterfall in, 102, 111, 204
  nitrogen fixation in, 188–189
  nutrient cycling in, 202, 206, 214
  organic matter budget, 204
  productivity of, 22, 111
  role in riparian zone, 281–282, 284
Alnus rubra. *See* Alder, red
Andrews, H.J., Experimental Forest
  climate, 12
  general description, 9
  location, 11
  reference stands, 37, 40
  soils, 9
  vegetation, 9

Bacteria
  free-living N fixers in logs, 189
  in lakes, 343, 349
Basal area
  diurnal changes in, 161
  on environmental grid sites, 52
  relationship to moisture stress,
    62–63
Biomass
  of fish
    in lakes, 363–369
    in streams, 324–327
  of forests
    foliage, 22, 90–99
    roots, 105
    stems and branches, 99
    understory, 99–102
  of phytoplankton

  in lakes, 366
  in streams, 307–308
  of stream invertebrates, 300
Black spruce
  photosynthesis, 58–60
  productivity, 56

Calcium cycling, 188–215
Canopy
  development of stand canopies,
    96–99
  development of individual crowns,
    90–96
  rate of closure, 23, 97
  relation of canopy closure to
    productivity, 23, 99
Carbon. *See also* Organic matter
  budgets in lakes, 340–352
  budgets in streams, 293–295,
    304–321
  incorporation in trees, 141–144
Carbon:Adenosine Triphosphate ratio
  (C:ATP), 352, 356–358
Carbon dioxide, influence on
  photosynthesis, 139–141
Carbon:Nitrogen ratio (C:N)
  in lake sediments, 338–341,
    345–346, 352
  relation to litter processing in
    streams, 298–301
  relation to terrestrial litter
    decomposition, 206–207
Chester Morse Lake
  description, 18–19
  elemental content of, 336–341
Chlorophyll, in lakes, 352–354
Clearcutting, impacts of,
  on erosion, 26, 258
  on forest structure, 25
  on nutrient cycling, 26, 216–218

on productivity, 25, 217
on streams, 26, 257, 323–330
Climate
  at H. J. Andrews Forest, 12
  in the biome, 3
  at Findley Lake, 12
  at A. E. Thompson site, 12
  west of the Cascade Mountain crest,
    3
Colorado blue spruce, photosynthesis
    in, 59–60
Cottus asper (prickly sculpin),
    biomass and productivity, 363

Daphnia, in Lake Washington, 364
Decomposition
  effects of moisture on, 192,
    204–206
  effects of substrate quality on, 192,
    206
  effects of temperature on, 192,
    204–206
  in relation to stand development,
    212
  in streams, 295–301
  in terrestrial ecosystems, 202–206
Diversity, of plants in relation to stand
    age, 99
Douglas-fir
  biomass of
    foliage, 22, 91–99, 200–201, 209
    roots, 105, 200–201
    stems and branches, 99, 200–201
  decomposition
    in forests, 202–206, 212
    in streams, 297–301
  development of crowns and stands,
    90–99
  erosion in old-growth forests,
    233–266
  litter production in, 102–105
  niche of, 73–78
  nutrient cycling
    processes, 187–199
    in relation to stand development,
    209–214
  organic matter budgets in, 200–201
  photosynthesis in 58–61, 127–144

productivity of, 22, 59, 105–110
respiration in old-growth forests,
    118
riparian zone in, 267–291
simulated growth of, 79–86
stream ecosystems in, 292–332
understory in, 99–102

Ecological indexes, 45, 54–64
Environmental grid, study site
    descriptions, 47–54
Erosion. *See* Material transport

Fertilization, effects of
  on lakes. *See* Sewage diversion
  on nutrient cycling, 219–221
Findley Lake
  elemental content of, 336–341
  nutrient cycling in, 341–348
  site description (including
    vegetation), 16–19
  soils, 18
Fire, effects of
  on erosion, 259
  on nutrient cycling, 218
  on riparian zone, 286
  on streams, 328
  on vegetation, 28
Fish
  productivity in lakes, 363
  productivity in streams, 323–327
  species occurring in biome, 8, 325,
    362–363
Foliage. *See also* Leaf surface area
  biomass 79–88, 91–99, 200–201,
    204
  effect of light on, 98
  effect of moisture on, 99
  effect of nutrition on, 99
  relationships between foliar biomass
    and sapwood cross-sectional
    area, 90, 147
Forest floor
  accumulation, 102–105
  decomposition, 202–206
Fungi, immobilization of nutrients
  in lakes, 343
  in terrestrial ecosystems, 206–207

Gasterosteus aculeatus (three spine stickleback), biomass and productivity, 363
Gaultheria shallon (salal), biomass, 101
Geology
  in the biome, 2
  at Findley Lake, 18
Growth. *See also* Productivity
  processes in Douglas-fir
    shoot and cambial growth, 144–148
    spatial variations, 162–170
    temporal variations, 148–162
  simulation of, 79–86

Insects. *See* Invertebrates
Invertebrates, in streams, 282, 293–301
Iron precipitation, in Lake Sammamish, 349

Lakes. *See also* Chester Morse Lake; Findley Lake; Lake Sammamish; Lake Washington
  carbon transfer in, 341–343 366–367
  C:N ratios in sediments, 338, 346
  descriptions of
    in biome, 8
    in Lake Washington drainage, 14
  elemental contents of, 336–341
  nitrogen cycling in, 343, 346, 348–352
    nitrification, 346
    nitrogen immobilization, 343
  nutrient cycling in, 333–362
  phosphorus cycling in, 346, 348–352
  phytoplankton responses, 352–362
  productivity of
    comparison of aquatic and terrestrial ecosystems, 369–375
    fish productivity, 362–369
  terrestrial inputs
    leaching, 336
    litterfall, 335
    weathering, 336

trophic status of, 334
Lake Sammamish
  description, 18–19
  elemental content of, 336–341
  nutrient cycling in, 348–352
Lake Washington
  description, 18–19
  elemental content of, 336–341
  fish production in, 362–369
Leaching
  effects of harvesting on, 218
  influence on lakes, 336
  soil leaching processes, 195–198
Leaf surface area, 114–117
  effect of moisture on, 114
  effect of nutrition on, 116
  effect of temperature on, 116
  effect of wind on, 116
  relation to productivity, 22
  of western conifers, 114–117
Lichens
  nitrogen fixation in tree canopies, 189
  relation to snowpack depth, 36
  relation to vegetation distribution, 36
Light, effects of
  on foliar biomass, 98
  on photosynthesis, 132, 141, 163
  on species niches, 78
  on stream primary production, 302
Lignin, effects on decomposition, 206
Litter
  accumulation. *See* Forest floor
  decomposition. *See* Decomposition
  in lakes, 335
  nutrient returns in, 190–192
  production, 102–105
  in streams, 294–301

Material transport, 233–266
  in old-growth Douglas-fir forests, 240–252
  processes, 234–240
  in total watersheds, 252–259
Mean residence time
  of forest floor, 208–209
  of nitrogen, 208–209

Mineral cycling. *See* Nutrient cycling,
     processes in forests
Modeling
  of canopy nitrogen flow, 193
  of carbon flow in Douglas-fir
     seedlings, 142
  decomposition model (exponential
     decay), 202
  of nutrient cycling, 188
  stream model, 325
  SUCSIM (SUCcession SIMulator),
     74–88
  of tree growth, 79–86
Moisture stress
  indexes of, 46, 55–57
  relation to foliar biomass, 99
  relation to leaf surface area, 114
  in relation to physiological
     processes, 126–185
  in relation to vegetation distribution,
     33–41
Mountain hemlock zone, 3, 6, 28
Myocheilus caurinus (peamouth),
     biomass and productivity, 363
Mycorrhizae, 199, 207

Niche
  of Douglas-fir, 77–78
  fundamental, 69
  of ponderosa pine, 73
  realized, 69
  relation to succession, 72–74
  theory, 69–72
  of western red cedar, 77–78
Nitrate reductase, in phytoplankton,
     358, 362
Nitrification
  in lakes, 346
  in terrestrial ecosystems, 221
Nitrogen cycling
  accumulation in soil, 202–204
  in canopies, 189
  internal translocation, 208
  in lakes, 336, 343–346, 348–352
  in litterfall, 76
  nitrogen transformation after
     fertilization, 221

nitrogen uptake by Douglas-fir,
     192–195
  processes, 187–199
  in streams, 298–304
Nitrogen fixation
  by *Ceanothus*, 189
  by free living bacteria, 189
  by lichens, 189
  by red alder, 188–189
Nutrient cycling
  in lakes, 336–362
  processes in forests, 187–199
  in streams, 293–304
  in terrestrial ecosystems, 186–232
    in different ecosystems, 199–209
    in relation to acid rain, 221
    in relation to fertilization, 219
    in relation to fire, 218
    in relation to harvesting, 216
    in relation to stand development,
       209–214

Oncorrhynchus nerka (sockeye
     salmon), biomass and
     productivity, 363
Organic matter. *See also* Biomass;
     Carbon; Productivity
  in forests, 89–125, 198–204
    Douglas-fir budget, 198–202
    Pacific silver fir budget, 198–202
    western hemlock budget, 198–202
  in lakes, 341–345, 366–367
  in streams, 304–321
Ordination, SIMORD, 30. *See also*
     Vegetation

Pacific silver fir
  foliar biomass, 98
  nutrient cycling in, 199, 209
  organic matter distribution in,
     200–201
  productivity of, 57
  stomatal activity in, 134
  zone, 3, 6, 28, 32–37
Parent material
  at H. J. Andrews Forest, 9
  at Findley Lake, 18

at A. E. Thompson site, 16
Perca flavescens (yellow perch),
    biomass and productivity,
    363
Phosphorus cycling, in lakes,
    346–352, 358–361
Photosynthesis
    in Douglas-fir, 58–61, 127–144,
        154–161, 162–170
    in ecosystems across the biome,
        58–61, 127–170
    in lakes, 353–356
    limiting factors in forests
        CO_2, 139
        light, 132
        temperature, 131
        water and stomates, 133
    in streams, 301–304
Photosynthesis:Respiration ratio (P:R)
    in lakes, 354–356
    in streams, 321–323
Phytoplankton
    in lakes
        biomass, 366
        C:ATP ratio, 356–358, 362
        C:P ratio, 359, 362
        nitrate reductase, 358, 362
        phosphorus flux, 358
        P:R, 354
        physiological response to
            nutrients, 352–354
        productivity, 334, 352–354
    in streams, 301–304
Picea mariana. See Black spruce
Picea sitchensis. See Sitka spruce
Pinus ponderosa. See Ponderosa pine
Ponderosa pine
    niche of, 73
    photosynthesis in, 59–61
    productivity of, 56–57
    simulated growth of, 80–82
Potassium cycling, 188–215
Predator-prey interactions, in Lake
    Washington, 364–369
Productivity
    aquatic and terrestrial ecosystems,
        comparison of, 369–375

of Douglas-fir, 22, 56–57, 105–110
indexes, in ecosystems across the
    biome, 59–64
of lakes, 334, 352–354, 363
of Pacific silver fir, 57
of ponderosa pine, 56–57
production efficiencies, 117–118
of red alder, 22, 111
relation to photosynthesis, 141–144
of Sitka spruce, 57
of streams, 323–327
of western coniferous forests, 22,
    56–57, 89–125
of western hemlock, 22, 56–57,
    111
Pseudotsuga menziesii. See
    Douglas-fir
Ptyocheilus oregonensis (northern
    sqawfish), biomass and
    productivity, 363

Red alder. *See* Alder, red
Redwood, coast, biomass, 22
Reference stands, in the H. J.
    Andrews Forest, 37, 40
Research site descriptions
    H. J. Andrews Experimental Forest,
        9–14
    environmental grid sites, 47–54
    Lake Washington drainage, 14–19
    other sites, 20
Respiration
    comparison of terrestrial and aquatic
        ecosystems, 369–375
    in forests
        autotrophic, 118
        heterotrophic, 118
Riparian zone, 267–291
    effects of clearcutting on, 284
    effects of fire on, 286
    function of, 274–282
    vegetation in, 268–274
        spatial variation in, 282–283
        temporal variation in, 283–288
Roots
    biomass of, 105
    decomposition of, 206

Salmo clarki (Cutthroat trout), 325
Sequoia sempervirens. See Redwood,
    coast
Sewage diversion
  Lake Sammamish, 348
  Lake Washington, 341
Site index, 62
Sitka spruce
  leaf conductance in, 134
  productivity of, 57
  zone 3, 6
Soil(s)
  cation exchange capacity of, 191
  descriptions
    in H. J. Andrews Forest, 9
    general, in biome, 3
    in Lake Washington drainage, 16
  leaching process. *See* Leaching
  profiles of typical soils
    at H. J. Andrews Forest, 13
    at Findley Lake, 18
    at A. E. Thompson site, 17
  water potential, 165
  weathering, 75, 189, 336
Species distribution, in biome, factors
    influencing, 45–67
Spirinchus thaleichthys (longfin
    smelt), biomass and
    productivity, 363
Stemflow, 192
Stomatal conductance, 133–141,
    169–170
Streams, 8, 13, 233–332
  effects of erosion on, 233–266
  effects of forest management
    (including clearcutting) on,
    323–330
  fish biomass in, 324–325
  function of
    autotrophic, 301
    heterotrophic, 295
  influence of riparian zone on,
    267–291
  organic matter in, 304–321
  production:respiration ratios,
    321–323
  spatial aspects, 314–323
  temporal aspects, 311–314

Succession
  modeling (SUCSIM), 74–88
  in relation to niche theory, 72–74

Temperature, in relation to
  decomposition, 206
  photosynthesis, 131
  phytoplankton activity, 353
  trout production in streams, 325
Temperature Growth Index
  as an ecological index, 46, 57
  in relation to succession modeling,
    77
  in relation to vegetation distribution,
    38–41
Thompson, A. E., Research Center
  site description, 15–16
  soils, 17
Thuja plicata. See Western red cedar
Transpiration
  diurnal and seasonal trends,
    158–161
  indexes of, 47–61
  ratio, in relation to niche, 72
Tsuga heterophylla. See Western
    hemlock
Tsuga mertensiana. See Mountain
    hemlock

Understory
  development and biomass, 99–102
  nutrient cycling in, 215

Vegetation
  in H. J. Andrews Forest, 9, 37–41
  biomass. *See* Biomass
  in the biome, 3–5, 28–44, 47–54
  classification, 30–32
  distribution along environmental
    gradients
    in H. J. Andrews Forest, 37–41
    in Cedar River drainage, 32–37
  dominance of conifers in biome, 20,
    64
  ecological indexes and species
    distribution, 45–67
  in Lake Washington drainage, 16,
    32–37

ordination, 30–32
productivity. *See* Productivity
in relation to environment, 28–44

Water, effects on stomates, 133–139.
   See also Moisture stress;
   Transpiration
Watershed 10
clearcutting in, 218, 258
material transport in, 240–259
stream
   description, 13
   location, 11
   organic matter budget, 306
Weight loss. *See* Decomposition
Western hemlock
decomposition of logs, 206
decomposition of needles, 202

foliar biomass of, 98
organic matter budget in, 200–201
photosynthesis in, 58
productivity in, 22, 56–57, 111
zone, 3, 6, 28, 33
Western red cedar, niche of, 73, 77
Wood
biomass of, 91, 99–100, 198–201
decomposition of logs, 206
importance for material transport,
   274–275
importance in streams, 274, 280,
   295
litter production, 102–104
production of, 106–110

Yield-density relations, 112